The Principalship

■

The Principalship

Vision to Action

Fred C. Lunenburg
Sam Houston State University

Beverly J. Irby
Sam Houston State University

WADSWORTH
CENGAGE Learning·

Australia • Brazil • Japan • Korea • Mexico • Singapore • Spain • United Kingdom • United States

The Principalship: Vision to Action
Fred C. Lunenburg and Beverly J. Irby

Publisher: Vicki Knight

Acquisitions Editor: Dan Alpert

Development Editor: Tangelique Williams

Assistant Editor: Dan Moneypenny

Editorial Assistant: Larkin Page-Jacobs

Technology Project Manager: Barry Connolly

Marketing Manager: Terra Schultz

Marketing Assistant: Rebecca Weisman

Marketing Communications Manager: Tami Strang

Senior Project Manager, Editorial Production:
    Kimberly Adams

Executive Art Director: Maria Epes

Print Buyer: Doreen Suruki

Permissions Editor: Joohee Lee

Production Service: Scratchgravel Publishing
    Services

Copy Editor: Chris Thillen

Cover Designer: Harold Burch

Cover Image Photographer: Harold Burch

Compositor: Cadmus Professional Communications

For product information and technology assistance, contact us at
Cengage Learning Customer & Sales Support, 1-800-354-9706
For permission to use material from this text or product,
submit all requests online at **www.cengage.com/permissions**
Further permissions questions can be emailed to
permissionrequest@cengage.com

Library of Congress Control Number: 2005923119

ISBN-13: 978-0-534-62595-5

ISBN-10: 0-534-62595-9

Wadsworth
10 Davis Drive
Belmont, CA 94002-3098
USA

Cengage Learning is a leading provider of customized learning solutions with office locations around the globe, including Singapore, the United Kingdom, Australia, Mexico, Brazil and Japan. Locate your local office at: **international.cengage.com/region**

Cengage Learning products are represented in Canada by Nelson Education, Ltd.

For your course and learning solutions, visit **academic.cengage.com**

Purchase any of our products at your local college store or at our preferred online store **www.ichapters.com**

Printed in the United States of America
4 5 6 7 11

Contents

Part I

Skills for Effective Leadership

1 ■ Cultivating Community, Culture, and Learning 1

Focusing Questions   1

Introduction   1

    Educational Leadership Constituent Council (ELCC) Standards   2

Reframing the Role of the Principal   5

    A New Approach to the Principalship   5

Creating a Professional Learning Community   6

    Creating a Mission Statement   7

    Developing a Vision   7

    Developing Value Statements   8

    Establishing Goals   9

Developing a Culture: Learning for All   10

    Definition and Characteristics   10

    Heroes, Traditions, and Networks   11

    Maintaining School Culture   12

The Principal as Instructional Leader   14

    Focusing on Learning   14

    Encouraging Collaboration   15

    Analyzing Results   15

    Providing Support   16

    Aligning Curriculum, Instruction, and Assessment   17

Summary   17

Field-Based Activities   18

Suggested Readings   18

Overview of Context for Case Studies   20

Part I Case Study: A New Role   21

Part II

ELCC Standard 1

2 ■ Creating a Vision for Learning 24

Focusing Questions   24

Gaining a Perspective on the Vision: Considering the Future   25

    Considerations of the Present and the Future: The Global Society   26

    Understanding Our World and Our Position as a Principal in the Challenges for Learning   26

    Bringing the Vision Home to the School Culture   28

The Systemic Vision   29

Creating a Vision   30

    The Principal's Vision   30

    Beliefs, Values, and Attitudes   30

    The Leadership Framework   32

    Benefits of Articulating the Vision   33

Shepherding the Vision   33

    Vision Detractors   33

    Vision Maintainers   34

Mission Statements   35

Goal Statements   36

    Hierarchy of Goals   36

    Criteria for Effective Goals   38

    The Goal-Setting Process   40

Problems With Goal Setting 41

Making Goal Setting Effective 42

Developing Plans for Attaining Goals 44

Strategic Plans 44

Tactical Plans 44

Operational Plans 44

Standing Plans 45

Single-Use Plans 46

How Some Schools Have Used Goal
Setting to Improve Test Scores 46

Summary 47

Field-Based Activities 48

Suggested Readings 48

Part II Case Study: Creating a Vision 50

Part III

ELCC Standard 2

3 ■ Curriculum Development and Implementation 53

Focusing Questions 53

Concepts and Models of Curriculum 54

Concepts of Curriculum 54

Models of Curriculum 55

Modern Models of Curriculum 61

Relationship of Curriculum to Instruction 69

The Principal as Curriculum and
Instructional Leader 71

Curriculum Goals and
Instructional Objectives 72

Writing Effective Instructional
Objectives 74

Developing a Needs Assessment 78

How to Conduct a Curriculum
Needs Assessment Considering
Standards 79

Assessment Tools 80

Curriculum Alignment Process 80

Focusing the Vision and the School's
Mission Through Curriculum 82

Aligning the Curriculum to the
Vision and Mission 82

Summary 83

Field-Based Activities 83

Suggested Readings 84

4 ■ Teaching and Learning 86

Focusing Questions 86

The Principal's Role in Teaching
and Learning 86

The Principal's Role in Instructional
Planning 87

Promoting Teacher Reflection in
Instructional Planning 88

Using Student Data and Evidence in
Instructional Planning 89

Using Students' Cultural Backgrounds
in Instructional Planning 91

Using Theoretical Frames for
Instructional Planning 92

The Effective Schools Model 102

Clear and Focused Mission 104

Instructional Leadership 104

High Expectations 104

Opportunity to Learn and
Time on Task 105

Frequent Monitoring and
Assessment 106

Safe and Orderly Environment 106

Positive Home-School Relations 107

Effective Teaching Practices 107

Twelve Principles of Effective
Teaching 108

Conditions for Learning 111

Best Practices for the Classroom 112

Models of Evaluation   113

    Formative and Summative Evaluation   113

    Classroom Observations   114

    Walk-Through Observations   114

    Peer Coaching   116

Summary   116

Field-Based Activities   117

Suggested Readings   118

5 ■ Professional Development   120

Focusing Questions   120

The Principal's Mission Related to Professional Development   120

The Principal's Mission for Teachers' Professional Development   121

High-Quality Professional Development   122

The Principal's Mission for Personal Professional Development   128

    The Professional Development Portfolio   128

    Using the Professional Development Portfolio   130

Ethics of Professional Development   132

Summary   132

Field-Based Activities   133

Suggested Readings   133

6 ■ Student Services   135

Focusing Questions   135

Guidance and Counseling Services   136

    Aims of Guidance and Counseling Programs   136

    The Role of the Counselor   137

    Major Guidance and Counseling Services   137

    Methods of Counseling   138

    Evaluation of Guidance and Counseling Programs   139

Attendance and Student Records   140

    The Cumulative Record   141

    The Use of Assessment Data to Improve Learning   141

Evaluating Student Progress   142

    Purposes of Assessment   142

    Establishing Information Criteria   143

    Creating Effective Tests   143

    Components of a Testing Program   145

Reporting to Parents and Families   147

    Difficulties in Grading   147

    Methods of Reporting Student Progress   148

Extracurricular Activities   149

    Goals of Education   149

    Functions of Extracurricular Activities   149

Special Education Services   150

    Related Services   151

    Due Process Protections   151

    Discipline   152

Gifted Education   153

    Administrative Arrangements for Gifted Education Programs   156

    Definitions of Giftedness   156

    What Principals Can Do for Gifted Education   160

    Curriculum Models for Gifted Education   161

Bilingual Education   162

    Program Descriptions   163

    Administrative Arrangements for Service Delivery of Bilingual Education   164

    Bilingual Education Models   165

    English as a Second Language Program Models   166

Summary   168

Field-Based Activities   168

Suggested Readings 169

Part III Case Study: Learning for All 171

Part IV
ELCC Standard 3

7 ■ Organizational Structures 174

Focusing Questions 174

Key Concepts of Organizational Structure 175
    Job Specialization 175
    Departmentalization 176
    Delegation 176
    Decentralization 178
    Span of Management 179
    Line and Staff Positions 179
Schools as Open Systems 181
    Inputs 181
    Transformation Process 181
    Outputs 182
    Feedback 182
Leadership Functions 182
    Planning 183
    Organizing 183
    Leading 184
    Monitoring 184
Administrative Roles 184
Management Skills 185
    Conceptual Skills 185
    Human Skills 186
    Technical Skills 187
Effective Principals 187
    Task Dimensions 187
    Human Resource Activities 187
    Behavioral Profiles of
    Effective Versus Successful
    Administrators 189

The Demise of Bureaucracy 189
Emergent Models of Organizational
   Structure 191
    System 4 Design 191
    Site-Based Management 192
    Transformational Leadership 193
    Synergistic Leadership Theory 194
    Total Quality Management 196
Summary 198
Field-Based Activities 199
Suggested Readings 200

8 ■ The Principal as Decision Maker 202

Focusing Questions 202

The Nature of Decision Making 202
The Decision-Making Process 204
    Identifying the Problem 204
    Generating Alternatives 205
    Evaluating Alternatives 206
    Choosing an Alternative 206
    Implementing the Decision 206
    Evaluating Decision Effectiveness 207
The Rational Decision Maker 207
    Assumptions of Rationality 207
    Limits to Rationality 209
Shared Decision Making 211
    Advantages and Disadvantages
    of Shared Decision Making 212
The Decision Tree Model 213
The Decision Making–Pattern
   Choice Model 216
The Synergistic Decision-Making
   Model 217
Summary 219
Field-Based Activities 219
Suggested Readings 220

9 ■ Developing Effective Communications 222

Focusing Questions 222

The Communication Process 222

Elements of the Communication Process 223

Planning a School-wide Communications Program 224

Organizational Communication 224

Direction of Communication Flow 224

Communication Networks 227

Managing Communication 229

Barriers to Communication 229

Improving Communication Effectiveness 231

Summary 235

Field-Based Activities 236

Suggested Readings 236

10 ■ The Principal and Change 238

Focusing Questions 238

The Nature of Organizational Change 238

Forces for Change 239

Resistance to Change 240

Overcoming Resistance to Change 240

Understanding Resistance to Change 243

Getting Reform Right: What Works and What Doesn't 244

Managing Change 244

The Principal as Change Agent 244

The Change Process 247

Key Principal Behaviors That Promote Successful School Change 249

Change Strategies 249

Process Strategies 249

Structural Strategies 251

Summary 253

Field-Based Activities 253

Suggested Readings 254

11 ■ Budgeting and School Facilities 256

Focusing Questions 256

School Budgeting 256

Expenditures and Revenue 257

The Budgeting Process 259

Financial Controls 261

Zero-Based Budgeting 262

Planning-Programming-Budgeting Systems 263

School Facilities Management 264

School Infrastructure Costs 265

Financing School Construction 267

Environmental Hazards 268

Summary 273

Field-Based Activities 273

Suggested Readings 274

12 ■ Creating Safe Schools 276

Focusing Questions 276

School Violence and Alcohol and Drug Use 277

Creating a Safe Environment 277

Research: School Violence and Alcohol and Drug Use 277

Applying Research to Practice: Developing an Action Plan 280

Strategy 1: Predict School Violence 280

Strategy 2: Prevent School Violence 281

Strategy 3: Focus Resources on Schools 284

Strategy 4: Strengthen the System 285

Strategy 5: Develop a Crisis Management Plan 285

Strategy 6: Create an Orderly
   Climate for Learning   287
Summary 292
Field-Based Activities 293
Suggested Readings 293

13 ■ Human Resource Management   295

Focusing Questions 295

The Human Resource Management
   Process   296
Recruitment   296
   Job Analysis   296
   Legal Constraints   297
   Personnel Sources   298
   Teacher Recruitment Consortium 299
Selection   299
   Interviews   299
   Components of a Good
      Interview Process   301
   Testing   302
   Assessment Centers   303
Staff Development   304
   Assessing Staff Development
      Needs   305
   Setting Staff Development
      Objectives   305
   Selecting Staff Development
      Methods   306
   Evaluating the Staff Development
      Program   306
   Orientation and Induction of
      the Beginning Teacher   307
   Guidelines for Improving Support
      for Beginning Teachers   308
Performance Appraisal   309
   Appraisal Techniques   309
   Common Rating Errors   312
   Modern Appraisal Techniques   313

Supervision and Evaluation   313
Improving Teacher Performance
   Appraisals   315
Union-Management Relations   316
   The Importance of Good Union-
      Management Relations   316
   The Collective Bargaining Process 317
Summary 317
Field-Based Activities 319
Suggested Readings 319

**Part IV Case Study: The New
   Math Program**   321

Part V

ELCC Standard 4

14 ■ Community Relations   324

Focusing Questions 324

Principals as "Boundary Spanners" 325
School, Family, and Community
   Involvement   325
   Principals Leading Community
      Efforts During Catastrophes 326
   Principals Leading School, Family,
      and Community Involvement 328
   More Family Involvement
      Information for Principals
      to Consider   329
Principals, School-Community Relations,
   and Public Relations   331
   The Politics of Internal and
      External Publics   333
   Consideration of the Media and
      Community Relations   333
   NSPRA Standards for Educational
      Public Relations Programs 334
Public Relations Plan   336

The Four-Step Public Relations
  Process 336
  Public Relations Planning Process 337
Summary 338
Field-Based Activities 340
Suggested Readings 340

**Part V Case Study: Building
  Bridges Again 342**

Part VI
ELCC Standard 5

15 ■ The Principal and Ethics 345

Focusing Questions 345
The Ethical Principal 346
Principals and Philosophical Concepts
  of Ethics 346
  Rights 347
  Freedom 347
  Responsibility and Authority 348
  Duty 349
  Justice 349
  Equity 349
  Caring 350
  Character, Commitment, and
    Formality 350
  Conflict of Interest 350
  Loyalty 351
  Prudence 351
  Critique 352
  Profession 352
  Moral Imperative 352
Principals and Ethical Behavior in Schools 353
  Principals Promoting Ethical
    Behavior in Athletic Programs 353

  Principals Promoting Ethical
    Behavior Through Character
    Education 354
  Policies and Procedures That
    Promote Ethical Behavior
    in Schools 355
National and State Codes of Ethics
  for Principals 357
  National Ethical Codes 357
  State Codes 360
Summary 362
Field-Based Activities 364
Suggested Readings 365

Part VI Case Study: Tough Decisions 367

Part VII
ELCC Standard 6

16 ■ Political and Policy
     Context 370

Focusing Questions 370
Society, Policy, and Politics 370
Policy, Politics, and the Principal 372
What Is a Policy? 372
  The Examination of Policy 374
  Conceptual Framework for
    Understanding Policy 377
What Is Meant by *Politics*? 379
  Types of Educational Politics 382
Politics in the District: Working With
  the Superintendent and Other
  External Forces 384
Summary 387
Field-Based Activities 389
Suggested Readings 389

17 ■ Legal Issues 392

Focusing Questions 392
Legal Basis for Public Education 393
Sources of Law 393
    Federal Level 393
    State Level 396
    Local Level 397
The American Judicial System 398
    Federal Courts 398
    State Courts 399
Schools and the State 400
    Compulsory School Attendance 400
    Church-State Relations 401
    State Aid to Private Schools 403
    School Fees 405
    The School Curriculum 407
    State-Mandated Performance
        Testing 409
Students and the Law 412
    Freedom of Expression 412
    Student Appearance 414

    Extracurricular Activities 415
    Student Discipline 416
    Students With Disabilities 419
Teachers and the Law 420
    Licensure and Certification 421
    Contracts 421
    Termination of Employment 422
    Discrimination in Employment 424
    Collective Bargaining 428
    Tort Liability 433
Summary 435
Field-Based Activities 436
Suggested Readings 436

**Part VII Case Study: A Case for
    the Attorney** 438

References 441
Name Index I-1
Subject Index I-9

Preface

Student learning is the main reason for the school's existence. The focus on results, the focus on student achievement, and the focus on students learning at high levels can happen only if teaching and learning become the central focus of the school and the central focus of the principal. The emphasis on student learning (the outcome rather than the process of schooling), coupled with federal legislation to that end, has placed more demands on the role of the principal than ever before in our nation's history.

To address the heightened demands on the principal for greater accountability for student learning, *The Principalship: Vision to Action* has woven the new Educational Leadership Constituent Council (ELCC) Standards into the material provided in the text. The ELCC Standards, created jointly by the National Council for the Accreditation of Teacher Education (NCATE) and the Interstate School Leaders Licensure Consortium (ISLLC), represent a common core of knowledge, dispositions, and performances that help link principal leadership more forcefully to student outcomes. The ELCC Standards have been endorsed by 10 national education organizations under the umbrella of the National Policy Board for Educational Administration (NPBEA).

Numerous textbooks have been written on the principalship. Where this text breaks new ground is that it is the first to connect the new standards to the philosophy and implementation of the principal as the steward of the school's vision: learning for all. Moreover, the separate administrative standards and guidelines of the NCATE and the ISLLC have merged into one set of collaboratively developed and agreed-upon standards for the preparation and development of school principals. These practical, applied components make this book a unique entry in the literature and a resource that we believe will enhance the skill and competence of future and current principals to become effective leaders of our nation's schools.

Organization of the Text

The book contains 17 chapters organized into seven parts. Part I contains one chapter (Chapter 1). This introductory chapter describes the ELCC Standards and introduces a new approach to the principalship, including how the principal creates a professional learning community, develops a culture for learning, and performs the role of instructional leader. Each of the six parts following is framed with one of the ELCC Standards as its major theme. Chapters contained in each part deal with the content of one of the ELCC Standards.

After the foundation is provided in the first part, Part II is framed with ELCC Standard 1 as its major theme. This part consists of one chapter (Chapter 2), which examines how the principal creates a vision for learning. Part III is framed with ELCC Standard 2 as its major theme. It contains four chapters, which focus on curriculum development and implementation (Chapter 3), teaching and learning (Chapter 4), professional development (Chapter 5), and student services (Chapter 6). Part IV is framed with ELCC Standard 3 as its major theme. It consists of seven chapters, which deal with organizational structures (Chapter 7), the principal as decision maker (Chapter 8), developing effective communications (Chapter 9), the principal and change (Chapter 10), budgeting and school facilities (Chapter 11), creating safe schools (Chapter 12), and human resource management (Chapter 13). Part V is framed with ELCC Standard 4 as its major theme. It contains one chapter (Chapter 14), which deals with the principal's role in school-community relations. Part VI is framed with ELCC Standard 5 as it major theme. It contains one chapter (Chapter 15), which examines the principal and ethics. Part VII is framed with ELCC Standard 6 as its major theme. It contains two chapters, which deal with the political and policy context (Chapter 16), followed by legal issues (Chapter 17).

Special Features of the Text

In the past, textbooks on the principalship have focused mainly on theory and research as a way of providing a knowledge base and preparation for future principals. This book is unique in that it goes beyond this tradition by including, in addition to comprehensive coverage of theory and research, a third component: practical applications that help principals make use of the knowledge base they acquire. Furthermore, a set of national standards now exists, providing a common core of knowledge, dispositions, and performances for the preparation and development of school principals. These standards, known as the Educational Leadership Constituent Council (ELCC) Standards, incorporate the political, social, economic, legal, and cultural contexts of schooling.

This applied and focused component of *The Principalship: Vision to Action* can be found in many aspects of this text.

- **Standards.** Each chapter of the book is framed with one of the ELCC Standards as it major theme.

- **Focusing questions.** Each chapter begins with six to eight focusing questions designed to draw the reader's attention to major topics within the chapter.

- **Examples.** Hundreds of examples of real school situations are sprinkled throughout the text. We believe that a well-constructed example can illuminate the most complex concept.

- **Illustrations.** Each chapter contains descriptive figures and tables to visually clarify important concepts covered in the chapter.

- **Summary.** At the end of each chapter, a brief point-by-point summary recaps critical and especially major issues of theory, research, and practice.

- **Field-based activities.** At the end of each chapter, activities for discussion are included to help stimulate application of concepts and foster greater understanding of the material.

- **Case studies.** A case from the world of practice is included at the end of each part of the book. In addition, a case for each chapter of the book is available online through the Wadsworth Cengage Learning Book Companion Website.

- **Suggested readings.** An annotated list of readings on chapter topics is provided at the end of each chapter. These are current and popular readings that principals and prospective principals will find helpful in operating and understanding the operation of schools.

- **Citations.** Our book is documented extensively throughout, so that those who wish to follow up on certain matters and obtain more detail can do so. References appear at the end of the book in American Psychological Association (APA) style. This provides the reader with a quick and easy reference to documented material cited in the book.

- **Unique coverage.** We include in our book several topics not found in many other principalship texts. These topics include school safety, special education, gifted education, bilingual education, nontraditional organizational structures, gender-inclusive theories, women and minorities in the principalship, ethics, the political and policy context, human resource management, budget development and facilities management, legal issues, and collective bargaining.

Acknowledgments

This book has been a cooperative effort between scholars of the field and experienced editors and publishers. We wish to express our appreciation to the reviewers and others whose suggestions led to improvements in this book:

Jeanette Hagelskamp, University of San Francisco

Jackson Flanigan, Clemson University

Pam Salazar, University of Nevada–Las Vegas

Keith Rose, Pennsylvania State University

Saul Grossman, Temple University

Wade Nelson, Winona State University

Frank Adams, Wayne State University

Christee Jenlink, Northeastern State University

Irwin Blumer, Boston College

Anthony Normore, Florida International University

Rayton Sianjina, Delaware State University

James Mitchell, National University

Janice Buck, Lamar University

Anthony Avina, California State University–Pomona

We also wish to thank the people at Wadsworth whose contributions made this a much better book: Vicki Knight, Publisher; Dan Alpert, Acquisitions Editor; Tangelique Williams, Development Editor; Larkin Page-Jacobs, Editorial Assistant; Kim Adams, Senior Project Manager; Terra Schultz, Marketing Manager; Tami Strang, Marketing Communications Manager; and Rebecca Weisman, Marketing Assistant.

We wish to thank Marion Czaja for conducting and writing the seven cases that appear at the end of each part of the book. We are grateful to our dean, Genevieve Brown, for creating an environment conducive to research and contributing the necessary resources to complete this book. Special thanks are also extended to Jessica Holleman and Shirley Jackson, who each typed portions of the book.

Fred C. Lunenburg
Beverly J. Irby

About the Authors

Fred C. Lunenburg is Professor and Senior Research Fellow in the Center for Research and Doctoral Studies in Educational Leadership at Sam Houston State University. He was previously Professor of Educational Leadership and Policy Studies at the University of Louisville, Distinguished Visiting Professor at the University of Utrecht, and Professor and Dean of the College of Education at Southern Utah University. Prior to moving to the university, he served as a high school principal and superintendent of schools in Minnesota and Wisconsin. He has authored or coauthored 18 books, including *Educational Administration: Concepts and Practices,* Fourth Edition (Wadsworth, 2004), and more than 150 articles in education.

Beverly J. Irby is Professor and Chair of the Department of Educational Leadership and Counseling at Sam Houston State University. Previously Director of Field Experiences, she has been a school psychologist, educational diagnostician, director of special education, elementary school principal, assistant superintendent, and superintendent of schools. She has authored or coauthored 12 books and more than 200 articles in education. In addition, she has secured grants totaling more than $25 million and often serves as a consultant to school districts. She is a member of the International Who's Who of Women and has received the Texas Council of Women School Educators' Outstanding Educator Award, the Renaissance Group Research Fellow Award, and the AERA Willystine Goodsell Award.

The Principalship

1. Cultivating Community, Culture, and Learning

FOCUSING QUESTIONS

1 How have the Educational Leadership Constituent Council (ELCC) standards changed the way in which principals are prepared, developed, and evaluated?

2 How has the role of the principal changed over time, and what is the appropriate role of the principal today?

3 How can the principal develop a professional learning community that transforms a school from a teaching organization to a learning organization?

4 How can the principal develop a positive school culture that promotes a professional learning community and the achievement of *all* students?

5 How can principals assume the role of instructional leader to ensure that school improvement efforts impact teaching and learning?

In this chapter, we respond to these questions concerning the principalship. We begin the chapter with an introduction to standards for school leaders. We discuss the ISLLC standards as the forerunner of the new ELCC standards and their impact on the preparation, development, and evaluation of today's principals. Then we review briefly the reconceptualization of the role of the principal. Next, we consider the way in which principals develop the capacity of the people within their schools to function as professional learning communities. We then examine the elements of school culture that encourage the learning of all students and the professional growth of faculty. Finally, we conclude the chapter with a discussion of the principal's role as instructional leader, the primary focus of which is to promote the learning and success of *all* students.

Introduction

Every educational reform report since *A Nation at Risk* (National Commission on Excellence in Education, 1983) has concluded that schools are only as good as their principals. The prospect of inadequately trained school principals is serious when one considers the public schools' struggle with such problems as declining test scores, gaps in performance among various student groups, drug abuse, school violence and vandalism, and at-risk youngsters. It is not surprising, therefore, that calls for reform of principal preparation programs based on standards have resounded throughout the nation.

In 1996, working in collaboration with the National Policy Board for Educational Administration (NPBEA) and using the work of personnel from 24 states and 10 professional associations, the Council of Chief State School Officers (CCSSO; 1996) published *Interstate School Leaders Licensure Consortium (ISLLC): Standards for School Leaders.* The ISLLC standards, aimed directly at building principals, are based on three underlying premises: a renewed struggle to redefine teaching and learning for all students; movement away from the established bureaucracies and hierarchies that have dominated school environments; and the increased impact and partnerships with parents, the corporate sector, and varied community agencies and groupings.

The ISLLC standards promised to have a considerable impact on the ways in which principals were prepared, developed, and evaluated. Fueled by external pressures for accountability, an increasing number of states have adapted the ISLLC standards and have used a test geared to those standards, developed by the Educational Testing Service (ETS), as a criterion for certification. ISLLC presents six standards for school principals; these standards are very similar to the National Council for the Accreditation of Teacher Education's (NCATE; 1995) *Curriculum Guidelines for School Administrators.*

In 2002, the National Policy Board for Educational Administration published the Educational Leadership Constituent Council (ELCC) *Standards for Advanced Programs in Educational Leadership,* which modified slightly the ISLLC standards' language and added a seventh standard — the Internship. More recently, in July 2004, the National Policy Board for Educational Administration (NPBEA) and the Educational Leadership Constituent Council (ELCC) merged, constituting a coalition of 10 national education organizations including the American Association of Colleges for Teacher Education (AACTE), American Association of School Administrators

(AASA), American Educational Research Association (AERA), Association for Supervision and Curriculum Development (ASCD), Council of Chief State School Officers (CCSSO), National Association of Elementary School Principals (NAESP), National Association of Secondary School Principals (NASSP), National Council for the Accreditation of Teacher Education (NCATE), National Council of Professors of Educational Administration (NCPEA), National School Boards Association (NSBA), and the University Council for Educational Administration (UCEA).

The aforementioned 10 national education organizations financially and philosophically support the NPBEA/ELCC standards-based approach to improving the development of principals, who will lead our nation's elementary and secondary schools in the future. The new ELCC Standards, adopted in 2002 and supported by the coalition of 10 national education organizations, provide a useful format for assisting principal development and are the framework of this book.

Educational Leadership Constituent Council (ELCC) Standards

The new *Standards for Advanced Programs in Educational Leadership* are stated as candidate proficiencies, because program assessment by the ELCC is based on results criteria. The ELCC standards and a brief description of each one follow:

> **Standard 1.0:** *Candidates who complete the program are educational leaders who have the knowledge and ability to promote the success of all students by facilitating the development, articulation, implementation, and stewardship of a school or district vision of learning supported by the school community.*

This standard addresses the need to prepare principals who value and are committed to educating all students to become successful adults. Each principal is responsible for creating and articulating a vision of high standards for learning within the school that can be shared by all employees and is supported by the broader school community of parents and citizens. Creating this vision requires that principals be willing to examine their own assumptions, beliefs, and practices; understand and apply research; and foster a climate of continuous improvement among all members of the educational staff. Such principals will commit themselves to high levels of personal and organizational performance in order to ensure implementation of this vision of learning.

> **Standard 2.0:** *Candidates who complete the program are educational leaders who have the knowledge and ability to promote the success of all students by promoting a positive school culture, providing an effective instructional program, applying best practice to student learning, and designing comprehensive professional growth plans for staff.*

This standard addresses the need for principals to position teaching and learning at the focal point of schools. It accepts the proposition that all students can learn and that student learning is the fundamental purpose of schools. To this end, principals are responsible for ensuring that decisions about curriculum, instructional strategies (including instructional technology), assessment, and professional development are based on sound research, best practice, school and district data, and other contextual information. They must also ensure that observation and collaboration are used to design meaningful and effective experiences that improve student achievement. Principals must capitalize on diversity to create a school culture that promotes respect and success for all students. All members of the school community should have confidence in the integrity of the decision-making process for school improvement and the appropriateness of that process, thus ensuring dignity and respect for all. Successful principals must be able to identify, clarify, and address barriers to student learning and communicate the importance of developing learning strategies for diverse populations. In addition, this standard requires that principals be learners who model and encourage lifelong learning. They should establish a culture of high expectations for themselves, their students, and their staff. Candidates preparing to be principals must be able to assess the culture and climate on a regular basis. They must also understand the importance of supervision and be able and willing to evaluate teacher and staff performance using a variety of supervisory models.

> **Standard 3.0:** *Candidates who complete the program are educational leaders who have the knowledge and ability to promote the success of all students by managing the organization, operations, and resources in a way that promotes a safe, efficient, and effective learning environment.*

This standard addresses the need to enhance student learning through effective, efficient, and equitable utilization of resources. Principals must use their knowledge of organizations to create a learning environment conducive to the success of all students. Proper allocation of resources such as personnel, facilities, and technology are essential to creating an effective learning environment. Resource management decisions should give priority to teaching, student achievement, and student development.

Also, operational procedures and policies must be established to maintain school safety and security and to strengthen the academic environment. All management decisions, including those regarding human resources, fiscal operation, facilities, legal issues, time management, scheduling, technology, and equipment, should be based on sound organizational practice. Principals must monitor and evaluate operational systems to ensure that they enhance student learning and reflect the school's accountability to the community. Skills in job analysis, supervision, recruitment, selection, professional development, and appraisal of staff positions, as well as an understanding of relevant collective bargaining agreements, strengthen the ability to use personnel resources. Effective principals define job roles, assign tasks, delegate appropriately, and require accountability. They also actively seek additional sources of financial, human, and physical support. They involve stakeholders to ensure that management and operational decisions take into consideration the needs of multiple constituencies while at the same time focusing the entire community on student achievement as the ultimate goal. To include stakeholders in management decisions, principals must be competent in conflict resolution, consensus building, group processes, and effective communication.

> **Standard 4.0:** *Candidates who complete the program are educational leaders who have the knowledge and ability to promote the success of all students by collaborating with families and other community members, responding to diverse community interests and needs, and mobilizing community resources.*

This standard addresses the fact that cooperation among schools, the district, and the larger community is essential to the success of principals and students. Principals must see schools as an integral part of the larger community. Collaboration and communication with families, businesses, governmental agencies, social service organizations, the media, and higher-education institutions are critical to effective schooling. The ability to analyze emerging issues and trends that might affect schools enables principals to plan effective instructional programs and school services. Effective and appropriate communications, coupled with the involvement of families and other stakeholders in decisions, helps to ensure continued community support for schools. Seeing families as partners in the education of their youngsters, and believing that families have the best interests of their children in mind, encourages principals to involve families in decisions at the school. Family and student issues that negatively affect student learning must be addressed through collaboration with community agencies that can integrate health, social, and other services. Such

collaboration relies on good relationships with community leaders and outreach to a wide array of business, religious, political, and service agencies. Providing leadership to programs serving all students, including those with special and exceptional needs, further communicates to internal and external audiences the importance of diversity. To work with all elements of the community, school principals must recognize, value, and communicate effectively with various cultural, ethnic, racial, and special interest groups. Modeling community collaboration for staff and then offering opportunities for staff to develop collaborative skills maximizes positive interactions between schools and the community.

> **Standard 5.0:** *Candidates who complete the program are educational leaders who have the knowledge and ability to promote the success of all students by acting with integrity, fairly, and in an ethical manner.*

This standard addresses the principal's role as the "first citizen" of the school community. Principals should set the tone for how employees and students interact with one another and with members of the school, district, and larger community. The principal's contacts with students, parents, and employees must reflect concern for others as well as for the school and the position. School principals must develop the ability to examine personal and professional values that reflect a code of ethics. They must be able to serve as role models, accepting responsibility for using their position ethically and constructively on behalf of the school community. Principals must act as advocates for all children, including those with special needs who may be underserved.

> **Standard 6.0:** *Candidates who complete the program are educational leaders who have the knowledge and ability to promote the success of all students by understanding, responding to, and influencing the larger political, social, economic, legal, and cultural context.*

This standard addresses the need for principals to understand and be able to operate within the larger context of the community and beyond, realizing that doing so affects opportunities for all students. Principals must respond to and influence this larger political, social, economic, and cultural context. Of vital importance is the ability to develop a continuing dialogue with economic and political decision makers concerning the role of schools and to build collaborative relationships that support improved social and educational opportunities for children. Principals must be able to participate actively in the political and policy-making context in the service of education, including proactive use of the legal and political systems to protect students' rights and improve their opportunities to learn.

> **Standard 7.0: *Internship.*** *The internship provides significant opportunities for candidates to synthesize and apply the knowledge and practice and develop the skills identified in Standards 1–6 through substantial, sustained, standards-based work in real settings, planned and guided cooperatively by the institution and school district personnel for graduate credit.*

This standard addresses the importance of structured, sustained, standards-based experiences in authentic settings. The internship is defined as the process and product that result from applying the knowledge and skills described in the previous standards in a workplace environment. Application of standards-based knowledge, skills, and research in real settings over time is a critical aspect of any institutional program. The provision of graduate credit allows institutions to underscore the importance of this activity. Generally, the internship experience should be a total of 6 months in length. However, the 6-month internship experience need not be consecutive, and may include experiences of different lengths. However, all internships must include an extended, capstone experience to maximize the candidates' opportunities to practice and refine their skills and knowledge. This culminating experience may be two noncon-

tiguous internships of 3 months each, a 4-month internship and two field practicums of 1 month each, or another equivalent combination. Full-time experience is defined as the number of hours per week required for attendance by a full-time student, receiving federal financial assistance (generally 9–12 hours per week).

Reframing the Role of the Principal

Despite some influential work of the effective schools research (Levine & Lezotte, 1990; National Center for Effective Schools Research and Development, 2000) and substitutes for leadership (Hovell & Dorfman, 1986; Kerr & Jermier, 1978), the principalship has historically been defined as position or role based and hierarchical in nature (Murphy, 2002; Murphy & Datnow, 2003). This means that those higher in the organizational structure are seen as more powerful than those below them and that the right to lead is limited to those provided with legitimate authority, that is, superintendent, principal, and so forth.

A New Approach to the Principalship

The type of principal needed in tomorrow's schools calls for a new approach to managing schools. The principal, faculty, staff, parents, and community work together sharing a vision of how to help all students achieve. Each school is considered a professional learning community. Management is less hierarchical (Goldring & Greenfield, 2002). Important decisions are made as much by site-level stakeholders as by state- or district-level participants. This emerging view of the principalship accounts for the centrality of organic (Weick & McDaniel, 1989) and adaptive (Louis & Kruse, 2000) models of organization and the importance of site-based management. That is, decisions about school programs are decentralized to the school level, and leadership is no longer limited to formal organizational positions. Leadership and management are based on ability rather than role (Smylie, Conley, & Marks, 2002; Crow,

Hausman, & Scribner, 2002). Leadership activities are dispersed according to competence for required tasks rather than authority. This altered view of the principalship explains the centrality of the empowerment of teachers, parents, and students; the importance of site-based decision making; and the development of professional learning communities.

Reframing the role of the principal for the future is best captured by the rubric of transformational leadership (Bass, 1985; Bass & Avolio, 1994; Burns, 1978; Leithwood, 1994). Central to this emerging view of the principalship is a movement from a "power over" approach to a "power to" approach (Brunner, 1999; Hartsock, 1987; Irby, Brown, Duffy, & Trautman, 2002). Principals are expected to be change agents and facilitators, who improve conditions for learning through the creation of cultures that allow schools to operate as professional learning communities. That is, principals are considered leaders of leaders. They are expected to bring out the leadership potential of every teacher and employee in the building and to work collaboratively with them, so that the school as a whole ends up making better decisions and is committed to continuous improvement (Lambert, 2003). Today's effective principals share leadership. They empower teachers to lead school projects and initiatives rather than serving as the chief problem solvers. They lead from the center rather than from the top, and they create an environment where teachers can continually learn and grow (Leithwood & Louis, 2000; Murphy & Datnow, 2003; Sarason, 2004; Senge, 2001).

Leading from the center, teacher empowerment, site-based decision making, and professional learning communities then are at the very core of a redefinition of the role of today's principal. In the more successful schools, today's principals clearly defined themselves as at the center of the school's staff rather than at the top. Instead of occupying an authoritative position, they preferred instead to give leadership to others and to guide by example and by indirectly inducing thoughtfulness, rather than by making direct suggestions. In each instance, their role as an authority figure was downplayed

and their role as a source of support and assistance was emphasized. These emergent principals believed in delegation; in developing collaborative decision-making processes; and in stepping back from being the chief problem solver in a school, by linking these roles more explicitly to the development of a professional learning community (Louis & Kruse, 2000).

Creating a Professional Learning Community

Since their inception, schools have continually sought to improve, whether in response to demands from teachers, administrators, parents, policymakers, or legislators. When we look at the research on improving schools over a long period and examine what were the keys to school improvement, invariably it boils down to the ability of people within that school to function as a professional learning community (DuFour & Eaker, 1998; Hord, 2003; Huffman & Hipp, 2003; Martin-Kniep, 2003; Norris, Barnett, Basom, & Yerkes, 2002; Roberts & Pruitt, 2003; Senge, 1990, 2001; Wald & Castleberry, 2000; Walsh & Sattes, 2000).

The principal is the key player in creating a professional learning community. A professional learning community shares a vision. They share a common understanding of how to go about getting to that vision, and they share a common commitment to a vision. When you walk into a professional learning community, you have a sense that people understand what is important, what the priorities are; and they are working together in a collaborative way to advance the school toward those goals and priorities. For example, you can walk around the building on any given day and see teachers talking to one another, discussing curriculum goals, discussing what activities they are going to engage in that day. There is an attitude of cooperation. There is never fear of asking for help. It is obvious that the support felt by participants working in a professional learning community is systemic (Senge, 1990, 2001). The ability to explore — to ask questions, ask peers, ask supervisors — is possible only when it comes from the top.

The whole philosophy of a professional learning community is people working together. Each member of the professional learning community wants to help the other succeed in daily interactions between staff and school principals. Members work together to achieve the goals they have for themselves — what they want to become. All stakeholders — board of education, superintendent, faculty, support staff — move together to achieve that shared vision. Teachers are empowered to do what is best for their students. Involving others in decision-making processes and empowering them to act on their ideas are two of the most significant and effective strategies used by capable leaders (Glickman, 2002; Kouzes & Posner, 2002; Lambert, 2003; Sergiovanni, 2000).

The principal plays a vital role in the creation of a professional learning community. The principal begins by bringing people together to engage in a four-step process: (1) creating a mission statement, (2) developing a vision, (3) developing value statements, and (4) establishing goals (DuFour & Eaker, 1998). Each step will be discussed in turn.

Creating a Mission Statement

The first step is to create a mission statement that identifies the school's purpose. The first question the faculty needs to consider is: What is our mission, our fundamental purpose? For example, the school's purpose may be to identify proven strategies to teach children how to learn. That phrase captures something people can hold in their minds and hearts as they perform their duties. It begins to influence the day-to-day teaching and learning that take place in the school.

To make the mission statement relevant, the principal must engage the faculty in a deeper discussion; for example, why do we exist? Typically, the response will be that we exist to help all students learn. For example, successful professional learning communities believe that all students can learn. That statement becomes meaningful only if

faculty are willing to engage in some deeper questions. For example, if we believe that all students can learn, we expect them to learn. How will faculty respond when students do not learn?

Other deeper questions that faculty must engage in to create a mission statement include the following: What does it mean to help students learn how to learn? That goes beyond reading and mathematics to how students organize their time and their materials. How do they work together? A professional learning community involves all stakeholders working together, including students. What kinds of skills do students have for working together? What kinds of skills do they have for understanding themselves, their own learning style, and being able to evaluate themselves? How good are they in applying their learning to other contexts in the school and outside? And how do students use technology and other resources in order to learn on their own (Adams et al., 2004; Lockard et al., 2004; Shelley et al., 2004; Torr, 2004)?

Developing a Vision

After clarifying the school's mission, the principal and faculty's next step in creating a professional learning community is to develop a vision. (Creating a vision for learning is addressed in greater detail in Chapter 2.) A vision is an attempt to describe the school that faculty members are hoping to create. It's a picture of what this place is about: what the school looks like; how the pieces fit together; and how the people fit in where the school is trying to go — not just where it is now; not just a particular goal for the future but sort of here's how the school looks now. Here are the people; here are the systems; here are the students; here are the community issues; here is the budget. Now where does the faculty want all of this to come out five years from now?

In an exemplary school, students (a) accept responsibility for their learning, decisions, and actions; (b) develop skills to become more self-directed learners as they progress through the grades; and (c) actively engage in and give effort to academic and extracurricular pursuits (DuFour & Eaker, 1998; Lunenburg & Ornstein, 2004).

Here are some tips for developing a vision for your school that professional learning community advocates recommend. Engage the faculty in a general agreement about what they hope their school will become. Enlist a faculty task force to identify the major findings of research studies on school improvement. Share the research findings with the faculty. Conduct small-group discussion sessions that enable the faculty to review the research and discuss their hopes for the future of the school. Discussions should also include criticisms of the traditional structure and culture of schools (DuFour & Eaker, 1998; Hord, 2003; Huffman & Hipp, 2003; Martin-Kniep, 2003; Norris et al., 2002; Roberts & Pruitt, 2003; Senge, 1990, 2001; Wald & Castleberry, 2000; Walsh & Sattes, 2000).

A traditional obstacle to schools moving forward is the inherent tradition of teacher isolation in schools (Elmore, 2000; Leithwood & Louis, 2000; Sarason, 2004; Senge, 2001). This must be addressed and overcome in order for a school to become a professional learning community. At all levels of the system, isolation is seen as the enemy of school improvement. Thus, most day-to-day activities in the school need to be specifically designed to connect teachers, principals, and district administrators with one another and with outside experts in regard to school improvement. Another tradition is that schools are very often run as top-down hierarchies, where faculty are not given a voice in decision making (Murphy, 2002; Murphy & Datnow, 2003). Faculty need to address these structural and cultural traditions in schools that present obstacles and barriers to substantive improvements.

Using this formula, gradually the faculty should be able to identify commonalities, a school all stakeholders can endorse. With the vision statement, with the ability to describe the school all participants are trying to create, the principal then needs to work with students, teachers, parents, and others to discover or invent the structures, policies, and processes that will enable the school to move in that direction (Sharp & Walter, 2003).

It should be noted that although the principal remains a valued participant in the development of a vision, "vision is embodied by the process rather than by individuals" (Goldman, Dunlap, & Conley, 1991, p. 9). Principals must help to keep their colleagues from narrowing their vision and assist the school to maintain "a broader perspective" (Conley, 1991, p. 39). Excellence is a moving target; therefore, the vision should be revisited periodically to ensure that the vision remains relevant. Principals, in a sense, are keepers of the vision. The principal's modeling and reinforcing of vision-related behaviors appear critical to the success of the professional learning community (Leithwood, 1994; Leithwood, Aitken, & Jantzi, 2001).

Developing Value Statements

The next stage in the process is to develop value statements. At this point, the members of another faculty task force might begin working with their colleagues to identify shared values — the attitudes, behaviors, and commitments — all teachers would pledge to demonstrate so as to move the school closer to their shared vision. The board of education, support staff, administrative team, students, parents, and community members also engage in discussions of the attitudes, behaviors, and commitments the school needs from them to advance the vision. For example, what attitudes, behaviors, and commitments must the board of education make to enable the school to achieve the vision statement? What attitudes, behaviors, and commitments must the parents make to become contributors in creating the school described in the vision statement? The process continues until all stakeholders are addressed.

DuFour and Eaker (1998) recommend a process for developing shared value statements. Each group begins by examining the vision statement and identifying what each group must do to bring it into existence. For example, what can the board of education, the superintendent, the principal, the teachers, the parents, and the students do to advance the school toward the vision statement?

Each group works in two teams of five. When all the ideas are listed, the five members review each idea. The ideas are shared between the two teams in each group. All ideas generated by each group are then broken down into four, five, or six general themes or categories. The groups do not need to have hundreds of value statements. A handful of value statements is most effective. Throughout this process, it is more powerful to articulate behaviors than beliefs. It is more important for each group to articulate what its members are prepared to do than to state what they believe.

The challenge for each group as it goes through the process is to get the members to understand the need to focus on themselves. They must ask, "What attitudes, behaviors, and commitments are we individually prepared to make in order to move this school forward?" After every group engages in this discussion, each one articulates the commitments it is prepared to make. At this point, the school has reached its first important milestone in the improvement process. Then a school can become more specific about where it goes from there.

Establishing Goals

To achieve the school's vision, school stakeholders must establish goals based on the adopted value statements. Goals are the results that a school tries to achieve (Locke & Latham, 1995). This definition implies at least three relationships between goals and the principal. First, in terms of laying a foundation for a professional learning community, goals represent the implementation phase of school improvement. The determination of school goals is a primary responsibility of principals. In a professional learning community, faculty are active and valued participants in establishing goals with the principal and other stakeholders. Goals become guideposts in defining standards of school improvement efforts. Without clearly stated goals, there is no way to determine if acceptable standards of school improvement have been met (Lunenburg & Irby, 1999; Lunenburg & Ornstein, 2004).

Second, goals are influenced by the aspirations of a school district's key administrators. For example, the goal of a school to be connected to the Internet; to have a computer lab in every school; to have computers in every classroom; and to provide professional development for faculty assumes that the district has or can obtain adequate resources to achieve the goal and that the school district's top administrators desire the goal. This is more likely to happen in a professional learning community, because all stakeholders were involved in developing a mission statement, vision, values, and goals.

Third, goals reflect a desired end result of school actions—what they wish to accomplish. It is important when formulating goals not to confuse means with ends. A powerful goal, and an appropriate one for school improvement, would be as specified here: "Every student in the school will be reading at grade level by third grade." It is direct. It is stating exactly what you want to accomplish. It is measurable. It is an end. It should be noted that because the vision statement is rather broad and tends to point to many different areas in the school, the principal and faculty are not going to be able to attack every area at once. They must make some decisions about which areas will take priority.

The focus may need to be narrowed, and goals help us narrow focus. Principals can provide a faculty with parameters for identifying goals that directly impact teaching and learning. And learning has to be the focus. Reading, writing, mathematics, and helping students learn how to learn are worthy goals. The next step is to plan activities and monitor progress on the stated goals.

Establishing explicit goals benefits all stakeholders by fostering commitment, providing performance standards and targets, and enhancing motivation (Drucker, 2004). Each of these benefits will be discussed in turn.

Commitment. Goal statements describe the school's purpose to participants. The process of getting participants to agree to pursue a specific goal gives those individuals a personal stake in the outcome. Thus, goals are helpful in encouraging personal commitment to collective ends.

Standards. Because goals define desired outcomes for the school, they also serve as performance criteria. When appraising performance, principals need goals as an established standard against which they can measure performance. Clearly defined goals enable principals to weigh performance objectively on the basis of accomplishment rather than subjectively on the basis of personality. For example, if a school wishes to increase test scores by 10% and the actual increase is 20%, the principal and faculty have exceeded the prescribed standard.

Targets. School goals provide principals with specific targets and direct collegial efforts toward given outcomes. People tend to pursue their own ends in the absence of formal organizational goals.

Motivation. In addition to serving as targets, standards, and commitment, goals perform a role in encouraging colleagues to perform at their highest levels. Moreover, goals give principals a rational basis for rewarding performance. If colleagues receive rewards equal to their levels of performance, they should continue to exert high levels of effort (Vroom, 1994).

To make the school's mission, vision, values, and goals something more than words on paper, the principal needs to communicate and model them so that they are embedded in the daily life of the school. The principal is the keeper of the vision and the one who keeps articulating it; when people are at the point where they say they can't go anymore, the principal is the one who comes out and says, "Let me remind you why we can do it." It is the principal's role to repeat such messages, over and over. It is his or her role to remind people: This is where we started; this is where we are now; and this is where we're headed. The principal does this in a variety of ways — writing about it in the weekly newsletter, talking about it at Parent-Teacher Organizations and faculty meetings — to show the school community that this is the way we do business in this school.

Communication is important, but it's not enough. The thing that is necessary is the day-to-day work. It means when a principal sits down with a faculty member to talk about a lesson observed, she may bring up the mission and how the lesson connects to that mission. The principal may bring up the mission when the budget is discussed with faculty. When the principal is hiring faculty or making faculty changes, or if the principal is engaged in curriculum changes or implementing new courses, she is always using the vision as the filter. When the principal is doing that, the people involved in a professional learning community — students, parents, faculty, district office administrators — can see, through the principal's behavior and actions, that what is most important is this mission. Thus the principal, as a change agent, helps to create new programs and procedures that evolve from the shared vision and goals (DuFour & Eaker, 1998; Hord, 2003; Huffman & Hipp, 2003; Martin-Kniep, 2003; Norris et al., 2002; Senge, 1990, 2001; Wald & Castleberry, 2000; Walsh & Sattes, 2000).

Developing a Culture: Learning for All

Regardless of population size or location, wherever people spend a considerable amount of time together, a culture emerges — a set of customs, beliefs, values, and norms — that can either create a sense of mutual purpose — mission, vision, values, goals — or perpetuate discord that precludes even the possibility of any unity or shared meaning. Every school has a culture, whether it is being attended to or not (Barth, 2003; Deal & Peterson, 2003).

Definition and Characteristics

Culture consists of all the beliefs, feelings, behaviors, and symbols that are characteristic of an organization. More specifically, culture is defined as shared philosophies, ideologies, beliefs, feelings, assumptions, expectations, attitudes, norms, and values (Alvesson, 2002). Although there is considerable variation in the definitions of school culture, it appears that most contain the following characteristics.

Observed Behavioral Regularities. When organizational members interact, they use common language, terminology, and rituals and ceremonies related to deference and demeanor.

Norms. Standards of behavior evolve in work groups, such as "a fair day's work for a fair day's pay," or "going beyond the call of duty." The impact of work-group behavior, sanctioned by group norms, results in standards and yardsticks.

Dominant Values. An organization espouses and expects its members to share major values. Typical examples in schools are high performance levels of faculty and students, low absence and dropout rates, and high efficiency and effectiveness.

Philosophy. Policies guide an organization's beliefs about how employees and clients are to be treated. For example, most school districts and schools have statements of philosophy or mission statements.

Rules. Guidelines exist for getting along in the organization, or the "ropes" that a newcomer must learn in order to become an accepted member.

Feelings. This characteristic applies to an overall atmosphere conveyed in an organization by the physical layout as well as the way in which members interact with clients or other outsiders (Schein, 1996).

None of the aforementioned characteristics by itself represents the essence of culture. However, the characteristics taken collectively reflect and give meaning to the concept of culture. And the culture of a school is interrelated with most other concepts in managing schools, including organizational structures, motivation, leadership, decision making, communication, and change. The challenge for the principal is to create a culture that is advancing the school toward its vision and reinforcing the behaviors that are necessary for moving the school forward. The principal as developer of culture is to be a support and visionary.

In a professional learning community, principals work with all stakeholders to develop the school's culture. Developing culture is a conscious endeavor, and principals must be proactive in doing so. They begin by having people articulate in specific terms the kinds of behaviors and commitments they think are necessary to move their school forward. This is a challenge, for every school faces the issue of developing school culture. In developing a culture for school improvement, the principal can pose the following questions: What is the school trying to become? What is our vision of the school we are trying to create? What attitudes, behaviors, and commitments must we demonstrate for our vision to be realized? What goals should we establish to move closer to the school we desire? Are we clear on what is to be accomplished and the criteria we will use in assessing our efforts? Are the current policies, programs, procedures, and practices of our school congruent with our stated vision and values? What are our plans to reduce discrepancies (DuFour & Eaker, 1998; Hord, 2003; Huffman & Hipp, 2003; Martin-Kniep, 2003; Norris et al., 2002; Roberts & Pruitt, 2003; Senge, 1990, 2001; Wald & Castleberry, 2000; Walsh & Sattes, 2000)?

Heroes, Traditions, and Networks

The process of developing school cultures is complex. Heroes and heroines, traditions and rituals, and cultural networks play key roles in developing school cultures (Deal & Kennedy, 1984; Deal & Peterson, 2003). Each role will be discussed in turn.

Heroes and Heroines   Most successful organizations have their heroes and heroines. Heroes and heroines are born and created. The born hero or heroine is the visionary institution builder like Henry Ford, founder of Ford Motor Company, and Mary Kay Ash, founder of Mary Kay Cosmetics. Created heroes and heroines, on the other hand, are those the institution has made by noticing and celebrating memorable moments occurring in the organization's day-to-day situational life. Thomas Watson, head of IBM, is an example of a situation hero. Other well-known heroes include Lee Iacocca at Chrysler,

Sam Walton at Wal-Mart, and Vince Lombardi, the legendary coach of the Green Bay Packers. Heroes and heroines perpetuate the organization's underlying values, provide role models, symbolize the organization to others, and set performance standards that motivate participant achievement.

In many schools, local heroes and heroines, exemplars of core values, provide models of what everyone should be striving for. These deeply committed staff come in early; they are always willing to meet with students and parents; and they are constantly upgrading their skills (Barth, 2003; Deal & Peterson, 2003; Sergiovanni, 2000).

Traditions and Rituals   Another key aspect in creating organizational cultures involves the everyday activities and celebrations that characterize the organization. Most successful organizations feel that these rituals and symbolic actions should be managed. Through traditions and rituals, recognition of achievement is possible (Barth, 2003; Deal & Peterson, 2003). The Teacher of the Year Award and National Merit Schools are examples. Similarly, a number of ceremonial rituals may accompany the appointment of a new superintendent of schools or building principal, including press and other announcements, banquets, meetings, and speeches.

Some schools have even created their own reward rituals. At Hollibrook Elementary School in Spring Branch, Texas, traditions and rituals reinforce students' learning. Under the leadership of former principal Suzanne Still and her faculty, and supported through ties to the Accelerated Schools Model, the school developed numerous traditions to create a powerful professional culture and foster increased student success (Hopfenberg, 1995). For example, faculty meetings became a hotbed of professional dialogues and discussion of practice and published research. "Fabulous Friday" was created to provide students with a wide assortment of courses and activities. A "Parent University" furnished courses and material while building trust between the school and the largely Hispanic community. Norms of collegiality, improvement, and connection

reinforce and symbolize what the school is about (Barth, 2003; Deal & Peterson, 2003).

Cultural Networks   Stories or myths of heroes are transmitted by means of the communications network. This network is characterized by various individuals, who play a role in the culture of the school. Each school has *storytellers* who interpret what is going on in the organization. Their interpretation of the information influences the perceptions of others. *Priests* are the worriers of the school and the guardians of the culture's values. These individuals always have time to listen and provide alternative solutions to problems. *Whisperers* are the powers behind the throne because they have the boss's ear. Anyone who wants something done will go to the whisperer. *Gossips* carry the trivial day-to-day activities of the school through the communications network. Gossips are important in building and maintaining heroes. They embellish the heroes' past feats and exaggerate their latest accomplishments. And, finally, *spies* are buddies in the woodwork. They keep everyone well informed about what is going on in the school. Each of these individuals plays a key role in building and maintaining a school's culture. It should be noted that the role names used here are those ascribed by Deal and Kennedy (1984) to emphasize the importance of communication networks in creating an institution's organizational culture.

Maintaining School Culture

Once a school's culture is created, a number of mechanisms help solidify the acceptance of the values and ensure that the culture is maintained or reinforced (organizational socialization). These mechanisms are described in the following steps for socializing employees (Pascale, 1985).

Step 1: *Hiring Staff.* The socialization process starts with the careful selection of employees. Trained recruiters use standardized procedures and focus on values that are important in the culture. Those candidates whose personal values do not fit with the underlying values of the school are given ample opportunity to opt out (deselect).

Step 2: *Orientation.* After the chosen candidate is hired, considerable training ensues to expose the person to the culture. Many forms of orientation are also provided to incoming students to a school, for example, transitions from elementary school to middle school and transitions from middle school to high school.

Step 3: *Job Mastery.* Whereas step 2 is intended to foster cultural learning, step 3 is designed to develop the employee's technological knowledge. As employees move along a career path, the organization assesses their performance and assigns other responsibilities on the basis of their progress. Frequently, schools establish a step-by-step approach to this career plan. For example, the Holmes Group recommends a three-step career ladder for teachers: (1) instructors, (2) professional teachers, and (3) career professionals (Holmes Group, 1986). The Carnegie Task Force on Teaching as a Profession proposes another approach consisting of four steps: (1) licensed teachers, (2) certified teachers, (3) advanced certified teachers, and (4) lead teachers (Carnegie Task Force, 1986).

Step 4: *Reward and Control Systems.* The school pays meticulous attention to measuring results and to rewarding individual performance. Reward systems are comprehensive, consistent, and focus on those aspects of the school that are tied to success and the values of the culture. For example, a school will specify the factors that are considered important for success. Operational measures are used to assess these factors, and performance appraisals of employees are tied to the accomplishment of these factors. Promotion and merit pay are determined by success on each of the predetermined critical factors. For example, teachers who do not fit the school's culture are either transferred to another school or dismissed. It should be noted that collective bargaining agreements may stipulate procedures for teacher transfer or grounds for dismissal (American Arbitration Association, 2004; Korney et al., 2000; Sharp, 2003).

Step 5: *Adherence to Values.* As personnel continue to work for the school, their behavior closely matches the underlying values of the culture. Identification with underlying values helps employees reconcile personal sacrifices caused by their membership in the school. Personnel learn to accept the school's values and place their trust in the school not to hurt them. For instance, teachers work long hours on a multiplicity of fragmented tasks, for which they sometimes receive little recognition from their superiors, subordinates, and community. They sometimes endure ineffective school board members and supervisors and job assignments that are undesirable and inconvenient. Identification with the common values of the school allows these teachers to justify such personal sacrifices.

Step 6: *Reinforcing Folklore.* Throughout the socialization process, the school exposes its members to rites and rituals, stories or myths, and heroes that portray and reinforce the culture. For example, in one educational institution, the story is told of a principal who was fired because of his harsh handling of teachers. The principal had incorrectly believed a myth that being "tough" with his teachers would enhance his image in the eyes of his superiors. The school district deemed such leadership behavior to be inconsistent with its school district philosophy of cultivating good interpersonal relationships and high levels of morale and job satisfaction among all its employees.

Step 7: *Consistent Role Models.* Those individuals who have performed well in the school serve as role models to newcomers to the school. By identifying these teachers as symbolizing success, the school encourages others to do likewise. Role models in strong-culture schools can be thought of as one type of ongoing staff development for all teachers.

As developers of culture, principals ensure that their school's culture reflects its vision and values. They do this by engaging all members of the professional learning community. Together they reflect on what they value and envision and how they will act to support those values. They regularly audit their culture. They orient new staff and incoming students. They recognize heroes and heroines, share stories, and celebrate people whose contributions reinforce their culture. Teachers can do many things to help facilitate the culture of a building; but if you don't have that leader, if you don't have that person (the principal) who is willing to absorb and buy into the culture and climate to make a difference, then you are not going to have a very positive culture.

Every school has a culture whether it is being attended to or not. If a school does nothing to develop a culture, it will create itself. Students will create it. Faculty will create it. Students will create their little piece of the climate. Teachers will create their little piece of the climate. Support staff will create their little piece of the climate. Ultimately, there will be a school culture. Will everyone be moving in the same direction with that culture? Will all stakeholders share the same mission, vision, values, and goals? Not very likely.

In a professional learning community, principals work with all stakeholders to develop the school's culture. Culture is a conscious endeavor, and principals must be proactive as they go about creating a culture that is advancing the school toward its vision and reinforcing the behaviors necessary for moving the school forward. Throughout the development of a school culture, student achievement must be paramount. A school should be a place where students come to learn (Danielson, 2002; Duffy, 2003, 2004; Langer, Colton, & Goff, 2003). Principals can make that happen by functioning as instructional leaders while guiding the development of their school's culture.

The Principal as Instructional Leader

Demands for greater accountability, especially appeals for the use of more outcome-based measures, require the principal to be instruction oriented. Are the students learning? If the students are not learning, what are we going to do about it? The focus on results, the focus on student achievement, the focus on students learning at

high levels can happen only if teaching and learning become the central focus of the school and the central focus of the principal (Blase & Blase, 2003; Castallo, 2001; Lambert, 2003).

How can principals help teachers to clarify instructional goals and work collaboratively to improve teaching and learning to meet those goals? Principals need to help teachers shift their focus from what they are teaching to what students are learning. We cannot continue to accept the teachers' premise that I taught it; they just didn't learn it. The role of instructional leader helps the school to maintain a focus on why the school exists, and that is to help all students learn (Glickman, 2002; Scheurich & Skrla, 2003).

Shifting the focus of instruction from teaching to learning, forming collaborative structures and processes for faculty to work together to improve instruction, and ensuring that professional development is ongoing and focused toward school goals are among the key tasks that principals must perform to be effective instructional leaders in a professional learning community (Hawley & Rollie, 2002; Joyce & Showers, 2002; Murphy & Lick, 2001; Speck & Knipe, 2001). This effort will require districtwide leadership, focused directly on learning. School principals can accomplish this goal by (1) focusing on learning, (2) encouraging collaboration, (3) analyzing results, (4) providing support, and (5) aligning curriculum, instruction, and assessment. Taken together, these five dimensions provide a compelling framework for accomplishing sustained districtwide success for all children (Lunenburg, 2003).

Focusing on Learning

Principals can help shift the focus from teaching to learning if they insist that certain critical questions are being considered in that school, and principals are in a key position to pose those questions. What do we want our students to know and be able to do? The focus in a professional learning community is not: Are you teaching? but: Are the students learning? How will you know if the students are learning? And that question points to student progress. How will we respond when students do not learn? What criteria will we use to evaluate student progress? How can we more effectively use the time and resources available to help students learn? How can we engage parents in helping our students learn? Have we established systematic collaboration as the norm in our school?

Encouraging Collaboration

A key task for principals is to create a collective expectation among teachers concerning student performance. That is, principals need to raise the collective sense of teachers about student learning. Then principals must work to ensure that teacher expectations are aligned with the school's instructional goals (Glickman, 2002; Lunenburg, 2002, 2003). Furthermore, principals need to eliminate teacher isolation so that discussions about student learning become a collective mission of the school (Elmore, 2000; Sarason, 2004; Senge, 2001).

Principals must develop and sustain school structures and cultures that foster individual and group learning. That is, principals must stimulate an environment in which new information and practices are eagerly incorporated into the system. Teachers are more likely to pursue their group and individual learning when the school provides supportive conditions, such as particularly effective leadership (Leithwood, 1994; Leithwood & Louis, 2000). Schools where teachers collaborate in discussing issues related to student learning are more likely to be able to take advantage of internally and externally generated information. Teachers can become willing recipients of research information if they are embedded in a setting where meaningful and sustained interaction with researchers occurs in an egalitarian context (Huberman, 1993).

One popular collaboration structure is teacher teams. Schools are recognizing that teachers should be working together in teams as opposed to working individually in isolation in their classrooms. High-performing teams will accomplish

four different things: (1) They will clarify exactly what students should know and be able to do as a result of each unit of instruction. We know that if teachers are clear on the intended results of instruction, they will be more effective (Cotton, 2003; Marzano, Pickering, & Pollock, 2001). (2) They will then design curriculum and share instructional strategies to achieve those outcomes. (3) They will develop valid assessment strategies that measure how well students are performing. (4) Then they will analyze those results and work together to come up with new ideas for improving those results. Regular assessment and analysis of student learning are key parts of the team's process.

Analyzing Results

How can schools gauge their progress in achieving student learning? Three factors can increase a school's progress in achieving learning for all students (Sclafani, 2001). The primary factor is the availability of performance data connected to each student. Performance data need to be broken down by specific objectives and target levels in the school curriculum. Then the school is able to connect what is taught to what is learned. The curriculum goals should be clear enough to specify what each teacher should teach. And an assessment measure, aligned with the curriculum, will indicate what students have learned (English & Steffy, 2001). Also, teachers need access to longitudinal data on each student in their classroom. With such data, teachers are able to develop individual and small-group education plans to ensure mastery of areas of weakness from previous years while also moving students forward in the school curriculum.

The second factor is the public nature of the assessment system. Annually, the school district should publish a matrix of schools and honor those schools that have performed at high levels. This activity provides role models for other schools to emulate. At the school and classroom levels, it provides a blueprint of those areas where teachers should focus their individual education plans (IEPs) and where grade levels or schools should focus the school's professional development plans. The public nature of the data from the accountability system makes clear where schools are. Data should be disaggregated by race/ethnicity, socioeconomic status, English language proficiency, and disability. Performance of each subgroup of students on assessment measures makes the school community aware of which students are well served and which students are not well served by the school's curriculum and instruction.

The third factor in gauging progress toward achieving student learning is the specifically targeted assistance provided to schools that are performing at low levels. Before the advent of accountability systems, it was not evident which schools and students needed help. The first step is to target the schools in need of help based on student performance data. Each targeted school is paired with a team of principals, curriculum specialists/instructional coaches, and researchers to observe current practices, discuss student performance data with staff, and assist in the development and implementation of an improvement plan. The targeted schools learn how to align their program of professional development with the weaknesses identified by the data. They learn how to develop an improvement plan to guide their activities and monitor the outcomes of the activities, all of which are designed to raise student performance levels (Lunenburg & Ornstein, 2004).

Next, once a team of teachers has worked together and identified students who are having difficulty, the school faces the challenge of how the teachers are going to respond to the students who are not learning (Williams, 2003). The challenge is not simply reteaching in the same way that the teachers taught before, but in providing support for teachers to expand their repertoire of skills and providing support and time for students to get additional assistance they need in order to master those skills (Tomlinson, 2003). When students are not learning, principals must ensure not only that professional development programs are in place to give additional support to teachers but

also that intervention strategies are in place to give additional support to students (Glickman, 2002; Joyce & Showers, 2002).

Providing Support

Teachers need to be provided with the training, teaching tools, and support they need to help all students reach high performance levels. Specifically, teachers need access to curriculum guides, textbooks, or specific training connected to the school curriculum. They need access to lessons or teaching units that match curriculum goals. They need training on using assessment results to diagnose learning gaps (Lunenburg & Irby, 1999). Teachers must know how each student performed on every multiple-choice item and other questions on the assessment measure. And training must be in the teachers' subject areas. Only then can teachers be prepared to help students achieve at high levels.

In addition to professional development for teachers, all schools need an intervention and support system for students who lag behind in learning the curriculum (Williams, 2003). Schools need to provide additional help—either in school, after school, on weekends, or during the summer—to students who lag behind in core subjects. Boards of education and school superintendents need to supply the financial resources to fulfill this mandate. This involves acquiring materials, information, or technology; manipulating schedules or release time to create opportunities for teachers to learn; facilitating professional networks; and creating an environment that supports school improvement efforts (Lunenburg & Ornstein, 2004).

A focus on student learning usually means changes in curriculum, instruction, and assessment—that is, changes in teaching. The history of school reform indicates that innovations in teaching and learning seldom penetrate more than a few schools and seldom endure when they do (Cuban & Usdan, 2003; Elmore, 2000; Fink, 2000). Innovations frequently fail because the individuals who make it happen—those closest to the firing line, the classroom teachers—may not be committed to the effort or may not have the skills to grapple with the basic challenge being posed (Fullan, 2001). Principals need to ensure that teachers have the skills to help all students perform at high levels (Glickman, 2002).

Aligning Curriculum, Instruction, and Assessment

Principals need to ensure that assessment of student learning is aligned with both the school's curriculum and the teachers' instruction (Carr & Harris, 2001; English & Steffy, 2001). When they are well constructed and implemented, assessments can change the nature of teaching and learning. They can lead to a richer, more challenging curriculum; foster discussion and collaboration among teachers within and across schools; create more productive conversations among teachers and parents; and focus stakeholders' attention on increasing student achievement (Lunenburg & Ornstein, 2004).

For curriculum goals to have an impact on what happens in classrooms, they must be clear. When school districts, administrators, and students are held accountable for results, more specificity is needed in implementing the curriculum (Wiles & Bondi, 2002). In a high-stakes accountability environment, teachers require that the curriculum contain enough detail and precision to allow them to know what the students need to learn (Hoy & Hoy, 2003).

Professional learning communities attempt to align their assessment measures with their curriculum. Lunenburg and Ornstein (2004) encourage schools to consider three principles in this endeavor. First, assessments not based on the curriculum are neither fair nor helpful to parents or students. Schools that have developed their own assessment measures have done a good job of ensuring that the content of the assessment can be found in the curriculum. That is, children will not be assessed on knowledge and skills they have not been taught. This is what Fenwick English and Betty Steffy (2001) refer to as "the doctrine of no surprises." However, the same is not true when schools use generic, off-the-shelf standardized

tests. Such tests cannot measure the breadth and depth of the school's curriculum. Second, when the curriculum is rich and rigorous, the assessments must be as well. Assessments must tap both the breadth and depth of the content and skills in the curriculum. Third, assessments must become more challenging in each successive grade. The solid foundation of knowledge and skills developed in the early grades should evolve into more complex skills in the later grades.

If one accepts the premise that assessment drives curriculum and instruction, perhaps the easiest way to improve instruction and increase student achievement is to construct better assessments (Popham, 2003; Yeh, 2001). According to Yeh (2001), it is possible to design force-choice items (multiple-choice items) that test reasoning and critical thinking. Such assessments could require students to *use* facts, rather than *recall* them. And questions could elicit content knowledge that is worth learning.

To prepare students to think critically, teachers could teach children to identify what is significant (Strong, Silver, & Perini, 2001). Teachers could model the critical thinking process in the classroom, during instruction, through assignments, in preparing for assessments, and in the content of the assessment itself. By aligning content with worthwhile questions in core subject areas, it may be possible to rescue assessment and instruction from the current focus on the recall of trivial factual knowledge. Assessment items could be created for a range of subjects and levels of difficulty. Then there would be little incentive for teachers to drill students on factual knowledge.

Summary

1. Adherence to the Standards for Advanced Programs in Educational Leadership developed by the Educational Leadership Constituent Council (ELCC) can foster the organizational dynamics and the context of shared values that promote the learning and success of all students.

2. The role of the principal has changed over time from a hierarchical, bureaucratic image to one of devolved decision making and school self-determination.

3. Principals foster a school's improvement, enhance its overall effectiveness, and promote student learning and success by developing the capacity of staff to function as a professional learning community.

4. Developing and maintaining a positive school culture cultivates a professional learning community, the learning and success of all students, and the professional growth of faculty.

5. The instructional leadership of the principal is a critical factor in the success of a school's improvement initiatives and the overall effectiveness of the school. The principal's primary responsibility is to promote the learning and success of *all* students.

Field-Based Activities

1. Get a copy of your school district's District Improvement Plan (DIP) or strategic plan. Examine the content of the DIP as to (a) content, including vision, mission, values, and goals; and (b) participation of stakeholders in development of the DIP, including administrators, teachers, students, parents, and community. Discuss your findings.

2. Get a copy of your school's Campus Improvement Plan (CIP). Examine the CIP as to (a) content, including vision, mission, values, and goals; (b) participation of stakeholders in development of the CIP, including principals, teachers, staff, students, parents; and (c) whether the CIP content is based on the DIP. Discuss your findings.

3. Interview a school board member, a district administrator, your building principal, a teacher in your school, and the president of the Student Association to determine each person's perception of the culture that exists in your school district and in your school. Note

any similarities and differences between your school district's culture and your individual school's culture. Discuss the implications of these findings.

Suggested Readings

Barth, R. S. (2003). *Lessons learned: Shaping relationships and the culture of the workplace.* Thousand Oaks, CA: Corwin Press. Barth's seemingly simple stories of interactions among colleagues and companions provide rich, humorous, and often poignant insights into the subtlety and complexity of human relationships that shape teams and leaders. The resulting "rules" provide a practical and delightfully conversational guide to cultivating and fortifying working relationships.

Blase, J., & Blase, J. (2003). *Handbook of instructional leadership: How successful principals promote teaching and learning* (2nd ed.). Thousand Oaks, CA: Corwin Press. Successful instructional leaders inspire their staff to develop "professional learning communities" dedicated to effective teaching practices. Time-tested practices of instructional leadership are central features of the text. Principals can use these keys to success to build teachers' trust through continual communication, encourage teachers to continue their self-improvement efforts, motivate teachers with constructive feedback, promote and participate in reflective practices, and support and encourage teachers' professional development.

Deal, T. E., & Peterson, K. D. (2003). *Shaping school culture: The heart of leadership.* San Francisco: Jossey-Bass. Deal and Peterson discuss how a principal can harness the power of school culture to build a lively, cooperative spirit and a sense of school identity. The reader will gain insight into the critical elements of culture and how a positive culture can make school reforms work.

Hord, S. M. (2003). *Learning together, leading together: Changing schools through professional learning communities*. New York: Teachers College Press. Increasingly, the education world is recognizing that the development of professional learning communities is an effective means for improving schools without increasing the budget or adding new programs. This volume offers practical advice gathered from 22 schools (elementary, middle, and high schools) that have successfully modeled or are creating professional learning communities. This authoritative volume clearly defines the professional learning community — what it looks like and how it operates; identifies the benefits that accrue to staff and students; outlines the strategies required to launch, develop, and sustain a community of professional learners that will promote student learning; and examines the construction of learning communities, including the roles and perspectives of teachers, students, principals, superintendents, and community participants.

Lambert, L. (2003). *Leadership capacity for lasting school improvement*. Alexandria, VA: Association for Supervision and Curriculum Development. In this follow-up to her ASCD best seller *Building Leadership Capacity in Schools*, Linda Lambert explains how to sustain a professional learning community where everyone takes ownership of improvement efforts and acts with a shared sense of purpose. Charts, action steps, and surveys help you analyze a school's leadership capacity and guide a professional learning community toward sustainable, continuous improvement.

Popham, W. J. (2003). *Test better, teacher better: The instructional role of assessment*. Alexandria, VA: Association for Supervision and Curriculum Development. This "crash course" on the basic principles of instructionally focused testing explains how tests can tell you what to teach and how to teach it; what to put on a test and why, including the rules for choosing and writing good test items; and how to avoid "teaching to the test" and the five most common mistakes in test writing. Sample test items, tips, and test-building steps help you design tests that reveal whether teaching practices are achieving the results you want.

Sarason, S. B. (2004). *And what do you mean by learning?* Portsmouth, NH: Heinemann. *Learning* is the word most used in educational literature, and yet educators have great difficulty in defining it. Sarason demonstrates that lack of clarity about the concept of learning is at the root of the disappointments of educational reform, inadequacies of preparatory programs, and proclamations of policy. He takes a good look at another question as well: Why are the principles of learning implied by what parents of preschoolers say and do so different from the principles educators employ? And he goes a step further when he asks, "Why is it that no one, educators or otherwise, has ever said that schools are places where *teachers* learn?"

Overview of Context for Case Studies

The case studies are set in a suburban/urban school district. Although the town was once a bedroom community for those who worked in the metropolitan area, in recent years the population has been growing and changing membership. The town has become a city through incorporating several small towns nearby. Students used to be mostly Caucasian. Now the student population of the district is 29.7% African American, 29.5% Hispanic, 34.7% Caucasian, 6% Asian/Pacific Islands, and 0.2% Native American. The district has never-ending challenges to build and maintain a vision, and to keep increasing the percentage of students mastering skills as tested on the state exam—whether through curriculum alignment, professional development of teachers, or improving the leadership of the schools. Turnovers in teaching staff and in school and district leadership positions create problems in moving smoothly through the change process.

In the case studies the superintendent, Dr. Petrovsky, has been in place for 20 years. You will find a new principal, Dr. Ted Caruthers, struggling with leadership and management issues. You will find one high school principal, Dr. Alice March, working with professional development and struggling with ethical issues. A second high school principal, Mr. Gary Jones, is dealing with legal issues ranging from theft to sexual harassment. An elementary principal, Glenna Greene, and her colleagues have been working to serve as leaders of change despite little support from the higher administration.

At the end of each case study, questions are raised that relate to the Educational Leadership Constituent Council (ELCC) standard examined in each part of this text (I–VII). Certainly additional questions may be posed to include more than one standard, and there is flexibility in cases reflecting real-life experiences.

A New Role

Setting: Eisenhower School District is a fairly large district with two high schools. Three junior high schools feed into each of these schools. Muskie Junior High School is one of the feeder schools for Dover High School. Because this junior high has been a school with an unusually large number of student problems, administrators have come and gone frequently. Teachers with 1–5 years of experience form 19.8% of the staff; those with 6–10 years of experience form 32.1% of the staff; those with 11–20 years form 17.9%, and those with over 20 years experience form 14.8%. The ethnic breakdown for students shows that 39.5% are African American, 30.7% are Hispanic, and 29.8% are White.

Scenario: It is the second day of January in a new year, the day before the staff and teachers return for a workday. Dr. Ted Caruthers, the very recently appointed principal of Muskie Junior High School, is mulling over options for starting his new job effectively. Martha Spieler, one of the assistant principals, finds him reviewing the most recent testing data, staff evaluations from last year, a two-year-old survey on climate at the school, and a three-year-old survey of school needs as perceived by parents and other stakeholders.

"Good Morning, Martha," says Dr. Caruthers, "I am trying to get a better understanding of our school. It seems that viewing this school from afar can lead to different conclusions about what's most needed compared to the conclusions I've reached after reviewing this data. I'm not sure how much of this data should be used. Changes have occurred so rapidly around here that even the staff evaluations of last year leave large gaps in the information I need to formulate a plan of action. I know there was at least a 19% turnover of staff this last summer. Certainly that will have changed the climate and the list of school needs that are indicated in these older documents. You've been around here for five years. What do you think the major needs are?"

"Well, I think one of the major needs was met when the superintendent and school board decided you needed to be the principal here," Martha replies. "They all know that you stand for law and order. Your record as the assistant principal at the high school is what got you this job. You are fair, and you respect the students, the teachers, and the parents. That has allowed you to take a strong stance on discipline. We need that here at the junior high, where all three groups of students — White, African American, and Hispanic — are trying to gain control or be top dog. Our teachers and staff really need a boost in morale. Last year the staff tried to take the discipline problems in hand. I tried to help, but our former principal would not make the tough decisions. Now we all suffer the consequences. The students feel as though they are in charge. Teachers are not willing to address discipline problems. We really have no sense of direction in discipline, or in anything else. Every teacher is just trying to make it through the day."

"Are you saying that discipline is the number one issue?" Caruthers asks. "At an even deeper level, are you perhaps saying that with a sense of direction or vision, discipline would fall in place? Am I reading you correctly?"

"Dr. Caruthers, we need a sense of direction, a sense of community, and a sense of order so that we can build a true learning community."

"How would you suggest I start, Martha?"

"First, I think you should ask the staff about their perceptions. Then I would ask some student leaders, some parents, and some community leaders. I know all of this will take time, but I'm afraid if we jump in and make changes too rapidly that we will create more problems. It might be wiser to limp along and gather fresh data as rapidly as possible."

"One thing I do know, Martha. I plan to be very visible and vocal. I am going to address the student body on the first day they return to school. On the teacher workday that's scheduled for tomorrow, I plan to address the faculty and staff. I also plan to start meeting with department groups. I want to have each person list the 10 best points of this school and the 10 areas needing immediate attention. I'd also like each staff member to prioritize his or her list. That way, I can see if there's a strong pattern for action in one direction or another."

"I think you're going to be surprised at the response, Dr. Caruthers. We were seldom asked what our thoughts were on any topic. I think you may get answers that vary tremendously. Some answers may be facetious. Others will be very serious. You had better be ready to listen and act on what you hear."

"I intend to listen very carefully," Caruthers responds, "sort all the input, and then call a planning team together. That team will plan for gathering a more extensive, updated set of information, and they'll analyze the information and make recommendations to me about what action needs to be taken. I think it would help to use Stufflebeam's model of context, input, process, and product evaluations (CIPP). We have to understand what needs to be done, and in what order. We also have to understand how these things should be done compared to how they are being done. Finally, we need to learn if our efforts succeed. All this activity must be carefully planned and documented. The entire learning community must understand what's being done, and why it's being done. We're facing a massive task. You and I are just two small pieces in the picture."

"Yes, we are," Martha agrees, "but you as leader have a much greater part than I do. Remember that we have had little direction. We need a leader, and we need a manager too. Unless we have a structured response to the obvious needs such as discipline management, I don't think we'll succeed. Do you think you can persuade the superintendent to give us more help with this effort? After all, we now have a history of changing principals every year, and sometimes even sooner. Those changes haven't helped anyone, as far as I can see. I hang in here because I think that basically, we have a great staff. They just need help in joining together in their efforts. Right now, everyone is acting like the lone ranger."

"Before I ask for any more help, monetarily or otherwise, I need to have a basic plan of action written out—like a position paper that I can use to help anyone see the picture that I see." Caruthers smiles at Martha. "Because we've had a chance to visit about this, I'd like you to review the proposal I am going to draft this afternoon. I plan to use it tomorrow, and in the future too. Of course, I expect my plan to be modified as we gather input and see what successes and/or failures we have. As an assistant principal to Dr. March, I was constantly reflecting and asking myself what I would do if I were in her shoes. Now that I am in the principalship or leadership position, I want you to do much the same. I encourage you to reflect and to share with me as we move along in the process of building a learning team. I hope you feel comfortable enough to do this with me. I will encourage the other assistant to interact with me at the same level, too."

"I can give you some feedback right now," Martha says. "If you mention the CIPP process to others as you did to me, I think it would be better if you used other terms. All that sounds too academic. Even with my basic understanding, I have questions. For one, I want to hear more about how you're going to get input from the community. The parents and some of the business leaders have been very active in this school, helping through the Parent-Teacher Association and the Boosters Club. You will need help in thinking this out."

Questions

1. How is Dr. Caruthers exhibiting leadership?

2. What do you think of Martha's advice to Dr. Caruthers?

3. If you were in Dr. Caruthers's position, what first steps would you take to help your school become a learning community?

4. How would you as a new principal begin to build morale? Shape culture?

5. What evidence, if any, do you see for each of the ELCC standards (1–7) in this case study?

2. Creating a Vision for Learning

Standard 1.0: *Candidates who complete the program are educational leaders who have the knowledge and ability to promote the success of all students by facilitating the development, articulation, implementation, and stewardship of a school or district vision of learning supported by the school community.*

FOCUSING QUESTIONS

1 Why is it important to focus on the future when establishing a vision?

2 Why is a systemic vision important?

3 How are visions created?

4 Why is it important for principals to shepherd the vision?

5 How are mission statements developed?

6 What role do goal statements play in creating a vision for learning?

7 How are plans for attaining goals developed?

In this chapter, we respond to these questions concerning the principal's role in creating a vision for learning. We begin the chapter by considering the future of society to gain a perspective on the potential constitution of the school's vision. Then we discuss the importance of principals having a systemic vision. This is followed by a discussion of how visions are created. Next, we explore the principal's role in shepherding the vision. Then we consider the importance of mission statements. This is followed by a discussion of the role goal statements play in creating a vision for learning. Finally, we conclude the chapter with a discussion of the principal's role in developing plans for attaining goals.

Gaining a Perspective on the Vision: Considering the Future

Einstein was criticized for saying that $E = mc^2$. Einstein's vision of matter and energy, bound together with space and time in a four-dimensional universe, was published in 1905; however, it was not until 14 years into the future that his vision would be realized. Then technology caught up to his imagination; and during a solar eclipse, astronomers were able to record the path of light (curved) in relation to the sun's gravitational force. Gorbachev was condemned for mentioning capitalism; but his vision of Soviet reform led to the future dismantling of the Soviet Union. DeKlerk was chastised for saying apartheid must end. DeKlerk's vision of a multiethnic government and antiapartheid began to form when he was elected president of South Africa in 1989. His vision was realized five years later in 1994, when Nelson Mandela assumed the presidency.

Others have been criticized for envisioning a new future. Admonished for educational experiences being too structured and an educational environment being too prepared or stilted, Maria Montessori focused on "the pupil's liberty as the basis for developing independence, his freedom to work when and for as long as he wants to on a given task and to progress at his own rate" (Kramer, 1976, pp. 295–296). This method is now used in over 7,000 certified schools internationally, with thousands more using Montessori concepts. Upon opening her first school in the slums of Rome, Montessori dreamed of helping children who were mentally challenged; but she never realized that a century later, her method would be central in educating not only children with special needs but also those who are special in that they are gifted, second-language learners, or from low and high socioeconomic status.

Piaget also was ridiculed for his research techniques of observation, description, and analysis of child behavior that began in the early 1950s; however, his research was the foundation of his vision for the future of education for children. A result of Piaget's research was his theory of cognitive development. Approximately 20 years later, beginning in the mid-1970s, this theory alone has altered not only how teachers and curriculum developers have created curriculum and instructional strategies within U.S. classrooms but also how they view observational research. The groundswell of acceptance for Piaget's work has added to the base support for qualitative research, which has reached an all-time high in publications approximately a half-century later.

Lev Vygotsky lived during the Stalinist period, when psychology was heavily influenced by Pavlovian theory. His own theory promoting the quality as well as quantity of social relationships, which he believed influenced cognitive functioning or development, was denigrated. Vygotsky's vision of cognition continued to be advanced and influenced the thinking of Albert Bandura in his theory of social learning. Much of Vygotsky's vision began to be taken seriously in child development and in language and literacy development only in the latter part of the 20th century.

Though they were criticized, all of these individuals had gained a perspective on their vision, had taken risks, and had considered the future. They were visionaries and were able to (a) reflect on what *was* in order to gain a perspective on what *could be,* (b) provide a perspective on their visions through clear articulation of them, (c) share their visions though criticisms emerged, and (d) consider the impact of their visions on the future.

What then does it mean for a school principal to gain a perspective on his or her vision while considering the future? To gain a perspective on a vision, a principal must use imagination as well as consequential and critical thinking. When considering vision, we can be certain its value is just as Einstein stated: "Imagination is more important than knowledge." In a sense, a vision comes out of a vivid imagination and dreams that consider future implications and consequences of that pictured vision. The vision that the principal develops expresses the ideals of standards for future judgment and educational conduct that ultimately impact the advancement of the society.

Considerations of the Present and the Future: The Global Society

Society is considered to be a global society, characterized by diversity in cultures, religions, and languages. With technology our world is becoming borderless. Teachers and students are able to access people and information in a matter of minutes. With immediacy, our students are able to witness events from every point on the globe. With this view of the world in their living rooms, our students are able to observe inequities and exclusions at home and abroad. The 2002 United Nations Development Report and the 2003 United Nations Millenium Report illustrate such globalization and inequities and are combined with data from the U.S. Census Bureau from 2002:

- The number of people on earth living in extreme poverty is slowly declining, from 29% in 1990 to 23% in 1999. (Nationally, the official poverty rate grew from 11.7% in 2001 to 12.1% in 2002, and the real median household income shows no change between 2002 and 2003. A total of 34.6 million people were classified as poor in 2002, representing a 1.7-million rise (Proctor & Dalaker, 2003; DeNavas-Walt, Procter, & Mills, 2003).

- Primary school enrollments have risen worldwide, from 80% in 1990 to 84% in 1998. However, of the 680 million children of primary school age, 115 million school-age children were still not in school, 94% were in developing countries, and 56% of them were girls (Millennium Development Goals, 2003a).

- Since 1990, 800 million people have had improved water supplies, and 750 million have benefited from improved sanitation.

- Since 1980, 81 countries have worked toward developing democratic governments, and civilian governments have replaced 33 military commands.

- A Japanese baby may have a 50% chance of seeing the 22nd century, while a baby born in Afghanistan has a 25% chance of dying before age 5.

- The richest 5% of the world's population have incomes 114 times those of the poorest 5%.

- Daily, over 30,000 of the world's children die of preventable diseases, while nearly 14,000 people are infected with HIV/AIDS.

- Nearly one in five Americans speaks a language other than English at home, compared to one in seven in 1990. Most speak Spanish, followed by Chinese. Some 47 million Americans 5 and older used a language other than English in 2000 (U.S. Bureau of the Census, 2000).

- In 1999, there were 2.8 billion people living on less than $2 a day, with 1.2 billion of them barely surviving on less than $1 a day.

- In the world's richest country (the United States), 16.5% of the people live in poverty, 20% of adults are illiterate, and 13% of the population has a life expectancy of shorter than 60 years.

- The richest 10% of the U.S. population has an income equal to that of the poorest 43% of the world. Put another way, the income of the richest 25 million Americans is equal to that of almost 2 billion people (Millennium Development Goals, 2003).

To many who have not witnessed firsthand such events, nor lived those as previously described, they are hard to comprehend. However, once again, we are living in this global society where students from our schools are exposed to the events of the world on television daily — or, in some instances, live these events daily. It behooves principals to address issues of learning related to such events within our global society.

Understanding Our World and Our Position as a Principal in the Challenges for Learning

As fast as the world is changing, so too is the United States. At current rates of immigration, minorities will make up almost half of the U.S. population by the middle of this century. According to the 2002 estimates by the U.S. Department of Commerce, as reported in 2003, the number of people who identified with one race, regardless of whether they also reported any other races, was as follows: 236.2 million for Whites, 38.3 million for African Americans, 13.1 million for Asians, 4.3 million for American Indians and Alaska Natives, and 943,000 for native Hawaiians and other Pacific Islanders. Because Hispanics are classified as an ethnic group, they can identify with any race; however, there were reportedly 38.8 million Hispanics accounted for in the Census. This number surpasses the African American minority population. According to *The Social Context of Education* (1997), published by the National Center for Education Statistics, it is projected that between 2000 and 2020, there will be 61% more Hispanic children ages 14–17 and 47% more Hispanic children ages 5–13. The numbers of Asian/Pacific Islander, American Indian, and Alaskan Native children ages 14–17 are projected to increase by 73%, while the numbers of those children ages 5–13 are projected to grow by 67%. Between 2000 and 2020, the number of White children ages 5–13 is projected to decrease by 11%, with White children ages 14–17 decreasing by 10%. With Hispanics being the largest ethnic majority and with a native language of Spanish, there is increased awareness of the growing numbers of English language learner (ELL) students in schools (U.S. Census Bureau, 2000).

These changing demographic figures present an intricate picture of education in the United States, which faces the challenge of needing teachers who understand the various ethnic or racial groups with which they work. The changes in the demographics contrast with the number of teachers who serve these ethnically, racially, and linguistically diverse students. Nationally, according to the National Education Association (2002), the shortage of minority teachers represents a discrepancy with the student population demographics: Only 5% of teachers are minority in this first part of the century, but the student population is 40% minority. Additionally, there are discouraging achievement findings among racial groups. For example, results from the National Assessment of Educational Progress (NAEP) show that both African American and Latino students perform significantly lower than White students in reading

(Donahue, Voelkl, Campbell, & Mazzeo, 1999), writing (Greenwald, Persky, Campbell, & Mazzeo, 1999), and math and science (Campbell, Hombo, & Mazzeo, 2000). These patterns are recurring at all three grade levels in which the NAEP is administered and, according to Meece and Kurtz-Costes (2001), are present even when controlling for parent income and housing value. The challenge for principals is to ensure that the minority children will receive an equitable education and will be prepared to compete economically in this changing world.

In addition to minority teacher shortages and the apparent achievement gaps, many more factors affect the nation's global society and may perpetuate the exclusion of certain groups. For example, currently over 75 million children under the age of 19 are living in poverty and have no health insurance (Proctor & Dalaker, 2003). Poverty leads to social exclusion and generates the lack of requisite knowledge to get work. According to Barton (2003), poverty is one of 14 correlates contributing to the achievement gap among racial/ethnic groups.

A recent Urban Institute study revealed that about 3.5 million people, 1.35 million of them children, are likely to experience homelessness in a given year (Urban Institute, 2000). This finding presents a challenge to principals: to provide as much support as possible to increase the learning capability of these children while they are in school.

Another challenge to principals in the learning situation is educating children who face abuse and/or neglect. In 1993 an estimated 1,553,800 children in the United States were abused or neglected under the Harm Standard. The Third National Incidence Study total reflects a 67% increase since the Second National Incidence Study estimate, which indicated that the total was 931,000 children in 1986 (Sedlak & Broadhurst, 1996). Furthermore, in 2001 the National Household Survey on Drug Abuse determined that more than six million children lived with at least one parent who abused or was dependent on alcohol or an illicit drug within that year. This total involved about 10% of children aged five or younger, 8% of children aged 6 to 11, and 9% of youths aged 12 to 17 (U.S. Department of Health and Human Services, 2003). Approximately 6 million children with disabilities were served in 1999 in federally supported programs (Digest of Education Statistics, 1999).

Although the conditions of children present challenges to principals who care about their students' learning, the changing technological society does so as well. Dias de Figueiredo (1995) suggested that several challenges, such as learning, cannot be equated only with schooling, because the key issue of education has become the much broader one of supporting the lifelong learners of a society adjusting to ever-changing knowledge. He suggested that education is currently in the age of the learning societies. Within these learning societies, public schools no longer have the monopoly on educating children and youth. There are many choice systems for education, and more are on the horizon. The author further suggested that traditional schools are badly equipped to face challenges of interactivity, mobility, convertibility, connectivity, ubiquity, and globalization. This means that principals must think nontraditionally — outside the box. Dias de Figueiredo proposed that another challenge for the school of the 21st century is its ability to include the human component and to transmit the culture. He said that culture can be understood as a unifying force.

The challenges in education are many for the principals as they plan an educational vision for the schools full of children under their care. Principals must reflect on broader social issues and where they find themselves in the present, in order to build a vision that is socially responsible for the future. A socially responsible vision challenges principals to educate and assess all children, with their diverse needs, who enter through the schoolhouse doors — which open from the opposite direction to a myriad of diverse situations and needs of the society at large.

Bringing the Vision Home to the School Culture

The No Child Left Behind Act of 2001 (NCLB) admonishes principals to hold all students accountable to high academic standards. The 2001 legislation expanded the federal role in public education by (a) requiring schools to be accountable to achievement in that all students must meet state standards by 2014 and all gaps be closed, (b) mandating schools to hire highly qualified teachers, and (c) emphasizing that schools put into place programs and strategies with demonstrated effectiveness based upon research. In effect, NCLB mandated data-driven decision making regarding program implementation in schools.

According to Learning Points Associates (n.d.a), the NCLB goals challenge states, districts, and schools in ways that require them to create visions that rethink the structure, organization, and delivery of education in public schools. One of the first steps in rethinking the structure and establishing the vision for the restructured school is to consider several aspects of the school culture. School culture, as defined by Smith and Stolp (1995), refers to the historically transmitted patterns of meaning, including understood norms, values, beliefs, ceremonies, rituals, traditions, and myths. These authors suggested that cultural understanding often shapes what people think and how they act. According to Stolp (1994), a vision determines the values and beliefs that will guide policy and practice on a school campus. He said the creation of a vision is not a static event, because the vision must change as culture changes; the principal who can develop a vision related to the new challenges society brings will be more successful in building strong school cultures than the principal whose vision does not reflect cultural change.

Considering the challenges as previously described while couching them in the context of the lived culture (the community, the place, in the present), Browder (2001) aptly shared a story of a high school principal.

> With thoughts of the definition of moral poverty in her head, the principal concludes that she feels a better sense of understanding a complex shift in American society, one that unfortunately leaves a growing number of children-on-their-own. She senses that the best way to deal with this phenomenon is to focus the school's resources for involving

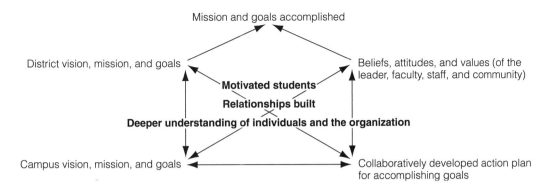

Figure 2.1

Systemic Vision and Its Connection to Context and Relationships

parents and engaging teachers and students. She believes it will be necessary for her to assume a leadership role as a moving force and cheerleader for establishing the school's institutional attitude — a positive one anchored in academic achievement and a firm sense of right and wrong. While this approach seems very traditional and may not work well today, the principal senses that, for her community, it is perhaps the most appropriate choice.

Meanwhile, more study will be necessary on determining ways of injecting "contagious" moral attitudes into adolescent peer groups. She realizes it is far easier to offer such a prescription than it is do to so. It is our obligation, however, to try, thinks the principal. (p. 258)

The principal that Browder portrayed considered her culture and saw herself as the facilitator in moving the vision with many stakeholders involved and including very human and moral factors that obviously had been neglected within her setting. Because she was about to embark on a collective venture with parents and teachers, she was setting out to create relationships while promoting her vision. Wheatley (1994) stated:

> To live in a quantum world, to wave here and there with ease and grace, we will need to change what we do. We will need to stop describing tasks and instead facilitate process. We will need to become savvy about how to build relationships. . . . The quantum world has demolished the concept

of the unconnected individual. More and more relationships are in store for us, out there in the vast web of universal connections. (p. 38)

The Systemic Vision

Figure 2.1 depicts a *systemic vision*, placed within the context of the school, which of course is within the district. Systemic vision is not only contextual but also dependent upon relationships. The systemic vision includes relationships between and among the following factors: (a) the district's vision, mission, and goals, (b) the school's vision, mission, and goals, (c) the school's strategic action plan, and (d) the considered values of the principal, teachers, staff, and community. Each factor is grounded in professional relationships, because such relationships are established as teachers, administrators, support staff, and other stakeholders develop and collectively understand each factor. Systemically and cyclically, these relational factors lead to the accomplishment of the mission and goals. The process of the systemic vision in developing these factors leads to more highly motivated students; better person-to-person relationships among faculty, administrators, and community; and a more sensitive or deeper understanding of each person in the organization, the organization itself, the vision, the mission, and the goals.

Creating a Vision

A vision statement for schools is a convincing description of how students are improved in various ways through numerous school services. Every principal can facilitate the creation of a vision and, in so doing, be a visionary. Like Einstein and other visionaries, the principal can recognize a need or opportunity for her students and school and, regardless of critics or cynics, can do something about it. Vision is the portrait the principal paints as she creates the future by acting in the present. Another way of considering vision is to think of it like a compass—it is the guide that gets us to where we want to go.

The Principal's Vision

For a principal to create a vision or even to facilitate the school community to create a vision, the first step is reflection. The principal must carve out ample reflective time to consider (a) where the school has been, (b) where it is presently, and (c) where he wants it to be or what he wants it to become. This reflective activity is critical to developing a more effective school.

Where the School Has Been   Review a history of the school. Take into account the community and how it has changed over time—economically, demographically, culturally. Has the school population grown or decreased? What success stories have been told in the community? What has the "talk" about the school focused on—students, faculty, sports, curriculum? What types of leaders (principals and teachers) has the school had?

Where the School Is Presently   Review current achievement reports in relation to past achievement. Review current demographics of the school's students, teachers, and community. What are the leader's current behaviors and styles? What is the current focus of the school, and what led to that focus? How are teachers and other stakeholders currently involved in making decisions about the school? How are decisions made—upon what are they based?

What the School Is to Become   Dream big; dream outside the box; get on top of the box and dance; dream with students at the center. Imagine, with no boundaries and based on the data analyzed, just what the school could become—this is the seed of the vision.

For the Vision to Grow   We suggest that for the school leader's vision to grow and become established in the school, six conditions are necessary, as outlined in Table 2.1. The first necessary condition involves the understanding of self—the principal must know herself in terms of beliefs, values, and philosophy. The second condition is so critical to formulating a vision and moving the vision forward that we discuss the second condition more extensively later in the chapter: Because of the changing society, as discussed earlier, the principal must value students' diverse backgrounds and understand and embrace them. Third, because our students are diverse and because schools are places for students to grow and learn, the vision must be centered always on the students and their needs. The fourth condition is that the principal must be perceived as authentic. She must exude a genuine commitment to the vision, and ultimately to the mission and goals, leading to the fifth condition—the principal must be able to effectively articulate the vision to all the stakeholders. The principal must, at all times, keep the vision in the forefront for all stakeholders. The dialogue and the message the principal states should always be centered in the vision. When she talks to parents, to the clubs and organizations in town, to the superintendent, to the custodial staff, to the businesses and industry executives, to members of the church, mosque, or synagogues—wherever the principal is and whatever she says related to school business—the vision should be the focal point. Then, *all* will know in which direction the school is headed, and the vision can stay alive in their minds and in their conversation.

Beliefs, Values, and Attitudes

Why is it important for the principal to know his own beliefs and values, and how they are portrayed in his attitude? Senge (1994) strongly

Table 2.1	**Conditions to Grow a Vision**

The Principal's Necessary Conditions to Grow a Vision

1. The principal must be able to know what he or she believes and values.
2. The principal and the stakeholders must value students' diverse backgrounds.
3. The vision must be centered in the needs of the students.
4. There must be a genuine personal commitment from the principal.
5. The principal must be able to clearly articulate the vision.
6. Continuous and repetitive dialogue and actions focusing on the vision are critical to the life of the vision.

urged that the vision be aligned with values and daily life of the people involved; if not, the vision would fail, would not foster enthusiasm, and would actually spawn cynicism. He illustrated the importance of knowing personal beliefs and values as well as values of the school community.

Why is it important to know the beliefs and values of the school community? The beliefs of individuals or stakeholders within the school organization are manifested in its actions and decisions. The principal must determine how those beliefs and values are reflected in her organization and exhibited in behaviors of the faculty and staff within the school culture. It is critical for the principal to assess whether her personal beliefs and values are aligned or misaligned with her organization.

You may have seen a set of values a school has printed, framed, and mounted on the office wall and in every classroom. Is there alignment of what is espoused and what is actually valued? The principal must be astute and aware of the alignment between the way the faculty and staff behave and what is printed and framed. Following is an example of visible awareness of such an alignment.

We recently saw a stated value of "respect for all" in a public Montessori prekindergarten school. During several visits, we noted "respect" that extended from the front office to the hallways to the classroom. What we saw was an amazing display of this behavior. It was exhibited, for example, in the cleanliness and orderliness of the building, from the hallways to the bathrooms and the classrooms; in the front office staff, as they greeted and assisted parents; in the hallways and classrooms, as teachers used quiet and understanding voices with children as they taught or provided corrective feedback; in the library, as the librarian demonstrated with the children the respect for books and reading; and in the principal's office, as she met with the assistant principal to provide corrective feedback on paperwork. Adults and children were respected; things were respected; and conflict was handled in the classrooms by teachers teaching children how to respect each other. This was an amazing display of alignment of behavior of an entire campus, from the principal to the students, with a value of "respect." This Montessori school's belief statements follow:

- All students can be successful learners.
- Students are capable of learning all material.
- Parents are an important part of our school.
- Respect is key on our campus — respect for all.
- We believe in continuous learning.

Another situation we have all observed lately is the misalignment of the value of trust in the case of the recent demise of a major energy corporation. In that corporation, the value of trust was underserved and not exhibited by the leaders. The leaders' values were not aligned with the values of the organization's members. Ultimately, this basic core value was violated — as demonstrated by actions that led to illegal, unethical, and destructive behaviors—and ultimately, the system failed.

Alignment of values between the principal and teachers produces a fruitful yield of trust and open communication at all levels and is seen in quality decisions, motivated teachers, enthusiasm, respect, an ethic of care and social responsibility, development of strategic alliances, openness to change, accountability for mistakes, and a focus on quality (Collins & Porras, 2002).

The Leadership Framework

Alignment of the principal's values with those of the organization (or the teachers within it) is one of the keys to a successful and quality school. To accomplish this alignment, according to Irby and Brown (2000), the principal must first assess her own beliefs through the development of a *leadership framework*. Irby and Brown described the leadership framework as "a comprehensive analysis of primary beliefs and attitudes regarding students, teachers, schools, learning, and leadership" (p. 18). Further, they iterated that a personal leadership framework helps in clarifying who we are as leaders, not only to ourselves but also to our employees. The principal's actions are predicated on her beliefs and values; therefore, it is important to know herself well and to express her beliefs clearly in writing. The leadership framework compels a principal to reflect on her philosophy of leaders, learning, and teaching and offers opportunities for personal and professional growth and prepares the leader for sharing her belief system. This step must be done before a leader can move forward in developing and creating a shared vision. Components of the leadership framework follow:

1. Philosophy of Education. The initial component provides insights into basic beliefs about the purposes of education and the importance of schools to society from the leader's perspective—forming the foundation not only for the principal's practice but also for subsequent components of the framework.

2. Philosophy of Leadership. What the individual believes about effective leadership and its impact is stated here. Students address such questions as: What constitutes effective, purposeful leadership? How is effective, purposeful leadership sustained? How do principals lead from the heart as well as from the mind?

3. Vision for Learners. An in-depth analysis of what the principal believes about how children or adolescents learn and about his or her role in promoting learning is essential to the development of this component.

4. Vision for Teachers. Here individuals examine and share views on teachers; that is, what it means to be a teacher, what a teacher's role is in the lives of children in the classroom and within the campus community, as well as how teachers should relate to students and others. The principal includes how he or she will empower teachers to develop and use their talents to be productive team members.

5. Vision for the Organization. A discussion of the principal's vision for the organization or school campus is important because this provides an image of how he or she thinks the campus "should be or could be." Within this component, the principal should reflect and comment on:

   ■ Climate
   ■ Community
   ■ Collaboration
   ■ Communication

   Additionally, the principal should address how to implement one's vision for fostering spirit within the workplace. Here he or she may discuss commitment to quality and equality, valuing diversity, connectedness, the spirit of service ethic and integrity, compassion, and stewardship to the community.

6. Vision for Professional Growth. This component addresses how the principal perceives professional growth impacts student achievement and effective schools. Here, the principal discusses personal views on the significance of professional development as well as disclosing how professional growth needs will be determined and addressed.

7. Method of Vision Attainment. All visions are merely cryptic illusions without a strategy for

attaining the vision. In discussing how to move the organization toward the vision, the principal will need to address the following:

- Decision making
- Encouragement, initiation, and facilitation of change
- Support during change
- Development of a shared mission
- How the students will work with others to achieve a school's mission and goals

(Brown, Irby, & Fisher, 2001, pp. 128–129)

Benefits of Articulating the Vision

The principal, as leader, must effectively articulate and communicate the vision for the school. With such a clearly communicated and future-focused vision that is attuned to the whole system of the school and community, the principal will be able to facilitate interest, buy-in, and commitment from the stakeholders and to create a sense of shared vision that will enable the school to realize the benefits associated with a strong sense of vision. Licata, Teddlie, and Greenfield (1990) suggested that teachers are more likely to support a school vision when it emanates from authentic dialogue among the principal, teachers, and others. Licata and Harper (2001) found more recent works that support this notion; see Blase & Blase, 1997; Greenfield, 1988; Jantzi & Leithwood, 1996; Johnson, 1992; and Smith & Stolp, 1995.

Long-term benefits of developing a clear, shared vision include

- Value and respect for human diversity and the breakdown of prejudices through analysis of personal values in the context of the school community and the global society
- Definition of the values of the school and its stakeholders
- Guidance of the behavior of the stakeholders
- A productive and efficient school
- Consequential, reflective, and critical thinkers, going beyond what is to what could be
- A continuity and a focus to planning efforts
- Direction and purpose of the school

- An alertness of stakeholders to needed changes
- Open communication
- Creativity and imagination in problem solving
- Encouragement and confidence enhancement among stakeholders
- Ownership and loyalty through continuous involvement

The principal is ultimately accountable for the vision, but is not the individual solely responsible for it. When the principal can give up the power and share it with teachers and others within the school community, the vision is more likely to be accomplished.

Shepherding the Vision

The principal must be the shepherd of the vision and the one who facilitates development of it, the mission, and the goals for accomplishing the mission. There are some points for maintaining the vision that the principal can remember as he goes about the shepherding process, and some detractors to consider along the way.

Vision Detractors

Vision detractors can impede progress of the school. Beware of these vision detractors, and consider what can be done to avoid them.

Beware of Tradition   Tradition and cultural mores will raise their heads at times and attempt to keep the principal off the path of the vision. Be prepared to question tradition, such as the traditional structure and culture of the school. On the other hand, consider how to use tradition and culture to benefit the vision.

Beware of Scorn   Some may ridicule the vision. Stay focused; keep repeating the vision and the mission of the school. That is part of the focus—to stay focused!

Beware of Naysayers   Naysayers will say things can't change; they will then proceed to tell the principal how she can't change and how she, herself, can't get things changed. Stay focused on the vision.

Beware of Complacency   The principal must keep the stakeholders motivated toward realizing the school's vision. This can be done by keeping the vision and mission at the front and center of all decisions.

Beware of Weariness   Keep focused on the dream, the vision. Envision the future; envision success. When you are weary, focusing on the vision will lift your spirits.

Beware of Short-Range Thinking   Short ranges yield little; sights set too low or short are very limiting and stifling; sights must be set long for far-reaching results, allowing room for mistakes and corrections.

Vision Maintainers

Stay centered on the vision maintainers. They will assist the principal in leading the way for the vision to be realized and success to be celebrated.

Build Ownership in the Vision   The principal must be able to articulate the vision well and must be able to bring the faculty together to support the vision. Building ownership means talking about the vision and involving the teachers in developing the mission and goals to attain the vision. The more they are involved, the more they will own the vision. Keeping the vision in the dialogue, keeping them focused and talking about the vision, and sending them out into the community to share the vision, all help in building ownership.

Think of the Long-Term Benefits   Think about how the vision will ultimately benefit the students. An example of one principal's vision was to create a climate of care where everyone is valued and where everyone can succeed. Imagine how that vision led to many wonderful outcomes for students, teachers, custodians, and parents. Just think of all the benefits that could emerge from such a vision.

Seek Input from Stakeholders on How to Achieve the Vision   Seek input. The old adage of "two heads are better than one" is true. Ask teachers, parents, and students how the vision could be accomplished. This, again, is a way to build ownership in the vision. Address isolation by designing activities that will connect teachers to teachers, and teachers to administrators. As Sarason (1994) indicated, isolation, particularly of teachers, may hinder moving forward with the vision.

Build Confidence in the Stakeholders That the Vision Can Be Accomplished   The principal has to be the mainstay. The principal must keep the vision alive by continuously encouraging others regarding attainment of the vision.

Stay With the Vision — It Will Keep All Decisions Focused and Will Provide Direction and Purpose   As all decisions are made, the principal must be the one to keep the focus on the vision. Bring the vision into all decisions. The decisions, then, will have a purpose and be guided by the vision.

Stay Focused; Let All Conversations Related to Public Speaking Focus on the Vision and Mission of the School   Follow the example of candidates in a public campaign — they stay focused on their platform. Good campaigners keep the platform in front of the voters in every stump speech and every public appearance. This is also the job of the principal — be a good campaigner for the vision.

Keep Stakeholders Alert to Any Changes That Are Needed   If unforeseen circumstances arise that would deter you from your vision, alert all stakeholders. Open communication is important to maintaining the vision.

Demonstrate How the Focus Has Resulted in Efficiency, Effectiveness, and Productive Teachers, Administrators, and Students   At the end of the year, provide all stakeholders with a formative progress report. Measure the progress toward attaining the vision, and share the accomplishments. Share this information with the superintendent and the community, as well. Excellence is a moving target; therefore, once the progress has been checked, determine how to continue moving forward and decide what remains relevant.

Mission Statements

Although the vision statement projects the school into the future and shares the stakeholders' desires for the direction of the school, the mission statement is different. It is, of course, related to the vision; in a sense, it is the "why" of the vision. The mission is a brief description of the purpose of the school.

The brief mission statement should, like the vision, guide the decision-making process for the school. It should be aligned not only with the vision, but with the core values or principles of the school. When this alignment occurs, stability ensues. Actions and resources should be assessed for alignment with the mission. The mission allows teachers, administrators, and other members of the school community to assess their personal actions with respect to the core values and purpose of the school. The mission depicts an image to the public regarding the purpose of the school and focuses the entire school community toward that purpose.

Mission statements often include two parts. The first part is a brief outline of the purpose of the school. For example, the Sharon Christa McAuliffe Elementary School's mission is "to provide appropriate strategies enabling each student to take an active and responsible role for learning" ("McAuliffe Elementary," 2003). The first part of the mission enables the teachers and school community to stay focused, and it serves as the purpose of the school.

The second part of the mission statement usually provides more detail, as in the McAuliffe Elementary mission: "This will allow them to become productive citizens, capable of competing in a global society." The vision statement of McAuliffe Elementary is "To create a positive learning environment that provides for continuous academic growth." It is easy to see the connection, yet the differences, between the vision

and mission of this school. This school further delineates its vision and mission with a statement of core beliefs as follows:

> Sharon Christa McAuliffe Elementary School is dedicated to providing our students with a strong, comprehensive core of academics and the development of an attitude that learning is a life long process. Integrated learning is aimed at developing the student's ability to discover, to interpret critically, and to understand connections between ideas. There are, through applications of reflective observation and critical analysis, opportunities for choice and decision making and the art of questioning. ("McAuliffe Elementary," 2003)

Another example of a school mission statement that depicts the two parts is from the Merriam School in Massachusetts. "The mission of the Merriam School Community is *to create and sustain an environment* that promotes academic excellence, encourages social development, fosters emotional well-being and instills a passion for lifelong learning." The Merriam School, like McAuliffe Elementary, has a vision and belief statement.

> The Merriam School strives to combine the thought provoking, enriching qualities of a children's museum with the nurturing and support of a family and the focused learning of a school. The Merriam School holds community at its center. Merriam parents, teachers and students learn and work closely together. Deeply rooted in Merriam's philosophy is the idea that students, teachers and parents share an active role in decision making and feel empowered through their involvement with the school. Students have opportunities to make choices in their classrooms that really affect them, from creating classroom constitutions to deciding what to sell in the school store. Teachers are empowered to make significant decisions, including those regarding the school's budget, curriculum and operation. By design, parents are also deeply involved in making a wide range of important decisions, such as setting the school's goals, evaluating the school's progress, hiring new teachers and designing the plans for school improvement.

> The staff at Merriam believes:

> ■ All learners can have successful and satisfying experiences through active participation in the educational process.

- Learning takes place in a dynamic environment which arouses curiosity, supports innovation and promotes a love of learning.
- Education prepares the learner for effective participation in communities beyond the school.
- The school is a central member of a community and family team that shares responsibility for the development of children.
- Learning takes place through experiences which link the learner's world to the great chain of ideas, past to future.
- Every learner comes with personal gifts. ("Merriam School," 2003)

To write a mission statement, principals should ask the following questions of the teachers in collaborative group settings. They need to have time to discuss these questions and share their thoughts:

- What is the vision, and is our purpose aligned with where we want to be?
- What is our purpose?
- What is important about our purpose?
- What is the most critical point of our purpose in this school?
- Will what we do help us realize our vision?

We suggest that in addition, the belief statements be turned into belief action statements. For example, the previous belief statement, "All learners can have successful and satisfying experiences through active participation in the educational process," might be reconsidered as a belief action statement in this way: "We will provide interesting lessons with satisfying experiences that engage the learners in the educational process."

Goal Statements

Once the vision, mission, and belief action statements have been articulated, a plan is needed to move the organization forward. Goals can assist in that movement. Schmoker (1996) indicated that specific, measurable goals are among the most promising yet underused strategies to improve schools. Goals are the results that a school or school district tries to achieve (Locke & Latham, 1994). Goals equal the vision and mission, with measurable outcomes and a timetable for implementation. Goals are outcomes that the school tries to accomplish and are aligned to the vision and mission.

Hierarchy of Goals

According to O'Neill (2000), there are process-oriented and results-oriented goals. Principals should consider process-oriented goals related to activities, programs, and instructional methods. O'Neill provided principals with examples of process-oriented goals, such as (a) developing a balanced literacy program for primary students, (b) implementing an integrated math/science curriculum for incoming freshmen, and (c) adopting a zero tolerance policy toward violence. She suggested that such goals fit nicely into methods or strategies sections of action plans. Alternatively, she indicated that results goals provide better feedback on how well teachers help students learn. A test score, a rubric system, or some other quantifiable tool or method evidences results goals. She provided examples of results goals, such as (a) increasing numbers of students who are reading by the end of third grade, (b) reducing failure rate of incoming freshmen, and (c) eliminating violent behavioral incidents.

Schools may have multiple goals, that is, to increase test scores, decrease the dropout rate, develop people, and improve community relations. There may be a hierarchy of goals that refers to the interrelationships between general, overall goals and specific instructional objectives or between upper and lower organizational units.

The starting point in the task of managing a school, for example, is to review the definition of the school district's overall goals. This definition is the first critical activity of strategic planning. All other planning, organizing, leading, and monitoring should implement the school district's goals for the school year and should align with the school's vision and mission. Long-range goals can be set for multiple school years as well. Unless goals are set, agreed on, and performed on all

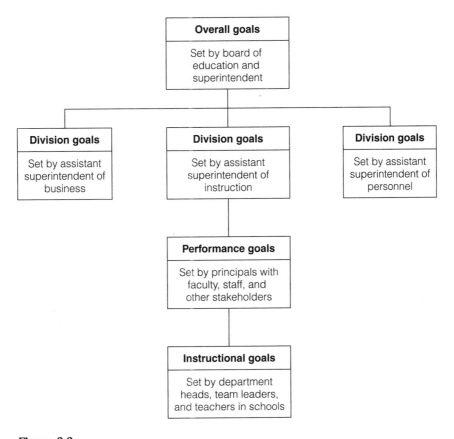

Figure 2.2

Hierarchy for Setting Goals

levels of operating the school district, there will be little basis for measuring the effectiveness of the school and school district outcomes.

A means-ends analysis, or developing a hierarchy of objectives, is the process of translating school-system goals into contributing subsidiary goals and objectives for central office administrators, principals, and teachers within the school district (Saaty, 1990). Figure 2.2 depicts the hierarchy of district and school goals, as well as classroom instructional objectives. The hierarchy of goals can be viewed as means that contribute to a single end—the school system's outcomes.

As Figure 2.2 indicates, each school is an end in the goal set for that building; it is also a means

to achieve the school district's goals. The school-system goals suggest a framework within which the hierarchy of contributing subsidiary goals and instructional objectives can be set. The responsibility for setting overall goals rests with the board of education and superintendent of schools. Assistant superintendents in turn generate subsidiary goals. School principals have responsibility for identifying the performance goals for their schools; but, again, with the input of teachers, staff, and stakeholders and with the analysis of data for development of such goals. Finally, department heads, team leaders, and teachers within the grade levels or content areas in the schools produce instructional objectives collaboratively.

Applying the concept at all levels of the school district achieves the benefits derived from developing a hierarchy of goals on a means-ends chain. For example, if the board of education and the superintendent set a goal "to increase the number of students reading on grade level," all efforts of district personnel will be exerted in that direction. Assistant superintendents, directors, building principals, assistant principals, library media specialists, department heads, and teachers will set and synchronize goals and instructional objectives with those of the board of education.

School districts need a comprehensive, long-range blueprint for their total operation. The goal-objective hierarchy allows them to become systematic in design and operation. Although there have been many proponents of goals and objectives, few have proposed a logical sequence of development from school district goals to instructional objectives. Bailey and Littrell (1981) described the benefits of a hierarchy of goals as follows:

- Teachers, administrators, students, and lay people can realize a sense of direction.

- Teachers and administrators are able to sense a common purpose and understand how each person is helping achieve the goals of the total school district. Responsibility for the goals, competencies, and objectives is determined.

- With the goal-objective hierarchy, articulation between and among the organization levels is highly probable.

- A sense of unity of working as a total group toward a common purpose becomes apparent.

- Systematic decision making based on how well those decisions will assist in accomplishing the goals and objectives is potentially greater.

- The goal-objective hierarchy makes the direction for evaluating the curriculum much clearer and exact. Evaluation becomes an ongoing practice rather than a piecemeal effort. As a consequence, curriculum revision should not have to be radical or upsetting to personnel.

Criteria for Effective Goals

To ensure goal-setting benefits for the school district, certain characteristics and guidelines need to be met. In most applications, a criterion holds true regardless of the environment in which the goal is actually being set. For example, goals determined for a teacher may be completely different from those set for a principal—yet they both must meet the same criteria (performance on the job) in order to be effective. Murray (1991) provided criteria for effective goals.

Clarity and Specificity Whenever possible, principals should be able to express goals in quantifiable terms, such as increasing student achievement on standardized tests by 5%, decreasing dropouts by 10%, or increasing average daily attendance by 4%. Clear and specific goals make it known to all employees where their efforts should lead them. Unclear and nonspecific goals create confusion and conflict among employees.

Time Frame Goals should have time frames within which they will be accomplished. A time frame usually is a deadline specifying the date on which goal attainment will be measured. A goal of increasing average daily attendance could have a deadline such as the end of the school year. If a goal involves a two- to three-year time period, specific dates for achieving parts of it can be developed. For example, reading improvement goals could be established on a three-year time period: (a) 50% of students will be reading on grade level in year one, (b) 55% of students will be reading on grade level in year two, and (c) 60% of students will be reading on grade level in year three. Within a school building or classroom, goals may be set for shorter time frames including daily, weekly, monthly, and yearly.

Key Areas Goals cannot be derived for every aspect of teacher and staff behavior or from each facet of school performance. Instead, principals should identify a few critical success areas, not to exceed four or five for the school, department, or job. For example, a high school might specify four goals for a given school year: 5% increase in standardized test scores, 10% decrease in student dropouts, 4% increase in average daily attendance, and 20% decrease in discipline referrals to the office. The principal is the leader in the process of goal setting, ensuring that the number of goals set can feasibly be attained. Goals reached equals increased motivation for teachers, staff, students, and community. Therefore, it is helpful to limit goals to four categories (Lunenburg, 1994): *professional skill goals,* which are clearly defined statements describing critical aspects of administrative or teaching performance; *problem-solving goals,* which are designed to correct areas in which performance is below standard; *innovative goals,* which pertain to improvement projects; and *personal development goals,* which are designed for the purpose of projecting an annual program for personal growth and development.

Challenging but Realistic Although goals should be made challenging, they should be realistic enough to accomplish. Easily attainable goals may lead to complacency. Goals that are too difficult may create frustration. Moreover, with two given employees of equal talent and ability, a given goal might be viewed as entirely possible by one and utterly impossible by the other. One value of limiting goals to professional skill, problem solving, innovation, and personal development goals is that these offer special challenges to a variety of employees.

Linked to Rewards People who attain goals should be rewarded. Rewards give significance to goals and help energize employees to achieve goals. However, failure to achieve goals may be due to factors outside the employee's control. For example, failure of a school to attain a goal regarding student achievement on standardized tests may be associated with the socioeconomic status of the student body, population shifts in school attendance areas, or some other phenomena. However, during such times, the principal and faculty should be anticipating changes, planning for changes, and setting subgoals in

response, even though factors may be outside their control regarding the overarching goal. A positive reward would be appropriate as employees reach subgoals. Celebrate the small wins, along with the big wins.

Principals must ensure that goals are communicated to all members of the school district. Organization members should understand how their performance goals relate to the overall school district goals. Goals should not be so numerous or complex that they confuse rather than direct organization members, and the principal must be prepared periodically to refine or even replace some goals. As the school and its environment change, goals may require adjustments to reflect these changes.

Educational goals should be as changeable as the social conditions and the groups that formulate them. Panels and commissions are often organized for purposes of formulating goals. They may operate at various government and educational levels. Ornstein (1986) recommended that task forces formulate educational goals, and that principals include the following stakeholders as representatives.

Students. Most secondary students are mature and responsible enough to provide appropriate input in developing educational goals; moreover, they have the most at stake and thus deserve to be represented.

Parents. In addition to providing the students and taxes that support schools, parents are becoming involved due to a recent movement toward school-based management.

Educators. Teachers and administrators must assume major responsibility in developing educational goals. To relinquish this responsibility is to surrender their professional roles.

Research community. Researchers and social scientists must provide objective data concerning trends and issues; they should not, however, serve in the role of advocate.

Community members. Citizens and taxpayers, regardless of whether they have children in school, have a civic responsibility to provide input in school matters. Their support is crucial because they vote on school and fiscal matters.

Business community. Businesspeople are natural allies of school people. They should be aggressively enlisted in school affairs because of their economic and political influence and their stake in the outcomes of schooling as regards industrial output.

Government officials. Political officials are also natural allies of schools; they, too, should be enlisted because of their political and economic influence. Indeed, educational policy and politics go hand in hand, as do school finance and governance.

Pressure groups. People have the greatest impact by organizing into groups to promote special interests. The operation of such groups is clearly valid within the democratic process, but extreme views must be tempered.

Professional organizations. The input of professional organizations is important in obtaining support from the educational establishment. The professional roles and responsibilities of the members warrant that what is good for schools should prevail.

Governing bodies. Representatives from governing and legislative groups — at the federal, state, and/or local levels — should be included because they have the power and authority to enact legislation (including the recommendations or policy statements) of commissions or panels designed to formulate educational goals.

It is motivational to involve many and varied stakeholders in the establishment of goals, just as when working through the school's vision, mission, and belief action statements. The activity is motivational because its participatory goal-setting and feedback components can enhance the employees' and the school community's motivation. It is also an integral part of the *performance-appraisal* method the school uses: teachers and employees are evaluated on the basis of how well they accomplish the jointly set goals and outcomes of the school and school district.

Goal setting is also a *monitoring* technique, because the jointly set goals become monitoring standards.

The Goal-Setting Process

Although there are many variations of goal setting, the cyclical process consists of four main steps: setting goals, developing action plans, monitoring performance, and evaluating results (Bryson, 1994). Figure 2.3 illustrates these steps as they apply to a districtwide goal-setting program.

Step 1: *Setting Goals.* Goal setting begins at the top administrative level — the superintendent and board of education meet and develop the long-range goals and plans for the school district, frequently with input from lower levels. An example of a goal they might set would be to increase student performance on standardized achievement tests. Then, each successive level in the school district develops its own set of goals and instructional objectives that dovetail with school district goals. At all points in the process, a check for alignment with the district vision and mission and the school vision and mission are necessary — this keeps the goals focused on the purpose. Discussions at each level among the administrators and the stakeholders result in an agreed-on set of goals. These goals should be written and measurable.

Step 2: *Developing Action Plans.* Once goals are agreed on, individuals at each level of the district develop collaborative action plans. Action plans identify how ends are to be achieved. This includes identifying the activities necessary to accomplish the goal, establishing the critical relationships among these activities, assigning responsibility for each activity, estimating the time requirement for each activity, and determining the resources required to complete each activity.

Step 3: *Monitoring Performance.* As members of the school district work toward goal attainment, attention turns to monitoring performance. If the goals are established for a one-year interval, goal-setting advocates recommend that the supervisor and subordinate meet quarterly to review

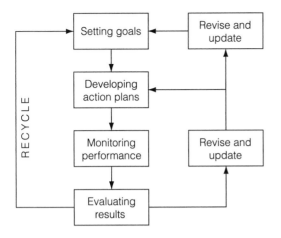

Figure 2.3

The Goal-Setting Process

progress to date. It may be necessary to revise goals, especially if districtwide goals have changed or if necessary resources are unavailable. Otherwise, progress toward valid goals is assessed. Periodic reviews give administrators the opportunity to give subordinates feedback on their performance.

Step 4: *Evaluating Results.* During the year, the principal and the superintendent or the assistant superintendent should hold formative evaluation meetings to mark progress toward the goals. At the end of one complete goal-setting cycle (usually one year), the principal and the superintendent hold another face-to-face meeting to evaluate the ultimate degree of goal attainment. They discuss which goals the principal was able to meet and which were not met. Principals are rewarded for goal attainment, and future corrective action is planned for goals that were not met during the goal-setting cycle. The emphasis should be constructive and directed toward how to improve future performance rather than dwelling on deficiencies. Finally, a new set of goals is established for the next cycle. The same process should be conducted on the school campus between the principal and the teachers.

Problems With Goal Setting

Goal setting has been used in schools for a number of years. Despite widespread use of this method, many principals seem to have difficulty implementing goal setting in their organizations. Several predictable problems prevent goal-setting programs from achieving maximum results (Lovejoy, 1992).

Lack of Top-Management Support   Sometimes central administrators, including the superintendent, do not set overall goals for the system; rather, they delegate the responsibility for goal setting to principals, directors, and coordinators. This limits the program's effectiveness, because the goals set at each lower level of the organization may be incongruent with the actual goals of the central administration as well as the board. This failure to develop and support overall goals results in confusion and a lack of common direction for all of the school's members.

Time-Consuming   The goal-setting process can be very time-consuming, especially during the first cycle. Principals who are unsure of the new system need to request meetings with their direct supervisors to clarify issues. The quarterly monitoring reviews and end-of-cycle evaluations also take time, especially for principals or directors who have large schools or areas of control.

Excessive Paperwork   Goal setting sometimes results in a great deal of paperwork and record keeping. Often, the central administrators allow principals to function largely on their own in determining how goals will be achieved and do not meet during formative stages of the evaluation. For these reasons, many supervisors attempt to stay abreast of what is going on by having principals submit volumes of data, reports, and other performance indicators.

Overemphasis on Quantitative Goals   The need for specific, measurable goals results in a built-in emphasis on quantifiable outcomes such as achievement test scores, numbers of dropouts, attendance figures, costs, and the like. Factors such as school-community relations, union-management relations, student attitudes, and employee job satisfaction—because they are all difficult to quantify—often are omitted in setting goals. This tends to displace work efforts toward limited and sometimes inappropriate ends.

Administrative Style　Goal setting is easily stalled by authoritarian administrators and inflexible, bureaucratic policies and procedures. For many administrators, both at the central level and the campus level, goal setting requires a 180-degree turn from their current ways of thinking and doing things. In many instances superintendents have relegated, have suggested, or even have assigned goals to principals. Principals are to have input, and must garner faculty and stakeholder input, in establishing school goals jointly with their supervisors.

Prepackaged Programs　External consultants who follow standard models used in other organizations frequently implement goal setting in schools. This practice spreads the mechanization of goal setting. Any goal-setting package usually requires substantial modification to fit the unique needs of a school campus organization.

Making Goal Setting Effective

Although goal setting has its problems, it can be an effective administrative technique if it is properly used and if it is incorporated into the system. In fact, goals must be part of a total system in order to be effective. Because many principals encounter some type of formal goal-setting program in their school districts, we examine some of the elements required for goal-setting effectiveness (Kraus, 1992; Bernhardt, 1999).

Develop a Participative Organization Structure

The formal organization structure must be compatible with the goal-setting process. For example, school districts that emphasize bureaucratic or mechanistic systems—with rigid hierarchies,

high degrees of functional specialization, many written rules and procedures, and impersonal human relationships—respond inadequately to goal setting. New organizational structures that are flexible and adaptive are needed, as are systems that both require and allow greater commitment and use of the creative talent of all employees within the system.

Create a Positive Leadership Climate　The leadership climate experienced by a particular work group or hierarchical level in a school district is determined primarily by the leadership behavior of echelons above it. Moreover, the behavior of leaders at the very top echelon (superintendent and his cabinet) exerts by far the greatest influence on lower levels of the organization. In specific terms, the values, attitudes, and perceptions of leaders at the top of the school district hierarchy act as either constraining or adapting forces affecting the successful implementation of goal setting and affecting the systemic outcomes of goals of the district and those of the school campuses.

Maintain the Means-Ends Chain of Goals　Goal setting needs to be structured in an interlocking network of means-ends chains to the organization's overall purpose and strategy. In so doing, every member at every level in the school district is a key link in the goal-setting process. Organization members link goals at one level (i.e., the means) to those at the next higher level (i.e., the ends). This ensures that the various levels within the school district have a common direction that is centered in the vision and mission of both the district and the campus.

Train Principals　For goal setting to succeed, principals and teachers must understand and be fully committed to it. They must be trained concerning the procedures and advantages of the program, the skills required, and the benefits goal setting provides individuals and the organization. Particularly, if the principal, as leader, is resistant, a goal-setting program is doomed to failure.

Table 2.2   The Delphi Dialog Technique: A Goal-Setting Process

Round I	Round II	Round III	Round IV
The School-Community Dialog	Individual Reflection Delphi	Team Reflection Dialog	Student Council Reflection Dialog
Group wishing each goal subsystem	State a concern for goal recommendations	Organize individual recommendations	Organize team goal by subsystem
Group reflection: Our school	State a goal for each goal subsystem	Analyze goal themes	Analyze goal themes
Selection: Most promising goal subsystems		Synthesize goal themes into inconclusive goal recommendations	Synthesize goal themes into inconclusive goal recommendations
Outcome I:	Outcome II:	Outcome III:	Outcome IV:
Recommended areas for school improvement	Goal statements from each school member	A team goal recommendation for each goal subsystem	Council recommendations for school goals

Source: Adapted from Karolyn J. Snyder, Richard Krieger, & Robert McCormick, "School Improvement Goal Setting: A Collaborative Model," 1983, *NASSP Bulletin, 67*, pp. 60–65. Used by permission.

Emphasize Periodic Feedback Sessions   The essence of goal setting is regular task-relevant communication among members of the school organization. This includes giving each member feedback on actual performance as compared with planned performance (goals). If goal setting is to work, this practice must occur throughout the organization — and repeatedly. How feedback is given is also important. If it is hostile, performance may actually be reduced. Feedback should not be used to degrade the individual, but instead should focus on constructive ways to improve performance.

Collaboration may create the conditions necessary for improving employee productivity. Collaboration in schools has been identified as the key schooling process variable for increasing the norms of student achievement. Effective schools research confirms that schoolwide collaboration is a characteristic of effective programs (Levine & Lezotte, 1990).

For use with their faculty in soliciting consensus for school achievement goals, Snyder, Krieger, and McCormick (1983) developed a methodology

called the Delphi Dialog Technique for principals. An example is presented in Table 2.2. The four-step process is designed to foster faculty dialogue about substantive issues through a series of individual and small-group tasks.

In Round 1 of the Delphi process, faculty members present relevant data to each other relating to pressures for school improvement. Using the data, the entire faculty engages in a series of small- and large-group activities until consensus is reached regarding the general direction for school improvement.

In Round 2, each faculty member reflects on the selected directions, identifying his own concerns and making recommendations for the dimensions of the improvement effort (a goal). Each faculty member is assigned to a group (four to eight persons) for Round 3. The task in Round 3 is to listen to individual recommendations and to formulate one team recommendation for each direction that reflects individual faculty member concerns.

In Round 4, a representative from each team and a principal form a council. Their task is to

listen to each group recommendation and to formulate one council recommendation for each direction that represents all concerns. Rounds 2, 3,
and 4 are repeated until faculty consensus (not
majority vote) is achieved on the improvement efforts for the year.

Developing Plans for Attaining Goals

Once organizational goals have been established,
the next step is to develop plans for meeting goals.
Goals mean little if organization members do not
plan how to attain them. In this section, several
commonly used plans are discussed: strategic
plans, tactical plans, operational plans, standing
plans, and single-use plans. As shown in Figure 2.4,
these plans can be described in terms of different
levels of scope and different time frames.

Strategic Plans

Strategic plans define the means by which the
goals of the school district are to be attained
(Kaufman & Herman, 1990). As shown in Figure
2.4, they are broad in scope, cover a relatively
long time frame, and are developed by top-level
administrators and policymakers (superintendent
with the board of education). The purpose of the
strategic plan is to turn school district goals into
reality during a given time frame. The key components of the strategy define the school district
activities and resources — money, personnel,
space, and facilities — required for meeting the
district's goals. For example, if a school district's
goal is to improve student performance in mathematics and science, the strategic plan may prescribe in-service training for math and science
teachers, identification of instructional technology needed, and allocation of resources for supporting an instructional program to meet the
needs of all students. The strategic plan provides
the basis for more detailed plans at middle and
lower school district levels.

Tactical Plans

Tactical plans are designed to help execute strategic plans and to accomplish a specific part of the
school district's strategy (Holbrook, 1994). Tactical
plans typically have a shorter time frame and a
more moderate scope than strategic plans do. The
term *tactical* derives from the military. Although
single battles may be won or lost due to tactical
plans, wars are guided by an overall strategic plan.
For example, General Norman Schwarzkopf de-
ployed strategic weapons systems, such as intercon-
tinental ballistic missiles and B1 bombers, to deliver
major blows to the enemy during the Persian Gulf
War. Strategic weapons systems reflect the country's overall strategic plans. Tactical weapons systems, such as fighter planes, tanks, and infantry
soldiers, were used to achieve just one part of the
overall strategic plan. In a school system, new
teaching techniques may be a part of the strategic
plan to increase student performance in math and
science, but the use of one piece of media production equipment is part of the tactical plan.

Principals use tactical plans to allocate school
district resources and to coordinate their system's
internal subdivisions or building units. These
plans, therefore, are associated with the organizational responsibility of middle managers, such as
building principals. Planning at this level —
resource allocation, integrating the visions of top-
level administrators with the day-to-day activities
of classroom teachers — reflects tactical planning.
Although strategic and tactical planning are different, both should be integrated into an overall
system designed to accomplish school district
goals and outcomes.

Operational Plans

Operational plans are developed at the lower levels
of the school district to specify the means toward
achieving operational goals and supporting tactical
planning activities (Daft, 1993). These plans are
associated with the organizational responsibilities
of department heads or team leaders. Operational
planning frequently is the outcome of a goal-setting

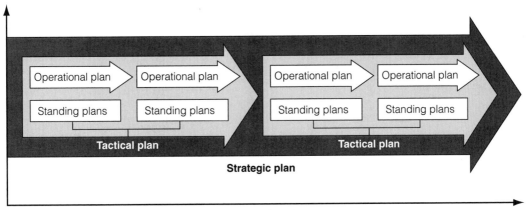

Figure 2.4

Types of Plans

system; it specifies plans for supervisors, department heads, and classroom teachers.

As shown in Figure 2.4, operational plans have a narrower focus and shorter time frame than tactical plans do. Schedules are an important component of operational plans. Schedules define precise time frames for the completion of each goal required for the school district's tactical and strategic goals.

Standing Plans

Schools and school districts repeatedly face similar or identical situations. Examples include student tardiness and absenteeism, smoking in the school building, requests by outside groups to use school facilities, and the like. *Standing plans* are predetermined statements that help decision makers handle repetitive situations in a consistent manner. These plans, once established, continue to apply until they are modified or abandoned. The major types of standing plans are policies, procedures, and rules (Carlson & Awkerman, 1991).

Policies   The broadest and most fundamental type of standing plans, *policies,* serve as guides to administrative decision making or to supervising the actions of subordinates. Sometimes policies are formally determined by the board of education; they may also be informally set by the superintendent, building principals, or classroom teachers. They may be written or unwritten, spoken or unspoken. They may be initiated at any level of the school district.

There are many types of policies — instructional policies, financial policies, and personnel policies, to name a few. Within each of these areas, more specific policies are developed. For example, personnel policies may include selection, recruitment, promotion, retirement, collective bargaining, and training and development policies. Instructional policies may encompass policies on class size, grouping for instruction, school hours, grading, and so on.

Procedures   There is a relationship between policies and procedures. *Procedures* indicate how policies are to be carried out. Procedures specify a chronological sequence of steps that must be taken to accomplish a particular task. For example, universities have procedures for registering, for adding and dropping courses, for applying to graduate school, and the like. The essential purpose of procedures is to ensure consistent action. Moreover, they enable administrators to "manage by exception," that is, to establish policies and procedures to handle recurring problems and to take other action only when exceptional or extraordinary events occur.

Rules   The simplest though usually the most detailed of all standing plans, *rules,* specifically state what can and cannot be done under a given set of circumstances. Rules, unlike procedures, do not specify a time sequence. Rules do not allow for deviations. Unlike policies, rules limit discretion; people use judgment in applying policies. The only choice a rule leaves is whether or not to apply it to a particular situation. Some examples of rules include the following: no smoking permitted on school grounds; no drugs permitted on the premises; a student may enroll in no more than seven courses in a given semester.

Single-Use Plans

Standing plans, in the form of policies, procedures, and rules, provide continued guidelines to the actions of school district members. School districts also use other types of plans, called *single-use plans,* that are predetermined courses of action developed for relatively unique, nonrepetitive situations. The major types of single-use plans are programs, projects, and budgets (Chowdhury & Kirkpatrick, 1994).

Programs   A *program* is a mixture of goals, strategies, policies, rules, and job assignments, as well as the fiscal, physical, and human resources required to implement them. The program typically specifies the goals, major steps necessary to achieve the goals, individuals' or departments' responsibility for each step, the sequence of the various steps, and the resources to be employed. Programs may be as large in scope as landing a person on the moon or as small as improving the reading level of fourth-grade students in a school district or improving teacher morale in a particular school.

Projects   A *project* is a single-use plan that is a component of a program and is usually more limited in scope. In a university, business administration students speak of being in the finance, industrial relations, or management "program." Each of these programs stipulates a sequence of courses that must be taken to fulfill the requirements of the major. However, as part of the course requirements, students may have to complete "projects" in specific courses. The time horizons for projects may be long or short.

Budgets   A *budget* is a single-use plan, expressed in numerical terms, that specifies in detail the resources or funds assigned to a particular program, project, division, or school building. Although budgets are normally expressed in monetary terms, they can be used to plan allocations of personnel, space, and facilities. Developing budgets is clearly a planning process, because it takes strategic goals into account in deciding in advance how to allocate resources among alternative activities. Budgets, then, serve two major purposes: planning and control. In the planning phase, budgets force principals to evaluate programs and activities in relation to cost effectiveness. In the control phase, budgets let principals know how well operations are conforming to plan, the vision, and the mission.

How Some Schools Have Used Goal Setting to Improve Scores

According to J. F. Johnson Jr. (1998), the Charles A. Dana Center at the University of Texas studied 10 medium-to-large districts in which more than one-third of the high-poverty schools had earned recognized or exemplary ratings according to the state criteria for rating schools. A finding was that these districts make academic success a nonnegotiable goal. These districts established clear, tangible, measurable, and challenging academic goals, and they insisted that the campuses develop believable plans for attaining those goals. They regularly used data to maintain focus on progress made toward meeting academic goals. Another finding was that the leaders—the superintendent and the principals—keep a focus on improving teaching and learning, the primary purpose or mission. In these schools there was evidence of strong support from the central administration and a strong relationship with the community of each school. The schools also were able to focus state and federal policy and resources toward attaining their goals.

Johnson (1998) reported another Dana Center study that occurred in 1996. Similar results were found. The following seven themes emerged from the 1996 study:

1. Strong focus on ensuring the academic success of each student. The 26 schools in the study established measurable goals that focused on student achievement. The focus was on what was best for the students.

2. A "no excuses" attitude. The teachers believed that any student could be successful, and no excuses were allowed for low student performances. There was no blaming of parents, economic status, or any other issue surrounding the student.

3. A variety of instructional strategies. The same instructional approaches that had been used in the past and had been unsuccessful were reevaluated for use. Experimentation with a variety of approaches was encouraged.

4. A community of responsible adults. These schools solicited assistance from many responsible adults to reach the goal. They utilized many volunteers. The teachers of various subject areas or special subjects, and the support staff, all maintained important roles in working with the students. A systemic approach was used with school personnel, as well as parent and community volunteers. The approach was welcoming to all who came to the school to assist with students' academic improvement.

5. An environment of family. These schools tended to act more like families and less like institutions. People involved felt valued and respected. Diversity was celebrated.

6. Openness, honesty, and trust. Teachers and staff felt comfortable sharing concerns, ideas, and accomplishments. Principals planned sharing and meeting times, both formal and informal.

7. Passion for continuous improvement, professional growth, and learning. These schools not only celebrated when success was the result, but they also challenged themselves with higher goals.

Summary

1. Vision is critical to the success and future of the school.
2. A mission defines the purpose of the school.
3. The belief, values, and attitudes of the principal, as leader, and the stakeholders are important to ascertain an alignment with the vision and mission.
4. Goals are the starting point for any school district. In addition to providing direction for the school district, they also serve as standards by which individual performance and district outcomes can be measured. Finally, they serve as motivators for organizational members who are given clear aims for which to strive.
5. Goals within the school district are defined in a hierarchical fashion, beginning with strategic goals followed by subsidiary goals, performance goals, and instructional objectives.
6. Some criteria for evaluating the effectiveness of goals are (a) clarity and specificity, (b) time frames, (c) challenging and realistic key areas, and (d) linkage to rewards.
7. One useful technique for systematizing system goals is the goal-setting process. Basic steps are setting goals, developing action plans, monitoring performance, and evaluating results.
8. Many goal-setting programs fail due to lack of top-management support, time commitment involved, excessive paperwork, overemphasis on quantitative goals, inappropriate

management style, and the use of prepack-aged programs.

9. Developing a participative organization structure, creating a positive leadership climate, maintaining the means-ends chain of goals, and emphasizing periodic feedback should increase the likelihood of success of a goal-setting program.

10. Several types of plans for meeting goals include strategic plans, tactical plans, operational plans, standing plans, and single-use plans.

11. Strategic plans focus on what the school district will do in the future; they involve determining strategic goals, adapting courses of action, and allocating the resources necessary to achieve these objectives.

12. Tactical plans are much narrower in scope; their primary purpose centers on how the activities specified by strategic plans are to be accomplished.

13. Operational plans are developed at lower levels of the school district to specify the means toward achieving operational goals and supporting tactical planning activities.

14. Standing plans provide standardized responses for recurring situations; they include policies, procedures, and rules.

15. Single-use plans are established for unique situations; they include programs, projects, and budgets.

Field-Based Activities

1. Analyze your school's vision, mission, beliefs, and goals. Are they aligned? Take field notes for one week and observe (a) the demonstrations within the school of its vision, mission, and beliefs; and (b) the principal's actions as to how he or she is focused on the vision and mission.

2. Write your own leadership framework. It should be single-spaced, in no smaller than 10-point font and no larger than 12-point font, and about one page long. Have two other teachers review your leadership framework. Ask them to tell you how they have observed you demonstrating those beliefs and values you have written.

3. Interview the principal of your school. Determine how goals are set on the campus and how those goals are assessed. Determine which strategic goal plan best aligns with what the principal does to set goals.

Suggested Readings

Barth, R. (1991). *Improving schools from within: Teachers, parents, and principals can make the difference.* San Francisco: Jossey-Bass. This book is a classic for developing a vision and community, and Barth stresses the relationship between teacher and principal and the importance of collegiality in fostering an active community of teachers who then become leaders themselves. Barth believes this will create a better climate for student learning. By calling attention to the principal as a factor in the school situation, Barth makes a definite contribution to the literature on the subject.

Bell, D. L. (2003, April). A team approach to building a new school. *The School Administrator, 60,* 4, 32. This article reviews an appropriate way in which vision and mission are developed through teams.

Covey, S. (1992). *Principle-centered leadership.* New York: Simon and Schuster. This book offers insights and guidelines that can help the reader apply leadership principles to increase quality and productivity, to build personal and professional relationships, and to enjoy a more balanced, more rewarding, more effective life.

Hoyle, J. (1995). *Leadership and futuring: Making visions happen.* Thousand Oaks, CA: Corwin Press. This book provides an overview of futurism as a field of study and shows how futuring, a process based on motivating others, can be used to create shared visions and stimulate the creativity of other people. This hands-on book includes group and individual futuring activities and a variety of step-by-step futuring techniques designed to enliven group workshops and help group members create real-world programs. Hoyle offers practical challenges and suggestions to help you become a better visionary leader.

Nanus, B. (1995). *Visionary leadership.* San Francisco, CA: Jossey-Bass. The author demonstrates why vision is the key to leadership. Additionally, he shares how any leader can develop his or her own vision statement. This book guides readers through the mechanics of forming a vision, guidelines for developing the scope of the vision, and processes for implementing that vision.

NASSP Bulletin, 87. (2003, December). This entire volume is devoted to visionary leadership.

Senge, P. M., McCabe, N. H. C., Lucas, T., Kleiner, A., Dutton, J., & Smith, B. (2000). *Schools that learn: A fifth discipline fieldbook for educators, parents, and everyone who cares about education.* New York: Currency. This book focuses specifically on schools and education to help reclaim schools, even in economically depressed or turbulent districts. A great strength of *Schools That Learn* is its description of practices that are meeting success across the country and around the world, as schools attempt to learn, grow, and reinvent themselves using the principles of organizational learning.

Wallace, R. C., Engel, D. E., & Mooney, J. E. (1997). *The learning school: A guide to vision-based leadership.* Thousand Oaks, CA: Corwin Press. The reader can use the guidelines in this book to implement the kind of vision-based leadership that will help educators create dramatic gains in their school's learning and teaching—education's bottom line. Take your vision-based goals for your school, and turn them into the reality of educational excellence for your students.

Creating a Vision

Setting: The action occurs at Muskie Junior High School in the fall following the Part I Case Study.

Scenario: Dr. Caruthers has served as principal of the junior high for half a year. His assistant principals, Martha Spieler and Bob Perez, are sharing impressions about the recent retreat held by their school. The previous spring, the superintendent charged each school to develop a campus vision to support the broad district vision of *Quality for All*. In response, the planning committee scheduled a two-day retreat for all faculty at the start of the new school year. Martha missed a portion of the retreat due to an emergency appendectomy, so Bob is explaining his experience.

"What a time we had at the retreat!" Bob exclaims. "All the teachers were there for both days. We reviewed the very broad district vision of *Quality for All*, and then we talked about what that meant for each of our roles. We shared how we might see the vision in place at our campus. It was very exciting to see people who have not spoken up in years perk up and add to the conversation. The small groups probably were responsible for that. Maybe Dr. Caruthers's emphasis on trust and listening really is helping to make a difference. People felt comfortable in sharing their viewpoints and their own smaller visions for individual classrooms. Yet we really had a difficult time coming up with a vision statement for our campus. You know how secondary teachers usually are — the focus is usually the content of their course. We made great progress, but we still don't have a statement that is acceptable to all."

"I heard that most of the time, the meeting moved along smoothly," Martha says. "But there were some sticky points. What happened when Ms. Whipple decided to speak out about what nonsense this was? Did you hear that? I'm beginning to think she has a difficult time finding anything positive to say about anything or anyone at any time. I know she's been around for 35 years, but does that give her carte blanche in her speech and actions? And then there was Mr. Cousins, who said all this talk would lead nowhere. He thought the process was a waste of time! I thought just getting all that data in front of the teachers would be very helpful. How can someone argue with the student learning data or the recent climate inventories?"

"I was wondering why our principal, Dr. Caruthers, didn't respond," Bob replies. "Maybe he was just trying to let all viewpoints be expressed. I really don't know."

"So, Bob, where are we now with the process of developing our vision? What do we have to do next? Let's talk to Dr. Caruthers and see how we can help."

Later that afternoon, Martha and Bob ask to visit with Dr. Caruthers. He invites them into his office and inquires, "How can I help you two?"

"We really want to help you if we can," Bob says, "or perhaps it's better to say we want to help everyone at this school. We want to know what we can do to help the campus complete the development of a vision. How do we proceed?"

Caruthers reflects for a moment and then answers. "A vision is really a picture of the future that can be shared by the entire learning community. This means that the best vision must incorporate input from parents, students, and staff as well as the administration. We have heard from the teachers in several ways. First there was my initial meeting with them last January, when they listed the perceived strengths and weaknesses of the school. Secondly, we have the climate inventories. Now we have a pretty good idea about the predominant beliefs, values, and attitudes that most of them share. We need to sound out other people in our community too. We must have a collaboratively developed vision if it is to be effective as a unifying force. So, you ask, what must we do next? Again and always, we must listen. This time we'll bring in teacher representatives to meet with some parents and share the teachers' thoughts as revealed in the two-day retreat. The parents will be those who have responded to our campus survey indicating a desire to serve on some committee. We'll also select some student representatives from each class — freshman, sophomore, junior, and senior — to meet with all of us. We'll go through a process similar to the one you experienced at the retreat. However, we must break the process into smaller units. We'll have to hold some night meetings for awhile, because most parents cannot give entire days to such an effort. Also, we do not want students missing large numbers of classes. That would reflect badly on the administration and the planning. You can remain upbeat about the entire process, and

sound out and listen to reflections from teachers who participated in the retreat."

Martha asks if the data needed for these meetings were readily available. "I'm not sure what else we might need," she says, "but I can see that if we get a grandparent like Colonel Sorenson, we'll certainly need the most up-to-date information. Otherwise, he'll be criticizing us in *The Town Crier.* I know he wants to be helpful, but he seems to want to take charge and dictate what's needed as well as how the process will go."

"You're right. We need everything up to date. I think the data we provided the teachers are fine. We'll plan to use that set of data again with the parent group. If we find that the process takes so long that the data shift, we'll note that," Caruthers says with a smile. He adds, "I'm not anticipating that lengthy a process. I do recognize that the vision will change over time as the issues and attitudes and emphasis on certain values change."

Bob says, "I've heard in some of my master's courses that it's helpful when the principal can share stories from the past about values and beliefs that have been instrumental in making the school what it is today. Although we've had some difficulties recently, we have had some great teachers and principals in the past. I don't remember hearing about these during the retreat days. Do you think we could give some of that information to the parents and students? Could we get some of the teacher representatives who have been here a long time to share these? What do you think, Dr. Caruthers?"

"I think that's a very good idea, Bob. Will you research that for me, please?" Caruthers asks. "We'll need stories to emphasize the values highlighted in the teacher discussions. We talked about the meaning of the district vision, *Quality for All,* but we didn't clarify it with examples from the past. Let's see what we can come up with for the next series of meetings. This could be a very important step. I am sorry I didn't think of this earlier. I guess that goes to show you that anyone can get so busy doing his job that he forgets to sound out others. We should have had this session much earlier. Well, I am learning too. I'm counting on you both to help throughout the process. Come to think of it, perhaps the superintendent could shed some light on these stories, Bob. Dr. Petrovsky has been here for twenty years, and I am sure he would have some ideas for us. Please include him too. He certainly is on our team."

Questions

1. Why is the creation of a campus vision important for Muskie Junior High School?

2. What do you think of the process for developing a vision as suggested by Dr. Caruthers? How would you improve it?

3. What stories have helped illustrate shared values for your campus?

4. If you were Dr. Caruthers, would you have confronted Mrs. Whipple or Mr. Cousins in the two-day retreat? If so, how? If not, why not?

5. Once the vision is completed, what will Dr. Caruthers have to do to help keep the vision alive?

3.
Curriculum Development and Implementation

Standard 2.0: *Candidates who complete the program are educational leaders who have the knowledge and ability to promote the success of all students by promoting a positive school culture, providing an effective instructional program, applying best practice to student learning, and designing comprehensive professional growth plans for staff.*

FOCUSING QUESTIONS

1 What are some concepts and models of the curriculum?

2 What is the relationship of curriculum to instruction?

3 How is the principal a curriculum and instructional leader?

4 How does the principal develop a needs assessment?

5 How are the school's vision and mission focused through the curriculum?

6 How are the school's vision and mission aligned to the curriculum?

In this chapter, we address these questions concerning the principal's role in curriculum development and implementation. We begin the chapter by discussing some concepts and models of curriculum. Then we consider the relationship of curriculum to instruction. Next, we discuss the role of the principal as curriculum and instructional leader. We then examine how the principal develops a needs assessment. This is followed by a discussion of how the school's vision and mission are focused through the curriculum. Finally, we conclude the chapter with a discussion of the alignment of the curriculum to the school's vision and mission.

Concepts and Models of Curriculum

Principals have most likely reviewed textbooks on curriculum and certainly many treatises on educational theory that have offered a particular concept or model of the curriculum. Many of these concepts and models have contained similar elements. Some authors refer to the curriculum as a formal course of study, emphasizing content or subject matter. Others define the curriculum as the totality of experiences of each learner, stressing how subject matter is learned or the process of instruction. Still others point out the importance of statements of expected learning outcomes or behavioral objectives. Behavioral objectives are typically identified within some framework such as the subjects offered in the school program. And some describe the curriculum as a plan for instruction specific to a particular school or student population. Still, there are others who present concepts of curriculum holistically or categorically. Our own analysis of the many conceptions and models of the curriculum, which have evolved during the 20th century, embodies all of the aforementioned definitions.

Concepts of Curriculum

Over the years and currently, the dominant concept of the curriculum is that of content or subject matter taught by teachers and learned by students. For example, Phenix (1962) defined the curriculum as *what* is studied, the "content" or "subject matter" of instruction. The concept of the curriculum as the experiences of the learner, complemented by organized content or subject matter, was introduced in many curriculum publications beginning in the 1960s. Selecting the content, with accompanying learning experiences, is one of the central decisions in curriculum making; therefore, a rational method of going about it was a matter of great concern to Taba (1971) and has remained so for 40 years. In addition, past and present efforts at conceptualizing the curriculum have made much use of goals and objectives as bases for curriculum planning.

Principals continue to use the work of Benjamin Bloom (1956), who attempted to devise some means that would permit greater precision of communication with respect to educational objectives. The taxonomy of objectives was this means. The movement toward outcome-based education complements and builds on the pioneering work of Bloom and his associates. Additionally, program goals, classroom objectives, and learning outcomes more recently have become integrated with teaching strategies that focus on higher-order thinking skills in Bloom's taxonomy and the use of authentic assessment procedures, including constructed response, performance testing, and portfolios (Boschee & Baron, 1994).

McNeil (1996) presented a holistic view of the prevailing concepts of curriculum. He classified curriculum concepts into four major categories: humanistic, social reconstructionist, technological, and academic. The *humanistic concept* suggests that the curriculum should include experiences that are personally satisfying for the students. These experiences should meet the students' needs for growth and personal integrity and should develop the creative individual who can solve problems of the future. The *social reconstructionist concept* stresses societal needs over individual interests. The curriculum presented should impact social reform and improve the prospects for the future of society through offering the learner many problems that society faces. There is an emphasis on social values and using those values in critical thinking processes. The *technological concept* promotes technological processes for accomplishing the goals of policymakers. This concept is concerned with efficiency, predictability, and accountability. It is focused on the identified goal, objective, and outcome. The *academic concept* promotes curriculum as the means by which students are introduced to content in the disciplines and organized fields of study. The content or subject matter is critical and central in this concept and outweighs societal or personal needs.

Models of Curriculum

To determine which curriculum model best aligns with the school in which the principal serves, it is important to review some of the most prominent models over the past and those that are becoming more prominent today. In the early 20th century, Bobbitt (1918) proposed a view of schooling as related to production processes in factories; he indicated that this process could be reduced to an efficient technique. Mid-century, Tyler (1949) introduced a disciplined approach to curriculum design. Behavioral objectives upon which curriculum could be built grew out of educational psychology and gained substantially in the 1950s and 1960s, and this approach is still practiced broadly today. Around the same time, curriculum theory was introduced by Goodlad (1958); he purported the need for a comprehensive and coherent framework in curriculum design (Hansen, 1995).

Hansen (1995) indicated that curriculum is a complex concept that is maladroitly linked to theory and practice. Hansen's notion about the complexity of curriculum was supported by Apple (1990) and Goodson (1991), who stated that the relationship of curriculum theory to educational change was complex and that ideas about how the theory guides the change have been too simplistic. Hansen reported:

> Often what appears on the surface to be a very coherent and rational argument for a curriculum policy direction in schools may never materialize, or if it does, the final result differs from what was envisioned. Whether one adopts Goodson's notion that curriculum theory, to be of use, must begin with studies of schools and teaching, or Apple's view that our ability to illuminate the interdependence and interaction of factors associated with curriculum reform is limited by political and cultural forces deeply embedded in the schools, the end result is the same. (Hansen, 1995)

The various concepts, past and present, of the curriculum have been reflected in theories of curriculum development. In its most simplified form, curriculum development is the process of planning, implementing, and evaluating curriculum that ultimately results in a curriculum plan.

Following is a brief description of some selected historical models or theories of the curriculum development process, followed by a more modern or emerging view of curriculum models.

Tyler: Classical Model   Probably the most frequently quoted theoretical formulation in the field of curriculum has been that published originally by Ralph Tyler in 1949. Tyler (1969) stated his curriculum rationale in terms of four questions that, he argued, must be answered in developing any curriculum and plan of instruction:

1. What educational purposes should the school seek to attain?

2. What educational experiences can be provided that are likely to attain these purposes?

3. How can these educational experiences be effectively organized?

4. How can we determine whether these purposes are being attained?

These questions may be reformulated into a four-step process: stating objectives, selecting learning experiences, organizing learning experiences, and evaluating the curriculum. The Tyler rationale is essentially an explication of these steps. Figure 3.1 depicts the Tyler curriculum process.

Tyler proposed that educational objectives originate from three sources: studies of society, studies of learners, and subject-matter specialists. These data are systematically collected and analyzed to form the basis of initial objectives to be tested for their attainability and their efforts in real curriculum situations. The tentative objectives from the three sources are filtered through two screens — the school's educational philosophy and the knowledge of the psychology of learning — resulting in a final set of educational objectives.

Once the first step of stating and refining objectives is accomplished, the rationale proceeds through the steps of selection and organization of learning experiences as the means for achieving outcomes and, finally, evaluating in terms of those learning outcomes. Tyler recognized a problem in connection with the selection of learning experiences by a teacher or curriculum designer. The

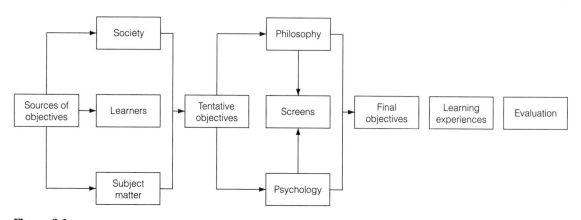

Figure 3.1

Designing the Curriculum

problem is that by definition, a learning experience is the interaction between a student and her environment; that is, a learning experience is to some degree a function of the student's perceptions, interests, and previous experiences. Thus selecting a learning experience is not totally within the power. Nevertheless, Tyler maintained that the teacher can control the learning experience by manipulating the environment, which results in stimulating situations sufficient to evoke the kind of learning outcomes desired.

The final step in Tyler's rationale, evaluation, is the process of determining to what extent the educational objectives are being realized by the curriculum. Stated another way, the statement of objectives serves not only as the basis for selecting and organizing the learning experiences but also as a standard against which the program of curriculum and instruction is appraised. Thus, according to Tyler, curriculum evaluation is the process of matching initial expectations in the form of behavioral objectives with outcomes achieved by the learner.

Beauchamp: Managerial Model   In his managerial model George Beauchamp (1981) recognized the following procedures for curriculum development described by Tyler: the process of determining objectives, selecting and organizing learning

experiences, and evaluating the program of curriculum and instruction. Two additional ingredients are included in Beauchamp's design model: a set of rules designating how the curriculum is to be used and an evaluation scheme outlining how the curriculum is to be evaluated. The essential dimensions of his position on curriculum development are shown in Figure 3.2.

According to Beauchamp, a curriculum possesses five properties or characteristics: (a) It is a written document; (b) it contains statements outlining the goals for the school for which the curriculum was designed; (c) it contains a body of culture content or subject matter that tentatively has the potential for the realization of the school's goals; (d) it contains a statement of intention for use of the document to guide and direct the planning of instructional strategies; and (e) it contains an evaluation scheme. Thus, by definition, a curriculum is a written plan depicting the scope and arrangement of the projected educational program for a school.

As shown in Figure 3.2, provision is made for a statement of goals, or purposes, for the school. Beauchamp argued that at the level of curriculum planning, it is recommended that these goal statements be phrased in general terms, whereas the preparation of specific behavioral objectives should be left to the level of instructional planning.

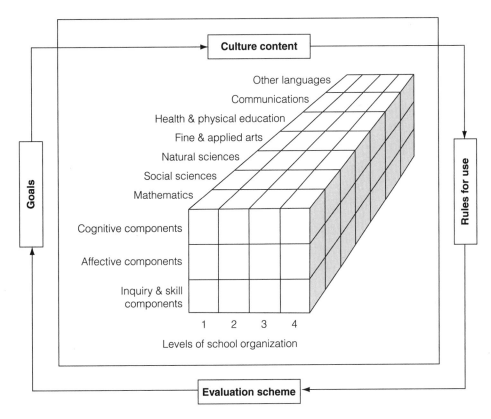

Figure 3.2

A Model for Curriculum Design
Source: Reproduced from *Curriculum Theory* (p. 129), by G. A. Beauchamp, 1981, Itasca, IL: Peacock.

A large part of a curriculum would consist of the organization of the culture content. Beauchamp designated the realms of culture content as languages, communications, health and physical education, fine and applied arts, natural sciences, social sciences, and mathematics. The culture content is also identified in terms of characteristics other than school subjects. These he refers to as cognitive components, affective components, and inquiry and skill components consistent with Bloom's and others' taxonomy domains. These characteristic components are included so that culture content may be more specifically related to goals and ultimately to behavioral objectives during the instructional planning stage.

Across the bottom of the model in Figure 3.2, four levels of school organization are shown. Typically these would be labeled in terms of the administrative organization of the school district or individual school, such as grade levels (primary, elementary school, middle school, high school) or ordinal years. This three-way organization of the culture content would require decision makers and curriculum planners to be cognizant of such design characteristics as scope, sequence, and vertical and horizontal articulation.

Two additional components are included in Beauchamp's model. One is a set of rules or statements designating how the curriculum is to be used and how it is to be modified based on experience in using the curriculum. An evaluation scheme constitutes the final component of the model. The evaluation scheme is designed to provide feedback data for the products and processes of the curriculum system and the instructional system. Outputs immediately lead back to the curriculum system and the instructional system, thus providing a dynamic cycle of feedback and correction to the fundamental processes of schooling: curriculum and instruction.

Taba: Applicative Model   Hilda Taba (1971) suggested that instead of developing a general plan for the school program, as Tyler and Beauchamp did, it would be more profitable to begin with the planning of teaching-learning units. In such a system, teaching-learning units would provide the basis for the curriculum design. Thus the curriculum would emerge from the instructional strategies.

Taba developed a social studies curriculum for grades 1 through 8, organized around teaching-learning units. In the process, a curriculum model evolved that is applicable to many types of curricula and that can be used in many different kinds of school settings and school levels: elementary, middle, and high school.

The model includes an organization of, and relationships among, five mutually interactive elements — objectives, content, learning activities, teaching strategies, and evaluative measures — so that a system of teaching and learning is represented. The model is depicted in Figure 3.3.

Taba's model contained within it a number of innovative aspects: specificity in determining objectives and content, learning activities selected and organized in accordance with specified criteria, teaching strategies that specify a variety of methods and technology, and an elaborate array of evaluative procedures and measures. Factors external to the model that may affect its internal components are also represented. Such factors include (a) the nature of the community in which the school is located — its pressures, values, and resources; (b) the policies of the school district; (c) the nature of a particular school — its goals, resources, and administrative structure; (d) the personal style and characteristics of the teachers

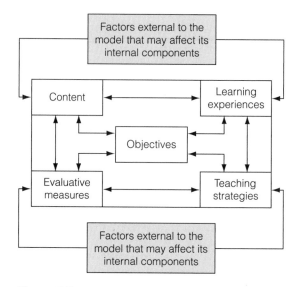

Figure 3.3

A Curriculum Model for the Social Studies

involved; and (e) the nature of the student population. Taba's model is recaptured by more recent philosophers and scholars in curriculum; that is, Boyer (1991), Slattery (1995), and Corrigan (1995).

More specifically, Taba (1962) asserted that to develop criteria for rational priorities in selecting learning experiences, it is necessary to clarify some significant issues. She pointed out the importance of understanding that the curriculum consists of two different things: the content (subject matter) and the learning experiences (the mental operations that students employ in learning subject matter). Although in the actual learning act the two are in constant interaction, one cannot deal with content without having a learning experience. Nevertheless, the two, content and learning experiences, need to be distinguished. According to Taba, it is possible to deal with significant content in a manner that results in inadequate teaching, or to apply fruitful learning processes to content that in itself is not worth knowing. One can speak of effective learning then as consisting of both content and processes that are fruitful and significant.

Taba stressed that the failure to make this distinction has caused many misunderstandings in the discussion of curriculum theories. Many reasonable criteria for selecting and organizing curricula have been misapplied or misunderstood by critics, because what was intended as a criterion for selecting learning experiences was also used as a criterion for selecting curriculum content or even for organizing the entire curriculum. For example, the discussion of the role of subjects as a means for training in disciplined thought has been obscured because of the assumption that disciplined thought is the direct function of the content rather than of the mental operations employed while learning it. Taba argued that it is possible to learn mathematics by rote, and to learn welding by analyzing and applying some basic principles. In other words, depending on the nature of learning experiences, any subject can be reduced to *learning about something* or become the means for the learning of the *how* of disciplined thinking. A clearer distinction between the content of the curriculum and the learning experiences (or the processes that students employ in dealing with content) would be helpful in classifying such problems of selection as determining which criteria apply to which aspect of curriculum — content or learning experiences.

The discussion of behavioral objectives, according to Taba, also showed that some educational objectives are served by the content, whereas others are best implemented by certain learning experiences. On the one hand, the objectives described as acquisition of knowledge — the concepts, ideas, and facts to be learned — can be implemented by the selection of content. On the other hand, the attainment of objectives such as thinking skills, attitudes, and values cannot be implemented by selection and organization of content alone. To attain them, students need to undergo certain experiences that give them an opportunity to practice the desired behavior. If curriculum is a plan for learning, and if objectives determine what learning is important, then it follows that adequate curriculum planning involves selecting and organizing both the content and learning experiences.

Objectives help to provide a consistent focus for the curriculum, to establish criteria for the selection of content and learning experiences, and to guide and direct evaluation of learning outcomes. At the same time that objectives, content, and learning experiences are being selected and organized, teaching strategies must also be planned and developed.

The process of determining objectives begins with the development of overall goals, originating from a variety of sources (for example, the demands of society, the needs of students, and the social science disciplines); is broken down into behavioral statements, classified in terms of the kinds of student outcomes expected (for example, the development of thinking skills, the acquisition, understanding, and use of important elements of knowledge, and the like); and is justified on the basis of a clearly thought-out rationale.

The content for each grade level in the curriculum is contained within a number of teaching-learning units, all emphasizing to some degree a yearly theme. Each unit consists of three kinds of knowledge: key concepts (for example, interdependence, cooperation, cultural change, and social control), main ideas (that is, generalizations derived from key concepts), and specific facts (that is, content samples chosen to illustrate, explain, and develop the main ideas).

The content provided in the units within a year's work is incorporated into learning experiences that are selected and organized in accordance with clearly specified criteria (for example, justifiability, transferability, variety of function, open-mindedness, etc.). Care is taken to ensure that the learning experiences develop multiple objectives: thinking, attitudes, knowledge, and skills.

Specially designed teaching strategies that identify specific procedures that teachers may use are included within the curriculum. (This makes Taba's model unique.) Some have been designed to encourage students to examine their individual attitudes and values. Particularly innovative are certain strategies that promote the development of children's cognitive skills, such as comparing and contrasting, conceptualizing, generalizing, and applying previously learned relationships to new and different situations.

A variety of objective format devices have been prepared to measure the effectiveness of the curriculum in helping students to explain or recognize causal relationships, to apply in new settings important generalizations developed in the curriculum, and to interpret social science data. Several open-ended devices have been designed to measure the quality of students' generalizations, the flexibility and variety of students' conceptualizations, and the variety and nature of the content that students use in response to open-ended questions. A coding scheme has been developed and used to analyze teacher-student discussions as to the levels of thinking that they exhibit, similar to Bloom's and others' taxonomies.

Saylor and Colleagues: Systems Model Galen Saylor, William Alexander, and Arthur Lewis (1981) adopted a systems approach to curriculum development. They describe and analyze curriculum plans in terms of the relations of ends and means, the attention to pertinent facts and data, and the flow of activities or procedures from beginning to end. Figure 3.4 depicts their conceptual model of the curriculum development process.

As shown in Figure 3.4, the selection of educational goals and objectives is influenced by (a) external forces, including legal requirements, research data, professional associations, and state guidelines; and (b) bases of curriculum, such as society, learners, and knowledge. (Note the similarity to Tyler's and Taba's sources.) Curriculum developers then choose the combinations of curriculum design, implementation strategies, and evaluation procedures that are calculated to maximize the attainment of goals; review feedback from the plan in effect through instruction; and replan the elements of the curriculum as indicated by the data.

Curriculum design involves decisions made by the responsible curriculum planning group(s) for a particular school center and student population. Having collected and analyzed essential data and identified goals and objectives, curriculum planners create or select a general pattern — a

curriculum design — for the learning opportunities to be provided to students. Among their alternatives is a subject design utilizing specific studies in the specified curriculum area, a scope and sequence plan built around a selection of persistent topics or themes, an analysis of the essential skills necessary for knowledge and competence in the subject area, and a selection of problems (in cooperation with students) related to the area of study. The design plan ultimately anticipates the entire range of learning opportunities for a specified population.

Curriculum implementation involves decisions regarding instruction. Various teaching strategies are included in the curriculum plan so that teachers have options. Instruction is thus the implementation of the curriculum plan. There would be no reason for developing curriculum plans if there were no instruction. Curriculum plans, by their very nature, are efforts to guide and direct the nature and character of learning opportunities in which students participate. All curriculum planning is worthless unless it influences the things that students do in school. Saylor argues that curriculum planners must see instruction and teaching as the summation of their efforts.

Curriculum evaluation involves the process of evaluating expected learning outcomes and the entire curriculum plan. Saylor and his colleagues recognize both formative and summative evaluation. Formative procedures are the feedback arrangements that enable the curriculum planners to make adjustments and improvements at every stage of the curriculum development process: goals and objectives, curriculum development, and curriculum implementation. The summative evaluation comes at the end of the process and deals with the evaluation of the total curriculum plan. This evaluation becomes feedback for curriculum developers to use in deciding whether to continue, modify, or eliminate the curriculum plan with another student population. The provision for systematic feedback during each step in the curriculum system — and from students in each instructional situation — constitutes a major contribution to Saylor's systems model of curriculum development.

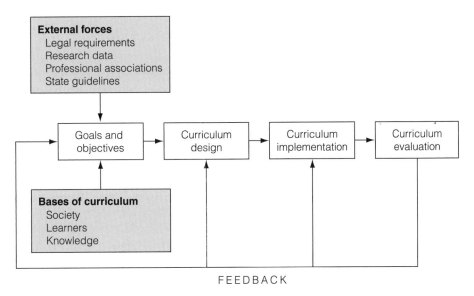

Figure 3.4

Elements of the Curriculum System
Source: Adapted from *Curriculum for Better Teaching and Learning* (pp. 29–30), by J. G. Saylor, W. M. Alexander, & A. J. Lewis, 1981, New York: Holt, Rinehart, & Winston.

Business leaders complain about the poor skills of high school graduates. Should the school curriculum prepare students specifically to earn a living, or should schools provide a broader curriculum that teaches students how to think?

Modern Models of Curriculum

McNabb (1995), reporting on the modern curriculum and pulling from Boyer (1991, 1995) and Slattery (1995), contended that the promising curriculum models are ones that include interdisciplinary courses, open-ended systems, intergenerational and inter-professional relationships, Socratic dialogue, multi-dimensional assessments, and multicultural infusion. The emerging curriculum models are systemic, relational, centered in a learning community, and reflective of society today.

Curriculum, as discussed by Boyer (1995), is a stabilizing force, one that imparts to the school the responsibility to stabilize the community of the child in every way possible. Corrigan (1995) outlined three purposes for schools considering societal conditions: "To teach relevant knowledge . . . To connect children and their families with other [health and human service] agencies . . . To collaborate with local, state, and national policy makers in developing policies that support integrated service programs and interprofessional education" (p. 10). He, like Boyer, considered the community of the student as central to what is taught in schools and suggested that technology could bring the world into the schoolroom to build the concept of community. For example, Boyer suggested bringing intergenerational relationships into curriculum. One such intergenerational curriculum, developed by Joyce McCauley at Sam Houston State University, brings residents of nursing homes or assisted living facilities and at-risk students together to improve literacy. The residents are bused to school during the day to work with the students — usually the sessions are housed in the school library. Additionally, the secondary students in the district work with the residents and teach them computer skills. The residents who learn the skills must share their newly learned information with another resident in the facility. McCauley has named this curriculum "Full Circle Literacy" (personal communication, January 15, 2004).

A principal characteristic of an emergent, postmodern curriculum is an open, rather than a closed, educational system (Slattery, 1995). A closed system might be viewed through the traditional standardized tests, rooted in Tylerian curriculum, which was inclined to over-assess students' static knowledge and under-assess students' higher-order thinking skills as well as process knowledge related to performing tasks (Corrigan, 1995; Wiggins, 1992). The traditional behavioral objectives are viewed by some of today's curriculum theorists as confining and fostering lower-order thinking; however, we contend that behavioral objectives can and must be written for higher-order thinking. Many curriculum modernists consider that it is authentic assessment within the curriculum that develops the student's cognitive strategies for self-assessment, fosters higher-order thinking, and accurately assesses the student against his or her own progress (Boyer, 1995; Cole, Struyk, Kinder, Sheehan, & Kish, 1997; Slattery, 1995; Wiggins, 1992).

Slattery (1995) reviewed features of emerging curriculum models. He stated:

> Laboratories, interviews, multisensory projects, seminars, workshops, playshops, and field experiences involving groups of students, teachers, and other community members will become the norm rather than the exception. Socratic dialogue that seeks understanding, respect, and synthesis rather than predetermined answers will be the hallmark of the postmodern theological curriculum. (p. 97)

More specifically, the following are offered as late 20th century definitions:

1. "The curriculum of a school, or a course, or a classroom can be conceived of as a series of planned events that are intended to have educational consequences for one or more students" (Eisner, 1985, p. 45).

2. "Curriculum is an explicitly and implicitly intentional set of interactions designed to facilitate learning and development and to impose meaning on experience" (Miller & Seller, 1990, p. 3).

3. "*Currere* is derived from the Latin infinitive verb that means 'to run the racecourse.' Curriculum is a verb, an activity, or for [William] Pinar, an inward journey. The modern curriculum development rationale has truncated the etymological meaning and reduced curriculum to a noun, the racecourse itself. Thus, generations of educators have been schooled to believe that the curriculum is a tangible object, the lesson plans we implement, or the course guides we follow, rather than the process of running the racecourse" (Slattery, 1995, p. 56).

4. "Curriculum understood as symbolic representation refers to those institutional and discursive practices, structures, images, and experiences that can be identified and analyzed in various ways, i.e., politically, racially, autobiographically, phenomenologically, theologically, internationally, and in terms of gender and deconstruction" (Pinar, Reynolds, Slattery, & Taubman, 1996, p. 16).

5. "A plan or program for all the experiences that the leader encounters under the direction of the school" (Oliva, 2001, p. 7).

6. "The 'curriculum,' as we use the term in this book, refers not only to the official list of courses offered by the school — we call that the 'official curriculum' — but also to the purposes, content, activities, and organization of the educational program actually created in schools by teachers, students, and administrators" (Walker & Soltis, 1997, p. 1).

7. "Curriculum development is a process whereby the choices of designing a learning experience for students are made and then activated through a set of coordinated activities" (Wiles & Bondi, 1998, p. 3).

8. Curriculum has the following four components: objectives, content, experiences, and evaluation means. Instruction refers only to experiences (Ornstein & Hunkins, 1998).

9. Curriculum is the central focus of the school as it entails accountability for all that each

student is, all each student brings to the learning situation, and all knowledge, skills, and dispositions that are planned, imparted, or facilitated via the instructional process.

Irby and Lunenburg Model We contend that with high-stakes testing dominating national and state agendas, the modern curriculum that is emerging must also include connected and aligned content objectives. Careful attention to the types of objectives written and the instructional delivery mode can take into account the issues brought forth by current curriculum philosophers. Our view for principals is that an integrated modern curriculum must be (a) led by the principal and developed collaboratively with teachers and community members; (b) considerate of the community; (c) responsive to the needs of the students related to academic needs, language needs, and social needs; (d) connected to the vision and mission of the school, which is usually focused on increased academic advancement of the students; (e) reflective of the needs of a global society; (f) able to be assessed in terms of how well the students are performing based on standards of performance; and (g) integrated systemically into the "whole" of the campus culture, programs, and instruction. This model is presented in Figure 3.5.

Principal acts as leader of curriculum efforts
There a strong relationship between the level of the building principal's leadership in curriculum project efforts and the success of both teachers and students. March and Peters (2002) studied the results of the Ohio Proficiency Test in six school districts. In one of those districts on all but one subtest, the proportion of students passing in one elementary building, where the principal was heavily involved leading curriculum efforts, exceeded by 5 to 15% the proportion of students who passed in a neighboring building where the principal provided limited leadership. It is the principal's primary role to focus the entire staff on curriculum development, revision, or reform and empower them in their work.

According to Allen (1995a), one strategy for empowering teachers is to provide a "highly

interrelated set of three resource elements to support teachers as curriculum constructors" (p. 2). Such resources include (a) guiding frameworks (representative of various sources of input), (b) examples of other teachers' and schools' curricular practice, and (c) formal, collaborative protocols that provide for teacher discussion, reflection, and critique. Allen (1995b) provides the example of the *tuning protocol* to represent the third type of resource. The tuning protocol helps structure teacher feedback and asks teachers to be "critical friends" to one another, to be their own best guides to reform. The protocol provides a safe, focused process for looking at students' and teachers' work and providing informed feedback on it (Allen, 1995b). The principal or lead teacher can facilitate a discussion within the parameters of preset norms. Wasley, Hampel, and Clark (1996) claimed that if a faculty can develop skills of rigorous self-analysis, they will have added a valuable critical tool to their repertoire of curriculum change. Furthermore, they suggested that schools need to develop habits of "civil discourse"—that is, new norms of conversation. Reflection about practice and about the curriculum is beneficial to teacher growth. The principal who engages faculty in this practice can improve the climate of the school, and it will **become** more professional, less subversive, and more respectful of real intellectual dialogue that fosters the development of shared understandings and more coherent action. As the principal facilitates critical self-reflection and analysis with colleagues, both the capacity for self-analysis among teachers and ways of critiquing each other's work presume a primary responsibility and knowledge on the part of teachers to carry (with assistance from the principal) the work of reform. The principal's primary goal in leading the curriculum is to empower teachers regarding curriculum development or reform.

As principals lead critical reflection, it is also their responsibility to encourage teachers to seriously examine curriculum that exists in the form of textbooks or other standards frameworks from the state or district. Sleeter (2002) provided an example of critical examination of History–Social Science Framework for California Public Schools,

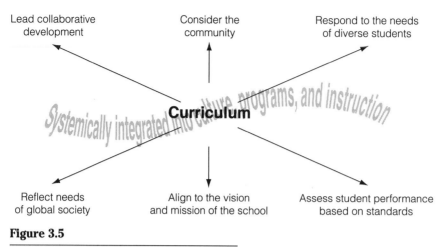

Figure 3.5

Irby and Lunenburg Model of Curriculum

first adopted by the California State Board of Education in 1987 and then readopted in 1994, 1998, and 2001 with only minor revisions. The examples follow and are self-revealing as to why it is of utmost import to critically examine such documents.

> By claiming to tell a multicultural story, the Framework masks the ideology of its own story. One way to identify whose experiences center a narrative is to examine the people who appear in it. I counted people who were named for study in the Framework's course descriptions. Of the 96 named Americans, 82% were male and 18% were female. They were 77% white, 18% African American, 4% Native American, 1% Latino, and 0% Asian American. All of the Latino and all but one of the Native American names appeared at the elementary level. At the secondary level, 79% of the named people were white, mostly either U.S. presidents or famous artists and authors. This analysis suggests that the narrative is centered on experiences of white men.
>
> Another way to identify whose experiences center a narrative is to examine the main topics and ask to whom they most closely relate. For the study of U.S. history, the progression of topics in the Framework traces the movement of Europeans and Euro-Americans west, and the expansion of the political boundaries of the U.S. People of color and women appear throughout, but within a storyline framed by this westward movement. Urging teach-

ers to tell the stories of multiple groups within a structure of topics that is based on Euro-American experiences, and especially those of English descent, masks the fact that multiple groups' stories are not being told.

> Consider, for example, how indigenous people appear. In third grade, students study local history, beginning with local topography and landforms, then briefly indigenous people of the past, and then move on. In fourth grade, students study the history of California, and in that context, briefly study American Indian nations in California's past. In fifth grade, students begin to study U.S. history, starting with a unit devoted to pre-Columbian indigenous people. After that unit, indigenous people appear only sporadically, in relationship to the story of the westward movement of Euro-Americans. Even when events such as the Trail of Tears are described as a tragedy, the basic cause of the displacement of indigenous people is not seriously problematized. (Sleeter, 2002, p. 8)

Curriculum is considerate of the community As curriculum is developed or reformed, principals must indicate to teachers that community is taken into consideration on several counts. First, the community should be taken into consideration when considering subject matter. For example, in the curriculum needs assessment, the community can be surveyed on several items generated by the teachers. An example would be work transfer skills needed in the community. Those skills would then become important in the curriculum planning. Another example here would be community interests in terms of service learning projects, which is an authentic curriculum and a concern that the community be involved in the learning itself. What community partners would best support significant service learning projects or community learning projects for the students?

Second, community members need to be included in the curriculum planning itself. Perhaps community members, including parents, may not be in on all the specific writing of the curriculum, but certainly they should be included in the assessment of it. Third, the type of community and needs must be considered. For example, Reid (1999) indicated it is unlikely that curriculum change in a rural secondary school, closely integrated with community interests, is explained in the same way as change in a suburban school with a cosmopolitan orientation and a heavy investment in college preparatory programs. Conversely, urban schools might deal with funding, access, or safety as basic needs that will need to be addressed in the curriculum. Reid further indicated that consideration of varying contexts has current significance, in that modern society is tending to become more diversified. Because curriculum and instructional strategies will likely differ from community to community, curriculum actions must be viewed within the context of a community, and such an activity demands that community members be involved.

Curriculum responds to the needs of the students Considering students' needs and interests presents a challenge to principals as they lead their faculty in curriculum reform. Consideration of student needs encourages more shared inquiry about special needs, such as inquiry about needs of students with disabilities and how to best serve them, students who are classified as gifted, students who are language minority, students who are economically deprived, and students from other cultures (none of these classifications is mutually exclusive from the others). The curriculum must also

consider more shared inquiry between teachers and students, as opposed to fitting the program to the students. Choice in the curriculum must be considered as student interests are considered. Within the curriculum, the principal must note how students will be assessed and evaluated. Principals must keep in mind that curriculum needs to meet the students' needs, but it must also conform to some reasonably consistent guidelines and goals for what students should know.

Curriculum is connected to the school's vision and mission Principals must keep the curriculum focused on the vision and mission of the school. They must always ask teachers how the curriculum is moving the school toward the vision and how it is accomplishing the mission.

Curriculum reflects the needs of a global society The principal must not only promote the needs of the immediate community but also be attuned to and share the reflections of the global society. He can do so (a) by promoting authentic curriculum; (b) by including service learning projects; (c) by incorporating and obtaining access to technology and its advances in hardware and knowledge generation; (d) by advancing critical thinking; (e) by problem finding and problem solving; (f) by bringing in cooperative learning; (g) by encouraging democratic, responsible, and politically and culturally aware citizenship; and (h) by incorporating multiple languages — or at least two, one native and one international.

Curriculum can be assessed based on academic performance standards The principal promotes an aligned curriculum with the skills and content to be tested as well as a curriculum map or sequence of skills necessary for success at each proximate grade level. The standards-based assessments are grounded in basic academic skills across all populations. They provide for a clear and uniform benchmark for what all children (based locally, by state or in the nation) should know and be able to do at specified points in their academic development. Principals who maintain a standards-based curriculum address societal expectations, focusing on how students will be judged by the state and the nation beyond the classroom and the school district. Alternative assessments can provide valuable insights into student progress in the curriculum.

There is systemic integration of culture, programs, and instruction The principal is responsible for synthesizing the total of the six components and ensuring that (a) they run through all programs and (b) they are observable in instruction. Additionally, the culture of the school should reflect these components from the curriculum, and all programs should be connected through the curriculum. No program should be an "isolationist" program on the campus. The principal should be able to articulate to the teachers, parents, central administration, and the community the path analysis of how one program relates to the other and how they are tied together by the curriculum of the campus.

Ornstein's Model   Ornstein's model of curriculum is systemic and takes into account society and schools today. As presented in Figure 3.6, there is an overview of the procedures and steps to consider for planning, developing, and evaluating the curriculum. The model is based on a behavioral/managerial model, rooted in the Tyler-Taba (behavioral) and Saylor-Alexander (managerial) approaches.

Overall, the model reflects a systemic approach because decisions and actions take place within the organization and recognize the impact of the organization, as well as other factors, on the curriculum decisions. In joining the school (or school district), participants accept an authority relation and understand certain roles, limits, and expectations of behavior, and certain policies and procedures for communication, collegiality, and change (the three Cs).

As part of *curriculum planning,* the political forces (Category 1 in Figure 3.6) are considered, the situation as it "really is" — or more precisely, as it appears to the participants. National, state, and local issues and opinion in general are reflected in the aims, goals, and objectives of the curriculum, but they will change over time. Specialists, consultants,

and experts can provide knowledge or expertise (Category 2) for modifying the school district or school's goals and objectives. These people will most likely be subject, learning, technological, or testing specialists. In determining what to teach, external groups (Category 3) play a major role in influencing curriculum participants, organizational norms and policies, and criteria for the selection of content. Major external groups are from the testing industry, textbook companies, professional associations, and colleges. The connection between the external forces and individual participants is virtually "one way"; that is, external groups influence participants' decisions and actions, but the reverse influence is almost nonexistent or slight. Viewed as "experts," those involved in determining the content of tests (and now standards), the content of textbooks, the college requirements (or Carnegie units), and/or the standards and policies of professional associations transmit, from one generation to the next, many of the major ideas of content (Category 4).

"Experts" from external groups may see the world quite differently than teachers and administrators do, but the latter have little influence in determining the content domain; basically, their job is to implement the curriculum. Curriculum implementation involves the what and how of curriculum. The content is the *what,* sometimes called the heart of the curriculum, and the instructional activities represent the *how.* Content is divided into knowledge, skills, concepts, research methods, ideas, and values.

Instructional activities (Category 5) — methods, materials, and media — usually take place in the classroom (although they can take place in the local and larger community) and represent the processes through which the teacher delivers the content. Activities are part of the implementation process. Although the activities are well entrenched by traditions, different methods, materials, and media evolve and replace traditional modes of instruction. The tension between traditional and progressive ideas of education is clearly depicted in Dewey's compact book, *Experience and Education* (1938). The term *activities* closely resembles what Dewy called

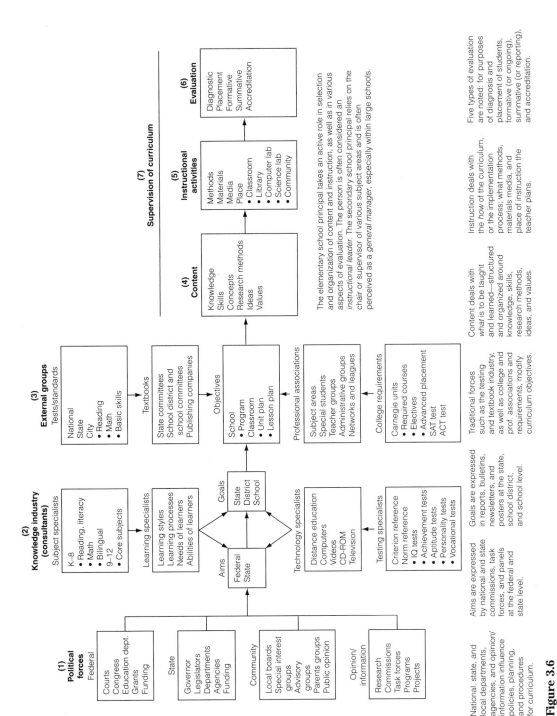

Figure 3.6

Ornstein's Model of Curriculum

"techniques and practices," what Kilpatrick called "purposeful methods," what Taba and Tyler referred to as "experiences," and what Bruner termed "processes." In short, instruction (Category 5) deals with ways in which content (subject matter) is taught by the teacher and learned by the student—that is, the *how* of implementation.

Curriculum evaluation (Category 6) provides information for the purpose of making judgments and decisions about students, teachers, and programs—or whether to postpone, modify, continue, and/or maintain the curriculum. Such decisions can be made at the classroom, school, and school district level. The principal's role is crucial at this stage. She provides direction, oversees content and instruction, and then, based on some form of evaluation, makes recommendations and decisions for maintaining, improving, or terminating the program. Five purposes and forms of evaluation (Category 6) are listed: diagnosis of problems; placement of students; formative, that is, during the implementation stage; summative, or at the end of the program; and accreditation, when the whole program is assessed.

Principals are responsible for overseeing curriculum instruction and evaluation. In Figure 3.6, this is represented by the term *supervision of curriculum* (Category 7).

Eisner's Model Eisner (1991) has offered a systemic and dimensional view of curriculum, as depicted in Figure 3.7, that could incorporate a postmodern view of curriculum while maintaining balance with evaluation of it. He indicated that if America is going to have the kind of schools it needs, it needs to pursue the following five dimensions.

■ *The intentional.* This refers to the serious, studied examination of what really matters in schools. To realize our intentions, we will need to address the characteristics of our curriculum, the features of our teaching, the forms of our evaluative practices, and the nature of our workplace.

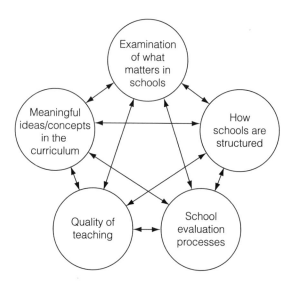

Figure 3.7

Eisner's Systemic and Dimensional Model of Curriculum

■ *The structural.* This dimension refers to how schools are structured, how roles are defined, and how time is allocated. All are important in facilitating and constraining educational opportunities. According to Eisner, the structural organization of schools has not changed much in the past 100 years. We start school in September and end in June; school lasts 12 years with a prescribed curriculum for everyone; 30 students per class are taught by a single teacher; grades are given several times a year; and students are promoted to the next grade. Such a structure is restrictive.

■ *The curriculum.* The significance of ideas in a curriculum is of great importance. We need to think about those ideas more deeply, and about the means through which students will engage them. The design of curriculum includes attention to ideas that matter, skills that count, and the means by which students and programs interact.

■ *The pedagogical.* Whatever the virtues of a school's curriculum, the quality of teaching ought to be a primary concern of school improvement. To treat teaching as an art requires a level of scrutiny, assistance, and support that any performing art deserves. Schools need to be places that serve teachers, so that teachers can serve students.

■ *The evaluative.* School evaluation practices operationally define what really matters for students and teachers. Schools need to approach evaluation not simply as a way of scoring students, but as a way of finding out how well we and our students are doing in order to better do what we do.

Relationship of Curriculum to Instruction

Principals dealing with issues of curriculum development or improvement often focus on the production of curricula. A few resources for the principal have reflected thinking about curriculum implementation and evaluation. The processes of developing, implementing, and evaluating a curriculum may be considered as the essential elements of a curriculum plan. A *curriculum plan* is a system for both decision making and action with respect to curriculum functions directed at a specified population. Thus a curriculum plan has three primary functions: (a) to produce a curriculum for an identifiable population, (b) to implement the curriculum in a specific school, and (c) to appraise the effectiveness of the curriculum developed.

The curriculum functions are particularly important in today's society due to the multicultural environments in which our schools are situated contextually. In our *contextual model of curriculum* (Figure 3.8), we consider it critical for the principal to have a plan that considers the population of the school community, the culture of the community, the specific needs of the school, and an evaluation plan for measuring the effectiveness of the curriculum. The curriculum must be related to the classroom instruction. It is imperative that the curriculum, the instruction, and the evalua-

tion of the students—all—be connected and aligned. Use the components as a checklist to determine if the curriculum is effective within the context. For example, ask "In what ways is the curriculum related to the population served in the school?" or "What is the relationship between the community's culture and the curriculum—how is that reflected in the curriculum?" or "How are curriculum and instruction related—how can we determine the connection? What instruments do we have available to connect the two?"

An example of disconnects between population served, community, curriculum, and instruction follows. Suppose that a teacher has a class of Hispanic children in her classroom. Hispanic culture is generally considered to be a collaborative, cooperative group culture. The children live this within their culture, and the parents expect this to happen at school as well. The curriculum has been developed to include cooperative learning groups, share pairs, and teamed learning centers; however, the teacher veers from the curriculum and teaches in a very non-collaborative way, using only independent work time, no pairing, and no teamed learning centers. This practice continues until an evaluation of the relationship between the curriculum and instruction in context is conducted. The disconnects in this fictitious scenario are between population served, expectations of community culture, and curriculum and the instructional delivery mode by the teacher.

The theory and research of John Goodlad supported the contextual model as depicted in Figure 3.8. Goodlad (1990) argued that curriculum development results in a plan for instruction, including elements of evaluation and the potential for school improvement. He also held that the key unit for educational change is the individual school and that the chief decision makers in effectuating a curriculum plan are the school principal, teachers, students, parents, and local community.

Tomlinson and Allan (2000) outlined essential characteristics in the connection of curriculum to instruction for delivering high quality in both. They stated that

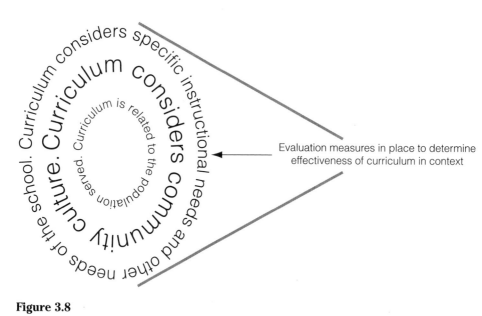

Figure 3.8

Contextual Model Addressing the Relationship between Curriculum and Instruction

a high-quality curriculum and instruction (a) is clearly focused on the essential understanding and skills of the discipline that a professional would value, (b) is mentally and affectively engaging to learners, (c) is joyful — or least satisfying, (d) provides choices, (e) is clear in expectations, (f) allows for meaningful collaboration, (g) is focused on products (something students make or do) that matter to students, (h) connects with students' lives and world, (i) is fresh and surprising, (j) seems real (is real) to the student, (k) is coherent (organized, unified, sensible) to the student, (l) is rich, deals with profound ideas, (m) stretches the students, (n) calls on students to use what they learn in interesting and important ways, and (o) involves the students in setting goals for their learning and assessing progress toward those goals. (p. 37)

Principals must assess these characteristics in order to make positive changes in the curriculum. Tomlinson and Allan (2000) avowed that many classrooms contradict the characteristics, specifically, stating that teachers are ill prepared to structure and

deliver high-quality classrooms. Therefore, it is incumbent upon the principal to develop the skills of his or her teachers through planned professional development that has been aligned to the curriculum needs and observations of instruction. Tomlinson and Allan also indicated that teachers are provided little time for reflection, observation, or discussion of their practice or to consider alternative and better ways to teach. (Much of this discussion on reflection may be found in Chapter 5, Professional Development.) Furthermore, Tomlinson and Allan indicated that left alone, teachers are not likely to become reflective practitioners and alter their classroom instruction.

Principals must structure the days so that teachers are provided time to reflect on their practice and on the curriculum they teach and on how that impacts student learning. Principals need to teach teachers how to reflect upon their practice or provide professional development that structures such reflection; therefore, it is incumbent on the principal to know the process of reflection and practice it also.

The Principal as Curriculum and Instructional Leader

Effective schools research has indicated that the principal, as the instructional leader, is critical to keeping a school focused on instruction, to setting a constructive climate and high expectations in standards and goals toward improved student achievement, to working to ensure a common curriculum, and to providing leadership for teachers (Brookover, Beady, Flood, Schweitzer, & Wisenbaker, 1979; Christie, 2000; Edmonds, 1979). The question we raise here is, does the principal have to provide all the leadership for the curriculum? Our response is no. However, it is the role of the principal to empower others and provide resources for others to perform instructional leadership tasks. Thayer-Bacon (2003) indicated that all principals should be like "Sister Katherine," a principal she worked with during one of her teaching assignments. She stated that Sister Katherine was one who supported teachers, empowered teachers, and found the resources to help them teach better. Principals have the role of supporter and facilitator in the development, alignment, and revision of curriculum. They have the responsibility to determine what curriculum model best fits within the campus and community culture.

Instructional or curriculum leadership tasks should be shared. According to Wildy and Dimmock (1993), instructional leaders (principals) do not perceive that they bear the major responsibility for instructional leadership tasks related to curriculum. In fact, few principals collect information about curriculum implementation or use such information to guide ongoing curriculum improvement and to identify needed support for teachers (Majkowski, 2000). This finding is contrary to what we have observed in effective schools; we found that principals did collect information and used it to guide ongoing curriculum improvement.

So that the instructional or curriculum leadership within the school can be shared, the principal must consider the following his or her responsibility:

1. Allow teachers to take on responsibility for leadership of the curriculum.
2. Arrange schedules so that teachers have the time to work on curriculum issues.
3. Provide staff development for teachers so that knowledge can empower their curriculum leadership.
4. Provide resources teachers need in their leading of curricular issues.
5. Create a community of learners where all share the vision for student achievement.

The concept of the school as a community of learners is a significant change from the paradigm in which schools are places where only instructional delivery occurs. Changing that paradigm requires a leader who is thoughtful of the common good and whose actions are expressed in democracy. Developing a community of learners requires that the principal be a team player and a team leader. It is critical for the principal to involve teachers, parents, or community members who have (a) expertise related to specific school issues, (b) something to share, and (c) a willing spirit to spend the time and effort to improve the particular curriculum issue at hand.

The principal cannot force team members to participate, nor can she appoint the members or force a topic, particularly one that is seen as unimportant, routine, or mundane. The principal must provide opportunities for the team members to learn as they tackle serious topics related to the vision, mission, and goals of the school. In building community, the principal and the campus team need to verbalize what the roles and relationships are between the school and community itself.

In developing a community of learners, it is the principal's role to assist teachers in how to filter that same development to their own classrooms and beyond. Prawat (1992) supported this notion of the community of learners in the classroom; the focus of the principal's evaluation would then move from the delivery of good lessons to judging the teacher on his ability to create a classroom learning community. Lieberman and Miller (1986) offered 14 ideas for consideration of building a community of learners, as depicted in Table 3.1.

Linda Lambert (2002) advocated for principals to build leadership capacity. She has defined leadership capacity as follows:

> broad-based, skillful participation in the work of leadership. In schools with high leadership capacity, learning and instructional leadership become fused into professional practice. Such schools have some important features in common.

> ■ *Principal and teachers, as well as many parents and students, participate together as mutual learners and leaders* in study groups, action research teams, vertical learning communities, and learning-focused staff meetings.

> ■ *Shared vision results in program coherence.* Participants reflect on their core values and weave those values into a shared vision to which all can commit themselves. All members of the community continually ask, "How does this instructional practice connect to our vision?"

> ■ *Inquiry-based use of information guides decisions and practice.* Generating shared knowledge becomes the energy force of the school. Teachers, principal, students, and parents examine data to find answers and to pose new questions. Together they reflect, discuss, analyze, plan, and act.

> ■ *Roles and actions reflect broad involvement, collaboration, and collective responsibility.* Participants engage in collaborative work across grade levels through reflection, dialogue, and inquiry. This work creates the sense that "I share responsibly for the learning of all students and adults in the school."

> ■ *Reflective practice consistently leads to innovation.* Reflection enables participants to consider and reconsider how they do things, which leads to new and better ways. Participants reflect through journaling, coaching, dialogue, networking, and their own thought processes.

> ■ *Student achievement is high or steadily improving.* "Student achievement" in the context of leadership capacity is much broader than test scores; it includes self-knowledge, social maturity, personal resiliency, and civic development. It also requires attention to closing the gap in achievement among diverse groups of students by gender, race, ethnicity, and socioeconomic status. (Lambert, 2002, pp. 37–40)

Table 3.1　Building a Community of Learners

14 Considerations for Principals as They Build a Community of Learners

1. Work with people rather than on people.
2. Recognize the complexity and nature of teachers' work.
3. Understand that there are unique cultural differences in each school and that they affect development efforts.
4. Provide time to learn.
5. Build collaboration and cooperation, involving the provisions for people to do things together—talking together and sharing concerns.
6. Start where people are, not where you are.
7. Make private knowledge public by being sensitive to the effects of teacher isolation and the power of trial and error.
8. Resist simplistic solutions to complex problems; get comfortable with reworking issues and finding enhanced understanding and enlightenment.
9. Appreciate that there are so many variations of development efforts that there is no one best way.
10. Use knowledge as a way of helping people grow rather than pointing up their deficits.
11. Support development efforts by protecting ideas, announcing expectations, and making provisions for necessary resources.
12. Organize development efforts around a particular focus.
13. Understand that content and process are both essential, that you cannot have one without the other.
14. Be aware of and sensitive to the differences in the worlds of teachers and other actors within or outside of the school setting.

Curriculum Goals and Instructional Objectives

How can the principal lead the formation or reformation of curriculum goals and instructional objectives? Principals must be able to motivate, encourage, and persuade teachers about the necessity for curricular change. Such motivation calls for principals to offer: (a) data that support the need for change; (b) evidence from other similar contexts that supports the proposed changes; (c) a link between proposed goals and achievement measures; (d) an emphasis on usability and time effectiveness in classrooms; (e) clear relationships between proposed changes and the vision, mission, and belief action statements; and (f) ample opportunities for all stakeholders to participate in determining goals and objectives (McGreal, 1980; Weick, 1982).

It is the principal who is the leader of the curriculum team, which in turn determines the curriculum goals and objectives related to the mission of the school. These goals may be derived from three sources and may focus on one of these in a more conceptual way: studies of society, studies of learners, suggestions from subject-matter specialists, and from standards. From studies of society, the principal may lead teachers to derive information about the needs of contemporary life, diversity, tradition, enduring values, and aspirations. From studies of the learner, the principal and the staff may learn about needs, interests, diversity, ability levels, and learning styles. From subject-matter specialists, the principal and the teachers may gain knowledge of best practices. From standards, the principal ensures that the goals and objectives are aligned to some benchmark, whether the perfor-mance standards are state or national ones.

The performance standards define the degree to which a student must master the content. National standards may be set by such organizations as the National Council of Teachers of Mathematics and, according to Noddings (1997), can certainly provide invaluable guidance; but she also indicated that local educators must decide what the sequence of study will be and why. The best plan would be for the principal and teachers to work closely with community colleges, local four-year institutions, trade schools, and businesses to establish performance standards that will enable students to make well-informed decisions. These may be aligned with the mandatory state standards.

Course content is very important. According to Campbell (1996), most teachers utilize textbooks as their curriculum. We have experience with school districts that allow for the adoption of a textbook and teacher's edition and supplemental materials as the "curriculum." Therefore, it is critical to bring textbooks into the arena of curriculum development as the investigation and development of goals and objectives are formulated; they should be scrutinized for their contribution to the diversity of the learners as reflected in society. Ultimately, the goals of the curriculum that reflects today's society were summarized by Campbell (1996):

> All students need to learn that they belong, that they are participants in the democratic project. The curriculum should help students to learn that they are important. They need to learn the skills, information, and attitudes that will protect and extend democracy and allow them to participate in the economy. (p. 291)

Curriculum goals are broad and general statements helpful in the development of programs of instruction or for general goals toward which several years of education might be aimed, such as elementary, middle, and high school courses of study. Examples of curriculum goals may be found in Table 3.2.

In contrast to the broad and general goal statements, instructional objectives are precise statements that indicate what students will be able to do as a consequence of instruction. According to Popham (1998), instructional objectives provide two key advantages to teachers. First, such objectives set forth in unmistakable terms what the student is to be able to do after instruction, making it easier for the teacher to provide on-target instructional activities for students. The more clearly a teacher understands what the end point of instruction is, the more relevant are the teacher's explanations, modeling, and practice activities. A second advantage of instructional objectives is that they permit teachers to evaluate whether their instructional efforts have been effective. Instead of teachers instructing in a haphazard way and hoping for the best, they can see whether their efforts were successful by finding out if students have, in fact, acquired the post-instruction behaviors set forth in their objectives (Popham, 1998). The word *evaluate* is critical to instructional objectives,

Table 3.2 **Examples of Curriculum Goals**

- To understand the rights and duties of citizens in American society
- To create a living history of personal stories of families' migration to the United States
- To attain an appreciation for literature, art, music, and nature
- To develop skills in reading, writing, speaking, and listening
- To learn to respect and get along with people of different cultures

Table 3.3 **Examples of Instructional Objectives**

- The student will learn to respect and get along with people of different cultures.
- Shown the letters of the alphabet in random order (in both upper- and lowercase form), the student will be able to say the name of each letter with 100% accuracy.
- Given 20 sentences containing a variety of mistakes in capitalization, the student will be able, with at least 90% accuracy, to identify and rewrite correctly each word that has a mistake in capitalization.
- Given a 12-bar Autoharp and the score (including the chord symbols in the form of letters) of a familiar 16-measure melody harmonized with two chords, the student will be able to provide accompaniment to group singing of the melody by locating by letter and playing correctly the required chords ("correctly" being defined as the proper channel sounded with rhythmic accuracy).
- Given the stylistic category of Renaissance, together with at least one example each of the musical, literary, and architectural achievements of the period, the student will be able within one-half hour, without the use of verbal reference sources, to write a 200-word essay comparing and contrasting in terms of style the given examples.

for without assessing and evaluating the students, the objectives are nothing more than curriculum rhetoric. Without assessment instruments to determine whether the objectives are actually achieved, the instructional impact of instructional objectives are decisively underwhelming (Popham, 1998).

Examples of instructional objectives may be viewed in Table 3.3.

Writing Effective Instructional Objectives

Well-written instructional objectives identify three important elements about learner behavior:

1. The *performance* that is required of the learner
2. The *conditions* under which the behavior will be performed
3. The *extent* or level of performance

Stated in one sentence, a well-written instructional objective should specify under what conditions and to what extent a certain kind of student performance can be expected to transpire.

For example, in Table 3.3, look at the second instructional objective again: Shown the letters of the alphabet in random order in both upper- and lowercase form (condition), the student will be able to say the name of each letter (performance) with 100% accuracy (extent). The three elements about learner behavior are incorporated in this instructional objective. You may now wish to identify the three important elements about

learner behavior in each of the subsequent instructional objectives.

Classifying Objectives   It is important for the school curriculum team to learn how to develop instructional objectives and assess learner outcomes. To that purpose, considerable effort has been devoted to the study of cognitive, affective, and psychomotor processes. Bloom's (1956) taxonomy is a scheme for classifying educational objectives into categories descriptive of the kinds of behavior that educators seek from students in schools. It is based on the assumption that the educational program can be conceived of as an attempt to change the behavior of students with respect to some subject matter. When we describe the behavior and the subject matter, we construct an educational objective. For instance: The student should be able to recall the major features of Japanese culture; he should be able to recognize form and pattern in literary works. The two parts of the objective, the subject matter and what is to be done with respect to the subject matter by the student, are both categorizable. It is, however, the latter—what is to be *done* with the subject matter—that constitutes the categories of the taxonomy.

The taxonomy is divided into three domains: cognitive, affective, and psychomotor. The cognitive includes those objectives having to do with thinking, knowing, and problem solving. The affective includes those objectives dealing with attitudes, values, interests, and appreciations. The psychomotor covers objectives having to do with manual and motor skills.

The classification scheme in each of the three domains is hierarchical in nature; that is, each category is assumed to involve behavior that is more complex and abstract than the previous category. Thus, the categories are arranged from simple to more complex behavior, and from concrete to more abstract behavior.

According to Bloom and his associates, there are at least four values of using the taxonomy for curriculum making. First, the taxonomy provides a basis for working with objectives with a specificity and a precision that are not generally typical of such statements. Second, this specificity and precision in the description of a student behavior make it easier to select the kinds of learning experiences that are appropriate to developing the desired behavior. Third, the hierarchical nature of the taxonomy facilitates scope and sequence in curriculum planning. And, finally, the taxonomy may be useful in evaluating teaching. Specifically, the content of norm-referenced and criterion-referenced tests, in addition to educational experiences and innovations in teaching, can be analyzed using the taxonomy as a framework of cognitive processes, which may reveal an over- or underemphasis on particular objectives.

As shown in Figure 3.9, the cognitive processes are classified in a hierarchical order, from simple to complex levels of thinking: (a) knowledge, (b) comprehension, (c) application, (d) analysis, (e) synthesis, and (f) evaluation. In the life of the student, the affective processes—interests, attitudes, appreciations, and values—are inseparable from the cognitive processes. The affective processes are classified in hierarchical order, from

simple to complex levels of feeling: (a) receiving, (b) responding, (c) valuing, (d) organization, and (e) characterization. Integrally related to the cognitive and affective processes are the psychomotor processes. From lowest to highest levels of the schema are the (a) reflex movements, (b) perceptual abilities, (c) basic-fundamental movements, (d) physical abilities, (e) skilled movements, and (f) nondiscursive communications.

The higher psychomotor processes—perceptual and physical abilities, skilled movements, and nondiscursive communication—operate cooperatively with the cognitive and affective processes. For instance, whether students are concerned with learning handwriting, improving their swimming strokes, learning a new art technique, playing a musical instrument, developing interpretive movements in ballet, or learning a surgical technique, the cognitive and affective processes are interdependent with the psychomotor processes.

Relationship of Objectives and Content The school curriculum team will need to be keenly aware of how the objectives relate to the content. This begins a process of curriculum alignment in which objectives are correlated within a scope and sequence of the content of the subject. Objectives are usually stated in terms of expected outcomes. For example, a high school science teacher might develop a chronological list of topics to be covered: functions of human organisms, use of plant and animal resources, evolution and development, and the like. This type of list shows what the science teacher intends to teach, but not what the expected outcomes of instruction will be. The content outline is useful for the teacher in planning and guiding instruction, but it is insufficient for the statement of behavioral objectives. To be useful in teaching, behavioral objectives must be linked to content.

The real contribution of stating objectives for learning is to think of how each objective can be achieved by students through the content or subject matter they learn. Tyler (1969) devised a two-dimensional chart for specifying varied types of objectives according to the subject-matter content and the behavioral aspects of the objectives (see Table 3.4).

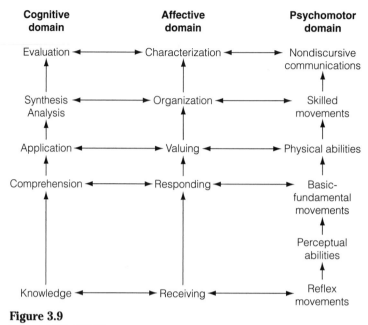

Figure 3.9

Relationships Among Cognitive, Affective, and Psychomotor Domains

As shown in Table 3.4, seven types of behavior are aimed at in the biological science course: (1) to develop understanding of important facts and principles; (2) to develop familiarity with dependable sources of information; (3) to develop the ability to interpret data; (4) to develop the ability to apply principles that are taught in biological science to concrete biological problems in life; (5) to develop the ability to study and report the results of investigation; (6) to develop broad and mature interests as they relate to biological science; and (7) to develop social attitudes.

However, the listing of the behavioral aspects is not a sufficient formulation of objectives to be most useful in teaching. Hence, Table 3.4 also includes a statement of the content aspects of the objectives. Note that the course is viewed as developing these seven behaviors in relation to the functions of human organisms: nutrition, digestion, circulation, respiration, and reproduction. Moreover, note that the course deals with the use of plant and animal resources including energy relationships, environmental factors conditioning plant and animal

growth, heredity and genetics, and land utilization. Finally, note that the behavioral objectives relate to evolution and development.

Formulation of the content aspects of the objectives has served still further to clarify the job to be done by the biological science course. Furthermore, the table indicates the relationship of the two aspects of the objectives: behavioral and content. The intersections of the behavioral columns and the content rows are marked with X's when it is implied that the behavioral aspect applies to a particular area of content.

Relationship of Objectives to Learning Experiences
In his classic text on curriculum, Tyler (1949) defined the term *learning experiences:*

> The term "learning experience" is not the same as the content with which a course deals nor the activities performed by the teacher. The term "learning experience" refers to the interaction between the learner and the external conditions in the environment to which he can react. Learning takes place through the active behavior of the student. (p. 63)

Table 3.4   Two-Dimensional Chart for Stating Objectives for a High School Course in Biological Science

Content Aspects of the Objectives	1. Understanding of important facts and principles	2. Familiarity with dependable sources of information	3. Ability to interpret	4. Ability to apply principles	5. Ability to study and report results of study	6. Broad and mature interests	7. Social attitudes
Behavioral Aspects of the Objectives							
A. Functions of human organisms:							
1. Nutrition	X	X	X	X	X	X	X
2. Digestion	X		X	X	X	X	
3. Circulation	X		X	X	X	X	
4. Respiration	X		X	X	X	X	
5. Reproduction	X	X	X	X	X	X	X
B. Use of plant and animal resources:							
1. Energy relationships	X		X	X	X	X	X
2. Environmental factors conditioning plant and animal growth	X	X	X	X	X	X	X
3. Heredity and genetics	X	X	X	X	X	X	X
4. Land utilization	X	X	X	X	X	X	X
C. Evolution and development	X	X	X	X	X	X	X

Tyler argued that the teacher's problem is to select learning experiences that will foster active involvement in the learning process in order to accomplish the expected learning outcomes. Tyler outlined five general principles in selecting learning experiences:

1. The learning experience must give students the opportunity to practice the desired behavior. If the objective is to develop problem-solving skills, then students should have ample opportunity to solve problems.

2. The learning experience must give the students satisfaction. Students need satisfying experiences to develop and maintain interest in learning; unsatisfying experiences hinder learning.

3. The learning experience must "fit" the students' needs and abilities. This infers that the teacher must begin where the student is ability-wise and that prior knowledge is the starting point for new knowledge.

4. Multiple learning experiences can achieve the same objective. There are many ways of

learning the same thing. A wide range of experiences is more effective for learning than a limited range.

5. The learning experience should accomplish several learning outcomes. While students are acquiring knowledge of one subject or concept, they are able to integrate that knowledge in several related fields and satisfy more than one objective. (Hollingsworth & Hoover, 1991)

We add these additional principles related to student learning:

6. We believe it is necessary to encourage learning experiences that enhance students' self-assessment skills; they should be taught to assess their own learning and progress as well as the teacher assessing it.

7. The learning experiences should be appropriate to the student's culture, ethnicity, and linguistic background.

Returning to the objectives of the biological science course (see Table 3.4), we illustrate several learning experiences that will help the high school science teacher achieve the first behavioral objective.

Objective Number 1: After studying the functions of human organisms, the students will be able to understand the important facts and principles of nutrition.

Learning Experiences:

1. Students study nutrition by classifying foods into four basic groups.

2. Students discuss the properties and nutritional values inherent in each grouping.

3. Students view a film on nutrition.

4. Students read research reports on the relation between nutrition and health.

5. Students write an essay relating the effects of poor nutrition and the incidence of various common diseases.

6. Students chart relationships between principles of nutrition and good health.

7. Students evaluate the many causes of health problems in America.

The mission of educators is to help students make valuable connections while learning. Educators can achieve this mission, in part, by integrating the curriculum.

For necessary curriculum integration, Banks (1988) provided four levels of curriculum. The first level is the *contributions approach* in which the curriculum or textbook simply adds a few ethnic characters from history or specific topics from history related to an ethnic group. This is a simple addition to the current curriculum and in no way changes the existing curriculum. The second level is the *additive approach;* like the contributions approach, it segregates ethnic history and societal and historical issues from mainstream curriculum. Ethnic content or learning units are added to the curriculum; but, again, no real reform is seen in the curriculum itself. The third level, the *transformative approach,* first considers that curriculum and textbooks written from a Eurocentric viewpoint do not reflect the truth. This approach, based on critical theory, requires that students are involved in the curriculum as they determine their own perspectives from their own worldview. This approach will require the principal to provide many professional development sessions for teachers to become competent in ethnic, multicultural, and cross-cultural studies. The *social action approach* is the fourth level provided by Banks. It includes the concept of social participation and employs empowerment strategies, critical thinking issues, and decision-making processes. In this curriculum the textbook is laid aside, or at least used at a minimum, and teachers pull from many resources to create, with their students, authentic material that revolves around societal issues.

Developing a Needs Assessment

In determining the effectiveness of the currently used curriculum and prior to revising or developing a new curriculum, the principal or the curriculum team must determine needs. According to Ornstein and Hunkins (1998), a "needs assessment contributes to curricular renewal when it exists as an ongoing process, rather than an intermittent activity. Needs assessment is integral in the planning and the change process" (p. 312). The established community of learners can take responsibility for the needs assessment by determining what data need to be collected, how it should be collected and by whom, and how it should be processed. Ornstein and Hunkins (1998) indicated that the data gathered should consist of both student and teacher performance, opinions, understanding, and desires.

As principals facilitate a needs assessment of the curriculum, several positive outgrowths can be seen. A needs assessment (a) assists with developing or revising curriculum and accompanying assessment and with implementing various instructional designs; (b) ensures the curriculum is fluid, dynamic, and responsive, rather than static and unresponsive; and (c) gives teachers information about learners, what they have learned, and what needs to be changed for greater achievement.

In our teaching of curriculum planning to prospective principals who are teachers, we have found that they, as teachers, are especially effective at conducting curriculum needs assessments. They are able to generate specific items to assess within the texts, with the teachers, and with the curriculum documents. Recently, in our classes, they have assessed such items as (a) how the curriculum addresses the needs of English language learners, (b) equity issues within the curriculum in its portrayal and treatment of gender, race, religion, ethnicity, disability, and language, (c) how the curriculum is aligned with state or national standards, (d) how English as a second language strategies are included within classes for English language learners, and (e) what teachers believe should be most relevant to be taught in the curriculum — that is, whether the curriculum is meeting the needs of the learners.

How to Conduct a Curriculum Needs Assessment Considering Standards

Today, high-stakes testing takes a center stage in many campuses across the country. How do the standards, the backdrop for high-stakes testing, figure into the needs assessment of the curriculum?

First, a needs assessment of the curriculum and the test must occur. Are the content of the test and the cognitive processes used in taking the test integral to the curriculum? The American Educational Research Association stated the following in its policy on high-stakes testing:

> High-stakes tests should not be limited to that portion of the relevant curriculum that is easiest to measure. When testing is for school accountability or to influence the curriculum, the test should be aligned with the curriculum as set forth in standards documents representing intended goals of instruction. Because high-stakes testing inevitably creates incentives for inappropriate methods of test preparation, multiple test forms should be used or new test forms should be introduced on a regular basis, to avoid a narrowing of the curriculum toward just the content sampled on a particular form. ("AERA Position Statement Concerning High-Stakes Testing in PreK–12 Education," 2000)

In this process, each teacher and the teachers collectively must be assisted by the principal to establish high expectations or standards for the students, and those standards should be published so that each student, each parent, and each community member knows what is expected. Doing so is part of further developing the learning community so that all can share in accomplishing the standards. The effective schools research of the early 1980s determined that schools are more effective when high expectations are set. Standards, whether they are at the local, state, or national level, help in setting those high expectations and assist teachers in assessing the alignment of their curriculum, instruction, resources, and evaluation practices to the standards. We suggest that principals consider local standards as well as state and national ones. Cohesion of the curriculum, including instruction, resources, and evaluation, or the lack of it, becomes apparent as the needs assessment is conducted related to high expectations and an established set of standards.

Content standards indicate what students should be able to know related to the subject matter; basically, content standards relate to the knowledge and skills of the learner. Content standards have been developed by many national organizations, such as the National Council of Teachers of Mathematics, National Council for Social Studies, and the National Science Teachers Association. Performance standards indicate to what degree the students attain competency in the subject matter as established by the content standards. Many states across the country now have content and performance standards by which schools are judged. If that is the case in a state in which the principal practices, then he must ensure that those standards are integrated into the curriculum that is taught and tested.

Assessment Tools

If students, teachers, or parents are involved in the needs assessment, they will have to understand the purpose of the assessment. Needs assessments can take various forms, including interest interviews or surveys on which learners assess their areas of interest; parent interviews to determine their perception of how well the child is progressing and what can be done with the parents to incorporate their support in the learning process; surveys in which teachers provide their perceptions of the curriculum as it relates to meeting the standards or to issues of gender, race, ethnicity, language, and so forth; open-ended interviews with teachers to garner their input on curriculum needs; document analysis of current curriculum documents or textbooks; and/or observations of performance. Needs assessment techniques selected should be appropriate for the learners and the teachers. For example, the interest interviews in English would be translated into the native language(s) of the child and parent. At an early grade level, using "smiley faces" for responses would be appropriate, and reading the questions aloud in the native language to the child or using rebus pictures on the inventory would be helpful.

Needs assessment at the curriculum level includes the following techniques:

1. Review and analyze the standards for the curriculum.
2. Review curriculum from other districts or schools that have been successful.

3. Interview or survey students, teachers, parents, professors, and employees.
4. Review current students' work.
5. Review the literature related to the curriculum area and consider best practices in the field.

Curriculum Alignment Process

Once the needs assessment is complete, the actual curriculum alignment process begins. This is a process in which teachers and principals check the curriculum against the standards and what is being taught and assessed.

Curriculum Alignment Curriculum alignment shows what will be taught in all subject areas and at each grade level. To begin, teachers put together their curriculum for the grade levels and align it with the state's standards or a selected national set of standards. Then they organize the curriculum and list the skills students should be able to demonstrate in every subject at each grade level.

Curriculum Mapping The curriculum map provides a scope and sequence of when skills will be taught. It lists the skills in the order they will be taught in each grade level, by subject area, and indicates to which standard they are aligned. It is necessary then to determine if the curriculum is aligned with the standards by reviewing the curriculum map for the assignment of specific standards to specific curriculum activities.

Curriculum Benchmarking The school should develop periodic assessments and minimum standards of achievement for all grade levels to determine how well students are moving toward the achievement goal. These multiple assessments, which are correlated with the curriculum alignment and curriculum map, allow teachers to collect objective data throughout the year. This helps them determine where children are — and where they need to be — to successfully pass the state assessment tests. Further, it gives teachers the opportunity to provide timely interventions in the classroom or even enroll students in special programs to deliver assistance wherever they need it (Decker, 2003).

It is critical to assess the timing or sequence to determine if and when the skill is taught prior to the test. This will require a horizontal alignment that takes a close assessment of the curriculum across a grade level or subject, as well as a vertical alignment that assesses the skills through the grade levels or subjects. For example, for an eighth-grade math curriculum, teachers would need to determine what skills have been taught before the eighth grade and what skills are to follow, so that students can spiral through a comprehensive and cohesive curriculum.

Curriculum Audit   "A curriculum audit helps to identify current strengths and gaps in instructional practices and can help align the district curriculum to state standards" (Chrispeels, 2002, p. 382). At the campus level, the principal leads the team to determine to what extent the standards are being met. This can be done by checking the state criterion test results or by checking the nationally standardized tests, such as the Iowa Test of Basic Skills (ITBS) or the California Achievement Test (CAT). Curriculum auditing allows the principal to determine "what is" and "what is to be," or as English (2000) indicated, to review the state between the actual and the desired and then to determine gaps between the desired and actual performance of the students. Once gaps are determined, the team prioritizes the gaps and establishes an action plan to effectively change what needs to be altered within the curriculum and instructional process.

Based on the curriculum audit standards (Phi Delta Kappa, 2004), the principal can guide the teachers in critically reflecting on the progress of the campus. The first standard deals with control of resources, programs, and personnel. The principal can ask, "What are the strengths and needs of the current educational program in our school? Does the evidence support our assertions about strengths and needs? What more do we need to know? If more information is needed, how will we follow up? What priorities does the information suggest?" The

second standard relates to the establishment of clear and valid objectives for students. The principal might ask, "Does the curriculum map indicate any gaps in objectives for students in general or for students with special needs?" The third standard relates to internal connectivity and rational equity in its program development and implementation. The principal should be concerned with asking, "What did we learn about how needs vary for different groups in our school—for example, among girls and boys, various ethnic groups, students with limited English proficiency or with disabilities, migrant students, or new immigrants? Are all our programs equitable? Are our expectations equitable?" The fourth standard deals with results or evidence from system-designed and/or adopted assessment to adjust, improve, or terminate ineffective practices or programs. The principal will ask here, "From our review of the data, can we state student needs in ways that specify goals, benchmarks for progress, and outcome expectations in measurable terms? Do we need to continue with this program?" The final standard is centered in improved productivity. This is productivity with student outcomes, as well as teacher outcomes. The principal would ask, "To what extent have students improved? How have the benchmark assessments indicated growth? Has teacher performance improved and how?"

Instructional Differentiation   As teachers review the assessment data and evaluate student performance, they try to determine what instructional methods are best for all learners. Determine how the curriculum addresses the needs of the gifted child, the students with disabilities, gender, and English language learners.

The description of the curriculum alignment process is an internal one whereby the principal takes the lead. English (2000), who conducted the first curriculum audit in 1979, called the process as just described a backloading process—moving from the test results to the curriculum—analyzing the results in comparison to the scope and sequence of the curriculum. Quality of instruction can be brought into the alignment by analyzing, as a whole, teachers' observational performances over the year and connecting the content to the test results.

Focusing the Vision and the School's Mission Through Curriculum

Curriculum alignment has an additional piece that we believe to be central, but that is rarely talked about in the alignment process. It relates to the school's vision and mission. The focus of the vision and the school's mission should always be the students, and it is the "student" that is at the heart of schooling. The vision and the mission must be aligned to the curriculum and instruction. Successful differences in a school are made in having a systemic relationship between vision and mission and the curriculum and instruction as reflected in the society, the students, and a culturally sensitive knowledge base. Wiles and Bondi (1998) stated, "few curriculum specialists have had the understanding of philosophy, the clarity of vision, and the technical skills to direct school programs toward consistently meaningful activity" (p. 37). We believe that the principal is the curriculum or instructional specialist or leader who does have the understanding of philosophy, the clarity of vision, and the technical skills to move his or her programs toward meaningful activity.

Aligning the Curriculum to the Vision and Mission

Curriculum is the central focus of the school as it entails accountability for all that each student is, all that each student brings to the learning situation, and all knowledge, skills, and dispositions that are planned, imparted, or facilitated via the instructional process.

Therefore, a vision for a school *would include* an interconnected system of (a) quality, culturally and linguistically sensitive curriculum; (b) effective instructional practices; (c) ongoing professional development; and (d) meaningful accountability measures for the benefit of all learners. The mission and goals of an action plan would follow that would actualize the vision. It is possible that a school could have an overall vision and a curriculum vision as well.

A good example of a connected vision and mission to curriculum can be observed through the following information on the Mauka Lani (2004) Elementary School in Hawaii.

Mauka Lani Elementary School's Vision Statement
Mauka Lani Elementary School is a safe, caring, and stimulating environment where learning is a shared responsibility of teachers, administrators, parents, students, and community.

Mauka Lani Elementary School's Mission Statement
The purpose of Mauka Lani Elementary School is to help educate children for the future and to prepare them to be productive members of our democratic society. All of us must answer three basic questions to be fully human.

1. Who am I?
2. Why am I here?
3. Where am I going?

The answers to these questions help to clarify our beliefs and values. Those beliefs and values determine our actions and conduct.

The 'Ohana Management System has evolved through a dynamic process of operating by values in the relationship structure of an 'Ohana and together learning how to work in a fashion that would benefit all members, not just a few.

In the process of learning to operate as 'Ohana, members have become clearer about their answers to those primary questions stated above.

Although the processes, activities, and manner of learning the 'Ohana Management System is synthetic, the cultural model is authentic.

'Ohana Management System utilizes and facilitates the positive group dynamics that exist in every group. The teacher is the minority. There is only one teacher, whereas, there are many students. Students are given opportunities to share in the responsibilities of learning together, while they develop a sense of ownership in class. Therefore, the teacher has a team of students working for the same goal of optimizing learning and begins to enjoy teaching, learning with the students.

The 'Ohana Management System has been compared with cooperative learning. The significant difference is that the 'Ohana Management System is values-driven. The learning of the values and the processes utilized to reinforce the values is at the core of the system. It is an inside-out approach which insures ownership and accountability. The values are universal and holistic, but are taken from the host culture of Hawaii, the Hawaiian culture.

For many in our diverse cultures, the structuring of relationships determines positive or negative outcomes. The 'Ohana Management System offers a way to structure relationships in a way that all can pursue the common mission of optimum learning opportunities. The System allows every individual to be significant and disallows anonymity in a group or class. It enables individuals to realize their potential without negatively impacting others, while understanding and appreciating diversity. (Mauka Lani Elementary School, 2004)

Based on this excerpt from the Mauka Lani Elementary School website, it is clear that if we were to investigate the school's curriculum, we would find it to be open to diversity, aligned to the community culture, incorporating core values, and centered in democracy. The general curriculum statement within the overall mission is clearly aligned with the stated values, beliefs, vision, and mission of the school.

The principal, as the instructional leader, is focused on accomplishing the mission through the development of teacher and student potential. The vision and mission through the establishment of goals related to the curriculum are focused on improving student achievement through improving curriculum and instruction and taking the learner's context into account.

Summary

1. There are many conceptions of the curriculum: as content, as learning experiences, as behavioral objectives, and as a plan for instruction.

2. There are several curriculum development models: classical, managerial, applicative, and systems. All models have merit for curriculum leaders.

3. Curriculum goals, in general, are derived from three sources: studies of society, studies of learners, and subject-matter specialists.

4. To be useful in teaching, objectives must be linked to content. Tyler has devised a two-dimensional chart for specifying varied types of

objectives according to the subject-matter content and the behavioral aspects of the objectives.

5. Curriculum must be aligned to the vision and mission of the school. There is a systemic relationship.

6. Although the principal is the curriculum and instructional leader, decisions on the curriculum must be shared with the teachers and other stakeholders.

7. Principals need to be cognizant of the global society when developing the curriculum.

8. Curriculum alignment begins with a needs assessment.

9. In the day of high-stakes testing, much of the curriculum alignment and audit processes will move from an analysis of the test alone to the results of the test and their connection to the curriculum and instruction.

Field-Based Activities

1. Review the curriculum on your campus. With what model does it most closely align? How does it differ? Present this review and discuss it at the next departmental or team meeting with your colleagues.

2. (a) Perform a curriculum needs assessment on your campus. Analyze your assessment data; discuss this analysis with your principal. How can you use these data to assist in improving the curriculum? Develop a plan and share it with your principal or supervisor. (b) Develop a plan to conduct a curriculum alignment in one area of the curriculum. What are the critical alignment elements you would include? Review your plan with your supervisor or the Director of Curriculum in the district. Conduct the curriculum alignment.

3. Have this debate with your team or grade-level colleagues. Record your responses.

Debate Question

Should preparation for a job be the new thrust of curriculum development and instructional reform?

Arguments Pro

1. Inherent in the notion of an education is the expectation that an educated person will be a productive, well-paid member of society.

2. Today's students do not perceive that the curriculum and the way it is taught prepare them for success in real life.

3. Both teachers and administrators recognize that present curricula and instructional practices are not congruent with the way that work is done in the "real world."

4. Recent developments in the cognitive sciences pervasively challenge standard educational practice. This research informs us that intelligence and expertise emerge from learners' interaction with the environment, not their isolation from it.

Arguments Con

1. An education prepares people for living their lives, not simply for earning a living.

2. Today's students are tomorrow's citizens. The curriculum must transmit the collective wisdom of the culture. The requirements of the workplace should not dictate the content of the curriculum.

3. Although there is something to be learned from businesses and industries that typify "earning organizations," schools need not mimic them in every way to successfully meet their goals.

4. Thinking is more important and more useful than doing. Schooling is designed to teach students to think. Well-prepared high school graduates should be able to enter any job and do well because they know how to think about it.

Suggested Readings

Dewey, J. (1966). *Democracy and education.* New York: Macmillan/Free Press. (Originally published in 1916). This is a classic book upon which reflective curriculum is based and has application for today. It is a must-read for all administrators.

English, F. W. (2000). *Deciding what to teach and test: Developing, aligning, and auditing the curriculum.* Thousand Oaks, CA: Corwin Press. This book combines strong curriculum and management theory with proven practice to offer curriculum design and delivery guidelines that the reader can use to ensure maximum student learning.

Hamilton, R., & Ghatala, E. (1994). *Learning and instruction.* New York: McGraw-Hill. The authors present the major contemporary learning theories: classical and operant conditioning, information processing theory, Piagetian and neo-Piagetian theories of cognitive development, Vygotsky's theory of cognitive development, social learning theory, and traditional and current views of motivation.

Jackson, P. W. (ed.). (1992). *Handbook of research on curriculum.* New York: Macmillan. This handbook covers conceptual and methodological perspectives, how the curriculum is shaped, the curriculum as a shaping force, and topics and issues within curricular categories.

Ornstein, A. C., & Hunkins, F. P. (1998). *Curriculum: Foundations, principles, and issues,* 3rd ed. Needham Heights, MA: Allyn & Bacon. The authors provide strong coverage of curriculum issues such as multicultural issues, education of at-risk students, and the national reform movement; and give students an in-depth analysis of curriculum development and design that covers many technical aspects of curriculum making.

Scriven, M., & Fisher, A. (1993). *Critical thinking: Designing and assessing it.* Thousand Oaks, CA: Corwin Press. This text addresses the difficulties in adequately defining and assessing critical thinking. It goes on to provide a more useful framework for both conceptual and practical applications.

Teddlie, C. B., & Stringfield, S. C. (1993). *Schools make a difference: Lessons learned from a ten-year study of school effects.* New York: Teachers College Press. The authors address evidence of school effects and characteristics of more effective schools: role of context, relationship among teachers' and principals' roles, naturally occurring school improvement efforts, and longitudinal issues in building and sustaining more and less effective schools.

Tomlinson, C. A., & Allan, S. D. (2000). *Leadership for differentiating schools & classrooms.* Alexandria, VA: Association for Supervision and Curriculum Development. This book addresses the needs in curriculum for academically diverse learners in diverse classrooms and schools. Change in curriculum is discussed for a changing society.

4. Teaching and Learning

Standard 2.0: *Candidates who complete the program are educational leaders who have the knowledge and ability to promote the success of all students by promoting a positive school culture, providing an effective instructional program, applying best practice to student learning, and designing comprehensive professional growth plans for staff.*

FOCUSING QUESTIONS

1 What is the principal's role in teaching and learning?

2 What data are necessary to assist principals in instructional planning?

3 How does the effective schools model relate to teaching and learning?

4 What effective teaching practices are important for student learning?

5 What models of evaluation exist that can improve instruction?

In this chapter, we address questions concerning teaching and learning in schools. "Within an educational context, the two phenomena [teaching and learning] are so inextricably intertwined that it often is difficult to imagine one without the other" (Shuell, 1993, p. 291). Because teaching and learning are the critical centers of schools, we have placed this chapter early in the book, following the chapter on curriculum and implementation. It is the principal who must facilitate and monitor the curriculum — *and the implementation of it, instruction* — because this is the powerful vehicle by which students are transported to learning.

The Principal's Role in Teaching and Learning

Teaching and learning are appreciably connected. All principals understand that learning is the primary goal of education, and that teaching is the vehicle to accomplish that goal. It is important for principals to realize that teaching is not a lock-step activity that is a one-size-fits-all routine; rather, teaching strategies must be varied to accommodate different learning strategies, goals, types of learners, and different subjects. The principal's role in the teaching and learning process is

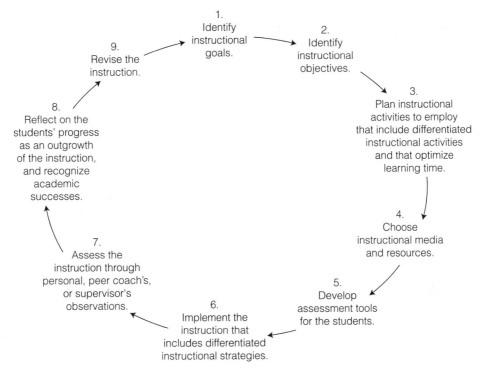

Figure 4.1

Cyclical Systemic Steps in Instructional Planning
Source: Adapted from *Instructional Planning: A Guide for Teaching* (2nd ed.), by R. A. Reiser & W. Dick. Needham Heights, MA: Allyn & Bacon, 1996.

(a) to accommodate teachers in their quest for gaining knowledge related to how the diverse student body learns best, (b) to assess the teaching as it relates to the outcome — learning, and (c) to facilitate the instructional planning process. Successful education can occur only if teachers are prepared to meet rigorous learning demands and the different needs of students (Darling-Hammond, 1995).

The Principal's Role in Instructional Planning

As the effective schools research of the 1980s determined, principals are the key to improved instruction, and a large portion of the principal's time is spent in the classrooms observing and providing feedback on instruction (Cooper & Good,

1983). Beyond the 1980s, Hallinger and Heck (1996) reviewed research from 1980 to 1995 on the principal's role in school effectiveness to determine if the principal made a difference; their research supported the notion that the principal's efforts to sustain a school-wide focus centered on student learning made a positive impact. Principals can help teachers shape their instruction by using instructional planning as a self-reflective tool (Baylor, Kitsantas, & Chung, 2001), and principals can facilitate instructional planning that provides teachers with a framework for developing a personal lesson-planning style (Clark & Peterson, 1986). Figure 4.1 offers nine cyclical, systemic steps the principal can take to assist teachers with their instructional planning. Many of these steps will have been accomplished during the curriculum alignment process on the campus.

Principals should encourage teachers to follow the steps in Figure 4.1 progressively, while considering the overall instructional design of the lesson. Effective instructional planning is a skill that teachers learn, and such planning requires purposeful practice (Baylor et al., 2001). It is important to encourage teachers to work with fellow teachers as peer coaches (trained in peer coaching and mentoring) throughout the campus or district to better determine if they are meeting their instructional objectives and the students' learning objectives.

The principal may share with teachers why instructional planning is important. First, planning provides the teacher with a daily map. Because discipline is tied closely to instruction, it is important that the teacher has planned the classes and activities for the students. If a teacher goes in unprepared, then problems with discipline may ensue.

Second, daily planning is important as well for targeting learner benchmarks as a part of the curriculum alignment process. How well are the students meeting the objectives of the grade level, the district, and the state? Daily planning and assessment of students and instruction can aid in answering that question.

A third reason for planning is so that the teacher can make certain she is following up on identified weaknesses of the students. From one day to the next and sometimes with multiple sections or classes, it is necessary to keep a daily planning system to stay on target with student needs in the various classes.

Fourth, instructional planning includes the teachers' understanding of the content necessary to succeed in facilitating the students' learning and in knowing how the content is connected to student goals, the community's resources, and the learning goals set by the campus, district, and state.

Fifth, instructional planning is intertwined with the curriculum alignment process. Usually, districts provide teachers with a curriculum guide for each subject area. Sometimes the school board adopts a textbook as the curriculum guide. The curriculum guide or textbook should be aligned with the district and state standards for learning in the particular subject area. This will be the first place to point a teacher in determining his learner-centered goals for developing his own instructional plans. Often the district will provide an aligned curriculum map or a learning scope and sequence with a timeline for instructional objectives; this is an excellent tool for teachers to use as they plan their instruction.

Promoting Teacher Reflection in Instructional Planning

Principals can use instructional planning to promote reflection among teachers (Baylor et al., 2001). To assist in reflection, Zimmerman (1999) developed the Instructional Planning Self-Reflective Tool (IPSRT), designed to facilitate reflective thinking through the instructional planning process. It consists of several questions teachers can ask themselves as they plan. The IPSRT follows closely Reiser and Dick's (1996) adapted phases of planning as previously depicted in Figure 4.1: (a) goals, (b) objectives, (c) instructional activities, (d) assessment, (e) revision, and (f) implementation. Some questions for reflection that are included in the IPSRT follow and are related to the first four phases of planning. These are the types of questions the principal would ask teachers related to their planning in order to assist them in becoming more reflective in their instructional planning.

1. *Goals.* Is the goal statement relatively general and broad, stating what the learner should achieve? Does it state *what* you want the learner to achieve, not *how* you are going to do it?

2. *Objectives.* Does each objective derive directly and logically from one of the instructional goals? Are audience, behavior, condition, and degree present for each objective? Does the objective state who will be doing the performance? Is it stated from the *learner's* perspective, *not* the *instructor's* perspective? Is the behavior specific and explicit? Is the behavior measurable and observable? Does the behavior state what the learner will

do at the *end* of instruction, not *during* instruction? Is there one active verb? Is the context for the behavior specified? Do the objectives clarify the conditions under which the performance will be done? Do the objectives clarify how well and/or to what extent the performance must be done? Are they specific and measurable?

3. *Materials/preparation.* Is everything included that is needed for the instructional activities?

4. *Level and learner characteristics.* Are all relevant characteristics of the students included (e.g., general characteristics, ethnicity, gender, grade level, preferences or learning styles, perceptual preferences, group size)? Are the objectives appropriate for these particular learners?

5. *Procedure.* Does this activity motivate these particular learners? Do you gain the learners' attention? Do you inform the students of what it is that they are going to be able to do when they finish the instructional process? Have you reminded students of any relevant prior knowledge about the new topic? Have you provided all necessary information about the subject in order for students to eventually perform the objectives? Have you provided examples so that the students can see how they can use the information? Have you provided practice opportunities that are directly related to the skills, knowledge, and attitudes reflected in the objectives? Have you provided feedback to the students? Have you summarized the lesson to bring closure and help reinforce the skills and knowledge that the students have just acquired?

6. *Assessment.* Does your assessment clearly align with your objectives? Do the active verbs of the test items *match* the active verbs of the objectives? Is each objective effectively taught and assessed? Does the lesson flow logically and easily through each section from goals to assessment? Is there an instructional purpose for each activity? Are the materials appropriate for the learners? Have you included all the materials necessary for the activities? Are the instructional media that you chose appropriate for each activity? Do you think your assessment items reflect what you think students should have learned?

Using Student Data and Evidence in Instructional Planning

The No Child Left Behind Act (NCLB) dramatically increases the principal's accountability toward student learning and focuses the principal on the importance of learning from student data (U.S. Department of Education, 2002). NCLB requires principals to disaggregate student achievement data, track the achievement of all students over time, and show demonstrable progress in raising the percentage of students who are proficient in math and reading. Principals and teachers must examine assessment results to identify problems and plan appropriate instructional interventions (Houlihan, 2002; Mason, 2002). NCLB expects principals to know how to learn from student data, and the law expects principals to provide teachers the time and support that they need to accomplish such tasks.

Supporting Teachers in the Use of NCLB to Improve Achievement Sharkey and Murnane (2003) suggested ways that principals could support the teachers in accomplishing NCLB requirements. Student achievement data must be obtained quickly. Access to *user-friendly software* that provides graphic summaries of achievement results for specific groups of students is necessary so that teachers can incorporate the information in their planning. Additionally, having access to student mobility data is important to teachers during instructional planning; therefore, student databases must be updated often to reflect student mobility. Sharkey and Murnane reported:

> The most useful district database stores the data centrally but enables teachers and administrators to look at test results for specific groups of students in their school, such as those participating in tutoring programs or review sessions. An effective data system also makes it easy for teachers to look at results on end-of-year summative assessments, not

only for their current students, but also for the students whom they taught the previous year. (p. 79)

The principal should be able to give designated members of the school's data team full access to school assessment results. Sharkey and Murnane purported that the software should enable teachers to compare performances of their students with the averages for the district and state. Some states, such as Texas, provide state achievement data that allow teachers to compare their students' performance with other students' performance in similar school districts.

Sharkey and Murnane (2003) further addressed compliance with NCLB through the provision of training. They indicated that training in the software was important, and that "teachers and administrators also need to learn a more difficult set of skills: how to ask instructionally relevant questions of data and how to answer such questions. Most educators have not learned these skills in preservice training" (p. 79). The authors provided this example:

> a common pattern in Massachusetts Comprehensive Assessment System results is that students tend to skip math questions requiring open-ended responses. Does this mean that the students did not understand the questions? That they could not do the math required? Or that they did not know how to write about their responses? To find the answer, teachers must not only think creatively about what patterns of test responses might throw light on why students did not respond to open-ended math questions but also recognize that answering the question may require data obtained by different methods — by interviewing students, for example. (p. 79)

Sharkey and Murnane found that opportunities to get together to analyze data are rare, and even when schools did find time for teachers to work together on examining student assessment results, teachers' feelings of vulnerability could have jeopardized the activity. Teachers need to plan together and analyze data together to be able to develop a coherent instructional program (Newmann, Smith, Allensworth, & Bryk, 2001). Sharkey and Murnane found that formative assessments were helpful in providing timely information on students' mastery of skills and the effectiveness of the instruction; however, they can present challenges such as (a) reliability in scoring student work, and (b) alignment, reliability, and validity of district- or campus-developed assessments as compared to the state assessment instrument.

Using Evidence-Driven Decision Making to Improve Achievement   In his book, *Leading from the Below the Surface* (2004), Creighton addressed the principal's need to evaluate student data or school data to make decisions. In this book, the author actually moves principals beyond "data-driven decision making" to "evidence-driven decision making." He has provided several examples of what he means by this (see the following example of Dr. Barrera, which we have paraphrased from one of Creighton's stories).

Creighton stated that many schools receiving the highest accountability rating (Exemplary) report average daily attendance (ADA) in a range of 92 to 98%. He said that 92% sounded pretty good and denoted a grade of A. So schools report that on average, they have 92% of their students in attendance. However, Creighton provided the example of Dr. John Barrera, the principal at Las Americas School in the Houston Independent School District.

Barrera exemplifies what Creighton calls "leading from below the surface," as Barrera perceives attendance in a different way: He is examining instructional planning, not state funding; he is concerned with quality instruction. Barrera asks, "If the ADA is 92%, what about the absence rate?" That's simple — 8%. So Barrera brings a different question to the surface: "On average, how many of our students are absent?" Investigating a little further below the surface, Barrera comes up with this important issue related to "evidence-based" decision making. The point is that if on average 8% of the students are absent, then based on a 180-day instruction year, these students are missing approximately two weeks of school per year (8% of 180 days equals 14.4 days). Barrera concludes that his school's state "Exemplary Rating," based on a 92% attendance rate, is one thing; but students missing two weeks of school per year is quite another.

Creighton argued that focusing on attendance may be no different from focusing on absence, but he stated that it is all a matter of perspective and reflects a characteristic of principals who lead from below the surface. He shares Barrera's story — a principal who cares deeply for the marginal students — and believes that looking at the absence rate rather than the attendance rate gives Barrera a better chance of focusing on students at risk of educational failure. Creighton said that yes, Barrera concerns himself with data; but he also digs deeper for further *evidence* to more effectively lead his school.

Once evidence has been gathered on the components of the curriculum and instruction, an action plan is needed to document the activities for improvement. The action plan, facilitated by the principal and developed by teams of teachers, should consist of (a) specific goals or objectives based on data or evidence; (b) connections to the vision or mission or overall school or district goal; (c) activities to accomplish the goal or objective; (d) person(s) responsible; (e) timelines; (f) targeted skills, standards, or benchmarks; and (g) evaluation format, or how the goal will be evaluated and documented to show that it has been accomplished (or to what degree it has been achieved).

Using Students' Cultural Backgrounds in Instructional Planning

Principal Barrera's story brings us to our next discussion on using students' cultural backgrounds in instructional planning; this concept is part of the *Irby and Lunenburg curriculum model* presented in Chapter 3. Here, it is explained in more detail and related to instruction as well as curriculum. Instructional planning calls not only for using the curriculum and student achievement data but also for using other types of student information such as their cultural backgrounds as well as their needs and interests.

Ethnoinstruction Ethnoinstruction takes into account the lived experiences and the cultural significance of the students with whom teachers work. Lara-Alecio, Bass, and Irby (2001) reported an example of using the students' cultural backgrounds

in teaching science. They indicated that according to Banks (1995), a leading authority in multicultural education, there are four dimensions to consider in instructional planning as related to cultural aspects of the students: (a) the integration of content, such as the integration of ethnoastronomy, ethnobotany, and ethnopharmacology; (b) the construction of knowledge, such as comparing how indigenous peoples and modern scientists differ in the ways they use evidence, build models, and generate explanations; (c) the reduction of prejudice, such as gaining a deeper understanding of culture, heritage, and contributions of the ancestors; and (d) pedagogical equity, which calls for the inclusion of interesting and challenging science opportunities for all students, regardless of age, gender, cultural, or ethnic background, abilities, or interests.

Lara-Alecio, Bass, and Irby provided an example of how ethnoscience can be incorporated into teachers' instructional planning. Principals can take these ideas and incorporate them into other subject areas with their teachers: (a) Select a topic in the study of nature and compare the knowledge generated on the topic among various cultures; (b) note that cultures generate knowledge, but that knowledge does not necessarily look the same from one culture to another — have the students study this concept; (c) tell the students that all cultures have systems of worldviews that describe natural phenomena; (d) emphasize to students that scientific observations that came before modern science have value; (e) ask the students to compare aspects of the indigenous worldviews, such as Mayan cosmology, with modern scientific worldviews. Principals who encourage teachers to infuse cultural sensitivity into the instructional planning can offer a broader and richer view of the world for their students by extending the content beyond the narrow scope of the traditional Western thought.

Differentiated Instruction Principals recognize that classrooms today increasingly reflect an image of diversity in a variety of ways. Responsible instructional planning cannot treat students as if they all learn in one way at the same speed. Such knowledge demands that principals must increase efforts to ensure that instruction is differentiated. Differentiated instruction assists students having a wide range of ability levels (Neber, Finsterwald, & Urban, 2001), learning styles, and cultural/linguistic backgrounds (Convery & Coyle, 1993).

According to Lawrence-Brown (n.d.), "differentiated instructional planning recognizes and supports the classroom as a community to which age peers belong, where they can and should be nourished as individual learners." What is differentiated instruction? Tomlinson and Kalbfleisch (1998) defined differentiated classrooms as "responsive to students' varying readiness levels, varying interests, and varying learning profiles" (p. 54). Waldron and McLeskey (2001) stated that "differentiating instruction means that teachers will create different levels of expectations for task completion within a lesson or unit" (p. 176). Waldron and McLeskey noted that schools need to create environments with differentiated instruction where all learners are benefited and where they can be successful.

We define *differentiated instruction* as instruction that reduces prejudice, that is equitable, that is sensitive to a variety of learning levels and styles, and that addresses cultural and linguistic diversity. All students benefit from differentiated instruction, through the availability of a variety of methods and supports and an appropriate balance of challenge and success.

Using Theoretical Frames for Instructional Planning

The best instructional planning and designs are based on the teacher's knowledge of theoretical frames of learning. Theoretical frames, although not prescriptive, are useful to teachers because they make them more aware of how learning takes place and how students acquire, retain, and recall knowledge. Additionally, teachers can use the learning theories as guidelines to help them in instructional planning, specifically in selecting instructional tools, techniques, and strategies to enable students to successfully complete course objectives.

In this section we share three broad categories of learning theories: (a) information processing, (b) cognitive, and (c) constructivist. Information processing theorists consider that learning occurs as information passes through short-term memory to long-term memory. Such theorists believe in scaffolded learning, by which students move from low to high, from easy to more difficult. Cognitive theorists consider learning to occur when students are able learn by doing through experiences or are able to add new concepts to their cognitive structure by recognizing a relationship between their prior knowledge and what they are learning. Constructivists believe that students construct knowledge for themselves — each learner individually (and socially) constructs meaning through the learning process. They believe that constructing meaning is the basis of learning.

Information Processing Theory
Conditions of learning   The principal should consider conditions of learning as he leads efforts for all children to learn. Gagné (1964) considered the objectives of learning when he indicated it was possible to divide objectives into categories that differ in their implications for learning. To do this, the principal must understand and lead teachers in putting together a selected set of learning conditions on the one hand and an abstracted set of characteristics of learner tasks on the other. The objective is to distinguish not the tasks themselves (which are infinitely variable), but the inferred behaviors that presumably require different conditions of learning.

Gagné presented eight learning-outcome categories that are a blending of behavioral psychology and cognitive theory; the first four are related to behavioral psychology and the last four to cognitive psychological theory. His categories are hierarchical in the sense that having any one capability usually depends on the previous learning of some other, simpler one. Thus, his two top categories of problem solving and strategy using require the prelearning successively of principles, concepts, associations, chains, identifications, and responses. Gagné's eight categories of conditions of learning include the following:

1. *Response learning.* A very basic form of behavior is called response learning, or it is sometimes given other names, such as *echoic behavior.* The individual learns to respond to a stimulus that is essentially the same as that produced by the response itself. For example, the child learns that fire burns and responds accordingly by withdrawing his hand from the heat.

2. *Identification learning.* In this form of behavior, the individual acquires the capability of making different responses to several different stimuli. Of course, she does this when she identifies letters of the alphabet, colors, numerals, late-model cars, or any of a great variety of specific stimuli.

3. *Chains or sequences.* Long chains of responses can most readily be identified in motor activities of various sorts. But many kinds of short sequences are very important to the individual's performance. One of the most prominent is a chain of two activities, the first of which is an observing response. If a teacher is concerned, for example, with getting a student to put the numeral 18 in the numerator, this activity has two main parts: First, finding the location of the numerator (an observing response); and second, writing in that place the numeral 18. In establishing such behavior as part of larger and more complex performances like simplifying fractions or figuring percentages, the teacher has to see that the student has learned such a chain or sequence.

4. *Associations.* For many years, psychologists appeared to be considering this category the most basic form of learning, but such is no longer the case. It is now fairly generally agreed, and supported by a good deal of research, that the learning of associations involves more than a stimulus-response (S-R) connection. Instead, an association is perhaps best considered as a three-step chain, containing in order: first, an observing response that distinguishes the stimulus; second, a coding response that usually is implicit; and third, the response that is to be expected as the outcome of the association.

5. *Concepts.* A concept is acquired when a set of objects or events differing in physical appearance is identified as a class. The class names for common objects like houses, chairs, and hats are more familiar examples. If one can assume these more basic forms as having been acquired, then the procedure of concept learning is fairly simple. It consists mainly in establishing associations in which the variety of specific stimuli that make up the class to be acquired are represented.

6. *Principles.* The next, more complex, form of learning pertains to the acquisition of principles. In their basic form, principles can be considered as a chain of concepts of the form "if A, then B," and the like. Again, it is evident that the important set of conditions necessary for principle learning is previous learning, this time of the concepts that make up the principle. It is assumed either that the learner already knows the concepts liquid, gas, and heating, in acquiring the principle, or that these concepts must first be learned. But when it can truly be assumed that concept learning has previously been completed, the conditions for principle learning become clear. The proposed chain of events is presented by means of particular objects representing the concept making up the chain.

7. *Problem solving.* Problem solving is a kind of learning through which principles are put together in chains to form what may be called higher-order principles. Typically, the higher-order principles are induced from sets of events presented to the learner in instruction. If carried out properly, these become the generalizations that enable the student to think about an ever-broadening set of new problems.

8. *Strategies.* Are there forms of behavior that are more complex than principles, or more complex than the higher-order principles acquired in problem solving? Some authors seem to imply that another form of learned organization is evident in the strategies with which

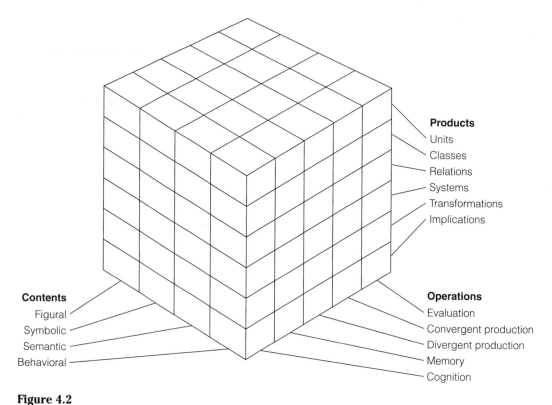

Figure 4.2

Structure of the Intellect Model
Source: From J. P. Guilford, "The Three Faces of Intellect," 1959, *American Psychologist, 14,* 470.

an individual approaches a problem. There can be little doubt as to the existence of such strategies in problem solving. It may be that strategies are mediating principles that do not appear directly in performance of the task given to the individual, but that they may nevertheless affect the speed or excellence of that performance. But it is possible to conceive of strategies as being principles in their fundamental nature, and of being made up of chains of concepts (Gagne, 1985).

Structure of intellect   For many years, there has been a tendency to think of the intellect as a generalized entity that functions on a generalized

level in all situations. In contrast, J. P. Guilford (1967) identified three primary mental abilities, broken down into 120 intellectual factors that may be considered necessary to perform well on a particular task. These primary mental abilities are depicted in Figure 4.2.

In his *structure of intellect* model, Guilford classified and organized the primary mental abilities according to (a) contents or type of information dealt with, (b) the operations to be performed on the information, and (c) the products resulting from the processing of the information. Instructionally, Guilford's second classification is probably most useful from the standpoint of principals sharing with teachers, because operations performed on the information refer directly to the major kinds of intellectual processes. The intellectual processes (operations) are as follows:

1. *Cognition.* Intellectual abilities concerned with the discovery or rediscovery of information; these abilities include comprehension and understanding.

2. *Memory.* Intellectual abilities associated with the retention or storage of information cognized.

3. *Divergent thinking.* Intellectual abilities related to the generation of new information from known information, with the emphasis on variety and quantity of information. In this case, thinking goes in varying directions, with no real "right" answer being sought.

4. *Convergent thinking.* Intellectual abilities related to the generation of new information that leads to the right or conventionally accepted answer. In this case, the given or known information usually determines the correct response.

5. *Evaluation.* Intellectual abilities related to the intellectual process by which judgments and decisions are made regarding the goodness, correctness, adequacy, or suitability of information, based on some criterion of consistency or goal satisfaction that resulted from productive thinking.

Guilford's thinking abilities (operations) can be thought of in terms of both their products (units, classes, relations, systems, transformations, and implications) and their content (behavioral, semantic, symbolic, or figural). A major shortcoming in much curriculum planning and instruction is that too much attention is directed toward the products of thinking and not enough to the operations and contents as indicated in the Guilford model. This deficiency needs to be corrected if the precision in planning instructional strategies is to result in predictable behavior changes in students who are exposed to purposeful teaching.

Note in Guilford's model that each of the intellectual processes (operations) is used to deal with processing products in various contents. For instance, students can be taught to comprehend units, classes, relations, systems, transformations, and implications in different content (behavioral, semantic, symbolic, or figural mediums). In the case of comprehending units (segregated items of information that have a single character), the teacher is primarily concerned with informational items or facts. The comprehension of units involves the recognition of visual, auditory, and even emotional units. With respect to instruction, this involves recognizing word structure and knowing the meanings of words in a variety of contexts.

The comprehension of classes (sets of items of information that are grouped by common properties) involves classifying groups of objects or ideas according to a prescribed criterion. At this point, the teacher is concerned with the process of concept formation as discussed previously by Gagné. At this point, students are in the most critical phase of instructional activity: If students do not learn how to deal intellectually with units and classes, they will be unable to deal effectively with the remaining products (relations, systems, transformations, and implications) depicted in the Guilford model. This appears to be one of the most important keys to ensuring instructional effectiveness and developing basic understanding in pupils at all levels of instruction.

The comprehension of relations (connections between the units of information based on certain points of contact that are applicable to them) involves helping students to discover relationships that exist among objects, symbols, or conceptual material when arranged according to some pattern.

The comprehension of systems (organized complexities of interrelated or interacting items of information) involves the abilities to structurally arrange objects in a given space; to discover patterns or systems among figural, symbolic, semantic, or behavioral elements; and to cognize or structure a problem preparatory to solving it. The comprehension of systems is more involved than the activity suggested in being able to see simple relationships, for it has to do with the organized total of a given structure. Frequently, this involves several simple relationships, fitted together in a conceptual structure that forms the system under consideration.

The comprehension of transformations (changes in existing, known information or in the actual use of information) involves the ability to form a mental image of patterns that would be possible if objects were rearranged in some way. An example is when a player creates a mental projection of a chessboard through several moves. Another ability required in the comprehension of transformations is predictive manipulation of available data to suggest a solution to a future problem. If students are to be taught to deal intellectually with transformations, they must be instructed in the processing of data, the detection of trends, and the development of strategies for theoretical formulation of plausible solutions to problems gleaned from the interpretation of selected data and trends.

The comprehension of implications (extrapolations of information, which can take the form of expectancies, predictions, concomitants, or consequences) involves attempts to plan or predict outcomes that might result from present conditions. In order to deal with implications, students must be taught to select the most effective solution to a problem from among a number of alternatives, to validate the process, and to anticipate the likely consequences given a particular situation and a certain arrangement of events (Rodgers, 1975).

Knowledge of Guilford's primary mental abilities is potentially useful in analyzing the kinds of instructional activities practiced and planned. In observing classroom activities, a principal can determine whether balanced intellectual development is being encouraged. In analyzing curriculum guides and textbooks, a principal can discover whether balanced intellectual development is an objective, and if it is planned adequately. Of course, this does not imply that intellectual factors should be sought in every teaching unit or daily lesson plan. Nevertheless, awareness of the factors should enable a principal, formally or informally, to analyze curriculum planning and practice.

The teaching of higher-level thinking skills is a topic that appeals to most teachers. These skills include comprehension of text, scientific processes, and problem solving. Although much has been written about the need for students to perform higher-level thinking operations in all subject areas, the teaching of these operations often fails because the instruction is inadequate.

How does one teach cognitive strategies? According to Rosenshine and Meister (1992), successful teachers of such strategies frequently use instructional procedures called scaffolds. The authors defined *scaffolds* as forms of support provided by the teacher (or student) to help students bridge the gap between their current abilities and the intended goal. Scaffolds may be tools, such as cue cards; or techniques, such as teacher modeling. A sample for the principal to use with teachers is found in Figure 4.3.

Stages of moral development   Numerous efforts have been made to examine systematically moral behavior as a developmental process. Kohlberg, a Harvard psychologist, developed a typological scheme describing general structures of moral thought. Like Piaget's framework, it is a cognitive-developmental theory that proceeds through a series of qualitatively distinct stages. In this regard, Kohlberg postulated that the sequence of stages is invariant and that each stage represents a reorganization and displacement of preceding stages. He believed that cognitive conflict is the central condition for reorganization. Unlike Piaget's stages of development, Kohlberg's stages are not strictly linked to ages and extend into the late twenties. However, according to Kohlberg, many people never reach the highest stages of moral development.

Kohlberg identified three distinct levels of moral thinking. Within each level there are two stages, thus making a total of six stages that may be considered as separate moral philosophies (Kohlberg & Likona, 1986).

- ***Preconventional level.*** Although Kohlberg's scheme is not strictly linked to ages, the individual at the preconventional level is typically a preadolescent. To a person at this level, moral value resides in externally imposed cultural rules and labels of good and bad or right

Present the new cognitive strategies.

- Introduce the concrete prompt.
- Model the skill.
- Think aloud as choices are made.

Regulate difficulty during guided practice.

- Start with simplified material and gradually increase the complexity of the task.
- Complete part of the task for the student.
- Provide cue cards.
- Present the material in small steps.
- Anticipate student errors and difficult areas.

Provide varying contexts for student practice.

- Provide teacher-led practice.
- Engage in reciprocal teaching.
- Have students work in small groups.

Provide feedback.

- Offer teacher-led feedback.
- Provide checklists.
- Provide models of expert work.

Increase student responsibility.

- Diminish prompts and models.
- Gradually increase complexity and difficulty of the material.
- Diminish student support.
- Practice putting all the steps together (consolidation).
- Check for student mastery.

Provide independent practice.

- Provide extensive practice.
- Facilitate application to new examples.

Figure 4.3

Using Scaffolds to Teach Higher-Level Cognitive Strategies

Source: Adapted from B. Rosenshine and C. Meister, "The Use of Scaffolds for Teaching Higher-Level Cognitive Strategies," 1992, *Educational Leadership, 49*(7), 26–33.

and wrong. Thus the individual interprets moral value in terms of physical or hedonistic consequences of action, such as punishment, reward, and exchange of favors; or in terms of the physical power of those who enunciate the rules. The stage 1 individual embraces an *obedience-punishment* orientation; that is, the person has an egocentric deference to superior power and authority, or a trouble-avoiding set. The stage 2 individual has a *naively egoistic orientation*. This individual believes that right action is that which instrumentally satisfies the self's need and occasionally the needs of others. Naive egalitarianism and orientation to exchange and reciprocity along the lines of "you scratch my back and I'll scratch yours" are representative of such a focus.

- ■ *Conventional level.* Chronologically, the individual at the conventional level is an adolescent. To a person at this level, moral value resides in good or right roles, in maintaining and conforming to the conventional order and the expectations of others. The stage 3 individual embraces an interpersonal concordance orientation in the good boy–nice girl vein. Thus, the person has an orientation to approval and pleasing and helping others. Conformity to stereotypical images of majority behavior and approval by being "nice" are typical manifestations. The stage 4 individual has an authority and social-order orientation. Orientation to authority, fixed rules, "doing duty," and maintaining the social order for its own sake are representative behaviors.

- ■ *Postconventional level.* The individual at the postconventional level is of adult age; however, Kohlberg believed that less than 20% of adult society act at the principled level, as it is also called. To a person at this level, moral values and principles are validated and applied apart from authority or conformity to group membership, though these values and principles are seen as shareable. The stage 5 individual embraces a contractual-legalistic orientation. Thus, the person has an awareness of the relativism of personal values and opinions and a corresponding emphasis on procedural rules for reaching consensus. Duty defined in terms of contract, general avoidance, of violation of the will or rights of others, and majority will and welfare are manifestations of such an orientation. The stage 6 individual has a conscience or principle orientation. Orientation to principles of choice involving appeal to logical universality and consistency, and to mutual respect and trust with conscience as a directing agent, are representative of such a focus.

Many contemporary educators view morality as something beyond intelligence. Such a perspective creates a schism between the two. Is not an intelligent person a moral being? Dewey pointed out that if subject matter is treated merely as knowledge acquisition, then it has only limited technical worth, but when subject matter is engaged in "under conditions where its social significance is realized, it feeds moral interests and develops moral insights" (Dewey, 1916/1966, p. 414).

Some researchers have found an association between moral reasoning and measured intelligence. However, Kohlberg asserted that although a person has to be cognitively mature to reason morally, he or she can be intelligent and never reason morally. He connects moral growth with social development, especially in relation to the amount of opportunity for role taking (Colby, Kohlberg, & DeVries, 1987).

Kohlberg's findings suggest implications for teaching. The social life of school and classrooms provides numerous opportunities for moral learning, especially if educators deliberately structure programs that facilitate movement from one developmental stage to another. Moral development demands an intimate knowledge of the individual and a program that involves discussion and problem solving (Kohlberg, 1989).

Gilligan (1982) examined the limitations of several theories, especially Kohlberg's stages of moral development, and concluded that developmental theory has not given adequate attention to the concerns and experience of women. Through a review of the literature and from her own research, she derived an alternative sequence for the development of women's moral judgments. She argued for an expanded conception of adulthood that would result from an integration of the "feminine voice" into developmental theory.

In her book, Gilligan challenged the notion that moral development is the same for girls and boys (Gilligan, 1982). For boys, the higher stages of moral development recognize notions of the rights of individuals; girls tend to view issues in terms of care, responsibility, and relationships. She pinpointed adolescence as a critical time in women's lives. By incorporating gender differences into their work, which Gilligan suggested, principals can more effectively address adolescent development, prevent psychological suffering, and strengthen women's voices in the world.

Cognitive Theories
Stages of intellectual development   Piaget, a Swiss psychologist, theorized that intellective capability undergoes qualitative developmental changes linked to the child's maturation. In this connection, Piaget identified four developmental stages, each one a necessary condition for subsequent intellective development. Although all children pass through these stages, it is important to recognize that all students in a given classroom will not be at the same cognitive developmental stage. Piaget's (1950) stages of cognitive development are the following:

1. ***Sensory motor stage.*** The sensory motor stage, which lasts from birth to about two years, is the prelanguage stage; it is vital to the development of thinking. During this stage, the child learns the rudimentary concepts of space, time, causality, and intentionality.

2. ***Preoperational stage.*** True language begins during the preoperational stage, which extends between the representative ages of two to six years. During this stage, the child learns to label with words the external world around him and to express his own feelings through language. He learns to adjust to the world through trial and error, to extract concepts from experience, and later to make perceptual and intuitive judgments. However, the child

adopts an egocentric orientation, a cognitive state in which the cognizer sees the world from a single point of view only — his own — unaware of the existence of viewpoints or perspectives of others. Instruction during this stage must focus on repeated and forced social interaction with others in order to fortify reflective thought and help the child to relinquish his egocentric orientation.

3. *Concrete operational stage.* During the concrete operational stage, which occurs in the range of seven and eleven years, the child can move things around and make them fit properly with developed fine motor skills. She can attack physical problems by anticipating consequences perceptually. However, because the student is dependent on personal experience during this stage, instruction must be appropriately arranged and must be concrete. For example, an urban student who sees a movie, videotape, or picture depicting farms, tractors, barns, and silos can understand the concept of a rural environment; but she cannot understand the concept by hearing a verbal description only.

4. *Formal operational stage.* During the formal operational stage, which takes place between the ages of 12 and 16 years, the child is no longer tied to concrete reasoning about objects. The child can think hypothetically, reason through the possible process of a logical solution, perform a controlled experiment, and reach some possible conclusion. Instruction can be organized by classifying, seriating, and corresponding. The results of these operations for learners are logical thinking and the intellectual processes of inference, implication, identity, conjunction, and disjunction (Smith, 1992).

Each successive stage of Piagetian theory requires more abstract thinking; therefore, a prime difficulty for the teacher involves selecting subject matter content that is abstract enough to challenge without being so abstract as to frustrate the student. When course content is properly selected, it is possible to build a spiral curriculum in which basic concepts are structured so that they can be used at different levels of abstraction, dependent on the students' ages and abilities. For example, Taba (1971) illustrated a hierarchical arrangement of concepts that allows each level to be prerequisite to the subsequent level. Concepts are taught at increasing levels of complexity and abstraction in a continuous thread through the curriculum.

Constructivist Theories

Learning styles   More than a decade of continuing research on student learning styles has revealed that, when taught through methods that complemented their learning characteristics, students at all levels became increasingly motivated and performed better academically. Essentially, learning style can be defined as a consistent pattern of behavior that gives general direction to learning. However, rather than simply looking at learning styles in isolation, teachers need to understand styles as they are exhibited in the classroom, interacting and influencing one another in a variety of ways.

Rita Dunn and Kenneth Dunn identified 18 elements of learning style that they further subdivided into four stimuli areas: environmental, emotional, sociological, and physical (Dunn & Dunn, 1992a, b). These are shown in Figure 4.4.

1. *Environmental elements.* According to Dunn and Dunn, studies have revealed that regardless of age, ability, socioeconomic status, or achievement level, individuals respond uniquely to their immediate environment. For example, some students require absolute silence when concentrating; others do not. Students also respond differently to temperature; some require a cool environment, and others prefer to feel comfortably warm. Learners also respond differently to the amount of light available; some require soft light when concentrating, and others prefer bright illumination. Finally, some students perform better in an informal physical environment (carpeting, lounge chairs, couches); others achieve better

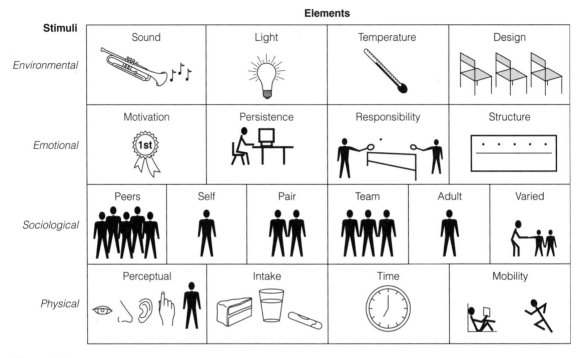

Figure 4.4

Diagnosing Learning Styles

in a formal setting (desks, "hard" chairs, and tables).

2. ***Emotional elements.*** Motivated, persistent, responsible students need to be told what they are required to learn, what resources to use, how to demonstrate their acquired knowledge, and where to get help if needed. They welcome praise and feedback when the assignment has been completed. The unmotivated, less persistent, less responsible students require short assignments, frequent feedback, a lot of supervision, and praise as they are working.

Structure is another vital element of learning style. Students who require specific directions, sequential tasks, frequent feedback, and continuing support usually achieve well using programmed learning—if they are highly visual or visual-tactual and able to work alone.

If youngsters are tactual-kinesthetic and also peer oriented, programmed material may not hold their attention. If they need structure, are tactual-kinesthetic (but not highly auditory or visual), and find learning difficult, they may do better with multisensory instructional packages.

Learners who tend to be creative, self-structured, or responsive to making choices appear to perform best when using a Contract Activity Package (CAP). Teachers experienced in the effective use of CAPs can decrease the amount of flexibility and the number of options provided, thus making contracts suitable for youngsters who require imposed structure.

3. ***Sociological elements.*** Some students learn best alone. For them, depending on whether they are auditory, visual, tactual, or kinesthetic as well as on whether they need structure, a

CAP, a program, an instructional package, or various tactual-kinesthetic resources (task cards, learning circles, or electroboards) should be prescribed.

Other learners achieve best when among their peers. For these students, Circles of Knowledge, cooperative learning groups, case studies, brainstorming exercises, and other small-group techniques tend to facilitate learning.

Youngsters who require interaction with an adult will benefit from lectures, discussions, or teacher-directed studies. However, it should be determined whether the relationship that is sought is authoritarian or collegial before suggesting whether large or small groups would be more effective.

4. *Physical elements.* During the past few years, researchers have found that only about 20 to 30% of school-age children appear to be auditory. Approximately 40% are visual, and the remaining 30 to 40% are either tactual-kinesthetic, visual-tactual, or some combination of these four senses (Dunn & Dunn, 1992a, b).

Other elements that either permit or inhibit learning are the need to eat or drink, the time of day, and the ability to remain stationary for longer or shorter periods of time. Teachers mistakenly label some students "hyperactive" when they are either light sensitive or require a great deal of mobility. Many of these students can learn well when they are assigned tasks that require them to move from area to area, or when they are permitted to take frequent breaks.

Most of the 18 elements of learning style can be accommodated easily by developing students' awareness of their own styles, permitting some flexibility, and then gradually developing the types of resources that complement learning styles.

Multiple intelligences   Gardner (1999), like Guilford, contended that a variety of mental operations are associated with intelligence. First, he stated that the theory is an account of human cognition in its fullness. He promoted the intelligences as a new definition of cognitive human nature. He said there are many different types of intelligences, although the society tends to focus on verbal or linguistic factors. He has described human beings as organisms who possess a basic set of seven, eight, or a dozen intelligences (Gardner, 1999).

Gardner (1985) proposed seven relatively independent forms of competence: linguistic, logical-mathematical, spatial, musical, bodily-kinesthetic, interpersonal, and intrapersonal. He later added an eighth intelligence, the naturalist (Gardner, 1999). Although Sternberg (1994) noted the lack of empirical support for the theory, Gardner's theory has been widely received by educators and provides a useful framework for understanding the basic skill level of all people as well as the unique strengths of individuals. An individual's uniqueness and cognitive competence are based on a combination of the multiple intelligences.

■ *Linguistic intelligence* is the capacity to use language, native language and other languages, to express oneself and to understand other people. Poets, writers, orators, speakers, lawyers, or a person for whom language is a strong part of her livelihood demonstrates linguistic intelligence.

■ *Logical-mathematical intelligence* is the ability to understand the underlying principles of some kind of a causal system—to manipulate numbers, quantities, and operations, like scientists and mathematicians do.

■ *Spatial intelligence* is the ability to represent the spatial world mentally, as when a sailor or pilot navigates large space or when a painter, a sculptor, or an architect envisions a design.

■ *Bodily kinesthetic intelligence* is the capacity to use the whole body or parts of the body to solve a problem, make something, or perform. This intelligence is seen in people who are athletic or who are in the performing arts in dance and theater.

■ *Musical intelligence* is the ability to think in music; to hear patterns, recognize them, remember them, and maneuver them.

- *Interpersonal intelligence* is the ability to understand others. People who excel in this intelligence are usually teachers, clinicians, salespersons, and politicians.

- *Intrapersonal intelligence* is having an understanding of yourself; knowing who you are, what you can do, what you want, when you need help, how you respond to events, what to avoid, and what to do.

- *Naturalist intelligence* designates the human ability to differentiate among living things (plants, animals) as well as to demonstrate sensitivity to the natural world (clouds, rock configurations) as seen in farmers, botanists, chefs, or meteorologists. The type of pattern recognition ability respected in some of the sciences may also relate to naturalist intelligence (Gardner, 1999).

The Effective Schools Model

Principals should be aware of how the Effective Schools Model or Process is a framework for school reform. This model is based on studies of schools across the country that have been successful in teaching the intended curriculum of basic skills to *all* their students. It is directly connected to learning through the acknowledgment of the need to acquire basic skills that may include comprehensive reading skills, oral and written communication skills, computing skills, problem solving, higher-order thinking skills, and social skills (National Center for Effective Schools Research and Development, 2000).

Every principal wants an Effective School because it is a place where *all* children learn. Faculty in Effective Schools teach all children, because they believe that they have a moral obligation to teach all children—a responsibility not just to the child, but to the parent, the community, and the society as a whole. Faculty in Effective Schools believe they are accountable and want to be accountable, insisting on regular testing and monitoring of their classrooms. An Effective School is an outcome-based operation, with specific mission statements and goals (Schmoker, 2001).

The schools insist on instructional leadership that models behavior and performance: leadership that gets involved with the staff and the students; leadership that spends time in the classrooms, observing and assessing teachers and students; leadership that understands organization and management skills; and leadership that is not afraid to take a stand or take risks (Blase & Blase, 2003; Glickman, 2002; Lambert, 2003). Change is ongoing; maintenance of the status quo is unacceptable (Duke, 2004).

The moral imperative of Effective Schools is the belief that *all* children can learn. That belief inspires the faculty and staff to be accountable for that learning. Accountability is welcomed. In fact, it seems that accountability becomes its own motivator (Sergiovanni, 2000).

By teaching *all* children, the school implements a process that begins to improve the school. Achievement scores rise. Teacher and student morale improves. The school becomes a more productive, accountable, professional learning community because it is following a precise process of change based on every child learning (Huffman & Hipp, 2003).

Two premises of Effective Schools are quality and equity. Quality assures that the level of achievement in a school is high. Equity assures that the high achievement does not vary significantly across the subsets of the school's population (Scheurich & Skrla, 2003). Educational equity is a precondition for excellence (Gordon, 1999). According to Gordon, we must achieve equal educational results for all children. Failure to do so will hamper specific groups from attaining the fundamental, primary goods and services distributed by society—rights, liberties, self-respect, power, opportunities, income, and wealth. Education is a social institution, controlling access to important opportunities and resources (Lunenburg, 2003).

The call for equity must begin at tracking. Tracking is denounced in Effective Schools. In Effective Schools there is no limit to the learning ability of all students. All children can learn, given the time and tools. And if schools operate on this premise, they will produce higher achievement scores and higher levels of satisfaction for the entire school community than will those schools that track (Oakes, 1985). Deciding whether a child is educable and then deciding what that child is entitled to learn, and operating a school that reinforces those decisions in policy and procedure produces ineffective schools. The policy of tracking, of selecting and sorting, is a major contributing factor to the failure of this country's public schools (Lunenburg, 2002).

Another essential component of Effective Schools is the disaggregation of test scores, the breakdown of test results according to specific criteria. Students are tested frequently, and the scores are disaggregated according to socioeconomic status, race/ethnicity, English language proficiency, and disability.

Disaggregation of test scores was not common in the public schools prior to the passage of the *No Child Left Behind Act of 2001*. For example, in 1994 only 42% of this country's 16,000 school districts had a program of school improvement, and of that 42%, only 11% (or 740) disaggregated their scores (Bullard & Taylor, 1994). The No Child Left Behind Act of 2001 now requires that states must disaggregate test results for all students based on socioeconomic status, race/ethnicity, English language proficiency, and disability.

Effective Schools recognize that it is unfair to ask teachers to accomplish a task they are not prepared to perform. A common complaint from teachers today is that they were never properly trained to deal with the learning needs of today's heterogeneous population. For that reason, staff development is another key component of the Effective Schools Improvement Process (Joyce & Showers, 2002). Through instructional changes like Teacher Expectation and Student Achievement (TESA), Mastery Learning, Cooperative Learning, Outcome-Based Education, Multiple Intelligences (MI), and other strategies, teachers can learn how students who previously would have been classified as low achievers can compete with some of the best students in the class (Tomlinson, 2003; Williams, 2003). It happens in Effective Schools all across the country.

"What gets measured gets done. What gets measured and fed back is what gets done well." This is a familiar slogan around Effective Schools. It is a matter of outcomes. The push for results is

the appeal of legislators and other policymakers, business leaders, parents, and the community (Schmoker, 2001). It makes sense. You create a plan with goals. You implement it. You aim for results. You evaluate the results (Carr & Harris, 2001). It seems to work for business; why not for education? Effective Schools are results oriented.

Effective Schools believe in site-based decision making (SBDM). Leadership is dispersed. The power to run schools is placed in the hands of those who actually do it. Teachers design their own school mission statement, the school goals, and the plan for the school to attain those goals. The teachers work on the school's curriculum. They choose the professional development they want. Teachers take courses in group process skills and decision making in order to become more effective at SBDM.

The school creates its own improvement team, which is elected rather than selected by the principal. Parents and business leaders serve on the improvement team, meeting regularly. The team discusses the needs of the students. They articulate a means of addressing those needs and present the plan to the entire community for approval (Langer, Colton, & Goff, 2003). The principal functions as an instructional leader: a leader who supports teachers; a leader who understands instructional techniques; a leader who is a team player; a leader who trusts teachers and gives them autonomy (Blase & Blase, 2003). This principal knows about adult learning, leadership of professionals, and student behavior (Cotton, 2003). This principal is a cheerleader, an inspiration, and the driving force for the school (Lunenburg & Ornstein, 2004).

Ron Edmonds (1979) published an article that brought together some of the most powerful and all-conclusive data on successful schools serving lower socioeconomic populations. This article, still cited today, became the clarion call for the Effective Schools Model — a call for teaching for learning for all children.

In the article, Edmonds set forth what he believed the research concluded were six correlates for an Effective School: (a) clear and focused mission, (b) instructional leadership, (c) high expectations, (d) opportunity to learn and time on task, (e) frequent monitoring of student progress, and (f) safe

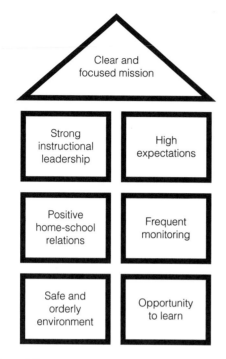

Figure 4.5

Effective Schools Correlates

and orderly environment. A seventh correlate was later added by Edmonds: positive home-school relations. These correlates are illustrated in Figure 4.5.

It is these same correlates, based on the philosophy that *all children can learn*, that have become the guiding principles of Effective Schools over the last 35 years. These correlates are in place in hundreds of school districts and thousands of schools throughout the United States. School people claim it is these correlates that lay the foundation for healthy environments for the teaching and learning for all children (National Center for Effective Schools Research and Development, 2000).

Clear and Focused Mission

The school board creates a district mission statement that publicly states their district's dedication to the needs of its population, with an emphasis on preparing students for the 21st century. Then schools reference their district's mission statement to create their own mission statements, in which each school's site-based team sets yearly goals and strategies. The result is a clearly articulated mission for the school, through which the faculty and support staff share a common understanding of and a commitment to instructional goals, priorities, assessment procedures, and accountability.

Instructional Leadership

The instructional leadership correlate recognizes that an effective school must have an effective leader. Each school operates like an independent company, with principals as visionary CEOs. Principals are hands-on leaders, as comfortable in the classroom discussing curriculum as they are in the community dealing with parents and business leaders. They are not afraid to take risks. They are buffers for their teachers and their students. They are respected and trusted. They know how to inspire, how to lead. The principal must see herself not just as an effective manager or as the leader per se, but as a leader of leaders. It is not a question of doing things right, but of doing the right things (Bennis & Nanus, 1985).

The principal uses whatever data she can to determine what she needs to do. Test scores and other types of data are indicators of how well the school is doing, and the principal uses that data to set goals for the improvement of student achievement (Phelps & Warren, 2004; Streifer, 2002). The principal empowers teachers within her school to become instructional leaders, so that she is engaging in a shared leadership. True effectiveness means that instructional leadership in the classroom is allowed. Teachers are better teachers when they are empowered, treated with respect, and held accountable for the achievement of their students.

High Expectations

Effectiveness demands high expectations. It pushes every child to be his or her best. It nourishes and builds confidence. As with all the correlates, it is data driven. Research indicates that a policy of tracking and low expectations greatly diminishes student achievement (Oakes, 1985). We have seen the harmful effects of tracking. We teachers track the students in our heads: The mother is a drug user. They are poor. They are this; they are that. We make excuses for students. We do not expect them to do very much, so we give them simple tasks. Most of the ditto sheets do not go to the brighter students. They go to the students we expect the least from, those we want to sit and be quiet. If teachers demonstrate low expectations by failing to give students a challenging curriculum, these students are not going to progress academically at the same rate as peers in other settings (Williams, 2003). Students are going to fulfill that prophecy. They will either drop out of school or walk across the stage at graduation and not be able to make a contribution to society.

The climate of high expectations reflects heterogeneous grouping of different levels of learners. This is probably a change in the educational culture, and it may require some re-learning by some teachers (Hall & Hord, 2001; Huffman & Hipp, 2003; Williams, 2003). Nonetheless, replacing tracking with heterogeneous grouping often alarms parents who fear the system dummies down, lowering standards to make the less productive students competitive. In fact, test scores reflect just the opposite (Oakes, 1985; Lezotte, 1997).

Staff development is essential to Effective Schools (Joyce & Showers, 2002) for learning about high expectations. Tools mentioned earlier, such as Cooperative Learning, Mastery Learning, Outcome Based Education, MI and TESA, aid teachers in realizing the power of high expectations (Tomlinson, 2003). Not only are students helped by the use of these tools as teachers provide more equal opportunity for all, but the students themselves, through the use of such tools, can also become more tolerant and understanding of one another's weaknesses, strengths, and differences.

It is possible to accelerate the curriculum in classes where teachers have children with different abilities. Effective Schools do not teach to the average, they teach to the top. Effective Schools can actually increase the abilities of children who previously may have been in a remedial group. The curriculum is actually accelerated. Effective Schools have a mission statement and goals. They have curriculum guidelines that must be met. Testing is done at the end of every semester over goals that were written in the beginning of the school year. That is, curriculum goals are in place. The curriculum is taught and learned by all students (Carr & Harris, 2001).

Opportunity to Learn and Time on Task

The Effective Schools correlate of opportunity to learn and time on task stresses new alternatives and teaching techniques in an interdisciplinary curriculum. The most significant change here goes from the behavioral psychological model that highlights the view of students as relatively passive accumulators of material—that is, students as products—to cognitive or constructivist psychology and newer sociological perspectives on learning, the conception of students as active constructors of their own understanding (Cohen, 1988).

Constructivism may be the most significant recent trend in education relative to the dynamic relationship between how teachers teach and how children learn (Brooks & Brooks, 2003). One foundational premise of constructivism is that children actively construct their knowledge, rather than simply absorbing ideas spoken to them by teachers. For example, more than 30 years ago Jean Piaget (1970) proposed that children make sense in ways very different from adults; children learn through the process of trying to make things happen, of trying to manipulate their environment. Theories such as these, which assert that "people are not recorders of information, but builders of knowledge structures," have been grouped under the heading of *constructivism* (Brooks & Brooks, 2003). Thus students are ultimately responsible for their own learning within a learning atmosphere in which teachers value student thinking, initiate lessons that foster cooperative learning, provide opportunities for students to be exposed to interdisciplinary curriculum, structure learning around primary concepts, and facilitate authentic assessment for student understanding. Under this approach to learning, schools that historically have been in the business of promoting student adaptation to the existing social order are being transformed to ensure equality of opportunity for all learners (Murphy, 2002).

Teaching today recognizes that there is a less formal, but at the same time a more intense and more focused atmosphere. A struggling child is never abandoned, but is coaxed along by teachers. Accepting that all students from prekindergarten to high school learn at different paces as well as in different ways from each other, teachers attempt to get all students involved (Tomlinson, 2003). Once students have learned to research materials, once they have learned to find information, they are equipped with research tools that will be helpful to them during their entire school career.

Frequent Monitoring and Assessment

You cannot correct a problem until you identify it. That is why a key correlate of Effective Schools is frequent monitoring and assessment (Carr & Harris, 2001; Lissitz & Schafer, 2002; Popham, 2003b). Feedback on student achievement is frequently obtained. Multiple assessment methods are used, including teacher-made tests, portfolios, mastery skills checklists, criterion-referenced tests, and norm-referenced tests. Effective Schools take testing a step further, requiring the disaggregation of scores — that is, breaking down scores by race/ethnicity, socioeconomic status, English language proficiency, and disability. This monitoring then tells the teachers not only what the students are learning but also who is learning what and, therefore, how instruction must be adjusted to reach those students who are not learning (Leithwood, Aitken, & Jantzi, 2001; Tomlinson, 2003; Williams, 2003).

Monitoring is critical if schools are going to have success with all their students, because monitoring is the feedback loop that determines the effectiveness of instruction (Hoy & Hoy,

2003; Wiles & Bondi, 2002). No matter how good a teacher is, if students are not learning, the teacher must question the effectiveness of the delivery of instruction. A teacher instructs; the students practice; the teacher monitors the practice. Where gaps in understanding are identified, the teacher may go back and re-teach (Williams, 2003). It may take just five minutes in that day's lesson, or the teacher may decide to teach another lesson the next day. All students do not learn in the same way (Tomlinson, 2003). Frequent monitoring and feedback are used to improve individual student performance as well as the school's instructional program (Danielson, 2002).

Safe and Orderly Environment

The correlate of a safe and orderly environment seems to grow more and more important in America. Schools cannot do the work of learning without clearly defined rules, discipline, and codes of conduct. Effective Schools are often very strict; every student knows what is expected and understands the parameters of behavior. A safe and orderly environment is essential not just in establishing grading practices, but in keeping violence outside of the school.

What has worked well for some schools is their zero tolerance policy for gang activity; for anything that looks like gang activity; for anything that disrupts the learning process. These schools have decreased significantly the number of fights and the number of weapons brought to school (Duke, 2002). The message is: This is an orderly, purposeful atmosphere that is free from threat of physical harm for both students and staff. A principal cannot change the environment surrounding the school; he cannot change the fact that there is violence in the community; and he cannot change the fact that impoverished children live in the attendance area. But the principal can work with parents, the community, churches, social agencies, and law enforcement to improve these conditions (Epstein, 2001; Rubin, 2002).

In addition, the principal can change what happens in the school from the opening bell to the end of the school day. Both approaches require collaboration within the school community to achieve an orderly, purposeful environment conducive to learning.

Positive Home-School Relations

This last correlate, positive home-school relations, was not included initially, because the Effective Schools Process holds as its base only those variables that the school can control. Edmonds was fearful that schools would use the lack of parental involvement as an excuse for failure. However, the positive home-school relations correlate is strongly encouraged and worked for by teachers and staff at Effective Schools (Epstein, 2001; Rubin, 2002). Parents are empowered in Effective Schools. They understand and support the school's mission and are given opportunity to play an important role in helping the school achieve its mission. The positive home-school relations correlate is now considered a vital Effective Schools correlate and a major inducement to community support. However, the original premise still holds: The involvement of parents in the school is encouraged, but the absence of parent involvement cannot be used as an excuse for failure.

These seven correlates, first laid out by Edmonds in 1979, have been reinforced by years of extensive research and data collection. The National Center for Effective Schools Research and Development at the University of Wisconsin–Madison uses the capitalized phrases *Effective Schools Research* and *Effective Schools Model or Process* to denote the comprehensive model espoused by the National Center and founded upon the research literature. "Effective Schools" is a service mark (SM) of the National Center for Effective Schools Research and Development. Currently, the seven correlates are in place in thousands of schools throughout the United States.

Effective Teaching Practices

Research continues to indicate that teachers have the greatest potential to influence children's education. More recently, research has suggested that the quality of a teacher is *the most important* predictor of student success (Darling-Hammond, 1998); therefore, it is critical for the principal to hire good teachers and lead teachers on the campus in effective teaching practices. In Tennessee, it was discovered that low-achieving students increased their achievement level by as much as 53% when taught by a highly effective teacher (Haycock, 1998). Research on teacher effectiveness has yielded a wealth of understanding about the impact that teacher ability has on student growth. For example, Cotton (1995) related the positive impact of teachers when they focus on instruction and produce concomitant effective instructional practices, as outlined in Table 4.1.

Several findings from the teacher effectiveness research follow and should impact how principals assist teachers in improving their teaching practices: (a) When teachers employ systematic teaching procedures, achievement improves; (b) effective teachers spend more time working with small groups throughout the day; (c) greater academic progress occurs when teachers begin their lessons with review; (d) effective teachers use systematic feedback with students about their performance; (e) teachers who have higher rates of communication with parents are viewed as more effective; (f) effective teachers run more orderly classrooms (achievement has been higher in classrooms where the climate is neither harsh nor overly lavish with praise); (g) teachers who adjust the difficulty level of material to student ability have higher rates of achievement in their classes; (h) effective teachers have more students in their classes on task and engaged in learning throughout the day; (i) classrooms in which engaged learning occurs have higher levels of student cooperation, student success, and task involvement; (j) effective teachers clearly articulate rules and include children in discussions about rules and procedures; (k) effective

Table 4.1   Instructional Focus and Effective Instructional Practices

Instructional Focus	Effective Instructional Practices
Planning and Learning Goals	Teachers use a preplanned curriculum to guide instruction.
Classroom Management and Organization	Teachers form instructional groups that fit students' academic and affective needs.
Instruction	Teachers make efficient use of learning time.
	Teachers routinely provide student feedback and reinforcement regarding their learning progress.
	Teachers review and reteach as necessary.
Teacher-Student Interactions	Teachers hold high expectations for student learning.
	Teachers provide incentives to promote excellence.
Equity	Teachers give high-needs students the extra time and instruction they need to succeed.
	Teachers promote respect and empathy among students of different socioeconomic and cultural backgrounds.
Assessment	Teachers monitor student progress closely.
	Teachers make use of alternative assessments as well as traditional tests.

teachers provide a variety of opportunities for students to apply and use knowledge and skills in different learning situations; and (l) effective teachers are able to pace the amount of information presented to the class, check student progress continually by asking questions of all students, and relate new learning to prior learning (Kemp & Hall, 1992; Taylor, Pearson, Clark, & Walpole, 1999).

Twelve Principles of Effective Teaching

It is important for a principal to be able to understand Brophy's (1999) principles of effective teaching, which cross grade levels and school subjects and focus on the basics of formal schooling. Principals need to be able to share these principles with teachers and to indicate that all 12 should be understood as a comprehensive approach to teaching. Applied as a whole, these principles are a means of helping students attain intended outcomes. The principles can serve as a useful guide for principals

who are working with beginning or experienced teachers; they can serve as a basis for dialogue about instruction.

Principle 1   *Students can learn best within cohesive and caring communities.* Productive contexts for learning feature an ethic of caring that pervades teacher-student and student-student interactions and transcends gender, race, ethnicity, culture, socioeconomic status, disabilities, languages, and all other individual differences. Brophy indicated that teachers need to display personal attributes that will make them effective as models and socializers: a cheerful disposition, friendliness, emotional maturity, sincerity, and caring about students as individuals as well as learners. The teacher needs to demonstrate concern and affection for students, be attentive to learner needs and emotions, and socialize them to display these same characteristics in their interactions with one another. In developing bulletin boards and other types of displays and in developing content during lessons, the teacher needs to connect with and build on the students' prior knowledge and experiences, including their home cultures. Extending the learning community from the school to the home, the teacher needs to establish and maintain collaborative relationships with parents and encourage their active involvement in their children's learning. Additionally, the teacher (a) promotes a learning orientation by introducing lessons with a description of what students will learn; (b) responds to mistakes as a natural part of learning—as someone once said, "celebrate mistakes, for in them, we learn"; (c) encourages collaborative learning; and (d) promotes risk taking (Good & Brophy, 2003; Sergiovanni, 1994).

Principle 2   *Students learn more when most of the available time is allocated to curriculum-related activities, and when the classroom management system emphasizes maintaining the students' engagement in those activities.* Effective teachers allocate most of the available time to activities designed to accomplish instructional goals. Research indicates that teachers who approach management as a process of establishing an effective learning environment tend to be more successful than teachers who emphasize their roles as disciplinarians. Effective teachers do not need to spend much time in responding to behavior problems, because they use management techniques that elicit students' cooperation and sustain their engagement in activities. A learning community is implied in this principle: The teacher articulates clear expectations concerning classroom behavior and participation in lessons and learning activities in particular. He fosters productive engagement during activities and smooth transitions between them, and follows through with any needed cues or reminders. Effective teachers plan well, not only in order to use their time efficiently within lessons and as they move from one activity to another but also to ensure that the lessons are engaging. During the lessons, effective teachers constantly monitor and continuously adjust. They engage students in learning actively (Brophy, 1983; Denham & Lieberman, 1980; Doyle, 1986).

Principle 3   *All components of the curriculum are aligned to create a cohesive program for accomplishing instructional purposes and goals.* Effective teachers know the underlying beliefs of the campus, district, and community; and they ensure, through careful and collaborative planning, that those beliefs are aligned within the curriculum. The teachers work toward developing a connected curriculum, so that learning is viewed within a meaningful system and not as a fragmented juncture in time (Beck & McKeown, 1988; Clark & Peterson, 1986; Wang, Haertel, & Walberg, 1993).

Principle 4   *Teachers can prepare students for learning by providing an initial structure to clarify intended outcomes and cue desired learning strategies.* Research indicates the value of establishing a learning orientation by beginning lessons and activities with advance organizers or previews. Effective teachers use advance organizers or call attention to the goals or objectives of the lesson (Ausubel, 1968; Brophy, 1998; Meichenbaum & Biemiller, 1998).

Principle 5   *To facilitate meaningful learning and retention, content is explained clearly and developed with emphasis on its structure and connections.* Effective teachers sequence ideas or events and help students make sense of them and understand the relationships among them. They (a) present new information based on previously learned information; (b) proceed with small bits of information, sequenced carefully so that students can follow; (c) use good pacing, gesturing, and communication; (d) do not digress or "birdwalk" off the topic; (e) frequently engage the learners in the topic by eliciting responses from them; (f) summarize the main objectives or what was learned from the lesson; and (g) follow up with authentic learning activities and assessment strategies (Beck & McKeown, 1988; Good & Brophy, 2003; Rosenshine, 1968).

Principle 6   *Questions are planned to engage students in sustained discourse structured around powerful ideas.* Effective teachers structure content-based discourse. They use questions to stimulate students to process and reflect on content; to recognize relationships among and implications of its key ideas; to think critically about it; and to use it in problem solving, decision making, or other higher-order applications. The discourse is not limited to rapidly paced recitation that elicits short answers to miscellaneous questions. Instead, it features sustained and thoughtful development of key ideas. Through participation in such discourse, students construct and communicate content-related understandings. In the process, they abandon naïve ideas or misconceptions and adopt the more sophisticated and valid ideas embedded in the instructional goals (Good & Brophy, 2003; Newmann, 1990; Rowe, 1986).

Principle 7 *Students need sufficient opportunities to practice and apply what they are learning and to receive improvement-oriented feedback.* Research indicates that skills practiced to a peak of smoothness and automaticity tend to be retained indefinitely, whereas skills that are mastered only partially tend to deteriorate. Most skills included in school curricula are learned best when practice is distributed across time and embedded within a variety of tasks. Practice should be embedded within application contexts that feature conceptual understanding of knowledge and self-regulated application of skills. Homework can be a time for practice, as well. Students should not only be allowed to practice, but they should also receive timely and effective feedback on the practice. The feedback on practice should be instructive rather than evaluative. Effective teachers may use not only themselves but also paraprofessionals, volunteers, or self-checking systems to provide such feedback (Brophy & Alleman, 1991; Cooper, 1994; Dempster, 1991; Knapp, 1995).

Principle 8 *The teacher provides whatever assistance students need to enable them to engage productively in learning activities.* Research on learning tasks suggests that activities and assignments should be sufficiently varied and interesting

to motivate student engagement, sufficiently new or challenging to constitute meaningful learning experiences rather than needless repetition, and yet sufficiently easy to allow students to achieve high rates of success if they invest reasonable time and effort. Teachers must select purposeful activities and effectively present, monitor, and follow up on them if they are to have their full impact. This means preparing students for an activity in advance, providing guidance and feedback during the activity, and leading the class in post-activity reflection (Brophy & Alleman, 1991; Rosenshine & Meister, 1992; Shuell, 1996; Tharp & Gallimore, 1988).

Principle 9 *The teacher models and instructs students in learning and self-regulation strategies.* Students can develop problem-solving skills by observing the teacher's modeling and instruction. Teachers who think aloud during the process of solving a problem (cognitive modeling) are the most effective in teaching such strategies. Students can then adapt this type of "self-talk" as they work on problems. Effective teachers also work with students on study skills, organizational skills, and self-monitoring skills (Meichenbaum & Biemiller, 1998; Pressley & Beard El-Dinary, 1993; Weinstein & Mayer, 1986). Even the very youngest child, at age four, can be taught self-monitoring or reflective skills to assess his or her own work (Irby & Brown, 2003).

Principle 10 *Students often benefit from working in pairs or small groups to construct understandings or help one another master skills.* Cooperative learning promotes affective and social benefits, such as increased student interest in and valuing of subject matter as well as increases in positive attitudes and social interactions among students who differ in gender, race, ethnicity, achievement levels, and other characteristics. Cooperative learning also creates the potential for cognitive and metacognitive benefits by engaging students in discourse that requires them to make their task-related information processing and problem-solving strategies explicit (Bennett & Dunne, 1992; Johnson & Johnson, 1994; Slavin, 1990).

Principle 11 *The teacher uses a variety of formal and informal assessment methods to monitor progress towards learning goals.* The assessments should be aligned to the curriculum. Not only should the assessments document to what degree the student is accomplishing the objectives, they should also assess reasoning and problem-solving abilities. Effective teachers use both formal and authentic assessments within their classrooms routinely. They scrutinize the results to develop plans for student, assessment, and instructional improvement (Dempster, 1991; Irby & Brown, 2003; Stiggins, 2000; Wiggins, 1993).

Principle 12 *The teacher establishes and follows through on appropriate expectations for learning outcomes.* Effective teachers should form and project expectations that are as positive as they can be while still remaining realistic. These teachers hold all students accountable for participating in lessons and learning activities and for turning in careful and completed work on assignments. They hold themselves accountable for providing effective instruction, as outlined here in the 12 principles and more thoroughly in Brophy's 1999 report (Brophy, 1998, 1999; Creemers & Scheerens, 1989; Good & Brophy, 2000; Shuell, 1996; Teddlie & Stringfield, 1993).

Lara-Alecio and Parker (1994) provided additional guidance for teachers of second-language learners. They suggested the following pedagogical principles for effective bilingual classrooms:

■ Provide an emotionally supportive environment.

■ Emphasize and provide quality of social interactions between teacher and student.

■ Ensure "bilingual" status is not considered a disability.

■ Provide multi-modality interactions with students.

■ Incorporate minority students' cultures into teaching.

■ Guide and facilitate, rather than control student learning.

■ Encourage student talk and independent learning.

■ Structure activities for quality interactions among students.

■ Encourage community participation in schooling.

■ Promote student intrinsic motivation.

■ Teach meaningful content.

■ Appreciate and develop prior competency in home language.

■ Continue to develop competencies in both languages. (pp. 119–120)

Conditions for Learning

The principal is concerned about providing the appropriate conditions for learning related to culture and climate. Some conditions should be attended to by the principal as she assists teachers in providing appropriate learning environments, or as she develops a full learning community. The principal should see that conditions in the school are such that when the student and parent enter the school, it is *warm and inviting*. Actually, this environment begins with the bus driver, the receptionist in the front office, and the custodian in the hallway. The United Nations Declaration of a Child's Rights document alludes to this condition in its statement that the child shall be given an education that will promote his general culture and enable him, on a basis of equal opportunity, to develop his abilities, his individual judgment, and his sense of moral and social responsibility; and to become a useful member of society.

Another condition for learning should be the inclusion of *fine arts* in the school curriculum. Fine arts aid students in understanding the society, culture, and history not only of the United States, but of the world. Often, we forget that the fine arts are essential to the development of individual potential, social responsibility, and cultural awareness and contribute significantly to the individual's intellectual, aesthetic, emotional, social, and physical development.

The development of *effective citizens* is another condition for learning. To be effective citizens in a democracy, students should be knowledgeable about the United States and the world, be aware of history and trends, and understand democratic values. This condition for learning is essential for preparing our youth to meet the diverse challenges of the 21st century. Another important condition for learning is the access *to develop skills for the workplace*. The school curriculum must include opportunities for developing communication, problem solving, positive attitudes and behaviors, adaptability, working with others, and science, technology, and mathematics skills.

Ensuring the condition for learning in an environment that has *smaller class size* is critical. Teachers can devote more individual attention to each student, answering questions and helping to solve small problems before they become large ones (Achilles, 1997).

Create optimum conditions for learning with *support staff*. Counselors, nurses, educational diagnosticians, psychologists, social workers, special education teachers, gifted education teachers, and bilingual/ESL teachers are all important to a student's optimal learning.

A condition for learning should be established in the *review of the school* as a whole. The school should be assessed annually to determine if it is meeting the mission and goals established. Are the activities and instruction within the classroom aligned with the vision? *Data or evidence* should drive decisions as a condition for learning.

Other conditions for learning that principals should be aware of are (a) a strong commitment to *early childhood* development, (b) support in transitions from childhood to youth to adulthood (the *work world*), (c) increased *economic equality* in programmic provisions (for example, a Montessori education, usually reserved for the economically advantaged, placed in a public early childhood program), (d) extensive *parent and community volunteer* programs, (e) *grant and foundation funds* that can enhance the economic supports at the campus, and (f) *safe, risk-free, and caring communities* within and around the school.

Best Practices for the Classroom

According to Tileston (2000), there are 10 best practices for the classroom that principals need to assist teachers in developing. The author indicated that teachers must attend to threats that impact learning, such as stress, embarrassment, deadlines, different learning styles, and classroom culture. The teacher must encourage students to (a) be engaged in active learning, (b) be creative, (c) make connections from content to content and from content to the world, and (d) have respect for learning.

Principals should encourage teachers to develop their classrooms and the school into an environment that is enriched with hands-on experiences and literacy opportunities. The school and classroom should promote a sense of belonging with high levels of support and a sense of empowerment. Teachers must monitor and assess frequently to keep students on target and engaged. The entire campus team can work toward providing students with choices and being aware of multiple intelligences as lessons and activities are developed.

Additionally, as teachers develop lessons, they will need to keep in mind the three learning styles (visual, kinesthetic, and auditory). Teachers need to consider chunking material for the purpose of aiding students to retain the information (it is suggested that preschool students can chunk two to three pieces of information at a time; preadolescents, three to seven pieces; through adulthood, seven to nine pieces). Critical and creative thinking and problem solving need to be incorporated into lessons, as also indicated in Brophy's 12 Principles of Effective Teaching. In teaching higher-order skills, teachers must consider the many content-area subjects that lend themselves to cause and effect, analysis, making inferences, and deductive and inductive reasoning.

Teachers need to learn to be facilitators and guides—a guide on the side, not a sage on the stage. Tileston said the teacher should act as a catalyst, not as a textbook. She also indicated that all students can learn, but all students are not equal. They are not equal in intelligences, interests, and time it takes for learning. Principals must help teachers to understand that through knowing their students fully — their interests, their motivations, their priorities, and their parents and culture — teachers can increase students' learning.

Teachers should also be aware of assessment; it should be continuous and part of the instruction, connect directly to learning, do more than require simple memorization, and be driven, in part, by student questions. Tie authentic assessment to rubrics and guidelines for success, and let the students help develop those guidelines so they know what they are responsible for learning.

Schools should incorporate technology into teaching. Technology can help create a research- or knowledge-rich environment. With technology, the world becomes the classroom. It will be the principal's responsibility to see that teachers have the necessary tools, including the computers, the infrastructure, and the training.

Models of Evaluation

According to Weiss and Weiss (1998), conventional "evaluation practices stress accountability and frequently are based upon teacher-directed models of learning such as lecture, demonstration, recitation, and modeling designed primarily to transmit knowledge and cognitive skills to students" (p. 1). The authors indicated that these practices are based on research from the 1980s in which specific teaching behaviors in a direct instruction format predict high scores on standardized tests (Brophy & Good, 1986). Sclan (1994) indicated that principals often use minimal teaching competencies as criteria to judge teachers' performance. Furthermore, such evaluations could become meaningless exercises for those teachers who are already performing at or beyond the minimal level (McLaughlin, 1990; Searfoss & Enz, 1996). Just as Brown and Irby (2001) indicated for principals, Weiss and Weiss stated that for teachers traditional summative evaluation models are not structured to support dynamic and constantly improving school environments. They

purported that new evaluation models include teacher involvement for self-development or for the development of collaborative school cultures. Sclan (1994) suggested that evaluations systems that recognize evaluation as an authentic part of teachers' daily practice, with supports for regular reflection, are becoming more accepted. Such environments sustain collegial communication.

Weiss and Weiss further noted that the National Commission on Teaching and America's Future (NCTAF) created a blueprint for recruiting, preparing, and supporting excellence in all of America's schools and recommended that the standards from the National Board for Professional Teaching Standards (NBPTS; n.d.) become the cornerstone for teacher evaluation (Darling-Hammond, 1996; NCTAF, 1996). NBPTS assessments help teachers reflect and learn from their practice. The NBPTS assessments are based on their five propositions that educators agree are essential to accomplished teaching:

1. Teachers are committed to students and their learning;
2. Teachers know the subjects they teach and how to teach those subjects to students;
3. Teachers are responsible for managing and mentoring student learning;
4. Teachers think systematically about their practice and learn from experience;
5. Teachers are members of learning communities.

Formative and Summative Evaluation

According to Brown and Irby (2001), formative evaluation provides an opportunity for principals to discuss teachers' instructional progress with them. During this stage, principals can offer clarification and assistance. Brown and Irby contend that a portfolio evaluation system is a vehicle for supporting a comprehensive evaluation system for teachers and principals. The summative evaluation in such a system takes place when the portfolio is presented. The portfolio contains evidence of how well the teacher has accomplished his goals as well as evidence that the teacher has reflected on his own progress and has suggestions for improvement. The summative evaluation is a time for additional growth, renewal, and planning. The newer models for evaluation emphasize continuous improvement through reflection, mentoring, and self-assessment.

Classroom Observations

The clinical supervision model developed by Goldhammer (1969) (refined by Robert Anderson [Goldhammer, Anderson, & Krajewski, 1980] after Goldhammer's untimely death) and Cogan (1973) is a classroom observation model that promotes continuous improvement evaluative models. Clinical supervision consists of three major stages that the principal can use for developing reflective practice with the teachers: (a) the preobservation conference, (b) the observation, and (c) the postobservation conference. In stage one, the preobservation conference, the principal sits with the teacher to discuss the parameters of what is to be observed and how. For example, the two may determine the lesson to be observed, the content of the lesson, the time period for the observation, and the concerns related to specific student needs and abilities. This preconference allows the principal to gain an insight into the learning environment or context that she is about to enter. The teacher may determine some specific areas of growth or improvement that he has been working on and might request specific attention to those areas.

Stage 2 is the actual observation. The principal will need to arrive at the classroom on time, give her undivided attention to the observation and the ground rules that have been established collaboratively with the teacher, and collect specific data to provide feedback. The principal may use a seating chart to assist her in observing teacher-student interaction; the specifics of work done in small or large groups or by individuals; cooperative learning; and teacher-student behaviors, such as lecture-listen or demonstrate-perform. Other observation specifics may be mandated by the state or by the collaborative arrangement developed between the principal and the teacher.

Stage 3 is the postobservation conference. Here the principal presents to the teacher what she observed, so that both the principal and the teacher can process the information in an analytical and reflective fashion. The principal should present what was observed and not formulate judgments— rather, she should allow the teacher to formulate the response through his own reflection about his practice. A good discussion about teaching and learning should be generated through this postconference. Conclusions about the observation must be determined together, and next steps for improvement need to be created by the teacher with assistance from the principal. The observation, the notes, and the improvement plan can become a part of the evaluation portfolio as evidence of growth throughout the year. The principal, in this role, acts as a supervisor who is ultimately on site to improve instruction. The administrative role of the principal is undertaken when a teacher does not show marked improvement or is not willing to improve. In this role, the principal must take action by gathering all relevant data to support or to reject renewal of a contract.

Walk-Through Observations

Time is critical for the busy principal, who has to work not only as the instructional leader but also as the school manager. Time management is always a challenge. The walk-through observation can assist the principal in keeping touch with the classroom, being in the classroom, and providing feedback needed for continous improvement. According to Fink and Resnik (2001), *walk-through observations* are organized observations from the principal, who observes specific instructional practices and subsequent student learning. When combined, all walk-through observations can provide an overall picture of the functioning of instruction within the building, and they can become a part of the evidence for areas of overall school improvement and correlated staff development.

Davidson-Taylor (2002) said that walk-through information can create focus dialogue with teachers about best practices, effective teaching principles, and student learning. The principal should develop a plan for walk-thoughs; that is, when, how often, how long (suggested 5- to 10-minute snapshots). In addition, the principal should develop a short duplicate feedback form to be completed "on the spot." This technique works best when the principal places the walk-throughs on his calendar and honors the time. The principal should train the teachers in the process of walk-throughs, because this will not be a typical classroom observation. During their training, teachers may be informed about what might be observed during walk-throughs. The focus is generally on student work and their behavior as a result of instruction. At times the principal may choose to share the results of walk-throughs with an entire department, including general observations that are repeatedly recorded in a pattern so that the team can address the issue and improve the teachers' instructional techniques. Grade-level or department meetings can include a time to address the following topics in depth: improving student learning, current research, learning expectations for students, and student performance.

According to Davidson-Taylor (2002), the following are key factors to be observed during a walk-through observation.

1. The principal should attempt to view the classroom from the student's perspective, because they are the recipients of the instruction. Observe the students and converse with them as appropriate about their classwork. Look at what students are doing. Are they actively engaged in learning? Do they understand the teacher's expectations? Can the students articulate what and why they are learning? Do students know the standard of excellence in this classroom? What evidence indicates that students have actually learned the targeted skill or objective(s)? These are questions that need to answered through evidence obtained from discussion with, or observation of, the students.

2. Look at the students' assignments to identify the work they complete. What is the level of thinking? Are students provided with quality samples of work? Are rubrics provided for the achieved criteria of the work completed?

3. Listen to student talk. Are they even allowed to talk? Is the teacher doing all the talking? What is the direction of their conversation? Are students asking questions of the teacher and other classmates? Do the conversations originate with the students as well as the teacher? Are the students talking about learning?

4. Is there evidence of student products in the classroom? Are the products authentic work samples?

5. As principals observe at a specific grade level, are the students overall progressing at the usual pace through the curriculum? Are they behind, or too far ahead? Are the curriculum and instructional plan being followed? Is there differentiation at the various grade levels? For example, students should not, with the same purpose, be planting a bean in first grade, again in second, and all the way through fourth grade. Nor should they be reading the same novels in English class in 9th, 10th, 11th, and 12th grades. If the curriculum map (scope and sequence) is being followed, then such lack of differentiation should not happen. Is instruction at the appropriate level? Are questions at an appropriate level for the students, and do students model the upper-level taxonomic questions?

6. Are technology standards integrated in instruction? These would have been integrated in the curriculum and the instructional plans; therefore, they should be observed during walk-throughs. Look for signs of how technology is being implemented in the classroom. Are students engaged in Web research, Microsoft PowerPoint presentations, and Web design?

7. What evidence is there that preassessments were given to determine prior knowledge so

that skill development can be at the appropriate level? Do teachers reteach needed skills?

8. Are students recognized for their superior work? Is work displayed?

Related to the walk-throughs, change the focus of faculty meetings from administrative issues (can be shared in e-mails, bulletins, or memos) to issues of teaching and learning. Discuss curriculum, new research, and best practices in instruction.

Peer Coaching

Peer Coaching (Costa & Garmston, 1994) is a technique that a principal can employ with teachers so that they can assist each other in improving instruction and create an environment in which risk taking is appreciated. This process involves a coach who mediates the thinking of the teacher. The coach (a) diagnoses and envisions desired stages for others, (b) constructs and uses clear and precise language in the facilitation of others' cognitive development, (c) devises an overall strategy through which individuals will move themselves toward desired states, (d) maintains faith in the potential for continued movment toward a more harmonious state of mind and behavior, and (e) possesses a belief in her own capacity to serve as an empowering catalyst of another's growth. The coaches are not experts; they are facilitors and mediators.

The coaching model is divided into two parts: planning and reflecting. In the face-to-face planning conference, the coach attempts to assist the teacher to specify the upcoming lesson in as much detail as possible, including student outcomes. The coach helps the teacher to establish goals for the lesson, for assessing the lesson, for teaching the methodology to be used, and for personal growth. The second part of coaching, reflection, begins after the lesson has occurred. The coach will ask the teacher to summarize his impression of the lesson and to provide data to support those impressions. The coach will help the teacher to consider cause-and-effect

relationships between himself and the students and between the content and format of the lesson and the results elicited from the students. Again, this type of model provides data for the teacher to include in an annual evaluation portfolio.

Summary

1. The principal's role in the teaching and learning process is (a) to accommodate teachers in their quest for gaining knowledge related to how the diverse student body learns best, (b) to assess the teaching as it relates to the outcome — learning, and (c) to facilitate the instructional planning process.

2. Principals can use instructional planning to promote reflection among teachers.

3. The No Child Left Behind Act (NCLB) dramatically increases the principal's accountability toward student learning and focuses the principal on the importance of learning from student data. NCLB requires principals to disaggregate student achievement data, track the achievement of all students over time, and show demonstrable progress in raising the percentage of students who are proficient in math and reading.

4. The teaching and learning action plan, facilitated by the principal and developed by teams of teachers, should consist of (a) specific goals or objectives based on data or evidence; (b) connection to the vision or mission, or to the overall school or district goal; (c) activities to accomplish the goal or objective, (d) person(s) responsible; (e) timeline; (f) targeted skills, standards, or benchmark; and (g) evaluation format, or how the goal will be evaluated and how its achievement (or the degree to which it has been achieved) will be documented.

5. Learning theories can facilitate further our understanding of the intellective process.

6. Gagné's eight categories of objectives — response learning, identification learning, chains, associations, concepts, principles, problem solving, and strategies — provide different conditions of learning in relation to learner tasks.

7. Guilford's structure of intellect model identifies three primary mental abilities, broken down into 120 intellectual factors.

8. Piaget theorizes that intellective capability undergoes qualitative developmental changes linked to the child's maturation.

9. Kohlberg developed a cognitive-developmental theory that proceeds through a series of qualitatively distinct moral stages. Carol Gilligan examines the limitations of Kohlberg's stages of moral development and concludes that moral development is not the same for girls and boys.

10. Dunn and Dunn identified 18 elements of learning style that have merit for increasing student motivation and learning.

11. Gardner introduced a nonpsychometric way of looking at cognition. He promoted eight multiple intelligences: linguistic, logical-mathematical, interpersonal, intrapersonal, musical, bodily-kinesthetic, spatial, and naturalistic.

12. Effective schools can provide guidance for the principal in reforming teaching and learning in a systemic way on the campus.

13. Research has suggested that the quality of a teacher is the *most important* predictor of student success.

14. Brophy presented 12 principles of effective teaching that cross grade levels and school subjects and focus on the basics of formal schooling.

15. The principal is concerned about providing the appropriate conditions for learning related to culture and climate.

16. There are 10 best practices for the classroom that principals need to assist teachers in developing.

17. Irby and Brown indicated that traditional summative evaluation models are not structured to support dynamic and constantly improving school environments.

18. Formative evaluation provides a time for principals to discuss with teachers their instructional progress, and summative evaluation should be another time for renewal and adjustment in teaching and in leading.

19. Clinical supervision consists of three major stages that the principal can use for developing reflective practice with the teachers: (a) the preobservation conference, (b) the observation, and (c) the postobservation conference.

20. Walk-through observations are organized observations from the principal, who observes specific instructional practices and subsequent student learning.

21. Peer coaching involves a coach who mediates the thinking of the teacher and helps the teacher to reflect on his or her own practice of teaching.

Field-Based Activities

1. Meet with three teachers in another grade level. Review the steps in instructional planning as depicted in Figure 4.1. Ask the teachers how they actually accomplish each step, individually and as a team. Reflect on this discussion. Briefly describe how you, as principal, would develop these steps with your teachers based on your recent discussion. Review your thoughts with a principal from another campus at your grade level.

2. Discuss with your principal the difference between data and evidence. Ask your principal to share how he or she uses data or evidence to make decisions with teachers about instructional planning. Ask, as a second question, how cultural components of the students are taken into consideration in instructional planning. Ask similar questions of two teachers on the campus. Compare the

responses of the principal with the responses of the two teachers. Are the principal and the teachers congruent in their thoughts? How would you respond if you were the principal?

3. (a) Use the clinical supervision model with a teacher from another campus. Implement all the steps. Were you able to provide instructionally sound feedback? (b) Develop a walk-through process and a feedback form with your team. Conduct 10 walk-throughs within a week. Are there any patterns? Discuss the results with your team. (c) Working with a peer, conduct a peer coaching episode. What did you learn? How can you instruct teachers about the peer coaching model?

Suggested Readings

Anderson, L.W., Krathwohl, D. R., Airasan, P. W., Cruikshank, K. A., Mayer, R. E., Pintrich, P. R., Raths, J., & Wittrock, M. C. (2001). *Taxonomy for learning, teaching, and assessing: A revision of Bloom's taxonomy of educational objectives* (Abridged Ed.). New York: Longman. This revision of Bloom's taxonomy can be a tool principals can use to help teachers understand and implement standards-based curricula. Cognitive psychologists, curriculum specialists, teacher educators, and researchers have developed a two-dimensional framework, focusing on knowledge and cognitive processes. This "revisited" framework allows principals to connect learning in all areas of curriculum.

Gardner, H. (1999). *Intelligence reframed: Multiple intelligences for the 21st century.* New York: Basic Books. Since its original description in *Frames of Mind* (Gardner 1983, 1993), the theory of multiple intelligences has taken its place as one of the seminal ideas of the 20th century. Further explicated in Gardner's 1993 book, *Multiple Intelligences,* these ideas continue to attract attention and generate controversy all over the world. Now, in *Intelligence Reframed,*

Gardner provides a much-needed state-of-the-art report on the theory. He describes how it has evolved and been revised. He introduces two new intelligences and argues that the concept of intelligence should be broadened, but not so much that it includes every human faculty and value. In addition, he offers practical guidance on the educational uses of the theory and responds in lively dialogue to the critiques leveled against it.

Marzano, R. J., Pickering, D., & Pollock, J. E. (2001). *Classroom instruction that works: Research-based strategies for increasing student achievement.* Alexandria, VA: Association of Supervision and Curriculum Development. The authors present, from decades of research, nine broad teaching *strategies that have positive effects on student learning:*

- Identifying similarities and differences
- Summarizing and note taking
- Reinforcing effort and providing recognition
- Homework and practice
- Nonlinguistic representations
- Cooperative learning
- Setting objectives and providing feedback
- Generating and testing hypotheses
- Questions, cues, and advance organizers

Scriven, M., & Fisher, A. (1993). *Critical thinking: Designing and assessing it.* Thousand Oaks, CA: Corwin Press. This book addresses the difficulties in adequately defining and assessing critical thinking. It goes on to provide a more useful framework for both conceptual and practical applications.

Shuell, T. J. (1993). Toward an integrated theory of teaching and learning. *Educational Psychologist, 28*(4), 291–312. This article provides an excellent history of teaching and learning for the principal and teachers.

Teddlie, C. B., & Stringfield, S. C. (1993). *Schools make a difference: Lessons learned from a ten-year study of school effects.* New York: Teachers

College Press. The authors address evidence of school effects and characteristics of more effective schools: the role of context, relationships among teachers' and principals' roles, naturally occurring school improvement efforts, and longitudinal issues in building and sustaining more and less effective schools.

Tileston, D. W. (2000). *10 Best teaching practices*. Thousand Oaks, CA: Corwin Press. The author presents research-based teaching practices. This would be an excellent book for principals to use with teachers in inquiry-discussion groups, or for teachers to use in peer coaching models.

5.

Professional Development

Standard 2.0: *Candidates who complete the program are educational leaders who have the knowledge and ability to promote the success of all students by promoting a positive school culture, providing an effective instructional program, applying best practice to student learning, and designing comprehensive professional growth plans for staff.*

FOCUSING QUESTIONS

1 What is the principal's mission as it relates to professional development in general?

2 What is the principal's mission as it relates to teachers' professional development?

3 What is the principal's mission for personal professional development?

4 What are the ethics of professional development?

In this chapter we respond to these questions concerning the importance of professional development and how it relates to student learning. We also examine the concept that schools are places where teachers learn. We begin the chapter with a general discussion of the mission of principals with respect to professional development. This is followed by a more specific discussion of the principal's mission as it relates to teachers' professional development. Next, we examine the principal's mission for her or his own professional development. Finally, we conclude the chapter with a discussion of the ethics of professional development.

The Principal's Mission Related to Professional Development

Imagine the unveiling of a painting titled "The Ideal Professional Development Situation in a School." What would it look like? Perhaps among the first things to be noticed would be high achievement by the students; high expectations by the principal, the teachers, and the staff; high morale among teachers; and high commitment by the principal, teachers, and staff. You may ask, what underlies this first impression? Come closer; there is a principal who . . .

- is well read, educated in the latest research and best practice; in particular, in leadership.
- defines her own personal, professional growth needs according to data received through feedback from teachers, parents, and staff.
- has analyzed her impact on the campus.
- is focused on solutions.
- is sensitive to the students and the community.
- thinks forward, and consequentially.
- scans the needs of the teachers, monitors instruction, and disaggregates data on student learning.
- initiates and implements a collaboratively derived professional development plan for continuous improvement.

The artist's intention is for the onlooker to view the painting of a reformed campus that is a purposefully planned, focused, cohesive, and executed system that yields positive results for all; and there—the focal point, the front and center of the painting—stands the principal.

What is the painter's message? Professional development is directly related to improved practice for principals and teachers, yielding subsequent increases in student achievement and overall reform of the school and campus. No reform can take place without a purposeful, coherent, focused, and sustained system that includes professional development. There are *two missions* of the principal related to professional development. First, there is the mission the principal must accomplish as it relates to her teachers' professional growth, and second, there is the mission the principal must attend to as it relates to her own professional growth.

The Principal's Mission for Teachers' Professional Development

The principal's mission related to his or her teachers' professional development is twofold. The first part of the mission is *to plan,* with teachers, a comprehensive professional development program targeted at identified individual and collective needs. The second part of the mission is *to provide* resources, including time and money, and to include time for teachers to reflect upon and participate in a dialogue about their practice. Darling-Hammond (1998) made a strong argument for quality professional development by stating that each dollar spent on improving teachers' qualifications nets greater gains in student learning than any other use of an education dollar.

The National Staff Development Council has called for a shift in the way that principals approach professional development. When the Council's recommendations include devoting a full 10% of the school budget and 25% of teacher time to professional development (Richardson, 1997), we consider a general gauge for spending education dollars in professional development to be the following. With 80% of a school budget being spent on personnel, it appears that a district and/or campus, in the most conservative way, would spend at least 10% of the remaining 20% on professional development. With either level of funding, principals must monitor the professional development and demand a return on the public's money.

Principals who promote successful professional development experiences for their teachers will, in turn, increase the teachers' interest in and commitment to the profession. Principals should encourage teachers to be the creators of their own professional development, but only when based upon the teachers' critical reflections and self-assessment of their work. When teachers collaborate on and personally plan their own professional development, they have better buy-in to the professional development activities; they see greater relevance in the activities; and, subsequently, they will commit the time required for the activities.

The plan that principals develop with their teachers should be connected to the overall campus improvement plan. Single, disconnected workshops do little to effectively alter instruction and improve learning. Workshops should be ongoing, connected, and imbedded in the campus improvement process. The complexity of instruction should be undergirded with inquiry, practice, implementation, reflection, and evaluation. All professional development should be supported by research. Teachers need to have time to make sense of experiences and transform professional knowledge into daily teaching habits (Bransford, Brown, & Cocking, 1999). Without inquiry that imparts the theory and rationale for new instructional techniques or methods, teachers will not understand the "why" of the practice in order to fully embrace it. When teachers (a) understand the practice, (b) have it modeled, and (c) practice it in a risk-free setting with feedback, they can internalize the practice, become comfortable with the practice, and attain the goals of the campus.

High-Quality Professional Development

There is a growing consensus in the literature regarding the elements of effective professional development for principals and teachers. Effective professional development is logically embedded in the reality of schools and teachers' work. It incorporates principles of adult learning, as reported by Knowles (1980): (a) Adult learners need to be self-directed; (b) they display readiness to learn when they have a perceived need; and (c) they desire immediate application of new skills and knowledge. Based on adult learning theory, then, principals and teachers would have a need for self-direction, for professional development based on their areas of needed improvement, and for application of what they learn in professional development. Time and created situations during which teachers can dialogue with other teachers, and principals can dialogue with other principals, are critical for effective application of the knowledge gained in professional development sessions.

To be effective, professional development must be internally coherent, rigorous, related to the campus and district vision and mission and the teacher's instructional goals, and sustained over time (Little, 1993; Renyi, 1996; Sparks & Hirsch, 1997). Any professional development that is not sustained and integrated will not be effective to the degree that the principal will desire. Some professional develop-

ment approaches include university-school partnerships (Darling-Hammond, 1997), teacher networks and collaboratives (Little, 1993; Renyi, 1996), teacher study or inquiry groups (Clair, 1995; 1998), university courses, school district teacher leader cohorts, teacher research, and portfolio development.

High-quality professional development refers to rigorous and relevant content, strategies, and organizational supports that ensure the preparation and career-long development of teachers and principals whose competence, expectations, and actions influence the teaching and learning environment. *The mission of professional development* is to prepare and support teachers and principals to help all students achieve to high standards of learning and development. The 10 principles of effective professional development are depicted in Table 5.1 and discussed in the following sections.

Principle 1 *Effective professional development focuses on teachers as central to student learning, yet includes all other members of the school community.* Many times, professional development is a one-size-fits-all approach; however, effective professional development takes into account instructional needs of the teacher as they relate *directly to students learning.* As the principal considers implementing a systemic approach to professional development on the campus, he will want to consider including support staff (instructional aides, counselors, psychologists, diagnosticians, auxiliary teachers) in those instructional professional development sessions. Instructional aides serve as an extension of the teacher while he works with the students; and other support staff should understand what the teacher is trying to accomplish with the students, so that they can strengthen the teacher's instruction in their own fields of support. For example, if a teacher is working on an instructional strategy in reading related to "main idea," other support staff might work on the same topic in their area. The counselor might meet in a group counseling session and support the concept of main idea through an activity. The health and physical education

---

Table 5.1   Ten Principles of Effective Professional Development

Effective professional development . . .

1. focuses on teachers as central to student learning, yet includes all other members of the school community;

2. focuses on individual, collegial, and organizational improvement;

3. respects and nurtures the intellectual and leadership capacity of teachers, principals, and others in the school community;

4. reflects best available research and practice in teaching, learning, and leadership;

5. enables teachers to develop further expertise in subject content, teaching strategies, uses of technologies, and other essential elements in teaching to high standards;

6. promotes continuous inquiry and improvement embedded in the daily life of schools;

7. is planned collaboratively by those who will participate in and facilitate that development;

8. requires substantial time and other resources;

9. is driven by a coherent long-term plan;

10. is evaluated ultimately on the basis of its impact on teacher effectiveness and student learning; and this assessment guides subsequent professional development efforts.

Source: From *The Mission and Principles of Professional Development,* retrieved December 13, 2003, from http://www.ed.gov/G2K/bridge.html

---

teacher might work with children on main idea through various physical activities.

Principle 2   *Effective professional development focuses on individual, collegial, and organizational improvement.* Consider here a teacher who might want to expand her knowledge of cooperative learning techniques. While her goal is valid, it becomes relevant only when it is seen in a larger context of school improvement, one that is focused on student learning, driven by data, and nested within school and district curriculum and instructional goals that have been formulated from the vision and mission. In this context, there is an explicit connection between this teacher's learning and the results for students.

Principle 3   *Effective professional development respects and nurtures the intellectual and leadership capacity of teachers, principals, and others in the school community.* Professional development in schools has traditionally consisted of activities such as attending conferences, one-day, one-shot workshops, and make-and-take workshops; or working on curriculum during teacher workshop days. According to Kelleher (2003), such strategies have proved to be inadequate in a number of ways. First, these strategies tend not to help teachers translate new learning into classroom instruction, nor do they nurture the teachers' intellectual capacity. A guest speaker, for example, may be interesting on a personal or professional level, but will the teachers employ the new information in the classroom? Second, these strategies are often not necessarily tied to specific building and district goals for student learning and most often are disconnected from the overall vision and mission of the campus. An example is that if literacy is the campus's top priority, then every workshop should be related to literacy issues. Third, there is usually no assessment mechanism to measure the results of the activities. The principal must, in effect, assess the intellectual capacity of professional development sessions by developing a plan with the teachers. For example, when a teacher attends a conference or a workshop and comes back to the classroom and experiments with the new idea, concepts, or programs, there should be a plan in place to determine how that idea, concept, or program will be assessed as to its effectiveness related to student learning.

The principal, through department, team, or grade-level meetings, inquiry groups, and other forums, can encourage teachers to discuss with colleagues what they have learned and to share materials they have developed through collaboration with peers, workshops, or assessment writing. Principals should keep the focus on connections to student learning by asking the question, "Based on what was learned in this experience, how will instructional practices and student learning change?" Both self-reflection and sharing with colleagues are integral components of professional development itself.

Principle 4 *Effective professional development reflects best available research and practice in teaching, learning, and leadership.* Little and Houston (2003) reported that the Florida State Department of Education and the University of Central Florida jointly developed a research-into-practice model for professional development through the Effective Instructional Practices (EIP) project. This comprehensive project, designated Project CENTRAL (Coordinating Existing Networks To Reach All Learners), was designed to identify and disseminate scientifically based instructional practices through professional development, resources, and research. The ultimate vision for the model was to provide quality professional development of scientifically based instructional practices and resources to teams of educators focused on the mastery of established standards and outcomes by all students in Florida. The four steps of the model include (a) identification of scientifically based instructional practices, (b) selection of teams of teachers to attend awareness-level professional development, (c) classroom implementation of scientifically based instructional practice from initial training to quality implementation for all students, and (d) data collection of the results of student learning through traditional and action research methodologies. Data collected during the implementation further inform the classroom instructional process and the identification and continued dissemination of the specific instructional practice. A principal on a campus could apply such a model, based in research.

Principle 5 *Effective professional development enables teachers to develop further expertise in subject content, teaching strategies, uses of technologies, and other essential elements in teaching to high standards.* Much of the time, we have seen professional development focused on general topics such as gifted education, self-esteem, communication with parents, or math education. It hardly ever is individualized, planned, and connected to the curriculum or the instructional needs of the teachers, subject matter, or technology needs of the teachers. It rarely connects teachers' reflections on their practice and on their students' achievement to professional development, and often the professional development we see is a one-time shot in the arm. There is no sustained effort to develop instructional knowledge and skills of the teachers that can ultimately lead to changed behaviors. Professional development is key in keeping teachers abreast of current issues in education, assisting them to implement new concepts or innovations, and improving their practice.

Peery (2002) suggested that principals should nudge teachers into seeing their subject matter from students' eyes. Principals can aid teachers in developing expertise in the content as well as in teaching strategies. Additionally, when teachers use technology just as students will do in the classroom, then teachers learn that skill to better share with students. Peery stated that becoming a student again is a good way to learn authentically and reexperience one's favorite subject, or to experience the world of technology or other elements related to state or national standards. The national teacher quality grants (former Eisenhower Math and Science grants) provide teachers the opportunity to become students again, learning new subject matter, experiencing firsthand the operation of power plants and waste water treatment facilities, or testing community water purity levels.

Principle 6 *Effective professional development promotes continuous inquiry and improvement embedded in the daily life of schools.* Research studies in the area of professional development have supported (a) determining how the newly learned instructional practice is implemented in the classroom, (b) specific guidelines and materials for initial implementation, and (c) ongoing peer coaching (Fullan, 1999; Glickman, 1993; Fullan & Hargreaves, 1992; Joyce, 1990; Sparks & Loucks-Horsley, 1992). Incorporating peer coaching into the professional development design dramatically increases the implementation of the training (Joyce & Showers, 1988). In a previous investigation of teachers who participated in professional development workshops but did not receive follow-up peer coaching, it was found that only 10% implemented the instructional strategy (Florida Department of Education, 1999).

Action research   Another way to promote continuous inquiry and improvement is through applied action research, conducted by teachers who want to study their own classroom to improve in their own situation (Little, 2001). In action research, the teacher is the decision maker, data collector, and information source in the research situated in the classroom. Action research is a continuous process of planned inquiry to determine the effects of the implementation of an instructional practice on the outcomes of the students in a classroom (Little, 2001). General components of the action research process include (a) define problems, (b) formulate research questions, (c) plan and implement interventions, (d) collect data, (e) draw conclusions, and (f) make changes accordingly.

According to the Wisconsin Center for Education Research (2001), action research, as a professional development experience, can significantly affect teaching and learning. The Center reported on Zeichner's recent meta-analysis of studies of action research activities nationwide, which shows teachers as researchers gaining a new sense of confidence from conducting research, beginning to see themselves as learners, and developing closer relationships with their students and colleagues. Action research involves teachers directly in the selection of immediate and compelling topics to explore with respect to their own practice. Among the many types of teacher research are journaling, video journaling, discussions of

practice, data analysis of observations, peer observations, interviews, document analysis, written essays, and/or investigation of specific questions related to student learning and/or teacher practices. The purpose of action research is to improve instruction and learning and impact or change procedures in the classroom, on the campus, or within the district. Action research can ultimately affect policy.

Evaluation portfolio   Some states, such as Texas, have developed a professional development and appraisal system (PDAS) for teachers. The Texas PDAS is comprised of eight domains and is aimed at advancing the level of teachers' professional practice and promoting their continuous professional development (Texas Education Agency [TEA], 1997). Principals can support teacher development by encouraging the inclusion of the teacher evaluation portfolio as an integral component of the PDAS or other like systems in various states. According to Marcoux, Rodriguez, Brown, and Irby (2001), by serving as a catalyst for revisions and modifications needed to improve the teacher's pedagogy and subsequent student achievement, the teacher portfolio can (a) provide an organized and systematic vehicle for documentation and reflection in all eight domains, (b) demonstrate strengths and target areas for needed improvement, and (c) offer teachers ownership of their own evaluations. The teacher's evaluation portfolio would include items similar to those suggested later for the professional development portfolio. In addition, the teacher could include artifacts and reflections on peer evaluations, parent follow-up letter to a conference, or a teaching unit collaboratively developed or singly developed. Other examples might be videotapes of lessons or lesson plans, certificates from workshops or staff development sessions, presentations to colleagues, and class newsletters or other examples that feature student achievement in the classroom or school (Brown & Irby, 1997).

The principal must understand that the key to the teacher portfolio process and teacher growth is the teacher's ability to self-evaluate and reflect upon experiences portrayed by selected artifacts that demonstrate actual teaching practices and that highlight and demonstrate the teacher's knowledge, skills, and attitudes in relation to his work. As a teacher reflects on his practice, he is able to critically self-assess the impact of a particular lesson or strategy and clarify future goals and plans for professional development aimed at improved pedagogy. Use of the Reflection Cycle (Brown & Irby, 2000) as described later in this chapter offers the structure for in-depth teacher reflection.

According to Marcoux, Rodriguez, Brown, and Irby (2001), improvement in the quality of teaching and learning depends largely on the commitment of teachers to continually assess and improve upon their own teaching as measured by student performance and established teaching criterion such as the PDAS. The portfolio should be comprehensive, containing documentation of the many facets of the teacher's work and achievement in relation to the state domains and campus and classroom goals. Artifacts for reflection that may demonstrate strengths or indicate areas for improvement may include administrator walk-through feedback; observation reports from supervisors and peers; profile sheets on student progress; staff development sessions related to professional goals; implementation of "new learnings" related to professional development goals; and/or feedback from students, parents, and others. Selecting artifacts or samples of work and writing accompanying reflections are beneficial in denoting areas of needed improvement, assisting in maintaining focus, and providing new perspectives and insights.

Using a teacher evaluation portfolio as a part of continuous improvement and professional growth/development is a positive, personal, and individualized approach to appraisal. In portfolio development, teachers must conceptualize their roles and become highly involved in their own evaluation and professional growth. Principals participate in a teacher's appraisal; but, according to Lambert (1998), their assessment simply adds to a teacher's performance portfolio—and, we add, to the teacher's professional development plans.

The portfolio evaluation process encourages collegial interaction among administrators and teachers, providing an avenue for two-way communication (Brogan, 1995; Brown & Irby, 2001). During the final evaluation conference the teacher, while referring to concrete examples in the portfolio, shares with the principal areas of professional growth over the course of the current school year, reflects on professional development goals that have been accomplished, and offers a proactive plan for new goals for the upcoming year. Additionally, the principal is able to seek clarification, give feedback, and offer suggestions for setting professional growth goals. Through this process, the principal empowers the teachers, who then can assume the major responsibility for their own growth and development. Collectively, the principal and the teachers can assess their evaluations and plan campus-wide needs related to instruction.

Principle 7 *Effective professional development is planned collaboratively by those who will participate in and facilitate that development.* Kelleher (2003) indicated that certain types of professional development are more likely to have an impact on student learning than others; therefore, it is imperative that the professional development system provides an incentive for teachers to pursue professional development activities that will easily translate into student learning. The principal should develop or offer various professional development strands, based on current research on effective professional development, to prioritize and categorize various pursuits. The four professional development strands are as follows:

1. *Peer collaboration.* This strand should be given the most importance, because it is job embedded and thus should have a bigger impact on student achievement. Teachers collaborate in writing curriculum and assessments, examining student work, working on committees, observing one another's classrooms and coaching, mentoring new teachers, and participating in study groups.

2. *Individualized professional growth.* A teacher participates in activities such as attending a conference, listening to a guest speaker, or taking a course at the college level.

3. *Research and leadership.* Teachers conduct action research and take leadership roles by sharing knowledge and practices through publications and other presentations.
4. *External experiences.* This strand includes many other activities, such as summer externships and visits to other schools.

The principal should help teachers choose among the various strands to ensure a range of appropriate professional development activities. The principal can allocate the budget to encourage teachers to focus heavily on activities related to peer collaboration. There may be some cases in which an activity applies to more than one strand, and in that case the principal (or possibly the assigned peer coach) may assist the teacher in determining which strand best fits her learning goals.

The North Central Regional Educational Laboratory (NCREL, 1996) provided suggestions for principals and teachers to collaborate in planning professional development as follows. They can (a) examine the current school philosophy regarding teaching and learning; (b) organize study groups to discuss contemporary views of learning and the research on effective instruction for different outcomes, articulating their beliefs about the ways in which learning occurs and discussing the implications for instructional practice; (c) use the discussions and conclusions of these groups to reach consensus on a collective vision that will provide a philosophical base for the consideration of new curricula and instructional practices; (d) understand principles for effective professional development; (e) examine and discuss current attitudes toward professional development; (f) create a school culture in which teachers feel free to critically assess their own practice; (g) examine the effective learning models and frameworks for designing professional development and discuss conditions in the school or district that facilitate or hinder the use of a variety of professional development strategies; and (h) evaluate the impact and effect of the professional development conducted throughout the school year and make recommendations for improving the professional development for the following year. In conducting the evaluation, the most important point to consider is the impact of professional development—first, on student achievement and, second, on teachers' instructional practices.

Principle 8 *Effective professional development requires substantial time and other resources.* Principals must devote the time for planning professional development that is systemically connected to the curriculum and instructional needs of the campus as well as to the vision and mission. Principals must advocate for funding to support professional development, and they need to propose that a full 10% of the school budget be devoted to professional development. The Council for School Performance (1998) determined that the most effective professional development programs related to time investment are long-term programs, implemented throughout the school year. Such investments of time require funds for hiring consultants, sending teachers to professional development sessions, and/or retaining high-quality substitutes as teachers are in training.

Principle 9 *Effective professional development is driven by a coherent long-term plan.* Leading an effective professional development program is a complex and comprehensive process, and it promotes change within a system. To achieve desired change, principals must develop a clearly articulated and communicated plan to address commonly identified goals (Fullan, 1993, 1999; Fullan & Hargreaves, 1992; Sparks & Richardson, 1997). In effect, principals create learning organizations where professional development and change become the norm of continuous improvement (Fullan, 2000; National Association of Secondary School Principals, 1996; U.S. Department of Education, 1996). According to Fullan (2000), professional development is a goal-oriented and continuous process, supported through mentoring, coaching, and feedback and developed to address the perceived needs of the students.

Principle 10 *Effective professional development is evaluated ultimately on the basis of its impact on teacher effectiveness and student learning, and* *this assessment guides subsequent professional development efforts.* According to Kelleher (2003):

> Current research on professional development, which has shown that professional development must be embedded in teachers' daily work to improve student learning, has led school boards and administrators across the country to evaluate the results of their investment in adult learning. The standards movement, along with the push to increase the use of data in educational decision making, has intensified the pressure on school administrators to prove that professional development is showing positive results. (p. 751)

Evaluating the professional development session through a survey at the end of the session is not sufficient. The issue is not how much the teachers liked the session; rather, the issue is what effect the professional development will have on student learning (Richardson, 2000).

The No Child Left Behind Act (NCLB) (U.S. Department of Education, 2002) requires states to have challenging academic standards; to test students annually in grades 3–8 and once in high school; and to increase student achievement so that all students reach proficient levels by the 2013–2014 school year. Some believe there is no link between professional development and student improvements in achievement; and perhaps there are no links in the one-time, shot-in-the-arm professional development strategies. However, when we look across the country and find entire school districts with students in every subgroup (Black, Hispanic, White, and economically disadvantaged) achieving at or above state or district standards in reading and math, we find that it is in those districts where the professional development is ongoing, sustained, and connected to the standards the teachers are trying to accomplish. According to the Iowa Association of School Boards (2003), a growing body of evidence indicates that teacher effectiveness is not fixed, and that when teachers of all experience levels learn powerful skills and methods to use with students in the classroom, student achievement increases. The association suggests that to accomplish this end result, professional development must be (a) grounded in student need in an academic content area; (b) research based; (c) collaborative and ongoing; (d) embedded in the system; (e) built on effective training processes; (f) structured to involve all administrative levels in support and planning; (g) connected to school improvement and aligned with the curriculum standards and assessed needs of the students, as well as the self-assessed needs of the teachers; and (h) monitored (effective professional development is monitored for implementation and results).

The Principal's Mission for Personal Professional Development

The second mission that principals have regarding professional development relates to their own professional growth. This mission is for principals to work with their supervisors to develop a personal, professional development plan including the resources, money, and time required. They should establish time for meetings with the supervisor and other principals that will allow for reflection on their leadership practice.

Principals can engage in their own long-term, ongoing professional development and become role models for their teaching staff. According to Brown and Irby (2002), one way that principals can effectively engage in their own improvement and serve as a model for their teachers is by producing a Professional Development Portfolio. The authors indicated that such a portfolio provides an excellent vehicle for organizing and documenting professional development experiences and subsequent improvement.

The Professional Development Portfolio

Brown and Irby (2000) defined the Professional Development Portfolio as a collection of thoughtfully selected exhibits or artifacts and reflections indicative of an individual's progress toward and/or attainment of established goals or criteria. In the process of developing a Professional Development Portfolio, principals can focus on

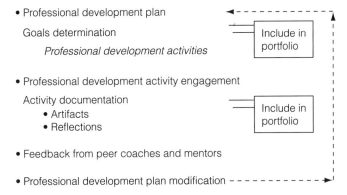

Pre-implementation phase: Basic assessment

- Assessment for data collection

  Artifacts from self and others

  - Assessment center feedback   Job-like
  - 360° feedback   Job-related
  - Inventory/survey results   Job-related
  - Evidences of leadership performance   Job-specific
  - Feedback from peers and mentors   Job-specific

- Reflections on artifacts

Use of Reflection Cycle

Implementation phase: Professional Development Portfolio

- Professional development plan

  Goals determination   Include in portfolio

  Professional development activities

- Professional development activity engagement

  Activity documentation   Include in portfolio
  - Artifacts
  - Reflections

- Feedback from peer coaches and mentors

- Professional development plan modification

Figure 5.1

Brown and Irby Model of Professional Development

Source: From G. Brown & B. J. Irby, "Documenting Continuing Professional Education Requirements Using the Professional Development Portfolio," 2002, *Texas Study, XI*(2), pp. 13–16. Reprinted with permission.

the documentation, through concrete examples (artifacts and reflections), of progress toward goals related to assessment results and their growth as leaders. The portfolio not only offers an effective system for organizing evidence of progress but also promotes self-assessment skills. As principals learn these skills, they can also assist their teachers in doing the same. When principals choose artifacts and write reflections for the portfolio, they become more reflective, more critical, and more able to determine their own strengths and weaknesses.

Brown and Irby (2002) offered a model for implementing the Professional Development Portfolio process over a five-year period. Figure 5.1 depicts the model that principals can use to improve their practice by considering multiple leadership assessment data, including self-assessment; by planning specific activities to enhance growth in targeted areas; and by reflecting on professional growth associated with those activities (Brown & Irby, 2000). This same model could be adapted by principals for use with teachers on their campuses.

Using the Professional Development Portfolio

Brown and Irby (2002) indicated that the Professional Development Portfolio Model facilitates continuous learning. Although assessment results reflect the performance of the individual at a specific point in time, the Professional Development Portfolio Model depicts assessment as occurring not only at certain points in time, but as continuous. The authors said that although portfolios are highly individualized, with specific contents usually determined by the individual or the district, the Professional Development Portfolio typically includes a table of contents, an introduction, assessment data, a current résumé, a Leadership Framework, a professional development plan based on assessment data, and artifacts and reflections related to professional development activities (organized by goals or standards). See Figure 5.2.

Table of Contents, Introduction, and Résumé

The table of contents should indicate clearly how the portfolio is organized, so that review of the portfolio is easily accomplished. The introduction briefly needs to (a) explain the purpose of the portfolio and (b) outline the results of the assessment. Including an updated résumé provides an opportunity for the principal to add recent accomplishments and the latest professional development experiences to the résumé. The résumé should also include a listing of certifications or endorsements, education, experience, areas of concentration, and strengths.

Leadership Framework

All actions are predicated on personal beliefs and values; therefore, it is important to express those clearly and concisely in writing. The Leadership Framework (Brown & Irby, 2001), a written statement of primary beliefs and attitudes regarding leadership, assists principals in analyzing why they do what they do as leaders; it also helps clarify who they are as leaders to others, including faculty, colleagues, community, and board. Because it compels principals to reflect on their philosophies of leadership, learning, and

Contents of the portfolio

• Table of contents
• Introduction
• Assessment data
• Résumé
• Leadership Framework
• Professional development
    ○ Goals
    ○ Plans
    ○ Activities
• Artifacts
• Reflections

Figure 5.2

Contents of the Professional Development Portfolio
Source: From G. Brown & B. J. Irby, "Documenting Continuing Professional Education Requirements Using the Professional Development Portfolio," 2002, *Texas Study, XI*(2), pp. 13–16. Reprinted with permission.

teaching, this self-analysis offers opportunities for personal and professional growth. Principals address seven important components as they develop their Leadership Framework: Philosophy of Education, Philosophy of Leadership, Vision for Learners, Vision for Teachers, Vision for the Organization, Vision for Professional Development, and Method of Vision Attainment.[1]

The Professional Development Plan

The professional development plan, viewed in Figure 5.3, provides direction for specific professional development goals based on assessment results. The principal then can align those goals with the state's principal standards and can select professional development activities accordingly. Although professional development experiences should be planned in advance, modifications should be made as new experiences become available. Next, timelines should be developed as well as brief notes related to securing appropriate artifacts from the experiences. Finally, feedback from colleagues, mentors, peer coaches, or supervisors

---

[1]For additional explanation and an example of a Leadership Framework, refer to *The Principal Portfolio,* Corwin Press, 2001.

Name: _____

Prioritized standards/ indicators	Professional goals	Professional development experiences	Timeline	Documentation (artifacts and reflections)	Feedback requested/ from whom

Figure 5.3

Brown and Irby Professional Development Plan

Source: From G. Brown & B. J. Irby, "Documenting Continuing Professional Education Requirements Using the Professional Development Portfolio," 2002, *Texas Study, XI*(2), pp. 13–16. Reprinted with permission.

regarding improvement in targeted areas may be included as further evidence of growth.

Related Professional Development Activity Artifacts and Reflection The artifacts and reflections are the heart of the Professional Development Portfolio. Principals who have developed portfolios report that the processes of selecting viable samples of their experiences and writing accompanying reflections are beneficial in maintaining focus on goals, in providing new perspectives and creative insights, and in developing satisfaction that specific goals related to improved leadership are being accomplished.

The artifacts and their accompanying reflections may be organized in the portfolio either by standard or by professional development goal. Figure 5.4 provides examples of artifacts related to professional development experiences.

Much of the current literature on successful leadership emphasizes the importance of self-assessment

for growth. The greatest benefit of portfolio development is realized through the process of reflection, as the leader assesses the effectiveness and impact of his leadership beliefs, style, and practices. The reflection inherent in the portfolio development process (a) provides insights into strengths and weaknesses, (b) encourages planning for professional growth, (c) leads to improved practice by the principal, and (d) ultimately, enhances school and teacher effectiveness and improves student learning.

Our research and our work with administrators has indicated the need for a structure for writing reflections. The Reflection Cycle (referred to here as the Cycle) (Brown & Irby, 2001) provides such a structure. The five steps of the Cycle offer critical prompts. Steps 1 and 2 of the Cycle focus on selecting the artifact and describing the circumstances surrounding it. (It is the selected artifact in the Professional Development Portfolio that serves as concrete evidence of the principal's

- Leadership workshop
- Group-leading skills training
- Inquiry group on teacher research and improvement
- Curriculum development
- Readings in school law
- Observations when conducting a group meeting
- Conflict resolution training

Figure 5.4

Brown and Irby Examples of Artifacts for
Professional Development Experiences
Source: From G. Brown & B. J. Irby, "Documenting Continuing
Professional Education Requirements Using the Professional
Development Portfolio," 2002, *Texas Study, XI*(2), pp. 13–16.
Reprinted with permission.

professional development experiences.) Step 3
asks the principal to analyze the experience illustrated by the artifact and the relation of it to issues, expectations, goals, and practice. Step 4 is
appraisal of the experience. Here the principal interprets events surrounding the experience; determines her impact or the impact the experiences
had on her leadership; determines effectiveness of
decisions made; and/or ascertains relationships to
her philosophy, values, and/or goals. Step 5 requires the principal to use the interpreted data
and develop projections for further improvement
and future goals. The Reflection Cycle should also
be taught to teachers; however, it is best if the
principal is using the Cycle to reflect on her practice and can share how she has used it to improve.

Ethics of Professional Development

The National Staff Development Council (2000)
adopted a Code of Ethics and divided the responsibilities into two categories: staff development
leader and staff development provider. The Council
considers professional development leaders as the
individuals within a school, school district, university, state education agency, or other educational
organization who plan, implement, coordinate,
and/or evaluate staff development efforts. They include but are not limited to directors of staff development, superintendents, school board members,
principals, curriculum coordinators, and teacher

leaders. Staff or professional development
providers use their knowledge and skills to promote adult learning or to assist groups and organizations to perform more effectively. They include
trainers, facilitators, consultants, mentors, and
instructional and leadership specialists or coaches.
The most critical person related to professional
development on a campus is the principal. It is the
principal who has a vantage point of the whole
school's needs and who can facilitate, collaboratively with teachers, the professional development
that addresses those needs.

Based on the Council's ethical code, the principal
should have the following responsibilities:
(a) be committed to achieving school goals, particularly those addressing high levels of learning and
performance for all students and teachers; (b) select
professional development content and processes
that are research based and proven in practice after
examining various types of information about student and educator learning needs; (c) improve his
work through the ongoing evaluation of professional development's effectiveness in achieving
school system and school goals for student learning;
(d) improve his own knowledge and skills; (e) ensure an equitable distribution of resources to accomplish school goals for student learning; (f) advocate
for policies and practices that ensure the continuous
learning of all students and teachers; and (g) conduct himself in a manner that avoids conflict of interest or the appearance of such conflict.

Summary

1. The principal's mission related to her teachers'
professional development is twofold. First, the
mission is *to plan,* with teachers, a comprehensive professional development program
targeted at identified individual and collective
needs; and second, the mission is *to provide*
resources, including time and money, and to
include time for teachers to reflect upon and
participate in dialogue about their practice.

2. There is a positive connection between professional development and student learning;

therefore, it is important to include in the budget funds for sustained professional development.

3. The best professional development is connected to the needs of the students and the teachers' related instructional concerns.

4. Principals who promote successful professional development experiences for their teachers will, in turn, increase the teachers' interest in and commitment to the profession.

5. Professional development should consider the data gathered related to student achievement and the types of professional development conducted throughout the school year. With these data, a principal and the teachers can plan more effective and sustained professional development programs.

6. Effective professional development is logically embedded in the reality of schools and teachers' work.

7. Principals can engage in their own long-term, ongoing professional development and become role models for their teaching staff.

8. Portfolios provide a means for self-assessment and evaluation. The reflection inherent in the portfolio development process (a) provides insights into strengths and weaknesses, (b) encourages planning for professional growth, (c) leads to improved practice by the principal, and (d) ultimately, enhances school and teacher effectiveness and improves student learning.

9. The principal has ethical responsibilities toward professional development.

Field-Based Activities

1. Determine, with your principal, the percentage of the school budget that is spent on professional development of administrators, faculty, and staff. Determine, with your business manager in the district, what percentage of the budget is spent on professional development throughout the district.

2. Based on the 10 principles of effective professional development, assess the professional

development activities on your campus. Do they meet these standards?

3. Develop a professional development portfolio. Use the components to build your portfolio as suggested in the text.

Suggested Readings

Brown, G., & Irby, B. J. (2001). *The principal portfolio.* Thousand Oaks, CA: Corwin Press. This book, in its first edition (1999), was the first to introduce four types of portfolios for principals: (a) Professional Development Portfolio, (b) Evaluation Portfolio, (c) Career Advancement Portfolio, and (d) Academic Portfolio. Benefits of each and how to develop each type of portfolio are included in the book.

Irby, B. J., & Brown, G. (2000). *The career advancement portfolio.* Thousand Oaks, CA: Corwin Press. This text offers teachers or administrators information on how to develop and use the Career Advancement Portfolio in obtaining a first or the next administrative position.

Joyce, B. R., Showers, B., & Fullan, M. G. (2002). *Student achievement through staff development* (3rd Ed.). Alexandria, VA: Association of Supervision and Curriculum Development. The focus of the book is on the potential for both personal and organizational growth inherent in staff development programs. School renewal ultimately depends on the individual development of all its members. The authors share a way of creating a community in which organizers, providers, teachers, administrators, and students learn and grow together to achieve the goal of lasting student achievement.

Kaagan, S. S. (2003). *30 reflective staff development exercises for educators.* Thousand Oaks, CA: Corwin. This author presents a unique guide for educators who enjoy challenging themselves and who hunger for new ideas and a fresh perspective on staff development. The book promotes individual and collective learning by all participants as they undertake formal staff development while enhancing the success and performance of the entire educational system. The 30 reflective exercises, designed to meet the specific needs of educators, include

- Fostering effective change
- Developing leadership skills
- Identifying and capitalizing on staff assets
- Gaining and using new perspectives

Koehler, M. (2002). *Administrator's staff development activities kit.* San Francisco: Jossey-Bass. This practical resource gives elementary and secondary school administrators a comprehensive, ready-to-use staff development activities program that integrates in-service training, supervision, and evaluation. The program encourages professional growth through self-assessment and includes over 120 reproducible forms, charts, models, and other aids that can be used "as is" in developmental activities.

Robb, L. (2000). *Redefining staff development: A collaborative model for teachers and administrators.* Portsmouth, NH: Heineman. In *Redefining Staff Development,* Robb advocates

for meaningful change that takes into account the culture of the school community and the diversity among its members.

Sparks, D., & Hirsch, S. (1997). *A new vision for staff development.* Alexandria, VA: Association of Supervision and Curriculum Development. Dennis Sparks and Stephanie Hirsh share in their book how effective staff development is targeting everyone who affects student learning, and how the total organization—not just the individual—is improving through multiple forms of learning. Sparks and Hirsh tell how "three powerful ideas"—results-driven education, systems thinking, and constructivism—are shaping the new staff development, and they describe how the focus has shifted from the district to the school, from fragmented efforts to comprehensive plans, from adult needs to student needs, from off-site training to job-embedded learning, and from generic skills to a combination that includes content-specific skills as well. At the heart of their discussion are examples of districts and schools throughout the nation that are at the forefront of the new staff development.

6. Student Services

Standard 2.0: *Candidates who complete the program are educational leaders who have the knowledge and ability to promote the success of all students by promoting a positive school culture, providing an effective educational program, applying best practice to student learning, and designing comprehensive professional growth plans for staff.*

FOCUSING QUESTIONS

1 Why is it important to provide guidance and counseling services in schools?

2 How do student attendance and record keeping support the overall function of the student services department?

3 Could the modern school operate effectively without some means of evaluating student progress?

4 What methods can be used to report student progress to parents/families?

5 What role does the extracurricular activities program play in relation to the overall goals of the school?

6 What are the special education services provided for exceptional children in today's schools? Why is it important for schools to offer such services?

7 What should principals know about gifted education in order to serve all learners?

8 What should principals know about bilingual education in order to serve all children?

In this chapter we respond to these questions concerning student services. We begin our discussion by examining the aims, services, and evaluation of guidance and counseling programs. Then we look at how student attendance and record keeping support the overall function of the student services department. Measuring and reporting student progress to parents/families are discussed next. Then we examine the role of extracurricular activities in relation to the overall mission of the school. Next, we discuss special education and explore some of the provisions of the 1997 reauthorization of the Individuals with Disabilities Act

(IDEA). Finally, we examine how gifted education and bilingual education programs benefit students with special needs.

Guidance and Counseling Services

One function of education is to provide opportunities for each student to reach his full potential in the areas of educational, vocational, personal, and emotional development. With continuous societal pressures upon students, the principal must ensure that guidance is an integral part of education and that it is centered *directly* on this function. Guidance and counseling services prepare students to assume increasing responsibility for their decisions and grow in their ability to understand and accept the results of their choices (Baker, 2004; Cobia et al., 2002; Sciarra, 2004; Thompson, 2002). Like other abilities, the ability to make such intelligent choices is not innate but must be developed. In this section, we examine the aims of guidance and counseling programs, major guidance and counseling services, methods of counseling, and evaluation of guidance programs. It is critical for principals to understand the basic concepts of guidance and counseling so that they can work with the counselor on their campuses to ensure quality services.

Aims of Guidance and Counseling Programs

The aims of the guidance and counseling service are similar to the purposes of education in general: to assist the student in fulfilling her basic physiological needs, understanding herself and displaying acceptance of others, developing associations with peers, balancing between permissiveness and controls in the educational setting, realizing successful achievement, and providing opportunities to gain independence (Davis, 2002; Dollarhide et al., 2002; Hitchner et al., 2002; Parsad, 2003; Sandu, 2001; Worzbyt et al., 2004). The purposes of guidance and counseling are to

provide emphasis and strength to the educational program. Some specific aims of the school guidance and counseling program follow:

1. *To provide for the realization of student potentialities.* To all students, the school offers a wide choice of courses and co-curricular activities. A significant function of education is to help students identify and develop their potentialities. The counselor's role is to assist students to distribute their energies into the many learning opportunities available to them. Every student needs help in planning his major course of study and pattern of co-curricular activities.

2. *To help children with developing problems.* Even those students who have chosen an appropriate educational program for themselves may have problems that require help. A teacher may need to spend from one-fifth to one-third of his time with a few students who require a great deal of help, which deprives the rest of the class from the teacher's full attention to their needs. The counselor, by helping these youngsters to resolve their difficulties, frees the classroom teacher to use his time more efficiently.

3. *To contribute to the development of the school's curriculum.* Counselors, in working with individual students, know their personal problems and aspirations, their talents and abilities as well as the social pressures confronting them. Counselors, therefore, can provide data that serve as a basis for curriculum development, and they can help curriculum developers shape courses of study that more accurately reflect the needs of students. Too often, counselors are not included in curriculum development efforts.

4. *To provide teachers with technical assistance.* Pre-service teacher training institutions typically provide very limited experience with the more technical aspects of guidance work. Thus, a need exists in most schools for assistance with guidance and counseling functions essential to the educational program. Specifically,

the guidance counselor is qualified to assist teachers with selecting, administering, and interpreting tests; selecting and using cumulative, anecdotal, and other types of records; providing help and suggestions relative to counseling techniques, which teachers can use in counseling their students; and displaying leadership in designing and conducting professional development of teachers in guidance functions.

5. *To contribute to the mutual adjustment of students and the school.* The guidance program has a responsibility for developing and maintaining a cooperative relationship between students and the school. Teachers and counselors must be cognizant of students' needs. Students also must make adjustments to the school. They have a responsibility to contribute something to the school. A major contribution of students is that of making appropriate use of the school's resources and working toward accomplishments. Such mutual adjustment of students and school is facilitated by providing suggestions for program improvements, conducting research for educational improvements, contributing to students' adjustment through counseling, and fostering wholesome school-home attitudes (Baker, 2004; Cobia et al., 2002; Sciarra, 2004; Thompson, 2002).

The Role of the Counselor

The major goals of counseling are to promote personal growth and to prepare students to become motivated workers and responsible citizens. Educators recognize that in addition to intellectual challenges, students encounter personal/social, educational, and career challenges. School guidance and counseling programs need to address these challenges and to promote educational success.

The guidance and counseling program is an integral part of a school's total educational program; it is developmental by design, focusing on needs, interests, and issues related to various stages of

student growth. The developmental guidance and counseling program in today's school has a broad scope that includes these components:

- *Personal/social.* In addition to providing guidance services for all students, counselors are expected to do personal and crisis counseling. Problems such as dropping out, substance abuse, suicide, irresponsible sexual behavior, eating disorders, and pregnancy must be addressed.

- *Educational.* Students must develop skills that will assist them as they learn. The counselor, through classroom guidance activities and individual and group counseling, can assist students in applying effective study skills, setting goals, learning effectively, and gaining test-taking skills. Counselors also may focus on helping students learn approaches to note taking, time management, memory techniques, relaxation techniques, overcoming test anxiety, and developing listening skills.

- *Career.* Planning for the future, combating career stereotyping, and analyzing skills and interests are some goals students must develop in school. Career information must be available to students, and representatives from business and industry must work closely with the school and the counselor in preparing students for the world of work (Cobia et al., 2002; Coy, 2004; Greenberg et al., 2002).

Major Guidance and Counseling Services

The primary mission of a school's guidance and counseling program is to provide a broad spectrum of personnel services to the students. These services include student assessment, the information service, placement and follow-up, and counseling assistance. These four areas should constitute the core of any guidance program and should be organized to facilitate the growth and development of all students from kindergarten through post–high school experiences.

Assessment   The *assessment* service is designed to collect, analyze, and use a variety of objective and subjective personal, psychological, and social data about each student. Its purpose is to help the individual to better understand herself. Conferences with students and parents, standardized test scores, academic records, anecdotal records, personal data forms, case studies, and portfolios are included. The school counselor interprets this information to students, parents, teachers, administrators, and other professionals. Students with special needs and abilities are thus identified.

Information   The *information* service is designed to provide accurate and current information in order that the students may make an intelligent choice of an educational program, an occupation, or a social activity. Essentially, the aim is that with such information students will make better choices and will engage in better planning in and out of the school setting. Students not only must be exposed to such information, but must also have an opportunity to react to it in a meaningful way with others.

Placement and Follow-up   The school assists the student in selecting and utilizing opportunities within the school as well as in the outside labor market. Counselors assist students in making appropriate choices of courses of study and in making transitions from one school level to another, from one school to another, and from school to employment. *Placement* thereby involves student assessment, informational services, and counseling assistance appropriate to the student's choices of school subjects, co-curricular activities, and employment. *Follow-up* is concerned with the development of a systematic plan for maintaining contact with former students. The data obtained from the follow-up studies aid the school in evaluating the school's curricular and guidance programs.

Counseling   The *counseling* service is designed to facilitate self-understanding and development through dyadic or small-group relationships. The aim of such relationships tends to be focused on personal development and decision making that is based on self-understanding and knowledge of the environment. The counselor (a) assists the student to understand and accept himself, thereby clarifying his ideas, perceptions, attitudes, and goals; (b) furnishes personal and environmental information to the student, as required, regarding his plans, choices, or problems; and (c) seeks to develop in the student the ability to cope with and solve problems and increased competence in making decisions and plans for the future. Counseling is generally accepted as the heart of the guidance service (Baker, 2004; Erford, 2003; Sciarra, 2004).

Methods of Counseling

Counseling students is a basic function of the school guidance program. Counseling skills are needed by school principals, teachers, teacher-advisors, athletic coaches, and club sponsors as well as by professional counselors. Although counseling of serious emotional problems is best handled by professional counselors, teachers and other faculty personnel find themselves in situations daily where counseling is necessary (Baker, 2004; Erford, 2003; Sciarra, 2004). Acquaintance with counseling methods and points of view is useful to them.

Counseling methods and points of view have developed from research and theories about how individuals grow and develop, change their behavior, and interact with their environment. These counseling methods are generally classified into three broad types or schools of thought: directive, nondirective, and eclectic (Baker, 2004; Cobia et al., 2002; Sciarra, 2004). One of the most fundamental philosophical and theoretical questions that confronts the counselor in the course of her training and professional practice is which method to select in counseling students.

Directive Counseling   The directive counselor is said to be more interested in the problem than he is in the counselee. This belief is an exaggeration. The student and her problem cannot be separated. All service professions are, by their very nature, concerned with the person to be helped. All teaching, for example, is student centered even when a teacher has 30 students in a class. The directive counselor, however, focuses attention on identifying and analyzing the problem and finding an appropriate solution to it. He tends to make use of test data, school records, and reports, and he is more disposed to giving advice and information based on such data. *Directive counseling* is the method most commonly used by counselors in school settings (Cobia et al., 2002).

Directive counseling seems to be most successful when the counselee is relatively well adjusted; the problem is in an intellectual area; a lack of information constituted the problem; the counselee has little insight into the problem; inner conflict is absent; and the client suffers from anxiety, insecurity, or impatience (Baker, 2004; Cobia et al., 2002; Sciarra, 2004).

Nondirective Counseling   The nondirective approach is more effective in the treatment of many types of emotional problems. However, many students who come to the counselor have few if any such emotional problems. Many cases merely call for information or some other routine assistance.

Although there are many proponents of nondirective counseling, Carl Rogers is best known because he started the movement and has given it leadership for about six decades (Rogers, 1942). The aim of *nondirective counseling* is, according to Rogers, to help the student "to become a better organized person, oriented around healthy goals which [he] has clearly seen and definitely chosen" (p. 227). It aims to provide the student with a united purpose, with the courage to meet life and the obstacles it presents. Consequently, the client takes from his counseling contacts not necessarily a neat solution for each of his problems, but the ability to meet his problems in a constructive way. Rogers defines effective counseling as a definitely structured, permissive relationship that allows the client to gain an understanding of himself to a degree that enables him to take positive steps in the light of his new orientation. This hypothesis has a natural corollary — that all the techniques used should aim toward developing

this free and permissive relationship, this understanding of self in the counseling and other relationships, and this tendency toward positive, self-initiated action (Cobia et al., 2002; Rogers, 1942).

Possibly the greatest contribution of the nondirective technique has been its influence in personalizing counseling. Nevertheless, even though this approach may be more effective in certain counseling situations, it is unlikely to be used in most schools because of the extensive training essential to its application in the counseling process (Baker, 2004; Sciarra, 2004).

Eclectic Counseling   Eclectic counseling is the result of selecting concepts from both directive and nondirective approaches. Thus, the eclectic counselor uses whatever approach seems best suited to the situation. Real help given to most students in schools would be located between the highly directive and the eclectic views rather than client centered (Baker, 2004; Cobia et al., 2002; Sciarra, 2004). The eclectic counselor's effectiveness will depend more on the relationship existing between the student and his counselors than on the method she chooses and how well she performs within the method she employs.

Evaluation of Guidance and Counseling Programs

Evaluation consists of making systematic judgments of the relative effectiveness with which goals are attained in relation to specified standards. In evaluating a function like guidance and counseling services, we attempt to determine to what extent the objectives of the service have been attained. The major objectives of guidance are to assist individuals in developing the ability to understand themselves, to solve their own problems, and to make appropriate adjustments to their environment as the situation dictates (Bor, 1993; Steege & Watson, 2004). Evaluation is the means by which school personnel can better judge the extent to which these objectives are being met. The following 10 characteristics provide criteria for evaluating the effectiveness of a school's guidance and counseling services.

1. *Student needs.* Effective guidance programs are based on student needs. Some needs are typical among students of a given age; others are specific to certain individuals in particular regions or schools. In effective guidance programs, teachers, counselors, and principals listen carefully to what students say, because they know the students are expressing either personal or situational inadequacies.

2. *Cooperation.* The staff of effective guidance programs work cooperatively. Cooperation is exhibited in the degree of active interest, mutual help, and collaboration among teachers, counselors, and principals.

3. *Process and product.* Effective guidance programs are concerned with both process and product. The questions "How well is the program operating?" and "What are the outcomes?" guide the focus in effective guidance programs. The most important outcome of a guidance program is desirable change in the behavior of students, such as improved school attendance, better study habits, better scholastic achievement, fewer scholastic failures, lower dropout rate, better educational planning, and better home-school relations.

4. *Balance.* Effective guidance programs balance corrective, preventive, and developmental functions. Personnel in such programs know when to extricate students from potentially harmful situations, when to anticipate student difficulties, and when to provide assistance necessary to a student's maximum development.

5. *Stability.* The ability to adjust to loss of personnel without loss of effectiveness is associated with program quality. Stability requires that the system be able to fill vacant positions quickly and satisfactorily.

6. *Flexibility.* Effective guidance programs manifest flexibility. Flexibility enables the program to expand or contract as the situation demands without significant loss of effectiveness.

7. *Qualified counselors.* Counselors hold a graduate degree in counseling and are fully certified by the state in which they practice.

8. *Adequate counselor-student ratio.* Most accrediting agencies (for example, the Southern Association and the North Central Association) require a counselor-student ratio of one full-time counselor for 250 to 300 students. A caseload of this magnitude is satisfactory if counselors are to have adequate time not only to counsel students individually and in small groups but also to consult with faculty, principals, and parents.

9. *Physical facilities.* Are the facilities for guidance work sufficient for an effective program? Physical facilities that are well planned and provide for adequate space, privacy, accessibility, and the like are characteristic of quality guidance programs.

10. *Records.* Appropriate records are maintained on each student, including achievement test scores as well as information supplied by teachers, principals, parents, employers, and other professional personnel (Bor, 1993; Steege & Watson, 2004).

Although many of these 10 characteristics are useful, they should not be accepted unquestioningly. To some extent, each guidance program is unique to its particular setting and consequently would either add other characteristics to the list or stress those cited previously in varying degrees.

Attendance and Student Records

Student accounting is the oldest area of student services. Its beginnings can be traced to enforcement of compulsory attendance in the Massachusetts law of 1642; much later, in 1852, Massachusetts enacted the first compulsory attendance law in the United States. From the beginning, this service was primarily an administrative one aimed at keeping students in school (Cobia et al., 2002).

Student accounting has gradually enlarged its administrative emphasis to one of understanding child behavior. In recent years attendance officers have brought about a separation of enforcement and correction, so that truancy is being treated as a symptom of some underlying difficulty. Counselors and principals are working together to determine the causes of nonattendance. School clerks handle routine aspects of truancy, and special cases are referred to personnel workers who have time to deal with them as guidance rather than as administrative problems. Thus nonattendance is becoming an essential part of personnel work, and its occurrences are viewed as opportunities to discover students who need special help (Crone et al., 2003; Kampwirth, 2002).

It is the aim of the compulsory attendance laws that have been passed by each of the 50 states that all children shall receive certain minimum essentials as their educational preparation for life. Teachers, principals, and counselors share responsibility for helping all children to secure these essentials. To assist in this process, careful records must be kept.

The Cumulative Record

What are some of the recorded data needed to develop a better educational program for each child? The following information is recommended for inclusion in a student's cumulative record (Cheung, Clements, & Pechman, 2000; Weckmueller et al., 1998):

1. *Personal data sheet.* Such a form will provide pertinent and up-to-date information about the child. This information, most of which can be utilized by the teacher, should include family history (parents, siblings, home conditions), health history (diseases, illnesses, injuries), and child's history (courses, grades, excused and unexcused absences, failures, activities).

2. *Parent's report.* The record should contain a brief report from the parents. This report might include a bit more information about the child's background, including what her problems in school might be, what sort of person she is at home, and any information that might help the teacher do a better job.

3. *Child's self-concept.* This information may be in the form of answers to standardized tests, such as interests and personality tests. The folder should also contain an autobiographical sketch. The following can be solicited from English teachers as part of a writing assignment: free writing or a discussion of specific areas, such as ideas about life at home, life at school, outside activities, and other things of importance to the students.

4. *Sociogram.* The record should contain a sociogram to show the degree of acceptance of the student by his peers. This provides valuable information to the teacher regarding peer group acceptance or rejection.

5. *Behavior reports.* The student's record folder should contain periodic, objective reports of his behavior. In the elementary school most of these reports would come from one teacher, whereas in the secondary school they would be compiled by many teachers. These reports should never be used against the child, but instead should always be used for the child's benefit.

6. *Standardized test data.* A major part of the cumulative record is data collected as part of the school testing program — intelligence, personality and adjustment, interests, aptitude, achievement, and the like, and interpretation of test results and recommendations for adjustments and remedial work (Cheung et al., 2000; Weckmueller et al., 1998). Such information may help the teacher to better understand each of his students, and it may alert him to some of the difficulties students may experience in the future.

The Use of Assessment Data to Improve Learning

Many schools have increased the value of their cumulative record by providing careful instructions for their maintenance and use. What outcomes may be reasonably expected from the use of these records? The following five are suggested (Weckmueller et al., 1998):

1. A clearer understanding that the master teacher is a teacher of students, not merely of subject matter

2. A more systematic focusing of attention on the needs of individual students in order to help them to become more self-sufficient and independent

3. A better adjustment of the school and the curriculum to the needs and capacities of every student

4. A practical use of the appraisal of children and their needs that may result in the solution of some of their problems in school

5. A better intellectual and social development of each child so that she may maximize her potential

The cumulative record has value for teachers, principals, and other personnel-service professionals. Such data provide a better understanding of the child — his needs, aspirations, interests, and potentialities. The cumulative record can help with the child's adjustment in school, in the transition from one school level to another, and in the selection of postsecondary education and vocational plans.

Evaluating Student Progress

Testing, evaluating, and measuring student progress is a part of every comprehensive student services program. Practically every faculty member in a school is involved in the appraisal service. Teachers spend a great deal of time testing, measuring, and evaluating their students, as do counselors, social workers, and school psychologists. Few people who work in schools would deny that the modern school could operate effectively without some means of measuring and evaluating student progress, particularly in light of the *No Child Left Behind Act, 2001* (NCLB), which requires schools to meet Adequate Yearly

Progress (AYP) standards in reading and math. Those schools failing to meet the standards for several years could undergo "restructuring."

Adequate Yearly Progress standards require schools and districts to have (a) the same high standards of academic achievement for all; (b) statistically valid and reliable tests; (c) continuous and substantial academic improvement for all students; (d) separate, measurable annual objectives for achievement for all students, racial/ethnic groups, economically disadvantaged students, students with disabilities (IDEA, §602), and students with limited English proficiency; and (e) graduation rates for high school and one other indicator for other schools. NCLB 1111(b)(2)(C)(vi) defined the percentage of students who graduate from secondary school with a regular diploma in the standard number of years, and the regulation clarifies that alternate definitions that accurately measure the graduation rate are permissible. For AYP, each group of students must meet or exceed the established statewide annual objective exception: The number below proficient is reduced 10% from the prior year, and the subgroup must make progress on other indicators; and for each group, 95% of students enrolled participate in the assessments on which AYP is based (see your state's guidelines for AYP). In this section, we examine the purposes of assessment, establishing information criteria, creating effective tests, and the components of a testing program.

Purposes of Assessment

The basic purpose of the assessment service is to help the student in school. More specifically, the six basic purposes of assessment are (1) to help the student understand herself; (2) to provide information for educational and vocational counseling; (3) to help principals, faculty, and personnel staff to understand the nature of their student population; (4) to evaluate the academic progress and personal development of students; (5) to help the principal staff appraise the educational program; and (6) to facilitate curriculum revision

(Arter et al., 2000; Bernhardt, 2003; Brown, 2003; Parsons, 2002; Wiggins, 2000).

Others suggest three basic purposes of testing students: to make instructional management decisions, to make decisions about screening students, and to make program decisions (Mathison, 2004; Soleo, 2004; Stake, 2003; Stiggins, 2000). (See Table 6.1.)

Table 6.1 describes the relationships among general purposes: assessment context, related decisions, necessary data, and appropriate decision makers. For example, diagnosis of student strengths and weaknesses is one of the decision areas listed under "Instructional Management." Because the purpose of testing in this case is to make decisions about individual students, any test that is adopted must provide information about specific skills and/or subject-matter understanding.

Establishing Information Criteria

After determining the purposes of testing students, the next step is to identify the type of information needed to make the desired decisions. The information provided by any testing program can be classified into one or more of three categories or domains: (1) the *affective domain,* which refers to attitudes, feelings, interests, and values (Krathwohl, Bloom, & Masia, 1964); (2) the *psychomotor domain,* which refers to those skills involving neuromuscular coordination such as handwriting skills and athletic skills (Harrow, 1972); and (3) the *cognitive domain,* which is identified in a variety of ways and is usually classified along a continuum. Knowledge (that is, knowledge of facts, rules, and sequences) is viewed as a lower-order cognitive skill; and higher-order skills include the ability to classify, to recognize relationships, to analyze, to synthesize, and to evaluate (Bloom, 1956).

For example, if the purpose of testing is to make decisions about placement of students into academic classes of differing ability levels, it will be necessary to collect data that will yield information about how students perform on specific cognitive objectives. However, if a program has explicit affective goals, and the decision is to determine how well those goals have been reached, it will be necessary to develop or purchase measures of student attitudes, feelings, values, or interests. Both teacher-constructed and standardized instruments can be used for this purpose.

Should tests be authentic simulations of how knowledge is tested in adult work and civic settings? Many educators believe so. Performance assessment, then, calls on test makers to be creative designers, not just technicians.

Creating Effective Tests

Grant Wiggins et al. (2000) offered the following eight basic design criteria as assistance to test designers.

- Assessment tasks should be, whenever possible, authentic and meaningful — worth mastering.
- The set of tasks should be a valid sample from which apt generalizations about overall performance of complex capacities can be made.
- The scoring criteria should be authentic, with points awarded or taken off for essential successes and errors, not for what is easy to count or observe.
- The performance standards that anchor the scoring should be genuine benchmarks, not arbitrary cut scores or provincial school norms.
- The context of the problems should be rich, realistic, and enticing — with the inevitable constraints on access to time, resources, and advance knowledge of the tasks and standards appropriately minimized.
- The tasks should be validated.
- The scoring should be feasible and reliable.
- Assessment results should be reported and used so that *all* customers for the data are satisfied.

Table 6.1   **Summary of Various Purposes for Testing**

Assessment Context	Types of Decisions	Type of Data Needed	Decision Makers					
			Students	Parents	Teachers	Administrators	Counselors	Public
Instructional Management Decisions								
Diagnosis	Decide students' strengths and weaknesses on specific skills	Individual student data on level of development of specific skills	✓		✓			
Placement	Place student into next most appropriate level of instruction	Scores that place students on relevant knowledge or skill continuum			✓	✓	✓	
Guidance and Counseling	Decide probability of success and satisfaction in given program of educational or vocational development	Data reflecting level of educational development of individual student relative to other students	✓	✓				✓
Student Screening Decisions								
Selection	Decide which students to be selected into or out of a program	Data that rank order individual students on relevant knowledge or skill scale			✓	✓	✓	
Certification	Determine mastery or nonmastery of specified body of knowledge or set of skills	Data reflecting individual student mastery of specified body of knowledge or set of skills			✓	✓		✓

(continues)

Table 6.1 **Continued**

Assessment Context	Types of Decisions	Type of Data Needed	Decision Makers					
Programmatic Decisions			Students	Parents	Teachers	Administrators	Counselors	Public
Survey	Make educational policy decisions: determine educational development of student group	Group achievement data gathered cyclically to show trends				✓		✓
Formative Evaluation	Decide program components in need of modification	Interim and final program outcomes attained and not attained by participating students considered as a group			✓	✓		
Summative Evaluation	Determine if program is to be adopted, expanded, or discontinued	Program outcomes attained and not attained by participating students considered as a group			✓	✓		✓

Components of a Testing Program

A comprehensive school-wide testing program begins in kindergarten and ends in the 12th grade. Tests administered throughout the school years include assessment of emerging reading; general learning readiness; and tests of general intelligence, achievement, and aptitude and interest. A typical testing program in a school district might resemble the one depicted in Table 6.2 (American Society for Testing and Materials, 2004; Carter et al., 2003; McDonnell, 2004).

In discussing the evaluation of student growth in schools, Popham (2003a) referred to three areas of measurement: (1) knowledge and understanding, (2) skills and competence, and (3) attitude and interest. For each of these areas, the author refers to a number of educational objectives and the appropriate means of evaluating them. It would seem, therefore, that every school should have at least the following components in the way of a testing battery:

1. *Emerging reading test.* An emerging reading test should be administered in kindergarten or first grade to determine the child's readiness to profit from reading. Examples include the Gates-MacGinitie Reading Tests (Houghton-Mifflin), Lee-Clark Emerging Reading Test (California Test Bureau), and the Murphy-Durrell Emerging Reading Analysis (Harcourt Brace Jovanovich). These tests measure speed and accuracy, vocabulary, comprehension, and recognition of similarities and differences in printed letters.

Table 6.2 Comprehensive School-wide Testing Program

Grade	Type of Test
K	Reading readiness
1 or 2	Learning readiness
	Reading ability
	Mental ability
3, 4, or 5	Achievement battery (language skills, including reading, mathematics, social studies, science)
6, 7, or 8	Mental ability (repeated at entrance to middle school or junior high)
	Multifactor aptitude
9, 10, or 11	Achievement battery
11 or 12	College aptitude
	Interests — personal
	Interests — vocational

2. *Learning readiness test.* A learning readiness test should be administered in grade one or two to demonstrate the student's ability to mark pictures and letters and to identify words that match given ones. Examples include the Metropolitan Readiness Test (a group test that assesses six important aspects of readiness for formal first-grade instruction: word meaning, listening, visual perception, alphabet, numbers, and copying) and Primary Mental Abilities Test (measures verbal meaning, number facility, reasoning, perceptual speed, and spatial relations).

3. *Intelligence test.* An intelligence test should be administered in grade one, again toward the end of the elementary grades, and again early in high school. An individual measure is better than a group measure. There is a wide discrepancy between tests concerning the accurate measurement of a child's intelligence. Among the best-known intelligence tests are the California Short Form Test of Mental Maturity, Lorge-Thorndike Intelligence Test, Otis-Lennon Mental Ability Test, Revised Stanford-Binet Scale, and the Wechsler Intelligence Scales.

4. *Achievement tests.* At a very minimum, an achievement test battery including language, reading, mathematics, and social studies should be given periodically during the student's 12 years of public school education. Examples include the Comprehensive Tests of Basic Skills, Iowa Tests of Basic Skills, Sequential Tests of Educational Progress, and Stanford Achievement Tests. Others include state-developed achievement tests. Generally, these tests measure the capacity to comprehend written material, to think scientifically and analytically, and to display some understanding of the process of history.

5. *Interest and aptitude tests.* Measures of interests and aptitudes might be administered periodically to individuals, or groups of students, for purposes of placement or selection. Examples of aptitude measures include the Differential Aptitude Tests, School and College Ability Test, American College Testing Program, and the Scholastic Aptitude Test. Generally, these tests measure basic verbal and mathematical ability and reasoning.

Perhaps the best reference available for a quick summary and review of nearly all tests on the market is the *Fifteenth Mental Measurements Yearbook* (Plake, Impara, & Spies, 2003). It should be noted, however, that not all of the tests that are published are available for use without the proper training. Many universities provide courses that are concerned with the understanding, interpretation, and use of one specific test.

There may be missing elements in the conceptualization on which standard test theory is based. Those elements are models for just how people know what they know and do what they can do, and the ways in which they increase these capacities. Different models are useful for different purposes; therefore, test experts are proposing broader or alternative student models. For example, three test experts from Educational Testing Service consider a variety of directions in which standard test theory might be extended. They discuss the role of test theory in light of recent work in cognitive and educational psychology, test design, student modeling, test analysis, and the integration of assessment and instruction (Fredrikson, Mislevy, & Bejar, 2002).

Reporting to Parents and Families

Principals must ensure a good school-home connection because the educational program of a school is limited by the amount of cooperation received from the home. Students are not educated by removing them from all of their activities for six hours each day and causing them to study English, mathematics, social studies, and science. They are educated as they live. This places a demand on the school to be interested in the whole of the student's life — her interests at home, her interests in the community, and her abilities and talents as demonstrated in school and in all of the interrelated activities of the school community. The more congruent the student's school life, home life, and community life, the more nearly the student will be accomplishing the fulfillment of a true education (Miller, 2002). School newspapers, monthly newsletters, parent-teacher conferences, and teacher and principal visits to the home are methods used to inform the home of school activities and student progress. The report card is another method of informing parents of the child's progress in school (Guskey, 2003).

The value of such reports is unquestionable. The time and effort involved in preparing them become one of the biggest clerical tasks the teacher must perform. In addition to recording school grades on the report cards, the teacher must devise a student rating system that is fair, accurate, and consistent (Guskey, 2000; Hirsch, 2000). In this section, we examine the difficulties in assigning grades and review some methods of reporting student progress.

Difficulties in Grading

Principals must be aware that teachers experience several fundamental difficulties in assigning grades to students. First, there is the variability of these measures from teacher to teacher. Research has shown that teachers vary in their grading of the same test by as much as four grade levels. That is, a sample of teachers rated a high school essay test from A to D. With more careful preparation of examinations and training of examiners, the reliability and validity of grades can be markedly improved (Farr & Trumbull, 2000; Gullickson, 2002).

The grades teachers assign to students not only show great variability but also do not measure the same kind of accomplishment as do standardized achievement tests in the same subject. Teachers' grades are an undefined composite into which enter estimates of effort and attitude. Thus, in addition to recording scholarship, grades usually include the teacher's personal feelings and reactions to the student. Standardized tests, on the other hand, provide a measure of achievement or aptitude not subject to personal bias. By definition, a *standardized achievement test* is a series of questions designed to provide a systematic sample of performance, administered in accordance with uniform (standard) directions, scored according to definite (standard) rules, and interpreted in reference to normative (standard) information. Furthermore, administration and scoring of standardized tests are determined so precisely that the same procedures could be conducted at different times and places. Both standardized tests and teacher grades are of significance in understanding the student, and neither should be eliminated as appraisal tools.

Another fundamental difficulty in grading is that relatively few schools have a reliable aptitude or IQ score for all of their students. Without this information, it is difficult for teachers to estimate a student's achievement in relation to his ability. Appraisals of students must somehow attempt to relate achievement and ability to determine if the student is performing up to his potential or beyond it.

Further, different grading policies appear to be in operation at various educational levels: elementary school, middle school, and high school. For example, at the elementary school level, a child's achievement may be judged based on her own ability, whereas in secondary schools a student may be graded on a strictly competitive basis.

Finally, new approaches to educational assessment — in particular, constructed response, performance testing, and portfolio assessment — provide a full range of alternatives to traditional testing methods. These new approaches are useful in all types of large-scale testing programs, including classroom use (Arter et al., 2000; Farr & Trumbull, 2000; Gullickson, 2002; Hargis, 2003; Soleo, 2004; Stiggins, 2000). To implement these new approaches effectively, however, teacher training will be necessary.

Methods of Reporting Student Progress

Over the years, several methods of reporting grades to parents and caregivers have evolved. In view of the aforementioned difficulties existing in various degrees in different communities, grading systems will vary with the situation. A few of the more common methods of measuring school progress follow.

Percentage Method   The *percentage method* is one of the oldest. Student ratings are based on a scale that ranges from zero to 100. For example, suppose that a mathematics test contains 10 problems. If all problems are answered correctly, the student would receive 100%. If half of the problems were performed correctly, the student would receive 50%. Each test given during a marking period would be averaged to determine an overall percentage grade for the period. The percentage method is difficult to use. There are so many points along the scale that the teacher must make fine discriminations among a class of students.

Letter Method   The *letter method* offers more flexibility in determining a student's grade. A letter grade on a five-point scale is commonly used: A, B, C, D, and F. To make these letters understandable, two practices have arisen. First, the letters are interpreted in terms of percentages, where, for instance, A = 90 to 100, B = 80 to 89, C = 70 to 79, D = 60 to 69, and F = any mark below 60. Second, definite standards are established for each of the five letter grades. For example, standards for an A might be (a) always hands work in on time, (b) completes all work assigned in a creditable manner, (c) completes more than the assigned work, (d) shows some cre-

ativity in mastering the work assigned, and (e) has an excellent record of attendance. Successively lower standards can be established for the remaining letter-grade categories.

Descriptive Method   Letters to or conferences with parents are used in place of percentages or letter grades in the *descriptive method*. Descriptive statements can also be used to supplement the previously mentioned estimates of achievement, providing explanations of grades or other open-ended information.

Percentile Method   A percentile score of 72 means that 72% of all students on whose test scores the scale is based have scores lower than the examinee. The *percentile method* is frequently used in interpreting standardized achievement test scores. The principal reason for using the percentile is that it enables the parent to know just where the child ranks in the group.

Three-Group Method   The *three-group method* involves reporting the student's achievement as "above average," "average," or "below average." Definition of these terms is based on the percentile technique. If a student rates among the middle 50% of his class group, he is considered an average student. This includes all students between the 25th and 75th percentiles. "Above average" means, therefore, that the student is in the upper quartile of his group. "Below average" means that he is in the lower fourth of the group.

Rank Method   The *rank method* indicates whether the student is in first, second, or any other position in her group. Most high schools rank their graduating seniors in this way. Some colleges and universities use rank in class as one criterion for admission. Parents of students in a college-bound track often want to know how their child ranks in the group.

T-Score Method   Like the percentile score, the *T-score method* is difficult to interpret. The T-score represents one-tenth of the standard deviation of the scores for the group considered. The

T-score is not based on the class group, nor on a grade group, but instead on a local or national norm for an entire age group. Use of these scores is more prevalent when reporting standardized achievement test data to parents than when reporting school grades (Farr & Trumbull, 2000; Guskey, 2000; Raebeck, 2002).

Each method of reporting student progress to parents and caregivers has merit. A school must decide, in light of all the factors, what type of report to adopt. The best kind of report appears to be the descriptive account, supplemented by quantitative estimates of achievement, aptitude, and personality.

Extracurricular Activities

Student activities are found at all levels of our school system, especially in secondary schools. The terms *extracurricular activities, cocurricular activities,* and *nonclassroom activities* have all been used interchangeably to mean experiences and activities such as debate, athletics, music, drama, school publications, student council, school clubs, contests, and various social events. This multitude of experiences forms a third curriculum — paralleling the required and the elective curricula — and it is well integrated into the daily school program. Generally, extracurricular activities are voluntary, are approved and sponsored by school officials, and carry no academic credit toward graduation (Emmer, 2001; Fashola, 2001; Klesse, 2004; Larson et al., 2004; Theobold, 2000). In this section, we discuss the role of extracurricular activities in relation to the overall goals of education and the functions of extracurricular activities.

Goals of Education

Extracurricular activities, by whatever name they are called, are an essential, vital, and extensive part of education in America. Developing skills in working in groups; cultivating hobbies and interests; producing yearbooks, newspapers, and plays; and participating in interscholastic athletics and intramural sports are some of the many opportunities students have for discovering and developing talents that approximate life in the adult community (Larson et al., 2004).

The legacy of including worthy use of leisure time as a valid part of educational goals is the foundation of the student activities program in American schools. Although the goals of secondary education had been variously stated for many years, one of the first concerted efforts to define the curriculum of secondary schools resulted in the Cardinal Principles of Secondary Education in 1918 (Commission on the Reorganization of Secondary Education). The seven cardinal principles have had a major impact on shaping the goals of education for nearly nine decades.

The importance of these objectives was demonstrated by a redefinition of the curriculum to include all activities that influence the way others think, feel, believe, and act. Social events, athletics, clubs, and all the many leisure activities have become a part of the values and virtues not only of American education, but of democratic life.

Functions of Extracurricular Activities

Extracurricular activities serve the same goals and functions as the required and elective courses in the curriculum. However, they provide experiences that are not included in the formal courses of study. They permit students to apply knowledge acquired in formal courses and to acquire concepts of democratic life. When managed properly, the extracurricular activities program allows for a well-rounded, balanced program by (a) reinforcing learning, (b) supplementing the required and elective curriculum (formal courses of study), (c) integrating knowledge, and (d) carrying out the objectives of democratic life.

Reinforcing Learning   One function of extracurricular activities is to reinforce the required course of studies. An activity is used to enrich and extend the work in the classroom. Clubs associated with a subject-matter discipline have considerable reinforcement value. The Spanish Club may be used as an example of reinforcing learning.

The Spanish Club extends the time students spend working on the Spanish language. During the course of club activities, specific linguistic lessons are reviewed or extended. The names of articles of clothing, of food, and of eating utensils are used in a natural setting. Mastery of the Spanish language is thus enriched, which is precisely the objective of the Spanish course.

Supplementing Coursework   Another function of extracurricular activities is to supplement the required and elective courses of study. This function supplements the curriculum with experiences that are not possible in regular classroom settings. Such activities as school dances, student council, chess, publications, and sports add opportunities to the total learning experience as well as worthwhile leisure-time activities to the total learning process. These nonsubject-related activities add to and enrich even the most innovative programs of required and elective courses.

Integrating Knowledge   An important objective of the total learning process is the integration of knowledge. Extracurricular activities are said to be integrative in nature because they tie together many areas of knowledge and experience. They do not provide abstract and isolated pieces of learning, but rather synthesize many aspects of real-life situations. For example, the school committee commissioned to select a site for the prom must consider such factors as size of the establishment, distance from the school, reputation of the facility, language in the contract, decor, and cost to the student. In the same way, the purchase of a home involves many of the same human, artistic, legal, and economic factors. Through the student activities program, the student learns to deal with many important aspects of a problem.

Democratization   The extracurricular activities program is effective because it carries out in an especially vital way the objectives of present-day democratic life. Generally, American schools devote a part of the required curriculum to study of the development, structure, and problems of American democracy. The actual living of a democratic life is seriously restricted within the formal classroom setting. A rich program of student activities can remove such barriers and provide for individual and group interaction in a natural environment.

The extracurricular activities program offers students an opportunity to participate in administration through the student council, teacher-advisory groups, and organized activities. The student council provides opportunities for administrative experience including planning, organizing, initiating, and controlling many aspects of school life. Through teacher-advisory groups, an advisory unit is created that becomes the source from which activities flow. In these groups, the teacher and students establish proper relationships that are somewhat analogous to those of a family, team, or department in an organization. Through the clubs, athletics, and intramural sports that emanate from subject-matter disciplines, students develop teamwork and cooperation — ideals of competitiveness in a democratic society (Emmer, 2001; Klesse, 2004; Larson et al., 2004; Theobold, 2000).

Special Education Services

Increased school enrollments over the last 50 years have resulted in an increased diversity of the school population. Whereas exceptional children with learning disabilities, social and emotional maladjustments, and physical disabilities formerly dropped out of school at an early age, they now remain in school until the compulsory age or beyond.

The issue of the exceptional child is not new. Special education services to accommodate these children have rapidly expanded their part in education since World War II. Among the forces responsible for this recent expansion are advances in the fields of psychology, sociology, and rehabilitation; growth of the humanitarian movement; new knowledge of medical diagnosis and treatment; educational methodologies for the exceptional child; and new federal and state laws (DeGroof et al., 2003; Maanum, 2004; Oliver, 2004; Reynolds et al., 2004).

Exceptional children are unlikely to achieve their full human potential without a special education program designed to capitalize on their abilities or help them overcome or compensate for their disabilities. Special education is specially designed instruction intended to meet the unique needs of students with disabilities. Special teaching procedures, materials, equipment, and facilities may be required. To that end, Congress has passed four landmark pieces of legislation: *Section 504 of the Rehabilitation Act of 1973*, the *Education for All Handicapped Act of 1975*, the *Americans with Disabilities Act of 1990 (ADA)*, and the *Individuals with Disabilities Act (IDEA)*.

Of these four laws, IDEA has had the most significant impact on public schools. Congress reauthorized IDEA in 1997, adding some new amendments and extended federal funding for special education services. The purposes of the 1997 IDEA are (a) to assure that all children with disabilities are provided a "free appropriate public education" that includes special education and related services tailored to their special needs, (b) to prepare such children for employment and independent living, (c) to assure that the rights of children with disabilities are protected, and (d) to assist states in providing appropriate special education and related services (20 U.S.C. §1401, 1997). School principals need to be familiar with all provisions of IDEA 1997.

Related Services

Under the 1997 IDEA, "related services" may include the following:

Transportation, and such developmental, corrective, and other supportive services (including speech-language pathology and audiology services, psychological services, physical and occupational therapy, recreation, including therapeutic recreation, social work services, counseling services, including rehabilitation counseling, orientation and mobility services, and medical services, except that such medical services shall be for diagnostic and evaluation purpose only) as may be required to assist a child with a disability to benefit from special education, and includes

the early identification and assessment of disabling conditions in children. (20 U.S.C. §1401, 1997)

This list of related services is illustrative, not exhaustive.

Due Process Protections

The 1997 IDEA provides significant due process protections. Procedural safeguards in IDEA include the following:

(1) an opportunity for the parents of a child with a disability to examine all records relating to such child and to participate in meetings with respect to the identification, evaluation, and educational placement of the child, and the provision of a free appropriate public education to such child, and to obtain an independent educational evaluation of the child;

(2) procedures to protect the rights of the child whenever the parents of the child are not known . . . ;

(3) written prior notice to the parents of the child whenever such agency—

A. proposes to initiate or change; or

B. refuses to initiate or change; the identification, evaluation, or educational placement of the child . . . or the provision of a free appropriate public education to the child.

(4) procedures designed to ensure that the notice required . . . is in the native language of the parents, unless it clearly is not feasible to do so;

(5) an opportunity for mediation . . . ;

(6) an opportunity to present complaints with respect to any matter relating to the identification, evaluation, or educational placement of the child, or the provision of a free appropriate public education to such child. (20 U.S.C. §1415, 1997)

The written prior notice referred to in Section 1415 of IDEA 1997 must include:

(1) a description of the action proposed or refused by the agency;

(2) an explanation of why the agency proposed or refused to take the action;

(3) a description of any other options that the agency considered and the reasons why those options were rejected;

(4) a description of each evaluation procedure, test, record, or report the agency used as a basis for the proposed or refused action;

(5) a description of any other factors that are relevant to the agency's proposal or refusal;

(6) a statement that the parents of a child with a disability have protection under the procedural safeguards of this part and, if this is not an initial referral for evaluation, the means by which a copy of a description of the procedural safeguards can be obtained; and

(7) sources for parents to contact to obtain assistance in understanding the provisions of the part. (20 U.S.C. §1415, 1997)

A document describing these procedural safeguards must be given to parents on initial referral, on notification of an individual education plan (IEP) meeting, and on registration of any complaint by a parent. IDEA 1997 requires that this document must contain a full explanation of the rights of students with disabilities related to:

(A) independent educational evaluation;

(B) prior written notice;

(C) parental consent;

(D) access to educational records;

(E) opportunity to present complaints;

(F) the child's placement during the pendency of due process proceedings;

(G) procedures for students who are subject to placement in an interim alternative educational setting;

(H) requirements for unilateral placement by parents of children in private schools at public expense;

(I) mediation;

(J) due process hearings, including requirements for disclosure of consultation results and recommendations;

(K) State-level appeals (if applicable in that State);

(L) civil actions; and

(M) attorneys' fees. (20 U.S.C. §1415, 1997)

One of the most significant procedural due process protections in the reauthorized IDEA is the right to an impartial due process hearing. Under IDEA 1997, any party to a hearing shall be given:

1. the right to be accompanied and advised by counsel and by individuals with special knowledge or training with respect to the problem of children with disabilities;

2. the right to present evidence and confront, cross-examine, and compel the attendance of witnesses;

3. the right to a written, or, at the option of the parents, electronic verbatim record of such hearing; and

4. the right to written, or, at the option of the parents, electronic findings of fact and decisions. (20 U.S.C. §1415, 1997)

IDEA 1997 also includes a "stay-put" provision:

During the pendency of any proceedings conducted pursuant to this section, unless the State or local educational agency and the parents otherwise agree, the child shall remain in the then-current educational placement for such child, or, if applying for initial admission to a public school shall, with the consent of the parents, be placed in the public school program until such proceedings have been completed. (20 U.S.C. §1415, 1997)

One exception to the stay-put provision is when a special education student poses a threat to safety or engages in other serious types of misconduct.

Discipline

All students are guaranteed due process of law, including notice and hearing prior to significant infringements of their property rights and liberty interests. However, special concerns exist in disciplining children with disabilities. When school officials seek to suspend or expel children with disabilities, IDEA imposes significant legal protections for these children, including a stay-put provision to protect them from being removed from their current placements. The U.S. Supreme Court addressed the issue of removing children with disabilities for disciplinary reasons and the effect of the stay-put provision in *Honig v. Doe*, 484 U.S. 305 (1988).

The Court held that the language of the stay-put provision states that during the pendency of any proceedings initiated under IDEA, unless the state or local educational agency and the parents or guardian of a disabled child agree, "the child shall remain in the then-current educational placement." The Court did recognize a "dangerousness" exception to the stay-put provision by stating that "while the child's placement may not be changed during any complaint proceeding, this does not preclude the agency from using its normal procedures for dealing with children who are endangering themselves and others," including the use of study carrels, timeouts, detention, or restriction of privileges. More drastic measures may be taken where a student poses an immediate threat to the safety of others. In such situations, school officials may temporarily suspend the disabled student for up to 10 school days.

With recent concerns over school violence and drug use, the revised 1997 IDEA provides school principals with additional authority to change the placement of special education students who carry weapons, sell or use drugs, or are a danger to themselves or others. IDEA 1997 amendments state:

> School personnel under this section may order a change in the placement of a child with a disability—
>
> (i) to an appropriate educational setting, another setting, or suspension, for not more than 10 school days (to the extent such alternatives would be applied to children without disabilities); and
>
> (ii) to an appropriate interim alternative educational setting for the same amount of time that a child without a disability would be subject to discipline, but for not more than 45 days—
>
> (iii) the child carries a weapon to school or to a school function . . .
>
> (iv) the child knowingly possesses or uses illegal drugs or sells or solicits the sale of a controlled substance while at school or a school function. (20 U.S.C. §1415, 1997)

If students with disabilities present a serious danger to themselves and others, school authorities may request a disciplinary transfer of the student to an alternative setting. The reauthorized IDEA provides that:

> A hearing officer . . . may order a change in the placement of a child with a disability to an appropriate interim alternative educational setting for not more than 45 days if the hearing officer—
>
> (a) determines that the public agency has demonstrated by substantial evidence that maintaining the current placement of such child is substantially likely to result in injury to the child or to others;
>
> (b) considers the appropriateness of the child's current placement;
>
> (c) considers whether the public agency has made reasonable efforts to minimize the risk of harm in the child's current placement, including the use of supplementary aids and services; and
>
> (d) determines that the interim alternative education setting meets [other requirements of the IDEA]. (20 U.S.C. §1415, 1997)

School officials, however, must establish by "substantial" evidence that maintaining the current placement of the student will likely result in injury.

Gifted Education

Appeals to provide the gifted with specialized instruction have received considerable impetus for over four decades. With the advent of space exploration, the need for the trained and creative mind was recognized. With the impact of Gardner's (1993) Multiple Intelligence Theory over the past several years, more inclusive concepts of giftedness have emerged; and principals and teachers increasingly have recognized the need to train giftedness in a variety of areas. This recognition, however, has brought no surge of legislative action. Education policy related to students who are gifted and talented is lacking at the federal level. Although there are federal mandates through Public Law (P.L.) 94-142 and the Individuals with Disabilities Education Act (IDEA) for free and appropriate public education for students with other types of exceptionalities, there are no specific federally mandated policies requiring action by states to enforce educational programming at the local level for gifted and talented students (Irby & Lara-Alecio, 2001).

It is critical for principals to note that during the 1970s and 1980s, attention was focused on providing gifted and talented education through what McDonnell (1994) referred to as capacity-building policies, not mandated policies. Capacity-building policies call for additional funding to enhance local or state efforts in their provision of gifted and talented education. Although the capacity-building policies, P.L. 95-561 and P.L. 100-297, gave special contingencies to children who were designated as gifted and aided significantly in supporting their education, again, neither of these laws were mandates; nor did these laws, themselves, lead to major systemic educational reform (Irby & Lara-Alecio, 2001). P.L. 100-297 continues today in its capacity-building mode, providing support through competitive grants to fund gifted and talented programs that emphasize economically disadvantaged students, English language learners (ELL), and students with disabilities who are gifted and talented (Federal Register, 1998).

Irby and Lara-Alecio (2001) indicated that because no federally mandated policy exists for programming for students designated as gifted and talented, educational policy at the state level is muddled, at best, in relation to students who are gifted and talented — and who furthermore are codified as minority in some way. Ortiz and Gonzalez (1989) testified, in a report from the U.S. Department of Education's Office of Civil Rights, that "minority groups such as Hispanics, Blacks, and Native Americans are underrepresented by as much as 70% in gifted programs" (p. 152). Moreover, Brown (1997) indicated that between 1980 and 1992, these same populations were constantly underrepresented in 34 of the 50 states. Those who live in rural areas continue to be overlooked and underrepresented, and those who are ELLs are further exploited.

Mandated programs, in some form, do exist in 64% of the states (Coleman & Gallagher, 1992; Seaburg, 1991). Passow and Rudnitski (1993) suggested that mandates are needed for program stability; however, they indicated that even if a state mandates a policy through law, the mandates may not be funded; and it is a fact that state funding does vary widely from state to state (Landrum, Katsiyannis, & DeWaard, 1998).

According to Irby and Lara-Alecio (2001), it is important for the principal to work toward contextual, systemic policy development in gifted education, observing how the policy situated within the district is impacted by the implementation and then by program redesign or policy revision. Policymakers and principals simply are unable to either predict or directly experience the results that policies will produce. However, over time, the most dangerous consequence of not providing appropriate educational experiences as a result of appropriate policy may be to undermine rather than advance the future of up to 25% of our population. What is needed is policy development that investigates potential consequences or outcomes based upon data input in the context of the state or district serving the population. What follows is an example of how a principal might work with the superintendent and board toward an equitable gifted education policy.

Policy development and implementation should include an examination of the impact of each of the following components upon each other within a state or school system: (a) the inventory of outcomes or consequences of identification, (b) a model program design that is sensitive to the population being served, (c) type of teacher training, (d) ongoing staff development, (e) parental involvement and training, and (f) needs-based curriculum and instruction. Further systemic examination would initiate model program redesign, which in turn would impact identification procedures and teacher training. This systemic type of policy development would examine the impact of all outcomes of gifted education services, not only for the ELLs but also for majority students. Principals should investigate policy and its implementation in a systemic manner to become more aware of the outcomes and impact it has on our society as a whole. A model for this systemic policy development plan is depicted in Figure 6.1, using as an example a program for gifted ELL students.

Irby and Lara-Alecio (2001) indicated that policy development and implementation entail at least five components, as suggested by Figure 6.1. First is the idea that there is a mandated policy for services to be provided to ELL students.

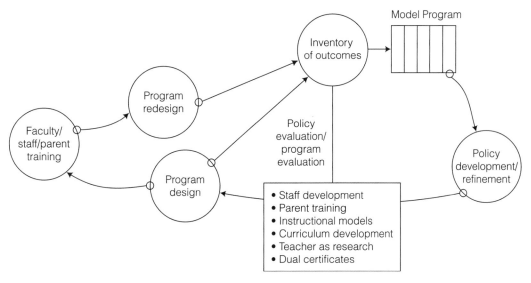

Figure 6.1

Systemic Model for Contextual Policy Development and Implementation for Gifted ELL Students
Source: Adapted from B. J. Irby & R. Lara-Alecio, "Educational Policy and Gifted/Talented, Linguistically Diverse Students," 2001, in J. A. Castellano & E. Díaz (Eds.), *Reaching New Horizons: Gifted and Talented Education for Culturally and Linguistically Diverse Students* (pp. 265–281). Needham Heights, MA: Allyn & Bacon.

From that point, state and district personnel can work on implementation. Note that the policy development and implementation process is both cyclical and systemic; therefore, as the system is complete, the outcomes may impact policy development or refinement, which in turn will impact the model used in the schools for service, and so on.

Model design suggests that there is input based on data from professionals who (a) are trained in the particular subject of educating linguistically diverse gifted children and (b) have based decisions on their own investigations. It also suggests that at the state level, model programs for the linguistically diverse gifted should require dual certificates of the teachers. For example, teachers should have a certificate in bilingual education, should speak the language of the child, and should have a certificate in gifted education. This may be made possible through a field-based teacher preparation program in conjunction with area universities, through distance education training programs,

or through some type of an effective alternative certification plan. Specialized programs that are sensitive to students' needs require a specialized teaching staff.

In addition, model programs should be based on input from parents who also have received training in supporting and enriching their linguistically diverse children. Parents should receive assistance in a model program for ELL students because the parents themselves are also linguistically diverse in the society and may need assistance to enhance their children's lives.

Model program design also includes appropriate identification techniques, instructional models for specific populations, and appropriate ethnolinguistic curriculum development. All of these components, along with those mentioned earlier, impact model design.

The developed model further determines the type of faculty, staff, and parental involvement and training from which new discussions, research, and new learnings emerge. This process, in turn, may lead to program *redesign*. Both the program and any redesign should require an evaluation, which should focus on an inventory of outcomes. From the inventory of outcomes, the policy should be analyzed for accuracy, inclusivity, and appropriateness. Then the program is implemented. From the preceding discussion, it is evident that (a) each component affects the others; (b) a systemic policy can determine numbers of students served in a program; and (c) such a program could further access, due to the appropriateness of accompanying training, identification, instruction, curriculum, and program evaluation (Irby & Lara-Alecio, 2001).

Administrative Arrangements for Gifted Education Programs

As the principal works to develop and implement policy for gifted students, there are several general administrative arrangements for service delivery that she, along with the teachers and central office administrators, may consider. Those arrangements and an explanation are given in Table 6.3.

Definitions of Giftedness

Principals must be aware of the varied definitions of giftedness. Because we have been discussing policy,

Table 6.3   **Administrative Arrangement for Gifted Education Service Delivery**

Type of Administrative Arrangement for Service Delivery	Description of the Arrangement
Ability Grouping	Students are grouped according to their ability in classes and/or subject area.
Acceleration	Refers to administrative practices designed to allow students to progress through the school grades at a rate faster than the average (e.g., early school entrance, content area acceleration, grade skipping, credit by examination, early graduation).
Advanced Placement	College-level courses provided at the secondary level for which students may receive college credit by examination (administered by the Advanced Placement Program of the College Board).
Alternative School	A school that provides an alternative to the traditional school structure and that is designed to meet the unique instructional needs of some gifted and talented students.
Cluster Grouping	Any classroom with a group of identified gifted and talented students purposefully organized to provide planned differentiated instruction most of the time.
Cluster Classroom	The intentional grouping of the grade level's top intellectually gifted students into a classroom with a teacher who has the desire and expertise to provide a supportive and challenging environment for this population of learners.
Competitions	Organized opportunities for gifted and talented students to enter local, regional, state, or national contests in a variety of subject areas (e.g., Quiz Bowl, Academic Games, Future Problem Solving, Spelling Bees, Science Olympiad).
Community & Business Resources	Continued sharing of resources to increase opportunities for high-ability students
Concurrent or Dual Enrollment	Usually refers to high school students taking some college courses at a nearby college or university before they graduate from high school, but may also refer to students at any level who are allowed to take some classes at the next school level (e.g., elementary/junior high/high school). Also includes correspondence courses.
Convocations, Seminars, Workshops	Special short-term sessions where the student focuses on one area of study (e.g., Young Authors Conference, Science Convocation).
Curriculum Adjustment	Experiences provided in the regular classroom that are additional and/or supplemental to the established curriculum and/or texts and that are purposefully planned with the needs, interests, and capabilities of particular students in mind.

(continues)

as well as state mandates, we will first look at state definitions for gifted. Table 6.4 presents 10 definitions that are fairly representative of the definitions from all points of the United States. Some definitions are short; others are extensive. Some use the word *gifted*, and others use the words *gifted and talented*. Many still use the basic Marland (1971) definition, which dates from the first time the federal government defined *gifted and talented*. It might be noted that four state legislatures or state education agencies have no definition: Massachusetts, Minnesota, New Hampshire, and South Dakota.

There are, of course, other definitions of giftedness. For example, Sternberg (1985) defined giftedness in terms of intelligence, as do most theorists. He suggested three dimensions to intelligence. "Compotential" intelligence consists of mental mechanisms for processing information. "Experiential" intelligence involves dealing with new tasks or situations and the ability to use mental processes automatically. "Contextual" intelligence is the ability to adapt to, select, and shape the environment.

Gardner (1999) developed his theory in 1983 by combining studies of the brain with research on the relative aspects of intelligence. He has identified eight different types of intelligence: logical-mathematical, linguistic, visual-spatial,

---

Table 6.3   Continued

Type of Administrative Arrangement for Service Delivery	Description of the Arrangement
Honors Classes	Courses, usually at the high school level, that are designed for able students.
Independent Study	Individually contracted, in-depth study of a topic.
Interest Groups	Any group organized from one or more classrooms on the basis of interest in a topic; usually of short-term duration.
Internships	Students who demonstrate high ability and need are placed in a professional setting for a specified period to learn skills of that profession.
Individualized Learning	Courses and curricula are altered to meet the specific needs of a high-ability student.
Local Teacher Consultant Services	The local consultant/helping teacher assists teachers in developing appropriate educational opportunities for high-ability students.
Magnet Schools	Specialized schools for high-ability students, usually with a specific focus (e.g., performing and/or visual arts, math and/or science, aviation school, etc.).
Mentorships	A program that pairs individual students with someone who has advanced skills and experiences in a particular discipline and can serve as a guide, advisor, counselor, and role model.
Ongoing Assessment and Planning	Students' abilities and needs are continually assessed through both formal and informal means designed to discover and nurture talent. The results are used as the basis for appropriate programming decisions.
Pacing	The content and pacing of curriculum and instruction are matched to students' abilities and needs. Students move ahead on the basis of mastery. Differentiation in pacing and/or depth is provided.
Pull-out Programs	A group organized from one or more classrooms that meets regularly to provide experiences beyond the established curriculum. This is enrichment of the regular curriculum.
Recognition	Student achievements are recognized through academic letters, awards, newspapers, and so forth.
Resource Room	Students are released from their regular classroom on a scheduled basis to work with a teacher specializing in education of the gifted in a resource room setting.

Table 6.4   Sample Definitions From States

State	Definition
Florida	(1) Gifted. One who has superior intellectual development and is capable of high performance.
	(2) Criteria for eligibility. A student is eligible for special instruction programs for the gifted if the student meets criteria under (2)(a) or (b) of this rule.
	(a) The student demonstrates: 1. Need for a special program, 2. A majority of characteristics of gifted students according to a standard scale or checklist, and 3. Superior intellectual development as measured by an intelligence quotient of two (2) standard deviations or more above the mean on an individually administered standardized test of intelligence.
	(b) The student is a member of an under-represented group and meets the criteria specific in an approved school district plan for increasing the participation of under-represented groups in programs for gifted students.
	1. For the purpose of this rule, under-represented groups are defined as groups: a. Who are limited English proficient, or b. Who are from low socio-economic status family.
	2. The Department of Education is authorized to approve school district plans for increasing the participation of students from under-represented groups in special instructional programs for the gifted. . . .
	(3) Procedures for student evaluation. The minimum evaluations for determining eligibility are the following: (a) Need for a special instruction program, (b) Characteristics of the gifted, (c) Intellectual development, and (d) May include those evaluation procedures specified in an approved district plan to increase the participation of students from under-represented groups in programs for the gifted. (Fla. Admin. Code Ann. r. 6A-6.03019)
Mississippi	"Gifted children" shall mean children who are found to have an exceptionally high degree of intellect, and/or academic, creative or artistic ability. (Miss. Code Ann. §37-23-175)
Virginia	"Gifted students" means those students in public elementary and secondary schools beginning with kindergarten through graduation whose abilities and potential for accomplishment are so outstanding that they require special programs to meet their educational needs. These students will be identified by professionally qualified persons through the use of multiple criteria as having potential or demonstrated abilities and who have evidence of high performance or capabilities, which may include leadership, in one or more of the following areas:
	1. Intellectual aptitude or aptitudes. Students with advanced aptitude or conceptualization whose development is accelerated beyond their age peers as demonstrated by advanced skills, concepts and creative expression in multiple general intellectual ability or in specific intellectual abilities.
	2. Specific academic aptitude. Students with specific aptitudes in selected academic areas: mathematics; the sciences; or the humanities as demonstrated by advanced skills, concepts, and the creative expression in those areas.
	3. Technical and practical arts aptitude. Students with specific aptitudes in selected technical or practical arts as demonstrated by advanced skills and creative expression in those areas to the extent they need and can benefit from specifically planned educational services differentiated from those provided by the general program experience.
	Visual or performing arts aptitude. Students with specific aptitudes in selected or visual performing arts as demonstrated by advanced skills and creative expression who excel consistently in the development of a product or performance in any of the visual and performing arts to the extent that they need and can benefit from specifically planned educational services differentiated from those generally provided by the general program experience. (8 Va. Admin. Code §20-40-20)
Oregon	"Talented and gifted children" means those children who require special educational programs or services, or both, beyond those normally provided by the regular school program in order to realize their contribution to self and society and who demonstrate outstanding ability or potential in one or more of the following areas:

(continues)

Table 6.4 Continued

State	Definition
	(a) General intellectual ability as commonly measured by measures of intelligence and aptitude.
	(b) Unusual academic ability in one or more academic areas.
	(c) Creative ability in using original or nontraditional methods of thinking and producing.
	(d) Leadership ability in motivating the performance of others either in educational or noneducational settings.
	Ability in the visual or performing arts, such as dance, music or art. (Or. Rev. Stat. §343.395)
California	Each district shall use one or more of these categories in identifying students as gifted and talented. In all categories, identification of a student's extraordinary capability shall be in relation to the student's chronological peers.
	(a) Intellectual Ability: A student demonstrates extraordinary or potential for extraordinary intellectual development.
	(b) Creative Ability: A student characteristically:
	(1) Perceives unusual relationships among aspects of the student's environment and among ideas;
	(2) Overcomes obstacles to thinking and doing;
	(3) Produces unique solutions to problems.
	(c) Specific Academic Ability: A student functions at highly advanced academic levels in particular subject areas.
	(d) Leadership Ability: A student displays the characteristic behaviors necessary for extraordinary leadership.
	(e) High Achievement: A student consistently produces advanced ideas and products and/or attains exceptionally high scores on achievement tests.
	(f) Visual and Performing Arts Talent: A student originates, performs, produces, or responds at extraordinarily high levels in the arts.
	Any other category which meets the standards set forth in these regulations. (Cal. Code Regs. title 5, §3822)
New York	As used in this article, the term "gifted students" shall mean those students who show evidence of high performance capability and exceptional potential in areas such as general intellectual ability, special academic aptitude and outstanding ability in visual and performing arts. Such definition shall include those students who require educational programs or services beyond those normally provided by the regular school program in order to realize their full potential. (N.Y. Educ. Law §4452)
Ohio	"Gifted" means students who perform or show potential for performing at remarkably high levels of accomplishment when compared to others of their age, experience, or environment and who are identified under division (A), (B), (C), or (D) of section 3324.03 of the revised code. (Ohio Rev. Code Ann. §3324.01)
Kansas	"Gifted" means performing or demonstrating the potential for performing at significantly higher levels of accomplishment in one or more academic fields due to intellectual ability, when compared to others of similar age, experience, and environment. (Kan. Admin. Regs. 91-40-1)

body-kinesthetic, musical, interpersonal, intrapersonal, and naturalistic. Mainly, schools will concentrate on the areas of logical-mathematical and linguistic intelligence.

Renzulli (1985) introduced a definition that denotes an interaction among the three clusters: above average intelligence, creativity, and task commitment. Each factor is important to contributing to giftedness (Renzulli, 1985). Irby and Lara-Alecio (2001) expanded Renzulli's definition in defining bilingual Hispanic students. The combined model can be viewed in Figure 6.2. They

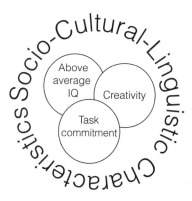

Figure 6.2

Irby and Lara-Alecio's (2001) Hispanic Bilingual Definition (adapted version of Renzulli)

suggested that there are socio-cultural-linguistic characteristics that encompass intelligence, creativity, and task commitment.

With the exception of Irby and Lara-Alecio's definition, gifted definitions are predominantly mainstream definitions. Ford and Thomas (1997) warned against definitions that were too narrow and that did not take into account the under-achieving gifted student. They provided some advice that principals can heed for reversing a segment of the gifted population:

> Reversing underachievement among gifted minority students requires intensive efforts on the part of teachers and counselors, as well as a partnership with parents and students. For optimal effects, teachers and counselors must tailor interventions to students' needs. Interventions for gifted minority students must consider social-psychological, family, peer, and school factors. Interventions must:

- Ensure that definitions of underachievement are both qualitative and quantitative, and that measures are valid and reliable

- Enhance self-perceptions, self-esteem, self-concept (academic and social), and racial identity

- Improve students' skills in studying, time management, organization, and taking tests

- Involve family members as partners in the educational process

- Address school-related factors, including providing teachers and counselors with gifted and multicultural training to meet both the academic and affective needs of gifted minority students. This training should include strategies for improving student-teacher relations, teacher expectations, and the classroom climate. (p. 1)

What Principals Can Do for Gifted Education

Besides ensuring that there is an adequate policy to serve gifted students, Hearne and Maurer (2002) suggested the following for principals:

- Understand program expectations.

- Be supportive of the educational model.

- Be an advocate for children to learn at their own level.

- Access appropriate resources to match the curriculum and instruction for the gifted learners.

- Allow for unique delivery of the curriculum that allows children to question, seek answers, and share information.

- Coach staff in a manner that encourages diversity, creativity, and high standards.

- Bridge the gap that can exist between staff and parents.

- Openly celebrate the success of all students.

- Support equity of educational services so that all children's needs are met.

- Modify policies and procedures to support a differentiated classroom.

- Learn the qualities of a high-quality, differentiated classroom.

Principals can help evaluate their gifted programs. VanTassel-Baska (1994) noted the importance of understanding the indicators of a quality program for gifted that could be used in evaluating the program. She indicated that the program should include the following:

1. Provides a written philosophy, goals, and anticipated outcomes for students

2. Presents multiple options at and across grade levels

3. Utilizes modified scheduling and differentiated staffing to achieve its goals

4. Utilizes multiple criteria for identification, appropriate instrumentation, and a process for ongoing admissions

5. Is comprehensive across years of schooling

6. Articulates the curriculum across years of schooling

7. Selects teachers according to key characteristics and trains them to work with gifted

8. Uses diverse and multiple resources, including the community, to carry out its goals

9. Uses models that respond to the needs of the students in the particular setting

10. Emphasizes problem solving, higher-level thought processes, inquiry-based discussion, and student-generated, high-quality products

11. Serves as a parent education component and an ongoing school/community awareness component

12. Utilizes curriculum development as an ongoing effort that actively involves teachers in the process

13. Monitors program implementation and revises the context as needed

Curriculum Models for Gifted Education

There are numerous curriculum models for gifted education. We share two that are used primarily at the elementary grade levels: Enrichment Triad Model and Creative Problem Solving. In most cases, the International Baccalaureate and Advanced Placement models are used at the secondary levels.

Enrichment Triad Model Renzulli, Sand, and Reis (1986) created the Enrichment Triad Model (ETM) that has three components: Type I enrichment (general exploratory experiences), Type II enrichment (group training activities), and Type III enrichment (individual and small-group investigations of real problems). Organizationally, ETM includes enrichment-planning teams, needs assessments, staff development, materials selection, and program evaluation. ETM also includes lessons to promote development of thinking processes, procedures to modify the regular curriculum, and curriculum compacting. ETM consists of three types of enrichment:

- *Type I—General Interest/Exploratory Activities.* The general interest and exploratory activities are designed to provide students with as wide a range of experiences as possible and include field trips, clubs, interest centers, visiting speakers, and brainstorming sessions.

- *Type II—Group Training Activities/Skills Development.* The group training activities are designed to develop thinking and feeling skills; and students are involved in designing, experimenting, comparing, analyzing, recording, and classifying. Skills development includes creative and critical thinking, learning how to learn, using advanced-level reference materials, and communicating effectively.

- *Type III—Individual and Small Group Investigation of Real Problems.* Students apply the knowledge and skills they have developed while working through Type I and Type II activities. They research real problems and then present the results to a real audience. Activities in Type III include researching, debating, surveying, making a presentation, writing a journal or newspaper article, or producing a book or play.

A significant feature of ETM is that *all* students can work at the first two levels. The activities generated within these levels support the third level. Type III activities are more appropriate for identified gifted students, because they allow for varying degrees of creativity. Type III does not preclude other students from participating, but the products generated should look different for gifted students—more sophisticated at a higher level of thought production.

Creative Problem Solving The Creative Problem Solving (Parnes, 1992) process is a flexible tool that can be used to examine real problems and issues. There are six stages to the model, providing a structured procedure for identifying challenges, generating ideas and implementing innovative solutions. Future problem solving grew out of this model. Through continued practice and use of the process students can strengthen their creative techniques and learn to generalize in new situations. The six steps are:

1. *Objective (Mess) Finding*—identifying the goal, challenge, and future direction.

2. *Fact Finding*—collecting data about the problem; observing the problem as objectively as possible.

3. *Problem Solving*—examining the various parts of the problem to isolate the major part; stating the problem in an open-ended way.

4. *Idea Finding*—generating as many ideas as possible regarding the problem; brainstorming.

5. *Solution Finding*—choosing the solution that would be most appropriate; developing and selecting criteria to evaluate the alternative solutions.

6. *Acceptance Finding*—creating a plan of action.

Unlike many other problem-solving methods, the Creative Problem Solving process emphasizes the need to defer judgment on possible ideas and solutions until a final decision is made. In this way, the flow of ideas in the third step is not interrupted, and possible solutions, however, bizarre, are accepted. The teacher's role at this step is important; she is creating an environment in which students can feel comfortable in making suggestions. Quantity of ideas is required in brainstorming, not quality of the initial idea and its solution.

Bilingual Education

The school population is becoming more and more diverse (Garrett & Morgan, 2002). Garrett (2002) stressed the importance for principals to be aware of the cultures and diversity on their campuses. In particular, it is critical for principals to keep projections on the numbers of diverse populations and their needs.

An increase in the Hispanic-language minority population and other language minority groups in the United States has provided principals many opportunities to meet the educational needs of non-English-speaking students through bilingual education programs. The ever-growing Hispanic student population has increased at five times the rate of the non-Hispanic population (Howe, 1994). This phenomenon has dramatically impacted public school systems, especially those in urban areas (Howe, 1994). Hispanics accounted for 9% of the total United States population in 1990, and their numbers increased to over 11% of the total population by 1998 (Lester, 1999). More than 30 million Hispanics currently live in the United States; this represents an increase of almost 8 million in only eight years (Gempel, 1999). It is projected that within the next five years Hispanics, the nation's fastest-growing minority group, will be the largest and likely the least educated minority (Sack, 2000). Hispanic expansion is permanent, and most Hispanics of all ages live in five states: California, Florida, Illinois, New York, and Texas (Gempel, 1999). In Houston, 37% of the population is Hispanic; in Los Angeles, 46.5% is Hispanic (U.S. Bureau of Census, 2001).

In seeking to address the educational needs of an ever-increasing Hispanic student population, educators are struggling. In a comprehensive address on bilingual education in March 2000, the U.S. Department of Education defended bilingual education and stressed the value of biliteracy, stating that language is at the core of the Hispanic experience in the United States, and it must be at the center of future opportunities. Only a few months later, the momentum continued, and the United States had a mandated policy for service to ELLs under the No Child Left Behind (NCLB) Act. Despite significant research that sound bilingual education programs work, and a federally mandated policy, bilingual education in America continues to be under attack (Supik, 1998), as witnessed by the virtual abolishment of bilingual education in California and Arizona. This situation complicates the principal's challenge to serve the needs of students in bilingual programs.

Program Descriptions

Several program models have been developed, although nonnative English speakers have been traditionally underserved. The following components should be considered when designing and implementing bilingual and English as a second language (ESL) programs: (a) state guidelines, (b) student population to be served, and (c) district resources.

Example of State Guidelines Texas will be used as the example for state guidelines under this section; we use this state because it has large numbers of students who are affected by this policy. It is critical for principals to be familiar with their own state's policy for English language learners (ELL). The statutory authority for services to ELLs falls under Subchapter BB, issued under Texas Education Code §§29.051–29.064, unless otherwise noted. Texas Education Code §89.1201(a) indicates that every student in the state who has a home language other than English and who is identified as limited English proficient (LEP) shall be provided a full opportunity to participate in a bilingual education or ESL program. To ensure equal educational opportunity as required in Texas Education Code §1.002(a), each school district shall:

1. Identify limited-English-proficient students based on criteria established by the state.

2. Provide bilingual education and English as a second language programs as integral parts of the regular program as described in the Texas Education Code, §4.002.

3. Seek certified teaching personnel to ensure that limited-English-proficient students are afforded full opportunity to master the essential skills and knowledge required by the state.

4. Assess achievement for essential skills and knowledge in accordance with the Texas Education Code, Chapter 39, to ensure accountability for limited-English-proficient students and the schools that serve them.

Furthermore, Texas Education Code §89.1201(b) promotes the goal of bilingual education programs: to enable limited English proficient (LEP) students to become competent in the comprehension, speaking, reading, and composition of the English language through the development of literacy and academic skills in the primary language and English. Such programs are to emphasize the mastery of English language skills—as well as mathematics, science, and social studies—as integral parts of the academic goals for all students to enable LEP students (or English language learners) to participate equitably in school.

The same policy, Texas Education Code §89.1201(c), addresses the goal of English as a second language, which is to enable LEP students to become competent in the comprehension, speaking, reading, and composition of the English language through the integrated use of second-language methods. Such programs shall emphasize the mastery of English-language skills—as well as mathematics, science, and social studies—as integral parts of the academic goals for all students to enable LEP students to participate equitably in school.

Texas Education Code §89.1201(d) states that bilingual education and ESL programs shall be integral parts of the total school program. Such programs shall use instructional approaches designed to meet the special needs of LEP students. The basic curriculum content of the programs shall be based on the essential skills and knowledge required by the state.

Texas Education Code §89.1205 requires the implementation of bilingual education and ESL programs. According to this section, a school district that has an enrollment of 20 or more LEP students in any language classification in the same grade level district-wide shall offer a bilingual education program for all elementary grade levels, including prekindergarten through fifth, and sixth when it is clustered with elementary grade levels. Cooperative arrangements with other districts may be developed for the provision of services. For bilingual education programs, the Texas Education Code requires the provision of a dual-language program in prekindergarten through the elementary grades, or an approved dual-language program that addresses the affective, linguistic, and cognitive needs of the LEP students. In addition, school districts are authorized to establish a bilingual education program at grade levels in which the bilingual education program is not required. All LEP students for whom a district is not required to offer a bilingual education program shall be provided an ESL program. Implementation of this type of program takes place regardless of the student's grade level and home language and the number of such students.

Should a district not be able to establish a bilingual or ESL program, the district may request from the commissioner of education an exception to the programs and an approval to offer an alternative program. Waivers of certification requirements may be requested on an individual basis and are valid only in the school year for which they are negotiated.

Texas Education Code §89.1210(b) indicates that the bilingual education program is to be a full-time program of instruction in which both the students' home language and English are used for instruction. The amount of instruction in each language should be commensurate with the students' level of proficiency in both languages as well as their level of academic achievement. The language proficiency assessment committee (LPAC) designates the students' level of language proficiency and academic achievement. According to Texas Education Code §89.1210(d), instruction in an ESL program may vary from the amount of time accorded to instruction in English language arts in the regular program for non-LEP students to total immersion in second-language approaches. In Grades 6 or 7 through 12, instruction in ESL may vary from one-third of the instructional day to total immersion in second-language approaches.

Student Population   Just as the law in Texas indicates that particular student language group populations should be considered when developing a program, all districts should determine the types of LEPs or ELLs to be served. Many campuses will find that their populations of language minority students are mobile, while others may be

fairly stable. The language groups may be from a variety of language groups, educational levels, and cultural backgrounds. In Texas, most of the immigrants are of the Spanish-speaking language group from Mexico or Central America. The principal must consider the numbers of students from the particular language group, the previous educational levels of the students, and the culture of the students when developing bilingual, dual-language, or ESL programs.

District Resources   Resources for provision of services to English-language learners vary from district to district and from state to state. For example, programs may depend upon geographic location, upsurges in immigrant settlements, district enrollment, physical space, availability of certified teachers, and/or the ability to attract certified teachers through stipends. These resources could significantly influence the types of services the district will provide. Garrett and Morgan (2002) suggested that districts and campuses could use specific instructional strategies to develop effective learning environments. Such strategies include (a) small-group instruction, (b) hands-on activities, (c) information exchange among students, (d) computer-based simulations, and (e) Internet-based activities for communication. The authors particularly addressed services that translate text and Web pages from English to other languages, or vice versa, as holding promise for assisting ELLs. Specifically, Garrett and Morgan indicated that teachers and principals could use such technology for improving one-to-one communications, both verbally and in writing, with students and parents not only in conferences but also in the classroom and for promoting clarity in classroom assignments.

Administrative Arrangements for Service Delivery of Bilingual Education

In this section we present, for a principal's consideration of his or her campus needs, a brief description of potential administrative arrangements that districts may choose in developing and implementing programs in (a) bilingual education and/or (b) English as a second language. When districts consider the type of program arrangement that best suits their population, the following should be taken into account:

- The program should meet the linguistic, academic, and affective needs of students.

- The program should provide students with the instruction necessary to allow them to progress through school at a rate commensurate with their native-English-speaking peers.

- The program should make the best use of district and community resources. (McKeon, 1987)

Districts need to have in place the following:

- Policies related to language minority students.
- A program design.
- Student identification procedures.
- An identified committee that assesses the language proficiency level.
- A means for student assessment.
- A formalized parent authority and responsibility policy, procedure, and plan.
- A plan for staffing and professional development.
- A summer school program.
- A plan for monitoring and evaluating programs. (Adapted from *Texas State Plan for Education of Limited English Proficient Students*, ESC §19, 2000)

All of these items should be on file and have documented evidence of implementation for compliance monitoring by the Texas Education Agency and for public consideration; other states have similar compliance components.

Bilingual Education Models

In 1997, the U.S. Department of Education indicated that bilingual education makes certain that children whose native language is other than English receive the necessary grounding in academics while transitioning to all-English classrooms (Supik, 1998). The goal of bilingual programs is the acquisition of English skills by language-minority children so they can succeed in mainstream, English-only classrooms (Ramirez, 1992). A variety of bilingual program models make use of students' primary language while developing English (Moran, 1993); following are models that principals can implement on their campuses.

Transitional   Transitional bilingual programs have been described as those in which the students' first language and English are used in some combination for instruction, and where the first language serves as a temporary bridge to instruction in English (Baca & Cervantes, 1989; Birman & Ginsburg, 1983; Bruce, Lara-Alecio, Parker, Hasbrouck, Weaver, & Irby, 1994; Peregoy & Boyle, 1993; Trueba, 1979). However, there is no single method for helping LEP students catch up with their peers, and there is no single definition for transitional bilingual education programs. According to Bruce et al. (1997), we must improve our understanding of bilingual education and provide descriptive accuracy. These descriptions should reflect actual instructional practices and be validated through reliable classroom observations.

Early-Exit   Early-exit programs provide some initial instruction, primarily for the introduction of reading, and instruction in the first language is phased out rapidly (Rennie, 1993). Ramirez (1992) described the early-exit program as one where children receive some instruction in their primary initial reading skills, with all other instruction in English. By the end of second grade, students participating in the early-exit model are expected to be exited from the program and mainstreamed into English-only classrooms (Ramirez, 1992).

The terms *early-exit* and *transitional bilingual education (TBE)* have been used interchangeably to define the model that uses more English instruction at an earlier time in an effort to move children quickly into mainstream English classrooms. In a discussion of the Ramirez study, Thomas (1992) referred to the early-exit program as transitional bilingual education and declared it the most commonly funded type of bilingual program.

Late-Exit   Late-exit programs serve ELL students in grades kindergarten through six, and students receive 40% of their instructional time in Spanish (Ramirez, 1992). In contrast to students in early-exit programs, the students in late-exit programs receive a minimum of 40% of their instructional time in Spanish-language arts, reading, and other content areas such as mathematics, social studies, and/or science (Ramirez, 1992).

English Immersion   Ramirez (1992) describes the immersion strategy as one in which instruction is almost exclusively in English. Teachers have specialized training to meet ELL students' needs, as well as strong skills in the students' receptive language. In an immersion program, English, the target language, is taught in the content areas; and a strong language development component is included in each content lesson. The child's home language is used primarily to clarify English and, on a case-to-case basis, a LEP student who begins the program in kindergarten is expected to be mainstreamed in two or three years. According to Moran (1993), confusion occurs when the immersion model is misinterpreted, programs are set up, minority children are placed in English-only programs with native English speakers, and the immersion concept is misused on submersion models.

Dual Immersion   Dual immersion is a bilingual program in which non-English-speaking students and native-English-speaking students learn together in the same class. Dual-immersion programs are a way to help students learn two languages at the same time.

Submersion   The submersion approach, often described as the "sink or swim" approach, calls for placement of ELL students in classrooms where only English is spoken. The student's first language is not used for instruction, and no special attempt is made to help overcome language problems (Ovando & Collier, 1998).

Dual Language   Moran (1993) described dual language as an adaptation of the French Immersion Model from Canada. In a dual-language program, native-English-speaking students are immersed in the minority language, Spanish, alongside native Spanish-speaking students. Dual-language programs are designed to help all participating students become fluent in both English and a second language. English-speaking children are placed in classrooms with non-English speakers, and all instruction is in both languages. As research has shown, the most successful programs begin in prekindergarten and continue through the sixth grade. According to Secretary Riley, students will develop high levels of proficiency in their first and second language. Academic performance will be at or above grade level in both languages, and students will develop greater cross-cultural awareness and knowledge.

Two-Way   Two-way bilingual programs (known also as two-way immersion), developmental bilingual, bilingual immersion, and dual-language programs have taken root in schools across the country (Two-Way Bilingual Education, 1994). These programs integrate two groups of students, language minority and language majority, and provide instruction through the minority students' target language and the majority students' language — English — with the goal of bilingualism for both groups (Christian, 1994). (In a one-way bilingual program the minority language group is taught in two languages, with no effort to teach the minority language to others.) Two-way programs cost slightly more than transitional programs to implement (Lara-Alecio, Galloway, Irby, Brown, & Gómez, 2004).

English as a Second Language Program Models

English as a second language (ESL) program models are generally classified as (a) specialized, pull-out ESL programs that focus on linguistics, or (b) English-plus programs, in which the native language may be used in instruction of content areas. English instruction is longer or may represent the entire instructional program (McKeon, 1987).

Pull-out Generally used in an elementary setting, pull-out is the most expensive of all program models (Crawford, 1997); yet, it is the most common and least effective (Thomas & Collier, 1997). The student receives specialized instruction in a separate classroom from her regular classroom during the day. The student is taken from her regular classroom for this special instruction. The teacher may be either stationary on a campus or itinerant (shared between several campuses). Students from different first-language backgrounds may be separated into groups for instruction. In Texas, the teacher must have an endorsement in ESL; however, in other states teachers may or may not be trained in this field (O'Malley & Waggoner, 1984). Most ESL teachers are not bilingual or bicultural.

Class Period This approach, in which ESL instruction is provided during a regular class period, is generally used in a middle or secondary school setting. Students generally receive credit for the course, just as they would for other courses in a departmentalized setting. Students may be grouped according to their level of English proficiency.

Sheltered English or Content-Based Programs To date, these programs have been used primarily with secondary school students. In such programs, ELLs from different language groups are placed together in classes where teachers use English as the language of instruction in the content areas of science, social studies, and sometimes mathematics. The language is adapted to the students' proficiency level. Teachers may use gestures and visual aids to help students understand. A teacher certified in ESL offers instruction in this effective program. (The program is effective due to accessibility to a broader curriculum; it is more cost-effective than the pull-out model.) Sheltered English or content-based programs may parallel virtually all mainstream academic curricular offerings, or they may consist of only one or two subjects (Chamot & Stewner-Manzanares, 1985; Ovando & Collier, 1998).

Structured English Immersion In the structured English immersion approach, instruction should be provided in the child's home language; but the second language, English, is not used at all until students have a mastery of the first language commensurate with their age and extent of formal schooling. This approach strictly focuses on providing sufficient oral, reading, and writing skills so LEP youngsters can eventually transition into mainstream programs (Pardo & Tinajero, 1993). Most students are mainstreamed after being in a structured immersion program for two or three years (Rennie, 1993); however, English-only proponents have misnamed this program model, have left out the native language, and use English only. This program has become another type of ESL content instruction in a self-contained classroom. *Structured* has become equated with highly structured materials that carry students through a step-by-step learning process. An example of such a program is Direct Instructional System for Teaching and Remediation (DISTAR) Reading. Structured immersion models have not proven effective, because the materials did not fit the process of natural second-language acquisition (Ovando & Collier, 1998).

High Intensity Language Training (HILT) Programs These programs are used primarily at the secondary level. According to McKeon (1987), in the HILT design students of various language backgrounds are grouped for a major part of the school day. Students receive intensive ESL instruction, usually for three hours a day in the first year of instruction and less in succeeding years (Chamot & Stewner-Manzanares, 1985). McKeon (1987) indicated that mainstreaming students into regular classrooms is accomplished on a subject-by-subject basis and usually begins with less linguistically demanding classes such as music, physical education, and art. She indicated that some models may include content-based or sheltered English classes.

Summary

1. The aims of guidance and counseling programs are to assist individuals to develop the ability to understand themselves, to solve their own problems, and to make appropriate adjustments to their environment.

2. Major guidance services include student appraisal, information giving, placement and follow-up, and counseling.

3. Broadly conceived, two methods of counseling include directive and nondirective approaches. On the one hand, directive counseling focuses attention on identifying and analyzing the problem and finding an appropriate solution to it using all available data. Nondirective counseling, on the other hand, provides the counselee not with a neat solution for her problem, but instead with the ability to meet her problem in a constructive way.

4. Ten criteria are used in evaluating guidance and counseling programs: student needs, cooperation, process and product, balance, flexibility, quality counselors, adequate counselor-student ratio, adequate physical facilities, and appropriate record keeping.

5. The student's cumulative record contains information beneficial to these school officials: administrators, counselors, school psychologists, social workers, and teachers. The cumulative record should include the following information: a student's data sheet, parent's report, child's self-concept appraisal, sociogram, behavior reports, and standardized test data.

6. The components of a school's testing battery should include the following tests: emerging reading, learning readiness, intelligence, achievement, and interests and aptitudes.

7. Methods of reporting grades include percentage, letter, descriptive, percentile, three-group, ranking, and T-score. Each method of reporting student progress to parents has merit.

8. Extracurricular activities fulfill the overall goals of education and the curriculum mission of the school. Functions of extracurricular activities include reinforcing learning, supplementing the curriculum, integrating knowledge, and fulfilling the objectives of democracy.

9. Special teaching practices, materials, equipment, and facilities may be required for children with disabilities to achieve their full potential. To that end, Congress has passed four landmark pieces of legislation: Section 504 of the Rehabilitation Act of 1973, the Education for All Handicapped Act of 1975, the Americans with Disabilities Act of 1990 (ADA), and the Individuals with Disabilities Act (IDEA).

10. Of these four laws, IDEA has had the most significant impact on public schools. Congress reauthorized IDEA in 1997, adding new amendments and extending federal funding for special education services.

11. Gifted education programs are not mandated by the federal government. Services to such students must be aligned with the district's definition and identification procedures.

12. Bilingual education has as its goal to successfully prepare all children to transition to English. This goal can be accomplished in a transitional bilingual classroom, a dual-language classroom, or an English as a second language (ESL) classroom.

Field-Based Activities

1. Interview the school counselor on the campus where you work. Determine what methods the counselor uses in counseling students. Review the curriculum the counselor uses in group settings; look for specific skills within the curriculum. Observe the counselor in a group session with students. Review the types of problems the counselor has dealt with over the past month; how did the counselor resolve these problems?

2. Review the district special education procedures. Develop a flowchart from the initiation

of an observed problem with a student to placement or non-placement in a special education classroom. Which specific services does the district provide? What tests are used to determine if a student has a disability? Are factors other than test results considered?

3. What are the identification procedures for students being placed in a gifted program or a bilingual program in your district? Is there a district policy on gifted education? What type of program is provided for gifted students at various grade levels? Is the district definition aligned with the identification procedures and with the program type offered? How does gifted education serve students who may also be disabled, or who may be ELL?

Suggested Readings

Calderón, M. E., & Minaya-Rowe, L. (2003). *Designing and implementing two-way bilingual programs*. Thousand Oaks, CA: Corwin Press. There is a strong need for comprehensive instruction for English-language learners that also develops genuine bilingualism among children of all backgrounds. This excellent resource provides essential elements to help your students gain literacy in two languages, increase cross-cultural understanding, and meet high levels of achievement in all core academic areas.

Gusky, T. R., & Bailey, J. M. (2001). *Developing grading and reporting systems for student learning*. Thousand Oaks, CA: Corwin Press. Written to help readers develop a deeper and more reflective understanding of the various aspects of the subjects, this work brings organization and clarity to a murky and disagreement-laden topic.

Klesse, E. J. (2004). *Student activities for today's schools*. Lanham, MD: Scarecrow Press. What are student activities? Why do schools have student activity groups? What are the benefits for students, schools, and communities? These are some questions addressed by Klesse, who has reviewed relevant educational research to provide an overview of the essential learning for all youth that is available through participation. What are those benefits, and who benefits? Are there ways to make student activity programs in schools more inclusive? What will these programs look like in 5, 10, and 15 years? Schools must educate and develop their students to meet the challenge of participation and survival in a global economy. The skills learned through student activities provide the foundation for adult participation as citizens of our democracy. So, how do we best prepare our young people for the future? Read this book to find out.

Kottler, J. A., & Kottler, E. (2000). *Counseling skills for teachers*. Thousand Oaks, CA: Corwin Press. Learn how to create a helping relationship with your students, understand problems, resolve critical classroom incidents, and make referrals when necessary.

Marzano, R. J. (2000). *Transforming classroom grading and reporting*. Arlington, VA: Association for Supervision and Curriculum Development. A renowned expert explains what grades are for, what they should include, and how to compute final scores that accurately reflect student learning. Explore seven basic forms of classroom assessment, the strengths and weaknesses of each, and how they provide a comprehensive picture of student knowledge and skill. Here is an authoritative guide that explains not only what's wrong with most grading systems, but how they can be fixed.

McLaughlin, M. L., & Nolet, V. (2004). *What every principal needs to know about special education*. Thousand Oaks, CA: Corwin Press. What is "effective" special education? How can I get better results for special education students? These are the questions that principals need to be asking. Special education law and practices are rapidly changing, and principals need to know what those changes mean for their schools. *What Every Principal Needs to Know About Special Education* is designed to provide that foundation. It contains the information that every principal needs to effectively educate students with disabilities and provides critical information to: (a) apply the features of "effective special education practices," (b) become comfortable with the core special education legal foundations, (c) include students with disabilities in assessments and new accountability systems, and (d) create collaborations between general and special education teachers.

Smutny, J. F. (Ed.). (2003). *Designing and developing programs for gifted students.* Thousand Oaks, CA: Corwin Press. Gifted programs have the potential to change lives, but they can be difficult to develop and sustain without the appropriate research and guidance. This book gives you the nuts and bolts needed to design and implement a gifted program to maximize the benefits to students, teachers, schools, and parents.

Learning for All

Setting: Dover High School is a large high school in a metropolitan area. At Dover, 189 teachers serve 2,086 students. Over 50% of the faculty has more than 10 years of experience. Most of that experience has been acquired on site. Approximately 8% of the teachers will be new in the next year. About 20% percent of the teachers now have 1–5 years of experience, 16% have 6–10 years of experience, 24% have 11–20 years of experience, and 32% have over 20 years of experience. Ethnic breakdown shows that over 90% of the teachers are White. Less than 4% are African American, and a similar percentage are Hispanic. Almost 63% of the teachers are female.

Scenario: The site-based decision-making (SBDM) committee of Dover High School is having a difficult time deciding how professional development days are to be used in the coming school year. A survey of all teachers taken late this spring has identified a large number of topics that staff members desire to learn about in some way. Committee members know that even attempting to provide small groups of teachers with an opportunity to improve using traditional staff development is doomed to fail. Budget cuts dictate that a new way of providing professional development for each teacher be found. On the other hand, the SBDM committee can reach no consensus. Many ideas have been proposed. SBDM committee chair Joan Abshire, who is also the English department chair, is telling committee members that she thinks it best to take the problem to the principal, Dr. March, and ask for advice. The reaction statements begin with Mr. Suarez's comments.

"Before we go running to Dr. March, I think we should network with our colleagues and come up with some solutions on our own. I am tired of having the administration dictate what we can or cannot do for professional development. Surely, as a group we ought to be able to think of some way to provide for our own in an effective way — effective for teachers and students as well as for the budget."

"Whatever we do will have to be approved by the principal anyway. Why not just go and ask her?" says Ms. Schwartz.

"First, let's summarize what we have discussed," Joan Abshire replies. "We've talked about hiring a presenter/trainer for each department. That may not be cost effective. Also, such an approach uses the old model for training, which research has shown to be ineffective. Another approach we've thought of is peer training. From two to six teachers, with varying teaching experience in the same content areas, could focus on how to improve the teaching and learning in their area of expertise. Some of you thought this seemed just like the department meetings you attend regularly anyway. And, we've also thought of the instructional training available over the satellite with interactive sites. Perhaps we could identify enough sites to make this type of training feasible on the learning side. We are not sure about the budget requirements. The last idea we have talked about is to have reading and discussion groups between and among our own teachers, and sometimes administrators too. Group activities may also include watching videotapes, to be followed with discussion and application of learning. Objections to this idea included the fact that some of you think your colleagues will lean on others and not do any reading or watching of videotapes. What else are you thinking about? Or should I go see Dr. March?"

Mr. Suarez, impatient with his peers, states, "We are all so socialized into this bureaucracy that we cannot see new ways to accomplish our goals. I can think of several ideas that you all might think are crazy. Instead of volunteering these at this time, I challenge each of you to go out and ask friends in business what they do for professional development. Ask our colleagues that do not serve on this committee, too. Let's come back in a week and revisit this issue."

After the committee votes to wait a week while seeking new ideas, Joan Abshire reports to Principal March. "I am not certain what ideas would be approved on up the line. Can you help me in bringing some new ideas to the committee?"

Dr. March indicates that as long as the mission and vision of the school are matched with the plan, and as long as the costs do not exceed the projected budget, approval should be forthcoming. She suggests that perhaps looking at data showing an overview of student performance by grade, group, and subject would be a starting point. Study groups in each department could then research best practices for strengthening areas of weakness. At the second in-service day, teachers could share what they have learned. From the principal's perspective, just that could provide a series of good learning sessions. She

thinks such efforts also might lead to curriculum alignment. Dr. March ends by encouraging Joan to listen carefully to all that is brought forth and to think about rewards, recognition, and reinforcements that might be built into a revised plan for professional development.

At the next SBDM committee meeting, Ms. Schwartz leads off with the reminder that staff development was meant to change teacher behavior and not student behavior. "I was reminded of this by my fiancé, who is in business. He said that when he was involved in professional development, the training emphasized not working to change the client, but to change his behavior in relation to the client. The other comment he made was that his superiors always provided support for his new learning in one way or another."

Joan immediately remembers what Dr. March had said about supporting staff with rewards, recognition, and/or reinforcement of some type. She tells the committee that she is sure the principal will support the teachers in their efforts as long as they remember the vision. Joan continues by saying, "Maybe we could use a combination of approaches that we have already discussed, and let the departments decide what they would like to do—have a set of peer coaching sessions, or a series of satellite sessions with interactive capabilities, or readings with discussion. I can see some modeling of teaching approaches coming out of this last suggestion. The modeling would probably be done by more experienced staff—such as you, Mr. Suarez. These collaborative sessions could be very beneficial. Dr. March thought that a review of data by department at the first staff development session might be a way to refocus on teachers' needs to use new strategies to reach all students. We are primarily an older, white group serving a very mixed population. After this first session, each department would have a couple of days to follow up on identified needs later in the year. Maybe if a department chose this activity as a group, they could earn so many dollars for research and/or reading."

Mr. Suarez comments, "Do you think this is really going to work? How is this team or the principal going to know that each department is going to plan well?"

"We don't know that going in, but we do know that we on the SBDM committee will have to approve the plan first, and then the principal must approve it. This sounds workable. Certainly it will be within the projected budget. The sessions will have to be structured fairly well by each department to make sure that all the teachers are involved. Also, each teacher must have an opportunity to receive an award — maybe that can be done on a team basis, so that bickering between individuals in the same department doesn't happen. What do some of the rest of you think?"

Following much discussion, the SBDM committee decides to move ahead with the plan as suggested. They believe that ultimately this approach will provide for individual teacher differences, roles, and needs. Certainly the collaboration should lead to a better climate. The focus on achievement needs of students is aligned strongly with the district vision. They draft a proposal to send to the principal and set the date for their next meeting.

Questions

1. What do you think about such a process to determine the professional development of a school team?

2. What would you do as principal to improve the process?

3. Do you agree with Ms. Schwartz's fiancé's comments? If not, why not?

4. What kinds of professional development have you found most meaningful?

5. How could Dr. March better use this opportunity to build leadership capacity? Explain.

7. Organizational Structures

> **Standard 3.0:** *Candidates who complete the program are educational leaders who have the knowledge and ability to promote the success of all students by managing the organization, operations, and resources in a way that promotes a safe, efficient, and effective learning environment.*

FOCUSING QUESTIONS

1 What are the key components of organizational structure?

2 Why is open systems theory important in understanding how schools function?

3 What are some different approaches to analyzing what principals do in terms of leadership functions, administrative roles, and management skills?

4 Why are some principals more effective than others?

5 How does bureaucracy differ from System 4, site-based management, transformational leadership, synergistic leadership theory, and total quality management?

In this chapter, we address these questions concerning organizational structure in schools. We begin our discussion by defining and describing six basic concepts of organizational structure: job specialization, departmentalization, delegation, decentralization, span of management, and line and staff authority. Then we discuss the importance of open systems theory in schools. Following that, we discuss three approaches to analyzing what principals do: leadership functions, administrative roles, and management skills. We then discuss effective principals in terms of task dimensions, human resource activities, and behavioral profiles of effective versus successful principals. Next we discuss the dysfunctions of bureaucracy, and we examine five alternatives to the bureaucratic form — the System 4 design, site-based management, transformational leadership, synergistic leadership theory, and total quality management (TQM).

Up to this point, we have concentrated on the principal's role as instructional leader. We have examined a host of processes for shaping schools as professional learning communities and have hinted at the implications of these initiatives for school improvement. But management is important in addition to instructional leadership (Louis & Kruse, 2000; Sharp & Walter, 2003). We know that when school improvements occur, principals play a central role in (a) ensuring that resources — money, time, and professional development — align with instructional goals, (b) supporting the professional growth of teachers in a variety of interconnected ways, (c) including teachers in the information loop, (d) cultivating the relationship between the school and community, and (e) managing the day-to-day tasks of running a school. Each of these is viewed as a management task in the sense that it involves daily or weekly attention to problem solving within the school and between the school and its immediate environment.

We think management is a prerequisite to leadership. You can't change something unless it is a viable system in the first place. It has to continue to survive while you take it to the next level. Management of the day-to-day operation of a school is essential. The leadership, though, is in asking: How are we going to make this work better? What is the business we are in? What is it we are trying to do? How are we going to put all of our resources together; to continue to grow; to continue to respond to new needs; to enable schools to be places where engaged teaching and learning occur? Very often good leaders, although they know the management skills, don't take the time personally to practice those skills. And part of leadership is in knowing what you do best and using all of the available resources. Thus principals work with students, teachers, parents, and others to set up organizational structures and help to develop other people in the school by delegating and very carefully monitoring the management functions in the school.

Key Concepts of Organizational Structure

Think of all the activities employees perform in a school: scheduling classes, ordering supplies, maintaining student records, teaching classes, cleaning classrooms, preparing food, driving buses, typing letters, photocopying, and the like. If you were to make a list, you would probably identify several hundred different tasks. Without some structures, policies, and processes, would all the required tasks be performed efficiently and effectively? Who will teach the classes, clean the classrooms, wash the chalkboards, serve lunch in the cafeteria, drive the buses, or mail student report cards? The management function of *organizational structure* is the process of deploying human and physical resources to carry out tasks and achieve school goals. How do principals manage the day-to-day activities of the school and, at the same time, work toward the school's improvement? They don't do it alone. In this section, we describe six basic concepts of organizational structure: job specialization, departmentalization, delegation, decentralization, span of management, and line and staff authority (Robbins, 2004b).

Job Specialization

The most basic concept of organizational structure is *job specialization* — the degree to which the overall task of the school is broken down and divided into smaller, component parts. For example, a school may employ principals, school psychologists, social workers, counselors, teachers, and many other support staff including secretaries, food service personnel, maintenance workers, bus drivers, and the like. This specialization of tasks provides an identity for the job and those performing it; and collectively, the tasks add back to the total. That is, the contributions of the individual jobs, including management coordination, equal the original overall job of the school — to educate all children.

Specialization is a key organizing concept for several reasons. First, repetition improves skill. By performing the same task repeatedly, the employee gains expertise and thus increases productivity. Second, wage economics may also arise through the development of various employee levels. Complex jobs can be staffed with skilled personnel, and simple tasks with unskilled labor. Third, whenever a sufficient volume of routine work is isolated, mechanization becomes a possibility; using computers for office work is an example. Finally, job specialization allows a variety of tasks to be performed simultaneously. For example, in a school, budgeting, counseling, typing, preparing lunch, and teaching can be performed concurrently by different people.

Despite the advantages, however, schools can overdo job specialization. When carried to extremes, job specialization can lead to fatigue, monotony, boredom, and job dissatisfaction, which can result in absenteeism, turnover, and a decrease in the quality of work performed. To counter these problems, school principals have begun to search for alternatives that will maintain the positive benefits of job specialization.

The three most common alternatives to job specialization are job rotation, job enlargement, and job enrichment (Herzberg, 1987). *Job rotation* involves systematically moving employees from one job to another. In large school districts, principals are often rotated among schools every five years. *Job enlargement* adds breadth to a job by increasing the number and variety of activities performed by an employee. *Job enrichment* adds depth to a job by adding "administrative" activities (decision making, staffing, budgeting, reporting) to a teacher's responsibilities. The latter two alternatives were recommended by the Carnegie Task Force on Teaching as a Profession (1986) and the Holmes Group (1986) as a way to restructure schools through shared governance, participatory management, and site-based management, whereby teachers play a more active role in the operation of the school.

Departmentalization

Once the overall task of a school is divided into specialized jobs, these jobs must be grouped into some logical organizational units such as teams, departments, or divisions—a concept known as *departmentalization*. The most common grouping in schools is by function. Departmentalization by function brings together, in a common organizational unit, people performing similar or closely related activities. For example, common departments in a school are English, social studies, mathematics, and science. Common divisions in school districts are personnel, instruction, business, and research and development. Similar activities are coordinated from a common place in the organizational hierarchy. The instructional division, for example, controls only instructional activities. Each functional unit may be broken down further for coordination and control purposes.

Because of its versatility, functional departmentalization is one of the most widely adopted approaches for grouping school district activities. This system can be used in both large and small school districts. It can be used at many different levels in the organizational hierarchy, at the central office level or further down to individual building levels, such as instructional grade-level teams in an elementary school or subject-matter departments within a high school.

Functional departmentalization offers a number of other advantages. Because people who perform similar functions work together, each department can be staffed by experts in that functional area. Decision making and coordination are easier, because division administrators or department heads need to be familiar with only a relatively narrow set of skills. Functional departments at the central office can use a school district's resources more efficiently, because a department's activity does not have to be repeated across several school district divisions. Functional departmentalization has certain disadvantages as well. Personnel can develop overly narrow and technical viewpoints that lose sight of the total system perspective; communication and coordination across departments can be difficult; and conflicts often emerge as each department or unit attempts to protect its own turf.

Delegation

Another key concept of organizational structure is *delegation*, the process principals use to transfer authority from one position to another within a school or school district. For example, superintendents delegate authority to associate or assistant superintendents, assistant superintendents delegate authority to principals, principals delegate authority to assistant principals, and so on. Delegating authority does not reduce the authority of the superintendents, assistant superintendents, or principals. To delegate means to grant or to confer. To delegate does not mean to surrender authority. A principal who delegates authority in no way abdicates the legitimate right to act on behalf of the school.

There are three steps in the delegation process. First, the principal assigns *responsibility*. For example, when a principal asks an assistant principal to prepare an enrollment projection, order supplies and materials, or hire a new teacher, she is assigning responsibility. Second, along with the assignment, the assistant principal is given the *authority* to do the job. The principal may give the assistant principal the power to access enrollment data, to negotiate on the price of supplies and materials, and to submit a hiring notice to the personnel department. Finally, the principal requires *accountability* from the assistant principal. That is, the assistant principal incurs an obligation to carry out the task assigned by the principal.

There are many reasons for delegating. For one, delegating tasks enables principals to accomplish more than if they attempted to handle every task personally. For example, in a large urban high school, a principal may have five or six associate or assistant principals, five or six counselors, a social worker, a school psychologist, and 300 teachers. Any one of these individuals is a potential delegatee. Moreover, delegation allows principals to focus their energies on the most crucial, high-priority tasks; for example, student achievement. Delegation also enables faculty to grow and develop. By participating in decision making and problem solving, faculty learn more about the overall operation of the school, which is the essence of site-based management.

Despite the positive reasons for delegating, problems often arise in the delegation process. For several reasons, principals may be reluctant to delegate. For one thing, some principals may be so disorganized that they are incapable of planning the activities to be assigned to others. For another, they may not want to delegate because they lack confidence in the abilities of faculty to do a task well, and they fear being held personally accountable for the work of others. Conversely, some principals

may fear that others will perform the delegated tasks so efficiently that their own positions will be threatened. And, some principals want so strongly to dominate and influence others that they refuse to delegate authority.

Not all barriers to effective delegation are found in superiors, however. Many faculty members try to avoid having authority delegated to them. First, delegation adds to a faculty member's responsibilities and accountabilities. Second, many faculty members fear criticism for mistakes. Third, some faculty members lack the necessary self-confidence to take on added responsibilities. Finally, faculty members may perceive that the rewards for assuming additional responsibilities are inadequate.

Delegation is critical to effective management. A principal can increase her effectiveness as a delegator by adhering to the following principles:

1. *Principals should not criticize colleagues.* Criticism makes colleagues reluctant to assume additional responsibilities in the future. When a mistake is made, the deficiency should be explained in such a way that improved performance results in the future, rather than defensiveness and a desire to avoid responsibility.

2. *Principals should ensure that colleagues have the necessary information and resources to do the job.* When there is a lack of necessary information and resources to do a good job, colleagues may hesitate to accept new assignments.

3. *Principals should provide incentives for assuming additional responsibilities.* Rewards for assuming additional assignments must be adequate.

4. *Principals should guard against letting the colleagues' task become theirs.* Frequently, a teacher will come to a principal and say, "I have a problem"; and after some conversation about the issue, the principal agrees to handle the matter. Being helpful in solving problems is important, but principals should get things done with and through other people.

5. *Principals should delegate to the point where the decision has a local focus.* In a school departmentalized by function, the principal

could delegate school instructional decisions to department heads, guidance and counseling-related decisions to counselors. For each of these colleagues, the decisions they make affect only their own school departments or divisions. Decisions having nonlocal, *district-wide* impact, such as those concerning system-wide collective bargaining agreements, could not be delegated locally but would have to be made in the superintendent's office.

Decentralization

Another key concept of organizational structure is the degree of decentralization of authority within the school district. In reality, authority can be centralized or decentralized.

The concept of decentralization, like the concept of delegation, has to do with the degree to which authority is dispersed or concentrated. Whereas the term *delegation* usually refers to the extent to which individual leaders delegate authority and responsibility to people reporting directly to them, *decentralization* is the systematic dispersal of power and decision making throughout the school district to middle- and lower-level leaders. Conversely, centralization is the systematic concentration of power and authority near the top, or in the head of a school (the principal) or school district (the superintendent). No organization is completely centralized or decentralized. Rather, these are extremes of a continuum, and school districts fall somewhere in between. The difference is one of relative degree; that is, a school district can be described as decentralized relative to other schools or school districts.

Several characteristics determine how decentralized a school is relative to others (Mescon, Albert, & Khedouri, 2004):

1. *Number of decisions made at lower levels.* The greater the number of decisions made by those lower in the organizational hierarchy (staff members), the more decentralized the school.

2. *Importance of decisions made at lower levels.* In a decentralized school, teachers can make

decisions involving substantial resources and increased people power, or they can commit the school to a new course of action.

3. *The scope of decisions made at lower levels.* If teachers can make decisions that affect more than one function, the school is probably decentralized.

4. *Amount of checking on school principals.* In a highly decentralized school district, top-level administrators (superintendents) seldom review day-to-day decisions of building principals. The presumption is that these decisions were made correctly. Evaluation is based on overall results of the school.

The advantages of decentralization are similar to the advantages of delegation: unburdening of top-level administrators; improved decision making because decisions are made closer to the firing line; better training, morale, and initiative at lower levels; and more flexibility to adjust to changing conditions. These advantages are so compelling that it is tempting to think of decentralization as "good" and centralization as "bad."

But total decentralization, with no coordination from the top, would be undesirable. The very purpose of organization—efficient integration of subunits for the good of the whole—would be diminished without some centralized control. Even in very decentralized school districts, top administrators such as superintendents retain a number of decisions: setting overall goals, strategic planning, school district policy formulation, bargaining with unions, and development of financial and accounting systems. The question for school leaders is not whether a school or school district should be decentralized, but to what extent it should be decentralized.

Decentralization has value only to the extent that it assists a school district or school to achieve its goals effectively. In determining the amount of decentralization appropriate for a school district, the following internal characteristics are usually considered (Stoner & Wankel, 2004):

1. *The cost and risk associated with the decision.* Principals may be wary of delegating authority

for decisions that could have an impact on the performance of their own subunits or the school as a whole. This caution is out of consideration not only for the school's welfare but also for their own, because the responsibility for results remains with the delegator.

2. *A principal's preference for a high degree of involvement and confidence in colleagues.* Some principals pride themselves on their detailed knowledge of everything that happens within their purview of responsibility. This has been referred to as running a tight ship. Conversely, other principals take pride in confidently delegating everything possible to their colleagues in order to avoid getting bogged down in petty details and to preserve their own expertise with the school's major goal of teaching and learning.

3. *The organizational culture.* The shared norms, values, and beliefs (culture) of members of some schools support tight control at the top. The culture of other schools supports the opposite approach. The history of the school's culture then will have some bearing on the amount of decentralization appropriate.

4. *The abilities of staff.* This characteristic is, in part, a circular process. If authority is not delegated due to lack of confidence in the talents below, the talent will not have an opportunity to develop. Furthermore, the lack of internal training and development will make it more difficult to find and hold talented and ambitious people. This, in turn, will make it more difficult to decentralize.

Span of Management

Another key concept of organizational structure is the *span of management* — the number of subordinates who report directly to a given principal. There is a limit to the number of persons one principal can effectively supervise. Care should be taken to keep the span of management, also called the *span of control,* within manageable limits.

Although there is agreement that there is a limit to the number of subordinates a principal can effectively supervise or manage, no agreement exists on the precise number. In fact, it is generally acknowledged that the optimum span of management varies greatly, even within the same school. Although principals may directly supervise only three to eight persons, assistant principals and department heads directing subordinates who are performing relatively similar activities may be able to manage much larger numbers efficiently.

Critical factors in determining the appropriate span of management include the following (Griffin, 2003):

1. *Similarity of functions.* Span of management should increase as the number of different functions to be supervised increases.

2. *Geographic proximity.* Span of management should decrease as the functions to be supervised become more geographically dispersed.

3. *Complexity of functions.* Span of management should be smaller for subordinates performing more complex tasks than for those performing simpler tasks.

4. *Degree of interdependence among units.* The greater the need for coordination of interdependent work units, the smaller the span of management.

5. *Level of motivation of subordinate personnel.* Increased motivation permits a larger span of management, and a larger span of management increases motivation.

6. *Competence of principals.* The ability of principals to delegate authority and responsibility varies. Span of management for those who can delegate more can be much larger than for those who can delegate little authority.

Line and Staff Positions

An important point in examining the key concepts of organizational structure is to distinguish between line and staff positions. *Line positions* are traditionally defined as those forming a part of the main line of authority (or chain of command) that flows throughout the school or school district.

Staff positions are positions outside the main line of authority or direct chain of command that are primarily advisory or supportive in nature.

Line positions are represented by a solid line in most organizational charts, starting with the superintendent and extending down through the various levels in the hierarchy to the point where the basic activities of the school district—teaching—are carried out. The roles of superintendent, assistant superintendents, directors, principals, and teachers are line positions. Each has goals that derive from and contribute to those of the overall school district. The positions of assistant to the superintendent and legal counsel are staff positions. These personnel perform specialized functions that are primarily intended to help line administrators. For example, the legal counsel is not expected to contribute to school district outcomes. Instead, he answers questions from and provides advice to the superintendent concerning legal matters that confront the school district. The assistant to the superintendent might be involved in such activities as computer programming, preparing enrollment projections, or conducting special studies that flow to the superintendent requiring information or advice. Staff positions are represented by dashed lines in organizational charts, implying that school district staff personnel communicate and advise line administrators.

The line and staff organization allows much more specialization and flexibility than the line organization alone. However, staff authority sometimes undermines the integrity of line departments and personnel who are accountable for results. Several factors may cause conflicts between and among line and staff departments and personnel (Mosley, Megginson, & Pietri, 2004). Due to the nature of this topic, we need to shift our focus to the school district.

1. Staff personnel may exceed their authority and attempt to give orders directly to line personnel.

2. Line personnel may feel that staff specialists do not fully understand line problems and think their advice is not workable.

3. Staff may attempt to take credit for ideas implemented by line; conversely, line may not acknowledge the role staff has played in helping to resolve problems.

4. Because staff is highly specialized, it may use technical terms and language that line cannot understand.

5. Top administration may not have communicated clearly the extent of authority staff has in its relationship with line.

6. Organizationally, staff departments and personnel are placed in relatively high positions close to top administration; lower-level line departments and personnel tend to resent this.

Basically, the line-staff conflict evident in many school districts is impossible to eliminate completely. However, it is possible to create conditions wherein line-staff conflicts are manageable. School districts can reduce the degree of line-staff conflict through the following strategies:

1. Create a public recognition of the reality of interdependence between the line and staff units, and develop a culture that attacks problems in a collaborative manner.

2. Do not allow organizational politics to mask true line-staff contributions. Cross-unit sabotage, backstabbing, spying, and intentional distortion can eliminate any hope of cooperation and lead to internal disintegration.

3. Develop an understanding of the broader organizational vision and goal and an associated recognition of each unit's responsibility to that goal.

4. Foster a climate in which leaders feel free to communicate their concerns, voice their perceptions, and discuss any apprehensions they have concerning actions of the other units.

5. Establish a team-based approach to problem solving that stresses the effective resolution of issues without undue concern over who will get "credit" for the solution.

6. Encourage nontask-related interaction between line and staff administrators to facilitate understanding of the different perspectives, values, needs, and goals held by both groups. (Schoderbeck, Cosier, & Aplin, 2004)

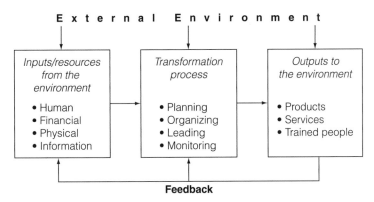

Figure 7.1

An Organizational System

The reduction of line-staff conflict is vital to overall school district performance. The creation of an organizational structure can unintentionally induce or minimize disruptive line-staff relationships.

Schools as Open Systems

Schools are social systems in which two or more persons work together in a coordinated manner to attain common goals. This definition is useful, for it specifies several important features of schools: (a) They consist, ultimately, of people; (b) they are goal-directed in nature; (c) they attain their goals through some form of coordinated effort; and (d) they interact with their external environment. Our definition, however, does not elaborate on one important feature of schools deserving special attention: All schools are *open systems,* although the degree of interaction with their environment may vary.

According to open systems views, schools constantly interact with their environments. In fact, they need to structure themselves to deal with forces in the world around them. In contrast, closed system theory views schools as sufficiently independent to solve most of their problems through their internal forces, without taking into account forces in the external environment (Miner, 2002). Consider a school closing or realignment of school boundaries, for example. It affects the people in the school and those outside it — in the community it's

moving from as well as the one it's moving to. Systems theory works on the inside and outside of the organization, as a way of understanding and anticipating the consequences of any decision.

A *system* can be defined as an interrelated set of elements functioning as an operating unit. As depicted in Figure 7.1, an organizational system consists of four basic elements: inputs, a transformation process, outputs, and feedback.

Inputs

Systems such as schools use four kinds of inputs or resources from the environment: human resources, financial resources, physical resources, and information resources. Human resources include administrative and staff talent, labor, and the like. Financial resources are the capital used by the school or the school district to finance both ongoing and long-term operations.

Physical resources include supplies, materials, facilities, and equipment. Information resources are knowledge, curricula, data, and other kinds of information utilized by the school or the school district.

Transformation Process

The principal's job involves combining and coordinating these various resources to attain the school's goals — learning for all. How do principals accomplish this? They do so by carrying out four basic management functions: planning, organizing, leading, and monitoring. In this way the principal, through the coordinated efforts of all members of the school community, transforms students into graduates.

Outputs

It is the principal's job to secure and use inputs to the schools and then transform them through the management functions of planning, organizing, leading, and monitoring — while considering external variables — to produce outputs. In social systems, outputs are usually labeled *goals* or *objectives* and are represented by the products, results, outcomes, or accomplishments of the system. Although the kinds of outputs will vary with a specific school, they usually include one or more of the following: growth and achievement levels of students and teachers, student dropout rates, employee performance and turnover, school-community relations, and job satisfaction. Most of these require no elaboration; only the last one is discussed. A school must provide "satisfaction" to members of the school community beyond the physiological needs (salary, working conditions, job security). Schools must provide for employees' needs for affiliation, acceptance, esteem, and perhaps even self-actualization if they hope to retain a motivated, committed workforce capable of performing at maximum levels.

Feedback

Finally, the external environment reacts to these outputs and provides feedback to the system. Feedback is crucial to the success of the school operation. Negative feedback, for example, can be used to correct deficiencies in the transformation process or the inputs or both, which in turn will have an effect on the school's future outputs.

Leadership Functions

Previously we noted that principals combine and coordinate various kinds of resources by carrying out four basic leadership functions: planning, organizing, leading, and monitoring. Our attention now turns to clarifying the four functions or activities that constitute the work performed by principals. The relationships among these functions are shown in Figure 7.2.

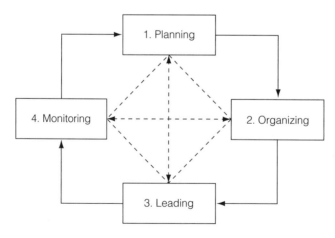

Figure 7.2

The Four Functions of Administration

Planning

Generally, *planning* defines where the school wants to be in the future and how to get there. Plans and the goals on which they are based give purpose and direction to the school, its subunits, and contributing staff. For example, suppose the principal in a large, urban school district decides that the school should attempt to increase the number of students reading at grade level by 20% by the year 2010. This goal and the methods needed to attain it would then serve as the planning framework for the school. School counselors, social workers, school psychologists, library media specialists, department heads, and teachers would set and synchronize individual objectives with those of the building principal.

Planning is important because it provides staff with a sense of purpose and direction, outlines the kinds of tasks they will be performing, and explains how their activities are related to the overall goals of the school. Without this information, staff would not know precisely how to use their time and energies efficiently and effectively. Subsequently, they would respond to their job responsibilities randomly, wasting valuable human resources.

Planning is also a prerequisite to other management functions. In particular, it becomes the basis for monitoring and evaluating actual performance. That is, plans made during the first step become benchmarks or criteria against which to measure actual performance in the monitoring step. Unless plans are formulated and mutually agreed on, there is relatively little value or basis for measuring the effectiveness of the school outcomes (Lunenburg & Irby, 1999; Lunenburg & Ornstein, 2004). In addition, comparing planned and actual results provides the principal with a sound basis on which to make necessary adjustments in the school's plan of action.

Since the 1970s, criticisms of traditional planning models have resulted in the development of the strategic planning approach (Kaufman, 2003). New ideas have arisen about the nature of educational organizations. Schools have been described as "loosely coupled systems" (Meyer & Rowan, 1977; Rowan, 1990; Weick, 1976) and "organized anarchies" (Cohen, March, & Olsen, 1972). The challenges facing schools have changed significantly as new demands have been placed on them. Their environment has become uncertain and even hostile.

Strategic planning, a subset of the public policy process, could be an ideal technology for shaping the future of education. Given the contextual constraints on educational policy (social, economic, and political), the challenge for educational strategic planners is to understand the internal and external boundaries and to use this understanding to design policies that could facilitate change in student achievement and the very structure of schools (Baker & Richards, 2004; Fowler, 2004).

Organizing

Once principals have developed workable plans and the methods for attaining them, they must design an organization that will successfully implement the plans. *Organizing* involves three essential elements: developing the structure of the organization, acquiring and developing human resources, and establishing common patterns and networks.

In a very basic sense, designing the structure of the organization involves creating the organizational chart for a school. The principal establishes policies and procedures for authority relationships, reporting patterns, the chain of command, departmentalization, and various administrative and subordinate responsibilities. Then the principal takes steps to hire competent personnel. When necessary, the principal establishes programs for training new personnel in the skills necessary to carry out their task assignments. Finally, the principal builds formal communication and information networks, including the types of information to be communicated, direction of communication flows, and reductions in barriers to effective communication.

Organizing at the upper levels of an organization usually includes designing the overall framework for the school district. At the building level, however, organizing is usually more specific and may involve the following specific activities: developing methods to help people understand what portion of the job is their responsibility; coordinating individual efforts through work schedules to avoid unnecessary delay in task accomplishment; designing an efficient system for making day-to-day work assignments should these be necessary; and cross-training personnel or providing for substitute personnel to avoid disruptions in the flow of work caused by absenteeism.

Leading

Once plans are formulated and activities are organized, the next step is leading staff members to achieve the school's goals. Although planning tells principals *what* to do and organizing tells principals *how* to do it, *leading* tells principals *why* the staff member should want to do it. Recently, the leading function is also called *facilitating, collaborating,* or *actuating*. No matter what it is called, leading entails guiding and influencing people.

The principal's role has been defined as getting things done by working with all school stakeholders in a professional learning community. Principals cannot do all of the work in schools alone. They must, therefore, influence the behavior of other people in a certain direction. To influence others, the principal needs to understand something about leadership, motivation, communication, and group dynamics. Leading means communicating goals to staff members and infusing them with the desire to perform at a high level (Kouzes & Posner, 2002; Sergiovanni, 2000). Because schools are composed largely of groups, leading involves motivating entire departments or teams as well as individuals toward the attainment of goals.

Monitoring

When principals compare expected results with actual results, and take the necessary corrective action, they are performing the *monitoring* function. Deviations from past plans should be considered when formulating new plans. As shown in Figure 7.2, monitoring completes the cycle of leadership functions.

Monitoring is the responsibility of every principal. It may simply consist of walking around the building to see how things are going, talking to students, visiting classrooms, and talking to faculty, or it may involve designing sophisticated information systems to check on the quality of performance, but it must be done if the principal is to be successful.

The success with which principals carry out these functions determines how effectively the school operates. A school is created to perform a set of tasks and achieve a number of stated goals, the most important of which is student learning. It is the principal's job to attain goals by working with all school stakeholders in an atmosphere of a professional learning community. This involves planning, organizing, leading, and monitoring.

Administrative Roles

Certain roles are required of all principals, whether they operate elementary, middle, or high schools. A principal does certain things, fulfills certain needs in the school district, has certain responsibilities, and is expected to behave in certain ways.

Thus far we have described how principals perform four basic functions that help ensure that school resources are used to attain high levels of performance. What do principals actually do to plan, organize, lead, and monitor on an hour-to-hour, day-to-day basis? A number of studies have been conducted in an attempt to describe what principals actually do on the job. Several researchers have followed principals around for long periods of time and recorded all of their activities (Doud, 1989a,b; Ferrandino, 2001; Fawcett et al., 2001; Kmetz & Willower, 1982; Martin & Willower, 1981; Ubben, Hughes, & Norris, 2004). They developed a description of the work of principals that can be divided into three general characteristics.

Heavy Workload at a Fast Pace   Principals' work is hectic and taxing. On the average, elementary school principals work 51 hours a week, from 7 to 9 hours a day. High school principals average about 53 hours a week, dividing 42 hours during the day and 11 hours on school-related activities in the evening. The principals observed processed over 20 pieces of mail a day, attended numerous meetings, and toured their buildings daily. Unexpected disturbances erupted, frequently requiring immediate action and unscheduled meetings. Free time was scarce; and even when time pressure was temporarily relieved, there were previously postponed activities that needed to be completed.

Variety, Fragmentation, and Brevity   Research on principal behavior is consistent in identifying the demands on the administrator as fragmented, rapid fire, voluminous, allowing little time for quiet reflection. The principals engaged in at least 149 different activities per day, half of which took less than five minutes each. This is in sharp contrast to many professional jobs, like engineering or law, which are characterized by long periods of concentration. Principals shift gears rapidly. There is no continuous pattern in their work. Significant crises are interspersed with trivial events in no predictable sequence. Each issue must be decided as quickly as possible.

Oral Communication   Principals spend 70 to 80% of their time in interpersonal communication. Personal contacts include colleagues in other schools, senior administrators, staff experts, teachers, and other personnel throughout the school. Effective principals also establish personal contacts outside the school, including principals in other school districts, legislators, state department of education personnel, parents, and people in the community. Most communication is face-to-face and by telephone rather than written. E-mail has added another dimension to the principal's communication patterns. Oral communication is fast and action oriented, and written communication is slow and time-consuming. In addition, principals depend heavily on gossip and hearsay, which travel quickly through oral communication. Finally, oral communication tends to

be more personal and satisfies people's needs for social interaction.

An analysis of the roles principals perform gives a clearer picture of what principals actually do on their jobs than does an analysis of leadership functions. By identifying a specific set of observable principal behaviors, the roles perspective also brings realism to the analysis of what principals do. Principals are the ones who make things happen in the school by doing the planning, organizing, leading, and monitoring that are required for the school to function. What skills are required of principals in order for them to function effectively?

Management Skills

Another approach to examining what principals do is based on the types of skills required to perform the job. The necessary skills for planning, organizing, leading, and monitoring have been placed in three categories that are especially important if principals are to perform their functions and roles adequately: conceptual, human, and technical (Katz, 1974). All school administrators must have these skills to be effective, but the amounts differ by hierarchical level (see Figure 7.3).

Conceptual Skills

All good school leaders have the ability to view the organization as a whole and solve problems to the benefit of everyone concerned. This is a *conceptual skill* that draws on one's mental abilities to acquire, analyze, and interpret information received from various sources and to make complex decisions that achieve the school's goals. In essence, it concerns the ability to see how the different parts of the school fit together and depend on each other, and how a change in any given part can cause a change in another part.

Conceptual skills are needed by all school leaders; but they are especially important for those at the top of the organization, such as school superintendents. These top-level administrators must perceive the significant elements in a situation

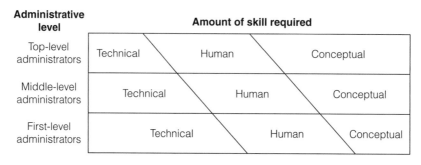

Figure 7.3

Relationship of Skills to Administrative Levels

and make decisions relevant to broad, conceptual patterns. Because they devote a large portion of their time to planning, they draw on conceptual skills to think in terms of relative tendencies, probabilities, patterns, and associations. Conceptual skills provide upper-level administrators with the ability to anticipate changes or to estimate the value of school district strategies. Many of the responsibilities of superintendents, such as decision making, resource allocation, and change, require a broad perspective.

In an era of school-based management, principals need to further develop their conceptual skills, to think "strategically"—to take a broad, long-term view. This ability will enable principals to see what goes on in their work environment and help them to react appropriately and reflectively to situations as they arise (Sergiovanni, 2004). Principals must consider environmental forces, resource flows, staff and administrative talent, board of education policies, reform mandates, parent complaints, and organizational change as significant inputs into the internal environment of the school (see Figure 7.1).

Human Skills

Principals spend considerable time interacting with people. Recall the researchers' descriptions of how principals spend their time: scheduled and unscheduled meetings, telephone calls, hallway and class-

room tours, and other face-to-face contacts. All these activities involve other people. For obvious reasons, the principal needs *human skills:* the ability to motivate, facilitate, coordinate, lead, communicate, manage conflict, and get along with others.

Human skills are important to school leaders at all levels. Upper-level administrators (superintendents) must use these skills to deal effectively with school boards, with groups outside of the school district, and with subordinate administrators. Middle-level administrators (principals) need human skills to manage individuals from a wide variety of departments or subject-matter areas and other technical experts (such as counselors, social workers, school psychologists, and department heads), and to interact productively with upper-level administrators. First-level supervisors (department heads, team leaders) must use human skills to challenge, to motivate, and to coordinate the work of teachers who are responsible for the education of the school district's clients—the students.

In recent years, the awareness of human skills has increased. The phenomenal appeal of such best-selling books as *In Search of Excellence, A Passion for Excellence,* and *Theory Z* attests to that fact. All three books stress the need for school administrators at all levels to take care of the human side of the enterprise. Excellent schools and excellent leaders provide warm, nurturing, caring, trusting, and challenging environments. In this view, effective principals are cheerleaders, facilitators, coaches, and nurturers of champions. They build their organizations through people. Effective human skills enable principals to unleash the energy within staff members and help them grow, ultimately resulting in maximum performance and goal attainment.

Technical Skills

The ability to use the knowledge, methods, and techniques of a specific discipline or field is referred to as a *technical skill*. Department heads and team leaders in schools are examples of people with technical skills — they are recognized as experts in their disciplines and are presumed to have the ability to supervise others. For the department head or team leader, the nature of technical skills is twofold. First, the supervisor has usually developed some expertise in a discipline or field of study. The department head in a high school, for example, has probably taught the subject she is supervising in an exemplary manner for a number of years. Second, the supervisor uses skills in the work being done. To successfully run an academic department, the chairperson must know how to teach the subject, how to organize the group, how to acquire resources, how to evaluate performance, and the like.

As shown in Figure 7.3, all school administrators need some knowledge of the technical functions they are supervising, although the amount of time they spend performing technical activities decreases as they move up the organizational hierarchy. The first-line supervisor in a school (department head, team leader) will need greater knowledge of the technical parts of the job than will either the superintendent of schools or the building principal. This is because first-line supervisors are closer to the actual work being performed; they often must train and develop teachers and answer questions about work-related problems. Every school district, school, and job has its special technical skill requirements.

Each approach to examining what a principal does looks at the job from a different perspective. Each has its merits. But in the final analysis, a successful principal must: (a) understand the work that is to be performed (management functions),

(b) understand the behavior needed to perform the job (administrative roles), and (c) master the skills involved in performing his role (management skills). Thus, these three approaches to analyzing what a principal does are not mutually exclusive; they are complementary perspectives.

Effective Principals

At several points in the discussion thus far, the notion of effective principals has been raised. Exactly what is an effective principal? In this section, we examine the notion of effective principals in terms of task dimensions, human resource activities, and behavioral profiles.

Task Dimensions

In analyzing the role of the principal, Marshall Sashkin and Gene Huddle (1986) identified 13 major task dimensions of the principal's job. They divided these task dimensions into two major categories. One category includes managerial tasks normally associated with the role of the principal — creating and enforcing policies, rules, procedures, and authority relationships. The other category, called "building cultural linkages," includes establishing behavioral norms, using symbols, instituting rituals, and telling stories designed to build the cultural foundations of school excellence.

Effective principals create more effective schools by deliberately designing their actions so that those actions build cultural as well as managerial linkages. Table 7.1 shows a number of tasks and related skills for effective management of schools.

Human Resource Activities

Earlier we noted that principals are responsible for getting things done by working with all school stakeholders. The principalship is, above all else, a social process. Principals spend a large portion of their time interacting with others, most often in face-to-face communication. Failure to interact

---

Table 7.1   Tasks and Skills for Effective Leadership of Schools

Building Bureaucratic Linkages

1. *Task: Building Sound Relations With the Central Office*
   Skills needed: liaison skills and negotiating skills.
2. *Task: Monitoring Organizational Information*
   Skills needed: scanning and monitoring information and using information networks.
3. *Task: Coordinating School Activities*
   Skills needed: time management, working with groups, and interpersonal skills.
4. *Task: Managing Financial Resources*
   Skills needed: developing budgets and mathematical skills.
5. *Task: Maintaining the School Building*
   Skills needed: developing maintenance schedules and using general management procedures and practices.
6. *Task: Directing School Support Services*
   Skills needed: designing policies, procedures, and rules and developing and monitoring contracts.
7. *Task: Staffing*
   Skills needed: use of selection methods, assessment and appraisal skills, and coaching and development skills.

Building Cultural Linkages

8. *Task: Establishing an Atmosphere Conducive to Learning*
   Skills needed: organizational communication, interpersonal communication and using symbols.
9. *Task: Setting High Expectations*
   Skills needed: goal setting, interpersonal communication, and interpersonal relationship skills.
10. *Task: Setting School Goals*
    Skills needed: goal setting and organizational communication.
11. *Task: Instructional Leadership*
    Skills needed: working with groups and committees, observational methods for assessment, and coaching skills.
12. *Task: Organizational Communication*
    Skills needed: using teams, committees, and task forces; using internal communication networks; and conflict management skills.
13. *Task: Building Parent and Community Support*
    Skills needed: representing the school to the community, public relations skills, and public communications skills.

---

well with others may hamper their careers. A study of 20 effective administrators and 21 ineffective ones emphasizes the importance of being able to work effectively with others. In contrast to their effective colleagues, the ineffective administrators were found to have the following shortcomings.

1. Insensitive to others; abrasive, intimidating, bullying style
2. Cold, aloof, arrogant
3. Betrayal of trust (failure to accomplish stated intentions)
4. Overly ambitious; thinking of the next job, playing politics
5. Over-managing: unable to delegate or build a team
6. Unable to staff effectively
7. Unable to plan and organize work

8. Unable to adapt to a superior with a different style

9. Unable to adjust to new and changing conditions

10. Overdependence on an advocate or mentor (Kreitner, 2004)

Note that all of these deficiencies are directly related to working effectively with others. People — whether superiors, colleagues, or subordinates — can make or break a principal's career.

Behavioral Profiles of Effective Versus Successful Administrators

Fred Luthans (2004) recently extended Doud's and others' work on administrative roles in two significant ways. First, he observed the behavior of 248 administrators at different hierarchical levels in a number of diverse organizations, including schools and universities. This was a much larger and more diverse sample than that used in Doud's and others' research. Second, Luthans contrasted the behavior of effective and ineffective administrators and successful and unsuccessful administrators — something not done by Doud and others.

The terms *effective* and *successful* are typically used interchangeably in the literature; therefore, Luthans made a clear distinction between the two by operationally defining each term. An administrator's *effectiveness* was measured by subordinates' evaluations of their satisfaction, commitment, and unit performance. Administrative *success* was determined by how fast the administrator had been promoted up the administrative hierarchy. Luthans then ranked the administrators in terms of relative effectiveness and relative success. Less than 10% of the administrators were labeled as both effective and successful. In fact, effective and successful administrators turned out to be behavioral opposites.

Results of Luthans's study revealed that effective administrators spent most of their time on task-related communication. Human resource management activities were an important part of the effective administrator's day. Successful administrators (those who enjoyed rapid promotions), on the other hand, spent relatively little time on human resource management activities. Instead, they proved to be good at networking (socializing, interacting with outsiders, politicking). That is, they were politically savvy and knew how to "play the game."

These conflicting findings may not be surprising to those who say, "It's not *what* you know, but *who* you know." However, Luthans notes that his research has broader implications. He suggests that his findings explain some of the performance problems facing American schools today. He argues that the successful administrators, the politically savvy ones who are being promoted into top-level positions, may not be the effective administrators who have satisfied, committed, and high-performing units. To achieve a more balanced administrative force, those who are both effective and successful, Luthans recommends performance-based evaluation and reward systems that place greater emphasis on human resource management activities (communicating, staffing, motivating, managing conflict, and developing staff and students) than on networking and politicking. We believe this is the direction we are headed with greater demands for accountability associated with the *No Child Left Behind* legislation.

The Demise of Bureaucracy

In a period of increasing demands for accountability, demographic changes in school population, and economic crisis, most schools are being forced to examine their fundamental structural assumptions. Bureaucracy — the basic infrastructure of schools in the industrial world — is ill suited to the demands of our postindustrial, demographically diverse information society (Lunenburg & Irby, 1999; Lunenburg & Ornstein, 2004; Murphy, 2002a,b). Bureaucratic characteristics not only are being viewed as less than useful but also are considered to be harmful. Some of these negative features of bureaucracy include the following:

1. *Division of labor and specialization.* A high degree of division of labor can reduce staff initiative. As jobs become narrower in scope

and well defined by procedures, individuals sacrifice autonomy and independence. Although specialization can lead to increased productivity and efficiency, it can also create conflict between specialized units, to the detriment of the overall goals of the school. For example, specialization may impede communication between units. Moreover, overspecialization may result in boredom and routine for some staff, which can lead to dissatisfaction, absenteeism, and turnover.

2. *Reliance on rules and procedures.* Weber (1947) claimed that the use of formal rules and procedures was adopted to help remove the uncertainty in attempting to coordinate a variety of activities in an organization. Reliance on rules can lead to the inability to cope with unique cases that do not conform to normal circumstances. In addition, the emphasis on rules and procedures can produce excessive red tape. The use of rules and procedures is only a limited strategy in trying to achieve coordinated actions. Other strategies may be required. But bureaucracy's approach is to create new rules to cover emerging situations and new contingencies. And, once established, ineffectual rules or procedures in a bureaucracy are difficult to remove.

3. *Emphasis on hierarchy of authority.* The functional attributes of a hierarchy are that it maintains an authority relationship, coordinates activities and personnel, and serves as the formal system of communication. In theory, the hierarchy has both a downward and an upward communication flow. In practice, it usually has only a downward emphasis. Thus upward communication is impeded, and there is no formal recognition of horizontal communication. This stifles individual initiative and participation in decision making.

4. *Lifelong careers and evaluation.* Weber's (1947) bureaucratic model stresses lifelong careers and evaluations based on merit. Because competence can be difficult to measure in bureaucratic jobs, and because a high degree of specialization enables most employees to master their jobs quickly, there is a tendency to base promotions and salary increments more on seniority and loyalty than on actual skill and performance. Thus the idea of having the most competent people in positions within the organization is not fully realized. Loyalty is obtained; but this loyalty is toward the protection of one's position, not to the effectiveness of the organization.

5. *Impersonality.* The impersonal nature of bureaucracy is probably its most serious shortcoming. Recent critics of bureaucracy attack it as emphasizing rigid, control-oriented structures over people found to be incompatible with professional learning communities (DuFour & Eaker, 1998; Louis & Kruse, 2000).

New viewpoints are leading to a decline in the use of bureaucratic structure in modern organizations (Stivers, 2001). School principals in the 21st century will see a change in some of their duties. One change will be a shift away from simply supervising the work of others to that of contributing directly to the school's goals. Instead of merely shuffling papers and writing reports, the modern principal will be a valued participant in a professional learning community (Glickman, 2002).

The renowned organization theorist, Warren Bennis, represents one of the extreme critics of bureaucratic structuring in organizations. More than three decades ago, he forecasted the demise of bureaucracy (Bennis, 1966). In a more recent book, *Managing the Dream,* he exposes the hidden obstacles in our organizations — and in society at large — that conspire against good leadership. According to Bennis (2000), within any organization an entrenched bureaucracy with a commitment to the status quo undermines the unwary leader. This creates an unconscious conspiracy in contemporary society, one that prevents leaders from taking charge and making changes.

In recent years, popular writers have expressed increasing dissatisfaction with bureaucratic structures. This is reflected in the phenomenal appeal of numerous best-selling books such as *In Search of Excellence, The Fifth Discipline, Schools That Learn,* and *Principle-Centered Leader-*

ship. The basic theme permeating these books is that there are viable alternatives to the bureaucratic model. There is a strong implication that warm, nurturing, caring, trusting, challenging organizations produce high productivity in people.

Emergent Models of Organizational Structure

What appears to be emerging to replace bureaucracy is a heterarchical model of organization capable of performing collective activities toward the achievement of school goals. Leadership in these heterarchical organizations will need to be considerably different. In particular, significant changes are envisioned in the principalship (Murphy & Datnow, 2002). Principals will lead from the center rather than from the top. The major focus of leadership will be in supporting teacher success in the classroom. Change management will be an integral part of the leadership role of the principal. The principal will provide intellectual leadership to support teachers' change efforts. The principal will manage a school culture that supports a professional learning community focused on learning for all. Whatever their title or formal role definition, it is clear that principals continue to be best positioned to help guide faculty toward new forms of organizational structure (Louis & Kruse, 2000).

System 4 Design

As the human relations movement emerged, new approaches to organization design were developed (Lunenburg & Ornstein, 2004). One of the more popular approaches was Rensis Likert's System 4 design. Likert (1961, 1967, 1979, 1987) argued that the bureaucratic approach to leadership fails to consider the human side of organizations. His work focused less on the rational and mechanistic aspects of organizational structure and more on its social and psychological components.

After studying many organizations, including schools, Likert found that there was a significant relationship between organizational structure and effectiveness. Organizations that hewed to the bureaucratic model tended to be less effective, whereas effective organizations emphasized incorporating individuals and groups into the system as an integral part of leading. Likert developed eight dimensions or processes for use in comparing organizations: leadership processes, motivational processes, communication processes, interaction processes, decision processes, goal-setting processes, control processes, and performance goals.

Using these eight dimensions, Likert observed four design approaches that incorporate these dimensions. At one extreme, Likert identified a form of organization he called System 1. In many ways, a System 1 design is similar to the ideal bureaucracy. In sharp contrast, he described a humanistic, interactive, group-oriented design, which he called System 4 (Likert, 1987). Intermediate designs, Systems 2 and 3, are variants of the two extremes, which have received little attention. Table 7.2 summarizes the characteristics of a System 4 organizational structure and contrasts them with a System 1 approach.

Likert viewed the *System 4 structure* as the ideal state toward which principals should try to move their schools. Trust and confidence in the principal are extremely high among System 4 members. A variety of economic, ego, and social factors are used as incentives in motivating participants. Communication flows freely in all directions — upward, downward, and horizontally. Decision making occurs throughout the school and involves all members equally. Cooperative teamwork is encouraged in setting goals, and members are expected to engage in self- and group control. Principals actively seek high performance goals and are committed to professional development.

The System 4 structure, according to Likert, rests on the notion of *supportive relationships*. The underlying theory is that if a school is to be highly effective, the leadership and other processes of the school must ensure that, in all interactions between the principal and faculty, each faculty member will perceive the relationship as enhancing his or her own sense of personal worth

Table 7.2   System 1 and System 4 Designs

System 1 Organization	System 4 Organization
1. *Leadership process* includes no perceived confidence and trust. Subordinates do not feel free to discuss job problems with their superiors, who in turn do not solicit their ideas and opinions.	1. *Leadership process* includes perceived confidence and trust between superiors and subordinates in all matters. Subordinates feel free to discuss job problems with their superiors, who in turn solicit their ideas and opinions.
2. *Motivational process* taps only physical, security, and economic motives through the use of fear and sanctions. Unfavorable attitudes toward the organization prevail among employees.	2. *Motivational process* taps a full range of motives through participatory methods. Attitudes are favorable toward the organization and its goals.
3. *Communication process* is such that information flows downward and tends to be distorted, inaccurate, and viewed with suspicion by subordinates.	3. *Communication process* is such that information flows freely throughout the organization upward, downward, and laterally. The information is accurate and undistorted.
4. *Interaction process* is closed and restricted; subordinates have little effect on departmental goals, methods, and activities.	4. *Interaction process* is open and extensive; both superiors and subordinates are able to affect departmental goals, methods, and activities.
5. *Decision process* occurs only at the top of the organization; it is relatively centralized.	5. *Decision process* occurs at all levels through group processes; it is relatively decentralized.
6. *Goal-setting process* is located at the top of the organization; discourages group participation.	6. *Goal-setting process* encourages group participation in setting high, realistic objectives.
7. *Control process* is centralized and emphasizes fixing of blame for mistakes.	7. *Control process* is dispersed throughout the organization and emphasizes self-control and problem solving.
8. *Performance goals* are low and actively sought by managers who make no commitment to developing the human resources of the organization.	8. *Performance goals* are high and actively sought by superiors, who recognize the necessity for making a full commitment to developing, through training, the human resources of the organization.

and importance in the organization. Furthermore, Likert considered the members of the organization as being brought together through what he called *linking pins*. Every leadership position is linked to two groups of positions: a higher-level group of which the leader is a member and a lower-level group of which the leader is the head. For example, the principal is the manager of school personnel but also a subordinate to a leader at the central office in another group at the next level in the organization. Thus the principal serves as an important communication link between two levels of organization — school and school district.

Likert's System 4 structure is probably more a prescription for an ideal school or school district than a description of existing organizations. According to Likert, a school's effectiveness increases as it moves from a System 1 to a System 4 structure. System 4, then, serves as an ideal organization model toward which principals and other school leaders may aspire. On the other hand, the System 1 structure, like the bureaucratic model, was based on the assumption that there is only one best way to structure organizations.

Site-Based Management

The general public's dissatisfaction with schools has moved some to support *site-based management* (SBM) as a solution to the educational quality control problem (Murphy, 2002; Murphy & Datnow, 2002). Related to this are widespread efforts to decentralize many large school systems, like the Chicago Public Schools, as a possible answer to their perceived administrative failings (Hess, 1991).

The rationale advanced for both decentralization and SBM is to improve performance by making those closest to the delivery of services — teachers and principals — more responsible for the results of their schools' operations. This change involves shifting the initiative from school boards, superintendents, and central office staff to individual school sites. The thinking is that if teachers had the authority to make decisions at the building level, without being subject to the school system's bureaucracy, much better progress could be made. Furthermore, the authority to run schools should be shared with parents in order to establish a coordinated home-school effort (Epstein, 2001).

Site-based management is what management experts Thomas Peters and Robert Waterman (2004) refer to when they recommend breaking large businesses into smaller units to improve productivity. And an examination of some programs touted under the SBM banner suggests the process parallels older models of parent-teacher-administrator collaboration that effective schools and school districts have practiced for years.

Transformational Leadership

Transformational leadership focuses on leaders who have exceptional impact on their organizations. These individuals may be called transformational leaders. This view of leadership is extremely rare. Although the number of leaders involved is minimal, the impact these leaders have on their institutions is significant.

James McGregor Burns's (1978) prize-winning book first drew widespread attention to the concept of transformational leadership. Burns claimed that transformational leadership represents the transcendence of self-interest by both leader and led. Later, in his examination of the concept of transformational leadership, Bernard Bass has contrasted two types of leadership behaviors: transactional and transformational (Bass, 1985, 1997). According to Bass, transactional leaders determine what subordinates need to do to achieve their own and organizational objectives, classify those requirements, help subordinates become

confident that they can reach their objectives by expending the necessary efforts, and reward them according to their accomplishments. Transformational leaders, in contrast, motivate their subordinates to do more than they originally expected to do. They accomplish this in three ways: (1) by raising followers' levels of consciousness about the importance and value of designated outcomes and about ways of reaching them; (2) by getting followers to transcend their own self-interest for the sake of the team, organization, or larger polity; and (3) by raising followers' need levels to the higher-order needs, such as self-actualization, or by expanding their portfolio of needs.

Bennis's (2000) modified notion of transformative leadership is the ability of a person to reach the souls of others in a fashion that raises human consciousness, builds meanings, and inspires human intent that is the source of power between leaders and followers. Leithwood (1994) used another modification of Burns, this one based on Bass's (1985) two-factor theory in which transactional and transformational leadership represent opposite ends of the leadership continuum. Bass maintained that the two actually can be complementary.

The most fully developed model of transformational leadership in schools has been provided by Leithwood (1994), who identified seven factors that constitute transformational and transactional leadership. His model conceptualizes transformational leadership along eight dimensions: building school vision, establishing school goals, providing intellectual stimulation, offering individualized support, modeling best practices and important organizational values, demonstrating high performance expectations, creating a productive school culture, and developing structures to foster participation in school decisions.

Alfred Sloan reformed General Motors into its divisional profit centers. Henry Ford revolutionized the Ford Motor Company by introducing the assembly line for the production of automobiles. More recently, John Welch of General Electric, Steven Jobs of Apple Computer, and Roberto Goizueta of Coca-Cola guided the metamorphosis of their companies during the 1980s. And Lee Iacocca saved Chrysler Corporation from bankruptcy and brought it to profitability. All have become transformational leaders by creating a vision of a desired future for their companies, by instilling that vision in their followers, and by transforming their vision into reality.

Restructuring initiatives is primarily about building a shared vision, improving communication, and developing collaborative decision-making processes. Transformational leadership provides such a focus. According to Kenneth Leithwood (1992), transformational principals are in continuous pursuit of three fundamental goals:

- *Maintaining a collaborative culture.* Strategies used by principals to assist teachers in building and maintaining collaborative professional cultures include involving faculty members in collaborative goal setting, reducing teachers' isolation by creating time for joint planning, and creating mechanisms to support cultural changes.

- *Fostering teacher development.* Teachers' motivation for development is enhanced when they adopt a set of internalized goals for professional growth. This process is facilitated when they become involved in establishing a school mission to which they feel strongly committed.

- *Improving group problem solving.* Strategies principals can use to solve problems collaboratively include ensuring a broad range of perspectives from which to interpret the problem by actively seeking different interpretations, being explicit about their own interpretations, and placing individual problems in the larger perspective of the whole school.

Synergistic Leadership Theory

Modernist theories in leadership were traditionally dominated by masculine incorporation and lacked feminine presence in development and language. The synergistic leadership theory (SLT) developed by Irby, Brown, Duffy, and Trautman (2002) seeks to explicate the need for a postmodernist leadership theory by providing an alternative to, and not a replacement for, traditional theories. SLT includes issues concerning diversity and the inclusion of the female voice in the

theory. In a tetrahedron model, the theory uses four factors: (1) attitudes, beliefs, and values; (2) leadership behavior; (3) external forces; and (4) organizational structure to demonstrate not only aspects leadership, but its effects on various institutions and positions (see Figure 7.4).

Factor 1: Attitudes, Beliefs, and Values As shown in Figure 7.4, attitudes, beliefs, and values are depicted as dichotomous, because an individual or group would either adhere or not adhere to specific attitudes, beliefs, or values at a certain time. Some dichotomous examples follow: (a) believes in the importance of professional growth for all individuals including self; does not believe that professional development is important; (b) has an openness to change; does not have an openness to change; (c) values diversity; does not value diversity; (d) believes that integrity is important for all involved in schooling; does not value integrity.

Factor 2: Leadership Behavior The second factor of the theory, leadership behavior, derives directly from the literature on male and female leadership behaviors and is depicted as a range of behaviors from autocratic to nurturer. The range of behaviors include those ascribed to female principals, such as interdependence, cooperation, receptivity, merging acceptance, and being aware of patterns, wholes, and context; as well as those ascribed to male principals, including self-assertion, separation, independence, control, and competition.

Factor 3: External Forces External forces, as depicted in the model, are those influencers outside the control of the school or the principal that interact with the school and the principal and that inherently embody a set of values, attitudes, and beliefs. Significant external influencers or forces relate to local, national, and international community and conditions, governmental regulations, laws, demographics, cultural climate, technological advances, economic situations, political climate, family conditions, and geography. These examples of external forces as well as others, including those listed in the model, interact in significant, nontrivial ways with the other factors in SLT.

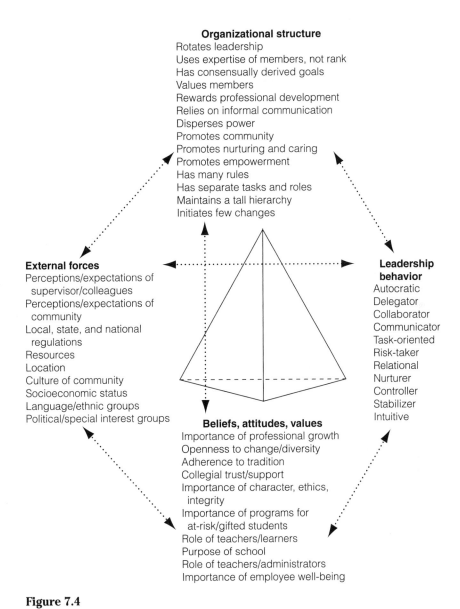

Organizational structure
Rotates leadership
Uses expertise of members, not rank
Has consensually derived goals
Values members
Rewards professional development
Relies on informal communication
Disperses power
Promotes community
Promotes nurturing and caring
Promotes empowerment
Has many rules
Has separate tasks and roles
Maintains a tall hierarchy
Initiates few changes

External forces
Perceptions/expectations of
  supervisor/colleagues
Perceptions/expectations of
  community
Local, state, and national
  regulations
Resources
Location
Culture of community
Socioeconomic status
Language/ethnic groups
Political/special interest groups

**Leadership
behavior**
Autocratic
Delegator
Collaborator
Communicator
Task-oriented
Risk-taker
Relational
Nurturer
Controller
Stabilizer
Intuitive

Beliefs, attitudes, values
Importance of professional growth
Openness to change/diversity
Adherence to tradition
Collegial trust/support
Importance of character, ethics,
  integrity
Importance of programs for
  at-risk/gifted students
Role of teachers/learners
Purpose of school
Role of teachers/administrators
Importance of employee well-being

Figure 7.4

Irby, Brown, Duffy, and Trautman's Synergistic Leadership Model
Source: Adapted from Beverly J. Irby, Genevieve Brown, Jo Ann Duffy, & Diane Trautman, "The Synergistic Leadership Theory," 2002, *Journal of Educational Administration, 40*, p. 313.

Factor 4: Organizational Structure   Organizational structure refers to characteristics of the school and how they operate. The SLT model (see Figure 7.4) depicts organizational structures as ranging from open, feminist organizations to tightly bureaucratic ones. Bureaucratic organizations include division of labor, rules, hierarchy of authority, impersonality, and competence;

whereas feminist organizations are characterized by practices such as participative decision making, systems of rotating leadership, promotion of community and cooperation, and power sharing.

In sum, SLT provides a framework for describing interactions and dynamic tensions among attitudes, beliefs, and values; leadership behaviors; external forces; and organizational structure. As a result, a principal can analyze and describe particular interactions that may account for tension, conflict, or harmony at specific points in time or over time. If it is discovered that tension exists between even two of the factors, then the effectiveness of the principal or the school itself can be negatively impacted. SLT is not only beneficial in determining "fit" while a principal is employed in a school district but also can be of assistance in job selection. Moreover, SLT can serve to build an understanding of the environment to aid in decisions made by the principal. And SLT fosters a reflective practice approach, because it encourages the leader to engage in self-assessment.

Total Quality Management

The Japanese transformed their economy and industry through a visionary management technique called *total quality management* (TQM). School leaders are finding that TQM principles can provide the formula for improving America's schools.

TQM, the latest business concept to reach the schools, is a systematic approach to education reform based on the philosophy of W. Edwards Deming (1988). Deming's work is not merely about productivity and quality control; it is a broad vision on the nature of organizations and how organizations should be changed.

Deming's philosophy provides a framework that can integrate many positive developments in education, such as team teaching, site-based management, cooperative learning, and outcomes-based education. Deming's 14 principles are based on the assumptions that people want to do their best and that it is the leader's job to enable them to do so by constantly improving the *system* in which they work (Deming, 1988, pp. 23–24). The framework for transforming an organization is outlined in the following 14 points:

1. *Create constancy of purpose for improvement of product and service.* For schools, constancy of purpose means thinking about the future. It requires expenditures in research and development and a continuous improvement of services for the client—the students.

2. *Adopt the new philosophy.* Implementation of Deming's principles will require a rethinking of the school's mission and priorities with everyone in agreement with them. What may be required is a total transformation of the American system of education as we know it.

3. *Cease dependence on inspection to achieve quality.* According to Deming, it always costs more to fix a problem than to prevent one. Examples of preventive approaches in schools are Head Start, Follow Through, preschool programs, and remedial interventions.

4. *End the practice of awarding business on the basis of price alone.* The lowest bid is rarely the most cost-efficient. Schools need to move toward a single supplier for any one time and develop long-term relationships of loyalty and trust with that supplier.

5. *Improve constantly and forever every activity in the organization, to improve quality and productivity.* For schools, this means requiring universal standards of achievement for all students before permitting them to move to the next level. Such provisions are stipulated in the *No Child Left Behind Act of 2001*.

6. *Institute training on the job.* For schools, this means providing continuous professional development activities for all teachers.

7. *Institute leadership.* The primary task of leadership is to narrow the amount of variation within the system, bringing everyone toward the goal of learning for *all*. It means removing achievement gaps for all population groups—a movement toward excellence and equity.

8. *Drive out fear.* Fear creates an insurmountable barrier to improvement of any system. In schools, faculty and staff are often afraid to point out problems because they fear they may be blamed. Principals need to communicate that staff suggestions are valued and rewarded.

9. *Break down barriers among staff areas.* In schools, different stakeholder groups have goals that conflict with each other. There needs to be collaboration between all stakeholders (students, staff, teachers, parents, community, and the principal) in promoting learning for all. It is the essence of initiating and maintaining a professional learning community.

10. *Eliminate slogans, exhortations, and targets that demand zero defects and new levels of productivity.* Implicit in most slogans, exhortations, and targets is the supposition that staff could do better if they tried harder. This offends rather than inspires the team. It creates adversarial relationships because the many causes of low quality and low productivity in schools are due to the system and not the staff. The system itself may need to be changed.

11. *Eliminate numerical quotas for the staff and goals for management.* Substitute aids and helpful supervision, using the methods described following.

12. *(a) Remove barriers that rob people of pride in their work. (b) Remove the barriers that rob people in leadership of their right to pride in their work.* Most people want to do a good job. Effective communication and the elimination of "de-motivators" — such as lack of involvement, poor information, the annual or merit rating, and supervisors who don't care — are critical.

13. *Institute a vigorous program of education and retraining for everyone.* The principal and staff must be retrained in new methods of school-based management, including group dynamics, consensus building, and collaborative styles of decision making. All stakeholders on the school's team must realize that improvements in student achievement will create higher levels of responsibility, not less responsibility.

14. *Put everyone in the organization to work to accomplish the transformation.* The school board and superintendent must have a clear plan of action to carry out the quality mission. The quality mission must be internalized by all members of the school organization (principal, faculty, staff, students, parents, community). The transformation is everybody's job.

A few years ago, the word *restructuring* was unheard of in education circles; today it is commonplace. Yet, few educators share a definition of what restructuring means. Most definitions incorporate the following ideas: school governance (including decentralized authority), new roles for educators (instructional leader), accountability (focus on student learning), and reforming the nature of the curriculum and how it is taught.

Regardless of how restructuring is defined, unless the entire reform agenda focuses on student achievement and on discussion of how to attain it, restructuring will produce only minimal changes in students' education.

Nothing is more fundamental to schooling than its content. School principals will find the following 10 concepts, culled from the many subject-matter organizations, helpful in their work on restructuring the content of schooling (Lunenburg, 1992).

1. *Heterogeneous grouping.* All of the recent reform documents call for ending tracking and reducing ability grouping.

2. *Cooperative learning.* This concept has worked very effectively with at-risk students. Students will engage in far less competitive learning. In heterogeneous groups, they will work democratically and collaboratively.

3. *High expectations for all.* All students, if motivated and provided adequate opportunities, can learn important, challenging, and interesting content. Important knowledge is no longer for an elite few. It is for all students,

regardless of their social circumstances or career aspirations.

4. *Responsiveness to student diversity.* Principals should view the increasing cultural, linguistic, and socioeconomic diversity of the student population as an opportunity as well as a challenge. Curriculum content and pedagogical approaches must build on and be respectful of the diversity.

5. *Emphasis on active learning.* Students will spend far less time passively receiving knowledge. They will spend far more time — sometimes individually, often in groups — doing, experimenting, and discovering knowledge and understanding for themselves.

6. *Essential curriculum.* Schools should select the most important concepts and skills to emphasize, so that they can concentrate on the quality of understanding rather than on the quantity of information presented. Students will acquire the tools to add to their knowledge independently.

7. *Authentic assessment.* The type of assessment employed will be determined by the learning being measured. This means there will be increased use of performance as a means of assessment. Educators as well as students will be held accountable for what students can do instead of relying solely on standardized test results.

8. *Technology as a tool.* Computers, videodiscs, satellite TV, and other state-of-the-art technologies should be viewed as resources to enhance learning, not as symbols of excellence or innovation.

9. *Time as a learning resource.* School time will need to be organized around learning, instead of the other way around. Teacher and principal needs will have to be secondary to the needs of learners. The typical 50-minute, seven-period school day may need to be restructured to fit the curricula content.

10. *Diverse pedagogy.* Educators will need to employ more diverse and more balanced kinds of teaching and learning experiences to implement curricula. This will require new kinds of teacher training and staff development for teachers and principals.

Summary

1. The internal structure of schools differs along a number of dimensions. Among the most important of these are job specialization, departmentalization, delegation, decentralization, span of management, and line and staff.

2. Job specialization, which involves grouping various jobs into units, can either contribute significantly to school effectiveness or create a problem. On the one hand, specialization provides the necessary mechanism for development of job skills and expertise. On the other hand, highly specialized jobs may increase employee boredom, dissatisfaction, absenteeism, and turnover.

3. Departmentalization involves the grouping of jobs according to some logical arrangement. Most schools employ functional departmentalization.

4. Delegation, the process of establishing a pattern of authority between a leader and a staff member, consists of three basic components: assigning responsibility, granting authority, and creating accountability.

5. At the overall organizational level, the establishment of patterns of authority is called decentralization. Factors influencing the degree of decentralization include cost, risk associated with the decision, leader's preference for involvement, confidence in staff, and organizational culture.

6. Span of management refers to the number of staff members who report directly to a leader. Critical factors in determining the appropriate span of management include similarity of functions, geographic proximity, complexity of function, degree of interdependence, level of motivation of staff, and competence of leaders.

7. Line and staff positions, as opposed to line positions exclusively, can enhance organizational effectiveness. Line positions are those that form a part of the main line of authority that flows throughout the school district. Staff positions are positions outside the main line of authority that are primarily advisory or supportive in nature. Examples in schools include the legal counsel and assistant to the superintendent.

8. The open systems view of schools provides an excellent framework for analyzing the process of education as consisting of the interaction of inputs, a transformation process, outputs, and feedback loops.

9. Every principal's goal is to ensure high performance of students and faculty in achieving the school's mission. High performance requires the effective use of organizational resources through the management functions of planning, organizing, leading, and monitoring.

10. Just looking at the principal's four leadership functions provides an incomplete picture of the principal's job. Researchers who observed principals on the job identified three characteristics of a principal's role: principals perform a heavy workload at an unrelenting pace; principals' activities are varied, fragmented, and brief; and principals prefer oral communication.

11. In order to perform these functions and roles, principals need three skills — conceptual, human, and technical. Conceptual skills are more important at the top of the school district's hierarchy; human skills are important at all levels; and technical skills are more important for first-line supervisors, such as department heads and team leaders.

12. Studies of effective principals reveal that the major reason for principal failure is the inability to deal with people. Effective principals have excellent people skills and focus on student learning.

13. There are many dysfunctions of the bureaucratic model, including those dealing with division of labor and specialization, uniform rules and procedures, hierarchy of authority, impersonality in interpersonal relations, and lifelong career and loyalty to the organization. New viewpoints are leading to a decline in the use of bureaucratic structure in schools.

14. Likert's System 4 design grew out of the human relations movement and is the antithesis of the ideal bureaucracy (which Likert calls System 1). An important component of System 4 is the linking-pin concept, relating levels of organization.

15. The general public's dissatisfaction with schools has moved some to support site-based management as a solution to improving performance, by making those closest to the delivery of services — teachers and principals — more accountable for the results of their schools' operations.

16. Other contemporary perspectives on organizational structures in schools, ones that are at the frontier, take several forms. They include transformational leadership, synergistic leadership theory (SLT), and total quality management (TQM).

Field-Based Activities

1. Analyze the internal structure of your school in terms of the following six concepts: job specialization, departmentalization, delegation, decentralization, span of management, and line and staff. Describe the evidence of the functioning of each of the six components operating in your school. What can you conclude from your analysis? Be specific.

2. Describe the existing administrative structure in your school using a continuum from bureaucratic, hierarchical management to System 4, site-based management (SBM), contingency organization design. Take field notes for one week and observe the existence of one or the other administrative structure. What can you conclude from your observations concerning

outcomes, such as teacher growth and development, job satisfaction and morale, student success, absenteeism, dropout rate, and so forth?

3. To what extent is your school an open system? Take field notes for one week. Analyze your observations in terms of the interactions of inputs, transformation process, outputs, and feedback loops. Describe how each component of the open systems model is functioning in your school. Be specific.

Suggested Readings

Fullan, M. (2001). *Leading in a culture of change.* San Francisco: Jossey-Bass. Good leadership is not innate. Leadership today requires the ability to mobilize constituents to do important but difficult work under conditions of constant change, overload, and fragmentation. Fullan offers new and seasoned leaders insights into the dynamics of change and presents a unique and imaginative approach for navigating the intricacies of the change process. *Leading in a Culture of Change* shows leaders how they can effectively accomplish their goals — by attending to their broader moral purpose, understanding the change process, cultivating relationships, sharing knowledge, and setting a vision and context for creating coherence in their organization.

Hanson, E. M. (2003). *Educational administration and organizational behavior* (5th ed.). Boston: Allyn & Bacon. This text makes a practical link between social science theory and the practice of leading educational systems. Hanson facilitates understanding of how educational organizations function as learning and sociopolitical systems, and then provides conceptual and analytical tools to facilitate real-world problem solving. Social and behavioral science frameworks are used to identify and explain three widely held perspectives on the administration of educational organizations: the school as a bureaucratic system, the

school as a social system, and the school as an open system.

Kouzes, J. M., & Posner, B. Z. (2002). *The leadership challenge* (3rd ed.). San Francisco: Jossey-Bass. Now in its third edition, this best-selling leadership book of all time explores the evolving essence of quality leadership in organizations around the world. This unprecedented resource includes more solid research and examples of real leaders than any other leadership book available.

Lambert, L., et al. (2002). *The constructivist leader* (2nd ed.). New York: Teachers College Press. Since publication of the first edition in 1995, *The Constructivist Leader* has provided educational leaders at all levels with a conceptual framework for leadership defined as reciprocal, purposeful learning in community. Today, learning communities based on constructivist principles are a major part of the school improvement landscape. The second edition of this best-selling book enables readers to carry this constructivist vision and purpose forward while effectively implementing standards-based reform, authentic assessment, and constructivist-based accountability.

Owens, R. G. (2004). *Organizational behavior in education: Adaptive leadership and school reform* (8th ed.). Boston: Allyn & Bacon. The eighth edition of *Organizational Behavior in Education* relates the study of educational leadership to the challenge of how leaders can participate effectively in school reform. Readers are challenged to develop and act upon a game plan for implementing school reform throughout the text. Issues arising from the No Child Left Behind Act of 2001 receive major emphasis in this edition. This edition continues to examine aspects of organizational behavior such as organizational culture, diversity, leadership, motivation, change, conflict, and decision making while maintaining high standards of scholarship and a lucid, readily accessible writing style.

Sergiovanni, T. J. (2000). *Leadership for the schoolhouse: How is it different? Why is it important?* San Francisco: Jossey-Bass. Sergiovanni believes education must develop its own theories and practices based on what schools are trying to do and the kinds of people schools serve.

Soder, R. (2001). *The language of leadership.* San Francisco: Jossey-Bass. Soder examines the relationship between language and effective leadership. Author Roger Soder shows leaders how to use ethical persuasion to cultivate public trust and build legitimacy for their case. And most important, *The Language of Leadership* clearly demonstrates how a leader can accomplish this within the context of democracy and the larger context of leadership.

8

The Principal as Decision Maker

> **Standard 3.0:** *Candidates who complete the program are educational leaders who have the knowledge and ability to promote the success of all students by managing the organization, operations, and resources in a way that promotes a safe, efficient, and effective learning environment.*

FOCUSING QUESTIONS

1 Why is decision making such an important activity for principals?

2 How do principals make decisions?

3 Why do schools make less than optimal decisions to solve their problems?

4 Why share decision making with others when one exceptional person may make more accurate decisions than a group?

5 When should a principal involve others in the decision-making process?

6 Are there decision-making techniques that can help to improve shared decision making?

In this chapter, we respond to these questions concerning decision making in school organizations. We begin our discussion by examining the nature of decision making in schools. Then we describe the major steps in the decision-making process. Next, we discuss the assumptions of rationality and identify factors that limit rationality. We explore the advantages and disadvantages of shared decision making and present a technique for increasing the advantages while simultaneously decreasing the disadvantages. Finally, we examine three models for determining the level of involvement of staff in the decision-making process.

The Nature of Decision Making

Decisions are made at all levels of school organization. The superintendent makes decisions concerning a school district's goals and strategies. Then principals make tactical decisions concerning those goals and strategies to accomplish them in relation to their own buildings. Department heads and team leaders then make curricular and operational decisions to carry out the day-to-day activities of a department or unit. And, finally, classroom teachers make decisions in their classrooms.

Consider the following decisions that need to be made at different organizational levels:

- How much inventory should be carried in the school district warehouse?
- Where should the newly proposed elementary school be located?
- Should the school district renovate the old high school or build a new one?
- How many classes of freshman English should our department offer next semester?
- What textbook series should the mathematics department adopt?
- Should all of our principals attend the conference on the use of technology?
- What minimum rules should I adopt in my classroom?

Questions such as these require an answer. Someone is going to have to do some decision making in order to provide answers.

Decision making is a process of making a choice from a number of alternatives to achieve a desired result (Bhushan, 2003). This definition has three key elements. First, decision making involves making a choice from a number of options—the school district can carry more or less inventory of school supplies, and the math department can choose the Macmillan or McGraw-Hill math series. Second, decision making is a process that involves more than simply a final choice from among alternatives—if the school district decides to renovate the existing high school rather than build a new one, we want to know how this decision was reached. Finally, the "desired result" mentioned in the definition involves a purpose or target resulting from the mental activity that the decision maker engages in to reach a final decision—to locate the new elementary school on the east side of town.

Decision making is a way of life for principals. Although everyone in a school makes some

decisions, principals are paid to make decisions. Their main responsibility lies in making decisions rather than performing routine operations. The quality of the decisions made is a predominant factor in how the superintendent views a principal's performance. Furthermore, decision making affects the performance of a school or school district and the welfare of its stakeholders: students, teachers, parents, and the community.

Decisions made in schools should result in changes that cause meaningful differences in student academic achievement. Student learning in the complex, multicultural environment of contemporary schools depends on more than a comfortable faculty lounge, ample supplies for teachers, and site-based management that avoids discussion of the real issues associated with teaching and learning.

Several years ago, Mac Bernd (1992) provided an excellent model of shared decision making that requires effective instructional leadership from the principal. According to Bernd, for schools to promote learning for all students and teacher involvement in decisions that increase student learning, today's principal must do the following:

- *Guide decisions that are consistent with the beliefs that all students can learn.* The belief that all students can learn is essential, because it holds faculty accountable for student success or failure. Faculty acceptance of responsibility for student achievement shifts responsibility away from factors beyond school control, like ethnicity or poverty, toward factors under school control—like school climate and culture, direct instruction, or cooperative learning.

- *Focus a majority of time on supervising instruction through classroom observation.* Effective principals spend considerable time observing and coaching teachers in the classroom, which enables teachers to more effectively practice the art and science of teaching.

- *Understand and apply conferencing and coaching techniques.* Instructional leadership depends on the principal's ability to teach teachers how to improve their instruction by understanding and applying specific behaviors.

■ *Encourage decisions that result in greater alignment among curriculum, instruction, and assessment.* Effective principals do more than insist that curriculum alignment takes place; they develop their own expertise, so they can lead teachers in these efforts. This means that principals must be familiar with state and district curricular goals, be able to recognize properly written instructional objectives, and be able to criticize written assessment items.

The Decision-Making Process

It is useful to conceptualize the decision-making process as a series of steps that a principal might take to solve a problem (Sioukas, 2003). (See Figure 8.1.)

After a problem is identified, alternative solutions to the problem are generated. These are carefully evaluated, and the best alternative is chosen for implementation. The implemented alternative is then evaluated over time to assure its immediate and continued effectiveness. If difficulties arise at any stage in the process, recycling may be required.

Thus we see that decision making is a logical sequence of activities. That is, before alternatives are generated, the problem must be identified, and so on. Furthermore, decision making is an iterative activity. As shown in Figure 8.1, decision making is a recurring event, and principals can learn from past decisions. In the following sections we elaborate on each of these steps and explain their interrelationships.

Identifying the Problem

Schools exist to achieve certain goals, such as educating students. Within the school, each department or subunit has goals, such as increasing test scores, reducing dropouts, and/or developing new approaches to teaching. Establishing these goals becomes the basis for identifying problem areas, deciding on courses of action, and evaluating the decision outcomes. A decision is said to be effective if it helps a principal to achieve a specific

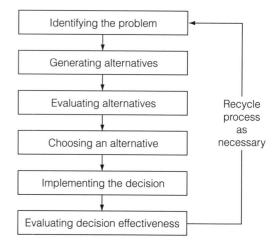

Figure 8.1

The Decision-Making Process

objective or set of goals for the school. Failure to achieve a desired goal becomes a problem, and the principal is ultimately responsible for solving it.

Effective decision makers are keenly aware of the importance of properly *identifying the problem* and understanding the problem situation. Kepner and Tregoe (2004) developed a method of problem analysis suggesting that the first step in decision making, identifying the problem, is the most important step. According to these authors, providing a good definition of the problem affects the quality of the decision. Their method suggests that it is often easier to define what the problem is not, rather than what it is. Also, the problem — and its solution — is prioritized with other problems, to clarify its relative importance. The final step is searching for cause-effect relationships. In summary, Kepner and Tregoe's method of problem analysis includes (a) problem identification, (b) definition of what the problem is and is not, (c) prioritizing the problem, and (d) testing for cause-effect relationships.

The process of identifying problems requires surveillance of the internal and external environment for issues that merit attention. Principals scan the world around them to determine whether the school is progressing satisfactorily toward its goals. For example, principals survey students, teachers, parents, and community members using instruments to measure satisfaction, organizational climate, and the like. Other information may come from formal information systems, such as periodic accounting reports, Management Information System (MIS) reports, and organizational plans designed to discover problems before they become too serious. Or the information may be gathered informally by talking over the situation and by personal observation. A principal, for example, might discuss a productivity problem with teachers, the superintendent, or other principals to obtain ideas and information. The principal must be plugged into an information system, whether formal or informal, that gathers these data as a means of identifying problems.

In addition to identifying problems, the principal must define the situation, which is partly a matter of determining how a specific problem arose. This is an important stage, because the situation definition plays a major role in subsequent steps. Suppose, for example, that a school has had decreasing test scores for the last two years. One principal might define this situation as the result of a changing student population in the school attendance area and then begin to search for new approaches to teaching these students, who come from lower socioeconomic backgrounds. Another principal might define the situation as a case of an inappropriate match between what is taught and what is measured—that is, placing the blame on the achievement test being used. The problem of declining test scores is the same in both cases, but the two different definitions of the situation call for two different solutions.

Generating Alternatives

Once the problem has been identified, the second step in the decision-making process is to *generate alternatives* to the problem. In developing these alternative solutions, principals first must specify the goals that they hope to achieve through their decision. Are they trying to reduce the dropout rate, improve the quality of instruction, increase test scores, or something else? Once principals

have determined their goals, they can search for alternative means of reaching them. Information must be collected regarding each of the alternatives and their likely consequences. More specifically, the principal must seek to learn as much as possible concerning (a) the likelihood that each alternative will result in the achievement of various outcomes and (b) the extent to which those outcomes will contribute to the achievement of the goals and objectives being sought.

Ideally, the principal should seek to generate as many alternatives as possible and should attempt to ensure that the alternatives are relatively diverse, that is, not highly similar to one another. The extent of the search for alternatives is limited by the importance of the decision, the cost and value of additional information needed to evaluate alternatives, and the number of people affected by the decision (Forgang, 2004).

The more important the decision, the more attention is directed to developing alternatives. For example, if the decision involves where to build a new multimillion-dollar high school, a great deal of time and effort will be devoted to identifying the best location. On the other hand, if the problem is to select a color to paint the classrooms in the new high school, less time and effort will be devoted to the activity.

The length and thoroughness of the search for alternatives depend on the cost of evaluating additional alternatives. For example, a 2% improvement in the solution of a $10 million problem may produce a profit margin of $200,000. However, if the cost of evaluating an additional alternative is $250,000, the evaluation costs $50,000 more than the possible savings. As a rule of thumb, the increase in the improvement of a solution should always be more than the cost of performing the additional evaluation of an alternative. Moreover, the greater the number of people affected by a problem, the more likely the organization will conduct a lengthy and thorough search for alternatives (Narayanan, 2004). However, when dealing with complex school problems affecting numerous people, it is often necessary to compromise on some points. Human benefits cannot be measured in dollars and cents (Shanteau, 2004).

Evaluating Alternatives

The third step in the decision-making process is *evaluating* each of the *alternatives* generated in step 2. In evaluating an alternative, principals must ask the following three questions: (1) "Is the alternative feasible?" (2) "Is it a satisfactory alternative?" (3) "What impact will it have on people?" (Adair, 2003).

The first question—whether the alternative is feasible—simply means "Can it be done?" For example, if one alternative requires a general layoff of school faculty but the school district has a collective bargaining agreement that prohibits such layoffs, that alternative is not feasible. Similarly, if a school district has limited capital, alternatives that require large capital outlays are not feasible unless funds can be borrowed to meet the capital outlay requirements.

The second question concerns the extent to which the alternative is satisfactory, that is, the extent to which it addresses the problem. For instance, suppose the principal wants to expand the curriculum by 25%. One alternative is to implement a trimester schedule. On closer examination, however, the principal may discover that the plan would expand the curriculum by only 15% and that such a modest expansion may also negatively affect the quality of the program. The principal may decide to implement the trimester plan anyway; he will then search for other ways to achieve the remaining 10% expansion in the curriculum and find ways to maintain the quality of the program. Or he may decide to drop the alternative from consideration entirely.

The third question addresses the impact of an alternative on school personnel. The alternative that is chosen must be acceptable to those who must live with the consequences of the decision. Failure to meet this condition is the single most likely reason for failure of the decision-making process to solve problems (Davidson et al., 2003). For this reason, questions of acceptability of a proposed alternative should be of great concern to the principal. On the one hand, even a mediocre solution to the problem may prove effective if it is implemented with enthusiasm and commitment. On the other hand, a technically correct alternative may fail to succeed if implementation is halfhearted.

Choosing an Alternative

Once the principal has evaluated all of the alternatives, he attempts to *choose* the best *alternative*. The evaluation phase will have eliminated some of the alternatives, but in most cases two or more will remain.

How does a principal decide which alternative is the best? One approach is to select the alternative that is feasible, satisfactory, and acceptable to the work group. Because most situations do not lend themselves to sophisticated mathematical analysis, the principal uses this available information in combination with judgment and intuition to make the decision (Davis & Davis, 2003). The basis of judgment should be how close the outcomes or consequences of the alternatives come to achieving the desired goals of the school. For example, if the original goal was to decrease the dropout rate as much as possible, regardless of the costs, the principal might choose an alternative that will decrease the dropout rate significantly but that carries a high cost, rather than an alternative that would reduce dropouts only moderately at a minimal cost. However, if the original goal was to reduce the dropout rate by a moderate amount and if that goal is more desirable now, the second alternative might be a better choice.

Finally, the principal may be able to choose several alternatives simultaneously. Suppose, for example, she is hiring an English teacher and has two strong candidates for the position. One frequently used strategy is to offer the position to one candidate and keep the other candidate on hold. Should the first offer be rejected, the principal still has an acceptable alternative to fill position.

Implementing the Decision

After choosing an alternative, the principal faces the challenge of *implementing the decision*. A sound decision can fail if implemented poorly. It is useful, therefore, to consider some suggestions for successful implementation (Kirton, 2003).

1. *Principals need to make sure that the alternative is clearly understood.* This is accomplished by communicating the decision to all involved

staff. Effective communication is necessary for effectively implementing decisions.

2. ***Principals need to encourage acceptance of the alternative as a necessary course of action.*** Committees can help a principal achieve commitment. If the people who must carry out a decision participate in the process, they are more likely to be enthusiastic about the outcome. Thus the degree to which persons have or have not been involved in prior steps may substantially affect the success of the total decision-making process (Lunenburg & Ornstein, 2004).

3. ***Principals need to provide enough resources to make the alternative succeed.*** Principals set up budgets and schedules for the actions they have decided to undertake. Specifically, the decision may require acquiring office space, hiring staff, procuring funds, and the like.

4. ***Principals need to establish workable timelines.*** The principal now faces a "how much" and "how soon" decision. As part of the process of implementation, he must ask himself whether to move forward step-by-step or whether to take the entire action at once.

5. ***Principals need to assign responsibilities clearly.*** In other words, what should be done by whom? Because the solution of most administrative problems requires the combined effort of many school members, each person should understand what role he or she is to play during each phase of the implementation process.

Evaluating Decision Effectiveness

The final step in the decision-making process is *evaluating the effectiveness* of the decision. When an implemented decision does not produce the desired results, there are probably a number of causes: incorrect definition of the problem, poor evaluation of alternatives, improper implementation, or any combination of these factors. Among these possible causes, the most common and serious error is an inadequate definition of the problem. When the problem is incorrectly defined, the

alternative that is selected and implemented will not produce the desired result.

Evaluation is important because decision making is a continuous process. Decision making does not end when a principal votes yes or no. Evaluation provides principals with information that can precipitate a new decision cycle. The decision alternative may fail, thus generating a new analysis of the problem, evaluation of alternatives, and selection of a new alternative. Some experts suggest that many large problems are solved by attempting several alternatives in sequence, each providing a modest improvement (Gelatt et al., 2003). Evaluation is the part of the decision-making process that assesses whether a new decision needs to be made.

The Rational Decision Maker

Administrative decision making is assumed to be *rational*. By this we mean that principals make decisions under certainty: They know their alternatives; they know their outcomes; they know their decision criteria; and they have the ability to make the optimum choice and then to implement it (Hardman et al., 2003). In this section, we examine the underlying assumptions of rationality and then determine how valid these assumptions are in school organizations.

Assumptions of Rationality

If a decision maker were completely rational, she would have perfect information: know all alternatives, determine every consequence, and establish a complete preference scale. Moreover, the steps in the decision-making process would consistently lead toward selecting the alternative that maximizes the solution to each decision problem (see Figure 8.2).

The following points summarize the assumptions of *rational decision making* (Robbins, 2004a).

■ ***Problem clarity.*** In rational decision making, the *problem identity* is clear and unambiguous. The principal is assumed to have complete

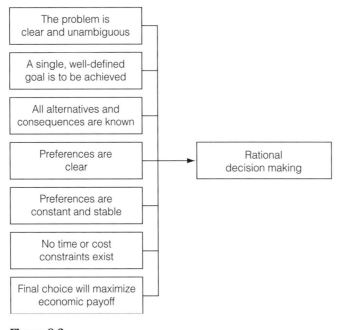

Figure 8.2

Assumptions of Rationality

information regarding the problem and the decision situation.

▪ **Goal orientation.** In rational decision making, there is no conflict concerning the *goal orientation.* Whether the decision involves increasing test scores, reducing dropouts, or developing new approaches to teaching, the principal has a single, well-defined goal that he is trying to reach.

▪ **Known options.** It is assumed that the principal is creative, can identify all relevant criteria, and can list all the viable alternatives; she *knows* all *options.* Further, the principal is aware of all the possible consequences for each alternative.

▪ **Clear preferences.** Rationality assumes that the criteria and alternatives can be ranked in order of importance, that there are *clear preferences.*

▪ **Constant preferences.** In addition to a clear goal and preferences, it is assumed that the specific decision criteria are *constant* and the

scales or weights assigned to them are stable over time.

▪ **No time or cost constraints.** The rational principal can obtain full information about criteria and alternatives because it is assumed there are no *time* or *cost constraints.*

▪ **Maximization.** The rational principal always chooses the alternative that will yield the maximum payoff to the school. It should be noted here that the principal is assumed to be *maximizing* the school's interests, not the interests of the principal.

Rational decision making assumes that decision makers have a tremendous mental capacity both for remembering and storing huge quantities of information and for processing that information in order to choose the optimum solution to each decision problem. Although administrative decision making can follow rational assumptions, most decisions that principals face do not meet all the criteria of complete rationality.

Limits to Rationality

Frequently, school principals are not aware that problems exist. Even when they are, they do not systematically search for all possible alternative solutions. They are limited by time constraints, cost, and the ability to process information. So they generate a partial list of alternative solutions to the problem based on their experience, intuition, advice from others, and perhaps even some creative thought. Rationality is, therefore, limited. Herbert Simon (1982, 1997) coined the term *bounded rationality* to describe the decision maker who would like to make the best decisions but normally settles for less than the optimal.

In contrast to complete rationality in decision making, bounded rationality implies the following (Zey, 1992):

1. Decisions will always be based on an incomplete and, to some degree, inadequate comprehension of the true nature of the problem being faced.

2. Decision makers will never succeed in generating all possible alternative solutions for consideration.

3. Alternatives are always evaluated incompletely because it is impossible to accurately predict all consequences associated with each alternative.

4. The ultimate decision regarding which alternative to choose must be based on some criterion other than maximization or optimization because it is impossible to ever determine which alternative is optimal.

Satisficing   One version of bounded rationality is the principle of *satisficing*. This approach to decision making involves choosing the first alternative that satisfies minimal standards of acceptability without exploring all possibilities. This is the usual approach taken by decision makers (Stirling, 2003). James March, another renowned decision theorist, expresses it this way: "Most human decision making, whether individual or organizational, is concerned with the discovery and selection of satisfactory alternatives; only in exceptional cases is it concerned with the discovery and selection of optimal alternatives" (March, 1978, p. 587).

Heuristics   When principals make satisficing decisions, they may use a set of heuristics to guide their decisions. A *heuristic* is a rule of thumb that can help the decision maker find a solution in a complex and uncertain situation (Moustakas, 1990). We use heuristics in our everyday lives. For example, a heuristic rule for dealing with other people is the Golden Rule: "Do unto others as you would have them do unto you." Football coaches use the rule, "When in doubt, punt." In playing chess, we follow the rule of "controlling the center of the board." And a heuristic for investors is that if a stock drops 10% or more below its purchased price, they should sell.

In management science, many well-known heuristics are used to make a wide variety of decisions: "'The customer is always right'; 'Treat employees as mature adults'; 'When in doubt, stick to the business you know best'" (Peters & Waterman, 2004). These are all rules that help simplify complex decision-making situations. Applying heuristics often helps principals make satisficing decisions possible. But the heuristic approach, as with judgment and intuition, has a tendency to oversimplify complex problems or introduce bias into decision making.

Primacy/Recency Effect   One bias that may decrease the effectiveness of a principal's information search behavior is the primacy/recency effect. In the decision-making process, the decision environment is searched for the following purposes: finding problems, identifying decision alternatives, determining consequences, and developing evaluation criteria. Although decision makers may have different strategies for these different purposes, the decision maker is often inordinately influenced by information discovered early in the search process (the *primacy effect*) or late in the search process (the *recency effect*). Thus, everything else being equal, the importance attached to information may be affected by its order in the search sequence (Brown & Moberg, 2004).

Bolstering the Alternative Another way in which the search for information is biased and inhibits decision optimization is the phenomenon of *bolstering the alternative* (Bubnicki, 2003). Even before accumulating the information on which to base a decision, the principal may prefer one alternative to all the others; the decision maker, therefore, searches for information that rationalizes the choice. Only information that supports the decision maker's preferred alternative is considered legitimate and acceptable.

A related bias in the search for information is the principal's professional training and identification with a particular department that may also bolster the alternative. For example, an assistant superintendent for curriculum may tend to view most problems with a curriculum bias, regardless of their nature, and an assistant superintendent of finance (business manager or chief financial officer) may perceive the same problems in terms of finance. Although such biases are bound to exist, it is important to understand that they can strongly influence a decision maker's ability to make accurate decisions.

Intuition Another aspect of bounded rationality, mentioned previously, is intuition. *Intuition* represents a quick apprehension of a decision situation based on past experiences and the reinforcement associated with these experiences, through a process that is devoid of conscious thought (Davis & Davis, 2003). For example, when you are driving an automobile the decision to apply the brakes is intuitive, because it comes almost automatically and without reasoning. Years of driving experience have taught us precisely when to apply the brakes. The same type of intuition often guides a principal's decisions. The decision to discipline a staff member or to buy an item for inventory may be quite intuitive for the principal and is based on years of experience.

Research on administrative behavior in schools is consistent in identifying the demands on the principal as fragmented, rapid-fire, and difficult to prioritize (Doud, 1989a,b; Doud & Keller, 1998; Ferrandino, 2001; Fawcett et al., 2001;

Kmetz & Willower, 1982; Martin & Willower, 1981; Ubben, Hughes, & Norris, 2004). Half of the activities of principals last less than 10 minutes, and only 8% exceed an hour (Estler, 1988; Leithwood & Duke, 1999). Researchers conclude that principals are action oriented and do not like reflective activities. These data support the observation that much decision making is intuitive. The fast and hectic pace of a principal's job makes the use of intuition almost a necessity.

Incrementalizing Another approach to decision making, sometimes referred to as *muddling through,* involves making small changes (increments) in the existing situation. Charles Lindblom (1993), in *The Science of Muddling Through,* distinguishes between completely rational decision making, based on the rational decision-making model, and *incrementalizing,* which is based on successive limited comparisons. On the one hand, the rational approach to decision making involves determining objectives, considering all possible alternative solutions, exploring all conceivable consequences of the alternative solutions, and finally choosing the optimal alternative solution that maximizes achievement of the agreed-on goals. Incrementalizing, on the other hand, does not require agreement on goals, an exhaustive search of all possible alternatives and their consequences, or selection of the optimal alternative. Instead, Lindblom argues, no more than taking small or incremental steps — that is, "muddling through" — is possible. In other words, incrementalizing is a process of successive limited comparisons of alternative courses of action with one another until decision makers arrive at an alternative on which they agree.

The Garbage-Can Model Earlier we noted that while the school principal wants to make optimal decisions, the realities of organizational life — including politics, time constraints, finances, and the inability to process information — limit purely rational decision making. Applying rational decision making is particularly troublesome for schools. The technologies of teaching are varied and not well understood. Moreover, schools have multiple and conflicting goals that are vague and ambiguous. And schools lack clearly defined success criteria (Elmore, 2000). Thus problems and solutions cannot be translated easily into a logical sequence of steps (rational decision-making model).

In accordance with this view, David Cohen, James March, and Johan Olsen (1972) conceptualized this decision-making process as a *garbage-can model*. As members of a school or school district generate problems and alternative solutions to problems, they deposit them into the garbage can. The mixture is seen as a collection of solutions that must be matched to problems. Participants are also deposited into the garbage can. Mixing problems, solutions, and decision participants results in interaction patterns leading to decisions that often do not follow purely rational decision making.

Shared Decision Making

Although the decision-making process focuses primarily on the individual decision maker, groups make many of the decisions in schools (Lunenburg & Ornstein, 2004). These groups may be called committees, teams, task forces, site-based councils, and the like. But, regardless of what they are called, they make decisions. And, very often, decisions are reached through some kind of consensus process rather than by majority vote (Straus, 2002). Making the move to shared decision making is not an easy process, but the positive results in terms of faculty commitment are encouraging. Ownership of and commitment to a decision are essential if we are to restructure schools and revamp curriculum to meet the needs of students in the 21st century (Lunenburg, 2002, 2003). Real, substantive change occurs with the teacher. Without committed teachers, reform efforts will be unsuccessful. Shared decision making then must capitalize on teacher expertise (Lunenburg & Irby, 1999).

Shared decision making has both advantages and disadvantages. A thorough understanding of these benefits and problems can help a principal determine when to encourage or discourage shared decision making and how to improve the quality of group decisions (Valesky, 2002).

Because it takes time to develop a comfort level for both the principal and faculty concerning shared decision making, a few years ago, Huddleston, Claspell, and Killion (1991) proposed a four-phase process to involve teachers in the school's decisions and developed some strategies principals can use to help teachers participate more fully in school decision making.

Phase One: Readiness. In this initial phase, principals plan for and begin to move toward shared decision making. While maintaining control over all phases of the process, they establish the school climate and culture in which the process can begin to develop. They determine what decisions will be shared, who will participate in the process, and how involved participants will be.

Phase Two: Experimentation. This phase focuses on building comfort and familiarity with faculty involvement in decisions. Because the faculty members and the principal are experimenting with shared decision making, the emphasis is on the evolving process rather than on the decisions themselves. The extent of involvement is the option of the faculty. In most cases, some teachers commit to the concept of shared decision making and work with the principal to begin defining the process for the school.

Phase Three: Refinement. In the third phase, principals begin to share with faculty the process for decision making as well as the decisions themselves. Teachers assist in determining what will be decided in a shared manner and who will be involved. They also assist in refining the process by which decisions are made.

Phase Four: Institutionalization. At this point, shared decision making becomes the norm in the school. Based on the school's history, the process of shared decision making may be formal or informal. The faculty and principal determine jointly which decisions will be shared and what process will be used to make decisions. The faculty assume the responsibility for their decisions and monitor their decision-making process.

Advantages and Disadvantages of Shared Decision Making

What advantages do groups have over individuals in making decisions? Some assets of shared decision making include the following (Baron et al., 2003; Galanes, 2003; Koutsoukis, 2003; Savage, 2003).

- *Greater sum total of knowledge.* When many people are involved in decision making, they apply a greater accumulation of information and experience to the decision than that possessed by any one member alone. Gaps in knowledge of one person can be filled by another.

- *Greater number of approaches to the problem.* Most people develop familiar patterns for decision making. If each person has a unique way of searching for information, analyzing problems, and the like, participatory decision processes provide more angles of attack at each stage of the decision-making process.

- *Greater number of alternatives.* Partly because of increased information and the use of varied decision-making patterns, groups typically can identify and evaluate more alternatives than one individual could. In listening to each other's ideas, group members may combine information to develop unique solutions that no single member could conceive.

- *Increased acceptance of a decision.* Shared decision making breeds ego involvement. That is, people tend to accept and support the decisions they make rather than those others make. The more people who accept a decision and are committed to it, the more likely the decision is to be implemented.

- *Better comprehension of a problem and decision.* More people understand a decision when it is reached by a group. This factor is particularly important when group members are to be involved in executing the decision.

Shared decision making also poses potential problems:

- *Social pressure toward conformity.* This phenomenon, known as *groupthink,* has received considerable attention. Groupthink occurs when the desire for cohesiveness and consensus becomes stronger than the desire to reach the best possible decisions (Janis, 1982). Because individuals fear being labeled uncooperative by other group members, they conform to the direction the group is taking even if they disagree with the group's position.

- *Individual domination.* Often one person will dominate the group because of difference in status or rank from other members, or through force of personality. This can cause resentment among other group members, who are prevented from participating fully. The problem is that what appears to emerge as a group decision may actually be the decision of one person.

- *Conflicting secondary goals.* Many times, participants in group decisions have their own axes to grind or their own turf to protect. Winning an issue becomes more important than making a quality decision. Too much energy is devoted to political maneuvering and infighting, and too little to reaching a quality decision.

- *Undesirable compromises.* Groups often make decisions that are simply compromises resulting from differing viewpoints of individual members. This is likely when a group must make a decision on a controversial issue. Controversial issues, by definition, result in opposing views. After a brief discussion, the group may conclude that a decision favoring either side is unacceptable; so they choose a compromise solution. Such an approach may result in a low-quality decision.

- *Ambiguous responsibility.* Group members share responsibility, but who is actually accountable for the final outcome? In individual decision making, it is clear who is responsible. In a group decision, the responsibility of any single member is diffused across the group participants. Furthermore, research has shown that group decisions are riskier on average than individual decisions. This phenomenon, known as *risky shift* (Stoner, 1968), is somewhat surprising because group pressures tend to inhibit the members. One possible explanation is that people feel less responsible for the outcome of a group decision than they do when acting alone. Risky decisions may be desirable in some situations; in others, the costs of risk may be too high.

■ *Time.* Groups often require more time to reach a final decision than do individuals. It takes time to assemble a group, and the interaction that takes place once the group is installed is frequently inefficient. This can limit a principal's ability to act quickly and decisively when necessary. It is also more costly because groups use more human resources.

The arguments for and against shared decision making suggest that choosing this approach requires careful thought. Principals must evaluate whether, for a particular situation, the assets outweigh the liabilities; and whether they can simultaneously take advantage of the assets and control the liabilities. Nevertheless, if principals intend to operate as professional learning communities, they must involve staff in the decision-making process.

Sheri Williams (2002), Communications Coordinator for the Adams Twelve Five Star Schools in Northglenn, Colorado, describes some effective practices in shared decision making. She collected these during train-the-trainer sessions with more than 300 local school principals in the southwestern United States. Although not exhaustive, the list represents the critical skills principals in the field identified as essential to more effective site-based decision making.

■ *Principals need to begin with a common vocabulary.* Coach team members in the predictable phases of group decision making.

■ *Principals need to put unwritten norms on paper.* Spend some time in the beginning establishing the norms of the group; then review the norms to make sure they are working.

■ *Principals need to get to know the demographics of the group.* Model acceptance and respect for a diversity of opinion. Provide interpreters for the full involvement of multilingual and multiethnic team members.

■ *Principals need to determine the strengths and future training needs of the team members.* Then provide training in those areas in which the group has the least ability and the greatest need.

■ *Principals need to avoid pushing for premature solutions.* Use brainstorming techniques to keep the dialogue open.

■ *Principals need to set the boundaries.* Seek agreement on the rules for a fair fight. Recognize cultural differences in conflict resolution.

■ *Principals need to recognize roadblocks to action.* Identify the ways groups can sabotage ideas.

■ *Principals need to look at the various methods groups use to solve problems.* Deal with conflict as it arises.

■ *Principals need to accept the notion that conflict can be a healthy change tool.* Use the consensus model to resolve conflicts.

■ *Principals need to keep the focus on practical problems.* Engage the team in substantive discussions to enhance their ability to move forward as a team of problem solvers.

■ *Principals need to make results visible.* Increase the team's commitment to action by setting high expectations for each team member. Ask team members to evaluate their progress in communicating results.

■ *Principals need to look at ways the site-based decision-making team can involve other agencies outside of the school.* Make coalitions work for you.

The Decision Tree Model

Victor Vroom, Philip Yetton, and Arthur Jago (1988) have developed a model to help principals decide when and to what extent they should involve others in the decision-making process. First, the authors identify characteristics of a given problem situation using a series of seven questions. Second, they isolate five decision-making styles that represent a continuum from authoritarian to participatory decision-making approaches. Finally, they combine the key problem aspects with the appropriate decision-making style to determine the optimum decision approach a principal should use in a given situation.

Characteristics of a Given Problem Situation

The key characteristics of a decision situation, according to the Vroom-Yetton-Jago model, are as follows:

1. Is there a quality requirement such that one solution is likely to be more rational than others?

2. Does a principal have sufficient information to make a high-quality decision?

3. Is the decision situation structured?

4. Is acceptance of the decision by the principal's subordinates critical to effective implementation of the decision?

5. Is it reasonably certain that the decision would be accepted by subordinates if the principal were to make it alone?

6. Do the principal's subordinates share the organizational goals to be achieved if the problem is solved?

7. Is the preferred solution likely to cause conflict among the subordinates?

In other words, these key variables should determine the extent to which a principal involves others in the decision process or makes the decision alone, without their input.

Decision-Making Styles

Five alternative decision-making styles, from which a principal can choose, include the following:

1. Principals solve the problems or make the decision themselves, using information available at that time.

2. Principals obtain the necessary information from others, then decide on the solution to the problem themselves. They may or may not tell others what the problem is when they request information. The role played by others in making the decision is clearly one of providing the necessary information to principals, rather than generating or evaluating alternative solutions.

3. Principals share the problem with relevant others individually, getting their ideas and suggestions without bringing them together as a group. Then principals make the decision that may or may not reflect others' influence.

4. Principals share the problem with other members as a group, collectively obtaining their ideas and suggestions. Then they make the decision that may or may not reflect others' influence.

5. Principals share a problem with others as a group. Principals and others together generate and evaluate alternatives and attempt to reach agreement [consensus] on a solution. Principals do not try to influence the group to adopt their preferred solution, and they accept and implement any solution that has the support of the entire group. (Vroom, Yetton, & Yago, 1988)

Choosing the Appropriate Style

Vroom, Yetton, and Jago match the decision styles to the situation as determined by answers to the seven questions. By answering these questions, the preferred decision style for each type of problem is identified. Figure 8.3 depicts how the Vroom-Yetton-Jago model works.

The flowchart provides the principal with a step-by-step approach to determining the most appropriate style of decision making under a given set of circumstances. To see how the model works, start at the left-hand side and work toward the right. When you reach a letter, the letter corresponds to the optimum decision-making style to use.

The *Vroom-Yetton-Jago* model represents an important improvement over rational decision-making theory, with implications for shared decision making. The authors have identified major decision strategies that are commonly used in making decisions, and they have established criteria for evaluating the success of the various strategies in a variety of situations. Moreover, they have developed an applied model for principals to use

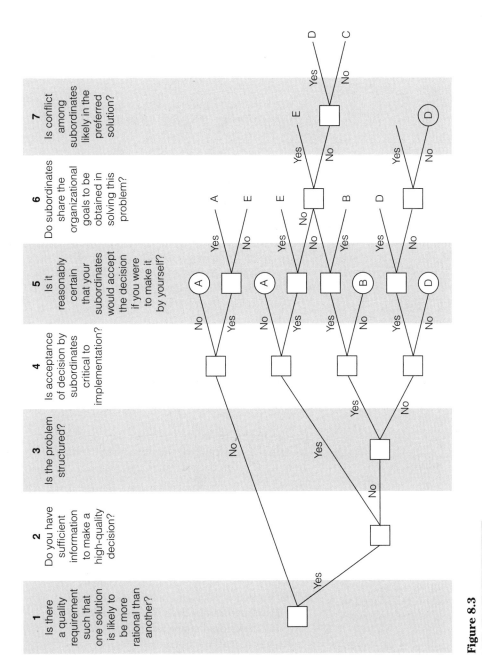

Figure 8.3

Effective Decision Styles

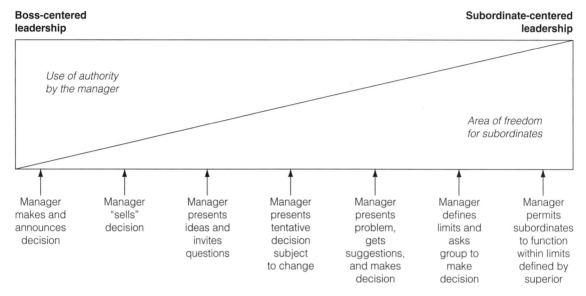

Figure 8.4

Leadership-Style Continuum

Source: Adapted from Robert Tannenbaum and Warren Schmidt, "How to Choose a Leadership Pattern," 1973, *Harvard Business Review, 51,* p. 167. Copyright © 1973 by the President and Fellows of Harvard College; all rights reserved.

in selecting decision strategies—one that improves the quality of decisions, increases acceptance of the decisions by others, and minimizes the time consumed in decision making.

The Decision Making–Pattern Choice Model

Another approach to shared decision making, which specifies under what circumstances participation should be used, was developed by Robert Tannenbaum and Warren Schmidt (1973). These authors posited seven different *decision-making patterns,* ranging on a continuum from what they call "boss-centered decision making" to "subordinate-centered decision making" (see Figure 8.4).

The theme of this approach is that a wide range of factors determine whether directive decision making, shared decision making, or something in between is best. These factors fall into

four broad categories: forces in the leader, forces in the subordinate, forces in the situation, and long-run goals and strategy.

Forces in the Leader   Factors operating in the principal's personality influence her choices among the seven decision-making patterns. These factors include the following:

1. *The principal's value system.* How strongly does the principal feel that individuals should have a share in making the decisions that affect them? Or, how convinced is the principal that the official who is paid or chosen to assume responsibility should personally carry the burden of decision making? Also, what relative importance does the principal attach to organizational efficiency and personal growth of staff members?

2. *The principal's confidence in the group members.* Principals differ in the amount of trust they generally have in other people. After

considering the knowledge and competence of a group with respect to a problem, a principal may (justifiably or not) have more confidence in his own capabilities than in those of the group members.

3. *The principal's own leadership inclinations.* Principals differ in the manner (e.g., telling or team role) in which they seem to function most comfortably and naturally.

4. *The principal's feelings of security in an uncertain situation.* The principal who releases control over the decision-making process reduces the predictability of the outcome. Principals who have a greater need than others for predictability and stability are more likely to "tell" or "sell" than to "join."

Forces in the Group Members　Before deciding how to lead a certain group, the principal will also want to remember that each member, like herself, is influenced by many personality variables and expectations. Generally speaking, the principal can permit the group greater freedom if the following essential conditions exist:

1. Members have relatively high needs for independence.

2. Members have readiness to assume responsibility.

3. Members have a relatively high tolerance for ambiguity.

4. Members are interested in the problem and feel that it is important.

5. Members understand and identify with the goals of the school.

6. Members have the necessary knowledge and experience to deal with the problem.

7. Members expect to share in decision making.

Forces in the Situation　Two of the critical environmental pressures on the principal are as follows:

1. *The problem itself.* Do the members have the kind of knowledge that is needed? Does the complexity of the problem require special experience or a one-person solution?

2. *The pressure of time.* The more the principal feels the need for an immediate decision, the more difficult it is to involve other people.

Long-Run Goals and Strategy　As the principal works on daily problems, his choice of a decision-making pattern is usually limited. But he may also begin to regard some of the forces mentioned as variables over which he has some control and to consider such long-range goals as the following:

1. Raising the level of member motivation

2. Improving the quality of all decisions

3. Developing teamwork and morale

4. Furthering the individual development of members

5. Increasing the readiness to accept change

Generally, a fairly high degree of member-centered behavior is more likely to achieve these long-range purposes. But the successful principal can be characterized neither as a strong leader nor as a permissive one. Rather, she is one who is sensitive to the forces that influence her in a given situation and one who can accurately assess those forces that should influence her.

The Synergistic Decision-Making Model

How can a principal effectively put the resources of a group (or a team) to work on a problem? Getting several people together in one location and using each of their strengths to facilitate decision making are always challenges to a principal. To accomplish this, the group must work smoothly in a team effort and not be dominated by one individual or by factions within the group.

The key to creating the proper environment for shared decision making is shown in Figure 8.5, and it is based to a great degree on effective communication skills (Lambert, 2004). We examine how each component of the model relates to each of the others when attempting shared decision making.

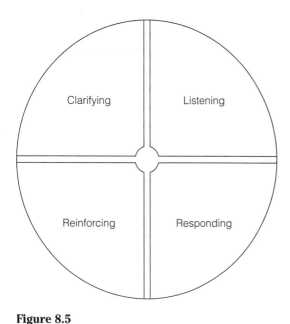

Figure 8.5

Synergistic Decision-Making Model

Listening   Active listening is not an automatic, easy process, especially when feelings are sensitized and frustration is evident within the group. To effectively accomplish the task, however, a listener should do the following:

- Always respect another's feelings.
- Never interrupt when another person is talking.
- Never prejudge.
- Always be considerate of someone else's remark.
- Never let rank or authority influence a comment.
- Always pay close attention to everything that is said.

Responding   Answering a remark that has been addressed to a group member occasionally requires a high degree of skill and tact. An often overlooked fact in shared decision making is that an *improper* response (even when it is merely *perceived* that way) can reduce the effects of positive synergism. Accordingly, when responding, an individual should take care to do the following:

- Paraphrase the remark, when applicable.
- Never respond in a disparaging manner.
- Keep the other person's feelings in mind at all times.
- Avoid any type of premature judgment.
- Always assume that the other person has spoken with sincerity.
- Avoid having the "final say" in the matter.

Reinforcing   The skill of reinforcing should not be confused with being condescending. The key here is to build on the previous remark(s) so as to encourage more creative thinking for all individuals on the team. To induce the best type of synergistic effect when reinforcing, an individual should do the following:

- Create the proper climate for a nonthreatening dialogue.
- Encourage free discussion by acknowledging appropriate remarks.
- Accept the other person's right to express themselves freely.
- Speak in a noncompetitive manner.
- Build on individual and group ideas.
- Encourage various viewpoints as they arise.

Clarifying   During the course of the decision-making process, a statement or remark made by another person may need clarification. Not to provide that clarification would be a serious mistake. What *is* important to the process is to get every possible confusing or unclear point clarified, so that some type of judgment can be made about it. When attempting to clarify, an individual should always take care to do the following:

- Phrase the question in a neutral way.
- Never imply that a foolish question has been raised.
- Not show any impatience in either voice tone or body language.
- Deal specifically with the question being addressed.

- Not generalize about the other person's intentions.

- Don't assume that you always have the answer.

Clearly, a variety of problems can influence decision-making processes. Individuals and groups have various biases and personal goals that may lead to suboptimal decisions. A technique such as the *synergistic decision-making approach* aims to minimize many of these problems by allowing individuals greater freedom of expression, and the group receives far less filtered information with which to make its decision. Thus, although not perfect, this technique can assist principals in need of mechanisms to improve both the quality and the timeliness of decisions made by groups in schools.

Summary

1. Decision making is one of the most important activities in which principals engage daily. The success of a school is critically linked to effective decisions.

2. Decision making is a process involving choices. The process generally consists of several steps: identifying problems, generating alternatives, evaluating alternatives, choosing an alternative, implementing the decision, and evaluating decision effectiveness.

3. Two major approaches to decision making have been identified. The rational model characterizes decision makers as completely searching through perfect information to make optimal decisions. The inherent imperfections of decision makers, and the social and organizational systems in which they are imbedded, impose limitations on decision makers' ability to process the information needed to make complex decisions (bounded rationality) and restrict decision makers to finding solutions that are less than optimal.

4. On the one hand, groups offer certain advantages in decision making: greater sum total of knowledge, greater number of approaches, more alternatives, increased acceptance of a decision,

and better comprehension of a problem and decision. On the other hand, groups create pressures to conform, can be dominated by one individual, result in conflicting secondary goals and undesirable compromises, cloud responsibility, and take more time. Nevertheless, if a principal wants to maintain a professional learning community, she must involve other stakeholder groups in the decision-making process.

5. The Vroom-Yetton-Jago model of determining the level of group involvement in the decision-making process requires the principal to diagnose a problem situation and the effect participation will have on the quality of the decision, level of staff members' acceptance, and the time available to make the decision.

6. Another approach to shared decision making, which specifies circumstances under which participation should be used, is the decision making–pattern choice model. The model posits seven different decision-making patterns, on a continuum ranging from "boss-centered decision making" to "subordinate-centered decision making."

7. The synergistic approach to decision making is a technique for increasing the advantages and limiting the disadvantages of shared decision making.

Field-Based Activities

1. Create a scenario that requires an educational decision, and run it through the six steps of the decision-making process: identifying the problem, generating alternatives, evaluating alternatives, choosing an alternative, implementing the decision, and evaluating decision effectiveness. Now reflect on the process. Discuss the advantages of running every important decision through each step in the decision-making process. Write your thoughts in your journal.

2. Examine the three decision-making models described in this book: the decision tree model, the decision making–pattern choice

model, and the synergistic decision-making model. Under what circumstances would each of these decision-making models be used? Take field notes for several weeks, and observe the extent to which any or all of the three models are used in your school or school district. Regardless of the outcome of your observation, how and when would *you* use each of the three models if you were a principal of a school? Be specific.

3. Why is it virtually impossible to use the rational decision-making model? Give some specific examples of how the effects of "bounded rationality" in schools can prevent principals from using purely rational decision making. Take field notes in your school for one week, during which you record reflections from your experience of incidents when bounded rationality was used in making decisions. Use the limits to rationality discussed in your text as a guide: satisficing, heuristics, primacy/recency effect, bolstering the alternative, intuition, incrementalizing, and the garbage-can model. Try to find at least one specific school-related incident when each of these limits to rationality has been used in your school or school district.

Suggested Readings

Cunningham, W. G., & Cordeiro, P. A. (2003). *Educational leadership: A problem-based approach* (2nd ed.). Boston: Allyn & Bacon. Thoroughly revised and updated, this text involves readers with the very latest thinking in the field and significant real-life problems of practice. Reflecting on current changes and thinking in educational leadership, this text includes updated expert analysis pieces by noted authorities in every chapter. This text uses a problem-based approach and provides readers with opportunities to analyze and apply their knowledge to authentic situations.

Davis, S. H., & Davis, P. B. (2003). *The intuitive dimensions of administrative decision making.* Lanham, MD: Scarecrow Press. The authors, with over 50 years of combined experience as principals and superintendents, provide educational leaders with a better understanding of how intuitive decision making may be effectively assessed, used, and enhanced as a powerful cognitive tool for resolving complex administrative problems. Contents include an in-depth examination of how intuition corresponds with rational and analytical approaches to complex problem solving and decision making in schools, a thorough investigation into the intuitive decision-making experiences of 90 California public school principals who participated in an empirical research study developed by the authors, and a comprehensive synthesis of ideas and suggestions about how school leaders can access and develop their intuitive decision-making skills.

Hanson, K. L. (2001). *Preparing for educational administration using case analysis.* Boston: Allyn & Bacon. This text combines 34 meaningful case studies and a case analysis framework to create a powerful resource that will be referenced long after being an assigned reading. The author offers a unique opportunity to participate in serious problem solving with relevant and realistic case material that captures the reader's interest. After being introduced to real-life situations and a case analysis framework, students are able to analyze and resolve the problems presented in each case.

Hoy, W. K., & Tarter, C. J. (2004). *Administrators solving problems of practice: Decision-making concepts, cases, and consequences* (2nd ed.). Boston: Allyn & Bacon. Using actual school cases, this text compares decision-making models and illustrates how to use each model. Frameworks include classical, administrative, incremental, mixed scanning, political, and garbage-can models, as well as two models of shared decision making. After illustrating how to use the strategies, the authors give students the opportunity to explore about 50 actual cases and build their own analyses and solution strategies.

Richetti, C. T., & Tregoe, B. B. (2001). *Analytic processes for school leaders.* Alexandria, VA: Association for Supervision and Curriculum Development. Discover how you, your colleagues, and your students can solve problems and make good decisions by following the research-based processes in this authoritative guide. Explore four key analytic processes that are involved in all decision making. Use the guiding steps and key questions to involve others in decisions and ensure the best outcomes. Over the past 40 years, more than 20 million people in 44 countries have been trained in these decision-making methods.

Shapiro, J. P., & Stefkovich, J. A. (2001). *Ethical leadership and decision making in education.* Mahwah, NJ: Lawrence Erlbaum. This textbook is designed to fill a gap in instructional materials for teaching the ethics component of the knowledge base that has been established for the profession. The text has several purposes: (a) It demonstrates the application of different ethical paradigms (the ethics of justice, care, critique, and the profession) through discussion and analysis of real-life moral dilemmas that educational leaders face in their schools and communities; (b) it addresses some of the practical, pedagogical, and curricular issues related to the teaching of ethics for educational leaders; and (c) it emphasizes the importance of ethics instruction from a variety of theoretical approaches.

Streifer, P. (2002). *Using data to make better decisions.* Lanham, MD: Scarecrow Press. Most of the business world has been using what is known as "data-driven" decision making for quite some time now. From retail to medicine to travel, the ability to access data from any point and cross-check it is commonplace—except in the educational sector. Striefer builds a case arguing that the correct use of data can help to answer the most complex questions facing education today. This process of analyzing evidence can help school administrators go to the public with the best and most accurate information they can quickly bring together.

9. Developing Effective Communications

FOCUSING QUESTIONS

1 What is communication?

2 How does the communication process operate?

3 How does communication flow in a school organization?

4 What are communication networks, and how do they operate?

5 What are the barriers to effective communication in schools?

6 How can principals overcome communication barriers?

7 What role does feedback play in communication?

8 Why must school principals pay attention to nonverbal communication?

In this chapter, we respond to these questions concerning communication in school organizations. We begin our discussion by defining communication and presenting a model of the communication process. Next, we look at the school district as a whole and consider upward, downward, and horizontal communications as well as various communication networks. Finally, we consider ways that principals can manage effective communication, including barriers to communication and techniques for overcoming them.

The Communication Process

Communication can be defined as the process of transmitting information and common understanding from one person to another. The word *communication* is derived from the Latin word *communis*, meaning "common." The definition underscores the fact that unless a common understanding results from the exchange of information,

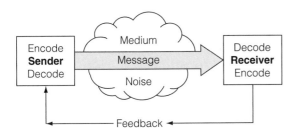

Figure 9.1

The Communication Process

there is no communication. Figure 9.1 reflects the definition and identifies the important elements of the communication process (Eisenberg, 2003).

Two common elements in every communication exchange are the sender and the receiver. The *sender* initiates the communication. In a school, the sender is a person who has a need or desire to convey an idea or concept to others. The *receiver* is the individual to whom the message is sent. The sender *encodes* the idea by selecting words, symbols, or gestures with which to compose a message. The *message* is the outcome of the encoding, which takes the form of verbal, nonverbal, or written language. The message is sent through a *medium* or channel, which is the carrier of the communication. The medium can be a face-to-face conversation, telephone call, or written report. The receiver *decodes* the received message into meaningful information. *Noise* is anything that distorts the message. Different perceptions of the message, language barriers, interruptions, emotions, and attitudes are examples of noise. Finally, *feedback* occurs when the receiver responds to the sender's message and returns the message to the sender. Feedback allows the sender to determine whether the message has been received and understood.

Elements of the Communication Process

The elements used in the communication process determine the quality of communication. A problem in any one of these elements can reduce communication effectiveness (Keyton et al., 2006).

For example, information must be encoded into a message that can be understood as the sender intended. Selection of the particular medium for transmitting the message can be critical, because there are many choices.

For written media, a principal or other organization member may choose from memos, letters, reports, bulletin boards, handbooks, newsletters, and the like. For verbal media, choices include face-to-face conversations, telephone, computer, public address systems, closed-circuit television, tape-recorded messages, sound or slide shows, e-mail, and so on. Nonverbal gestures, facial expressions, body position, and even clothing can transmit messages. People decode information selectively. Individuals are more likely to perceive information favorably when it conforms to their own beliefs, values, and needs. When feedback does not occur, the communication process is referred to as one-way communication. Two-way communication occurs with feedback and is more desirable.

The key for being successful in the contemporary school is the principal's ability to work with other school stakeholders (faculty, support staff, community members, parents, central office) and develop a shared sense of what the school is attempting to accomplish — where it wants to go, a shared sense of commitments that people have to make in order to advance the school toward that shared vision and clarity of goals. As principals are able to build that shared mission, vision, values, and goals, the school will become more effective. Building a relationship between the principal and other school stakeholders requires effective communication.

Principals spend 70 to 80% of their time in interpersonal communication with various stakeholders. Effective principals know how to communicate, and they understand the importance of ongoing communication, both formal and informal: faculty and department meetings; individual conversations with parents, teachers, and students; and telephone calls and e-mail messages with various stakeholder groups.

The one constant in the life of a principal is a lot of interruptions — they happen daily, with a number of one- and three-minute conversations in the course of the day. This type of communication in the work of the principal has to be done one on one—one phone call to one person at a time, one parent at a time, one teacher at a time, one student at a time; and a principal needs to make time for these conversations. For example, a principal may be talking with a parent with a very serious problem. She may be talking with a community member. She may be talking with the police about something that went on during the school day. The principal must be able to turn herself on and off in many different roles in any given day.

Planning a School-wide Communications Program

Communication is the lifeblood of a school. The principal plays a key role in developing a communications program in the school. Here are some essential steps a principal can take in planning a successful communications program (St. John, 2004).

- Do a needs assessment by analyzing current strengths and weaknesses.
- Define goals and priorities.
- Assign responsibility.
- Adopt a budget.
- Hire a communications consultant, if possible.
- Explain plans to the superintendent and win her support.
- Develop policies and procedures.
- Train staff to develop their communications skills.
- Establish communications channels and networks.
- Write and disseminate a communications section for faculty and staff handbooks.
- Survey faculty and staff attitudes regarding communications needs and problems. (Ask for their suggestions.)
- Select the best media to use for different communications purposes.
- Find out information needed by the faculty and staff surveys.

- Identify key individuals and positions on which to focus communications efforts.
- Develop emergency communications procedures.
- Check effectiveness of the total program.
- Revise as indicated by evaluation.

Organizational Communication

The purpose of organizational communication is to facilitate achievement of the school district's mission and goals. District-wide communications typically flow in three directions: downward, upward, and horizontally (Tourish et al., 2004). Principals are responsible for establishing and maintaining formal channels of communication in these three directions. Principals also use various communication networks, such as the grapevine, to coordinate activities that help to achieve the school's mission and goals.

Direction of Communication Flow

Downward, upward, and horizontal communication refers to the way that information flows down, up, and horizontally through the formal school district hierarchy; that is, it occurs between positions or task responsibilities defined by the organization. These communication flows are depicted in Figure 9.2.

Downward Communication   Traditional views of the communication process in school organizations have been dominated by *downward communication* flows. Such flows transmit information from higher to lower levels of the school district. School leaders, from central office administrators to building principals, communicate downward to group members through speeches, messages in school bulletins, school board policy manuals, and school procedure handbooks.

Richard Daft (2004) has identified five general purposes of downward communication:

1. *Implementation of goals, strategies, and objectives.* Communicating new strategies and

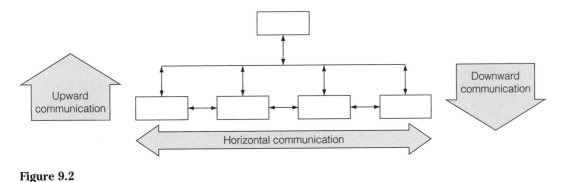

Figure 9.2

Downward, Upward, and Horizontal Communication Flows in School Districts

goals provides information about specific targets and expected behaviors. It gives direction for lower levels of the school district or school. For example: "The new reform mandate is for real. We must improve the quality of student learning if we are to succeed."

2. *Job instructions and rationale.* These are directives on how to do a specific task and how the job relates to other school district activities. Schools need to coordinate individual and departmental objectives with district-wide goals. We often fail to provide enough of this kind of information, leaving it to the individual staff member to get the big picture.

3. *Procedures and practices.* These are messages defining the school district's policies, rules, regulations, benefits, and structural arrangements in order to get some degree of uniformity in school district practices. In schools, this information is transmitted to staff members through school board and district policy manuals, school handbooks, and the day-to-day operation of the school.

4. *Performance feedback.* Departmental progress reports, individual performance appraisals, and other means are used to tell departments or individuals how well they are doing with respect to performance standards and goals. For example: "Mary, your work on the computer terminal has greatly

improved the efficiency of our guidance department."

5. *Socialization.* Every school district tries to motivate staff members to adopt the institution's mission and cultural values and to participate in special ceremonies, such as picnics and United Way campaigns. It is an attempt to get a commitment, a sense of belonging, and a unity of direction among staff members (Lunenburg & Ornstein, 2004). For example: "The school district thinks of its employees as family and would like to invite everyone to attend the annual picnic and fair on May 30."

The downward flow of communication provides a channel for directives, instructions, and information to organizational members. However, much information gets lost while being passed from one person to another. Moreover, the message can be distorted if it travels a great distance from its sender to the ultimate receiver down through the formal school district hierarchy (Tourish et al., 2004).

Upward Communication   The behaviorists have emphasized the establishment of *upward communication* flows. In a school, this term refers to communication that travels from staff member to principal. Upward communication is necessary not only to determine if staff members have understood information sent downward but also to meet the ego needs of staff. Five types of information communicated upward in a school are as follows (Daft, 2004):

1. *Problems and exceptions.* These messages describe serious problems and exceptions to routine performance in order to make the principal aware of difficulties.

2. *Suggestions for improvement.* These messages are ideas for improving task-related procedures to increase the quality or efficiency of teachers and other staff members.

3. *Performance reports.* These messages include periodic reports that inform the principal how individual teachers and departments are performing.

4. *Grievances and disputes.* These messages are employee complaints and conflicts that travel up the school district hierarchy for a hearing and possible resolution. If the grievance procedure is backed up by the presence of a collective bargaining agreement, staff members are even more encouraged to express true feelings.

5. *Financial and accounting information.* These messages pertain to costs, accounts receivable, interest on investments, tax levies, and other matters of interest to the school board, central administration, and building principals.

Ideally, the organizational structure should provide for both upward and downward communication flows. Communication should travel in both directions through the formal school district hierarchy. Unfortunately, communication from the bottom does not flow as freely as communication from the top. Some barriers to effective upward communication in a school are as follows (Cheney, Christensen, Zorn, & Ganesh, 2003):

1. Principals fail to respond when staff members bring up information or problems. Failure to respond will ultimately result in no communication.

2. Principals tend to be defensive about less-than-perfect actions. When staff members see this defensiveness, they will withhold information from the principal.

3. The principal's attitude plays a critical role in the upward communication flow. If the principal is really concerned and really listens, then upward communication improves.

4. Physical barriers can also inhibit upward communication flow. Separating a principal from his staff members creates common problems.

5. Time lags between the communication and the action can inhibit upward communication. If it takes months for the various levels of administration to approve a staff member's suggestion, upward communication is hindered.

The following are some methods of improving the effectiveness of upward communication in a school (Luthans, 2004):

1. *The open-door policy.* Taken literally, this means that the principal's door is always open to staff members. It is an invitation for staff to come in and talk about any problem they may have. In practice, the open-door policy is seldom used. The principal may say, "My door is always open"; but in many cases, both the staff member and the principal know the door is really closed. This does not occur in a professional learning community.

2. *Counseling, attitude questionnaires, and exit interviews.* The principal can greatly facilitate upward communication by conducting nondirective, confidential counseling sessions; periodically administering attitude surveys; and holding exit interviews for those who leave the school. Much valuable information can be gained from these forms of communication.

3. *Participative techniques.* Shared decision making can generate a great deal of upward communication. This may be accomplished by the use of union-management committees, quality circles, suggestion boxes, site-based councils, and the like.

4. *The ombudsperson.* The use of an ombudsperson has been utilized primarily in Scandinavia to provide an outlet for persons who have been treated unfairly or in a depersonalized manner

by large, bureaucratic government. More recently, this approach has gained popularity in American state governments, the military, universities, and some business firms. Xerox Corporation inaugurated the position in 1972, and General Electric followed shortly thereafter. If developed and maintained properly, it may work where the open-door policy has failed.

5. *The union contract.* A prime objective of the union is to convey to administration the feelings and demands of various employee groups. Collective bargaining sessions constitute a legal channel of communication for any aspect of employer-employee relations. A typical provision of every union contract is the grievance procedure. It is a mechanism for appeal beyond the authority of the immediate supervisor.

6. *The grapevine.* Although principals may be reluctant to use the grapevine, they should always listen to it. The grapevine is a natural phenomenon that serves as a means of emotional release for staff members and provides the principal with significant information concerning the attitudes and feelings of staff members.

In short, the upward flow of communication in a school building is intended to provide channels for the feedback of information up the school hierarchy. Some deterrents may prevent a good return flow, but there are ways to promote more effective principal-staff communications.

Horizontal Communication

Upward and downward communication flows generally follow the formal hierarchy within the school or school district. However, greater size and complexity of schools and school districts increase the need for communication laterally or diagonally across the lines of the formal chain of command. This is referred to as *horizontal communication*. These communications are informational too, but in a different way than downward and upward communication. Here information is basically for coordination — to tie together activities within or across either departments in a single school or divisions in a school district.

Horizontal communication falls into one of three categories (Daft, 2004):

1. *Intradepartmental problem solving.* These messages, which take place between members of the same department in a school or division in a school district, concern task accomplishment.

2. *Interdepartmental coordination.* Interdepartmental messages facilitate the accomplishment of joint projects or tasks in a school or divisions in a school district.

3. *Staff advice to line departments.* These messages often go from specialists in academic areas, finance, or computer service to building principals seeking help in these areas.

In brief, horizontal communication flows exist to enhance coordination. This horizontal channel permits a lateral or diagonal flow of messages, enabling units to work with other units without having to follow rigidly up and down channels. Many schools and school districts build in horizontal communications in the form of task forces, committees, liaison personnel, or matrix structures to facilitate coordination.

Communication Networks

Downward, upward, and horizontal communication flows can be combined into a variety of *communication networks*. Five common networks are shown in Figure 9.3: the chain, Y, wheel, circle, and all-channel (Shockley-Zalabak, 2002).

An understanding of communication networks can help principals improve their overall communication effectiveness.

Five Communication Networks   As shown in Figure 9.3, the *chain network* represents a five-level vertical hierarchy in which communications can move only upward and downward. In a school district, this type of network would be found in line-authority relations. For example, a teacher reports to the department head, who reports to the principal, who reports to the assistant superintendent, who reports to the superintendent. These five individuals would represent a chain network.

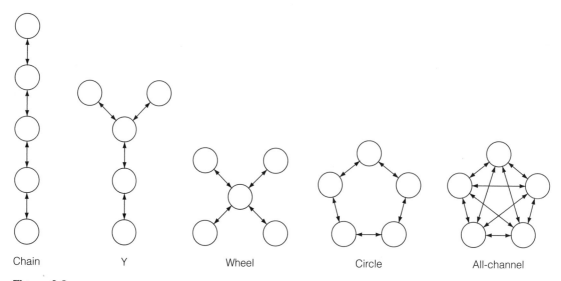

Figure 9.3

Common Communication Networks

If we turn the *Y network* upside down, we can see two staff members reporting to a leader, with two levels of authority above the leader. For instance, two high school assistant principals report to the principal, who in turn reports to the assistant superintendent for instruction, who reports to the superintendent. This is, in effect, a four-level hierarchy.

If we look at the *wheel network* as though we were standing above the diagram, we see that the wheel represents four staff members who report to a leader. For example, four assistant principals in a large high school report to the principal. There is no interaction between the assistant principals. All communications are channeled through the principal.

The *circle network* allows members to interact with adjoining members, but no further. It represents a three-level hierarchy in which there is vertical communication between the leader and staff members and horizontal communication only at the lowest level. In a large high school, the principal communicates with two assistant principals, who communicate separately with two different teachers. The two teachers communicate with each other.

Finally, the *all-channel network* allows each of the participants to communicate freely with the other four. Of the networks discussed, it is the least structured. Although it is like the circle in some respects, the all-channel network has no central position, and there are no restrictions; all members are equal. The all-channel network is best illustrated by a committee, in which no one member formally or informally assumes a leadership position. All members are free to share their viewpoints.

An Informal Network: The Grapevine Every school needs formal channels of communication to organize, control, and coordinate activity within the building. Coexisting with the formal channels is an informal communication network, commonly referred to as the grapevine (Shockley-Zalabak, 2004). The *grapevine* is simply the informal communication network among people in a school. Grapevines are present and highly active in virtually every school. They flow in all directions — up, down, or horizontally — in unpredictable patterns and are not fixed by any formal organization chart.

The grapevine serves as an emotional outlet for staff members' fears and anxieties; helps satisfy a natural desire for people to talk about their job, their institution, and their colleagues; gives staff a sense of belonging and a way of gaining social acceptance and recognition; and helps principals to learn how staff members feel about policies and programs.

Given these benefits, it is not surprising that grapevines exist in almost all schools. Surprising is the fact that the information transmitted through the grapevine is accurate and relevant to the school. About 80% of grapevine communications pertain to job-related topics rather than personal, vicious gossip. In addition, approximately 75% of the details passed through the grapevine are accurate. Moreover, five of every six important messages are carried by the grapevine rather than through formal communication channels (Newstrom & Davis, 2004). This has obvious implications for school principals. It means tuning into the grapevine, understanding what it is saying, and knowing and using its sources. Thus principals can use the energy of the grapevine to supplement formal communication channels. Management by wandering around is an excellent way to use the grapevine in a nonthreatening way (Frase et al., 2003).

Managing Communication

Problems of communication diminish the success of principals in the performance of their function. If messages are poorly transmitted or misinterpreted and if action is not effected, principals cannot plan and monitor school activities properly. Principals can do several things to improve communications in schools. In general, these center around understanding the barriers to communication and knowing how to overcome them.

Barriers to Communication

The sender, the receiver, and the medium are the basic elements of the communication process. But unless a message is interpreted as it was meant, we still do not have communication. Misinterpretation is always possible whenever two individuals interact. The four types of communication barriers are (a) process barriers, (b) physical barriers, (c) semantic barriers, and (d) psychosocial barriers (Gilbert, 2004).

Process Barriers Every step in the communication process is necessary for effective communication. Blocked steps become barriers. Consider the following situations:

- *Sender barrier.* A new principal with an innovative idea fails to speak up at a meeting, chaired by the superintendent, for fear of criticism.
- *Encoding barrier.* A Spanish-speaking teacher cannot get an English-speaking principal to understand a grievance about working conditions.
- *Medium barrier.* A very upset teacher sends an emotionally charged letter to the principal instead of transmitting her feelings face-to-face.
- *Decoding barrier.* An older principal is not sure what a young department head means when he refers to a teacher as "spaced out."
- *Receiver barrier.* A principal who is absorbed in preparing the annual budget asks a teacher to repeat a statement, because she was not listening attentively to the conversation.
- *Feedback barrier.* During a school district meeting, the failure of principals to ask any questions causes the superintendent to wonder if any real understanding has taken place.

Because communication is a complex, give-and-take process, breakdowns anywhere in the cycle can block the transfer of understanding.

Physical Barriers Any number of physical distractions can interfere with the effectiveness of communication, including a telephone call, drop-in visitors, distances between people, walls, and static on the radio. People often take physical barriers for granted, but sometimes they can be changed. For example, an inconveniently positioned wall can be removed. Interruptions such as telephone calls and drop-in visitors can be decreased by issuing instructions to a secretary.

An appropriate choice of media can overcome distance barriers between people.

Semantic Barriers   The words we choose, how we use them, and the meaning we attach to them cause many communication barriers. The problem is with semantics, or the meaning of the words we use. The same word may mean different things to different people. Words and phrases such as *efficiency, increased productivity, management prerogatives,* and *just cause* may mean one thing to the principal and something entirely different to staff.

Technology also plays a part in semantic barriers to communication. Today's complex school districts are highly specialized. Schools have staff and technical experts developing and using specialized terminology — jargon that only other similar staff and technical experts can understand. And if people don't understand the words, they cannot understand the message.

Psychosocial Barriers   Three important concepts are associated with psychological and social barriers: fields of experience, filtering, and psychological distance (Baldwin, 2003). *Fields of experience* include people's backgrounds, perceptions, values, biases, needs, and expectations. Senders can encode and receivers decode messages only in the context of their fields of experience. When the sender's field of experience overlaps very little with the receiver's, communication becomes difficult. *Filtering* means that more often than not, we see and hear what we are emotionally tuned in to see and hear. Filtering is caused by our own needs and interests, which guide our listening. Psychosocial barriers often involve a *psychological distance* between people that is similar to actual physical distance. For example, the principal talks down to a teacher, who resents this attitude; and this resentment separates them, thereby blocking opportunity for effective communication.

Successful communication by principals is the essence of a productive school. However, as discussed previously, communications do break down. Several communication theorists (Abrell, 2004; Baldwin, Perry, & Moffitt, 2003; Backlund & Ivy, 2003; Johnson, 2003; Kramer, 2003; Nelson, 2004; Stern et al., 2003) have focused on the major areas where failures in communication most frequently occur. In schools, communication breakdowns most frequently occur in these areas:

- *Sincerity.* Nearly all communication theorists assert that sincerity is the foundation on which all true communication rests. Without sincerity — honesty, straightforwardness, and authenticity — all attempts at communication are destined to fail.

- *Empathy.* Research shows that lack of empathy is a major obstacle to effective communication. Empathy is the ability to put yourself into another's shoes. The empathetic person is able to see the world through the eyes of the other person.

- *Self-perception.* How we see ourselves affects our ability to communicate effectively. A healthy but realistic self-perception is a necessary ingredient in communicating with others.

- *Role perception.* Unless people know what their role is, the importance of their role, and what is expected of them, they will not know what to communicate, when to communicate, or to whom to communicate.

- *Efforts to distort the message.* Pitfalls in communication often occur in our efforts — both consciously and unconsciously — to distort messages.

- *Images.* Another obstacle to successful communication is the sender's image of the receiver, and vice versa. For example, on the one hand, principals are sometimes viewed as not too well informed about teaching, seen as out of touch with the classroom, and looked on as paper shufflers. On the other hand, some principals view teachers as lazy, inconsiderate of administrative problems, and unrealistic about the strengths and weaknesses of their students. Such views lead to a "we-they" attitude.

- *Vehicle for message.* The vehicle by which we choose to send messages is important in successful communication. In most cases, the vehicle to be used is defined by the situation.

- *Ability to communicate.* Some of the ways we communicate raise barriers by inhibiting discussion or causing others to feel inferior, angry, hostile, dependent, compliant, or subservient.

- *Listening ability.* Frequently, people fail to appreciate the importance of listening, do not care enough to become actively involved with what others are saying, and are not sufficiently motivated to develop the skills necessary to acquire the art of listening.

- *Culture.* Our cultural heritage, biases, and prejudices often serve as barriers to communication. The facts that we are African American or White, young or old, male or female have all proved to be obstacles in communicating effectively.

- *Tradition.* Past practice in a school helps to determine how, when, and what we send and receive. For example, a principal who has an authoritative style may find that his faculty will not share information readily. If a new principal with a collaborative style replaces the authoritarian one, the new principal may find that it takes a while for her colleagues to speak out on important issues.

- *Conditioning.* The manner in which communication is conditioned by the environment influences the accuracy of messages sent and received. If we work for principals who set a climate in which we are encouraged to share information, we soon become conditioned to communicate accordingly.

- *Noise.* A major barrier to communication is what communication experts call noise. Noise consists of the external factors in the channels, and the internal perceptions and experiences within the source and the receiver, that affect communication.

- *Feedback.* Faculty and staff tell their leaders that they want feedback. However, feedback improperly given can impede communication rather than improve it. Principals and followers both need more training in how to use feedback more productively.

Improving Communication Effectiveness

Effective communication is a two-way process that requires effort and skill by both sender and receiver. Principals will at times assume each of these roles in the communication process. In this section, we discuss guidelines for improving communication effectiveness, including senders' and receivers' responsibilities, listening, feedback, and nonverbal communication.

Senders' Responsibilities   Several communication theorists (Dues, 2003; Gilbert, 2004; Johnson et al., 2003; Nelson, 2004) have gleaned 10 commandments of good communication that are particularly applicable to the sender. These commandments, together with a basic understanding of the communication process itself, should provide a good foundation for developing and maintaining an effective set of interpersonal communication skills, which principals can use when communicating with various school stakeholders.

1. *Principals need to clarify their ideas before communicating.* The more systematically principals analyze the problem or idea to be communicated, the clearer it becomes. This is the first step toward effective communication. Many communications fail because of inadequate planning. Good planning must consider the goals, attitudes, and needs of those who will receive the communication and those who will be affected by it.

2. *Principals need to examine the true purpose of each communication.* Before principals communicate, they must ask themselves what they really want to accomplish with their message— obtain information, initiate action, or change another person's attitude? Principals need to identify their most important goal and then adapt their language, tone, and total approach to serve that specific objective. Principals should not try to accomplish too much with each communication. The sharper the focus of their message, the greater are its chances of success.

3. *Principals need to consider the total physical and human setting.* Meaning and intent are

conveyed by more than words alone. Many other factors influence the overall impact of a communication, and principals must be sensitive to the total setting in which they communicate: the circumstances under which an announcement or decision is made; the physical setting—whether the communication is made in private or otherwise; the social climate that pervades work relationships within the school or department and sets the tone of its communications; and custom and practice—the degree to which the communication conforms to, or departs from, the expectations of the audience. Be constantly aware of the total setting in which you communicate. Like all living things, communication must be capable of adapting to its environment.

4. *Principals need to consult with others, when appropriate, in planning communications.* Frequently, it is desirable or necessary to seek the participation of others in planning a communication or in developing the facts on which to base the communication. Such consultation often lends additional insight and objectivity to the message. Moreover, those who have helped plan the communication will give it their active support.

5. *Principals need to be mindful, while communicating, of the overtones as well as the basic content of the message.* The principal's tone of voice, expression, and apparent receptiveness to the responses of others all have tremendous impact on those the principal wishes to reach. Frequently overlooked, these subtleties of communication often affect a listener's reaction to a message even more than its basic content. Similarly, the principal's choice of language—particularly his awareness of the fine shades of meaning and emotion in the words used—predetermine in large part the reactions of the listeners.

6. *Principals need to take the opportunity, when it arises, to convey something of help or value to the receiver.* Consideration of the other person's interests and needs—trying to look at things from the other person's point of view—frequently points up opportunities to convey something of immediate benefit or long-range value to the other person. Staff members are most responsive to principals whose messages take staff interests into account.

7. *Principals need to follow up their communication.* A principal's best efforts at communication may be wasted, and she may never know whether she has succeeded in expressing her true meaning and intent if she does not follow up to see how well she has put her message across. A principal can do this by asking questions, by encouraging the receiver to express his or her reactions, by follow-up contacts, and by subsequent review of performance. A principal needs to make certain that every important communication has feedback, so that complete understanding and appropriate action result.

8. *Principals need to communicate for tomorrow as well as today.* Although communications may be aimed primarily at meeting the demands of an immediate situation, they must be planned with the past in mind if they are to maintain consistency in the receiver's view. Most important, however, communications must be consistent with long-range interests and goals. For example, it is not easy to communicate frankly on such matters as poor performance or the shortcomings of a loyal teacher, but postponing disagreeable communications makes these matters more difficult in the long run and is actually unfair to the principal's staff and his school.

9. *Principals need to be sure that their actions support their communications.* In the final analysis, the most persuasive kind of communication is not what principals say, but what they do. When principals' actions or attitudes contradict their words, others tend to discount what they have said. For every principal, this means that good supervisory practices—such as clear assignment of responsibility and authority, fair rewards for effort, and sound policy enforcement—serve to communicate more than all the gifts of oratory.

10. *Principals need to seek not only to be understood, but to understand—be a good listener.* When a principal starts talking, he often ceases to listen, at least in that larger sense of being attuned to the other person's unspoken reactions and attitudes. Even more serious is the occasional inattentiveness a principal may be guilty of when others are attempting to communicate with him. Listening is one of the most important, most difficult, and most neglected skills in communication. For the principal, listening demands that he concentrate not only on the explicit meanings another person is expressing, but also on the implicit meanings, unspoken words, and undertones that may be far more significant. Thus, a principal must learn to listen with the inner ear if he is to know the inner person.

Receivers' Responsibilities Communication depends on the ability not only to send but also to receive messages. The ability to listen effectively thus greatly enhances the communication process; but many of us are not good listeners. Effective listening skills can be developed, however. Summarized following are 10 rules for good listening (Newstrom & Davis, 2004):

1. *Stop talking.* You cannot listen if you are talking. As Polonius in *Hamlet* said: "Give every man thine ear, but few thy voice."

2. *Put the talker at ease.* Help a person feel free to talk. This is often called a permissive environment.

3. *Show a talker that you want to listen.* Look and act interested. Do not read your mail while someone talks. Listen to understand rather than to oppose.

4. *Remove distractions.* Don't doodle, tap, or shuffle papers. Will it be quieter if you shut the door?

5. *Empathize with talkers.* Try to help yourself see the other person's point of view.

6. *Be patient.* Allow plenty of time. Do not interrupt a talker. Don't start for the door or walk away.

7. *Hold your temper.* An angry person takes the wrong meaning from words.

8. *Go easy on argument and criticism.* These approaches put people on the defensive, and they may clam up or become angry. Do not argue: Even if you win, you lose.

9. *Ask questions.* This encourages a talker and shows that you are listening. It helps to develop points further.

10. *Stop talking.* This rule is first and last, because all others depend on it. You cannot do an effective listening job while you are talking.

Nature gave people two ears but only one tongue, which may be considered a gentle hint that we should listen more than we talk. Listening requires two ears, one for meaning and one for feeling. Principals who do not listen have less information for making sound decisions.

Active Listening *Active listening* is a term popularized by the work of Carl Rogers and Richard Farson (n.d.) and advocated by counselors and therapists (Barker, 1991; Benward & Kolosick, 1995). The concept recognizes that a sender's message contains both verbal and nonverbal content as well as a feeling component. The receiver should be aware of both components in order to comprehend the total meaning of the message—for instance, when a school counselor says to the principal, "Next time you ask me to prepare a report, give me some advance notice." The content conveys that the counselor needs time, but the feeling component may indicate resentment for being pressured to meet a deadline with such short notice. The principal, therefore, must recognize this feeling to understand the counselor's message. Here are five guidelines that can help principals to become more active listeners (Rogers & Farson, n.d.):

1. *Listen for message content.* The receiver must try to hear exactly what the sender is saying in the message.

2. *Listen for feelings.* The receiver must try to identify how the sender feels regarding the message content. This can be done by asking, "What is he trying to say?"

3. *Respond to feelings.* The receiver must let the sender know that her feelings as well as the message content are recognized.

4. *Note all cues, verbal and nonverbal.* The receiver must be sensitive to the nonverbal messages as well as the verbal ones. If the receiver identifies mixed messages, he may ask for clarification.

5. *Rephrase the sender's message.* The receiver may restate or paraphrase the verbal and non-verbal messages as feedback to the sender. The receiver can do this by allowing the sender to respond with further information.

The last guideline, one of the most powerful of the active listening techniques, is used regularly by counselors and therapists. It helps the receiver avoid passing judgment or giving advice and encourages the sender to provide more information about what is really the problem.

The Art of Giving Feedback   *Feedback* is the process of telling other people how you feel about something they did or said. There are two types of feedback: responsive feedback and corrective feedback. *Responsive feedback* enables the sender to determine if the message has been correctly interpreted by the receiver. In any kind of oral communication, we can test understanding by asking the receiver to repeat the information. This helps to clarify any misunderstandings immediately.

Corrective feedback tells other people how you feel about their behavior or performance. Principals regularly give (corrective) feedback to other people; such feedback is often in the form of performance evaluations or appraisals. There is an art to giving corrective feedback; it must be phrased so that the receiver will accept and use it. Corrective feedback that is poorly given can be threatening and cause resentment instead of corrective behavior change. The following list summarizes some characteristics of effective feedback for staff performance (Luthans, 2004):

1. *Intention.* Effective feedback is directed toward improving job performance and making the staff member a more valuable asset. It is not a personal attack and should not compromise the individual's feeling of self-worth or image. Rather, effective feedback is directed toward aspects of the job.

2. *Specificity.* Effective feedback is designed to provide recipients with specific information so that they know what must be done to correct the situation. Ineffective feedback is general and leaves questions in the recipients' minds. For example, telling a staff member that he is doing a poor job is too general and will leave the recipient frustrated in seeking ways to correct the problem.

3. *Description.* Effective feedback can also be characterized as descriptive rather than evaluative. It tells the staff member what she has done in objective terms, rather than presenting a value judgment.

4. *Usefulness.* Effective feedback is information that a staff member can use to improve performance. It serves no purpose to berate staff for their lack of skill if they do not have the ability or training to perform properly. Thus the guideline is that if the feedback is not related to something the staff member can correct, it is not worth mentioning.

5. *Timeliness.* There are also considerations in timing feedback properly. As a rule, the more immediate the feedback, the better. This way the staff member has a better chance of knowing what the principal is talking about and can take corrective action.

6. *Readiness.* For feedback to be effective, staff must be ready to receive it. When feedback is imposed or forced on staff members, it is much less effective.

7. *Clarity.* Effective feedback must be clearly understood by the recipient. A good way of checking is to ask the recipient to restate the major points of the discussion. Also, principals can observe nonverbal facial expressions as indicators of understanding and acceptance.

8. *Validity.* To be effective, feedback must be reliable and valid. Of course, when the information is incorrect, the staff member will feel that

the principal is unnecessarily biased, or the staff member may take corrective action that is inappropriate and only compounds the problem.

Nonverbal Communication   A great deal of communication between a sender and receiver is carried on nonverbally. *Nonverbal communication* refers to the transmission of messages by some medium other than speech or writing. Facial expressions, tone of voice, posture, eye contact, manner of dress, and office furnishings are examples of nonverbal communication. Nonverbal messages can be very powerful in that they often convey feelings and emotions that can amplify or change the meaning of words.

Mark Knapp and Judy Hall (2001) have identified three important kinds of nonverbal communication practiced by principals and other school leaders: body language, object language, and paralanguage.

Body language consists of those body movements or actions that are not specifically intended to replace words, but nevertheless transmit meaning (Hassell, 2002; Hedwig, 2000). For example, senders communicate liking and interest in the receiver when they position themselves physically close to the receiver, touch the receiver during the interaction, maintain eye contact with the receiver, and lean forward during interactions. Furthermore, senders who feel themselves to be of higher status than the receiver assume a more relaxed body position than do those who perceive themselves to be of lower status. Relaxation is manifested by a casual placement of arms and legs, a reclining seated position, and a lack of fidgeting and nervous activity.

Object language consists of physical items such as clothing, furniture, awards, and other physical possessions that convey messages. A person's clothing can indicate status and position, particularly in work settings (Molloy, 1993; 1996). Awards displayed in an office indicate an occupant's accomplishments, whereas the size, furnishings, and location of the office indicate status. Even the arrangement of furnishings can act as object language. For example, some persons choose a closed-desk placement. Their desk faces the door

and serves as a barrier between themselves and visitors. Similarly, chairs for visitors are on one side of the desk, and the office holder sits on the other side. In contrast, other individuals select an open-desk placement. Their desk faces the wall, and chairs for visitors are next to their own, without any barrier between them. Research indicates that office visitors feel more welcome and comfortable when the office design demonstrates moderate tidiness and the office occupant uses an open-desk arrangement (Feldman, 2004).

Paralanguage relates to vocal sounds that influence how words are expressed. These include voice quality, volume, speech rate, pitch, nonfluences (saying "oh," "um," or "uh"), laughing, and yawning. How we say words can greatly alter their meaning (Hickson, 2002). What message is conveyed by a principal at a faculty meeting when he asks, "Do you have any ideas?" The spoken word, on the surface, is a clear request for suggestions. However, when delivered with a scowl in a harsh, authoritarian tone, it may mean instead, "Don't offer any ideas that contradict mine if you know what's good for you."

Summary

1. Communication is the process of transmitting information and common understanding from one person to another.

2. The elements of the communication process are sending the message, encoding the message, transmitting the message through a medium, receiving the message, decoding the message, feedback, and noise.

3. Communications flow in four directions—downward, upward, horizontally, and diagonally.

4. Downward communication consists of policies, rules, and procedures that flow from top administration to lower levels. Upward communication consists of the flow of performance reports, grievances, and other information from lower to higher levels. Horizontal communication is essentially coordinative and occurs between

departments or divisions on the same level. Diagonal communication cuts across the organization's formal chain of command.

5. Organizational communication also flows through a formal network. The five most common networks are the chain, Y, wheel, circle, and all-channel.

6. Also existing in schools is an informal communication network — the grapevine — that can serve as another important source of information to principals.

7. Many barriers retard effective communication. These can be divided into four categories: process barriers, physical barriers, semantic barriers, and psychosocial barriers.

8. To improve the effectiveness of communications, schools must develop an awareness of the importance of sender and receiver responsibilities, active listening skills, feedback, and nonverbal communication.

Field-Based Activities

1. Take field notes for one week and observe the organizational communication flow in your school in four directions: downward, upward, horizontally, and diagonally. Describe how each direction of communication flow is functioning in your school. What can you conclude from your observations? Write your responses in your journal. Be specific.

2. Using this text as your guide, consider the barriers to effective communication that exist in your school: process barriers, physical barriers, semantic barriers, and psychosocial barriers. For each category, discuss barriers to effective communication found in your school. Record your findings in your journal.

3. Imagine that you are the principal of a school. Assuming that communication can always be improved, consider the specific techniques you would use to improve communication in your school relative to (a) awareness of the importance of the sender's and receiver's

responsibilities, (b) active listening, (c) feedback, and (d) nonverbal communication. Address each of these areas. Write your communication improvement plan in your journal. Be specific.

Suggested Readings

benShea, N. (2003). *Inspire, enlighten, & motivate: Great thoughts to enrich your next speech and you.* Thousand Oaks, CA: Corwin Press. The next time you are asked to give a talk, leave your audience talking by drawing from best-selling author Noah benShea's new, original offering, *Inspire, Enlighten, & Motivate.* This valuable resource provides wise and touching thoughts, stories, humor, and one-liners designed to stimulate ideas and help you "punch up" your professional speeches. And, this book does more; it contains reflections to help spur and serve your thinking in daily life.

Gilbert, M. B. (2003). *Communicating effectively: Tools for educational leaders.* Lanham, MD: Scarecrow Press. Here is a unique perspective for aspiring and practicing educational leaders to expand their problem-solving and conflict-resolution strategies. Starting with an exploration of listening problems and solutions, this book evolves into an examination of how people perceive reality, what motivates them, and what happens when their needs are not met.

Kegan, R., & Lahey, L. L. (2002). *How the way we talk can change the way we work: Seven languages of transformation.* San Francisco, CA: Jossey-Bass. This is a how-to book for reflective practitioners. Step-by-step, it teaches educators and leaders how to build highly collaborative, creative, and caring communities.

Parker, D. A. (2003). *Confident communication: Speaking tips for educators.* Thousand Oaks, CA: Corwin Press. In his new easy-to-read resource, trained counselor and experienced educator Douglas A. Parker demonstrates a sensible, skills-based, humorous, and psychologically savvy approach to the strategies that every educator needs to develop as a public speaker. Parker also illustrates how to gain confidence and make nervousness work for you during a speech.

Powell, R. G., & Caseau, D. (2004). *Classroom communication and diversity: Enhancing institutional practice*. Mahwah, NJ: Lawrence Erlbaum. This textbook provides a useful framework for helping new and experienced teachers manage the communication challenges of today's classroom. Challenges that teachers face include the growing diversity of the student body, the impact of diversity on gender and classroom communication, the increasing numbers of students being educated in regular school classrooms annually, and the presence of students with learning disabilities. Authors Robert G. Powell and Dana Caseau believe it is important to challenge teachers to reflect on the ways their personal cultures influence their expectations about appropriate classroom communication and effective ways to demonstrate learning.

Ramsey, R. D. (2002). *How to say the right thing every time: Communicating well with students,* *staff, parents, and the public*. Thousand Oaks, CA: Corwin Press. This user-friendly guide empowers educators with the confidence and tools necessary to communicate effectively, efficiently, and honestly in all situations. The author includes strategies for avoiding the 20 most common communication barriers, with specific tips for delivering meaningful messages to students, parents, peers, and the public to foster understanding and support.

Tomlinson, G. (2002). *The school administrator's complete letter book* (2nd ed.). San Francisco: Jossey-Bass. Make your daily life smoother and your professional image sharper with this complete model-and-reference book for school administrators on the subject of school correspondence. Clearly organized, designed for easy use, and filled with the best letters of the best communicators in modern American education, *The School Administrator's Complete Letter Book* is a gold mine of tested, usable letters and other communiqués. Some of the letters can be used practically word for word from the book or CD-ROM; others can be adapted to your specific needs.

10. The Principal and Change

FOCUSING QUESTIONS

1 What are the forces that bring about the need for change?

2 Why are people likely to resist change?

3 What tactics can principals use to overcome resistance to change?

4 How can force-field analysis help principals better understand resistance to change?

5 What role do principals play in implementing change?

6 What steps must be followed in order for change to be successful?

7 What strategies can be used to improve schools?

In this chapter, we respond to these questions concerning change in school organizations. We begin our discussion by examining the nature of change, including the forces for change and resistance to it. Force-field analysis is described as a useful concept in understanding the complex nature of change. Then, after discussing the processes of planned change, we focus on the types, roles, and characteristics of principals as change agents. Finally, we explore several change strategies to improve schools.

The Nature of Organizational Change

The role of the principal is both intense and diverse. Paradoxically, the only constant in the principal's domain of ever-increasing responsibilities is that of change—change in the physical environment; change in the curriculum; change in faculty and staff; change in the student body; unexpected change; and most importantly, change that can bring about vast improvement in the growth and development of the entire school. The principal must be the primary catalyst in order for the change to be both positive and lasting (Barth, 2004; Cooper, Fusarelli, & Randall, 2004; Deal & Peterson, 2000, 2003; Duke, 2003; Meier, 2003; Sims et al., 2003).

In relation to a school building, we define *organizational change* as any modification in one or more elements of the school. Practically everything a principal does is in some way concerned with implementing change. Hiring a new teacher (changing the work group), purchasing a computer (changing work methods), and developing curriculum (changing subject-matter content) all require knowledge of how to manage change effectively. Virtually every time a principal makes a decision, some type of change occurs.

Forces for Change

Given a choice, most schools prefer stability to change. Why? Because the more predictable and routine activities are, the higher the level of efficiency that can be obtained. Thus the status quo is preferred in many cases. However, schools are not static, but continuously change in response to a variety of forces coming from both inside and outside the school (Hallinan, Gamoran, Kubitacheck, & Loveless, 2003). For principals, the challenge is to anticipate and direct change processes so that school performance is improved (Duke, 2003; Liston et al., 2003; Nata, 2003). Several important factors in each of these categories (internal and external forces) are considered next (Fullan, 2001).

External Forces The external forces for change originate in the school's environment. The *marketplace*, in recent years, has affected schools by introducing competition from within a school district — in the form of magnet schools, learning choice schools, and the like — and from outside the school district, in the form of private schools, storefront schools, and home instruction (Boyd & Miretzky, 2003; Bracey, 2002; Murphy & Datnow, 2002). *Government laws and regulations* are a

frequent impetus for change. As a case in point, strict enforcement of Equal Employment Opportunity Commission regulations causes many schools to carefully examine their hiring, promotion, and pay policies for women and minorities (Cihon & Castagnera, 2001). *Technology* creates the need for change. Computers have made possible high-speed data processing and retrieval of information and have created the need for new positions. The fluctuation of *labor markets* forces principals to initiate change. For instance, the education, talents, and attitudes of potential teachers play an important role in a school's effectiveness. Changes in these facets of the labor force can lead to a shortage or a surplus of qualified teachers. *Economic changes* affect schools as well. During periods of recession, inflation, or downturns in the local or national economy, the attitudes and morale of some teachers suffer, which may hinder school performance (Garner, 2004).

Internal Forces Pressures in the internal environment of the school can also stimulate change. The two most significant internal pressures for change come from *processes* and *people*. Processes that act as pressures for change include communications, decision making, leadership, and motivational strategies, to name only a few. Breakdowns or problems in any of these processes can create pressures for change. Communications may be inadequate; decisions may be of poor quality; leadership may be inappropriate for the situation; and staff motivation may be nonexistent. Such processes reflect breakdowns or problems in the school and may indicate the need for change (Ginsberg, 2003).

Some symptoms of people problems are poor performance levels of teachers and students, high absenteeism of teachers or students, high dropout rates of students, high teacher turnover, poor school-community relations, poor management-union relations, and low levels of teacher morale and job satisfaction (Lunenburg & Irby, 1999; Lunenburg & Ornstein, 2004). A teachers' strike, numerous employee complaints, and the filing of grievances are some tangible signs of problems in the internal environment (Alexander & Alexander, 2005; Essex, 2002; Fischer & Schimmel, 2003;

LaMorte, 2002; McCabe, McCarthy, & Thomas, 2004; Yudof, Kirp, Levin, & Moran, 2002). These factors provide a signal to principals that change is necessary. In addition, internal pressures for change occur in response to organizational changes that are designed to deal with pressures for change exerted by the external environment.

Resistance to Change

Forces for change are a recurring feature of school life. It is also inevitable that change will be resisted, at least to some extent, by both school leaders and staff. There is a human tendency to resist change, because it forces people to adopt new ways of doing things. To cope with this recurring problem, principals must understand why people resist change.

The following are some suggested reasons that people resist change (Argyris, 1985; Jones, 2003; McMillan, 2004):

1. *Uncertainty.* Teachers may resist change because they are worried about how their work and lives will be affected by the proposed change. Even if they have some appreciable dissatisfaction with their present jobs, they have learned their range of responsibilities and know how their principal will react to their behavior in certain situations. Any change creates some potential uncertainties.

2. *Concern over personal loss.* Appropriate change should benefit the school as a whole; but for some teachers, the cost of change in terms of lost power, prestige, salary, quality of work, or other benefits will not be sufficiently offset by the rewards of change. Teachers may feel that change will diminish not only their decision-making authority, accessibility to information, and autonomy but also the inherent characteristics of the job.

3. *Group resistance.* Groups establish norms of behavior and performance that are communicated to members. This communication establishes the boundaries of expected behaviors. Failure to comply with such norms usually results in sanctions against group members by the group. If principals initiate changes that are viewed as threatening to the staff's norms, they are likely to meet with resistance. The more cohesive the staff is, the greater its resistance to change will be. This may explain partially what causes wildcat strikes by teachers when school districts introduce changes without proper notification and preparation.

4. *Dependence.* All humans begin life in a dependent state. Thus, dependence is instilled in all people to a certain extent. Dependency, in and of itself, is not all bad; but if carried to extremes, dependency on others can lead to resistance to change. For instance, staff members who are highly dependent on their principal for feedback on their performance will probably not adopt any new methods or strategies unless the principal personally endorses their behavior and indicates how the proposed changes will improve the teacher's performance.

5. *Trust.* Schools vary substantially in the degree to which teachers trust the principal. On the one hand, if a change is proposed when trust is low, a natural first reaction is to resist it. On the other hand, when trust is high, teachers are more likely to support a proposed change. Further, under conditions of distrust teachers often resist changes, even when they are understood and they can benefit from them.

6. *Awareness of weaknesses in the proposed change.* Teachers may resist change because they are aware of potential problems in the proposed change. If teachers express their reasons for resistance to the principal clearly, along with adequate substantiation, this form of resistance can be beneficial to the school. Principals can use these suggestions to make their change proposals more effective.

Overcoming Resistance to Change

To better understand resistance to change, Kurt Lewin (1951/1975) developed the concept of *force-field analysis.* He looks on a level of behavior within a school not as a static custom, but as

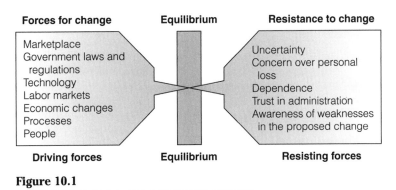

Figure 10.1

Forces for Change and Resistance to Change

a dynamic balance of forces working in opposite directions within the school. He believes that we should think about any change situation in terms of driving forces or factors acting to change the current condition (forces for change) and resisting forces or factors acting to inhibit change (resistance to change). These forces may originate in the internal or external environment of the school or in the behavior of the principal.

Principals must play an active role in initiating change and in attempting to reduce resistance to change. Principals can think of the current condition in a school as an equilibrium that is the result of driving forces and resisting forces working against each other. Principals must assess the change potential and resistance and then attempt to change the balance of forces so that there will be movement toward a desired condition. There are three ways principals can do this: increasing the driving forces, reducing the resisting forces, or considering new driving forces.

Lewin points out that increasing one set of forces without decreasing the other set of forces will increase tension and conflict in the school. Reducing the other set of forces may reduce the amount of tension. Although increasing driving forces is sometimes effective, it is usually better to reduce the resisting forces because increasing driving forces often tends to be offset by increased resistance. Put another way, when we push people, they are likely to push back. Figure 10.1 illustrates the two sets of forces discussed earlier:

forces for change—the marketplace, government laws and regulations, technology, labor markets, economic changes, and processes and people; and resistance to change—uncertainty, concern over personal loss, dependence, trust in the principal, and awareness of weaknesses in the proposed change. These are the types of situations that principals face and must work with every day when attempting to effect change.

As Figure 10.1 shows, change results when an imbalance occurs between the ratio of driving forces and resisting forces. Such an imbalance alters the existing condition—ideally, in the direction planned by the principal—into a new and desired condition. Once the new, desired condition is reached, the opposing forces are again brought into equilibrium. An imbalance may occur through a change in the velocity of any force, a change in the direction of a force, or the introduction of a new force.

Moreover, change involves a sequence of organizational processes that occur over time. Lewin suggests these processes typically require three steps: unfreezing, moving, and refreezing.

1. *Unfreezing.* This step usually means reducing the forces acting to keep the school in its current condition. *Unfreezing* might be accomplished by introducing new information that points out inadequacies in the current state or by decreasing the strength of current values, attitudes, and behaviors. Crises often stimulate unfreezing. Examples of crises are significant increases in

the student dropout rate, dramatic enrollment declines, shifts in population within a school, a sudden increase in teacher or principal turnover, a costly lawsuit, and an unexpected teacher strike. Unfreezing may occur without crises as well. Climate surveys, financial data, and enrollment projections can be used to determine problem areas in a school and initiate change to alleviate problems before crises erupt.

2. *Moving.* Once the school is unfrozen, it can be changed by *moving.* This step usually involves the development of new values, attitudes, and behaviors through internalization, identification, or change in structure. Some changes may be minor and involve a few members—such as changes in recruitment and selection procedures—and others may be major, involving many participants. Examples of the latter include a new evaluation system, restructuring of jobs and duties performed by staff, or restructuring the school district, which necessitates relocating faculty to different school sites within the system.

3. *Refreezing.* The final step in the change process involves stabilizing the change at a new quasistationary equilibrium, which is called *refreezing.* Changes in school culture, changes in staff norms, changes in school policy, or modifications in school structure often accomplish this.

Resistance to change may be overcome in several specific ways. Here are six of the most popular and frequently used approaches (Duke, 2003; Jones, 2003; Kirton, 2003; McMillan, 2004):

1. *Education and communication.* Resistance can be reduced when principals communicate with teachers to help them see the need for change as well as the logic behind it. This can be achieved through face-to-face discussions, formal group presentations, or special reports or publications. The approach works, providing that the source of resistance is inadequate communication and that principal-teacher relations are characterized by mutual trust. If trust does not exist, the change is unlikely to succeed.

2. *Participation and involvement.* Teachers who participate in planning and implementing a change are less likely to resist it. Before making a change, principals can allow those who oppose the change to express their view on the change, indicate potential problems, and suggest modifications. Such participant involvement can reduce resistance, obtain commitment, and increase the quality of the change decision.

3. *Facilitation and support.* It is important for principals to manifest supportive and facilitative leadership behaviors when change is being implemented. This type of leader behavior includes listening to teachers' ideas, being approachable, and using teachers' ideas that have merit. Supportive principals go out of their way to make the work environment more pleasant and enjoyable. For example, difficult changes may require staff development to acquire new skills necessary to implement the change. Such training will likely diminish resistance to the change.

4. *Negotiation and agreement.* Principals can neutralize potential or actual resistance by providing incentives for cooperation. For example, during collective bargaining between the board of education and the teachers' union, certain concessions can be given to teachers in exchange for support of a new program desired by principals. Such concessions may include salary increases, bonuses, or more union representation in decision making. Principals can also use standard rewards such as recognition, increased responsibility, praise, and status symbols.

5. *Manipulation and co-optation.* Manipulation occurs when principals choose to be selective about who gets what information and how much information, how accurate the information is, and when to disseminate the information to increase the chance that change will be successful. Co-optation involves giving the leaders of a resistance group (teachers or other staff members who represent their work group) a key role in the change decision.

The leaders' advice is sought not to arrive at a better decision, but to get their endorsement. Both manipulation and co-optation are inexpensive ways to influence potential resisters to accept change, but these techniques can backfire if the targets become aware they are being tricked. Once such tricks are discovered, the principal's credibility may suffer drastically.

6. *Explicit and implicit coercion.* When other approaches have failed, coercion can be used as a last resort. Some changes require immediate implementation. And change initiators may have considerable power. Such instances lend themselves more readily to the use of coercion to gain compliance to proposed changes. Teachers and other staff can be threatened with job loss, decreased promotional opportunities, salary freeze (this technique is used infrequently in public schools), or a job transfer. There are, however, negative effects of using coercion — including frustration, fear, revenge, and alienation, which in turn may lead to poor performance, dissatisfaction, and turnover.

Understanding Resistance to Change

Presented here are a series of questions, proposed by Howard Margolis (2004), that principals should answer from the perspective of individual teachers opposing proposed changes. The answers provide information to better understand the reasons behind a teacher's resistance, and they shed light on how to effectively address concerns and secure cooperation.

- How demanding are the proposed changes?
- Will the proposed changes give me relief from pain?
- Will the proposed changes lead to feelings of satisfaction?
- To what degree will the proposed changes benefit or harm me?
- What is the probability of my effectively instituting the proposed changes?
- What will others think of me if I fail?
- What will I think of myself if I fail?
- What will others think of me if I'm successful?
- Do I have the time and resources to institute the proposed changes?
- How important are the proposed changes to me?
- Are the proposed changes consistent with my values?
- Do I understand the proposed changes?
- Do those proposing the changes accurately understand what I'll have to do to ensure the changes work?
- Will implementing the proposed changes be interesting?
- What are the consequences of success?
- What are the consequences of failure?
- Have I had an opportunity to influence the proposed changes?
- How will the proposed changes affect other students in my class?
- Will I have ample opportunity to modify the proposed changes so they fit my way of doing things?
- How do other teachers feel about the proposed changes?
- Will I get the training I think I need?
- Will those providing support and feedback be understanding?
- What are the consequences of not making the proposed changes?
- Will people listen and act on my concerns?
- Can I return to the old ways if the proposed changes fail?
- If the proposed changes do not work, can I modify them or abandon them without a hassle?
- Ultimately, how important are the goals and objectives of the proposed changes to me?
- Will the proposed changes make life easier or more difficult for me in the short and long term?

- What is the long-term commitment of the administration and support staff?
- Are the proposed changes just another educational fad?

Getting Reform Right: What Works and What Doesn't

After years of failed educational reform, educators are saying that knowledge of the change process is crucial. To succeed, we need to cognize what we know about successful change both before and during the change process. According to Michael Fullan and Matthew Miles (1992), seven basic themes derived from current knowledge of successful change form a set and must be contemplated together when attempting change:

1. *Change is learning.* All change involves learning, and all learning involves coming to understand and be good at something new. Thus conditions that support learning must be part of any change effort. Such conditions are also necessary for the valid rejection of changes, because many people reject innovations before they fully understand them.

2. *Change is a journey, not a blueprint.* There can be no blueprints for change, because rational planning models for complex social change (such as educational reform) do not work. The message is not the traditional "Plan, then do," but "Do, then plan, and do and plan again." This perspective rests on the assumption that the environment both inside and outside schools is often chaotic.

3. *Problems are our friends.* We cannot develop effective responses to complex situations unless we actively seek and confront real problems that are difficult to solve. Only through immersing ourselves in problems can we come up with creative solutions. Problems are the route to deeper change and deeper satisfaction.

4. *Change is resource hungry.* Change demands additional resources for training, for substitutes, for new materials, for new space, and above all, for time. Change represents developing solutions to complex problems, learning new

skills, and arriving at new insights, all of which are carried out in a social setting already overloaded with demands.

5. *Change requires the power to manage it.* Change initiatives do not run themselves. They require substantial effort devoted to such tasks as monitoring implementation, keeping everyone informed of what's happening, linking multiple change projects, locating unsolved problems, and taking clear coping action.

6. *Change is systematic.* What does it mean to work systematically? There are two aspects: (a) Reform must simultaneously focus on the development and interrelationships of all main components of the system — curriculum, teaching and teacher development, community, student support systems, and the like; and (b) reform must focus not just on structure, policy, and regulations, but on the deeper issues of system culture.

7. *All large-scale change is implemented locally.* The ideas that change is learning, change is a journey, problems are our friends, change is resource hungry, change requires the power to manage, and change is systematic all embody the fact that local implementation by teachers, principals, parents, and students is the only way that change happens.

Managing Change

Because schools are beset by counteracting forces that simultaneously induce and resist change, managing change effectively is one of the principal's most difficult and challenging tasks. We examine the following issues in managing change: the principal as change agent (types, roles, and characteristics) and the process of change.

The Principal as Change Agent

Any principal can be a *change agent.* As we discuss the management of change, we assume that, for the most part, it is initiated and carried out by a principal within the school. However, the change agent can be an internal staff specialist, central office administrator, or outside consultant whose expertise is in implementing change. For major system-wide changes, internal administration will often hire outside consultants to provide advice and assistance. Because they are from the outside, they are not bound by the school district's culture, politics, or traditions. This can be a disadvantage though, because outside consultants lack an understanding of the school district's history, operating procedures, and personnel.

Change Agent Types   Although little research has explored what type of change agent is most effective in a given situation, some research has identified different types of change agents according to their characteristics and methods of implementing change (Burke et al., 2003; Duarte et al., 2003; Sims et al., 2003; Wasson, Ludwigsen, & Hopper, 2003). These include the following:

1. *Outside-pressure type.* These change agents work to change systems from outside the school. They are not members of the school they are trying to change; and they use various pressure tactics such as mass demonstrations, civil disobedience, and violence to accomplish their objectives. Typically, they offer options that are more radical than those the community might accept. This usually results in the possibility of examining many different alternatives.

2. *People-change-technology type.* The focus of activity for this type of change agent is the individual. The change agent may be concerned with teacher morale and motivation, including absenteeism, turnover, and quality of work performed. The methods used include job enrichment, goal setting, and behavior modification. The major assumption underlying this orientation is that if individuals change their behavior, the school will also change, providing that enough people change. A principal can certainly assume the role of people-change-technology type, and she often does.

3. *Analysis-for-the-top type.* The focus of this change agent is on changing the organizational structure so as to improve output and

efficiency. The change agent uses operations research, systems analysis, policy studies, and other forms of analytical approaches to change the school's structure or technology. For example, the change might include introducing computerized information processing systems. Many principals assume this role when implementing change.

4. *Organizational development type.* These change agents focus their attention on internal processes such as intergroup relations, communication, and decision making. Their intervention strategy is often called a cultural change approach, because they thoroughly analyze the culture of the targeted school. This approach grew out of such areas as sensitivity training, team building, and survey feedback. Many principals assume the role of organizational development type when implementing change.

Change Agent Roles   Change agents (including principals) play at least three distinct roles: consulting, training, and research (Carnall, 2003; Greve, 2003; Jackson, 2003; Stamm, 2003). A school principal can and often does perform each of these functions.

1. *Consulting.* As a *consultant,* the principal places the school staff in touch with data from outside the school or helps the school staff to generate data from within the school system. The overall purpose is to help the school staff find solutions to school problems through analysis of valid data.

2. *Training.* In addition to performing the role of consultant, the principal may function as a *trainer.* Here the principal helps the school staff learn how to use data to effect change. The principal, or outside change agent if one is used, has a dual purpose as trainer: (a) to help the school staff derive implications for action from the present data; and (b) to leave the school staff with a new set of skills — the ability to retrieve, translate, and use new data to solve future problems. Several school districts in Texas have hired outside consultants to instruct teachers on how to improve student achievement on state-mandated tests.

3. *Research.* Finally, and closely associated with the previous role, the principal may assume the role of *researcher* (Poole, Van De Ven, Dooley, & Holmes, 2000). As researcher, the principal may train the school staff in the skills needed for valid evaluation of the effectiveness of action plans that have been implemented. Furthermore, as part of the overall intervention strategy, the principal will design an evaluation component that can be used in solving current as well as future problems.

Characteristics of Successful Change Agentry

After an extensive review of the literature, several researchers have identified a set of 10 factors characteristic of effective change agentry (Havelock & Sashkin, 1983; Metcalfe et al., 2003; Tsoukas & Mylonopoulos, 2003; Tushman et al., 2004). These factors, briefly defined in the following list, refer to the way in which change agents manage change rather than to any personal characteristics they may possess. In most cases, the principal of the school building performs the role of change agent.

1. *Hemophily.* The more alike the principal and school staff are, the more likely it is that the principal will be successful. Similarity between the principal and school staff results in acceptance of the principal by the staff as well as understanding of the staff by the principal.

2. *Empathy.* This is the skill of understanding the feelings of another person. Empathy leads to improved communication and understanding between the principal and school staff.

3. *Linkage.* This refers to the extent to which the principal and school staff are tied together in collaborative activities. The greater the collaborative involvement (the tighter the linkage), the more likely the principal will be successful.

4. *Proximity.* This refers to the physical and psychological closeness of the principal and school staff. The greater the proximity between the principal and the school staff, the more likely the principal will be successful. Increasing proximity makes it easier to develop collaborative linkages. Proximity also facilitates the development of empathy between principal and school staff. Proximity has relevance to the principal's open-door policy and to his visibility during school hours.

5. *Structuring.* This factor refers to the ability of the principal and school staff to clearly plan and organize their activities concerning the change effort. A clearly designed change effort is more likely to be understood and implemented by the school staff.

6. *Capacity.* This factor is a characteristic of the school system. It refers to the school district's capability of providing the resources needed for a successful change effort. A successful change effort requires an adequate amount of resources.

7. *Openness.* This characteristic refers to the degree to which the principal and school staff are willing to hear, respond to, and be influenced by one another. The preceding six factors can all facilitate the development of such openness or, when absent, they can hinder the development of openness between principal and school staff.

8. *Reward.* This refers to the nature and variety of potential positive outcomes of the change effort that might accrue to the principal and school staff. Change efforts should be designed so that the staff is rewarded for changing.

9. *Energy.* This refers to the amount of physical and psychological effort the principal and school staff are able and willing to expend on the change effort. When day-to-day problems are so pressing that they sap most of the staff's energy, the staff has diminished energy to devote to the change effort.

10. *Synergy.* This characteristic refers to the positively reinforcing effects that the preceding nine factors have on one another. More specifically, synergy involves the variety of people, resources, energies, and activities involved in interacting in the change effort that mutually support success.

All changes involve a change agent, the person who initiates the change. This can be the existing principal, a new principal, a principal from another school, an internal staff specialist, or an outside consultant. Whichever approach is used, change agents make things happen. They facilitate creativity and innovation in schools and school districts (Stamm, 2003).

The Change Process

Management of change requires the use of some systematic process that can be broken down into steps or phases (Dawson, 2003). One of the most well-known and popular models of the change process emphasizes the role of the change agent (Greiner, 1967). As described in the previous section, a change agent is the individual, from inside or outside the school or school district, who takes a leadership role in initiating the change process. In many cases, the change agent is the building principal. As you study this change process, notice that it must involve two basic ideas for the change to be effective. First, successful change requires a redistribution of power within the existing structure. Successful change is characterized by a greater degree of shared power within the organizational hierarchy. Second, this redistribution of power occurs as a result of a developmental change process. In other words, it is a sequential process rather than a sudden shift (Barth, 2004; Conley, 2003; Liston et al., 2003; Marshall, 2003; Meier, 2003).

Figure 10.2 depicts six phases through which change may occur in schools. In this figure, top administration plays a key role as change agent. The potential for change also exists at all levels of leadership and operating responsibilities in the school or school district. Figure 10.2 shows change taking a top-down pattern; it may also occur from bottom-up or middle-outward patterns. In each case, however, school leaders play key change agent roles.

The following list summarizes the activities in each phase of the total developmental process. We will assume that the change process takes place in an individual school, and that the principal assumes the role of top management in the change process.

Phase 1: Pressure and Arousal. The process begins when the principal feels a need or pressure for change. This pressure can be exerted by external factors such as increased competition for students, economic changes, or federal and state mandates. Or it may be felt because of internal factors such as a sharp decline in test scores, reduced teacher productivity, high faculty turnover, increased student dropouts, serious student or teacher unrest, and excessive teacher grievances. The need for change is more readily apparent if there are both external and internal pressures that do not offset each other.

Phase 2: Intervention and Reorientation. Although school principals may sense the need for change, they may not be able to analyze its problems accurately and thereby make the correct changes. When under severe pressure, principals may rationalize the school's problems by blaming them on another group such as the teachers' union, the federal government, or the state legislature. Principals may be capable of managing the change process if they are perceived as expert and are trusted. If not, an outside consultant or change agent is often brought in to define the problem and begin the process of getting school members to focus on it.

Phase 3: Diagnosis and Recognition. In the third phase of successful change, the entire school becomes involved in determining the true causes of problems requiring change by gathering relevant information. A shared approach between the principal and staff is common in this stage. The decision-making process has been broadened as the principal shows her willingness to recognize tough problems and to change. Diagnosis of the problem areas leads to recognition of specific problems. This step tends to be avoided in efforts involving unsuccessful change.

Phase 4: Invention and Commitment. After the problem is recognized, the school moves toward creative solutions to the problems that have been identified. The shared approach again predominates in this phase. If teachers are encouraged to participate in this process, they will probably be more committed to the solutions.

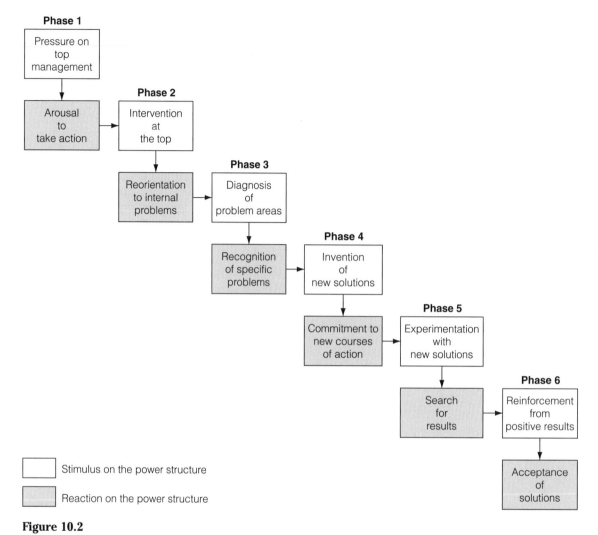

Figure 10.2

Model of Successful Organizational Change

Phase 5: Experimentation and Search. The solutions developed in phase 4 are usually tested
in small-scale pilot programs, and the results are
then analyzed. For example, in a high school,
one department may try out an idea before it is
attempted in the school as a whole. In this way,
the principal can work out the bugs before
introducing the change on a large scale. Through
control mechanisms, the principal determines to

what degree the planned change is succeeding in
remedying the problem, how well it is being
received, and how implementation can be
improved.

Phase 6: Reinforcement and Acceptance. Finally, if the course of action has been tested and
found desirable, it should be accepted more willingly. Furthermore, individuals need to be reinforced for making the change successful. The

positive feedback coming from the pilot programs in phase 5 adds reinforcement to the change process. Other techniques for reinforcing acceptance include praise, recognition, promotion, salary increases, and continued participation in the change process.

Key Principal Behaviors That Promote Successful School Change

Principals wishing to promote change in their schools need to know about effective leadership behaviors that contribute to successful school improvement. Recently, the New York State Task Force on Educational Reform (Possin, 2004) examined 60 cases of educational improvement in schools across New York State. The task force identified the following key behaviors of successful principals for change in schools:

1. *Build a vision.* Successful principals for change communicate a vision of reform goals throughout the school. This vision is a clear idea of where the school is headed.

2. *Create a positive climate.* Principals for change encourage experimentation and permit faculty to fail from time to time. Heavy-handed monitoring for mistakes and failures dampens innovation. Principals also recognize success in others, rather than claiming all the credit themselves. They understand that the faculty's success is the principal's success.

3. *Mobilize.* Principals demonstrate this behavior by sharing the responsibility for student success with their teachers. Sharing responsibility for improvement can rapidly multiply reform efforts by engaging many faculty members throughout the school to contribute energetic and creative leadership for change.

4. *Engage community support.* Engaging community support — from parents, business, and other community resources — makes change more enduring. Supportive parents protect the change process. Business and community agency linkages add resources and affirmation to reform.

5. *Train.* Change through shared decision making is complex and usually requires initial training in communication, group process, and decision making. Principals need to provide training in specific curricular improvements and assistance with problem solving during the implementation of a reform.

6. *Provide resources.* Successful change is characterized by a central office that supports program development with adequate funding, staffing, supplies, and other resources. Building principals must request additional resources during school improvement efforts.

7. *Remove barriers.* Faculty involved in change may run into policy barriers or opposition from the public or from other faculty members. Successful changes are supported by principals who remove such barriers by making policies flexible, finding creative ways to circumvent barriers imposed from the outside, and dealing with political opposition through power and persuasion (Cooper, Fusarelli, & Randall, 2004).

Change Strategies

School improvement programs include a broad range of behavioral science–based strategies. For convenience of discussion, we have categorized them into two groups: process strategies and structural strategies. We will discuss these strategies specifically in relation to a single school and its principal and teaching staff.

Process Strategies

The emphasis of process change strategies is on the *process* to accomplish change. Many of these strategies focus on improving individual and group processes in decision making, problem identification and problem solving, communication, working relationships, and the like. We examine four frequently used process strategies: survey feedback, team building, process consultation, and quality of work life (QWL).

Survey Feedback   Three basic steps are employed in *survey feedback* (Conlon & Short, 1984). First, a questionnaire is typically completed by all members of the school staff, or the school district if the change is initiated districtwide. The questionnaire asks staff for their perceptions and attitudes on a broad range of topics such as decision-making practices, communication effectiveness, coordination between units, job satisfaction, and the like. The school's principal receives a summary of the tabulated results from the survey. In some cases, a consultant (an internal or external change agent) meets with the principal to discuss the results. In the second step, data are fed back to the school staff, usually during group meetings. The organizational development consultant, usually the building principal, often attends the meeting to explain any technical aspects of the data. Finally, in the third step, specific plans for dealing with the problems identified by the survey are developed. Again, this process usually takes place in group sessions where open discussion is encouraged.

Survey feedback functions both as a change strategy and as a diagnostic process. Because of its value in organizational diagnosis, survey feedback is frequently used as part of large-scale, long-term change programs in conjunction with other strategies and techniques. It can be used to improve groups and teams, intergroup relations, and system-wide activities. The survey feedback technique is powerful because it provides feedback to staff members at all levels of the school on results for their units, and it engages them in constructive discussions with their principal for making improvements.

Team Building   Schools are made up of people working together to achieve some common goal. Because people are frequently required to work in groups, considerable attention has been focused on team building in recent years (Maeroff, 1993). Improving the team means better performance by the school in providing teaching and encouraging learning.

Team building is a process of diagnosing and improving the effectiveness of a staff, devoting particular attention to teaching and collaboration within staff — especially the principal's role in relation to other staff members. Team-building strategies are typically directed toward goal setting, development of interpersonal relations, role analysis, and team process analysis.

Team building may begin by having teachers define the school's goals. Different perceptions of what the school's purpose is may surface. Following this task, teachers can evaluate the school's performance: How effectively is the school achieving its goals? This evaluation may identify potential problem areas. Next, each team member's role can be identified and clarified. Previous ambiguities may be brought to the surface. And, finally, key processes that go on within the team are analyzed to identify how these processes might be improved, resulting in greater team effectiveness. This latter activity is similar to process consultation.

Process Consultation   A variation of the team-building technique is process consultation. In *process consultation,* often an outside consultant helps the principal perceive, understand, and act on process events that occur in his work environment (Schein, 1999). These might include work flow, informal relationships among faculty members, and formal communication channels. The consultant gives the principal insight into what is going on around him, within him, and between him and other people. The consultant is not there to solve the principal's problems. Instead, the consultant provides guidance to help the principal diagnose which processes need to be improved.

Process consultation usually addresses one or more of the following areas of concern: communication, leadership, decision making and problem solving, group norms and roles, and conflict resolution. Typical activities include gathering data about some organizational or group process, sharing this information with the staff members involved, and planning actions designed to improve the process. Ideally, the work-group intervention would be a combination of a team-building session followed by periodic process consultation to reinforce the improved work environment.

Quality of Work Life (QWL) In recent years, there has been a growing recognition of the importance of simultaneously improving the value of teachers' psychological experiences at work as well as their productivity. This philosophy is embodied in the quality of work life (QWL) approach to change. Such programs are typically broad based and lack the precise definition and focus of survey feedback and team building. *Quality of work life* can be defined as any activity undertaken by a school or school district for the express purpose of improving one or more of the following conditions that affect a staff member's experience with a school or school district: adequate and fair compensation; safe and healthy working conditions; opportunity to use and develop personal capabilities; opportunity to grow and progress in a career; opportunity to participate in decisions; protection from arbitrary and unfair treatment; and opportunity to satisfy social needs (Pasmore, 1985).

Successful QWL programs are being used in such organizations as GM, Ford, Chrysler, AT&T, Motorola, IBM, Texas Instruments, Xerox, GE, and many school districts. QWL programs often encompass a wide variety of specific techniques, such as team building, job restructuring, shared decision making, redesign of pay systems, Theory Z, and quality circles. Implementation of these techniques is expected to translate into improved faculty teaching performance and student learning.

Structural Strategies

Structural change strategies involve an adjustment in the school's structure to accomplish change goals. Structural adjustment may be the change goal or simply may lead to it. Some strategies focus on changes in the task, whereas others focus on the means of setting goals as well as strategic plans for attaining those goals. Here we discuss the more commonly used structural approaches to change: goal setting, job redesign, quality circles, and strategic planning.

Goal Setting A major problem confronting large school districts is the lack of identification by the individual staff member with the goals of the district. With specialization so highly developed in schools, many staff members are very much divorced from the direction and purpose of the larger system. *Goal setting* is a method of coordinating individual staff members' efforts toward overall school district goals (Locke & Latham, 1995). Getting staff to work toward school district goals is not just a matter of informing them what the goals are. Rather, staff members' support for system-wide goals is increased if they participate in the goal-setting process. When the goal-setting process is mutually influenced by leader and staff, the staff are given some control over their work environment (Barth, 2003; Marshall, 2003; Meier, 2003; Senge, 2001; Tsoukas et al., 2003).

A goal-setting program is system-wide, in order to achieve a better fit between individual and system goals. Top leaders (superintendent and her administrative team) set their operating goals, followed by meetings with the second level of administrators (building principals) during which their goals are mutually set. These principals then meet with their staff to help set their goals, and so on down the hierarchy to the lowest level in the school district. In this way, every level is linked with every other level. Short-run goals mesh with long-run goals; broad school district goals mesh with building goals, which in turn mesh with department and instructional objectives. This approach increases the chances that the school district will work as a coordinated unit, even in the face of change (Barth, 2004; Conley, 2003; Cooper, Fusarelli, & Randall, 2004; Liston, 2003).

Job Redesign The redesign of jobs has received increasing emphasis as a change strategy (Griffin & Woodman, 1985). *Job redesign* can be defined as a deliberate, planned restructuring of the way tasks are performed, with the purpose of improving performance. Job redesign includes a host of specific organizational change techniques, such as job enrichment, specialization, job engineering, job rotation, job enlargement, and autonomous task groups (Herzberg, 1987). These techniques are most successful when employed as a comprehensive school change program that examines the fit among the task, technology, structure, and people within the school system (Senge, 1990; 2001).

Boredom on the job experienced by blue-collar workers in industry precipitated much of the emphasis on job redesign. However, repetitive tasks affect all kinds of employees, from mass-production systems to management. Once workers' lower-level needs are satisfied, experienced employees begin to expect more from their jobs. They want them to be more challenging, expressive, and fulfilling. Job redesign techniques are attempts to add variety and challenge to jobs — bringing them more in line with staff expectations. In effect, increasing teachers' involvement in decision making through site-based management is an example of job redesign (Barth, 2004; Conley, 2003; Liston et al., 2003; Marshall, 2003; Meier, 2003; Senge, 2001). In many cases, these improvements should lead to increased motivation, teaching performance, and student learning (Ginsberg, 2003).

Quality Circles   Widely used by Japanese firms, quality circles have become increasingly popular in the United States (Bonstingl, 2001; Katzan, 1989). Like survey feedback, quality circles are designed to stimulate an upward communications flow, from first-line staff to principals and central office administrators. Quality circles also fit well into comprehensive QWL programs, in that they regularly and actively solicit greater staff involvement in decision making and problem solving.

A *quality circle* is a voluntary group of 5 to 10 members, typically from similar jobs or the same school, who meet periodically to identify and solve work-related problems. Each quality circle usually has an appointed group leader; and members are trained in techniques of problem solving and group process by a facilitator, who may be an internal or external change consultant. Groups focus on departmental and organizational goals and submit proposals for change to the principal. Recently, principals have acted as facilitators of quality circles. A steering committee consisting of people from all levels and areas of the school typically reviews proposals, accepts or rejects them, and allocates resources for implementation.

Strategic Planning   Constantly changing social and economic conditions affect schools, necessitating the imperative to plan ahead. Schools must anticipate the turbulence of future years and plan processes for achieving their goals (Burke et al., 2003; Drucker, 2001). Implicit in these processes for schools is environmental scanning (Cook, 1995).

Strategic planning involves identifying the mission of a school; recognizing internal and external forces that affect the school; analyzing those forces to determine the effects they have on the school's ability to accomplish its mission; developing strategies for dealing with them, including a framework for improving and restructuring programs, management, participation, and evaluation; and instituting action plans to carry out those strategies and achieve the school's mission (Kaufman, 2003).

Many authors do not discriminate between long-range planning and strategic planning. Strategic planning goes beyond a mechanistic series of planning procedures. Its power lies in its capacity to create dissonance in people, upset traditional views, identify new possibilities, and pose new questions. In this sense, "strategic planning is a management process for changing and transforming schools" (McCune & Brandt, 1986, p. 32).

Shirley McCune and Ronald Brandt (1986) outline the structural differences between strategic planning and long-range planning. On the one hand, although both types of planning are concerned with the future, long-range planning typically begins with an assumption that a school will remain comparatively stable; it seeks to develop internal goals and projections based on that assumption. Strategic planning, on the other hand, begins with a recognition of the external environment as an important consideration of the planning process; and the actions initiated to effect plans are based on an analysis, synthesis, and evaluation of this environment.

Business has devoted a great deal of attention to strategic planning (Bryson, 2004). Only recently has any emphasis been placed on the study of strategic planning in school settings. In a study of 127 school districts in Kentucky, Basham and Lunenburg (1989) found relationships between strategic planning and student achievement in reading, language arts, and mathematics at several grade levels. None of the relationships were strong, however. In addition, the researchers found a direct relationship between strategic planning and both school district wealth and per-pupil expenditures. That is, the higher the assessed property value per child and the greater the percentage of revenue from local sources supporting education, the more likely the school district is to be engaged in strategic planning efforts.

Summary

1. Both external and internal forces can create the need for change in schools. These include factors such as competition for students, government regulations, new technology, labor market fluctuations, economic changes, administrative processes, and fulfillment of people's needs.

2. People often resist change because of the uncertainty it creates, concern over personal loss, group norms, need for dependence, lack of trust in the principal, and awareness of weaknesses in the proposed change.

3. Force-field analysis can help principals understand resistance to change. Principals must encourage driving forces for change and reduce resisting forces to change. The change process also passes through three stages: refreezing, moving, and unfreezing.

4. Principals also can use specific tactics for overcoming resistance to change, including communication, participation, support, negotiation, manipulation and co-optation, and coercion.

5. A change agent is often utilized to help a principal manage a change effort, or the principal herself can act as a change agent. There are four types of change agents: outside-pressure type, people-change-technology type, analysis-for-the-top type, and organizational development type. The principal as change agent, or an outside change agent, plays three distinct roles: consultant, trainer, and researcher. Several factors characterize successful change agentry: hemophily,

empathy, linkage, proximity, structuring, capacity, openness, reward, energy, and synergy.

6. The change process should proceed through six steps: pressure and arousal, intervention and reorientation, diagnosis and recognition, intervention and commitment, experimentation and search, and reinforcement and acceptance.

7. Change strategies can be divided into two categories: process and structural. Process change strategies include survey feedback, team building, process consultation, and quality of work life (QWL). Structural change strategies include goal setting, job redesign, quality circles, and strategic planning. Both process strategies and structural strategies are designed to improve teaching and learning.

Field-Based Activities

1. What changes have occurred in your school or school district? People often resist change for a variety of reasons: the uncertainty it creates, concern over personal loss, group norms, the need for independence, lack of trust in the principal, and awareness of weaknesses in the proposed change. Observe and reflect on changes that have occurred in your school or school district. Take field notes for one week, during which time you analyze the type(s) of resistance to the change(s) that have occurred. In your journal, record the results of your observations, reflections, and analysis.

2. Principals use specific tactics for overcoming resistance to change: communication, participation, support, negotiation, manipulation and co-optation, and coercion. Which of these tactics does your principal use? Assuming you were the principal of a school, which tactics for overcoming resistance to change would you use? Write your response in your journal.

3. To accomplish change, principals can use several process change strategies (survey feedback, team building, process consultation, and quality of work life) and several structural change strategies (goal setting, job redesign, quality

circles, and strategic planning). Observe for one or more weeks and reflect on changes that have taken place in your school or school district. What strategies have your principal or central office administrators used to accomplish change in your school or school district? If you were principal of a school, what strategies would you use to accomplish change in your school? Support your position. Write your responses in your journal. Be specific.

Suggested Readings

Cuban, L. (2003). *Why is it so hard to get good schools?* New York: Teachers College Press. Providing a strong counter voice to today's standards-based reform, *Why Is It So Hard to Get Good Schools?* covers many concepts: (a) It features powerful ideas on teacher education, curriculum, and school administration in an accessible lecture style by Larry Cuban, an experienced teacher, administrator, and acclaimed author; (b) it offers vignettes of four "good" schools (traditional, progressive, community-based, and democratic) that clearly differ from one another, illustrating that there is no one type of schooling that is inherently better than another; (c) it discusses the centrality of teaching to substantial and lasting school improvement, helping us tackle the ongoing reform paradox of viewing teachers as both the problem in and solution to creating "good" schools; and (d) it illuminates the "messy linkages" between educational policy and classroom practice.

Fuhrman, S. H. (Ed.). (2004). *Redesigning accountability systems for education.* New York: Teachers College Press. Expert contributors examine and offer recommendations on crucial issues such as: (a) the effect of accountability policies on the ability of schools to improve over time, (b) the significant variation in the design and effect of accountability systems in different states, (c) the choice of accountability measures and the levels of progress to expect, (d) how to avoid penalizing schools for socioeconomic

problems and other factors out of their control, (e) the use of multiple measures of student achievement, (f) inclusion of students with disabilities and limited English proficiency in accountability systems, and (g) building teachers' capacity to use information provided by assessments to improve instruction.

Fullan, M. (2001). *The new meaning of educational change* (3rd ed.). New York: Teachers College Press. In 1982 an extraordinary book, *The New Meaning of Educational Change,* revolutionized the way educational reform was regarded. Now, Michael Fullan has greatly revised and expanded the ideas that make this book the definitive up-to-date reference for the educational innovator in the new millennium. It offers powerful insights into the complexity of reform and recommends inspiring and practical strategies for lasting improvement. Writing in clear, accessible language, Fullan provides a classic guide to reform.

Hargreaves, A., Early, L., Moore, S., & Manning, S. (2001). *Learning to change: Teaching beyond subjects and standards.* San Francisco: Jossey-Bass. In a compelling, highly readable book, the authors explain the factors that support and hinder the teachers' struggle to create higher standards for their students. The authors go beyond the technical and intellectual work of teaching, recognizing the highly emotional cultural aspects of change.

Oaks, J., Quartz, K. H., Ryan, S., & Lipton, M. (2000). *Becoming good American schools: The struggle for civic virtue in education reform.* San Francisco: Jossey-Bass. Gain valuable insight as you listen to the stories of schools that altered structures and practices to become places fostering innovative ideas, caring people, principles of social justice, and democratic ideals.

Sarason, S. B. (2002). *Educational reform: A self-scrutinizing memoir.* New York: Teachers College Press. In this "self-scrutinizing memoir," Professor Sarason candidly confronts his "errors of omission and commission, mistakes, and emphases" in his half-century involvement in educational reform. Sharing his thoughts about the future of education, Sarason discusses his thinking on charter schools, productive learning, motivation, high-stakes testing, the importance of working through change, the mistaken idea that we can clone reforms, and much more.

Schlechty, P. C. (2001). *Inventing better schools: An action plan for educational reform.* San Francisco: Jossey-Bass. In this powerful wake-up call to educators, Phillip Schlechty argues that schools must change or become obsolete—and that central to this change is a rethinking of old rules, roles, and relationships.

11. Budgeting and School Facilities

> **Standard 3.0:** *Candidates who complete the program are educational leaders who have the knowledge and ability to promote the success of all students by managing the organization, operations, and resources in a way that promotes a safe, efficient, and effective learning environment.*

FOCUSING QUESTIONS

1 How are school budgets developed?

2 Why are financial controls necessary in schools?

3 Are zero-base budgeting and planning-programming-budgeting systems, or variations thereof, suitable for schools?

4 What is the average age of schools in your district? What school infrastructure items are most costly in your district?

5 How are principals and other school personnel dealing with environmental hazards in their school buildings?

In this chapter, we address these questions pertaining to budgeting and school facilities. We begin our discussion with budgets, the budgeting process, and financial controls. Then we discuss the pros and cons of two budgeting methods: zero-based budgeting and planning-programming-budgeting systems as alternatives to line-item budgeting. We conclude the chapter with a discussion of school facilities, including school infrastructure costs, financing new construction, and environmental hazards.

School Budgeting

Budgets translate the school district's education plan into numerical terms (Garner, 2004; King, Swanson, & Sweetland, 2003; Odden & Picus, 2004). Thus budgets are statements of planned revenue and expenditures by category and period of time. School districts may establish budgets for building units, divisions, or the entire school district. The usual time period for a school district budget is one year.

Expenditures and Revenue

Expenditures   Education expenditures are divided for accounting purposes into current expenses, capital improvement, long-term and short-term debt payment, and interest payment. In addition, the U.S. Department of Education in conjunction with the Association of School Business Officials (ASBO) has developed a uniform system of classification of current expenses that most state departments of education have accepted and are using.

Current Expenses   Current expenses include all monies disbursed for the daily operation of schools. They are usually classified in the annual budget under the following four categories: *instruction,* including regular programs (elementary, middle/junior high school, high school), special programs, and adult/continuing education programs; *support services,* including attendance and health services, pupil transportation services, food services and student activities, plant maintenance, instructional staff and support services, and general administration; *community services,* including recreation, civic activities, and nonpublic school services; and *nonprogrammed charges,* including payments to other governmental units.

Capital Outlay   Items that are constructively consumable during a single fiscal year (e.g., salaries, textbooks, and supplies) are listed under current expenses; an item with a life expectancy of more than one year is considered a capital expense. Thus capital outlay includes all permanent additions to existing land, buildings, and equipment. It differs from expenditures for plant maintenance in that capital outlay represents an extension of the existing plant.

Debt Service   Debt service includes the payment of short- and long-term loans and revenue payments for the principal as well as interest on these debts. Principal payments are made directly, as in the case of serial bonds, or into a sinking fund for retiring long-term bonds.

If a school district pays for capital extension out of current tax revenues or on a pay-as-you-build basis, there is no need for a budget classification for debt service, except for short-term or floating debts. By law, school districts raise all their own revenue to meet the communities' needs, including capital extension, which sometimes necessitates borrowing funds for that purpose (Alexander & Alexander, 2005; Russo, 2004). The use of credit for plant extension, therefore, represents an additional handicap to school districts, because debt service is a prior budgetary obligation that may carry over from one year's budget to the next until the debt is paid. And the total expense of long-term borrowing for capital extension generally more than doubles the cost of the school plant. *Interest payments* are made as they fall due.

Revenue   Although in the past public schools depended chiefly on local sources of revenue for their support, the relative percentage of local and state contributions has changed greatly over nearly three-quarters of a century. In the 1929–1930 school year, local districts contributed 82.7% of the total revenue for the operation of public schools in the United States. In the 1999–2000 school year, local revenue for public education had declined to 44.2% and state appropriations were 48.7% nationally. The remaining balance of 7.1% was derived from federal funds (U.S. Department of Education, 2002a). The change has resulted in a better-balanced revenue system generally and, in many cases, better-equalized educational opportunity for all schoolchildren.

Current expenditures and debt payment remain largely dependent on the general property tax. State appropriations are derived primarily from the general property, sales, and income taxes. Regular federal contributions are taken from the general treasury and represent income from all sources of federal taxation. The local school district has comparatively little authority over the methods and sources of financing its schools; this is a state responsibility. The Tenth Amendment to the U.S. Constitution confers on the state the authority not only to regulate and control education but also to devise and implement its own system of taxation.

Thus the authority of local school districts to raise and collect taxes for schools is a power that the state legislature must confer on them. Furthermore, not all districts have the same taxing power. The legislature can classify school districts and delegate varied financial powers to those dependent on their classification.

Basically, with respect to their power to tax and raise funds for public schools, there are two broad classifications of school districts: fiscally independent and fiscally dependent. The vast majority of the nearly 15,000 public school districts in the nation are fiscally independent.

Fiscally independent school districts

The state legislature grants these school districts legal authority to set the tax rate on real property, within state constitutional and legislative limits; to levy and collect taxes for the support of local schools; and to approve the expenditure of the funds collected. States require local school boards to prepare budgets of proposed expenditures. In fiscally independent school districts then, boards of education have a relatively free hand in determining how and where expenditures are to be made, subject to limitations on the total amount by the state's constitution or statute. For example, in Florida local school authorities levy and collect taxes for school purposes, independent of the local county or city governments. However, Florida state law sets a legal limit on the tax rates that can be established by local boards of education (Alexander & Alexander, 2005; Russo, 2004). Similarly, in Kentucky, state statutes grant local school boards authority to tax property for the support of public schools (*Kentucky Revised Statutes* Chapter 160.593, 2002).

Fiscally dependent school districts

In this configuration, the board of education prepares and adopts a budget specifying the anticipated expenditures and projected revenue needs. Then a different municipal government may reduce the total budget or eliminate items not required by state law and apportion the school taxes. For example, in Chicago, statutory language authorizes the school tax levy to be a cooperative endeavor, joining the board of education and city officials. Although the local board performs all the preliminary steps in the budget process — preparation, review, and adoption — no school taxes can be forthcoming until the city council adopts an ordinance levying the tax (Alexander & Alexander, 2005; Russo, 2004). Similarly, in Alaska, Maryland, Massachusetts, New Hampshire, New York, and Pennsylvania, school districts are fiscally dependent on the municipal government to apportion taxes for school purposes (Alexander & Alexander, 2005; Russo, 2004).

Challenges to state finance schemes

Several states have challenged finance schemes as inequitable. These challenges were advanced using two separate standards: the *educational needs standard* and the *fiscal neutrality standard*. Using the *educational needs standard*, plaintiffs challenged the constitutionality of state finance schemes under the equal protection clause of the Fourteenth Amendment. Additionally, plaintiffs claimed that there were markedly inequitable per-pupil expenditures among school districts in various states. Using the *fiscal neutrality standard*, the U.S. Supreme Court rejected the federal constitutional theory that education is a right under the Constitution. The Court left in the hands of state legislatures the responsibility to remedy any existing inequities in state funding systems. Under the *fiscal neutrality standard*, the quality of a child's education could not be a function of the wealth of the child's local school district but rather must be based on the wealth of the state as a whole.

The fiscal neutrality standard represents an evolutionary step in the judicial expansion of equal rights protection under the federal Constitution regarding public school finance. Litigation in school finance issues continues to flourish. The federal courts have been abandoned as an arena for such litigation. The Supreme Court has made it clear that successful challenges to state finance schemes must be pursued on state constitutional grounds rather than on the provisions of the U.S. Constitution. Plaintiffs continue to pattern their arguments on the fiscal neutrality standard.

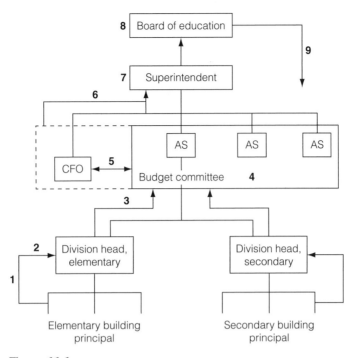

Figure 11.1

The Budgetary Process

The Budgeting Process

Traditionally budgets have been prepared by the school district's chief financial officer (CFO), with the approval of the superintendent, and then imposed on lower-level administrators. Although some school districts may still follow this pattern, many others now allow building principals to participate in the process of formulating the budget. This practice, known as *school-based budgeting*, helps principals to internalize budgets as their own and to use these budgets as operating guides to implement their educational plans. Although the process could begin in almost any area, school districts usually start with a revenue budget, which is derived from three sources — local, state, and federal revenues — based on projected enrollment figures for the fiscal year. Then, almost simultaneously, building principals prepare their own units' expenditure budgets and submit these

budgets to upper-level administration for approval. Figure 11.1 illustrates the steps involved in preparing a budget using a school-based budgeting approach.

In step 1, the building principals submit their budget requests to their appropriate division head. The division head takes the various budget requests from the building principals and integrates and consolidates them into one overall division budget request (step 2). Overlapping and/or inconsistent requests are corrected at this stage. For example, two principals might each request $10,000 to buy five computers. The division head knows that an order of 10 computers carries a 10% discount, so the school district will request $18,000 to buy 10 computers. Much interaction between administrators usually takes place as the division head works to integrate and coordinate the budgetary needs of the various building sites.

In step 3, division budget requests are forwarded to a budget committee. The budget committee itself, shown as step 4 in Figure 11.1, is composed of top-level administrators with line authority. The committee members are likely to be associate or assistant superintendents (AS). Budget requests from the two divisions are reviewed at this stage and, once again, overlapping and inconsistencies are corrected.

Step 5 of the process involves interaction between the budget committee and the chief financial officer (CFO). This interaction can take a variety of forms. The budgets could pass from the committee to the CFO for further evaluation and approval. Or the CFO could be a member of the budget committee. Or the CFO might evaluate the budget requests before they go to the budget committee.

In step 6, the final budget is sent to the superintendent of schools for approval. After undergoing her scrutiny (step 7), it is passed on to the board of education for review (step 8). Final budgets are then passed back down to the division heads and building principals (step 9). As the budget requests pass through these stages, some changes may be made. The budget that each building site ultimately has available may be more than, less than, or the same as what it initially requested.

This school-based budgeting approach is often advocated because it has two primary strengths. First, individual building principals are able to identify resource requirements about which top-level administrators are uninformed. Site leaders (principals) have information on efficiencies and opportunities in their specialized units. Second, school principals are motivated to meet the budget, because they participated in its formulation and therefore feel it is their responsibility (Garner, 2004).

There may be, however, disadvantages to site-based budgeting. Let's look at the advantages and disadvantages of site-based budgeting. The question is, should the building principal have total control of the budget? The school literature on quality supports decentralization of the budget to the site where the product is made or the service is delivered (Garner, 2004; Guenther, 2004;

King et al., 2003; Mort, 2004; Odden & Picus, 2004; Plecki & Monk, 2004; Rosenstengel, 2004). The thinking behind this recommendation is that those at the site are in a better position to know how to allocate resources in order to meet school goals. In a school setting, site-based budgeting means that the school's administrative team controls all funds necessary for the functioning of the school, including the largest budget category: personnel.

The advantages of site-based budgeting include the following:

1. Site-based budgeting is an enlightened approach. It empowers the educators at the school site.

2. Principals often feel their hands are tied by bureaucratic regulations originating from the central office.

3. Principals are more able to meet needs if they have control of important variables. Because they are accountable for outcomes of a school, they should have the option of allocating all resources as needed.

4. Only people at the site know exactly what resources are needed. For example, the superintendent has no idea how many teacher aides are needed in a building. The present way of doing things is ineffective.

Here are some disadvantages of site-based budgeting:

1. Site-based budgeting is inimical to district-wide coordination and quality control. Accountability is diffused and weakened.

2. Policy and regulation, including the teachers' contract, are safeguards that protect most people in the school district from the frivolous behavior of some.

3. People are comfortable with the traditional budgeting paradigm whereby the principal and department chairpersons indicate needs and make requests. Principals and department chairs would be extremely uncomfortable making all budget decisions and being held accountable for them.

4. Teachers and principals are generally not risk takers. Given full control of a school's budget, they would probably play it safe. They would be unlikely to invest in important but costly new ventures.

Financial Controls

Financial control techniques assist building principals and other school administrators in acquiring, allocating, and evaluating the use of financial resources — cash, accounts receivable, accounts payable, inventories, purchases, and long-term debt. Regardless of their size, school districts must be able to pay short-term obligations and long-term debts. They must also protect the school district's revenue from theft, unlawful conversion, and misuse. Control of financial resources in individual schools and school districts is implemented primarily through two methods: internal control and financial audits.

Internal Control   *Internal control* is an accounting function and responsibility. Through the efforts of the school district's accounting unit headed by the CFO, policies and procedures are adopted to safeguard assets and verify the accuracy and reliability of accounting data. The following are some characteristics of effective internal control (American Management Association, 2004; Calbom, 2003; Fertakis, 1999; Loader, 2003):

1. Formal organization should be clear. Definitions of job responsibilities must be estimated so as to fix accountability for every aspect of a financial transaction. The organizing function of administration must be the primary source for this important aspect of internal control.

2. Financial accounts must be set up for each division or other unit of administration. When expenses and income are readily traceable to specific administrators, they are more easily controlled. Such communication between accounts and divisions or building units is especially important in both the preparation of budgets and the evaluation phase of the accounting system.

3. Employees who handle assets should not also be responsible for record keeping of those assets. For example, employees who receive and store materials should not also verify the receipt of those materials.

4. No one person should have complete control over all phases of an important transaction. For example, the same individual should not be responsible for preparing purchase orders and for making out the checks in payment of those purchases.

5. The flow of work from employee to employee should not be duplicative, but the work of the second employee should provide a check on the work of the first. For example, the check drawn to pay for supplies and materials should be cosigned by a second employee who verifies the accuracy and legitimacy of the transaction.

Effective internal control procedures can be established for each distinct financial resource. Cash, accounts receivable, interest, inventories, accounts payable, payrolls, and purchases must be safeguarded through procedures that conform to the preceding five characteristics of effective internal control.

Financial Audits   Another major financial control technique is the *financial audit* — an independent appraisal of a school district's accounting, financial, and operational systems. Audits are of two types: external and internal (Carmichael et al., 2004).

An *external audit* is conducted outside the school district by experts such as bank examiners or certified public accountants (CPA). Their main purpose is not to prepare the school district's financial reports but to verify that the district, in preparing its own financial statements, has followed generally accepted accounting principles and applied them correctly. External audits are so important that some states require all public school districts to have their financial records examined and certified by outside accountants, as assurance to taxpayers that the school district's financial reports are accurate.

An *internal audit* is performed by school district employees who are trained to examine the accuracy of the school district's accounting and financial reports. Large school districts may have an accounting staff assigned to the internal audit function. Like external auditors, internal auditors verify the accuracy of financial and accounting procedures used by the school district. Internal audits also focus on the efficiency and appropriateness of the financial and accounting procedures. Besides appraising the school district's accounting and financial operations, internal audits sometimes involve assessment of operations in general, including policies, procedures, use of authority, quality of management, effectiveness of methods, special problems, and so forth.

Both external and internal audits should be thorough. Following are some of the areas examined by auditors (American Institute of Certified Public Accountants, 2000):

1. *Cash flow.* Confirm bank balances; review cash management procedures.

2. *Accounts receivable.* Obtain verification from vendors concerning amounts owed and anticipated payments; confirm bank balances.

3. *Inventory.* Count physical inventory to verify accuracy of the school district's financial reports.

4. *Fixed assets.* Check physical evidence of fixed assets (buildings, equipment); evaluate depreciation; determine whether insurance is adequate.

5. *Loans.* Review long- and short-term loan agreements; summarize the school district's obligations.

6. *Revenues and expenditures.* Evaluate proper matching; safeguard assets; prevent or detect fraud or theft.

Zero-Based Budgeting

In most school districts, the budgeting process begins with the previous year's budget; that is, administrators plan future expenditures as an increase or decrease over the previous year. Under *zero-based budgeting* (ZBB), administrators must start the budgeting process at zero every year, and they must substantiate all expenditures — new

and continuing (Hammond & Knott, 1980). Thus the entire expenditures budget must be justified, not merely the adjustments to an existing budget.

Zero-based budgeting was originally developed for use in government organizations as a way to justify budget requests for the coming year. The U.S. Department of Agriculture was the first to use ZBB in the 1960s. Texas Instruments adopted ZBB in 1970, and Jimmy Carter used ZBB while governor of Georgia. Later, as president, Carter ordered ZBB used in the executive branch of the federal government. Since then, many government agencies, business firms, state departments of education, and local school districts have adopted ZBB (or variations thereof).

The ingredients of ZBB are not new. The concept's founders extracted a viable budgetary technique from the following systems: management by objectives, performance budgeting, program budgeting, incremental budgeting, and line-item budgeting. These management techniques were integrated into a budgeting process, ZBB, which involves three steps (Odden & Picus, 2004): (1) identify decision units, (2) develop decision packages, and (3) rank the decision packages.

Identify Decision Units   As a first step, to prevent conflicts and assure complete budgeting for the entire school district, all possible decision units should be identified and the nature of their responsibilities and operation defined. At the district level, decision units might include the superintendent's office, the business office, personnel administration, curriculum and instruction, and the like. At the building level, decision units might include the principal's office, student services, curricular departments, teaching teams, attendance services, and other support service areas.

Develop Decision Packages   A decision package is a document that describes and justifies a specific program or activity in such a way that decision makers can evaluate it and rank it against other activities competing for available resources. Each package must include sufficient information about the program or activity to allow the next level of administration to properly understand and evaluate it. This information includes the following:

1. The purpose or function of the unit
2. Alternative means to carry out unit functions
3. The cost and benefits of each alternative
4. The technical and operational feasibility of each alternative
5. Performance measures to compare past and present productivity
6. The consequences of not funding a particular program or activity

Rank the Decision Packages   The final step in ZBB involves ranking decision packages. The initial ranking occurs at the lowest organizational level, where the packages are developed. In schools, for example, this might involve department chairpersons, head custodians, and building principals. This permits the unit leader to evaluate the importance of her own activities and to rank the decision packages affecting her unit accordingly. Next, the packages would be ranked by each succeeding administrative level (see Figure 11.1). Budget revenues are then distributed according to activities ranked as essential to meeting the school district's goals. Some departments or divisions may receive increases, some decreases, and others nothing at all.

On the one hand, ZBB provides a constant reassessment of all the school district's programs and divisions as regards their ongoing contribution to the organization's goals. ZBB facilitates the development of new programs. And it broadens the base of decision making by involving personnel at operating units in the budgeting process. On the other hand, the process of continual justification necessitates more paperwork at every level of administration, and administrators may tend to inflate the benefits of their programs in order to maintain funding.

The application of ZBB in schools is frequently more appropriate in support areas such as research and development, personnel, and finance—where programs are more likely to be discretionary—than in instructional areas. That is, administration can change such programs easily if cost-benefit analysis indicates that such action is warranted. However, ZBB is less applicable in instructional areas, because a prescribed curriculum may be mandated by the state and a core curriculum may be necessary to develop a student's essential and life skills.

Planning-Programming-Budgeting Systems

The planning-programming-budgeting system (PPBS) was pioneered at the Rand Corporation in connection with weapons system analysis for the United States Air Force in the 1950s; the Department of Defense implemented the system in 1961. A few years later, in 1965, President Lyndon B. Johnson popularized PPBS by directing all federal agencies to use this budgeting technique (Doh, 1971).

Planning-programming-budgeting systems were developed to provide school administrators with objective information to aid in planning educational programs and for choosing between alternative ways of allocating funds to achieve the school's goals (Garner, 2004; Guenther, 2004; Langdon et al., 2004). PPBS is very similar to zero-based budgeting (ZBB), but it does not assume that all programs must be re-justified during each budget cycle.

The essential steps of PPBS include the following:

1. *Specify goals.* The process begins by analyzing and specifying the basic goals in each major activity or program area. The starting point of PPBS is to answer such questions as "What is our basic purpose or mission?" and "What, specifically, are we trying to accomplish?" For example, a school district's goal might be to improve management information systems by implementing computer technology districtwide. A school building's goal might be to improve all students' performance on the state-mandated achievement test.

2. *Search for relevant alternatives.* Through PPBS, school administrators assess as fully as possible the total costs and benefits of various

alternatives. Program budgeting is an endeavor to determine the rates of return for programs as well as the rate of return to be forgone when one program is chosen over another. The implementation of a computer network, for example, may be the most efficient way to improve management information systems in the school district.

3. *Measure the costs of the program for several years.* An essential feature of PPBS is long-range planning and budgeting. For example, in budgeting for additional schools, decision makers would need to consider not only the initial costs of construction but also the costs of operating and maintaining the facilities in future years. In addition, long-term enrollment projections must be made to determine the future need for school facilities.

4. *Evaluate the output of each program.* PPBS focuses on the outputs of programs, whereas traditional budgeting approaches tend to emphasize expenditure inputs. Program budgeting enables school administrators to compare program proposals, relate them to current activities, evaluate their priority, and then increase or decrease allocations of resources to them. In other words, it is an attempt to answer the question, "How effectively and efficiently are we achieving our goals?"

The planning-programming-budgeting system has great potential benefit in education, where budgeting too often has been regarded as merely a technique for controlling the allocation and expenditure of revenues, rather than as a tool for planning (Garner, 2004; Guenther, 2004; Langdon et al., 2004). For too many years, public school budgeting has been handled largely on a line-item basis, allocating funds to such accounts as salaries, textbooks, supplies, equipment, and contracted services rather than earmarking money for programs designed to accomplish identifiable program objectives. Furthermore, because program responsibility is often fragmented among various divisions, buildings, or departments, and because most goals are expressed in such general terms as "providing adequate counseling services," budgeting has tended

to be an exercise by various divisions of competing and negotiating for funds rather than a unification of effort and support to accomplish specific program goals.

Despite its benefits, for most schools and school districts, PPBS has not been the great tool in practice that its logic would imply. There are several reasons for this. First, many school leaders do not understand the philosophy and theory of the technique. They have tended to provide lower-level administrators, including principals, with directives and forms without really understanding the system. Second, schools have multiple and conflicting goals that are vague and ambiguous. And schools lack clearly defined success criteria. Leaders cannot sensibly program, plan, and budget for an unknown or vague goal that is not easily measurable. Third, in many cases, there is a lack of attention to planning premises: Even with clear program goals, the decision maker needs to have a clear understanding of critical planning concepts. Fourth, schools have a long tradition of doing line-item budgeting, and most school board members, accustomed to this approach, often reject program budgets unless they are presented in a line-item format. Finally, because revenues are dispersed annually for the operation of schools, many school leaders have been reluctant to change from the practice of annual budgets to long-range program budgets.

School Facilities Management

Management of school facilities falls within the key duties of the school principal. Principals need to embrace this responsibility as they gain greater control and are held more accountable. Aging school buildings often create barriers that impede effective teaching and learning. This situation has resulted in escalating school infrastructure costs. A case can be made to renovate or build new facilities that maximize an optimal learning environment. Such a choice will necessitate financing school construction. Moreover, principals need to be cognizant of environmental hazards that can threaten the health and safety of students and staff. In this section, we discuss escalating school infrastructure costs, financing new school construction, and environmental hazards.

School Infrastructure Costs

The nation's school infrastructure is in a state of critical disrepair. By *infrastructure,* we mean the basic physical facilities that underpin the school plant (plumbing, sewer, heat, electric, roof, masonry, carpentry). Schools seem to be deteriorating at a faster rate than they can be repaired, and faster than most other public facilities (Drake & Roe, 2003; Ubben, Hughes, & Norris, 2004). Plumbing, electrical wiring, and heating systems in many schools are dangerously out of date, roofing is below code, and exterior materials (brickwork, stone, and wood) are chipped or cracked. The cost of deferred expenditures currently runs to over $100 million in Los Angeles, Detroit, Chicago, Seattle, and Miami's Dade County, with an enormous bill of $680 million for the New York City schools. The accumulated cost to repair the nation's public schools, according to knowledgeable sources, can now be conservatively placed at $50 billion and may run as high as $115 billion (U.S. Department of Education, 1995). In the year 2000, government sources estimated the nation's school repair bill to be $2,900 per student, and the cost per student for schools needing to make the repairs was $3,800 per student. Approximately 76% of public schools needed major repair or renovation (U.S. Department of Education, 2001a).

Although experts maintain that schools need to allocate 5% a year for repairs and replacement, recent findings suggest that schools allocate only 3%. The investment in new construction is equally insufficient. Whereas colleges and universities allocate 7% annually for new construction, and other public sectors allocate 8%, public schools allocate approximately 3.5%.

Schools in small towns and suburbs are in the best shape. Most of these school board members report their school buildings are in either better than

adequate (43%) or adequate (35%) condition. They say this even though their schools are aging. More than 60% report their schools are between 25 and 50 years old. Nearly 25% say their schools are between 10 and 25 years old (Moulton, Curcio, & Fortune, 1999).

Schools in cities and in the Frostbelt suffer the greatest infrastructure problems because they are the oldest and the most decayed. Nearly 35% of the schools in the older industrial cities of the Northeast and Midwest were built before 1930; a large number were constructed before 1900. For example, nearly half of Chicago's 597 school buildings were built before 1930, and as many as 80 schools still in existence in 1991 were built before 1900. In Akron, Buffalo, Houston, Kansas City (Missouri), Minneapolis, and Portland, 50% or more of the schools were built before 1930 (Ornstein & Cienkus, 1990).

A school building has five stages. It has lived its normal life during the first 20 years, especially in the Sunbelt where construction is cheaper. When the building is 20 to 30 years old, frequent replacement of equipment is needed. By the time it is 30 to 40 years old, most of the original equipment and materials should have been replaced — especially roofs, lighting fixtures, and heating equipment. Accelerated deterioration takes place when the building is 40 to 50 years old. A 50-year-old building is sometimes too new to abandon, especially in the Frostbelt, where construction is usually good; but after 60 years, many buildings are usually abandoned, reconstructed, or replaced (Lewis, 1989).

Nationwide, 29% of the public schools built before 1970 are considered in "inadequate condition." Sixty-one percent were built after 1970, but have been renovated since 1980, and are considered in "adequate" condition. Ten percent were built after 1984 and are considered in "good" condition. A larger percentage of schools in the Midwest (36%) and Northeast (33%) are considered inadequate and in need of major repair or renovation, compared to the Southeast (21%) and West (25%). Only 6% of schools in the Midwest and 5% in the Northeast are in the "new" category ("good" condition) compared to 11% in the

Southeast and 15% in the West (U.S. Department of Education, 2001b). The differences between regions reflect stagnant enrollments in the Midwest and Northeast and growing enrollments in the Southeast and West.

Small schools (fewer than 300 students) have an average age of 48 years, compared to large schools (1,000 or more students) with an average age of 39 years. City schools have a mean age of 46 years, compared to suburban (40 years) and rural schools (42 years). Nationwide, 26% of schools were built before 1950.

Interestingly, schools in poorer areas have a greater percentage of newer schools than do those in middle-class areas; this flies against the charges of reformers, who often refer to most inner-city schools as dilapidated. For example, among schools with less than 20% of students eligible for free or reduced-price lunch, 42% were built before 1950 (U.S. Department of Education, 2001a).

States leading the list of inadequate buildings are Connecticut (60%), California (55%), Washington, DC (50%), Illinois (50%), and Rhode Island (40%). Of the buildings that are inadequate, 61% need major repairs, 43% are obsolete, 25% are overcrowded, and 13% are structurally unsound (U.S. Department of Education, 2001b). Many, of course, have multiple problems.

In comparison with other public sectors, the construction and repair needs for schools rank among the most serious in the nation. Yet it is doubtful whether the public is willing to spend sufficient money to meet these needs. A nationwide survey of the largest 100 school districts (74% responded) identified in rank order the top three repair items on which schools are spending money: (1) roofs, averaging $21,555 per school and $29 per student; (2) heating and air conditioning at $17,652 per school and $24 per student; and (3) painting at $15,101 per school and $22 per student. Other costly repair items in descending order were plumbing and sewer repairs, electric repairs, carpentry, brick and mortar, carpet and tile, and insulation (Richman, 1988). Government estimates for the condition of the nation's schools are even grimmer. The top items rated as "inadequate" and in need of repair or

replacement in the year 2000 were as follows: (a) heating, air, and ventilation (29%), (b) plumbing (25%), (c) exterior walls, windows, or doors (24%), (d) roofs (22%), and (e) electricity (22%). As much as 50% of the nation's schools had at least one inadequate feature (U.S. Department of Education, 2001a).

Several factors other than age contribute to the deterioration of school buildings and the costs for repairs and renovation.

1. *Energy prices.* Although energy prices stabilized in the 1990s, they have dramatically increased since 2000. K–12 schools spend more than $7 billion a year on energy costs— or $125/student/year. Most schools, particularly in old Frostbelt communities, continue to be heated by inefficient boilers. Electrical costs are higher because the school design rarely takes advantage of sunlight. The operating funds devoted to increased energy costs and energy-saving devices have robbed schools of money for repairs and maintenance.

2. *Weather conditions.* The weather is severe in certain parts of the country—especially in the Frostbelt, where the 100- to 120-degree annual temperature range causes considerable contraction and expansion of school buildings, roofs, and pavement. The intense cold makes the water and sewer systems, as well as exterior brick, vulnerable to cracks and leaks. In addition, acid rain, common in heavily industrialized or polluted areas, causes deterioration of all structural surfaces.

3. *Density and vandalism.* Big-city schools are usually located in densely populated areas, resulting in concentrated use of and greater demand for facilities. Moreover, many of these schools are located in highly concentrated poverty areas and service youth populations that are more often involved in property destruction and theft than are youth from more affluent areas. All this results not only in higher costs and more frequent repairs but also in higher budgets for security measures, which deplete a system's financial resources and operating funds for repairs and maintenance.

4. *Newer buildings.* Many new schools were constructed during the last 25 years, especially in the Sunbelt and suburbs. Many of these schools were built hastily, to accommodate expanding enrollments. Quality suffered, and these buildings are now approaching the end of their life spans. In contrast, the problems with older buildings involve not only their quality but also their energy efficiency, their failure to meet health and safety codes, and the results of accumulated neglect.

For the most part, educators and the public alike are unaware of the ticking time bomb represented by the steady deterioration of U.S. school buildings. What typically catches our attention is student test scores and the need to reform or upgrade the curriculum; the safety and operating efficiency of the schools are not on the minds of the public unless there is a call for new taxes (Garner, 2004; King et al., 2003; Odden & Picus, 2004).

Many school board officials are aware of our schools' environmental and structural problems, but have left them for the next generation. Ignoring our inadequate school facilities has enormous costs and will potentially lead to inadequate schools. The longer we wait, the greater the cost for future educational services and the more difficult it becomes to sustain long-term educational growth and financial solvency among school districts. Either we devote, today, a greater share of local and state revenues to the repair and renovation of our educational facilities, or we burden our children and grandchildren with crippling educational expenses.

Financing School Construction

Public school investment in new schools, compared to other public sectors, has been minimal over the last 15 to 20 years because of previous taxpayer resistance and student enrollment declines. Nationwide, 61% of the schools were constructed during the 1950s and 1960s, and only 6% were built in the 1980s; more than 20% were over 50 years old in 1990, and the percentage is growing about 0.5% each year (King, Swanson,

& Sweetland, 2003; Lewis, 1989; Odden & Picus, 2004). As of 2000, the average age of the nation's schools was 40 years; and the average time since the last renovation was 11 years (U.S. Department of Education, 2001a).

Where will the money come from to build new schools? Although the states fund about 50% of the revenues for the maintenance and operation of schools, they contribute only 23% for construction. According to one study, 27 states use grant programs (equalized, flat, or matching) to finance new schools, 12 states rely on state or local bonds, and 2 states use fully funded capital programs; but 16 states provide no state financial assistance (National Association of State Directors of Education Plant Services, 1989). Based on these numbers, some states use more than one program.

The big-spending region for building is the Southeast, which includes the states of Alabama, Florida, Georgia, Kentucky, Mississippi, North Carolina, South Carolina, and Tennessee. These eight states spent more than $3.3 billion on education construction in 2002. Of that amount, 67% went for new buildings, 20% for additions, and 13% for modernizations. School officials predict school construction will continue to rise; it has been rising since 1985.

Public school enrollments for K–12 from 2000 to 2011 are expected to increase in the West (7.5%) compared to the South (1%), Midwest (−3.3%), and Northeast (−4.2%). All 13 states in the West are expected to show enrollment increases; Idaho (17%), New Mexico (14%), Nevada (13%), Alaska (13%), Hawaii (12%), and Arizona (10%) are expected to show the greatest amount (U.S. Department of Education, 2001b). In short, the western region of the country has replaced the South in K–12 student growth and construction. Nationwide school construction is expected to total approximately $30 to $40 billion per year from 2000 to 2011 and then level off, on the one hand reflecting a need to replace and renovate old buildings and on the other hand indicating a slowdown in public school enrollments: 3.5 million students from 1993 to 2000 compared to 125,000 students from 2000 to 2011 (U.S. Department of Education, 2002; U.S. Department of Education, 2001b).

Building a new school is no simple task. The rules are complex, the stakes are high, and the considerations are political. Consider these questions, for example: How many students will the school accommodate? Where will the building site be located? How will attendance boundaries be drawn? Have environmental concerns been fully addressed? How will the cost be funded? How will voters react? Which companies will get the contracts? How many minority contractors will be hired? The list of questions, along with the potential for vague answers, is endless.

Is it possible for one school serving the same number of students to be three or four times more expensive than another? You bet. Consider different building requirements (local construction codes, insulation factors, space requirements), building designs (open-air or enclosed, horizontal or vertical), land prices, professional fees, and labor and material expenses.

As of the year 2000, a downtown Chicago or New York City attorney charges $250 to $500 an hour compared to $150 to $250 for an attorney in New Orleans or Tampa, Florida. A union plumber makes more than $75 an hour in Northeast or Midwest urban areas, half that much in southern urban areas, and even less in rural areas. The cost of land can be from 2 to 10 times as high in one city (New York, Chicago, or Los Angeles) as another (Baton Rouge, Louisiana, or El Paso, Texas). In short, where you build is important. The cost of a school building can run from $75 to $100 per square foot in rural southern areas to $150 to $200 per foot in the major cities and adjacent metropolitan areas (Garner, 2004; King et al., 2003; Odden & Picus, 2004).

Another factor to consider is square footage. To adequately serve their clientele, high schools need more square footage per student (about 1.5 times more) than do elementary schools. The reason is related to specialization and additional facilities for older students — larger auditoriums, pools, theaters, cafeterias, indoor gyms, outdoor ball fields, student parking lots. Also, schools in cold climates cannot use outdoor areas as effectively as schools in warm climates can. A typical high school serving 1,000 students might provide 100 square feet per student (at $100 per square foot) in the rural South. Another high school serving the same number of students might provide 200 square feet per student (at $200 per square foot) in the urban Northeast or Midwest. The school's total cost in the urban Northeast or Midwest can run three to four times as high as in the rural sites: One school costs $5,000 per student, and the other costs $20,000 per student (King et al., 2003; Odden & Picus, 2004). To be sure, these differences in school construction costs have ramifications for property tax assessments.

Schools in the future will cost more than current prices because the designs will be more complex, built for varied functions using more sophisticated components and materials. There will probably be more (a) technological equipment, such as computers, videos, and satellite dishes; (b) school laboratories; (c) places for small-group and independent study; (d) flexible spaces, modular classrooms, and adaptable walls; (e) contrasting or great spaces such as common rooms, atriums, and open courtyards; (f) innovative spaces and materials such as underground structures and new plastic and prefabricated materials; (g) expensive lighting, heating, and communications equipment; (h) energy-conservation controls, solar features, heat pumps, and geothermal heating and cooling systems; (i) earth berms and high clerestory windows; (j) curved corners and curved furniture; (k) pitched roofs and arches; and (l) centers or wings to house child-care, elderly, and community services (Garner, 2004; Guenther, 2004; King et al., 2003; Odden & Picus, 2004; Rist, 1989). Increasingly, yesterday's "boxy" classrooms and rectangular buildings will be replaced by flexible spaces and a variety of exterior designs (Plecki & Monk, 2004).

Environmental Hazards

In many of America's schools, environmental hazards including asbestos, radon gas, school lead in paint and pipes, poor indoor air quality, and electromagnetic fields pose threats to the health and safety of students and staff. School principals need to be cognizant of these and other environmental hazards.

Asbestos   The U.S. Environmental Protection Agency (EPA) has ordered government and commercial property owners to clean up *asbestos-laden buildings* that have been housing people at work and in school for the last 25 to 50 years. Estimated costs to clean up these buildings are hard to come by, although one estimate was $100 billion for government and commercial buildings and $3.5 billion for some 45,000 schools in 31,000 school districts (Richman, 1988). Another nationwide study puts the estimate at $1.2 billion, or $22,858 per school and $31 per student (U.S. Environmental Protection Agency, 2000). The cost exceeded $150 per student in 10% of the schools, and the Oklahoma City School District had the greatest expenditures — or the dubious distinction of having a $65 million bill and $1,688 cost per student. These costs are based on an estimate of $15 to $20 per linear square foot to remove asbestos, depending on whether this once acclaimed "wonder fiber" is located in the ceilings, walls, floors, or basements. In 1999, some 8 to 10 million children and 1.1 million school employees were subject to asbestos exposure; this is a marked improvement from 10 years ago, when some 15–20 million children and 1.5 million employees were subject (Jones, 1999).

Estimates of people on the job who will die from direct exposure to asbestos-containing buildings are extremely low (25 per year) when compared to the 10,000 per year who die due to workplace accidents (Florio, 1988). The ultimate question is, do we need to spend all this money on asbestos removal? At what level of exposure is asbestos unsafe? If asbestos is intact, not flaking, and out of reach of students and employees, should it be removed? Although airborne asbestos can be deadly (when more than 1% is present in the air), the dangers of inert asbestos are minimal in most buildings. Nonetheless, children are considered to be especially vulnerable because their longer life expectancy means that a latent asbestos-related disease has more time to develop.

During the 1980s and 1990s, the federal government imposed many environmental requirements and regulations on the schools but did not provide funds for compliance. Many school

districts delayed in removing the asbestos, while others used funds from their school maintenance budget to comply with federal regulations. However, one EPA study reports that as much as 75% of all school cleanup work was done improperly up to 1985 (R. Garratt, Staff Specialist, Environmental Protection Agency, Region 5, personal communication, June 9, 2003). Rather than mitigating the problem, cleanup efforts may have exacerbated the problem in many cases; indeed, the cure may be worse than the disease, especially with a lot of "rip and skip" companies that do the work and move on to another school district or city.

Be aware that removal of asbestos is not the only form of abatement, although the great majority of school districts have chosen this option. Encapsulation, if done properly, can last for several years (10 or more years, depending on the materials applied and the method used) at an average cost of 10% of the removal bill (Probst, 1990). The savings to be realized by encapsulating are obvious; but in cases where asbestos is loose or crumbling, removal is the best solution. In still other cases, encapsulation is only a stop-gap measure until a school district can raise sufficient money for removal.

Radon Gas   Radon gas may pose as much of a threat to the health and safety of students and staff as asbestos does. *Radon gas* is considered the second leading cause of lung cancer among adults. EPA tests show dangerously high levels of this invisible, odorless gas in 54% of the 130 schools randomly checked; homes are also affected. In short, many of our children are exposed to a risk equivalent to smoking from $1/2$ to $1 1/2$ packs of cigarettes a day (U.S. Department of Education, 1989; Wright, 1989).

Radon gas (radon-222) seeps into buildings through the foundation from soil and rock as the radium-226 isotope decays. In some cases, well water may be a source of radon. No EPA, federal, or state guidelines exist for containment or abatement of the gas; however, the situation is considered dangerous, and levels are too high in schools to wait for the EPA. Basically, procedures for ascertaining radon levels include (a) testing all school rooms on and below ground level, (b) testing in the cold months of the year, and (c) testing for two days to four weeks depending on the type of test. Screening test results of over 4 pCi/L (picocuries/liter, or one-trillionth of a unit of radon) are considered dangerous enough to require a lengthy retest (9–12 months); levels over 100 pCi/L are considered sufficiently dangerous to call for relocating children (Harrington-Lucker, 1990; Schneider, 1993).

Average corrective costs per school run from as low as $1,000 if ventilation adjustment works to $10,000 if subventilation is needed. On the other hand, some observers contend that the cost for decontaminating the nation's schools runs into billions of dollars, and since the connection between radon and illness has not been firmly proven, it may not be worth the cost to ventilate schools.

School Lead   The water our children are drinking at home and school may be tainted with lead that accumulates in their blood and bones and eventually dulls the mind and causes severe behavior problems.

According to one U.S. government survey, 15 to 16% of the nation's children under the age of 14 years have blood levels high enough to cause academic and neurobehavioral problems in school, which eventually lead to school failure. The ratios of high lead levels are three times higher for poor White than for middle-class White children, and seven times higher for inner-city Blacks than for suburban Whites; these results are due largely to the differences in air quality and the age of the children's housing (U.S. Agency for Toxic Substances, 1988; Arfstrom, 1998).

The federal Centers for Disease Control and Prevention (CDC) maintains that lead poisoning is the nation's number-one preventable child health problem and that proper lead abatement would eventually reduce the cost of child medical care and special education as much as $38 billion annually (Centers for Disease Control, 1999). The CDC has revised its definition of lead poisoning, lowering the level at which lead is now considered dangerous from 25 micrograms (mcg) per deciliter in 1974 to 10 mcg in 1991. The last revision

resulted in a tenfold increase in the number of children now considered poisoned by lead — about 1.5%, which means lead poisoning now affects 15% of all U.S. preschoolers (Banham, 1994; Black, 2001). Moreover, at least 20 recent U.S. and international studies from industrialized nations show that levels of lead in children are associated with measures of low IQ, language and reading incompetency, limited attention span, inability to follow instructions, and behavioral impairment as well as with 40 other cognitive, social, psychological, and health problems (Bellinger, 1987; Needleman, 1992).

In a recent study one researcher found that first and second graders who had moderate quantities of lead (5.0 mcg or less) in their systems were six times as likely to exhibit reading problems and seven times more likely to drop out of high school when compared with children who were lead free (Lanphear, 2001). Although the lead variable possibly interacts with a social-class variable, the fact remains that lead infects multiple organs of the body.

In short, childhood lead poisoning may be one of the most important and least acknowledged causes of school failure and learning disorders. Given all the rhetoric and funding for school reform, which focuses on curriculum, instruction, teaching, and testing, we may have been myopic and even foolhardy not to realize that part of school failure may be related to the adverse effects of lead.

The major source of lead poisoning is old lead-based paint and the dust produced from it when windows are opened and closed or renovations take place. The problems exist in nearly all schools built before 1978 — and that's more than 65% of the nation's schools — the year Congress banned lead-based paint. Several layers beneath newer lead-free paint, because of cracking and flaking, the lead-based paint is not always sealed as we might believe; and it can be found in the air teachers and students breathe. Renovations cause bigger problems because these building areas are not properly sealed and monitored with sample air readings, as in the prescribed manner for asbestos removal.

And we have some more bad news. Dangerous traces of lead are sometimes found in the municipal water we drink. Even worse, lead gets into water from lead lines in our older water coolers, faucets (unless they are made from plastic, which most people feel is inferior in quality), and copper pipes (from the lead solder on the joints). Lead also comes from the cities and villages with old plumbing that connects the water main to our schools and homes. Allowing water to run for a couple of minutes before drinking it or using it for cleaning foods can flush out the lead that has collected, but that idea does not always sit well with budget-minded people who pay utility bills.

It costs about $50 to $75 for a laboratory to test each water faucet and cooler in our schools; however, this is not going to happen on a large scale unless schools are forced to budget this item. The National Education Association estimates that $30 million per year is needed for paint and water testing in our schools—a tiny sum for such an important safety measure (Natale, 1991; National Conference of State Legislatures, 1999). Because the problem is odorless and invisible, and because most parents are not aware the problem even exists, school officials are not under pressure to take appropriate measures.

No testing and reporting procedures are required for lead, and school authorities have been remiss in dealing with the problem. Furthermore, many school officials who are able to do something about it take the position that there is no problem (they believe it went away when lead was outlawed in paints and gasoline); or, they see the solutions as too expensive because eventually abatement and not testing will have to be done in many schools (and other government buildings). The cost of lead abatement is estimated at between $5,000 and $15,000 per 1,000 square feet of lead paint coverage. Most school boards (and owners of property) find the cost too expensive and just leave the problem as is, gambling that if a party files a claim due to lead injury, the district's insurance will pay for it. Verdicts run as high as $10 million, though most cases are settled in the range of $500,000 (Banham, 1994).

EPA or health requirements are needed to ensure adequate compliance. Like the tobacco industry, which fights facts about cigarette smoking and cancer, the lead industry has its spokespeople and lobbyists who obscure the health hazards of lead. The federal government, medical profession, and socially concerned groups need to come together to force cleanups of lead contamination in the same way they have acted to discourage cigarette smoking.

Indoor Air Quality Some schools suffer from what is known as sick building syndrome (SBS) and other indoor air quality (IAQ) shortcomings due to the trend to increase insulation and tighten schools (and office buildings) to save energy. The outcome, in extreme cases, is virtually no outside air infiltration.

Everything in a building has some form of toxic emission. The human body exhales carbon dioxide, and it emits body odors, gases, and other *bioeffluents*. Carbon monoxide, also colorless and highly poisonous, results from incomplete combustion of fuel. It can be a problem when auto engines are left running, say in school parking lots near open windows when parents pick up or drop off their children. Diesel exhaust from parked buses is also common, as drivers keep bus engines running while waiting for students or warm the bus in winter before students board. Carpets, plastics (most furniture and bathroom fixtures contain plastics), and pressed wood emit formaldehyde and other gases. Room dividers and window blinds emit a host of carbon chemicals. Copy machines give off ozone, spirit duplicators give off methyl alcohol, and fluorescent lights give off ultraviolet rays.

Then there is the dilemma of doing battle with pests—fleas, cockroaches, termites, wasps, and rodents. Although chemical pesticides are a critical component of successful pest control, there is the other side of the coin — our concern to limit or even rid schools of pesticides (Krieger, 2000). It's one thing to permit weeds to run amok on school playgrounds because of our concern to reduce pesticide exposure, but it's quite another to allow indoor pests to run wild with the likelihood of increasing. Nonetheless, educators and parents are concerned that students are unknowingly breathing in various poisonous chemicals used to kill vermin. As of 2000, 31 out of 50 states had school pesticide management policies that were considered "inadequate" or "unsatisfactory" for protecting children from pesticides that are harmful to children's central nervous system and have "very profound consequences for human beings" (Bushweller, 2000).

Even drywall, paints, and cleaning fluids have various fumes that are dangerous in sufficient quantities. Long-term exposure to chemicals and volatile compounds from art supplies, science labs, shop facilities, and indoor pools is potentially dangerous, and it affects all students because the vapors and dusts enter the heating and cooling systems. Excessive humidity found in locker rooms, pool areas, and school basements can lead to mold and fungus growths that multiply to potentially harmful levels—which they often do, unbeknownst to school authorities.

As schools become more insulated, the toxins from cigarette smoke, chalk dusts, science labs, art rooms, and shop facilities cannot escape and thus are circulated through the ventilation system. In addition, the entire duct system usually has dust or mold that spreads germs throughout the building. If vents are not cleaned regularly, the potential for Legionnaires' disease or other respiratory infections caused by bacteria and/or germs exists. The Occupational Safety and Health Administration (OSHA) requires that outside air be circulated into buildings to avoid the constant recirculation of viruses and bacteria.

Roughly one-third of the nation's schools (and offices) are considered to be afflicted with sick building syndrome. We need to follow the amended recommendations of the American Society for Heating, Refrigeration and Air Conditioning Engineers; they raised air circulation standards from 5 cubic feet per minute to 15 (Dunn, 1990; National Conference of State Legislatures, 1993). Two problems arise: More energy is consumed; and in some big cities, such as Los Angeles, Houston, and New York, it is even more damaging to bring in outside air at certain times of the year.

The human symptoms of poor IAQ are eye, nose, throat, or lung irritations. Students (and teachers) are drowsy, exhibit shorter attention spans, or become out of breath when walking up the stairs or playing in the gym. In searching for problems, one important consideration is whether people's symptoms disappear within a few hours after leaving school (Greim & Turner, 1991). Parents whose children suffer from respiratory problems often feel their children are being infected by classmates; such parents fail to consider the strong possibility that the air at school may be the culprit.

Unless symptoms are apparent, educators usually believe the school's IAQ is fine. But many air pollutants, including radon gas, carbon monoxide, asbestos particles, and lead dust, are not easily detectable by sight or smell. Other pollutants are obvious only in high concentrations. Formaldehyde, paint, and cleaning fluid vapors, and mold and fungus, for example, have an odor only at harmful levels.

Obviously, schools need to test air quality regularly and not assume the best-case scenario. But when was the last time your neighborhood school— or the school that your brother, sister, or children attend—tested the air to see whether it was "healthy"? Given the budget constraints of most school districts, the answer is probably, "Not since anyone can remember." So long as parental and public pressure is on improving the curriculum and teaching process, and minimal attention is directed at the air we breathe (which is merely taken for granted), and so long as there is no legislation requiring the testing and improvement of our air, the problem will be ignored. With lack of funds a common school problem, ventilation maintenance is not a top priority; in fact, the maintenance budget is often robbed to pay for curriculum and teaching reform—an unfortunate circumstance that threatens student health and learning conditions.

When the public becomes more aware of the hazards related to indoor pollutants, air quality within school buildings will become the focal point for student rights and litigation. Lack of responsiveness today by school officials can make a seemingly innocuous problem and noncontroversial issue into a serious issue in the future.

Electromagnetic Fields   Electromagnetic fields (EMF) are part of our complicated and growing technology: radio, television, computers, microwaves, fluorescent lights, and so on. The most controversial and visible electromagnetic fields are produced by the existence of transmission lines running through our communities — often near our schools, playgrounds, and homes. Only six states set limits on the strength of EMF around transmission lines. New York State, for example, requires a 350-yard corridor around its lines. The fear seems to coincide with growing research data: Children exposed to these power lines suffer from childhood cancer two to three times more frequently (depending on years of exposure) than do children who are not exposed (Burko, 1991).

What about our home appliances and school machines? The higher the strength of the magnetic field (in devices such as microwaves, ovens, stoves, and heaters), as well as the closer the object and the longer the exposure (as with electric blankets, computers, copy machines, televisions, and fluorescent lights), the greater the risk. Actually, objects with electric motors (such as air conditioners, electric clocks, hair dryers, and even telephones) present a possible risk to humans. In theory, because our bodies are often only inches away from them, these household and school objects may be more dangerous than transmission lines are.

To get an idea of the emission effects of these household and school objects, copy machines give off 4.0 milligauss (mG) units, computers 10.0 mG, and microwave ovens 15.0 mG ("Electromagnetic fields," 1991). The problem is, some of us sit at a computer for hours. In general, the research on EMF is highly complex and tentative.

Some scientists claim we are unsure what to measure to determine exposure. For right now, the best precaution is to have children keep their distance from all EMF emitters at home and in school, especially televisions and computers. Schools need to enforce this notion of distance and purchase computers and electronic equipment with screens or filters. Because there is little public pressure to spend money on screens or filters, and no legislation requiring schools to take corrective steps, few schools are considering these precautions.

Summary

1. School budgeting involves expressing statements of planned revenue and expenditures for a coming fiscal year in numerical terms.

2. Many school districts now allow subordinates to participate in the budgeting process, called school-based budgeting.

3. Financial control techniques, such as internal control and financial audits, assist administrators in acquiring, allocating, and evaluating the efficient and effective use of financial resources.

4. Two alternative methods for developing budgets are zero-based budgeting (ZBB) and planning-programming-budgeting systems (PPBS). ZBB requires that principals start from zero to justify budget needs every year. PPBS, a variation of ZBB, requires that budgets be developed from a program perspective rather than using the traditional line-item approach.

5. A key responsibility of school principals is facilities management. School buildings across the nation are aging and becoming a barrier to optimal learning and teaching. This results in escalating school infrastructure costs. A case can be made to renovate, or to build new facilities that maximize an effective learning environment. This will involve allocating funds for building renovation or new construction. Moreover, principals need to be sensitive to environmental hazards that can threaten the health and safety of students and staff.

Field-Based Activities

1. Many school districts now allow school staff to participate in the budgeting process. Interview your building principal concerning the budgeting process. Does your principal allow staff to participate in the budgeting process? If your principal uses a school-based budgeting process, what procedure does he or she use to get input from staff concerning both budget development and implementation? Outline the budgeting

procedures used in your journal. Interview the chief financial officer (CFO) in your school district. Determine from the interview what the district's philosophy is regarding staff participation in the budgeting process.

2. Interview the school principal, bookkeeper, and all other individuals who handle money in your school. Discuss with them their opinions concerning the importance of using effective financial control techniques, including internal control and external control and financial audits. Record the responses in your journal.

3. Due to the current recession, controversy over school infrastructure costs and the abatement of environmental hazards such as asbestos removal and radon gas are likely to continue to affect school expenditures in the future. Interview the superintendent and CFO in your school district, and your building principal, to secure each person's opinion concerning school infrastructure costs and expenditures for the removal of environmental hazards. Record their responses in your journal.

Suggested Readings

Brimley, V., & Garfield, R. R. (2002). *Financing education in a climate of change* (8th ed.). Boston: Allyn & Bacon. The writing in this book is both scholarly and engaging, appealing to a diverse audience of students, educational leaders, parents, and legislators. School finance is an ever-changing topic; this text has continued to cover all current trends, giving readers a firm grounding in educational finance issues that administrators often misunderstand.

King, R. A., Swanson, A. D., & Sweetland, S. R. (2003). *School finance: Achieving high standards with equity and efficiency* (3rd ed.). Boston: Allyn & Bacon. This new edition explores traditional economic and political models and contemporary issues within their current contexts. The authors enable students to see the political and judicial forces at work in shaping school finance policy. They also provide students with tools drawn from economics to analyze the impact of those policies in terms of equity, adequacy, efficiency, and liberty.

Levin, H. M., & McEwan, P. J. (Eds.) (2002). *Cost-effectiveness and educational policy*. Larchmont, NY: Eye on Education. This book presents a unique and original assessment of the state of the art of cost-effectiveness analysis in education. It identifies key issues and presents original empirical studies to serve as models.

Odden, A., & Picus, L. (2004). *School finance: A policy perspective* (3rd ed.). New York: McGraw-Hill. Completely updated, this clear, concise discussion of how recent research in school finance, resource allocation and use for higher performance, site-based management of schools, and teacher compensation may affect the funding of our nation's schools. As a core text for all masters and doctoral level students of educational administration, this text is the first to use computer simulations to extend the discussions of school finance formulas into the application stage. A Microsoft Excel (PC and Mac) simulation allows students to manipulate various school finance formulas and analyze their fiscal, political, and equity impacts. This financial simulation allows for state, district, and school-based data manipulation and encourages real-time comparisons of school finance equity.

Organisation for Economic Co-operation and Development (OECD). (2000). *Facilities: The appraisal of investments in educational facilities*. Washington, DC: Author. Appraisal of the substantial investments that are made in educational facilities remains a largely unexplored field of research. Is it possible to develop reliable and effective criteria for evaluation, given the wide range of parameters from planning and cost-effectiveness of buildings to their impact on the performance of the educational system as a whole? These questions, faced by every modern educational system, are of concern to investors and funding bodies as well as those who are responsible for planning, managing, and designing educational facilities.

Plecki, M., & Monk, D. H. (Eds.). (2003). *School finance and teacher quality: Exploring the connections*. Larchmont, NY: Eye on Education. This yearbook offers research insights to stimulate thought, inform debates, and consider future research directions.

Thompson, D. C., & Wood, R. C. (2003). *Money and schools* (2nd ed.). Larchmont, NY: Eye on Education. This book is for those who build school budgets, cut them, face angry constituents, hire and fire staff, and otherwise engage in school leadership. Data from the first edition have been updated, and a new chapter on policy perspectives has been added.

12. Creating Safe Schools

Standard 3.0: *Candidates who complete the program are educational leaders who have the knowledge and ability to promote the success of all students by managing the organization, operation, and resources in a way that promotes a safe, efficient, and effective environment.*

FOCUSING QUESTIONS

1 What does the research tell the principal about school violence and alcohol and drug abuse?

2 How can the principal predict school violence?

3 How can the principal prevent school violence?

4 What resources can the principal use to meet the needs of violence-prone youth in our schools?

5 How can the principal advocate the juvenile justice system to help deal with the problem of school violence?

6 What strategies can the principal use to create an orderly climate for learning, which may diminish school violence?

In this chapter, we respond to these questions concerning the creation of safe schools for all students. We begin our discussion with an overview of the research concerning violence as well as alcohol and drug use in our schools. Then we look at methods that can be used to predict school violence. Next, we examine ways to prevent school violence, including toughening weapons laws and dealing effectively with violent students. We then discuss additional resources that may be required to meet the needs of violence-prone students. We examine ways to strengthen the juvenile justice system, including improving the juvenile code and creating a state center for the prevention of school violence. And, finally, we provide several techniques for creating an orderly climate for learning, including establishing and emphasizing goals, establishing rules and procedures, and improving teacher-student relationships.

School Violence and Alcohol and Drug Use

Growing violence, chaos in classrooms, and access to drugs are a regular part of the school day for an increasing number of students (Babbit, 2001; Cruz, 2003; Gale Research Staff, 2003; Grimes et al., 2002; Hill, 2004; Marotto, 2004; Moore et al., 2003; Mosline, 2001). Consider some of the obstacles that are facing our schools. Gunshot wounds are a leading cause of death among high school students in the United States, second only to motor vehicle deaths (Cruz, 2003). Fifteen percent of all students report the presence of gangs in their schools. At least 30% of students nationwide find it easy to obtain cocaine. Forty-four percent of all teachers report that student misconduct interferes substantially with their teaching (Hill, 2004; Orr, 2004; U.S. Department of Education, 2004b).

Creating a Safe Environment

Frequently the violence in a community spills into the schools (McCann, 2004; Nicoletti & Spencer-Thomas, 2003). Although the situation in some schools and neighborhoods is more serious than in others, creating a safe, disciplined, and drug-free learning environment is a challenge for all school principals (Fishbaugh, Schroth, & Berkeley, 2003; Noble, 2003; Watson, 2002). Increasing the graduation rate, improving student achievement in challenging subject matter, and ensuring our students' ability to compete in a world economy and carry out their responsibilities of citizenship will be much more difficult to achieve if our schools and neighborhoods are unsafe for our children (Lunenburg & Irby, 1999).

Whether a school is urban, suburban, or rural, several questions can be asked to help understand how schools may be affected by violence, drugs, and class disruptions: How many students feel unsafe at school? Are acts of violence frequent? What is the overall drug use in schools? Is the sale of drugs in school a frequent occurrence? Are student disruptions of class perceived to be a problem by teachers and students? What violence is committed that relate to race, class, and gender? Answers to these questions can provide valuable clues not only to what kinds of problems exist in our schools but also to what school principals can do to make our schools violence free, drug free, and disciplined environments conducive to learning.

Research: School Violence and Alcohol and Drug Use

There has been a plethora of research and professional literature dealing with violence, drug use, and discipline problems in our schools. Some studies and reports bear directly on the questions posed earlier. We have chosen several reports and studies for examination here, based on their recency and their importance to school principals. Some of these reports have been highly visible; others are less well known.

School Violence What the research says about school violence follows:

1. The Phi Delta Kappa/Gallup polls on education over the past decade have cited lack of discipline, violence, and drug abuse as the worst problems confronting the public schools. Some authorities point out that public perception of the frequency of violent acts may be exaggerated somewhat by intense media attention when incidents of school violence do occur, and that most of the nation's schools are safe (National Education Goals Panel, 2000).

2. The number of crimes committed at or near the 85,000 U.S. public schools was estimated at more than 3 million annually, with 185,580 people injured. On any given day, more than 100,000 students are estimated to carry guns to school (National Crime Survey, 2004).

3. Nearly 6,000 violent incidents occurred in New York City schools alone in 2003, for an increase of 15% from the previous year (New York City Board of Education, 2004).

4. Principals from more than 1,500 school districts who were surveyed by researchers from Xavier University in Cincinnati revealed that violence is not solely a problem of urban schools: 64%, 54%, and 43% of principals in urban, suburban, and rural areas respectively reported that violence had increased in their schools during the past five years (Xavier University, 2000).

5. Approximately 40,000 students are physically attacked in America's schools each month. Approximately 8,000 of the nation's more than 2 million school teachers are physically attacked at school each month (National School Safety Center, 2004).

6. Estimated annual costs of school crime, including vandalism, are between $50 million and $700 million. Estimates of yearly replacement and repair costs due to crime are about $250 million (National School Safety Center, 2004).

7. About one in four students nationally report having very serious problems in their school with hostile or threatening remarks among different groups of students; physical fights among members of different groups of friends; threats or destructive acts other than physical fights; turf battles among different groups of students; and gang violence (Harris and Associates, 2004).

8. Age appears to be an important factor affecting the level of social tension and violence during the middle and high school years. Beginning in ninth grade, there is a steady decline in the proportion of students who report having serious problems with each of these social problems. In contrast to 8th graders, who see these as very serious problems, less than half of 12th graders express the same level of concern (U.S. Department of Education, National Center for Education Statistics, 2005). Perhaps as students get older, they merely get more accepting and tolerant of social tension and violence in school.

9. Eleven percent of eighth graders admitted that at least once during the previous month,

they had brought a weapon such as a gun, knife, or club to school. Percentages increased significantly from the previous year for both 8th and 12th graders, and 3–4% of the students at each grade reported that they habitually carried a weapon to school on 10 or more days in the previous month (U.S. Department of Education, 2004b).

10. Newly released data from state surveys conducted the same year show that in 20 of the 24 participating states and territories, at least 10% of public high school students reported carrying a weapon on school property at least once during the previous month (U.S. Department of Health and Human Services, 2004a).

Size of School   Size of school may be a factor in incidences of school violence:

1. Urban students are more likely to report having serious problems with hostile remarks, physical fights, threats or destructive acts, and gang violence than suburban or rural students are. African American and Hispanic students are twice as likely as White students to report experiencing very serious problems with turf battles and gang violence (U. S. Department of Education, National Center for Education Statistics, 2005).

2. One in five students report that the level of violence has decreased over the past year, yet an equal proportion report that it has increased. Two in five believe there has been no change in the level of violence over the past year. A larger percentage of students in urban schools report a decrease in violence than do students in suburban or rural schools. The proportions reporting an increase in violence are consistent (1 in 5) across geographic areas (Harris and Associates, 2004).

Teachers and the Educational System   The behavior of teachers and the educational climate of the school may be factors in school violence:

1. When teachers are supportive, encouraging, and caring about students' futures, students report less social tension and violence in their

schools. Among those who give their teachers A's on treating them with respect, smaller percentages report serious problems with each of the following, compared with those who give their teachers D's and F's: hostile or threatening remarks among different groups of students; physical fights among members of different groups of friends; threats or destructive acts other than physical fights; and turf battles among different groups of students (Harris and Associates, 2004).

2. Students are more likely to report a decrease rather than an increase in violence when they are satisfied with the quality of education and the lessons they learn from teachers on tolerance. Students who rate the quality of education high are more likely to report decreases than increases in violence over the past year; conversely, low raters are more likely to report increases than decreases. Students are more likely to report a decrease in violence compared with all students when their teachers do a good job of teaching tolerance (Harris and Associates, 2004).

Alcohol and Drug Use   There has been quite a lot of research on alcohol and drug use among school-age children. What the research says follows:

1. Between 2000 and 2002, the percentage of 10th graders who reported using alcohol during the previous year declined significantly, from 72% to 68% (U.S. Department of Education, 2004b).

2. Individual state data reported that some states witnessed a sharp decline in extreme episodes of alcohol consumption among public high school students, that is, the proportion who reported having five or more drinks in a row during the previous month (U.S. Department of Health and Human Services, 2004b). According to student reports, alcohol is by far the most commonly used drug. Alcohol is used by more than half of all 8th graders, seven out of ten 10th graders, and more than three-fourths of all 12th graders (U.S. Department of Education, 2004b).

3. While the overall student consumption of alcohol has declined, overall student drug use has increased. Between 2000 and 2002, the percentage of 10th graders who reported using any illicit drug during the previous year increased from 25% to 28%, reversing previous trends indicating that overall student drug use had been declining since 1980. Furthermore, additional data revealed significant two-year increases in the proportion of 8th and 10th graders who reported using cocaine (U.S. Department of Education, 2004b).

4. Students report that they rarely use alcohol, marijuana, and other illicit drugs at school during school hours. And the vast majority of students report never being intoxicated or being under the influence of other drugs while at school. Nevertheless, other data indicate that the percentages of 8th and 10th graders who reported using marijuana or other illicit drugs at school during school hours increased significantly between 2000 and 2002. The proportion of 8th graders who reported drinking alcohol at school during school hours also increased significantly over the same two-year period (U.S. Department of Education, 2004b).

5. In 2004 nearly 3 out of 10 students, and 4 out of 10 high school students, reported that obtaining alcohol and marijuana at school or on school grounds was easy. Thirteen percent of 8th graders, 20% of 10th graders, and 25% of 12th graders reported being approached at school by someone trying to sell them drugs during the school day (U.S. Department of Education, 2004b).

In addition to a desire to reduce overall student drug and alcohol use, reducing the sale of drugs at school is an indicator of progress toward eradicating drug abuse among school children and adolescents. Although schools cannot be held solely accountable for student behavior away from school, schools do have a major responsibility for eliminating the sale of drugs at school. School principals, in cooperation with law enforcement officials, need to exert considerable control in eliminating the sale of drugs at school (Dorn, 2003; Duhon-Sells & Agard-Jones, 2004).

Along with eliminating drugs, alcohol, and violence in schools, school principals aim to increase the proportion of the nation's schools that offer a disciplined environment conducive to learning (Council for Exceptional Children, 2000; Fishbaugh et al., 2003; Pepperl & Lezotte, 2000; Wessler & Preble, 2004). Annual *Phi Delta Kappa*/Gallup polls for the past four decades have identified "lack of discipline" as one of the worst problems confronting public schools. Minimizing classroom disruptions is a necessary—though not sufficient—condition to ensure that an environment conducive to learning exists in our schools and that students are learning. According to student reports, we have not made real improvement in reducing classroom misbehavior. One in three high school teachers report that student misbehavior interferes with their teaching (U.S. Department of Education, 2004a).

Applying Research to Practice: Developing an Action Plan

Interest in predicting school violence stems from a desire to prevent it rather than attempt to control it after it occurs (Wilde, 2003; Williams, 2004). Ideally, if teachers and school principals could determine the conditions that cause violence and the types of students most likely to engage in it, as well as those teachers whose behavior precipitates violence, timely corrective interventions could be initiated to prevent its occurrence (Allison, 2004; Begun & Huml, 2003; Goldstein & Conoley, 2004). This approach would be far better than waiting for violence to erupt and then having to deploy resources to quell the incident.

Strategy 1: Predict School Violence

Predicting violence in schools is not impossible. In fact, school administrators in the Milwaukee (Wisconsin) Public Schools district are using a school-violence tool that has enabled them to reduce attacks against teachers by almost 38% in two years. The program, entitled "Safe Schools — Better Schools," allows school security officials to identify behavior problems in schools and provide resources immediately to prevent violence from occurring. School security officials in Milwaukee Public Schools are taking a proactive stance. They plan in advance and anticipate problems.

In Milwaukee Public Schools, violence against teachers has decreased from 1,080 cases in 1998–1999 to 665 in 2002–2003. The Safe Schools — Better Schools program has a three-pronged strategy to predict violence: collect and analyze data, identify problem students, and identify problem teachers (National Alliance for Safe Schools, 2004).

Collect and Analyze Data Information on violence and discipline problems reported by teachers is collected, using standardized incident reporting forms, and analyzed by computer (Thomerson et al., 2003a,b). School administrators then look at where incidents are occurring, their frequency, and whether specific schools, teachers, or locations within schools are showing a pattern of repeated incidents. For example, if a particular school building is having difficulty during the beginning of school or at dismissal, then additional security officers can be marshaled to patrol the school during those times (Aspen Publishers Staff, 2004; Dorn, 2003; Mohondie, 2003; Turk, 2004).

Identify Problem Students Milwaukee public school administrators believe that little is accomplished simply by punishing students who are referred frequently to principals for acts of violence or disciplinary problems. Additional resources are provided to these disruptive students, such as counseling, referrals to social agencies, or assignments to alternative school programs. Milwaukee Public Schools provide a variety of alternative programs for weapon-carrying students, for those prone to violence, and for those with other behavior or learning problems (Hester, 2004; McCann, 2004; Smith, 2004).

Identify Problem Teachers Identifying problem teachers may sound a bit negative, but some teachers actually precipitate student violence. Much assault behavior by students can be diminished with good psychological preparation of teachers and consistent support of school policies and procedures (PITS et al., 2004). Milwaukee public school administrators observe that a disproportionate number of discipline referrals are made by a few teachers in a school. Typically, 3% of the faculty is responsible for about 50% of the discipline referrals. In response, school principals arrange for teachers with classroom management problems to attend the school district's Professional Development Academy in order to learn how to handle students (Barton, 2001; Blauvelt, 2001; Duke, 2002). On-site follow-up relative to effective management techniques designed for unique populations is also available through the academy (Meeks et al., 2000).

Another important part of the Safe Schools–Better Schools program is to develop "school teams" consisting of teachers, parents, university professors, and school principals from various school sites. These individuals agree to be part of a team. The team approach helps prevent cases from being thrown out of court due to being improperly prepared. Teams of educators working together can prevent that from happening. Milwaukee public school administrators claim that the Safe Schools — Better Schools program will work with schools of any size or type: urban, suburban, or rural. The program provides a planning system for administering school security resources.

Strategy 2: Prevent School Violence

Violence in America has increased substantially in the past few years (Andryzewski, 2004). In fact, the reported violent crime rate in the nation has increased by more than 35% in the last 10 years (from 1993 to 2003). That rate of increase in such a short period is greater than in any comparable period in history, or at least since reliable records

have been maintained by the Federal Bureau of Investigation's Uniform Crime Reports. During that same 10-year period, the number of reported arrests of young people 15 years of age and under for violent offenses increased by 100% (Brown & Merritt, 2002; Hasday, 2003; U.S. Department of Education, 2004b; Watson et al., 2003; Webber, 2004).

It is not surprising that the level of violence in public schools is increasing as well. Violence in schools cannot be separated from the larger problem of violence in communities. Studies have shown that the conditions of schools are strongly influenced by the conditions of their neighborhoods (Nicoletti & Spencer-Thomas, 2003; Turk, 2004). Violence in schools is endangering the health, welfare, and safety of students and teachers. Students cannot learn and teachers cannot teach in an atmosphere where fear and anxiety prevail (Orr, 2004). Two ways of preventing school violence are to toughen weapons laws and to deal with violent students (U.S. Department of Education, 2004b).

Toughen Weapons Laws School principals should advocate for state legislation and school board policies that address violence in schools. Tough measures have already been implemented in most states for dealing with violent behavior, especially regarding possession of weapons and initiation of a parent responsibility law for minors possessing weapons. School principals can be strong advocates of such legislation and school board policies.

Establish weapon-free school zones School boards might consider making their schools weapon-free zones. Efforts to do so would ideally involve the school, home, community, law enforcement, and health services (Dorn, 2003; Mohondie, 2003). Strategies would include apprehension, prevention, intervention, education, counseling, and student and public awareness programs (Garrett, 2002; Gulledge, Trump, & Beard, 2001; Kane, Avila, & Quiroz, 2002; Leonard, 2000; Mills, 2002; Schonfeld et al., 2003; Stevens, 2003; Wanko, 2002).

The following is a concise statement suggested by the National School Boards Association (2004):

> The Board of Education determines that possession and/or use of a weapon by a student is detrimental to the welfare and safety of the students and school personnel within the district. Possession and/or use of any dangerous or deadly weapon in any school building on school grounds, in any school vehicle, or at any school-sponsored activity is prohibited. Such weapons include but are not limited to any pistol, revolver, rifle, shotgun, air gun or spring gun; slingshot; bludgeon; brass knuckles or artificial knuckles of any kind; knives having a blade of greater than two inches, any knife the blade of which can be opened by a flick of a button or pressure on the handle, or any pocketknife where the blade is carried in a partially opened position. The possession or use of any such weapon will require that the proceeding for the suspension and or expulsion of the student involved will be initiated immediately by the principal.

In addition to a written school board policy, the following state legislation is recommended to provide for weapon-free schools: Make it a felony to knowingly and willfully bring a firearm on school property; make it a felony for any person to knowingly allow a minor to carry a weapon to school; provide that any person convicted of bringing a firearm on school property will lose his or her driver's license.

Limit access by minors to handguns
To provide for limited access by minors to handguns, the following laws are recommended: Make it a misdemeanor for any person to allow a minor to have access to a handgun without the consent and supervision of a parent, guardian, or other responsible adult; make possession of a handgun by a minor without the consent and supervision of a parent, guardian, or other responsible adult a misdemeanor.

Deal With Violent Students
Students cannot learn when they are in fear of harm from their classmates. Teachers cannot teach in an atmosphere of fear for their own safety, as well as that of their students (Bluestein, 2002). To provide a safe and secure learning atmosphere for children, school districts must be able to expel violent students to alternative schools; require schools to report violent offenders to law enforcement officials; require court counselors to confer with school officials; expand immediate school actions; and take privileges away from students.

Expel violent students
Most state statutes provide that a school board can expel a student, age 14 or older, only if he has been convicted of a felony *and* if his continued presence in the school constitutes a clear threat to the safety and health of other students or staff. State statutes should be amended so that when the principal and the superintendent can prove a student is a clear threat to the safety and health of other students or employees, the school board has the option of expelling the student, even though no felony has been committed. School officials are encouraged to use long-term suspension and alternative schools or programs in lieu of expulsions.

Transfer violent students to alternative schools
Under compulsory attendance laws, states have a duty to provide an education for all of their children, even those deemed violent by the juvenile justice system. In numerous instances a violent student has been placed in a regular school setting, and the results have been disruptive and even dangerous. To provide a safe and secure setting for all children and teachers, school districts must be able to transfer to another institution the juveniles who have been categorized as violent by the courts, as well as the juveniles whose presence poses a clear threat to others within the school. Transferring a juvenile to an alternative school for long-term supervision is a viable option to expulsion. The state fulfills its duty to provide an education; the school is made safer by removing the violent juvenile; the community is not burdened by juveniles who have been suspended from school and are roaming the streets; and the juvenile is provided a safe and structured setting in which to continue the educational process. For juveniles awaiting trial for violent acts, this approach would provide a supervised situation while preventing the juvenile's continued presence at a school from becoming disruptive.

Due to the expense of alternative schools, such placement should constitute a last step in a continuum of services for violent students. Placement should be temporary, with the goal being to return the student to the regular school setting at the appropriate time. Although the format of alternative programs varies from small, informal programs similar to homebound instruction in some systems to more formal school settings in larger systems, the focus must be on providing a strong, academic course of study with therapeutic emphasis. Other service agencies such as Public Health, Mental Health, Social Services, Juvenile Justice, and so forth must be an integral part of the team providing the alternative education program. School districts should consider using drug-free school funds, dropout prevention funds, juvenile justice and delinquency prevention funds, community-based alternative funds, in-school suspension funds, average daily membership positions, basic education program positions, and contributions from other agencies to staff alternative programs.

Report violent offenders to law officials
School violence is a community problem, not just a school problem (National School Boards Association Council of School Attorneys Staff, 2001). Violence in the schools will be stopped only when the schools join with local law enforcement, parents, juvenile court counselors, and other agencies to work together to solve the problem (Dorn, 2003; Mohondie, 2003). To obtain the support of law enforcement in curtailing school violence, principals must report all felonies and misdemeanors involving personal injury, sexual assault, possession or use of weapons, possession or sale of drugs occurring on school property. Schools can appropriately handle misdemeanors — which do not involve violence, sexual assault, weapons use, firearms, or drugs — without calling on law enforcement for help.

Require court counselors to confer with school officials Juvenile court counselors should be required to confer with school officials, the juvenile, and the juvenile's parents or guardian whenever

the minor is ordered to attend school as part of his probation after adjudication of a crime of violence. Juvenile court counselors should be given the resources needed to work more closely with the schools. The state's juvenile code should specify that minors placed on probation and required to attend school must maintain a passing grade.

Expand immediate school actions School districts should take immediate actions to make school safer. These actions should address a comprehensive approach to prevention, intervention, and crisis management. Use of school security officers, peer mediation, and crisis intervention teams is encouraged, as well as the development of policies and procedures governing student behavior (Aspen Publishers Staff, 2004; Hester, 2004; Lichtenstein et al., 2004; Marotto, 2004; McCann, 2004; Osher et al., 2004). The following recommendations will expand immediate school actions:

1. A student's right to park on school property can be conditioned upon agreeing to have her vehicle searched at any time by school officials.

2. Metal detectors, cameras, lights, handheld radio communications, and other security measures may be installed.

3. Cooperative arrangements with local law enforcement should be arranged to put trained resource officers in schools that need them.

4. Parent training and involvement programs should be established or strengthened.

5. Peer mediation and conflict resolution programs for students and teachers should be established.

6. Rules governing student behavior should be established, communicated, and enforced.

7. Warrants against students who commit violent acts in schools should be sought.

8. Rewards for information leading to the confiscation of weapons, drugs, firearms, and other dangerous items should be offered.

9. Anonymous reporting of weapons or drugs on school property must be encouraged.

10. Taking book bags to lockers should be restricted.

11. Intruder drills and other crisis management drills should be conducted periodically to ensure that students and other school employees are prepared for emergencies.

Take privileges away from students   Principals must have the authority to act immediately in ways that restrict meaningful student privileges. No appeal of these actions should delay implementation of the action. A prompt and meaningful response to student misconduct is an effective way to produce desired conduct (Council for Exceptional Children, 2000).

The department of education in each state needs to adopt procedures that enable principals to:

1. Suspend school bus transportation privileges for students who commit acts of violence;

2. Suspend parking privileges on school grounds for students who commit acts of violence;

3. Assign to an alternative school those students who commit acts of violence;

4. Remove from extracurricular activities (athletic and academic) students who commit acts of violence; and

5. At extracurricular activities, restrict attendance of students who commit acts of violence.

Strategy 3: Focus Resources on Schools

The number of dysfunctional and violence-prone youth in our schools is growing rapidly. These students require special attention. To meet their needs, additional resources may be required, including more assistant principals, guidance counselors, school psychologists, social workers, nurses, and teachers. Providing for the needs of violence-prone students also includes funding the basic education program, teaching violence prevention, and establishing local task forces (Beaty, 2004; Davis, 2004; Lincoln, 2003; Ross, 2004; Vasquez, Myhand, & Creighton, 2004; Wilde, 2003, 2004). Each one will be discussed in turn.

Fund the Basic Education Program   Providing smaller class sizes to deal with these special needs students will require the allocation of additional teaching positions in the regular school program. In addition, many schools are now assigning school resource officers to schools to prevent school violence. School districts that utilize these plainclothes police officers report significant reductions in school violence (National Alliance for Safe Schools, 2004). Alternative schools or programs must have additional staff members as well as intensive therapeutic support to serve violence-prone youth. Basic education program funding must be reviewed as "positive prevention," because our failure to serve the special needs population inevitably leads to incarcerations or welfare that will cost the taxpayers much more in the future.

Teach Violence Prevention   State departments of education need to ensure that violence prevention is included in their state's K–12 curriculum. Peer mediation, conflict resolution, multiculturalism, media literacy, and citizenship should be part of that curriculum (Carisson-Paige & Levin, 2004; Lincoln, 2003; Wilde, 2003; Williams, 2004). Principals need to advocate for the state department of education to encourage teacher training in these areas. In particular, the teaching of citizenship skills needs to be developed more fully in schools. Courses should include personal responsibility, cultural and racial differences, morals and ethics, and problem-solving strategies. However, merely teaching about these topics will not be sufficient; schools must work to develop these skills in students.

Establish Local Task Forces   Principals need to advocate for each school district to establish a school safety task force consisting of students, parents, teachers, school administrators, law enforcement officials, juvenile court personnel, local government representatives, and community leaders. Task force goals will be (a) to evaluate the extent of violence in the schools and the community and (b) to develop an action plan that includes both prevention and intervention strategies. In addition to these goals, the two most important contributions of the task force will be to develop a vision within the community that violence can be diminished and to model the collaboration among stakeholder groups.

Strategy 4: Strengthen the System

As noted previously, juvenile violence has increased substantially during the past few years. In some states, the juvenile justice system is not adequately dealing with the problem. Improving the state's juvenile code and creating a statewide center for the prevention of school violence may help strengthen the system.

Improve the Juvenile Code   School principals can be advocates for an examination of the state's juvenile code and the way its juvenile justice system handles crimes committed by juveniles. The review of issues should include fingerprinting of juveniles for violent crimes; submission of these fingerprints to the State Bureau of Investigation for inclusion in the Automated Fingerprint Identification System; the age at which a juvenile can be bound over to superior court for trial as an adult; and the access by superior court judges to prior juvenile convictions at sentencing.

Create a State Center for the Prevention of School Violence   School principals can be advocates for the governor of each state to establish a state center for the prevention of school violence. The center would function as the state clearinghouse and contact agency for technical assistance and program development. Specifically, the center would perform the following functions: serve as the point of contact for data and information about the number of violent incidents occurring in schools across the state; conduct periodic analysis of school violence trends, and assess the impact of programs initiated and legislation enacted to deal with the problem of violence; and provide direct service to those requesting to establish violence reduction programs in the schools.

Strategy 5: Develop a Crisis Management Plan

As discussed earlier, one of the most serious problems that principals face today is the increasing level of violence in schools. It is essential for principals and their staffs to be prepared for such incidents. Schools need to have a comprehensive crisis management plan. By adhering to the following steps, principals can ensure to the greatest degree possible that their schools are safe for students and staff alike (Rettig, 1999; Walker & Eaton-Walker, 2000).

Form a School-wide Crisis Management Team
The team should be made up of school staff and parents as well as representatives from social service and mental health agencies, the religious community, recreational organizations, and law enforcement. The charge of the crisis management team is to develop and evaluate a comprehensive plan for school safety.

Conduct an Ongoing, School-wide Safety Audit
A firm knowledge base has emerged, called Crime Prevention Through Environmental Design (CPTED), that examines the design and use of school spaces according to how well they enhance school safety. A CPTED evaluation prescribes changes in the design of the school building, in patterns of building use, and in supervision processes to reduce the likelihood of school crime and violence.

Items addressed in a CPTED analysis would include the design and location of bathrooms; the height of windows; how entrances and exits to the school are monitored and managed; the use of lighting, natural surveillance capabilities, and obstructions thereof; where locker bays are located and how they are managed; identification of low-traffic areas requiring an increased adult presence; identification of school sites that tend to be inhabited inappropriately by certain groups of students; scheduling procedures that result in large groups of students coming in contact with each other in crowded spaces; how students and other adults who belong in the school are recognized and identified; and procedures that allow students to communicate anonymously their concerns about other students or situations.

Develop Policies and Procedures for Various Emergencies   Specific policies and procedures must be developed to address a wide range of potential problems at the district, school, and classroom levels. These could include a violence prevention policy, a zero tolerance policy for weapons and drugs, a dress code, and an intruder policy.

It may be helpful if the principal divides policies and procedures into categories like the following:

1. The *people crisis* category could include medical emergencies, intruders, drive-by shootings, student runaways or abductions, deaths of students or staff members, and bomb threats.

2. The *natural disaster* category could include fires, tornados, earthquakes, other severe weather, or floods.

3. The *physical plant* category could include policies that address power outages, nonworking phone lines, gas leaks, hazardous materials, or explosions.

Conduct Safety Drills   Every aspect of the crisis management plan should have at least two people responsible for coordinating each task. Staff members should be assigned to respond to emergency teams, parents, and the press. Each school should carefully consider its physical plant and analyze where students should be directed to go from wherever they are in the school. Upon hearing a predetermined signal or tone, teachers should lock down classrooms. Every room should have two methods for communicating with the office (i.e., a two-way public announcement system and a phone, cell phone, or walkie-talkie).

Develop a School-wide Discipline Plan   School discipline should be consistent, predictable, and perceived as fair by students in the school. It is essential that every crisis management plan include a carefully developed school-wide discipline plan that has input from teachers, students, parents,

administrators, and other adults in the school. The plan should be posted throughout the school with clearly stated rules that govern classroom, cafeteria, playground, gym, and hallway behavior.

Provide a Means for Students to Communicate Information to Staff   A recent report from the U.S. Department of Education (2004b) notes that in several instances of school violence or student suicide, some students knew in advance of the activity but did not tell anyone. It is essential in such situations that children be able to communicate their concerns or fears to the staff in a way that maintains confidentiality, respect, and safety.

Teach Students Alternatives to Violence   In any program aimed at averting student violence, it is first necessary to focus attention on students' individual needs and problems. School staff should address such topics as self-esteem, conflict resolution, impulse control, consequences of gang membership, and stress management. Schools also need to foster a sense of belonging among students. One reason students join gangs is that these groups meet their need for belonging. Membership in after-school extracurricular activities and clubs also may help reduce violence.

Evaluate Administrative Practices of the School   How a school is operated can have a strong impact on its relative safety. Academically effective schools, for example, tend to be safer schools. Schools that provide a positive, inclusive climate tend to have less conflict and fewer instances of aggressive, bullying behavior. Schools attended by the number of students for which they were designed tend to have fewer behavioral incidents and problems. Safer schools tend to have clear behavioral and performance expectations for everyone.

Use Resources to Identify Students at Risk for Violent Behavior   School principals can use an excellent resource for identifying troubled youth and responding to their needs. It is called the *Early Warning/Timely Response Guide* for making schools safer and violence free. This guide was jointly developed by the U.S. Attorney General's Office and the U.S. Department of Education. It contains comprehensive guidelines and recommendations for the early profiling of troubled youth and the role that schools, teachers, parents, communities, and peers can play in responding to their problems and meeting their needs. It is a valuable tool for addressing the current crisis of school safety. The guide is a public domain publication, costs nothing, and can be downloaded from the Internet at http://www.ed.gov/about/offices/list/osers/osep/gtss.html. Table 12.1 provides a sample checklist that principals can use to identify violence-prone students.

Strategy 6: Create an Orderly Climate for Learning

Several authors suggest ways that schools may be able to reduce student violence by creating an orderly climate conducive to learning. According to these authors, research has indicated three important differences between schools that create an orderly climate for learning and those that fail to do so: goals, rules and procedures, and teacher-student relationships (Council for Exceptional Children, 2000; Fishbaugh et al., 2003; Meeks et al., 2000; Pepperl & Lezotte, 2000; Watson et al., 2003).

Establish and Emphasize Goals   In schools that emphasize academic goals, students are more engaged in schoolwork; that is, they spend more time on task. Teachers in these schools have higher expectations for their students and tend to have more positive interactions with them. These student and teacher characteristics make it more likely that students invest more time and energy in academic goals rather than in a peer culture that might sanction violence and disruptive behavior. Studies reveal that school violence is much more likely to occur when students feel that grades are punitive or impossible to obtain and if the school curriculum is irrelevant. Also, the level of violence increases with class size and the total number of students taught per week. Moreover, a

Table 12.1   Checklist for Identifying Students at Risk for Violent Behavior

Children and adolescents at risk may:

express self-destructive or homicidal ideation

have a history of self-destructive behavior

articulate specific plans to harm self or others

engage in "bullying" other children

have difficulty with impulse control

evidence significant changes in behavior

engage in substance abuse

become involved with gangs

evidence a preoccupation with fighting

have a history of antisocial behavior

evidence a low tolerance for frustration

externalize blame for their difficulties

evidence a preoccupation with guns and weapons

have engaged in fire setting

evidence persistent bed wetting

appear to be, or acknowledge, feeling depressed

talk about "not being around"

express feelings of hopelessness

give away possessions

appear withdrawn

evidence significant changes in mood

experience sleep and eating disturbances

have experienced prior trauma or tragedy

have been, or are, victims of child abuse

have experienced a significant loss

evidence a preoccupation with television programs and movies with violent themes

evidence a preoccupation with games with violent themes

have harmed small animals

have access to a firearm

have brought a weapon to school

evidence frequent disciplinary problems

exhibit poor academic performance

have frequently been truant from school

higher incidence of aggression against teachers occurs if the class consists largely of students with behavior problems, low achievers, or minority students (Hill, 2004; Meeks et al., 2000). This is one of many reasons for the elimination of tracking (George, 1992; Oakes, 1992).

Specific areas of the school program, as related to school violence, that should be evaluated include the curriculum and the instructional setting. For the curriculum, the following questions should be asked: Is the curriculum relevant? Does it meet the needs of students (Ornstein & Hunkins, 2004; Sowell, 2000; Wiles & Bondi, 2002)? Regarding the instructional setting, the following are significant questions: Are the class size and total students manageable for effective teaching? Are the instructional materials and procedures appropriate? Are grades attainable and fair? Are the students tracked by ability or other factors (Glickman, Gordon, & Ross-Gordon, 2004; Ornstein & Lasley, 2004; Wiles & Bondi, 2004)?

An effort should be made to improve the achievement of all students in schools. And schools must expand teaching beyond the basic skills to include citizenship, effective decision making, conflict-resolution skills, cooperation, and courtesy. Teachers and students alike should model the art of compromise. Students need to learn that these are acceptable ways to deal with their conflicts and to meet their individual needs (Allison, 2004; Beaty, 2004; Begun & Huml, 2003; Carisson-Paige & Levin, 2004; Goldstein & Conoley, 2004; Hester, 2004; Hill, 2004; Marotto, 2004; Vasquez et al., 2004; Wilde, 2003; Williams, 2004).

The need to reach children in the early years is important. Programs that provide support for young families should be enhanced. Head Start, Follow Through, day care, and after-school care for children of working or student parents should be funded. School districts must become involved in early childhood education by providing facilities and staff. Teachers need to be trained to work with infants, toddlers, and preschoolers. Parents may require assistance in acquiring parenting skills (Beaty, 2004; Begun & Huml, 2003).

Establish Rules and Procedures Students and teachers feel safe in schools with clear discipline standards that are enforced firmly, fairly,

and consistently (Council for Exceptional Children, 2000; Duke, 2004; Pepperl & Lezotte, 2000; Watson et al., 2003). This environment can be accomplished by developing a comprehensive student handbook that identifies expectations for student behavior and states the consequences for students who violate the rules. Student handbooks should unambiguously outline student rights and responsibilities. Suspension and expulsion procedures should be carefully explained, and the appeals process fully described. Due to the frequency of gang activity in schools, the handbook should include sections on dress codes, search and seizure, graffiti, beepers and pagers, and school design (Fishbaugh et al., 2003; Garrett, 2002; Grimes et al., 2002; Gulledge et al., 2001; Hester, 2004; Leonard, 2000; McCann, 2004; National School Boards Association, 2004; Noble, 2003; Osher et al., 2004; Reuter et al., 2002; Thomerson et al., 2003b; Wanko, 2002). We discuss each of these policies in turn.

Establish dress codes School boards should consider establishing policies regarding dress codes for students and teachers. For example, the Oakland (California) Board of Education banned clothing and jewelry denoting identification with a gang; expensive jogging suits often worn by drug dealers; and all hats and clothing designating membership in nonschool organizations. Detroit (Michigan) Public Schools have implemented a ban on expensive clothing and jewelry. Baltimore (Maryland) Public Schools are experimenting with school uniforms. The Dallas (Texas) Board of Education has adopted a policy opposing clothing and grooming that are considered distracting or disruptive. And school principals have been given the discretion to determine what are inappropriate dress and appearance at their school (National School Boards Association, 2004). Furthermore, there may be a relationship between the implementation of a standardized dress code policy and student achievement (Stallings, 2000) and student attendance (Creel, 2000).

School boards may enact reasonable regulations concerning student appearance in school. Such regulations have focused on male hairstyles and pupil attire. Student challenges to these regulations have relied on First Amendment constitutional freedoms to determine personal appearance. The U.S. Supreme Court has consistently refused to review the decisions of lower courts on these matters (*Karr v. Schmidt,* 401 U.S. 1201, 1972). Generally, courts tend to provide less protection to some forms of expression (e.g., pupil hairstyle and attire) than to others (e.g., symbolic expression and student publications). Nonetheless, awareness of constitutional freedoms places limits on school principals to regulate student dress, excluding special situations (e.g., graduation and physical education classes). Pupil attire can always be regulated to protect student health, safety, and school discipline. In short, the extent to which school principals may control student appearance depends more on different community mores and on "the times" than on strict principles of law.

Use search and seizure cautiously   The introduction of drugs, weapons, and other contraband in schools has placed school principals in the position of searching students' persons or lockers, and students claim that such acts violate their Fourth Amendment guarantees. A student's right to the Fourth Amendment's protection from unreasonable search and seizure must be balanced against the need for school principals to maintain discipline and to provide a safe environment conducive to learning. State and federal courts generally have relied on the doctrine of *in loco parentis,* reasoning that school principals stand in the place of a parent and are not subject to the constraints of the Fourth Amendment. In *New Jersey v. T.L.O.,* 469 U.S. 325 (1985), the U.S. Supreme Court held that searches by school officials in schools are within the constraints of the Fourteenth Amendment. The court concluded that the special needs of the school environment justified easing the warrant and probable cause requirement imposed in criminal cases, provided that school searches are based on "reasonable suspicion."

Pay attention to graffiti   Attending to symbols is an important way of controlling misbehavior. Graffiti is a form of vandalism (defacing school property) that frequently serves as gang symbolism.

Immediate removal of graffiti sends a message to students of the school principal's opposition to vandalism and gang symbols. It not only prevents conflict over potential gang territory but also tells students and staff alike that the principal cares about personnel safety and is taking appropriate steps to protect everyone's safety.

Ban beepers and pagers   Except for students who have severe medical problems or those who are members of rescue units, beepers and pagers should be prohibited on school grounds. Law enforcement officials maintain that frequently students with beepers and pagers are involved in drug trafficking. Undesirable behavior is less likely to occur when beepers and pagers are banned from schools.

Reconsider school design   School design and facility use can encourage undesirable behaviors. School policy should restrict student congregation in "blind spots"; recommend random spot checks of problem areas, such as restrooms, locker rooms, and parking lots; and increase physical security with fences, lights, and metal detectors. The least costly security measure is faculty supervision. When principals and teachers are visible throughout the buildings and school grounds, disruptive behavior is less likely to occur.

Improve Teacher-Student Relations in the Classroom   School principals may be able to reduce student violence and disruptive behavior by facilitating orderly and nurturing classroom learning environments. Quality teaching may avert violence and disruptive behavior in classrooms and throughout the school. By making sure that all students are actively engaged in meaningful, challenging learning every day, students are less likely to be disruptive. Furthermore, all teachers and students should be encouraged to treat others with respect at all times.

Teachers may utilize the following instructional techniques as they interact with and direct students within their classrooms (Glickman et al., 2004; Lunenburg & Irby, 1999; Lunenburg & Ornstein, 2004; Ornstein & Lasley, 2004; Wiles & Bondi, 2004).

Use anticipatory set Discipline of students is connected with the quality of instruction delivered by the teacher. Following is a discussion of what the literature suggests regarding improving instructional delivery and thereby improving classroom discipline among the students. Observers have noted that teachers usually do not spend much time preparing a class for an activity. They frequently say, "Read this story tonight for homework," or "Watch this demonstration carefully," and expect their classroom to be full of eager students who are anxious to learn as much as possible.

The problem that every teacher faces at least twice during each classroom period is to hit upon those introductory remarks (or procedures) that will produce the maximum payoff in learning. That is, when introducing an activity, what can a teacher say that will produce the maximum payoff in learning? What words can a teacher use to produce the maximum in subsequent learning?

The concept of *anticipatory set* comes from research on learning and the theory developed from that research (Emmer et al., 2003; Evertson et al., 2003; Good & Brophy, 2003). This research appears to indicate that the activities preceding a learning task influence the outcome of that task, and that some instructional sets are superior to others. If some instructional sets are superior to others, then each teacher is faced with the need to find those types of sets that will be most useful for his purposes and then to modify these sets to fit the specific classroom situation.

Activities for which anticipatory set is appropriate include the following: at the start of a unit; before a discussion; before question-answer recitation; before giving a homework assignment; before hearing a panel discussion; before students present reports; when assigning student reports; before viewing a filmstrip; in a discussion after viewing a filmstrip; before assigning homework based on the discussion following a filmstrip. Examples of set induction include (a) starting a lesson on tone in poetry by comparing the lyrics of a Joan Baez song with the song "Goldfinger," with a Rolling Stones song; (b) giving an assignment of creating a character as a set for noticing character in the reading of short stories; (c) using

the three hats that King Lear wore as facilitating sets to understand his three roles and the three stages of his change; (d) understanding the executive, legislative, and judicial branches of government by working through analogies to family, school, and the city; and (e) studying history from 1700 to 1900 by giving a set for developing "rules of history." Another example of anticipatory set is beginning a unit in physics with a demonstration involving a piece of wood overhanging the edge of a desk. The part on the desk is covered with a piece of paper. When the teacher gives a sharp blow to the part of the wood hanging over the edge (because of the air pressure), the paper is undisturbed and the wood snaps.

Use reinforcement Research has indicated that if teachers reinforce students both verbally and nonverbally when they participate in large- and small-group classroom discussions and do so whether their responses are correct or not, students will participate more often and more actively. If teachers wish to get students to participate more often and more actively in class, they must discover what is reinforcing for particular students and then reinforce the students for participating in class. It would seem that the more techniques a teacher has at her disposal for reinforcing students, the better his chances for getting good pupil participation.

For example, when a student makes a particularly good response, the teacher might say, "That's exactly it," and nod his head affirmatively as he moves toward the student. In this case, he combines one positive verbal reinforcer with two positive nonverbal reinforcers. Such a combination produces a cumulative effect. Examples of positive nonverbal reinforcement include the following: The teacher nods and smiles; the teacher moves toward the pupil; the teacher keeps his eyes on the pupil; and the teacher writes the pupil's response on the blackboard. Positive verbal reinforcement includes responses using words and phrases such as "Good," "Fine," "Excellent," "Correct," and the like, or otherwise verbally indicating pleasure at the pupil's response. Teacher actions and responses that act as negative reinforcement tend to decrease pupil participation and should be avoided. Examples follow: The teacher scowls or frowns; the teacher moves away from the pupil; the teacher fails to maintain eye contact with the pupil; the teacher responds with "No," "Wrong," and "That's not it"; the teacher manifests expressions of annoyance or impatience.

Recognize attending behavior   Related literature on pupil attending behavior indicates that pupil behavior can be classified as either work-oriented or nonwork-oriented behavior and that these pupil behaviors can be distinguished from each other. Two important variables, which are dimensions of total teacher behavior, were reported in the literature as instructional technique and the immediate effect of technique on pupil attending behavior. An inverse relationship has been found between pupil attending behavior and pupil disruptive behavior (Lunenburg & Ornstein, 2004; Ornstein & Lasley, 2004).

Suggested criteria for recognizing attending behavior include making eye contact with the teacher or the teaching media; actively engaging in the task assignment (such as reading, writing, or note taking); displaying a positive response to the teaching task; and participating in the class activity. Suggested criteria for recognizing nonattending behavior include appearing bored with the teaching task; not making eye contact with the teacher; not participating in the class activity; being involved in an activity other than the assigned task; and seeming to respond negatively to the teacher's direction.

Employ questioning techniques   The use of questioning techniques is basic to good teaching. Generally speaking, questions can be placed into four broad categories: initiating, probing, higher-order, and divergent (Hunkins, 1995).

Initiating questions elicit an initial response from the student. Once the student has responded, the teacher probes the student's response. Some of the *probing* questions the teacher asks require the students to remember facts or to describe something they see. The teacher also asks *higher-order* questions that require the students to make comparisons, inferences, and evaluations or to relate ideas.

Divergent questions have no "right" or "wrong" answers. When first asked divergent questions, many students are uncomfortable because there are no right answers for them to lean upon. Such students are reluctant to explore and hypothesize, for fear of giving wrong or foolish answers. As a result, they try to pick up cues from the teacher regarding what answer is wanted. If the teacher gives these kinds of cues, however, her questions are not truly divergent. If, on the other hand, the teacher is not giving cues, some students are likely to feel uncomfortable and uncertain. This should be viewed as a favorable sign — students are forced to think for themselves.

Establish appropriate frames of reference   A student's understanding of the lesson material can be increased if it is organized and taught from several appropriate viewpoints. A single frame of reference provides a structure through which the student can gain an understanding of the materials. The use of several frames of reference deepens and broadens the general field of understanding more completely than is possible with only one. Teachers can be trained to become more powerful teachers as they learn to identify many possible frames of reference that might be used in instruction, to select judiciously from among them, and then to present them effectively.

Use closure   The skills of set induction and closure are complementary. Unless the students achieve closure — that is, perception of the logical organization of the ideas presented in a lesson — the effects of an otherwise good lesson may be negated. By using closure techniques, the teacher can make sure that students understand the material and its relationship to what they have learned already.

Closure is not limited to the completion of a lesson. It is also needed at specific points within the lesson, so that pupils may know where they are now and where they will be going next. If the planned lesson is not completed, the teacher can still attain closure by drawing her students' attention to what has been accomplished up to the point where the lesson must end.

Examples of closure include drawing attention to the completion of the lesson or part of the lesson; making connections between previously known material, currently presented material, and future learning; allowing students opportunity to demonstrate what they have learned; and developing unsuspected closure by helping students to take the material that has been presented and develop it into a new, and unsuspected, synthesis.

Be attentive to race, class, and gender equity in the classroom   On the surface, the existence of nonequitable classrooms does not appear as violent against students, nor as being a matter with which teachers should contend; however, when one considers the societal baggage attached to each equity issue, perhaps then violent scenes can be brought to mind. The best method of achieving gender equity is to improve classroom learning generally (Meeks et al., 2000). We would suggest the same approach for handling race and class issues. Administrators should assist teachers in creating better learning environments where equity can be achieved. The following strategies can be used to assure race, class, and gender-equity classrooms (Lara-Alecio, Irby, & Ebener, 2000):

1. Conduct a gender-bias, race-bias, class-bias audit of the classroom (this should include an assessment of your feelings about your own race, class, and gender; knowing ourselves help to get a better perspective on how we relate to others).

2. Self-assess, and teach students to self-assess.

3. Encourage students to set goals and be risk takers.

4. Provide situations where inclusion is a natural consequence of a multicultural curriculum; that is, where special education students are included, and where language minority students are included rather than isolated. The latter can be achieved through a dual-language approach to schooling. To develop a truly inclusive and multicultural environment, total reform of the school curriculum and instruction may be necessary. Understanding goes

beyond awareness; understanding of others yields support of others and assists with a more cohesive faculty and student body and, consequently, fosters a safer learning environment.

5. Teach the teachers and students to celebrate mistakes, because we all learn from them, but also encourage everyone to take pride in their successes.

6. Avoid sending negative messages.

7. Retrain students and teachers in considering to what their successes and failures are attributed.

8. Provide positive, honest feedback.

9. Reduce stereotypical thinking.

10. Redirect selective attention.

11. Remember individual differences.

12. Use cooperative learning groups.

13. Teach concepts in the curriculum that are not brought out in the texts.

14. Focus on math and science.

The assurance of safe and orderly schools requires the commitment of each individual in the school and larger community. School principals have at hand the facts regarding physical and emotional school violence, drugs, and alcohol. Armed with this knowledge, they have access to many successful programs and suggestions for restructuring their schools to be safer and more orderly learning environments. It is impossible to overemphasize the importance that attitudes, understandings, and instructional techniques of teachers play in reducing violence in the classroom.

Summary

1. Growing violence, chaos in classrooms, and access to drugs are regular occurrences in the school day for an increasing number of students. Frequently, the violence in a community spills into the schools. Although the situation in some schools and neighborhoods is more serious than in others, creating a safe,

ment is a challenge for all schools.

2. Violence prediction strategies have reduced incidences of violence in our schools. The strategies include collecting and analyzing data, identifying problem students, and identifying problem teachers.

3. Violence in America has increased substantially over the past few years. It is not surprising that the level of violence in public schools is increasing as well. Violence in schools endangers the health, welfare, and safety of students and teachers. Strategies for preventing school violence include toughening weapons laws and dealing effectively with violent students.

4. Additional resources may be required to meet the needs of violence-prone students. Strategies include funding the basic education program, teaching violence prevention, and establishing task forces. In some states, the juvenile justice system is dealing inadequately with the problem of school violence. For those states, improving the juvenile code and creating a statewide center for the prevention of school violence may help strengthen the system.

5. Several researchers suggest ways that schools may be able to reduce student violence by creating an orderly climate conducive to learning. Some strategies are establishing and emphasizing goals, establishing rules and procedures, and improving teacher-student relationships.

Field-Based Activities

1. Take field notes for one week, during which time you will investigate your school's violence prediction strategies and violence prevention strategies. Record these in your journal. Then interview your building principal to determine how the violence prediction and prevention strategies are functioning in your school. If your school has no such strategies, find out if they exist in other schools in your district

and/or other school districts in your state or other states. That is, do a survey of effective violence prediction and violence prevention strategies in operation in schools. Record your findings in your journal.

2. Additional resources may be required to meet the needs of violence-prone students. Some strategies are funding the basic education program, teaching violence prevention, and establishing task forces. What additional resources and strategies exist in your school or school district to meet the needs of violence-prone students? Record these strategies in your journal. Next, interview a state official to learn how your state's juvenile code applies to violence in your state. Record your findings in your journal.

3. Student violence may be reduced in schools by creating an orderly climate conducive to learning. Some strategies are establishing and emphasizing goals, establishing and implementing rules and procedures fairly and consistently, and improving teacher-student relationships. Investigate which of the three strategies just mentioned are used successfully in your school to reduce student violence. Record your findings in your journal. Recommend other strategies not described in this text.

Suggested Readings

Burstyn, J. N., et al. (2001). *Preventing violence in schools*. Mahwah, NJ: Erlbaum. The author provides an in-depth analysis of violence prevention programs and assesses their effectiveness by using data from observations, individual interviews, and focus groups as well as published data from the schools. This book is distinguished by its focus on the cultural and structural context of school violence and violence prevention efforts.

Duke, D. L. (2002). *Creating safe schools for all children*. Boston: Allyn & Bacon. The author provides a set of standards that educators can use to evaluate their schools and then develop practical and systematic plans for ensuring orderly and caring learning environments. This book also addresses several theoretical perspectives through which readers can come to understand school safety. Attention is given to the distinction between preventing violence and promoting safety.

Fishbaugh, M. S. E., Berkeley, T. R., & Schroth, G. (2003). *Ensuring safe school environments: Exploring issues — seeking solutions.* Mahwah, NJ: Erlbaum. The authors present research findings and information about school violence, with a focus on strategies for increasing school safety. Based on a special topical issue of *Rural Special Education Quarterly,* this book contains rewrites of the authors' original journal articles, which address safe schools from the perspective of suburban and urban as well as rural environments. Topics include the frequency of violence in these different settings; violence as it directly affects school administrators; strategies for preventing and addressing violence at both the school and individual levels; and ways to work with the community both in and out of schools.

Kauffman, J. M. (2004). How we prevent the prevention of emotional and behavioral difficulties in education. In P. Garner, F. Yuen, P. Clough, & T. Pardeck (Eds.), *Handbook of emotional and behavioral difficulties.* London: Sage. Kauffman offers a realistic appraisal of reversing antisocial behavior once it is firmly established in a child's repertoire. The author highlights the importance of early intervention, but dismisses no youngster as hopeless. Even though students may present tough problems and need continuing support, the author maintains that teachers should not give up. It is an extraordinarily realistic yet hopeful book.

Teaching Tolerance. (2001). *Responding to hate at school: A guide for teachers, counselors, and administrators.* Boston: Allyn & Bacon. This step-by-step, easy-to-use guide is designed to help teachers, principals, and counselors react promptly and effectively whenever hate, bias, and prejudice strike. The handbook offers proven school-based strategies and concrete recommendations for addressing day-to-day problems, emergency situations, and long-term policy and development issues.

Walker, H. M., Ramsey, E., & Gresham, F. M. (2004). *Antisocial behavior in school: Evidence-based practices.* Belmont, CA: Wadsworth/Thomson Learning. This book will help teachers *identify* antisocial behavior, *understand why* students exhibit such behavior, and — more importantly — *know what to do about it when they see it.* This book should be read by everyone who cares about children's socialization.

Wessler, S. L., & Preble, W. (2003). *The respectful school: How educators and students can conquer hate and harassment.* Alexandria, VA: Association for Supervision and Curriculum Development. Protect students who are being teased and harassed in your school and preserve a respectful learning environment by following the strategies and advice in this guide. Know what to do when students use degrading language and slurs, how to intervene when students are being picked on, and what kinds of structures and policies promote respect and help students take a stand against hate and prejudice.

13. Human Resource Management

Standard 3.0: *Candidates who complete the program are educational leaders who have the knowledge and ability to promote the success of all students by managing the organization, operation, and resources in a way that promotes a safe, efficient, and effective environment.*

FOCUSING QUESTIONS

1 What are the steps in the human resource management process?

2 How do principals recruit personnel?

3 What steps do principals use in selecting personnel?

4 Why are staff development programs needed?

5 What are the most commonly used staff development methods?

6 Why is the appraisal of performance important?

7 How can staff performance be measured? What are some common errors principals make in evaluating personnel?

8 What is the impact of collective bargaining on the principal's role in operating schools?

In this chapter, we respond to these questions concerning human resource management in schools. We begin our discussion with an overview of the human resource management process. Then we look at recruitment, selection, and staff development of personnel. Next, we examine performance appraisal, including methods, rating errors, and programs specific to teaching personnel. And, finally, we provide a brief outline of union-management relations, including negotiation and administration of the collective bargaining agreement.

Who performs the human resource management function? In many large school districts, human resource management activities are carried out largely by a human resources department. However, not all principals work in school districts that have a human resources department; and even those that do still must be engaged in some human resource management functions. Principals in small- to medium-sized school districts are examples of individuals who must frequently do

their hiring without the assistance of a human resources department. But even principals in large
school districts are involved in recruiting, reviewing applications, interviewing applicants, developing faculty and staff, and appraising performance.
And with the advent of site-based management,
principals are becoming more involved in human
resource management decisions—involving both
certificated and classified employees—than in
the past.

The Human Resource Management Process

The human resource management process consists
of the following steps: (a) recruitment, (b) selection, (c) staff development, and (d) performance
appraisal (Bratton et al., 2003; Castetter &
Young, 2000; Dessler, 2002; Foot et al., 2002;
Ivancevich, 2003; Seyfarth, 2001; Webb &
Norton, 2004). Figure 13.1 illustrates these steps.
The figure also indicates that all of these various
activities are affected by legislative constraints
and union demands.

The focus of this chapter is on four main steps
in the human resource management process.

1. *Recruitment.* Internal and external sources
   are used to locate qualified applicants to satisfy the school's personnel needs.

2. *Selection.* Applicants in the recruiting pool
   are carefully screened. Candidates who meet
   the school's job requirements are selected.

3. *Staff development.* Staff development (professional development) involves teaching support
   staff (custodians, cooks, bus drivers, secretaries)
   the skills they need to fulfill the requirements of
   the job and faculty (teachers, counselors, social
   workers, school psychologists) to perfect their
   skills in the classroom and elsewhere.

4. *Performance appraisal.* This step involves
   evaluating personnel performance in relation to
   the school's job requirements and goals. Features of this step involve providing feedback to
   faculty and staff and improving the school's
   productivity with respect to student learning.

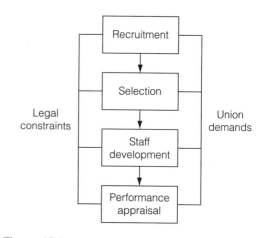

Figure 13.1

Human Resource Management Process

Legal constraints and union demands are discussed in relation to the preceding four steps.

Recruitment

Recruitment is the process of attracting a pool of
qualified applicants to replenish or expand a
school's human resources. To effectively recruit
applicants, principals must (a) have a thorough
analysis of job requirements; (b) know the legal
constraints that influence recruiting efforts; and
(c) cultivate the sources of potential employees.

Job Analysis

To recruit appropriate personnel to fill vacant
positions, the principal must know in detail what
tasks are to be performed and the personal characteristics necessary to perform the tasks. These
determinations are derived through *job analysis*
(U.S. Department of Labor, 2005). The information obtained through job analysis is used in most
subsequent personnel decisions, such as selection,
staff development, and performance appraisal.
But its most immediate use is to prepare job
descriptions and job specifications.

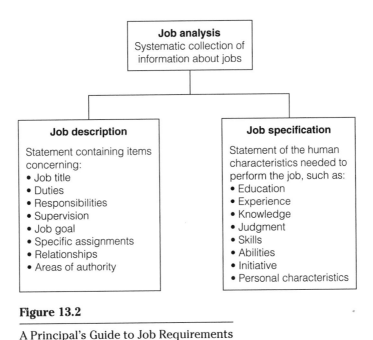

Figure 13.2

A Principal's Guide to Job Requirements

The *job description* is a written statement of the duties and responsibilities, relationships, and results expected of the job incumbent. It generally includes a job title, the person to whom the job incumbent reports, and a statement of the job goal. The *job specification,* also based on job analysis, specifies the minimum acceptable qualifications that an incumbent must possess to perform the job successfully. It identifies the degree of education required, the desirable amount of previous experience, and the skills, abilities, and physical requirements needed to do the job effectively. Figure 13.2 illustrates the relationships of job analysis to job description and job specification.

Legal Constraints

Every principal is affected to some extent by federal laws governing the recruitment and selection of employees. The laws governing *equal employment opportunity* (EEO) have had an especially long history in the United States; the laws prohibit employment decisions based on race, color, religion, sex, national origin, age, or disability (Walsh, 2003). This legal environment has increased the need for high-caliber principals who can deal with the complex legal requirements in human resource management (Marczely & Marczely, 2002).

Specific requirements of the most important EEO laws are shown in Table 13.1. The laws apply to recruitment and selection; wages, hours, and working conditions; classification, assignment, transfer, and promotion of employees; training and development; and performance appraisal.

These basic laws have been supplemented by numerous guidelines and regulations issued by the Equal Employment Opportunity Commission (EEOC), the Office of Federal Contract Compliance, and the Department of Labor. The regulations are too numerous and complex to mention here; however, their impact on employment decisions in schools has been significant. For example, job descriptions and job specifications must be written so as not to exclude any race, sex, age, or other factor prohibited by law. Applicant interviewing and testing, which we discuss later, also must be conducted carefully in order to meet legal

Table 13.1 Major Laws Affecting Hiring Practices

Law	Basic Requirements
Title VII of the Civil Rights Act of 1964 (as amended)	Prohibits discrimination in employment on the basis of race, color, religion, gender, or national origin
Age Discrimination in Employment Act of 1968 (as amended)	Prohibits discrimination in employment against any person 40 years of age or over
Equal Pay Act of 1963	Prohibits wage discrimination on the basis of gender; requires equal pay for equal work regardless of gender
Rehabilitation Act of 1973	Requires employers to take affirmative action to employ and promote qualified handicapped persons
Pregnancy Discrimination Act of 1978	Requires employers to treat pregnant women and new mothers the same as other employees for all employment-related purposes
Vietnam Era Veterans Readjustment Act of 1974	Requires employers to take affirmative action to employ disabled Vietnam War veterans
Occupational Safety & Health Act (OSHA) of 1970	Established mandatory safety and health standards in organizations

requirements. And *affirmative action programs*, designed to increase employment opportunities for women and minority groups, put pressure on principals to ensure that females and other minorities (including veterans, the aged, and the handicapped) are employed in proportion to their actual availability in the area labor market. Courts have ruled that religious schools may use religion as an employment consideration.

Personnel Sources

School districts have numerous sources available for obtaining personnel. When attempting to fill a position, most principals look within the school district first. Policies for promoting from within are widely used because they tend to increase employee morale and motivation while reducing recruitment costs (Bernardin, 2002; Fyack, 2004; Lundy et al., 2003; Schriesheim & Neider, 2003).

External sources of potential employees are used when personnel with specialized skills, such as teachers, counselors, social workers, and computer programmers, are required. Some of the most frequently used external sources include college and university placement offices, state employment services, private employment agencies, newspaper and radio advertisements, professional journals, employee referrals, and professional meetings and conventions (Baerdwell et al., 2001; Daley, 2001; Seyfarth, 2001; Torrington et al., 2002).

School districts committed to equal employment opportunities and affirmative action programs typically take additional steps to ensure that available positions are provided the broadest possible publicity. For instance, the district might try advertising in publications designed specifically for minority candidates; contacting colleges and universities that specialize in educating women or minorities; and contacting employment agencies that specialize in placing women and minority candidates. To reach minorities and women, the district may also contact neighborhood groups or national organizations, such as the Urban League or the National Organization for Women. These organizations, and groups like them, have newsletters or other media for contacting minority and female prospects.

Most school districts hire from a pool of candidates who apply to their individual school systems. Occasionally, someone might notify universities or colleges of the school district's specific needs; but all too often, the search for qualified candidates does not extend beyond the central office applicant file. Sometimes, the candidates are qualified and plentiful. Often, however, personnel doing the hiring find themselves making too many compromises (Lunenburg & Ornstein, 2004).

As a means of alleviating such recruiting problems, some school districts have formed a teacher recruiting consortium. To expand a school district's applicant pool, the consortium hires a consultant to help the district streamline its application procedure, increase its visibility, and orchestrate the logistics of recruiting for several different school systems.

Teacher Recruitment Consortium

Lindquist and Metzger (2004) describe the operation of the teacher recruitment consortium, which works through a consultant. The consultant puts a workable program in place.

1. *The consultant identifies which recruiting fairs the consortium should visit.* He makes sure each school district is properly registered for each recruiting fair.

2. *The consultant standardizes the recruiting process.* For example, applicants submit a single application form, credential file, transcripts, criminal clearance (required in some states), and teaching certificate to the consortium.

3. *The consultant trains teams of administrators from different school systems to serve as recruiters.* He develops a standardized process for interviewing and evaluating candidates.

4. *The consultant creates a computerized database of qualified applicants.* The database is updated twice a month, and updated disks are sent out to all school districts in the consortium regularly from April 1 through Labor Day. School districts review information on the disk (a brief biography of the candidate) and then decide which candidates to call for final interviews. The school districts also can review the candidate's complete file, which is kept in the consortium office.

Selection

Once applicants have been recruited, the next step is *selection*—the process of determining which candidates best meet the job specifications. Steps in a typical selection process include (a) preliminary screening of credentials, (b) preliminary interview, (c) testing, (d) reference checks, (e) in-depth interview, (f) physical examination, and (g) hiring decision. Table 13.2 lists the specific steps in the selection process and gives sample reasons for rejecting applicants at each stage.

The actual selection process varies with school districts and between hierarchical levels in the same school district. For instance, the in-depth interview for classified staff may be quite perfunctory; instead, heavy emphasis may be placed on the preliminary screening interview or on performance tests. In selecting certificated personnel, like teachers, the interview may be extensive—sometimes lasting an hour or more—and there may be little or no formal testing. Instead of completing an application blank, the candidate for a certificated position may submit a letter of application and/or a resume. Some school districts omit the physical examination. Three techniques often used in the selection process are interviews, testing, and assessment centers.

Interviews

The interview is perhaps the most widely used personnel technique in the selection process. It serves as a two-way exchange that allows both the principal and the applicant to gather information that would otherwise be difficult to secure. Unfortunately, despite its widespread use, the interview is a poor predictor of job performance.

Interviewing Problems The three major interviewing problems that should be avoided are as follows:

1. *Unfamiliarity with the job.* Interviewers frequently are unfamiliar with the job. When interviewers do not know what the job entails, they (a) do not ask the right questions;

Table 13.2   Procedures for Selecting Employees

Steps in the Selection Process	Reasons for Rejection
Preliminary screening from application blank or letter, vita, school records, and so forth	Inadequate educational or experience record for the job specifications
Preliminary interview	Obvious disinterest and unsuitability for the job
Testing	Failure to meet minimum standards on job-related measures
Reference checks	Unfavorable reports on past performance
In-depth interview	Inadequate ability, ambition, or other job-related qualities
Physical examination	Physically unfit for the job
Hiring decision	Overall inability to fit the job requirements

(b) interpret the obtained information differently; (c) have faulty impressions of the information supplied; and (d) spend time discussing matters irrelevant to the job.

2. *Premature decisions.* Interviewers tend to make a decision about an applicant during the first few minutes of the interview, before gathering all the relevant information. Then they spend the rest of the interview seeking information that confirms their initial impression.

3. *Personal biases.* Some interviewers tend to have preconceptions and prejudices about people. Other biases may reflect negatively against some minority groups or in favor of those candidates who have backgrounds similar to the interviewer(s). Furthermore, some interviewers are overly impressed with surface signs of composure, manner of speech, and physical appearance (Castetter & Young, 2000; Dessler, 2002; Fyack, 2004; Ivancevich, 2003).

Improving the Interview Process   School organizations will continue to use interviews regardless of the problems. Thus researchers have identified several techniques for improving the interview process:

1. *Use a structured interview format.* It has been widely suggested that interviews be more structured. In a structured interview, questions are written out in advance, rated on a standardized scale, and asked of all applicants for a job. The structured interview has three major advantages: It brings consistency to the interview process; it provides an opportunity to develop questions that are relevant to the job; and it allows screening and refinement of questions that may be discriminatory. In addition, the structured interview is more defensible in court. A less-structured method can be used when interviewing administrative personnel. That is, the interview is still carefully planned regarding content areas covered, but it allows the interviewer more flexibility in asking questions.

2. *Train interviewers.* One way to improve the validity and reliability of the interview is to train interviewers. Effective interviewing requires specific skills, including asking questions, probing, listening, observing, recording unbiased information, rating, and the like. Workshops can be specifically designed to teach these skills. A cadre of trained interviewers can then be used to interview job applicants.

3. *Use the interview as one aspect of the selection process.* Avoid using the interview as the sole criterion for selecting applicants. By the same token, the interviewer(s) should not be the sole decision maker(s) concerning who is hired or not hired. Supplement the interview with data from other sources, including biographical information, results of tests, written references, and oral telephone inquiries. Interviewers

cannot be privy to the telephone reference checks, which must rest exclusively in the hands of the top executive officer. When these suggestions are implemented, the interview can be a useful source of information in the selection process (Dubois, 2004; Fyack, 2004).

The most important part of the selection process begins and ends with the interview. By including several key components in this process, principals can ensure they will offer contracts to worthy candidates.

Components of a Good Interview Process

Several authors have studied and recommended the following major components of a good interview process (Castetter & Young, 2000; Dessler, 2002; Fyack, 2004; Mondy et al., 2004; Vansciver, 2004; Woodall, Lee, & Stewart, 2004):

1. *Give interviews to candidates only after checking their references.* This information gives the interviewer(s) some insight into prior experiences that shape the candidate's attitudes and work ethic.

2. *Screen candidates' files to ensure completeness, neatness, and lack of gaps in their employment history.* Experience has shown that an application that is incomplete, sloppy, or missing pieces of past employment is indicative of a candidate's work quality.

3. *Make time an important consideration during the interview.* Candidate interviews should not be scheduled close together, because the candidates may become anxious upon seeing the waiting room filled with other candidates.

4. *Before the interview, mail two or three questions to the candidates.* By getting some questions in advance, the candidates can reflect on their responses before they come in for the interview. This can make the beginning of the interview more productive.

5. *Place a name card in front of each interviewer for easy identification.* A host should greet each candidate before the interview.

6. *Make introductions at the outset.* Each member of the interview committee should be introduced, the position fully explained, and the process and timeline for the selection process outlined.

7. *After the interview, give each candidate an evaluation form regarding the interview experience.* This evaluation, which covers interview team preparation, attention to the process, and listening skills, should be accompanied with a stamped, self-addressed envelope. The evaluation should have room for the candidate to share any ideas for improving the interview process.

Interview Questions: Potential Problem Areas

What questions are permissible and impermissible during interviews? The basic principle in determining the acceptability of any applicant questions is whether the employer can demonstrate a job-related reason for asking the question. In asking the applicant questions, the interviewer should decide whether or not the information is truly necessary in order to evaluate the applicant's qualifications, skills level, and overall competence for the job in question. Problem areas arise with respect to questions, whether direct or indirect, about the applicant's gender, race, age, national origin, marital or parental status, handicap, or disability.

The following are some broad generalizations regarding permissible and impermissible approaches to a variety of employment questions. Because state and federal laws prohibiting discrimination in the employment arena can be vast and complex, it is imperative for the principal to consult with her legal counsel when reviewing the school district's or school's current employment application or when making changes to the application or questions asked by an interviewer.

To ensure that they are conducting a nonsexist, nonracist interview, interviewers should follow these guidelines:

- Ask the same general questions and require the same standards of all applicants.

- Treat all applicants with fairness, equality, and consistency.

■ Use a structured interview plan that will help achieve fairness in interviewing.

Questions That May Be Asked   The following are some of the questions that may be asked at an interview:

■ Why do you want to teach here?

■ What can you bring to the school or department that is uniquely yours?

■ What type of grading criteria do you use?

■ How do you keep current in your field?

■ In the last year, what have you done to develop professionally?

■ What is your view of the relationship between faculty and administration?

Questions That May Not Be Asked   A search committee cannot ask an applicant about the following:

■ Age, unless it is relevant to the job

■ Financial condition

■ Prior wage garnishments

■ Credit rating and bank accounts

■ Home ownership

■ Disabilities

■ Marital status

■ Where his or her spouse works or resides

■ Pregnancy or medical history concerning pregnancy

■ Ages of children

■ Military experience or discharge

■ Religious observance

■ Lineage, ancestry, national origin, descent, place of birth, original language, or the national origin of parents or spouse

■ How he or she learned to read, write, or speak a foreign language

■ Membership in clubs such as country clubs, social clubs, religious clubs, or fraternal orders that would indicate an applicant's race, color, sex, religion, and the like

■ Names and addresses of relatives other than those working for the school or school district

■ How long he or she intends to work

Testing

A wide range of instruments are available to examine applicants' abilities, skills, knowledge, and attitudes. The best tests assess those factors that the job analysis identifies as necessary for the applicant to perform well on the job. For instance, the three top candidates for a secretarial job could each be given a typing and shorthand test. In the states that use them, scores on the National Teachers Examination (NTE) and/or the Liberal Arts and Science Test (LAST), the Elementary and Secondary Assessment of Teaching Skills (ESATS) and the grade point averages (GPA) of the final candidates for a teaching position could be used as criteria in selecting certificated personnel.

School districts use tests infrequently as an employment device. Conversely, most United States firms give an hour-long test to entry-level, blue-collar employees; and applicants for professional and managerial positions take a battery of tests requiring a day or less. Toyota Motor Corporation in Georgetown, Kentucky, for example, puts applicants for entry-level jobs through 14 hours of testing. Many human resource experts believe that testing is the best selection device (Castetter & Young, 2000; Dessler, 2002; Dubois, 2004; Fyack, 2004; Ivancevich, 2003). Tests yield more information about an applicant than do preliminary screening of records and letters of recommendation, and they are less subject to bias than interviews are. School districts may need to take a closer look at testing as a valid criterion for selection, based on the evidence from business firms (Lunenburg & Ornstein, 2004). Many tests are available to school districts for use in the selection process (Fyack, 2004; Plake et al., 2003).

There are three major problems with using tests as an employment selection device (Aguinis, 2004): (a) They are time-consuming to administer; (b) some require training to administer and score; and (c) tests discriminate against minorities. Ethnic minorities, such as African Americans and Hispanic Americans, may score lower on certain paper-and-pencil tests because of cultural bias. EEOC guidelines and amendments to the Civil Rights Act prohibit employment practices that artificially discriminate against individuals on the basis of test scores (Gutman, 2000).

The objective of any employment test is to gather information that will help predict the applicant's future job success or performance. To do so, a test must be both valid and reliable. A *valid test* measures what it purports to measure relative to the job specifications. Selection of criteria to define job specifications is difficult, and its importance cannot be overemphasized. Obviously, test validity cannot be measured unless satisfactory criteria exist. A *reliable test* yields consistent results over time. Scores should remain fairly stable for an individual who takes the test several times.

Assessment Centers

NASSP Principals Assessment Center An approach to the selection and development of principals that has steadily gained in popularity is the National Association of Secondary School Principals (NASSP) Assessment and Development Center (National Association of Secondary School Principals, 2002). A typical NASSP Assessment Center session lasts two days, with groups of 6 to 12 assessees participating in various administrative exercises. NASSP Assessment Center sessions include two in-basket tests, two leaderless group activities, a fact-finding task, and a personal interview. Candidates are assessed individually by a panel of NASSP-trained assessors on several task-relevant dimensions using a standardized scale. Later, by consensus, a profile of each candidate is devised, and each assessee receives a written and oral report. Assessment centers are also used to help design appropriate training and development programs for high-potential employees interested in the principalship (NASSP, 2002). The centers are quite valid and reliable, providing NASSP guidelines are followed, and they are fair to women and members of minority groups (Schmitt & Cohen, 1990).

Pre-Teacher Assessment Program A recent extension of the NASSP Assessment and Development Center, designed to assess and develop a candidate's teaching potential, is the Pre-Teacher Assessment Program (Millward & Gerlach, 1991). Developed by a consortium composed of Indiana University of Pennsylvania, Millersville University, and Slippery Rock University, it is a method of predicting future teacher behavior by using behavioral simulations (similar to those at NASSP) that measure a candidate's ability to handle future responsibilities in teaching. Although the Pre-Teacher Assessment Project is discussed here primarily as an aid in selecting teachers, it is also used in the training and development of pre-service teachers.

How are Pre-Teacher Assessment activities developed? (a) Behaviors required for successful job performance are identified; (b) dimensions that represent those behaviors are defined; (c) simulations that require a candidate to exhibit selected dimensions are developed (these activities mirror the work activities of teachers); and (d) scoring techniques that can discriminate between high and low skill acquisition for each dimension are designed. Table 13.3 provides brief descriptions of the 13 Pre-Teacher Assessment Center dimensions.

Four simulations—classroom vignettes, actual teaching simulations, the educational fair, and the school museum—have been designed to assess the 13 skill dimensions. A brief description of these simulations follows:

1. *Classroom vignettes.* In this exercise, students view a series of five-minute videotapes portraying different classroom episodes. At selected intervals, students are asked to respond in writing to such questions as, "How would you react to this situation?"

2. *Actual teaching simulations.* In this exercise, students are given a lesson packet with content they will be required to teach. After two hours of preparation, the student teaches the lesson.

3. *The educational fair.* In this two-hour exercise, students are faced with the problem of organizing a districtwide educational fair. Students

Table 13.3   Thirteen Skill Dimensions of the Pre-Teacher Assessment Center

Planning and organizing	Establishing a course of action for self or others to achieve a specific goal; planning appropriate time, resources, setting, and sequence of activities for task accomplishment
Monitoring	Establishing procedures to monitor classroom activities and student progress
Leadership	Setting high standards, communicating a clear philosophy about learning, challenging students, reflecting on teaching
Sensitivity	Showing consideration for feelings and needs of others in verbal and nonverbal situations
Problem analysis	Identifying issues or problems; securing relevant information; identifying causes of problems; relating, comparing, or quantifying data from various sources
Strategic decision making	Developing alternative courses of action, making decisions, and setting goals when time for deliberation is available
Tactical decision making	Making appropriate decisions in ongoing situations where time for deliberation is limited and extensive information gathering may be inappropriate
Oral communication	Expressing ideas with clarity, style, appropriate volume and rate of speech, and appropriate grammar for classroom use
Oral presentation	Presenting ideas in an organized manner with an opening and a closing, while using persuasiveness, enthusiasm, and eye contact
Written communication	Expressing ideas clearly in writing (includes grammar, context, syntax)
Innovativeness	Generating or recognizing and adopting new or creative instructional approaches, techniques, and materials
Tolerance for stress	Performing with stability under pressure or opposition; ability to maintain attention on multiple tasks or activities
Initiative	Actively attempting to influence events to achieve goals; taking action beyond what is necessarily called for; self-starting

are given a packet of information that must be analyzed, reviewed, and then organized into an overall plan.

4. *The school museum.* This is another two-hour exercise that requires students to read and analyze data related to a problem. Students are asked to develop an educational museum exhibit that would be relevant for students and be educationally sound.

Following the assessment, each candidate meets with a trained assessor to discuss the assessment report. The report can be used for selection, placement, promotion, compensation, or further development of skills. If the report is used for development, the candidate will have an opportunity to improve these assessed dimensions through work in training modules or through other resources on a university campus.

Staff Development

Schools recruit and select people who match their job specifications as closely as possible, but the match is seldom perfect. Usually staff at all levels—maintenance, service, clerical, and professional—need to be taught how to apply their abilities to specific job requirements. This instruction, which teaches new employees the skills they need, is known as *training. Development* usually refers to teaching experienced professionals how to maintain and even improve those skills.

The training and development of faculty and staff are essentially a four-step process: (a) assessing needs, (b) setting objectives, (c) selecting methods, and (d) evaluating the program (Castetter & Young, 2000; Dessler, 2002; Ivancevich, 2003; Woodall et al., 2004). Figure 13.3 presents these steps, each of which we will discuss in turn.

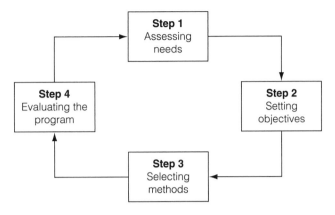

Figure 13.3

Steps in the Staff Development Process

Assessing Staff Development Needs

Before a principal can properly plan staff development activities, she must assess the staff development needs of both the employees and the school. The discrepancy between a job's skill requirements and the employee's job determines the specific training needs. For example, if a secretary lacks word processing skills, he should receive computer literacy training. If a teacher lacks proficiency in one or more teaching skills, she should attend a staff development program to improve those skills. Furthermore, staff development must be aimed at the achievement of some school district goal or school objective, such as improved teacher performance, more efficient operating methods, or increased student achievement. A school should commit its resources only to staff development that can help in achieving its objectives.

To determine the staff development needs of individuals in their school, principals can choose from three basic methods (Castetter & Young, 2000; Dessler, 2002; Ivancevich, 2003; Woodall et al., 2004):

1. *Reviewing performance appraisals.* Employees' work is measured against the performance standards established for the job (using the job description as a guide). If actual performance

is significantly below the acceptable standards, a performance deficiency exists. Those employees become candidates for a training and development program (Daley, 2001).

2. *Conducting organizational analyses.* The effectiveness of the school and its success in achieving its goals are analyzed to determine where discrepancies exist. For example, members of a department or grade-level team with low student achievement scores on a standardized test may require additional staff development (Seyfarth, 2001).

3. *Surveying human resources.* Interviews with employees, questionnaires, and group discussions can be used to determine staff development needs. Data from these sources can pinpoint areas, skills, or abilities that need improvement (Lundy et al., 2003).

Setting Staff Development Objectives

Once staff development needs have been identified, objectives must be set for meeting these needs. The objectives should be in writing and be meaningful, concise, and measurable. There are usually three major categories of objectives: transmitting information, changing attitudes, and developing skills (Castetter & Young, 2000; Dessler, 2002; Ivancevich, 2003; Webb & Norton, 2004; Woodall et al., 2004):

1. *Transmitting information.* This is typically a training objective rather than a development one. It may include a general orientation into the school's policies and procedures. For example, a teacher needs to learn board of education policies, local school policies, the union contract (if there is one), the school and school district's communication structure, and the like.

2. *Changing attitudes.* This is a kind of socialization. It is an attempt to change the employee's ideas about the school and/or the school district and the various jobs within it. Every school has a unique culture, and every employee — maintenance, service, clerical, and professional — at that school must understand its culture to perform effectively in it.

3. *Developing skills.* With the introduction of site-based management, teachers and other staff members need to develop three kinds of skills: human, technical, and conceptual. *Human skills* are essential to increase staff leadership, teamwork, and effective interactions with students, parents, and colleagues. *Technical skills* are essential to performing classroom teaching functions, such as preparing lessons, presenting information, diagnosing learning, reinforcing and correcting students, and evaluating learning. And *conceptual skills* are essential to decision making and strategic planning, that is, thinking about the school and school district as a system of interrelated parts rather than as isolated pieces of an organization (Senge, 1990; 2001). The development of human, technical, and, particularly, conceptual skills among the faculty and staff should help to facilitate the implementation of site-based management.

Selecting Staff Development Methods

Staff development goals establish a frame of reference for choosing appropriate instructional methods. Table 13.4 presents some of the more widely used staff development methods.

Selection of a particular method depends on many considerations, but perhaps most important are the goals of the staff development effort. For example, if the goal is for employees to learn about school policies and procedures, then assigned reading, lecture, and programmed learning might be an effective approach. If the goal is to teach professionals how to make decisions effectively, role playing, case discussion, conference, and sensitivity training might work best. If the goal is to teach a physical skill such as operating a new machine, then behavior modeling, vestibule training, or on-the-job training might be the most appropriate method. Other considerations in choosing a staff development method are cost, the time available, the number of persons to be trained, background and skill of the trainees, and whether the training is to be done by in-district personnel or contracted to an outside staff development firm or a university skilled in staff development methods.

Evaluating the Staff Development Program

The final step of the staff development effort is evaluation. Considering the cost investment of staff development programs — costs include training materials, trainer time, and time lost while employees are being trained — principals must make sure that the program goals are met.

Ideally, the best method to use in evaluating the effectiveness of staff development is the controlled experiment. In a controlled experiment, one or more groups that receive staff development (experimental groups) and a group that does not receive staff development (control group) are used. Relevant data — for example, some output variable(s) — should be secured before and after the training in both the experimental group(s) and the control group. Then a comparison is made of the performance of the groups to determine to what extent any change in the relevant variable(s) occurred due to training. One study, which used a quasi-experimental design, found no change in principals' leadership effectiveness before and immediately following situational leadership training, but did discover a

Table 13.4 Widely Used Staff Development Methods

Methods	Comments
Assigned readings	Readings may or may not be specially prepared for training purposes.
Behavior modeling	A videotaped model displays the correct behavior, then trainees role-play and discuss the correct behavior (used extensively for supervisor training in human relations).
Simulation	Both paper simulations (such as in-basket exercises) and computer-based games teach management skills.
Case discussion	Real or fictitious cases or incidents are discussed in small groups.
Conference	Trainees participate in small-group discussion of selected topics, usually with the trainer as leader.
Lecture	The trainer makes an oral presentation; audience participation is limited.
On the job	This method ranges from trainees receiving no instruction, to casual coaching by more experienced employees, to carefully structured explanation, demonstration, and supervised practice by a qualified trainer.
Programmed instruction	This is a self-paced method using text followed by questions and answers (expensive to develop).
Role playing	Trainees act out roles with other trainees, using scenarios such as "boss giving performance appraisal" and "subordinate reacting to appraisal" to gain experience in human relations.
Sensitivity training	Called T-group and laboratory training, this is an intensive experience in a small group. Individuals try new behaviors and give feedback (promotes trust, open communication, and understanding of group dynamics).
Vestibule training	Trainees participate in supervised practice on manual tasks in a separate work area with emphasis on safety, learning, and feedback.
On-line training	Many Web sites are available that can assist in staff development training.

change in their effectiveness three years after training (Pascarella & Lunenburg, 1988).

More specifically, four basic categories of staff development outcomes can be measured (Dessler, 2002; Ivancevich, 2003; Woodall et al., 2004):

1. *Reaction.* How well did the staff like the program?

2. *Learning.* What principles, facts, and concepts were learned in the program?

3. *Behavior.* Did the job behavior of staff members change because of the program?

4. *Results.* What were the results of the program?

The last category is probably the most important one. Staff members may say they enjoyed the staff development program and learned a great deal, but the true test is whether their job performance has improved after the development. For example, if a staff development program is designed to increase the proficiency of secretaries' word processing skills, the secretaries' performance should improve after

the training. Teachers who participate in many staff development activities and achieve high marks in those activities should improve their performance in the classroom. If these results are not achieved, then, in the final analysis, the staff development program has probably failed.

Orientation and Induction of the Beginning Teacher

What are the general needs of the beginning teacher? Most schools plan for teacher orientation, but despite efforts to help teachers succeed, many still encounter adjustment problems. A review of the research on problems of beginning teachers shows that feelings of isolation; poor understanding of what is expected of them; workload and extra assignments that they were unprepared to handle; lack of supplies, materials, or equipment; poor physical facilities; and lack of support or help from experienced teachers or supervisors contribute to their feelings of frustration and failure. The result is that many potentially talented and creative teachers find teaching unrewarding and difficult, especially in inner-city schools; and nearly 50% of newly hired teachers leave the profession within five years (U.S. Department of Education, 2001a).

There is recognition that the induction period, the first two or three years of teaching, is critical in developing teachers' capabilities, and that beginning teachers should not be left to sink or swim. Several state education agencies have recently developed internship programs for new teachers, while other states have increased staff development activities. However, most important for the professional development of new teachers are the internal support systems and strategies that the schools adopt (that is, the daily support activities and continual learning opportunities).

In general, having to learn by trial and error without support and supervision has been the most common problem faced by new teachers. Expecting teachers to function without support is based on the false assumptions that (a) teachers are well prepared for their initial classroom and school experiences, (b) teachers can develop professional expertise on their own, and (c) teaching can be mastered in a relatively short period of time. Researchers find there is little attempt to lighten the class load and limit extra-class assignments to make the beginning teacher's job easier. In the few schools that do limit these activities, teachers have reported that they have had the opportunity to "learn to teach" (Kennedy, 2002).

Unquestionably, new teachers need the feedback and encouragement experienced teachers can provide. Peer coaching or mentoring is gaining support as an effective supervision tool. *Peer coaching or mentoring* takes place when classroom teachers observe one another, provide feedback concerning their teaching, and together develop instructional plans. According to Joyce and Showers (2002), an experienced teacher who acts as a peer coach or mentor teacher for an inexperienced teacher performs five functions: (a) *companionship,* discussing ideas, problems, and successes; (b) *technical feedback,* especially related to lesson planning and classroom observations; (c) *analysis of application,*

integrating what happens or what works as part of the beginning teacher's repertoire; (d) *adaptation,* helping the beginning teacher adapt to particular situations; and (e) *personal facilitation,* helping the teacher feel good about himself after trying new strategies. Others suggest that the main features of a successful mentoring program include (a) proximity, (b) grade equivalence (at the elementary level), (c) subject equivalence (at the secondary level), and (d) compatibility regarding personality, experiences, and educational philosophy (Perkins, 1998; Wallace, 1998).

Perhaps the most important ingredient for a peer coach, mentor, or resource teacher is to allow new teachers to reflect, not react or defend. An integral part of any good program for helping novice teachers is for them to observe experienced teachers on a regular basis and then for experienced teachers to observe novice teachers. With both observational formats, there is need to discuss what facilitated or hindered the teaching-learning process and precisely what steps or recommendations are needed for improving instruction. The peer coach or mentor needs to serve as a friend and confidante (function in a nonevaluative role). The term *peer sharing and caring* among colleagues best describes the new spirit of collegial openness and learning advocated here.

Guidelines for Improving Support for Beginning Teachers

Whatever the existing policies regarding the induction period for beginning teachers, there is the need to improve provisions for their continued professional development, to make the job easier, to make them feel more confident in the classroom and school, to reduce the isolation of their work settings, and to enhance interaction with colleagues. Here are some recommendations that school principals can implement for achieving these goals (Lunenburg & Ornstein, 2004):

1. Principals need to schedule beginning teacher orientation in addition to regular teacher orientation. Beginning teachers need to attend both sessions.

2. Principals need to appoint someone to help beginning teachers set up their rooms.

3. Principals need to provide beginning teachers with a proper mix of courses, students, and facilities (not all leftovers). If possible, lighten their load for the first year.

4. Principals need to assign extra-class duties of moderate difficulty and requiring moderate amounts of time, duties that will not become too demanding for the beginning teacher.

5. Principals need to pair beginning teachers with master teachers to meet regularly to identify general problems before they become serious.

6. Principals need to provide coaching groups, tutor groups, or collaborative problem-solving groups for all beginning teachers to attend. Encourage beginning teachers to teach each other.

7. Principals need to provide for joint planning, team teaching, committee assignments, and other cooperative arrangements between new and experienced teachers.

8. Principals need to issue newsletters that report on accomplishments of all teachers, especially beginning teachers.

9. Principals need to schedule reinforcing events involving beginning and experienced teachers; examples are tutor-tutoree luncheons, parties, and awards.

10. Principals need to provide regular (monthly) meetings between the beginning teacher and supervisor (mentor) to identify problems as soon as possible and to make recommendations for improvement.

11. Principals need to plan special and continuing in-service activities with topics directly related to the needs and interests of beginning teachers. Eventually, beginning staff development activities should be integrated with regular staff development activities.

12. Principals need to carry on regular evaluation of beginning teachers; evaluate strengths and weaknesses, present new information, demonstrate new skills, and provide opportunities for practice and feedback.

Performance Appraisal

After employees have been recruited, selected, and trained, the next step in the human resource management process is *performance appraisal*—the process of evaluating the contribution employees have made toward attaining the school's goals. There are several reasons to evaluate employee performance. First, the school needs evidence to justify the selection techniques used in hiring personnel. Second, performance appraisal provides input for determining both individual and organizational staff development needs and later gauges whether these have been effective. Third, performance evaluation serves as the basis for making decisions about salary and merit increases, promotions, transfers, or terminations. Finally, it is used as a means of communicating to employees how they are performing and suggesting needed changes in behavior, attitudes, skills, or knowledge. Principals can use several different kinds of techniques for performance appraisal (Daley, 2002; Dubois, 2004; Fyack, 2004; Martocchio, 2002, 2003).

Appraisal Techniques

Job analysis is the foundation on which employee performance appraisal is based. A job analysis identifies the standards and expectations against which performance is later measured. Principals have two ways of comparing actual to expected performance: nonjudgmental and judgmental methods (Murphy & Cleveland, 2004).

Nonjudgmental Methods Performance indicators that can be counted, seen, touched, and so on, represent *nonjudgmental methods* of performance. No judgment is involved in obtaining these measures. Nonjudgmental methods can be quite useful because numbers are readily understandable, easy to explain, and in some cases may reflect the most important dimensions of an employee's performance. Nonjudgmental factors include indirect measurements such as absenteeism, tardiness, and number of complaints lodged against the employee by others. Direct measures of performance, however, are usually more important and include counts of the employee's actual output: number of pages typed, number of clients seen, or number of errors made. Nonjudgmental measures tend to be objective indicators of performance. In Table 13.5 we present some examples of direct, nonjudgmental measures of performance.

Performance measures like those in Table 13.5 are easy to obtain. But for most positions, objective measures are neither possible nor accurate. For instance, in some tasks, performance is the combined effort of many individuals. Winning a football game requires a team effort. In other cases, an objective count says nothing about quality of performance. A professor's performance is not judged solely on the number of books or journal articles published in a year. Such factors as quality must be taken into account. Furthermore, even though different observers are likely to agree on the numbers collected, different principals are likely to disagree on the importance of these measures of performance output. For example, "lines per week" may not be as important to the overall performance of a secretary as the ability to compose a professional-quality business letter. The ability to handle irate parents and to screen principals' calls may be equally important. For these reasons, principals often use judgmental methods to appraise performance rather than, or in addition to, objective methods.

Judgmental Methods   When one person (a supervisor) makes a judgment about the performance of another (the staff member), *judgmental methods* are involved, which include ranking and rating techniques. *Ranking,* as the term implies, requires the supervisor to list all employees in an order of performance from best to worst, usually based on overall performance. Ranking has several limitations. First, because a single, global assessment of performance is used, the various dimensions of behavior are frequently overlooked. Second, when there are a large number of employees, it may be difficult to place them into a simple ranking. Third, by forcing a principal to rank employees as high or low performers, it is possible that the highest performer still falls short

Table 13.5   Nonjudgmental Performance Measures for Different Positions

Position	Sample Measure
Bus driver	Accident-free miles driven
Custodian	Tasks completed per day and minutes taken per task
Secretary	Lines typed per week
Teacher	Higher- and lower-order questions asked per class period
Counselor	Number of students counseled per week
Principal	Number of teacher observations completed per semester

of the school's expectations. Conversely, the lowest-ranked employee could be meeting the school's goals quite well, if not as well as those ranked above him. Finally, because this method pits one employee against another, it creates jealousy and competition rather than teamwork.

Rating compares the performance of each employee to an absolute standard instead of to the performance of other employees. Thus principals rate the degree to which performance meets the standard. The rating scale provides the standard. Figure 13.4 presents an example of a rating scale for judging the performance of teachers. The rater is asked to assess a teacher on several criteria (classroom management and procedure, teacher-pupil relationship, staff relationships, and professional attributes) using some form of rating scale. As shown in Figure 13.4, these scales may range from "outstanding" to "unsatisfactory" or from "most desirable" to "least desirable" and the like.

Regardless of the scale used, evaluators are looking for some evidence of the quality of a teacher's performance in all aspects of the role description and the contract. From the many instruments reviewed, the characteristics delineated in Figure 13.4 are among the criteria school systems consider important (Educational Research Service, 2000). One problem with such rating scales is that performance criteria are so loosely defined that there is frequently no consistency in rating teachers. "Outstanding," "good," "satisfactory," and the like may mean different things

Teacher	Outstanding	Good	Satisfactory	Needs Improvement	Unsatisfactory	
School						
Assignment						
Classroom Management and Procedure						Comments
1. Shows evidence of planning						
2. Demonstrates initiative and adaptability in adjusting to circumstances and individuals						
3. Uses effective teaching techniques						
4. Maintains adequate and accurate pupil records						
Teacher-Pupil Relationship						
1. Encourages pupil participation in classroom activities						
2. Deals with behavior problems						
3. Shows evidence of pupils' respect and confidence						
4. Identifies the special needs of students						
5. Uses appropriate instructional materials						
6. Demonstrates willingness to spend time with students in addition to what is assigned						
Staff Relationships						
1. Cooperates with other members of the staff						
2. Demonstrates respect for the opinions and contributions of others						
3. Utilizes services of specialized personnel within the district						
Professional Attributes						
1. Manifests adequate preparation for teaching subject matter						
2. Enhances academic development through continued formal education and inservice activities						
3. Handles reports efficiently						
4. Fulfills obligations related to board policies and building regulations						
5. Uses discretion in releasing information gained from professional activities						

Figure 13.4

Rating Scale for Teachers

to different principals. Some principals are lenient and others are strict in applying the rating scale.

Common Rating Errors

A major objective in developing performance appraisal systems is to reduce errors and personal biases so that the most accurate portrayal of actual performance emerges. Several common sources of error found in performance appraisal systems that can jeopardize the validity of the rating include strictness or leniency, central tendency, single dimension, halo effect, recency of events, and personal biases and first impressions (Baker, 1988).

Strictness or Leniency   Every evaluator has her own value system that provides a standard against which appraisals are made. In university classrooms, for example, we know of professors who are notoriously tough graders and others who give easy A's. Similar situations exist in the schools, where some principals see most staff as not measuring up to their high standards, whereas other principals see most staff as deserving a high rating. These situations are referred to as *strictness* or *leniency* rating errors, respectively. The strict rater tends to give ratings that are lower than the average ratings usually given to staff. Conversely, the lenient rater tends to give higher ratings than those usually given. Strictness or leniency errors fail to adequately distinguish between good and poor performers, but instead relegate nearly everyone to the same or related categories.

Central Tendency   This error is similar to that of strictness and leniency, but in this case the principal's ratings cluster together at the middle of the scale. For example, if the rating scale ranges from one to five, many principals will tend to avoid the highs (four and five) and lows (one and two), and put most of their check marks in the three category—Satisfactory (see Figure 13.4). This *central tendency* error means that all staff members are simply rated average. As with strictness and leniency, central tendency errors make it difficult to separate good performers from poor ones. In addition, this error makes it

difficult to compare ratings from different principals. For example, a good performer who is evaluated by a principal committing central tendency errors could receive a lower rating than a poor performer who is rated by a principal committing leniency errors.

Single Dimension   An employee's job typically consists of many different tasks. A teacher's job, for example, includes preparing lessons, presenting information, diagnosing learning, reinforcing and correcting students, evaluating learning, and performing other administrative or supervisory duties. If performance on this job were evaluated on a *single dimension*—say, preparing lessons—the result would be a limited appraisal of that job. More important, teachers whose performance appraisal included evaluation solely on this single dimension would likely ignore those other tasks of the job. Similarly, if their superintendent appraised all the principals in a school district solely on their ability to perform management functions, they would likely attend to managerial tasks exclusively and ignore other instructional leadership duties required of today's principal. The point is that when staff are evaluated on a single dimension, and when successful performance in that position requires good performance on a number of dimensions, staff members will emphasize the dimension that is being evaluated to the exclusion of other job-relevant dimensions.

Halo Effect   The *halo effect* occurs when principals allow a single prominent characteristic of an employee to influence their judgment on all of the dimensions or characteristics being assessed. Thus the staff member who is rated high on quantity of performance will also be rated high on quality, initiative, cooperation, and the like. The result is that employees show no variation in ratings across dimensions—they are rated consistently high, medium, or low on all performance dimensions. The problem created by a halo effect is that it is impossible to identify areas of weakness that need development for staff who are generally strong, and conversely, the areas of strength for staff who are generally weak.

Recency of Events   Ideally, performance appraisals should be based on systematic observations of a staff member's performance over an entire rating period (say, six months or a year). Oftentimes, evaluators focus on a staff member's most recent behavior. That is, in an annual evaluation, a principal may give undue consideration to performance during the past two or three months and forget to include important past behaviors. Using only the most recent evaluatee behaviors to make evaluations can result in what is called the *recency of events* error. This practice, if known to employees, leads to a situation whereby employees become visible, motivated, productive, and cooperative just before the formal evaluation occurs. Hence, their performance during the entire evaluation cycle is uneven and inconsistent.

Personal Biases and First Impressions   Some principals allow their personal biases and first impressions to influence the appraisals they give staff members. The *personal biases* may be gross prejudices concerning not only gender, race, color, or religion but also other personal characteristics, such as age, social status, style of dress, or political viewpoint. In addition, principals have permitted *first impressions* to influence later judgments of a staff member. Although first impressions represent only a sample of behavior, people tend to retain these impressions even when confronted with contradictory evidence. Personal biases and first impressions can interfere with the fairness and accuracy of an evaluation.

Modern Appraisal Techniques

In an effort to minimize the rating errors just described, some school districts have used various behaviorally based and results-oriented appraisal systems. Behaviorally based systems attempt to examine what the employee does in performing the job. Results-oriented approaches typically examine the employee's results or accomplishments. Because teachers constitute the largest group of employees in schools, we limit our discussion to modern teacher performance appraisal techniques.

Bear in mind, however, that principals evaluate other certificated and classified employees as well.

Most teachers do not like to be evaluated, and they do not find it helpful to them professionally. For example, in several studies of teacher appraisal efforts, Morris Cogan (1961) concluded that teachers reacted defensively to evaluation and viewed it as a threat to their position. More recently, Jon Wiles and Joseph Bondi (2004), in a study of 2,500 teachers, found that only 1.5% of them perceived their principal (or supervisor) as helpful in improving their performance in the classroom.

One conclusion is that teachers' negative feelings about performance appraisals relate more to the way they are conducted than to the function of performance appraisal in general. Teachers might react more positively to a procedure that is responsive to their needs and professional aspirations. Clinical supervision, goal setting, and peer coaching and mentoring (discussed earlier) are examples of this approach to teacher performance appraisal.

Supervision and Evaluation

Teachers, especially beginning teachers, should welcome evaluation as a means of developing professionally. In general, the evaluation a teacher receives takes two forms. Some evaluation is formative and some evaluation is summative, just as good student evaluations are of both types. Formative evaluation is intended to reassure teachers, especially beginning teachers, that they can succeed and can foster student growth. Summative evaluation is intended to help teachers know how they are performing relative to the specific criteria of a school district's evaluation system (Peterson, 2000).

Viewed simplistically, evaluation is rating; it is judging the goodness of teaching. Evaluation is tough-minded, a quality assurance mechanism, a process principals carry out to compare one teacher to another and to the school district's standards. Painted in similar broad strokes, supervision is nonjudgmental, reflecting to the teacher the intended and sometimes unintended consequences of her behavior; it is a collegial, humane dialog. Administrators do evaluation; supervisors do supervision.

Of course, nothing is ever that simple. Supervision has an important role to play in evaluation. Moreover, supervisors often are called upon to judge, rate, compare, and decide issues such as promotion, tenure, transfer, and dismissal. Three approaches to supervision that school districts use to improve teacher performance are peer coaching or mentoring (discussed earlier), clinical supervision, and goal setting.

Clinical Supervision   Designed to improve the teacher's classroom performance, *clinical supervision* is a subcategory of instructional supervision. Instructional supervision is defined as "all of the activities, functions, maneuvers, and monitoring conditions that are intended to help teachers upgrade their performance." Adding the word *clinical* (as Morris Cogan did in creating the idea as a part of the Harvard Training Program in 1958) indicates that such efforts are based upon data collected in the actual classroom (or other instructional situations), where the teacher is working directly with the learner and the supervisor is present as a witness, if not a participant. Clinical supervision had its roots in the work of Morris Cogan (1961, 1973) and Robert Goldhammer and others (Goldhammer, Anderson, & Krajewski, 1969) at the Harvard School of Education in the late 1950s. Acheson and Gall (2003) have continued the early, pioneering work of Cogan and Goldhammer.

Basic to the model of clinical supervision is the notion that the clinical supervisor knows more about instruction and learning than the teacher(s) do. Robert Goldhammer and colleagues' clinical supervision model (1969) consists of five stages: (1) preobservation conference, (2) observation, (3) analysis and strategy, (4) supervision conference, and (5) postconference analysis. We discuss each of these stages in turn.

Stage 1: Preobservation conference. The principal (or supervisor) obtains information regarding the teacher's lesson objectives, instructional procedures, and criteria of evaluation; establishes a contract between the principal and teacher as to

the areas in which the teacher wants feedback; and establishes specific plans for carrying out the observation, such as time limits, instrumentation, and so on.

Stage 2: Observation. The principal views the lesson as planned in the preobservation conference.

Stage 3: Analysis and strategy. The principal assesses the observed lesson, considers supervisory implications, and develops a strategy for helping the teacher.

Stage 4: Supervision conference. The principal provides feedback and a basis for the improvement of future teaching by defining and authenticating issues in teaching, offering didactic help when appropriate, and training the teacher in the techniques of self-supervision.

Stage 5: Postconference analysis. The principal assesses the conference in relation to the principal's own intentions, supervisory criteria, and the value of the conference to the teacher.

At its best, clinical supervision is group supervision, that is, two or more supervisors working with the same teacher. Some schools with seasoned teaching teams practice clinical supervision at its finest. The purist would insist that stage 5, postconference analysis, cannot be done alone. Stage 5 is thought of as the superego of the sequence, the conscience of the clinical process. No matter whether it is conducted by one person or a team, clinical supervision is labor intensive, as the reader can well imagine.

Evaluation takes a somewhat different tack. The rationale behind evaluation is that the wise evaluator evaluates only as much as she has to. Whereas clinical supervision puts great stress on teacher behavior in the future, evaluation stresses the here and now. Evaluation is measuring or assessing progress toward predetermined objectives—the teacher performance criteria set as performance standards by the school district or individual school.

The major and continuing difference between supervision and evaluation is that the appraiser in the evaluation process must make performance comparisons, asking and answering these questions:

(a) Is this teacher's performance meeting the standards of my school? (b) Is the lesson appropriate for our curriculum and the intended learners? and (c) What can we do together to assure even better teaching and learning in the next cycle? (The last question is where clinical supervision, goal setting, and peer coaching or mentoring can come into play.) To do less would not meet the principals' responsibility for quality assurance in that school building and in the school community.

Goal Setting   Another popular technique for appraising teachers is *goal setting* (Locke & Latham, 1995). Goal setting defines job performance based on accomplishing specific task goals, such as student achievement, student growth, skill acquisition, or attitude change. Instead of being evaluated on observed teaching behaviors, teachers are evaluated on what they have accomplished (Glickman, Gordon, & Ross-Gordon, 2004; Ornstein & Lasley, 2004; Wiles & Bondi, 2004).

The goal-setting approach includes two major elements. First, at some point in the appraisal process, the principal (or supervisor) and teacher meet to determine jointly the teacher's performance goals over some specified time period. Second, the principal and teacher meet to appraise the teacher's performance in relation to the previously established goals. Individual teacher goals evolve at least in part from the school district's goals, which are established by the board of education and superintendent.

Goal setting as a performance appraisal technique has both strengths and weaknesses. Strengths of goal setting are that it stresses results rather than personality or personal traits, improves motivation due to knowledge of results, minimizes judgment errors, and improves commitment through participation. Major weaknesses of goal setting are that it emphasizes quantitative goals at the expense of qualitative goals, creates too much paperwork, lacks uniformity in performance measurements, and requires constant attention and administrative support.

Overall, for appraising performance, the approaches of goal setting, clinical supervision, and peer tutoring or mentoring are particularly well suited to result in better teaching; this is due mainly to the motivational and participative aspects of such programs. Used in the proper way, these techniques are interactive rather than directive, democratic rather than authoritarian, and teacher centered rather than principal centered.

Improving Teacher Performance Appraisals

Conducting performance appraisals is a difficult task. Principals cannot shirk their responsibility to conduct an accurate appraisal of their teachers. Teacher appraisal is an essential element in a principal's attempt to improve his school's instructional program. The following suggestions for improving teacher performance appraisals may help to improve the teacher evaluation process (Alkire, 2004; Daley, 2001; Dubois, 2004; Glickman et al., 2004; Wiles & Bondi, 2004):

1. *Principals need to read union contracts and board policies, and abide by them.* Contracts can place specific limitations on a principal's conduct of teacher evaluations, including the number of classroom observations, use of evaluation instruments, and the like.

2. *Principals need to ask teachers for self-evaluations.* A self-evaluation serves at least two purposes: First, if teachers rate themselves higher in an area than the principal thinks they deserve, she is prepared for a potential conflict before conducting postevaluation conferences with those teachers. Second, teachers may identify problems that the principal is not aware of. Their honesty allows the principal to provide assistance that she might not otherwise have offered.

3. *Principals need to plan classroom visits wisely.* Observing a teacher in the classroom is the heart of any successful evaluation, but only if it is done correctly. The authors recommend that principals observe all teachers at least three times a year, and marginal and beginning teachers as many times as needed.

4. *Principals need to make their observations correctly.* Principals need to spend at least a

full class period in order to identify a teacher's work habits. Observations should be scheduled for different times of the day.

5. *Principals need to take accurate notes.* The wise principal takes detailed notes, including names, dates, times, places, and a narrative account of what happens in the classroom. Such records are invaluable should a teacher be considered for termination in the future.

6. *Principals need to consider videotaping teachers.* A principal's comments make more sense when teachers can see themselves in action. However, videotaping may be restricted by contract. In many cases, written permission from the teacher is needed as a prior condition to videotaping.

7. *Principals should not limit themselves to ratings.* An evaluation approach that is limited to a 1-to-5 scale is ambiguous and misleading. A more informative evaluation uses a narrative approach. For example, "The teacher repeatedly demonstrated the ability to provide students with feedback by answering their questions and praising and correcting their performance."

8. *Principals need to make sure postobservation conferences mean something.* Principals should use the postobservation conference to discuss possible solutions to any problems cited in the evaluation. Compliment strengths also.

9. *Principals need to offer teachers a chance for rebuttal.* Discussion of the performance appraisal between the principal and teacher can often lead to compromise and changes in the evaluation that are mutually satisfactory. In any case, teachers should be allowed the opportunity to provide a rebuttal to the principal's report.

10. *Principals need to demonstrate that they take evaluations seriously.* There are at least two ways a principal can show he takes the evaluation seriously: (a) Put all recommendations in writing and (b) hire substitute teachers to free teachers for postobservation conferences during school hours.

11. *Principals need to have the teacher sign the evaluation report.* The signatures of both the observer and the teacher on the evaluation report, and the date, prove that the evaluation actually occurred. An explanatory sentence should appear below the signature line, stating that the teacher's signature does not indicate agreement with the evaluation, but signifies that the teacher received a copy of the evaluation and that the contents were discussed.

Union-Management Relations

The final aspect of human resource management to be discussed is *union-management relations,* which generally refers to formal interactions between unions and the school district's management. In this section, we first briefly address the importance of good union-management relations. Then we discuss and provide a schematic of the collective bargaining process.

The Importance of Good Union-Management Relations

Professional negotiation by teachers emerged as a new factor in human resource management in the early 1960s and has become an increasing concern to teachers, administrators, and school board members in the 2000s. Today, 41 states have enacted statutes permitting public school employees to bargain collectively with boards of education, and over 70% of the nation's teachers are covered by negotiated agreements (U.S. Department of Labor, 2005). In addition to certificated employees, noncertificated groups are demanding the right to negotiate with management as well. Thus many principals today work with employee groups that are represented by unions.

For many principals in unionized school districts, the human resource function is largely composed of following policies and procedures stipulated in the union contract. Decisions about salaries and employee benefits, hours and workloads, transfers, reductions in force, and disciplinary procedures are no longer unilateral prerogatives of principals. Such decisions are substantially made at the time the collective bargaining agreement is negotiated.

More than any other level of administration, a poor principal can harm union-management relations because she is the first-line administrator for most school employees. Good relations between and among the principal and her staff in the day-to-day operation of the school are likely to result in a favorable outcome for administration at the bargaining table. Changes in the union contract(s) can be agreed on that not only improve the school's productivity but also limit undue constraints placed on the principal's decision-making options while administering the contract.

The Collective Bargaining Process

The negotiation, administration, and interpretation of a union contract are achieved through collective bargaining (American Arbitration Association, 2003; Booth, 1993; Kerchner, Koppich, & Weers, 1998; Korney et al., 2000; Sharp, 1993; Troy, 2001). Figure 13.5 presents a model of how the process typically flows through various stages of negotiation, including assessing needs, setting goals, presenting proposals, defining the negotiation process, solving impasses, and reaching agreement.

Collective bargaining is the process of arriving at an agreement between the employer (school board) and employee union(s) on the terms and conditions of employment (American Arbitration Association, 2003). It is collective in that the employees, as a group, select representatives from their membership to meet with management to discuss issues that need to be resolved. Similarly, the school board selects its bargaining team. The union identifies and bargains on items that represent the concerns of its members (Korney et al., 2000; Sharp, 1993). The board tries to negotiate terms favorable to the school district (Booth, 1993).

Once each side has identified items to be bargained and has selected its negotiating teams, the bargaining process begins. Negotiations take place in face-to-face union-management meetings, where numerous proposals and counterproposals are exchanged and discussed. Several rounds of negotiations may be required to reach agreement on all issues. If the two parties agree on the issues, a new negotiated contract is presented to the union membership and the school board for their approval. This is called a *ratification vote*. If both groups vote to approve the agreement, it goes into effect. If they reject the agreement, they go back to the bargaining table for another round of negotiations.

An *impasse* is said to exist when the two parties are unable to reach agreement. State bargaining laws vary when the union and school board are deadlocked in negotiations. Most states have some provision for resolving impasses; the procedure typically involves three steps: mediation, fact finding, and arbitration (American Arbitration Association, 2003). Such a procedure forces the two contending parties to resolve the remaining issues on the bargaining table and arrive at an agreement.

From a behavioral standpoint, collective bargaining is a continuous process. Formal negotiations around a bargaining table take place periodically, when the existing contract has expired. However, after the contract is ratified, several other parts of the bargaining process remain to be performed. The contract must be communicated to the school board, administrators, and employees. Because principals must operate a school under the provisions of this document, they have an obligation not only to peruse the contract but also to understand it (Korney et al., 2000; Sharp, 1993). Finally, because disagreements such as grievances often arise, provisions must be made for interpreting the contract.

Summary

1. The human resource management process consists of the following steps: recruitment, selection, staff development, and performance appraisal. Today's principals must work within a growing body of laws regulating the personnel process.

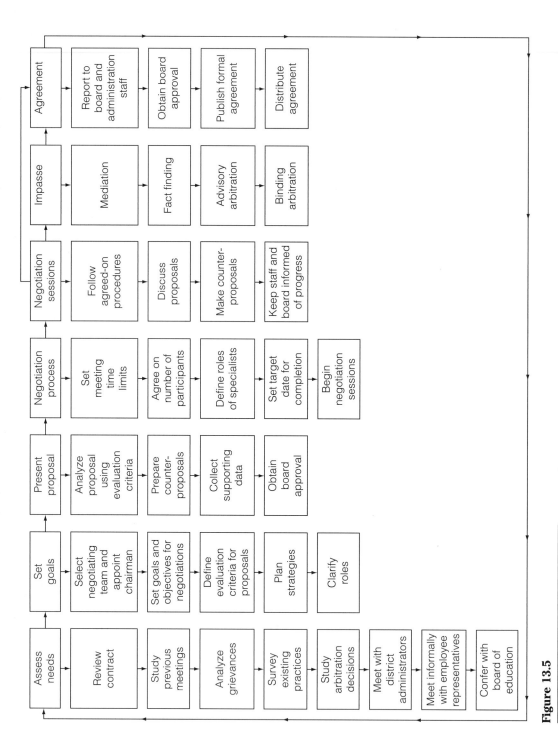

Figure 13.5

Collective Bargaining Process Model

2. Recruitment involves attracting a pool of qualified applicants to replenish or expand a school's human resources. To effectively recruit applicants, principals must know the job, know the legal constraints that influence recruiting efforts, and cultivate the sources of potential employees.

3. Selection involves the process of determining which candidates best meet the job requirements. Preliminary screening of credentials, preliminary interview, testing, reference checks, assessment centers, and in-depth interviews are often used as aids in the selection process.

4. Staff development programs are used to teach new employees the skills they need and to help experienced professionals maintain and improve those skills. The staff development process involves assessing needs, setting goals, selecting methods, and evaluating the program.

5. Performance appraisal is the process of evaluating the contribution employees have made toward attaining the school's goals. Appraisal techniques include the traditional nonjudgmental and judgmental approaches as well as modern appraisal techniques like clinical supervision, goal setting, and peer coaching or mentoring.

6. Most states have enacted laws that permit public school employees to bargain collectively with boards of education. Union-management relations refers to interactions with employees when they are organized into a union. Principals must learn to administer and interpret the contract in unionized school districts.

Field-Based Activities

1. Interview your building principal or the human resources department in your school district to determine what procedures they use to select personnel: administrators, faculty, and staff. Find out the answers to questions like these: What are the contents of preliminary screening of credentials? Are preliminary interviews held, and with whom? Are testing, reference checks, and assessment centers used? Are in-depth interviews held, and with whom? Describe these procedures in your journal.

2. Interview your building principal or the human resources department in your school district to determine the amount and type of professional development provided in your school and school district for school administrators, faculty, and staff. Report the results of these interviews in your journal.

3. Interview your building principal or other appropriate central office administrator to determine what procedures are used to evaluate school administrators, faculty, and staff. How often are evaluations done of each employee group? What types of instruments are used to evaluate administrators, faculty, and staff? How are the results of evaluations communicated to each employee group? Report your findings in your journal.

Suggested Readings

Castetter, W. B., & Young, P. (2000). *The human resource function in educational administration* (7th ed.). Upper Saddle River, NJ: Merrill/Prentice Hall. With its comprehensive approach, this classic core text is designed to cover each of the 11 processes related to the human resource function. The text focuses on management of the school system's human resources and discusses whose qualities and performance determine system outcomes in educational administration. Several important themes throughout the book provide a conceptual foundation for gaining insight into the human resource function.

Marczely, B., & Marczely, D. W. (2002). *Human resource and contract management in the public school: A legal perspective.* Lanham, MD: Scarecrow Press. Human resource management, an essential part of public school administration, is particularly vulnerable to legal interpretation and challenge. Like all other institutions that receive federal funds, public schools have a unique rulebook that sets the parameters for management, particularly with respect to human resource issues. This authoritative text is an essential resource for administrators. It will help new and experienced managers to navigate the practical and legal concerns likely to affect the many human resource functions: recruiting, hiring, and firing personnel; collective bargaining; staff development; and record keeping and reporting. Insightful discussion of the laws and policies currently structuring human resource management is augmented with examples of forms and procedures to be used in addressing particular human resource functions.

Rebore, R. W. (2004). *Human resources administration in education: A management approach* (7th ed.). Boston: Allyn & Bacon. The text uses a management approach organized around the processes and procedures necessary for implementing effective human resource administration. Treated in separate chapters are the eight essential dimensions of the human resource function: human resource planning, recruitment, selection, placement and induction, staff development, appraisal, rewarding, and collective negotiations.

Seyfarth, J. T. (2002). *Human resources management for effective schools* (3rd ed.). Boston: Allyn & Bacon. Many human resources management books emphasize only the functions of the area. This text emphasizes how human resource decisions affect student achievement. It also discusses human resource practice in schools with site-based management, addresses Interstate School Leaders Licensure Consortium (ISLLC) standards, and shows practical applications for research related to human resource practice.

Smith, R. E. (2001). *Human resources administration: A school-based perspective* (2nd ed.). Larchment, NY: Eye on Education. This field-based book provides easy-to-read checklists,

sample forms, and summary charts. The second edition contains new case studies on recruitment, induction, and dealing with marginal teachers. Topics include (a) strategic human resources planning, (b) recruitment, (c) selection, (d) orientation and induction, (e) supervision and evaluation, (f), assisting the marginal teacher, (g) staff development, (h) collective bargaining, and (i) continuity and legal issues.

Stronge, J. H., & Tucker, P. D. (2003). *Handbook on teacher evaluation: Assessing and improving performance.* Larchmont, NY: Eye on Education. This book and accompanying CD-ROM provide teacher evaluation "tools you can use." They have been adapted from materials developed over the last 15 years and field tested in over 500 schools. These tools will enable you to evaluate teachers based on current thinking and best practices. Among the tools included are (a) performance appraisal rubrics, (b) goal setting for student achievement, (c) portfolio guidelines and forms, (d) student and parent surveys, (e) improvement assistance plan, and (f) teacher performance feedback forms.

Webb, L. D., & Norton, M. S. (2004). *Human resources administration: Personnel issues and needs in education* (4th ed.). Upper Saddle River, NJ: Merrill/Prentice Hall. This comprehensive core text is based on the theme that human resource management is a shared responsibility among central human resources administrators and local principals. The book emphasizes coverage of selection, staff development, evaluation, climate, and legal considerations. Appropriate for the graduate level course in human resources administration, the text provides comprehensive, research-based coverage of the human resource function as it exists today in education and projects competencies that will be required of future human resource professionals.

The New Math Program

Setting: Garfield Elementary School, whose principal is Ms. Glenna Greene, is a feeder school to Johnson Middle School, where Mr. Bill Fripps serves as principal. This middle school feeds into Muskie Junior High School, where Dr. Ted Caruthers is completing his first year as principal. All three principals have been struggling with a mandated change in the teaching of mathematics.

Scenario: Ms. Greene, principal of Garfield Elementary School, isn't sure what Mr. Davis, the new assistant superintendent for curriculum and instruction, wants her to do. In the conference they have just completed, Mr. Davis's message was that the just-released math scores on the state exam are not satisfactory. As he emphasized to Ms. Greene, the school board had told the superintendent that unless each campus met the goal of 90% mastery on the math test at each grade level, the board would be requesting weekly progress reports from each principal.

Although Ms. Greene's school has shown an increased percentage of students mastering the exam (from 85% to 87% mastery), such a gain, evidently, is not enough. She wonders if the school board members know that changes in programs take a good deal of time to implement. The new math program was initiated just two years ago, after much planning and discussion. Ms. Greene thinks back to the data showing that all grades, 1–8, were lacking a strong program in mathematics. There had been some rather sharp discussions about how to address this need. A review of test results, personnel concerns, teaching strategies, differing philosophies, and more had led to some heated debate. Even some letters from concerned parents had been read during the council meeting. The few teachers who served on the curriculum council voiced their skepticism about how successful a new approach would be, especially with teachers who were experienced and felt they had reasonable success. Nevertheless, after all was said and done, the curriculum council finally recommended that the district adopt a new math textbook and implement new strategies to complement the text. The school board approved that recommendation.

In an unrelated action, the former assistant superintendent for curriculum and instruction had retired. The principals were left to follow up on introducing the new textbook and the accompanying strategies. The new assistant superintendent for curriculum and instruction, Mr. Davis, was hired after the start of the school year. Some of the more accomplished, younger teachers at the three schools favored the new approach and did not mind helping their colleagues; but most of the older teachers resisted adopting the new program. Those teachers would not *really* use the new text and strategies. Ostensibly, they did. When observed, they would have the correct textbook in hand; but they have never fully changed to the new teaching strategies — at least not yet.

Mr. Davis was not familiar with this new approach to mathematics. That left only a few teachers who were comfortable with the change. Teachers at the middle and junior high schools said they felt as though the curriculum council had sold them out. At the time of the vote, the curriculum council was composed of a math teacher from each school, an assistant principal or principal from each campus, and the assistant superintendent for curriculum and instruction. The former assistant superintendent for curriculum and instruction had handpicked the teachers who served on the council. He had sparked the whole move to a new program.

A new curriculum council reviewed the math test scores for last year and found some minimal improvement at the middle school and junior high levels. The elementary level had made the most gains, edging scores upward from 81% to 85% mastery in grade 3.

Next week, Ms. Greene thinks, the council will review this year's gains. At least her campus has improved again. She is proud of that, of her team, and of their effort to improve. Certainly, she will praise them all and share her pride with the curriculum council.

Ms. Greene wonders about the results at Johnson Middle School and Muskie Junior High School. Just as she is about to pick up the phone and call one of those principals, her phone rings.

"Glenna! Have you heard from our illustrious curriculum leader?" asks Bill Fripps, principal of the middle school. "I'm so mad I could pop! He told me that my campus was a failure, and that I'd better get busy finding out why. Our test results showed that our math scores have not improved substantially again. We did have some improvement, but not enough to please everyone. We moved from 65% mastery to 72% mastery. I think that's a substantial gain — and pretty good, given the fact that all this change has been imposed on us with no help from the central office. My math teachers are going to be proud of

that, not ashamed. I couldn't care less if I have to write another report for the board each week. More paperwork! Another reason I can't become the instructional leader they want me to be. Enough of this. Thanks for letting me blow off steam. How did you do?"

"We improved some, too," Ms. Greene replies. "I'm proud of my staff, just as you are. I think maybe we as principals and instructional leaders need to meet with Mr. Davis and review a few things. What do you think, Bill?"

"You may be on the right track, Glenna. Maybe you don't know that your neighbor at the junior high school is unhappy, too. Have you had a chance to talk to Ted?"

"No, I haven't talked to Ted. What happened with him?"

"His group improved from 77% mastery to 80% mastery," says Bill. "Still, he hasn't been greeted with congratulations. You know as well as I do that making sure the change went smoothly has really been left to us. We've worked our tails off trying to build a math team on each campus. We all want success for each student, but if you ask me, shooting for 90% mastery for all students in two years is too much. I mean, the goal is good; but with a program change like this, we can't expect such huge gains in such a short time."

"Whoops! My secretary is telling me Ted is on the other line. I'll call you back in a few minutes. Will you be there, Bill?"

"Yes. It seems that I have some paperwork to complete. Call me when you finish talking to Ted."

"Hello, Ted," says Glenna, "how can I help you? It's been a busy day. Have you met with Mr. Davis?"

"You bet I have, and he didn't make me very happy. I was just thinking that we should be getting our test results back; and if we succeeded in boosting our scores to 80% mastery, I was going to have a faculty party so the teachers could celebrate. Mr. Davis certainly threw cold water on that idea. We did raise our scores to 80% mastery, but it seems those results didn't make the central office happy. We've been using this new math textbook for less than two years. My teachers have gone all out, trying to help the students really understand all the tested material. Well, we may have a party anyway, even if I have to throw it off campus or at my home."

"Bill and I were just visiting about this very issue. What do you think of getting together with Mr. Davis soon, before the curriculum council meets? I think we need to explain a few things to him about the background on this, and about all that we and our teachers have done."

"OK. Why don't you try calling him and asking for a meeting before the end of this week? Then, maybe tomorrow, at least the three of us can get together and plan our presentation to him. I have copious notes on what we've done in the last year and a half to support this imposed change. You know, I think perhaps we need to go to the heart of the issue. We need to change the policy about how the curriculum council operates. We need to make certain that membership enables the teachers to have an adequate voice. That's one of my staff's main concerns. They feel that they are professionals and should be given an opportunity to provide input. In this case, only a very few teachers were involved in deciding to make a major change for the district."

"OK, Ted," says Glenna, "I'll set up a meeting for the three of us with Mr. Davis. I agree with you. We need to have more of our teachers involved when we plan such a major change. I'll be in touch with you about the meeting very soon."

Questions

1. What are some of the driving and restraining forces in this case study?

2. What do you think you would have done to support change had you been principal when the new math program was adopted?

3. If you were one of the principals, what assistance would you ask Mr. Davis to provide?

4. How might strategic planning aid in this whole effort?

5. Do you think the test results indicate that some major changes have occurred?

6. As a principal, what evidence would you seek to have in place to substantiate a successful change in the math program?

14 ∎ Community Relations

Standard 4.0: *Candidates who complete the program are educational leaders who have the knowledge and ability to promote the success of all students by collaborating with families and other community members, responding to diverse community interests and needs, and mobilizing community resources.*

FOCUSING QUESTIONS

1 What is the role of the principal as "boundary spanner"?

2 How can the principal promote school, community, and family involvement?

3 How can the principal promote effective internal and external public relations?

4 How does a principal develop a public relations plan?

In this chapter, we address the questions that deal with democracy and community. We respond to those questions with suggestions about how principals can involve the community in the functions of improving policy and purposefully educating students.

"Democratic education guarantees to all the members of its community the right to share in determining the purposes and policies of education" (Educational Policies Commission, 1940, p. 36). This resounding statement, made more than 60 years ago, is the foundation of community involvement in the schools. Today, principals appreciate and understand not only the learning potential in positive school-community relations but also the interdependence among schools, families, and communities. In addition to acknowledging this interdependence, principals are also beginning to realize that building social capital in the community is necessary. If the community is strengthened, the school is also strengthened for successful education. Principals today have a sense of even larger community issues, conditions, and needed investments such as housing quality, parks and recreation opportunities for after-school activities, employment and training, and law enforcement (Crowson, 1998).

Principals as "Boundary Spanners"

Goldring (1990) identified principals as a bridge between the school and external constituencies and referred to principals in this role as *boundary spanners*. Portin and Shen (1998, p. 93) indicated that principals serve as the individuals who market the school, who interpret the school's program to the parents and community. These authors indicated that principals are being called upon to form partnerships with the business community and to enter the discussion and debate regarding future policy directions for their schools. Bagin and Gallagher (2001) indicated that principals must be active and visible in the community and need to communicate with the overall community. This means reaching out or spanning boundaries with different business, religious, political, and service entities. Relationships must be established and nurtured with community leaders. Indeed, in addition to their ever-increasing responsibilities, principals must span the boundaries strengthening the link between the community and the school. Until recently, schools have done little to improve, empower, or revitalize the community or neighborhood (Cohen, 1995).

The school has viewed partnerships as minimally disenfranchising the community; in fact, schools are more likely to think of partnerships as doing crisis intervention with parents rather than sharing power with the community (Fine, 1993). The principal is the boundary spanner for ensuring that partnerships go beyond parents to include the community in interagency collaborations that can make decisions about the education of the "whole child." However, because interagency collaboratives—or coordinated service models, in some cases—have viewed some community problems, such as racism, crime, gangs, or poverty, as too difficult to handle, the traditionally empowering strategy of including the community to make decisions in policy and education of students sometimes amounts only to maintaining the status quo (Capper, 1996). Principals must respond to community politicization, particularly in the urban areas, that appreciates such elements as market

forces, choice, empowerment, enterprise strategies, self-reliance, and development above meeting needs, providing services, offering guidance, helping, involvement, and partnerships (Crowson, 1998). Epstein (1995) argued that although partnerships can "improve school programs and school climate, provide family services and support, increase parents' skills and leadership, connect families with others in the school and in the community, and help teachers with their work," their main benefit comes from helping "all youngsters succeed in school and in later life" (p. 701).

School, Family, and Community Involvement

The literature defines most of the community involvement in schools in relation to the parents; however, a broader definition of community involvement is needed. Community involvement is defined as volunteerism in the school by community members who devote their time to a variety of school needs. Those community members include local businesspersons, mayor, city council, urban planner, county judge, the media, police, firefighters, medical personnel, and/or clergy. How can these people be involved for a cogent, effective partnership?

In effect, principals must be involved in developing coordinated services, an array of partnered services extending from schools to families, which is a significant broadening of the mission of the public school (Crowson, 1998). Principals can consider many possibilities for spanning the boundaries and coordinating the services of community members; such services may range from volunteering time to providing resources. For example, businesses may adopt a school to fund an event, or to buy paper and pencils for economically disadvantaged students, or to provide coffee for "donuts with Dad" or "morning with Mom." The media, such as the local newspaper, may adopt a school and give the students newspapers once a week for improving their reading. Medical personnel may provide health workshops at the various grade levels for students and their parents. The police and firefighters may share important before- and after-school safety tips with youth. Clergy may assist students and families in a time of crisis at the school.

The coordinated services model is akin to the growing trend of community schools. Although they are a current trend, community schools date back to when Dewey (1966/1916) brought the school into the community, indicating that learning within the school should be continuous outside the school, and when Addams (1910) brought the community into the school. Dryfoos (2002) described community schools as follows:

> A community school, operating in a public school building, is open to students, families, and the community before, during, and after school, seven days a week, all year long. It is jointly operated and financed through a partnership between the school system and one or more community agencies. Families, young people, principals, teachers, youth workers, neighborhood residents, college faculty members, college students, and businesspeople all work together to design and implement a plan for transforming the school into a child-centered institution. Oriented toward the community, a community school encourages student learning through community service and service learning. A before-and after-school learning component encourages students to build on their classroom experiences, to expand their horizons, to explore their cultural heritage, to engage in sports and recreation, and just to have fun. A family support center helps families with child rearing, employment, housing, and other services. Medical, dental, and mental health services are also available on site. (p. 393)

Even though a district does not particularly house "community schools," the principal can take elements of coordinated services from the community school description by Dryfoos (2002) and incorporate those components into a school community relations plan.

Principals Leading Community Efforts During Catastrophes

When I (Beverly Irby) think of the principal as the person who is in charge of coordinated services, it takes me back to Tuesday, September 11, 2001. I was to conduct a full-day workshop for a regional group of teachers and principals that day, and had driven one hour from my home to the workshop site in College Station, Texas. Before entering the campus drive where I was to conduct the workshop, I happened to turn on the radio. I heard that a plane had crashed into the World Trade Center; I listened more closely, thinking what a terrible accident. I turned off the car, gathered my materials, and went into the school. There, I spoke with the workshop attendees about how horrible the accident was. We had begun the workshop when word arrived that a second plane had hit the other Trade Center tower; then another plane hit the Pentagon; and we heard that a fourth was headed for the White House. Of course, the workshop ceased. The principals in the audience were thinking of just one thing — responding to the attack some 2,000 miles away. They knew they had to return to their campuses and their communities. They had never faced the issue of a terrorist attack. First on their minds were the students and the teachers. They had to respond to parents, teachers, and community members.

According to Colvin (2002), in lower Manhattan, of course, principals and teachers faced an even more immediate set of issues. Schools near the devastated towers had to be evacuated and students rushed to safety, some of them ferried to Staten Island or to New Jersey. In the suburbs of New York and Washington, DC, the challenge was to figure out what to do with children whose parents might be trapped in the city and unable to get home — or whose parents might never come home again. In New York many telephones, both cellular and conventional — as well as Internet connections — were not working. Around DC, circuits were jammed and so were roads out of the city. In response to the disaster, the principals in Fairfax County, Virginia, kept the children in school because it was the safest place for them to be. The schools would stay open as long as they had to. Community support was overwhelming. The next day, schools were closed, and the DC area superintendents joined in a conference call with municipal leaders to discuss what should happen next with federal emergency and law enforcement officials (Colvin, 2002). Principals reported to work and determined collaborative and coordinated efforts that would go into effect to keep their students safe in the shadows of terrorism.

In times of catastrophe, schools often become the lifeline to the communities they serve. Lazarus and Gillespie (1996) determined some imperatives for principals following a natural disaster by interviewing principals, assistant principals, crisis intervention specialists, and district coordinators of psychological services one year after Hurricane Andrew, which struck in August 1992. The authors examined how these individuals coped in the aftermath of the hurricane and what they learned in the process. They concluded that principals should rapidly establish a means of communication. Often, when a natural disaster occurs, telephone service is interrupted or destroyed. The authors suggested that a telephone tree be developed before a crisis. They gave the following examples: One Florida principal sat on his roof, calling faculty members on a cellular telephone while others had to drive to locate staff and arrange assistance for them.

Another strategy is to quickly assess the damage and make appropriate accommodations. Principals and teachers can register the damage caused to their school and classrooms. Going through all buildings to determine their usability and safety is essential before students return. If there is structural damage, other accommodations will be needed for classes. Additionally, principals must prioritize needs and establish authority to make site-based decisions. Lazarus and Gillespie reported that after Hurricane Andrew, tent cities, medical assistance areas, and food distribution tents were established. Thousands of armed personnel and volunteers from all over the country arrived to help. There was a real display of coordinated services, and principals helped to facilitate those services. The military involvement enabled schools to open three weeks after the hurricane struck. Troops moved tons of building remnants, mangled fences, and uprooted trees from school campuses. Site-based decision making helped make areas accessible and reduced potential safely hazards.

Principals must address the emotional and survival needs of faculty, staff, and students after a disaster. Coordinating crisis counseling is imperative and must be provided to all affected schools to help not only students but also teachers, staff, and parents. Lazarus and Gillespie made the point that after Hurricane Andrew, the primary stress was on adults. Small and large group counseling sessions were organized by campus counselors.

Principals must arrange for training and support for mental health caregivers. According to Lazarus and Gillespie (1996), the National Organization for Victims Assistance, the American Psychological Association, and the American Red Cross have training programs to assist mental health personnel who work in schools following a disaster. These personnel can benefit from additional training in how to respond to a large-scale crisis specifically related to stress reactions, stress response, issues of loss and grief, coping skills, debriefing techniques, and crisis resolution.

Either the principal or a designee should provide feedback to the news media. This will ensure consistency of shared information, rumor control, and reduced interruptions to staff members. Media control can enlighten others to the impact and needs of the schools following a natural disaster and establish partnerships between citizens and schools. After Hurricane Andrew, schools in Miami were adopted by other schools across the nation.

Principals need to encourage creative instructional methods using lessons learned in the aftermath. Students' emotional needs must be addressed before beginning academic instruction. In interviews with principals, Lazarus and Gillespie found that daily discussions in which everyone relates their experience can create a strong bond and feeling of community among class members. The authors said that in dealing with lessons from disasters, teachers can use real-life examples to teach about math, weather, geology, history, geography, politics, economics, social science, psychology, and English.

Principals must identify and secure all available resources and implement systemic interventions to meet school and community needs. They can assess the needs of their school and help secure resources. Lazarus and Gillespie reported that one school created a "Teachers Helping Teachers" bulletin board, listing the needs of staff (e.g., food, child care, a place to do laundry, space to store items). A sign-up sheet was also posted, with names of volunteers willing to assist in specific areas. The PTA and the Student Council provided funds for gift certificates or household items. Donations were obtained from community businesses and schools across the country. The counseling and school psychology staff distributed gifts, thus gaining the opportunity to touch base with members of the school community who were most affected and to offer psychological assistance as needed. Guest speakers addressed parents and teachers on crisis reactions, stress reduction, and coping. The primary benefit of many of these interventions was to establish the school as a source of security and stability in a fearful and anxious community (Lazarus & Gillespie, 1996, p. 35).

Principals Leading School, Family, and Community Involvement

Epstein (1997) suggested that there are six types of school, family, and community involvement: (a) parenting, (b) communicating, (c) volunteering, (d) learning at home, (e) decision making, and (f) collaborating with the community. What can principals do to lead in these components? We discuss each type of involvement in turn.

1. *Parenting.* Families must provide for their children's health and safety, and they must maintain a home environment that encourages learning and good behavior in school. Principals must provide training and information to help families understand their children's development and how to support the changes they undergo.

2. *Communicating.* Principals must reach out to families with information about school programs and student progress. This includes encouraging teachers to make the traditional phone calls, send report cards, and hold parent conferences, as well as to send new information on topics such as magnet schools, transition from elementary school to higher grades, and involvement opportunities. Because communication must be in forms that families find understandable and useful, language translations are necessary. For example, principals must hire translators and interpreters to reach parents who do not speak English well.

3. *Volunteering.* Parents can make significant contributions to the environment and functions of a school. Principals can get the most out of this process by creating flexible schedules to enable more parents to participate and by working to match the talents and interests of parents to the needs of students, teachers, and administrators.

4. *Learning at home.* Principals should encourage teachers to train family members to assist the children at home with homework assignments and other school-related activities.

5. *Decision making.* Principals can give parents meaningful roles in the school decision-making process by providing parents with training and information so they can make the most of those opportunities. The opportunity to participate in decision making should be open to all segments of the community as well.

6. *Collaborating with the community.* Akin to the coordinated services model, Epstein's model suggested that principals help families gain access to support services offered by other agencies, such as health care, cultural events, tutoring services, and after-school child-care programs. Principals also can help families and community groups provide services such as recycling programs and food pantries.

Epstein (2001) further addressed the development of *comprehensive partnerships* with the family and community that are linked to school improvement goals. She suggested that as programs develop, (a) many ways should emerge for parents, other family members, community groups, and other citizens to gain and share information about parenting; (b) communication should become clearer with educators and each other about school programs and children's progress; (c) volunteerism at school, at home, or in the community should increase; (d) interactions with children regarding in-class work, homework, and academic decisions such as course choices should be observed in the home; (e) parents should become informed about and involved in school decisions; and (f) connections with organizations, services, and other opportunities in the community should be more apparent. Such partnerships should be reviewed annually and improved from year to year with more parents and community members becoming involved.

Schiller, Clements, and Lara-Alecio (2003) reminded principals that *family involvement* is a current, more inclusive term for what has always been referred to as parent involvement. They indicated that *family* is used in place of *parent* because it includes all students, even those living with someone other than their parents.

Family involvement includes family visits to the school for observation purposes, active roles by families in the classroom instruction, family education programs, family support from home, family volunteers, parent boards, family participation in special events, and family partnerships in advocacy for children and youth.

More Family Involvement Information for Principals to Consider

The research has been specific to parent involvement in the past; and it has been determined that the more actively involved in their children's educational activities the parents are, the better the children's academic achievement, self-confidence, and attitudes toward school (Beveridge & Jerrams, 1981; Chavkin & Williams, 1989; Comer, 1984; Epstein, 1983; Lightfoot, 1978; McDill & Rigsby, 1973; McLaughlin & Shields, 1987; Tizard, Schofield, & Hewison, 1982). Additionally, when parents are actively involved in their children's education, positive cognitive and affective changes in

their children can be observed, regardless of the parents' economic, ethnic, or cultural background (Flaxman & Inger, 1991). Researchers continuously have reported that parent participation in their children's education (a) enhances children's self-esteem, (b) improves children's academic achievement, (c) improves parent-child relationships, and (d) helps parents develop positive attitudes toward school and a better understanding of the schooling process (Schiller et al., 2003). However, parents may find it difficult to find the time or have the resources or energy to become involved or to coordinate their schedules with school events, particularly in today's engaged society.

Involvement of parents in their children's education, whether at home or at school, whether initiated at preschool age or later, has significant, long-lasting, and positive effects (Mowry, 1972). For example, home-based parental involvement is reported to have a positive, significant effect on achievement (Bermúdez & Padron, 1988; Chavkin & Williams, 1988; Comer, 1986; Dornbusch & Ritter, 1988), particularly for children of low-income parents (McLaughlin & Shields, 1987).

Some parents and families may feel uncomfortable when visiting school because of previously bad experiences or because of a language barrier; however, low-income and poorly educated parents want to become involved in their children's education (Chavkin & Williams, 1989; McLaughlin & Shields, 1987). But no matter how strong their desire, the Hispanic English-language-learning proficient parents are typically not involved for a number of reasons, including low levels of proficiency in English, little understanding of the relationship between home and school, little knowledge of how the school system operates, work schedule demands, negative experiences with schools, and lack of sensitivity and understanding on the part of school personnel (Bermúdez & Márquez, 1996). The involvement of language minority parents in their children's education is necessary for the reinforcement of native language development and for the communication of high expectations and emotional support regarding academic achievement (Crawford, 1989).

Because the need to increase the involvement of Hispanic parents in their children's schools is critical (Inger, 1992), many administrators and teachers have begun to address these issues by collaboratively developing strategic plans and goals for their campuses (Irby & Brown, 1996). They have begun to develop parent resource centers, where parents can review and develop materials to assist them in child rearing (Bermúdez & Márquez, 1996), and they have initiated parent involvement workshops (Minaya-Rowe, 1996). Yet many school district personnel lack the necessary skills to involve language minority parents effectively (Bermúdez & Márquez, 1996). A modest body of research exists regarding effective parenting or parent involvement strategies of disadvantaged and/or Hispanic students (Bronfenbrenner, 1974; Flaxman & Inger, 1991; Inger, 1992; Laosa, 1977, 1978, 1982; Laurea, 1989; Nicolau & Ramos, 1990; Parker, Lara-Alecio, Ochoa, Bigger, Hasbrouck, & Parker, 1996). However, Lara-Alecio, Irby, and Ebener (1997) found only one study (Clark, 1988) that investigated effective home practices of minority parents, including Hispanics, of higher-achieving students. Clark found various positive parental practices associated with standards, norms, rules, allowances, and sanctions, such as (a) a wide range of enriching materials during home instructional activities, (b) cooperation of parents with teachers, (c) adult and peer modeling of academic and social behaviors, (d) clear expressions of right and wrong, (e) support of the child's personal worth, and (f) reward and respect.

Principals must first be committed to involving families and parents, but principals must also motivate and encourage teachers to be committed to involving families and parents and to use as many ways as possible to involve the parents. To get parents and families involved, principals and teachers must find ways to increase communication with parents and encourage involvement in children's learning experiences (Brown, 1989).

Parent and family involvement may be school-based, including such activities as parent-teacher conferences, class parties, field-trip chaperone, school volunteer, classroom assistant, or parent-teacher organization meetings. Parent involvement may be home-based, focused on things that parents can do with their children at home. Parent involvement may be education-based, with parents attending classes to learn how to (a) improve discipline, (b) encourage children in reading or math improvement, (c) improve their own technology skills, (d) pass a high school equivalency test, or (e) learn to speak English. Such educational programs for parents are planned with flexible scheduling; some programs are held in the early morning, some during the school day, others in the evening, and yet others on Saturdays.

Schiller, Clements, and Lara-Alecio (2003) indicated that communication with families and parents falls into two broad categories — general information that applies to all students (about the school, curriculum, upcoming events, etc.) and specific information about individual students. Both types of communication are important in bringing the school and home together. All communication should be inclusive of the languages spoken at home and at school.

Schiller and colleagues (2003) recommend the following general communication avenues:

1. *Orientation meetings.* Orientation meetings can be held during the semester prior to student enrollment, during the first month of school, or at both times. This meeting provides opportunities for the teacher to communicate school policies and rules, bus schedules, emergency routines, and pick-up and drop-off requirements of families.

2. *Newsletters.* Newsletters allow teachers to stay in contact during the year. They can relay information about upcoming events, specific topics regarding child development, parenting tips, health and safety tips, and changes in procedures. They may describe changes in curriculum and suggest activities in which families and parents can become involved at home or in the community.

3. *School handbook.* The school handbook is a great way to get information to families before the first day of school. Handbooks can be provided during orientation, mailed to students' homes, or put up on the school

Web site. Handbooks will include the school calendar, faculty names, programs at the school, school services, and school policies and procedures.

4. *Programs for families.* Family seminars, meetings, and school programs are types of programs for families. Each program offers opportunities to share information with families. Some schools have Saturday programs for families and their children, particularly for those families who are English language learners.

5. *Suggestion box.* Families can make suggestions to school personnel through the use of a suggestion box.

6. *Home visits.* Home visits usually are reserved for the very young child, with the purpose of having the child meet the teacher in familiar surroundings.

7. *Conferences.* Conferences are the most formal way to meet with family members; they are recommended at least twice a year. Of course, for students with special needs, conferences will be required for reviewing their assessment, individual educational plans, placements, and transition-to-work plans. Encourage teachers to begin with successes in any conference and then discuss challenges. If problems are suggested, then offer the family an opportunity be involved in planning the solutions.

8. *Journals.* Principals can encourage teachers to have students take home a journal or a folder for exchanging information with parents or families. Additionally, children's class portfolios may be sent home periodically for review and comment.

9. *Personal notes.* A note to the families sharing their children's accomplishments is a good way to include them in the successes at school. In the secondary school, notes or letters sharing the students' successes are also welcomed.

10. *Phone calls.* Families expect telephone calls for bad news, but a telephone call about good news is an excellent way of staying in touch with parents and families. The principal and teacher can become liaisons for families, directing them to agencies that can assist in making their lives better.

Principals, School-Community Relations, and Public Relations

As principals engage in building cooperative and working relationships with teachers and the community, they are developing school-community relations. Good school-community relations foster *communications* and a *working relationship* between the school and the community, giving community members greater awareness of the school's purposes and achievements. By fostering involvement of the school and community, the principal can develop joint ventures for the mutual benefit of all parties. The principal will need to develop relationships with businesses, retired persons, human services, governmental agencies, and legislators. School-community relations create an image. It has been said that image is perception, and perception is everything. In public relations the effort is to transmit and create an image from the school to the community; in school-community relations, there is more emphasis on involvement of community groups and joint development of the image desired with various public sectors (Sybouts & Wendel, 1994, p. 292).

The National School Public Relations Association (NSPRA) has defined school public relations in the following way:

Educational public relations is a planned and systematic management function to help improve the programs and services of an educational organization. It relies on a comprehensive two-way communications process involving both internal and external publics, with a goal of stimulating a better understanding of the role, objectives, accomplishments, and needs of the organization. Educational public relations programs assist in interpreting public attitudes, identify and help shape policies and procedures in the public interest, and carry on involvement and information activities which earn public understanding and support. (National School Public Relations Association, 2003)

It is crucial for the principal to establish good community and public relations. Campus communication needs have increased dramatically and become more complex. The principal on the campus must either act as the public relations coordinator or assign that role to another individual. In any case, the public relations coordinator not only develops and executes the school's communication plans through print and electronic media as well as face-to-face communication but also handles relations with the multitude of media that call school districts weekly. Languages of parents must be taken into account when establishing communications and collaboration. Principals must realize that education is under attack from taxpayers, business groups, special interest groups, and others (Berliner & Biddle, 1995; Bracey, 2002). The campus needs to establish a two-way communication pattern allowing information to flow out about the school as well as allowing feedback to come into the school. Positive news about achievements by students, teachers, and staff as well as new or successful programs are the type of outward-flowing information that promotes positive feelings in the community about the school. Such information aids the principal in being on the offensive rather than the defensive in communications with the public. Principals may get help in promoting information about the school from district public relations, or they may do much of the work themselves. Many public relations persons suggest that principals arrange meetings with realtors, school open houses, or breakfasts with clergy, parents, legislators, city council members, or the Chamber of Commerce to develop an informed and supportive public.

Some districts have an employed public relations person, but not all of the principal's work will be done through the district. The NSPRA (2003) suggested the following examples for developing two-way communications and collaboration within the community:

1. Provide public relations counsel, taking a proactive stance. Anticipate problems and provide solutions.

2. Handle all aspects of the school's publications, such as its external and internal newsletters.

3. Write news releases for all local newspapers, TV, and radio; work to get media coverage of school district news. Serve as the media's liaison with the school.

4. Stay closely attuned to the entire budget-making process, and promote community input.

5. Write and develop a communications plan for the campus, detailing how to reach its internal and external publics; write and develop a crisis communications plan of reaching publics, gathering the facts and dealing with media in a crisis.

6. Conduct formal and informal research to determine public opinion and attitude as a basis for planning and action.

7. Promote the school's strengths and achievements and its solutions to problems.

8. Vigorously publicize student and staff achievement; develop staff and retirement recognition programs.

9. Answer public and new resident requests for information; maintain extensive background files; keep school's historical and budget passage records; and plan for school anniversary celebrations.

10. Provide public relations training to staff and PTOs in areas such as talking to the media, communicating in a crisis, and recognizing that nonteaching staff are part of the school public relations team.

11. Serve as the school's liaison with community groups such as civic associations and service clubs; help plan and publicize the school's parent, senior citizen, and community service programs. Develop ways to bring the community into the schools.

According to the NSPRA, true communication is a two-way process involving both inflow and outflow of information. The principal, in essence, helps keep both *I*'s of the school open, working to keep the public, in turn, both *Informed* and *Involved* in the schools.

The Politics of Internal and External Publics

Community and public relations begins at home and operates from the inside out; therefore, it is extremely important that the principal identify and communicate effectively with her internal and external publics. Internal publics refer to those groups of people directly associated with the campus or the school district, such as administrators, teachers, students, support staff, or the school board. External publics refer to those people who are outside of the campus or district or who have an indirect relationship with the campus or district; these include such groups as parents, community organizations, churches, government, businesses, or senior citizens.

The principal will want to draw the attention of both internal and external publics toward the school's faculty and student accomplishments as well as its effective programs. No principal can afford to be unmindful of the opinion and attitudes of those publics concerning the campus. The principal must develop a two-way communication system through which he or the teachers will not only inform people of its accomplishments and programs but also study the people's reactions to them. Carefully handled through competent professional techniques and media, a community relations process goes a long way in building a favorable school image and public satisfaction. However, complaints about the school or its personnel must also be handled carefully, through a two-way communication process. It is the principal's responsibility to correctly assess public opinion and reactions to the information being propagated; the principal must then react appropriately and thoughtfully toward public opinion. The faster the principal knows about concerns, the faster she can respond and take corrective actions. It may be wise to devise some early warning networks to monitor public opinion or reaction. Use of technology can aid not only in gathering information from the public but also in disseminating information and providing feedback. The politics of public or community relations basically becomes the ability to present complex issues in a way that makes sense to all publics. The principal must present his school in the best light.

Consideration of the Media and Community Relations

The media is an external public that keeps the remaining external public notified of daily happenings on the campus or in the school district. We are certain that you have repeatedly viewed the following scenario on your television screen. The television reporter sticks a microphone in front of anyone passing by, asking them questions to get the breaking story. The reporter states that the principal was unavailable for comment, or the principal walks by and the reporter catches the principal and pulls her into the report. The principal, unaware of how to deal with the media, says too much. Parents are outraged and come to protest the comments. In another scenario, the district's trained public relations coordinator is immediately on the scene, getting the answers from school officials and parents and seeking out the reporters to respond for the district and the campus.

Unfortunately, not every school system has a district-level media coordinator; this means that principals need to know how to deal with the media. Perhaps part of the crisis plan for the district is to have a district media liaison, particularly during times of crisis. In fact, Brock, Sandoval, and Lewis (1996) recommend that districts have such a person. Larger districts have media liaisons who also are usually the public relations director or coordinator; however, in smaller districts, as indicated, the liaison job falls to the principal.

If a crisis occurs on the campus, news reporters usually want to know who, what, when, where, why, and how. Lazarus, Brock, and Feinburg (1999) recommended that if at all possible when preparing to be interviewed, the principal should try to get a sense of what the topic or focus will be. The authors provided some examples: A print reporter may leave you a message that she is doing a story on empathy or the failure to develop empathy in teenagers for an article that will be printed in two days. She needs to speak with you if at all possible before 7:00 p.m. A national news network may tell you that they are doing a piece at 5:30 p.m.–6:00 p.m. on how crisis counselors respond to grieving children and want to know if you can be available in the studio for a live interview at that time.

Brock and colleagues (1996) provided six suggestions for dealing with news reporters. The authors suggest that the person being interviewed should: (a) display a high energy level, (b) use simple language rather than technical terms and speak in short sentences, (c) be brief, (d) be friendly; (e) be knowledgeable, sincere, and compassionate, and (f) use good nonverbal communication (p. 194).

Lazarus and colleagues (1999) stressed the importance of remembering that everything you say is on the record and that you should choose your words carefully; anything you say to a reporter may eventually be read by tens of thousands of individuals. Messages to newspaper reporters are usually more complex; therefore, the authors recommended that you check with the reporter to be sure he or she understood you correctly. Asking the reporter to repeat the information you have delivered can ensure its accuracy. When the news story appears in print, it should be read for accuracy, because it is possible to correct any inaccurate information in later editions (Brock et al., 1996).

Always remember to report only the facts, and try not to get into the attorney's job or the detective's job. Try to ensure that the media portray the situations accurately. Always try to emphasize what the school is doing to address the issues in question.

Lazarus and colleagues (1999) provided suggestions for avoiding some of the pitfalls presented by media coverage of crisis events. (a) Attempt to clarify the subject matter of the interview. If it appears to be sensationalistic, do not agree to participate. Some interviewers have well-established reputations for providing sensationalistic coverage of tragic events. Consider such reputations before agreeing to an interview. (b) Try to avoid playing the blame game. Placing blame does not give the general public the kind of information it needs on coping with tragedy. (c) Try to avoid participating in interviews that might give undue attention to the perpetrators of violent acts. (d) Establish some ground rules for what you will and will not discuss.

NSPRA Standards for Educational Public Relations Programs

Figure 14.1 is an excerpt of the standards from the National School Public Relations Association (NSPRA; available at http://www.nspra.org/). These are the standards by which a principal and teachers could collaboratively develop a public relations program, should one not already exist on the campus or in the district. If a program exists, the principal and a committee would want to review it based on the following standards.

Educational public relations is a planned and systematic management function designed to help improve the programs and services of an educational organization. It relies on a comprehensive two-way communications process involving both internal and external publics, with a goal of stimulating a better understanding of the role, objectives, accomplishments, and needs of the organization. Educational public relations programs assist in interpreting public attitudes, identifying and helping shape policies and procedures in the public interest, and carrying on involvement and information activities that earn public understanding and support.

A School District's Plan   The Tacoma (Washington) Public Schools Public Relation Plan adheres to the standards set forth by the NSPRA. The Tacoma Plan follows:

> The Board of Directors believes it is the responsibility of each Board member, as well as each employee of the District, to actively pursue a two-way communications program that highlights the educational experiences in the city's public schools and promotes effective school/home/community partnerships.
>
> The Board recognizes that citizens have a right to know what is occurring in their public school system; that Board members and all school administrators have an obligation to see that all publics are kept systematically and adequately informed; and that the District will benefit from seeing that citizens get all information, good and bad, directly from the system itself.
>
> The Board affirms the following objectives:
>
> 1. To maintain an effective two-way communication system between the District and its various publics which ensures:

I. Concept

A. Policy
1. The organization shall adopt a clear and concise public relations policy statement.
2. The policy statement shall be approved through formal action of the organization's governing body, shall be published in its policy manual, and shall be reviewed annually by the governing body.
3. The policy statement shall express the purposes of the organization's public relations program and shall provide for the delegation of authority to appropriate executives.

B. Procedures
1. Management shall clarify the public relations policies through the development of written operational procedures.
2. The procedures shall outline major components of the public relations program, detail rules and regulations, and specify employee roles and responsibilities.
3. The procedures shall be distributed to all employees and representatives of key external publics.

II. Resources

Commitment to the achievement of the purposes of the organization's public relations policy shall be demonstrated through the allocation of adequate human and financial resources to the public relations program.

A. Staff
1. The staffing of a public relations program will vary according to an organization's size, needs, and availability of resources. In every situation, however, the responsibility shall be assigned to an individual who reports directly to the chief executive officer and who participates as a full member of the administrative cabinet.
2. Recognition of public relations as a management function of primary importance shall be demonstrated through the existence of a unit staffed by full-time professional public relations personnel. Staff size shall be sufficient to accomplish the objectives of the organization and to cope with the variety of inherent conditions and problems.
3. The public relations staff shall meet NSPRA's Standards for Educational Public Relations Professionals.
4. Provision shall be made for continuous training and development for members of the public relations staff.

B. Budget
1. The organization's budget shall include a specific item for public relations staffing, services, and programs.
2. The amount of the public relations budget will vary according to organizational needs. However, in addition to staff, appropriate provisions shall be made for the following: materials and equipment; facilities; technical services (publications, advertising, audiovisual, radio, television, etc.); involvement activities; professional growth and development; research and evaluation.
3. Provisions shall be made for appropriate public relations activities in the budgets of each of the organization's major departments and programs.

III. Internal Communications

The basic foundation of the organization's public relations program shall be a sound and effective system of internal communications.

A. Planning
1. The organization shall develop a written plan which identifies key internal audiences, as well as procedures for determining the kind of information they need and desire.
2. Each major department, program, or unit in the organization shall develop appropriate communications strategies based on the overall plan.

B. Implementation
1. An appropriate variety of communications methods shall be used, including vehicles for encouraging, receiving, analyzing, and using feedback.
2. A continuing public relations training program shall be provided for the entire staff or membership of the organization.

IV. External Communications

The organization shall be committed to continuing and creative efforts to inform and involve external publics.

A. Planning
1. The organization shall develop a written plan which identifies key community individuals and groups, as well as procedures for determining the kind of information they need and desire.
2. Each major department, program, or unit in the organization shall develop appropriate communications strategies based on the overall plan.

B. Implementation
1. An appropriate variety of communications methods shall be used.
2. Special efforts shall be made to encourage, receive, analyze, and use feedback.
3. Strategies shall be developed to identify and involve community resources.

V. Accountability

A. Program Performance
1. The organization shall provide for evaluation of the public relations program based on proposed objectives and the degree to which they have been achieved.
2. The staff or membership of the organization shall be included in any evaluation process.

B. Development
1. The organization shall provide for long-range public relations planning.
2. The organization shall develop a plan for anticipating, preparing for, and dealing with the public relations aspects of unusual or crisis situations.
3. Emphasis shall be given to seeking and developing new and different avenues of communications and relationships.

Figure 14.1

Excerpt of National School Public Relations Association (NSPRA) Standards

a. Dissemination of accurate, timely information about school policies, programs, procedures, achievements, decisions, critical issues;

b. Interpretation of decisions and action;

c. Elimination of rumors and misinformation;

d. Programs and practices designed to provide an open climate which will elicit ideas, suggestions, reactions from the community and employees alike;

e. An effective working relationship with the news media.

2. To maintain a Public Information Office which will coordinate the District's communication efforts.

3. To develop and maintain an organizational environment where all District staff members are aware that they share the responsibility for communication of school policies, programs and activities to parents, members of the educational and other communities.

4. To maintain a written plan of communication policies and guidelines which will be available to employees and to the public upon request.

5. To support the establishment of a Communications Review Committee to review and evaluate District-wide two-way communication efforts.

Board members believe it is essential to the development of excellence in the education of youngsters that the maximum possible knowledge about the goals, achievements, activities and operations of the school district be conveyed to the students, staff and citizens. The Board therefore reaffirms its commitment to openness in relationships with its patrons. The Board further believes that the citizens, as well as the staff and students, should be consulted and involved in the problem-solving and decision-making processes at as early a stage as possible. This involvement should be solicited actively and honestly through a wide variety of means. A principal could model a public relations plan for the campus after the Tacoma Board plan.

Public Relations Plan

The National School Public Relations Association (NSPRA) published a model for establishing a community relations or public relations plan. The NSPRA indicated that the role of school public relations is to maintain mutually beneficial relationships between the school district and the many publics it serves. Each principal will have his or her own unique way of carrying out this role, but there is one common element of all successful public relations programs: They are planned.

A well-thought-out public relations plan will help ensure that a school district carries out its mission and meets its goals with the support of its staff and community. Where does the principal begin? The NSPRA provides a basic process for developing a district public relations plan; and from that plan, a principal can develop one at the campus level.

The Four-Step Public Relations Process

Exemplary public relations programs follow this four-step process:

1. *Research.* The principal conducts an up-front analysis on where the district (campus) stands in regard to all publics it wishes to reach.

2. *Action plan.* The principal develops public relations goals, objectives, and strategies that go hand in hand with the district's (campus's) overall mission and goals.

3. *Communicate.* The principal carries out the tactics that are necessary to meet the objectives and goals.

4. *Evaluate.* The principal reflects on actions taken to determine their effectiveness and to identify what changes are needed in the future.

Keeping these four basic public relations tenets in mind, the principal can follow this process to develop a public relations plan for her school or district. Box 14.1 presents a real story of how this plan can work (Johnson, personal communication, August 2004). The story moves through each step of the process.

Box 14.1   Dr. Shirley Johnson's Story of How a Principal Implemented a Community Relations Plan

---

A Young Principal's Story

A young principal was brought to an inner-city elementary that had experienced principals within a period of 12 years. The superintendents, of whom there had been two within that same period, were very frustrated because nothing they had done to date really helped the situation of poor climate, low achievement scores, and the very tight community surrounding the elementary that had become vocal and very unhappy.

The new principal had been briefed on the situation, but was not exactly sure where to start to remedy the problems. He found the faculty entirely uncooperative, the students some of the most wonderful kids he had ever seen, and the assistant principal totally lost for an idea. The superintendent said, "Do whatever you think will work!"

For a new principal, this was a rather large order; however, he began by looking first to the community. For the first month and a half of his principalship, and with no vision or assistance from the faculty, he organized coffee meetings with small groups from the community. He began his *research* by carefully listening to the parents, and he found several points of entry to the problems. The young principal then started listening to the businesses that had been in the small community for some time. He found the businesses open and very willing to help, even though they seemed very skeptical because the teachers had convinced them that the students were the problem.

Armed with lots of data, the principal pored over the data with a trusted central administrator in the district. They fashioned an *action plan* that called for a careful analysis of the school, beginning with the parents and the students. All meetings were conducted off campus and carefully scripted. Within weeks, very clear evidence began to emerge supporting the points of entry into solving the school's problems.

Using two parents, two faculty members, and two business partners, the principal created a final action plan. He *communicated* the objective of targeting improved student performance, but more important, an improved climate. What little budget the principal had was bolstered by the business partners to buy the consultants and materials needed for plan implementation. When the faculty began to resist, the principal called upon the community to support continued implementation of the plan and to provide support to the superintendent.

The first year was very difficult, but as the faculty began to understand that the school's problems involved considerations beyond the students' performance, they became more open to other considerations. By March of the first year, teachers began asking hard questions about their own performance without fearing retribution. The faculty voted to fully join the effort, helping with fund-raising and joining the community's efforts. The principal *evaluated* the progress and revised the planned strategies with the committee that now included more community members and teachers.

Public Relations Planning Process

The NSPRA also provides a planning process to assist in developing the public relations plan.

1. *Do variety assessment.* Begin by meeting with the superintendent and school board to discuss their priorities for district public relations objectives. Know the district mission and goals, and be prepared to discuss how your program can help achieve those goals.

2. *Develop internal and external research.* Before structuring the plan, you must be aware of where the district stands in the eyes of both staff and the community. There are a variety of questions to answer: Who are our publics? What are our publics' overall perceptions of our schools? What "hot issues" are circulating among staff and community? What issues affecting other school districts may soon be coming our way? . . . the list goes on and on.

Base your research on your district mission and goals, and use several methods. Tactics to consider: national studies, census data, telephone logs, media reports, interviews with community opinion leaders, focus groups, written or telephone surveys.

3. *Develop public relations goals and objectives.* Thinking first and foremost about facilitating achievement of district goals, develop short-term and long-term public relations goals to accomplish. It is advisable to develop these with input from a committee representing board, staff, parents, families, and outside community members. Remember, to make the objectives timed and measurable, so that you will know if you achieved them. Example: By the end of the school year, 75% of the district's teachers will be involved in projects to improve teacher-parent relations.

4. *Identify target publics.* These "targets" are the groups of people that need to be reached in order to achieve the goals. Primary publics are those most important to achieving goals. In schools, they are often students, staff, and parents. Secondary publics are those who could be reached if money or time permits, or those who are indirectly reached by public relations tactics.

5. *Identify desired behavior of publics.* This is a critical step! For the plan to succeed, you must decide what you want the program to do. Do you want to provide information? Or, do you want to reinforce or change the behavior of certain publics? These questions must be answered before tactics are created.

6. *Identify what is needed to achieve desired behavior.* Using research data, decide what actions must take place to create the behaviors you desire. For example, you could find out by taking attendance that only 50% of the parents and families at your school normally attend the fall open house. The desired behavior is to increase this number. A follow-up written survey could help you identify the reasons that 50% do not attend. Then you can decide what actions to take to change this percentage.

7. *Create strategies and tactics for reaching publics.* Strategies are overall procedures, like developing a media kit that provides general information about the school district. Tactics are the actions that must be taken to carry out the procedures, like writing the press release or printing the folder for the district media kit.

8. *Put your plan on paper.* This is where you develop the budget, create a timeline, and assign responsibility for all strategies and tactics.

9. *Implement the plan.* After management and board approval, put your plan into action. Keep your committee involved, and prepare to refine the plan along the way.

10. *Evaluate your efforts.* Using the same methods you used in the research phase, evaluate your plan. First, evaluate the planning process itself: What worked and what didn't? Continue to evaluate your program as it is implemented to determine what revisions may need to be made. Finally, measure your goals and objectives to determine whether you have reached them.

Several of the steps involved in the public relations planning process can be identified in the story presented in Box 14.2 (Johnson, personal communication, August 2004).

Summary

1. Today, principals appreciate and understand the learning potential in positive school-community relations and the interdependence among schools, families, and communities.

2. Principals are also beginning to realize that building social capital in the community is necessary because if the community is strengthened, the school will also be strengthened for successful education.

3. Principals are a bridge between the school and external constituencies, and they are called boundary spanners as they fulfill this role.

4. The principal is the boundary spanner for ensuring that partnerships go beyond parents

Box 14.2   Dr. Shirley Johnson's Story of How a Principal Implemented a Public Relations Planning Process

A Seasoned Principal's Story

A small town in East Texas had fired its fourth high school principal in five years. Money was very tight, and the community totally distrusting of the school board and their decision making but feeling powerless to do anything to help. The superintendent selected a seasoned veteran who was patient but clear about the task. She vowed that she would do nothing during the first year. Rather, she met with all the faculty, parents, and students and talked about what were pressing problems. She even visited with the custodial staff and the bus drivers who were community members, all the while taking very careful notes. Watching the principal, the superintendent and board could not figure what she was doing. Did she not trust their input?

During the summer of the first year, the veteran principal spent considerable time with the superintendent and the board. Her mission was to understand their value structure and find a point of commonality between herself, the community, the superintendent, and the faculty. After assembling the data, the principal brought together the school's major players, including the superintendent and the board, for a presentation on the state of the school.

Her delivery was direct, straightforward, and without cover. She was strategically correct, and her observations went to the heart of the problem. When finished with her address, the principal asked those assembled to join her in developing a comprehensive plan for addressing the problems. The entire presentation and plea were directed toward the agenda of improving the schools for students, not for disinterested employees and agenda-focused board members.

Sobered by the rather revealing presentation, at first the superintendent and the board were disgruntled; but as person by person began to come forward to accept the challenge, suddenly they were confronted by a large group of people in the schools and community who had ably accepted the challenge. Finding the support to do what was necessary, the principal established a meeting schedule with the volunteers and started the much-needed reconstruction of the school.

The principal had created a wonderful strategic implementation plan; but the success of her work was clearly the architecture of strategies that moved the board, the superintendent, and the teachers beyond their personal interests and focused their energies on the students and the school.

to include the community in interagency collaborations that can make decisions about the education of the "whole child."

5. A community school, operating in a public school building, is open to students, families, and the community before, during, and after school, seven days a week, all year long. It is jointly operated and financed through a partnership between the school system and one or more community agencies.

6. In times of catastrophe, schools often become a lifeline to the communities they serve.

7. There are six types of school, family, and community involvement: parenting,

communicating, volunteering, learning at home, decision making, and collaborating with the community.

8. Principals must first be committed to involving families and parents; but principals must also motivate and encourage teachers to be committed to involving families and parents and to use as many ways as possible to involve the parents.

9. Community and public relations begin at home and work from the inside out; therefore, it is extremely important for the principal to identify and communicate effectively with his or her internal and external publics.

Internal publics refer to those groups of people directly associated with the campus or the school district, such as administrators, teachers, students, support staff, or the school board. External publics refer to those people who are outside of the campus or district or who have an indirect relationship with the campus or district, such groups as parents, community organizations, churches, government, businesses, or senior citizens.

10. If a crisis occurs on the campus, news reporters usually want to know who, what, when, where, why, and how.

11. School public relations is a planned and systematic management function performed by the principal and designed to help improve school programs and services.

12. Exemplary public relations programs follow this basic four-step process: research, action plan, communicate, and evaluate.

Field-Based Activities

1. Interview your principal and determine how he or she incorporates a coordinated services model. If your principal does not use such a model, determine with him or her how to develop one for the campus.

2. Develop a family involvement plan for the campus. Include on your team other teachers and parents.

3. Develop a four-step public relations plan for your school. What steps will you take in its development? Work with your principal or assistant principal in developing this plan.

Suggested Readings

Bagin, D., & Gallagher, D. R. (2001). *The school and community relations* (7th ed.). Boston: Allyn & Bacon. This book enables school officials to communicate effectively with their staff and the community to improve school

quality and student learning. The authors continue to teach, research, and work extensively with school administrators. In this book the authors explain not only "why" but "how" to communicate to create a supportive environment in which students learn better. Focusing on every audience a school administrator will encounter, this book offers sound advice that is field tested and successful.

Epstein, J. L., Sanders, M. G., Simon, B. S., Salinas, K. C., Jansorn, N. R., & VanVoorhis, F. L. (2002). *School, family, and community partnerships: Your handbook for action* (2nd ed.). Thousand Oaks, CA: Corwin. Focus on improving achievement, aligning teaching and learning with student performance, creating secure facilities, and forging links with the community with this excellent resource.

Epstein, J. L. (2001). *School, family, and community partnerships: Preparing educators and improving schools.* Boulder, CO: Westview Press. In this comprehensive book, the author explains the theory, practice, and benefits of school and family partnerships, incorporating ideas and lesson plans that teachers and school officials may use to involve parents in their children's education. This book is a valuable research tool, college text, and professional handbook. In *School, Family, and Community Partnerships*, the author offers educators a framework for thinking about, talking about, and then actually building comprehensive programs for school and family partnerships. Epstein helps principals understand the theory of overlapping influences of family and school organizations that support children as students. She reviews the research on the implementation and effects of partnerships, and she offers a framework of six types of involvement for creating partnerships.

Fiore, D. (2002). *School community relations.* Fitchburg, MA: Eye on Education. It has been shown that our country's most successful school administrators place a high priority on effectively communicating with and involving the public. In this book, the author provides school leaders and other educators with background knowledge about school-community relations and describes practical techniques for improving principals' ability to understand and communicate with the many publics they serve. This book includes case studies.

Hughes, L., & Hooper, D. W. (1999). *Public relations for school leaders.* New York: Allyn & Bacon. This book provides both a conceptual and a research base in public relations for school leaders, and it demonstrates how these concepts can be practically implemented and put to good use in the schools. The authors include reality-based case studies that conclude most chapters and are based on actual experiences.

Kowalski, T. J. (2003). *Public relations in schools* (3rd ed.). Upper Saddle River, NJ: Prentice Hall. In this interesting and thoughtful book, the author explains and evaluates schools in relation to modern technology, prevailing social conditions, and political demands, treating public

relations as an integral part of school administration. Through real-life case studies and the most current thinking in this field, Kowalski provides readers with the issues and challenges at work in the educational sector today. Individual chapters convey the roles of public relations in the educational arena. Topics covered in the readings provided include contemporary conditions, public relations in districts and schools, and administrator responsibilities.

Stirling, D., McKay, L., Archibald, G., & Berg, S. (2000). *Character education connections: For school, home, and community.* National Professional Resources. The authors of this book offer clear, practical, holistic, and brilliant advice for teachers, administrators, parents, and anyone who wants to raise emotionally healthy, civic-minded children. It is a useful and inspiring guide that can be used at any grade level from K through 12. The authors include ideas, lessons, courses, activities, and approaches that have been proven in the field.

Building Bridges Again

Setting: The school board members for Eisenhower School District are about ready to start their regular monthly meeting. Dr. Petrovsky, superintendent of schools, is concerned because attendance of parents and community members is much higher than it has been in the past. Tension seems to be building during the opening moments of the school board meeting. A large group of parents is clustered along the wall and back section of the room. Teachers, too, are present in large numbers. All levels of the school district are represented.

Scenario: Dr. Petrovsky, superintendent, and the board members are sitting at the front table viewing the audience. Dr. Petrovsky sees that his assistant superintendent for curriculum and instruction, Mr. Davis, is present and sitting with a group of the principals. The superintendent remembers that it was the assistant superintendent who first received a number of complaints from parents about the gifted and talented (G/T) program. In response to the calls, Mr. Davis completed some research on his own and then started the task force to review new options. Later, Dr. Ted Caruthers, principal of Muskie Junior High, was elected chair of the G/T task force. Dr. Caruthers had expressed a desire for several changes in the G/T program. From his perspective as principal, he did not think that the district identified G/T students well. Dr. Petrovsky was anxious for the report to be made. He thought once the report was understood, the opportunity for conflict in the community and conflict on his board would be reduced.

Before discussing any item on the agenda, board policy allows public input. If several parties wish to speak, each can speak for only three minutes. Dr. Petrovsky wonders what speeches may be given tonight. He knows that two representatives from the parents and one representative from the teachers are signed up to speak. He does not have long to wait; Mr. Bounds, an African American parent, steps up to the microphone. Mr. Bounds shakes his fist and claims that once again most of the minority students are quite likely not going to receive the education promised by the district.

"You say you have a vision of *Quality for All.* I say you have a vision of quality for the nonminorities. Look at the gifted and talented program. How many African Americans are being identified and served? Very few. How many Hispanic students are being served? Even fewer. Just how do you justify that, when minorities form over one-third of the student population? We know that a large percentage of the dropouts from the secondary levels are minority students. I wonder how many of these are G/T students who have been denied access to the program for the elite. Maybe that's why we have such a large number dropping out. Their needs are not being met. Why haven't we had a public forum on this? It seems like all the work of planning for such a program is done in secret. I don't see any minority members on the task force. In fact, I don't see any minority members on the board deciding these issues. How can we get our points made without proper representation?"

A series of rumbles erupt from some of the parents. Dr. Petrovsky can hear some of the comments: "Yeah, tell them!" "You need to know what it's like on the other side!" and "Quality for *all*! Let's have it!"

Ms. Margeson, the parent of a student currently in the G/T program, speaks next. She praises the program highly, saying it has helped her child grow in all ways — intellectually, emotionally, and socially.

The teacher representative, also an African American, speaks last. "I have worked with the gifted and talented program for two years. I believe the program has worked well for most students. However," she says, "I have expressed concerns to my principal, Dr. Caruthers. The needs of some special students should be served by the gifted and talented program. Some of these are minority students." The representative goes on to say she feels confident that the task force that has examined the G/T program will address her concerns and any other concerns, too. Dr. Petrovsky observes that after this teacher representative speaks, the audience seems to settle down somewhat.

Board president, Hank Jones, thanks the speakers for their comments and then opens the meeting for board discussion of the agenda item titled "Task Force Report on the Gifted and Talented Program."

Dr. Petrovsky says, "The charge of this task force was to research the current G/T program, determine strengths and weaknesses, and come back to the school board with definite recommendations so that all children will be better served.

Now we shall see what the recommendations are. Dr. Caruthers, principal of the junior high, serves as chair. I would like to call on Dr. Caruthers to give the report from the task force."

Dr. Caruthers steps up to the microphone and begins by saying, "I appreciate the comments by all parties tonight. It is true that our task force had no minorities serving on it. However, I would like it noted that I wrote articles in the local newspaper and in the district newsletters seeking volunteers from the community to serve. The people you see here tonight responded. Our recommendations are too detailed to read. I will present the report in broad strokes and address any questions board members may have." As Dr. Caruthers goes on to explain, the task force has agreed on the following points:

1. New identification and selection procedures must be put in place. This means that the school board must adopt a new definition of gifted and talented. Details are in the board packet.

2. As a result of the new definition, we expect fewer students to be labeled G/T. Those identified will receive a truly differentiated program. Alternatives are presented in the board packet.

3. All teachers will become proficient in teaching strategies commonly used in a G/T program. Such strategies are to be used in teaching all students. Thus, we expect all students to have improved learning experiences.

4. Community members, parents, and businesses are encouraged to become actively involved with the G/T program.

Mr. Rogers, one of the board members, asks the first question: "Dr. Caruthers, do you think these recommendations will fully address the community concerns that you have heard expressed tonight?"

"I think it is a start, Mr. Rogers," Dr. Caruthers says. "In my opinion, we may need a team to follow up on our recommendations to finalize the design and implementation of the G/T program."

After Dr. Caruthers answers a few questions from other board members, Mr. Rogers asks a question that sets off another stir in the audience. "If you will have fewer G/T students, how do you plan to increase the number of minorities being served?"

Dr. Caruthers does his best to answer the question without getting caught up in too many details. However, tension begins to build again in the boardroom.

After the board votes to approve the task force recommendations, Dr. Petrovsky suggests two actions: (a) a public forum to answer all questions about the proposal just approved, and (b) a new task force to follow up on the final design and implementation of the program. He directs Dr. Caruthers to plan and schedule the public forum, and he charges Mr. Davis with the follow-up in design and implementation. Dr. Petrovsky concludes by saying that he hopes these efforts will bring a deeper understanding of the gifted and talented and of the school district's efforts to meet all students' needs.

After action on this agenda item, the remainder of the meeting proceeds smoothly. Many teachers and parents depart early. At the conclusion of the meeting, Dr. Caruthers finds Mr. Bounds and asks him to meet with him the next day. "Perhaps I can address some of your concerns directly, Mr. Bounds. Maybe we can help each other by building bridges to everyone in the community."

Questions

1. As principal of a campus where some concerns had been raised about the G/T program by an African American teacher, and later as chair of the task force, how could Dr. Caruthers have prevented the ill will voiced at the start of the meeting?

2. What strategies might have been employed by the superintendent to help the situation?

3. How could parent involvement in and with the schools improve a program such as this?

4. If you were Dr. Caruthers, how would you plan this public forum?

5. What is the principal's role in public relations when concerns about this and other programs are raised?

15. The Principal and Ethics

> **Standard 5.0:** *Candidates who complete the program are educational leaders who have the knowledge and ability to promote the success of all students by acting with integrity, fairness, and in an ethical manner.*

FOCUSING QUESTIONS

1 How is the ethical principal defined?

2 What are the philosophical concepts of ethics that the principal must consider on the job?

3 How does the principal promote ethical behavior in schools?

4 What are some examples of national and state codes of ethics for principals?

In this chapter, we respond to these questions concerning the principal and ethics. We begin the chapter with a discussion of several general definitions of the ethical principal. Then we examine several philosophical concepts of ethics that principals must consider on the job. This is followed by a discussion of how the principal promotes ethical behavior of all stakeholders in the school. Finally, we conclude the chapter with an examination of some examples of national and state codes of ethics for principals.

The unparalleled events at the turn of the 21st century cry out for ethical leaders worldwide. Some of those events have revealed leadership full of hate that has annihilated thousands with no remorse, leadership full of greed that has wrecked families with no guilt, leadership full of infidelity that has undermined the public's faith with no shame, and leadership full of desire for power that has stirred fear among innocents with no retraction.

When this type of leadership is witnessed 24/7 on the television, what greater calling is there for a school principal than to step forward and lead future generations to a better life, a better world? Starratt (1994) reminded principals of the importance for their leadership to demonstrate ethical behavior as a life's work in progress and action when he said, "Ethical education is a lifelong education" (p. 135). Society today is screaming for leaders who demonstrate integrity; who model ethical, moral, and caring behavior; and who can help others along their own life's journey. Although the cry is for ethical leadership, there is a paucity of research regarding whether principals, in particular, exhibit such ethical behavior (Craig, 1999; Michel, 1995).

The Ethical Principal

How is an ethical principal defined? The ethical principal is one who, in the face of adversity, ambiguity, and challenge, reflects on what is right by some set standard or code and acts in a rational and caring manner to resolve problems and conduct business. An ethical principal must know her own values and goals and how those are aligned with the campus and district's vision, mission, and goals. Additionally, an ethical principal will have already asked himself, "What is important? What is the purpose of my being here? What do I stand for?" The answers from the principal during a challenging situation, and during these uncertain times in our world, can help in providing stability to students and their parents, teachers, and the community.

The ethical principal acts in genuine ways and is not ostentatious. The ethical principal has to "face into the wind" as decisions are made, and she must be able to stand firm during such confrontations while remaining true to her moral compass. Marshall (1992) determined that what controls the moral compass in the face of ethical dilemmas are the moral principles instilled by the principal's church and family; she found principals were not guided by school policies or professional codes. Marshall indicated that principals must be trained in ethics in order to confront the issues of poverty, racism, sexism, and inequities. Hall (1986), who studied values development for over 20 years, indicated that skills development is necessary but not sufficient for ethical growth. Hall was not saying that skill development was not necessary; rather, he was also indicating that practice was needed for growth to occur (Craig, 1995).

Kidder (1995) instructed that "ethics defines the way we participate in the community around us. Yet it's also a deeply personal construct, developing powerful standards and practices in each of us" (p. 219). McKerrow (1997) extended Kidder's comments and wrote, "How one thinks and what one believes about leadership are translated into institutional values and practices" (p. 214).

Czaja and Lowe (2000) stated:

> If educational leaders cannot lead by example and do not know how to practice ethics, there is great cause for the "doom and gloom" mentality that has been evidenced in much of the press about public schools and the leadership. On the other hand, even the light from a small candle can banish the darkness. Preparing ethical leaders will do much the same. (p. 11)

Ethical principals must be able to motivate followers to use many of their innate talents in pursuing the school goals and mission. Principals as "moral leaders train, educate, and coach followers, provide motivation, involve them in appropriate networks, and then free them from situational constraints that may hamper their growth or transformation toward full effectiveness. They endow followers with the capacity to lead themselves in accomplishing the organization's ends" (Fairholm, 2000, p. 52). Rebore (2000) captured the essence of the ethical principal by stating, "the ethical administrator is a person who makes decisions with the dignity of each person in mind, who empowers others, who has a sense of solidarity with at-risk students, who promotes equality in all aspects of education, and who is a responsible steward of school-districts assets" (p. 275).

Principals and Philosophical Concepts of Ethics

According to Beckner (2004, pp. 25–40), ethical principals must be concerned with the following six philosophical concepts: (1) rights, (2) freedom, (3) responsibility, (4) duty, (5) justice, and (6) equity. Kimbrough (1995) listed several other practical concepts related to ethics for principals: (a) authority, (b) caring, (c) character, (d) commitment, (e) conflict of interest, (f) formality, (g) loyalty, and (h) prudence. Shapiro and Stefkovich (2001) noted four paradigms: (1) justice, (2) critique, (3) care, and (4) the profession.

We add a moral imperative to these lists. All of these principles, concepts, or paradigms reflect personal character traits, behaviors, and incidences involving ethical decision making. Shapiro and Stefkovich (2001) suggested that principals can become more aware of their own perspectives, and with such principles or paradigms they can be better equipped to solve the daily, complex dilemmas they encounter on their campuses.

Rights

Ethical principals have a responsibility to respect the rights of others, as moral decision makers and as role models. But disagreement occurs about what rights should apply in a given situation or what constitutes violation of another person's rights. Those are rights

> which God and nature have established, and are therefore called natural rights, such as are life, and liberty, need not the bid of human laws to be more effectual than they are . . . no human legislature has power to abridge or destroy them, unless their owner shall himself commit some act that amounts to forfeiture. (Blackstone, 1941, p. 21)

Absolute rights of individuals have withstood the test of time; and rights related to principals would include those indicated by Blackstone (1941) of personal security, personal liberty, and private property. The principal is responsible to all individuals on the campus to ensure the right of personal security. An example of personal security responsibility was published in September 2004 in the report, *Preparedness in America's Schools: A Comprehensive Look at Terrorism Preparedness in America's Twenty Largest School Districts*. In that report, Phinney (2004) equated principals as public officials who are accountable and responsible for the security of our children. She stated that "in light of the conclusions of the 9/11 Commission, it benefits none of us if we mince words about how the nation's school officials are fulfilling, or not fulfilling, their responsibility to protect our children from another terrorist attack" (p. 4).

Beckner (2004) recognized that absolute rights prevail in all circumstances; however, he indicated that if justified by circumstances, prima facie rights — such as the right to freedom of speech within the classroom or freedom of dress on the campus — may be overridden. Personal liberty is seen as an absolute right; but in the case of schools, it may become a prima facie right because it would be overridden if within the personal liberty there is potential for harm or harassment to others or for endangerment of the equal rights of others. Because "school" is a public property, the personal liberty of individuals is subject to the scrutiny of the law. The function of civil law is to protect the natural liberty of individuals, not to punish them for their sins.

Another right indicated by Beckner (2004) as an essential concern of principals is *negative rights*. This concept extends the right to be left alone, to not be interfered with when one wants to do something (i.e., teachers moonlighting after contract hours). Negative rights also relate to safety issues to which the principal must attend in the school; these issues are within the arenas of counseling, curriculum, and crisis management. For example, Wellman (1999) stated that an example of negative rights would be "one's right not to be killed, which imposes a duty upon others not to kill one" (p. 24).

Beckner (2004) related that *positive rights* require others to assist in their exercise, usually through some governmental entity (i.e., equal opportunity through affirmative action). These rights operate in a positive sense, in that they declare the right of an individual to have something (e.g., a humane standard of living; the right to an appropriate education). "In order to protect positive rights, the state must do or give something to improve the individual's life" (Devine & Hansen, 1999, p. 67); therefore, it is the principal's ethical duty to ensure that each child is educated in the best possible way.

Another set of rights that Beckner (2004) included were *human rights,* which are obtained because one is human. Negative human rights are life, physical property, due process, privacy, autonomy, freedom of thought and expression;

positive human rights include food, adequate housing, competent medical care, employment at a living wage, and education. Finally, Beckner reported that "particular rights" are dependent upon specific circumstances; for example, a person who is promised a specific thing has the right to receive it. If a child who has a learning deficit that must be addressed by a variety of instructional techniques is promised an education — meaning, in the basic sense, the ability to read, write, and do arithmetic — then the principal could be called into question regarding her responsibility and ethical obligation to protect and ensure the child's particular rights if the child cannot function at a basic level of education.

Freedom

Beckner (2004) suggested that the concept of freedom is related closely to that of rights, and it is aligned in Americans' minds with the notions of liberty, independence, and individuality. The *Washington Times* recently published an article that is related to freedom and how principals must engage in ensuring the freedom of all students. The article described the Civic Mission of Schools, a study from the Carnegie Corporation of New York and the University of Maryland's Center for Information and Research on Civic Learning and Engagement, which revealed that most formal civic education today comprises only a single course on government, with little emphasis on the rights and responsibilities of citizens and ways that they could work together and relate to government. However, the report cited research that children start to develop social responsibility and interest in politics before the age of nine.

These are critical teaching and learning principles for school principals to consider when dialoguing with their teachers. For example, the same *Washington Times* article reported increased class discussions and debates in some schools on the justification for forcibly disarming Saddam Hussein. Some principals have had to warn teachers to ensure that all sides are given equal opportunity to be heard.

Despite the fact that freedom of speech in class debates has to be pointed out to teachers, the newspaper reported, the teaching of our constitutional history has been sorely lacking. The newspaper reported that Charles Haynes, a senior scholar at the Freedom Forum First Amendment Center, said that this generation has been called upon to defend freedom at home and around the world. Our task is to ensure that they understand what they are defending and why ("Bringing the Constitution to Life," 2003, p. A23). Infusing an understanding of various freedoms into the curriculum and establishing such an understanding with the teachers and students are the ethical responsibility of the principal.

Responsibility and Authority

Rights and freedom carry with them responsibility. There is responsibility for the consequences of actions that may result from exercising various rights and freedoms. One major freedom enjoyed by all U.S. citizens is the freedom of speech. In relation to that freedom, the principal must consider consequences involving this right. Consequently, the principal's role in freedom of speech issues is one that has been scrutinized, such as in the following cases. Sybouts and Wendel (1994) stated that principals are often viewed as public figures and as such both enjoy and suffer from their status. They reported that the Georgia Supreme Court determined that high school principals were not public officials and as such did not need to prove malice on the part of a defendant in a libel suit. In Maryland and Mississippi, principals are held to be public officials, whereas the law in Illinois grants principals the same protections that private citizens enjoy. In general, principals do not stand in a confidential relationship with others, as do a husband and wife or attorney and client. Thus principals have the responsibility to limit their negative comments about students and staff members to those they have personally observed. Also, principals should report any statements that are possibly defamatory only to those who have a need to know (Sybouts & Wendel, p. 75).

Kimbrough (1985) stated that responsibility has two dimensions: (1) objective responsibility and (2) subjective responsibility. Cooper (1982) defined *objective responsibility* as the obligation to someone else for a particular standard or category of performance, and he contrasted objective and *subjective responsibility* as follows:

> Objective responsibility arises from legal, organizational, and societal demands upon our role as public administrator, but subjective responsibility is rooted in experience like loyalty, conscience, and identification. We feel inclined, or even compelled, to act in a particular way, not because we are required to do so by a supervisor or the law but because of an inner drive. (p. 51)

Related to responsibility is authority. Kimbrough (1995) defined *authority* as the power to influence the behavior of others. He said that excess in the arbitrary use of authority and the failure to exercise authority effectively both represent failure to meet acceptable ethical standards.

Duty

According to Beckner (2004), sometimes duty and responsibility are thought of as synonymous; however, duty tends to regard demands that override other values. The principal must perform duties that come with rules and regulations. Some of the prima facie duties are (a) fidelity, (b) reparation, (c) gratitude, (d) justice, (e) beneficence, (f) self-improvement, and (g) non-maleficence. Other duties that may take precedence in the school arena over the prima facie duties are (a) duty to students, (b) duty to colleagues, (c) duty to discipline, (d) duty to the school team, (e) duty to the profession, (f) duty to funding sources, (g) duty to parents, and (h) duty to community.

Justice

There are concerns for principals in dealing with justice — one concern is the equal treatment of non-equals or the unequal treatment of equals. Shapiro and Stefkovich (2001) indicated that the ethic of justice "focuses on rights and law and is part of a liberal democratic tradition" (p. 11). Many have defined justice; but more recently, Beckner (2004) defined justice using the term *fairness*, which implies that individuals could be just and fair if they would see clearly and think rationally and act in an uninterested and benevolent manner. Beckner shared from the literature five types of justice: (1) procedural justice — treatment people should receive in connection with the application of rules; (2) substantive justice — examines the "rightness" of rules and procedures and protects ownership of property, compensation for work, freedom, privacy, bodily safety, truth telling, citizenship, and copyright; (3) retributive justice — involves punishment for wrongdoing; (4) remedial justice or compensatory justice — involves wrongdoing in relation to the victim, not the perpetrator, and involves making amends; and (5) distributive justice — does not necessarily deal with a wrongdoing, but relates to benefits and burdens shared equally among people.

Equity

The words *justice* and *equity* are sometimes used interchangeably. *Equity* refers to the bending of rules to fit a situation. This implies treating equals equally and non-equals unequally to level the playing fields, but not to the point of being unfair. Beckner (2004) provided an excellent example: Applying the same standardized test score requirements for admission to a university or consideration for scholarships may be unfair to one whose native language is not English or to one whose cultural background is different from that on which the test is based. To do so may also create inaccurate results (prediction of academic success). Therefore, certain individuals would not have an equal opportunity to succeed in life. Recently, a large university changed its rules of providing extra points on its admissions criteria to those whose parents attended the university. This may not have been a popular decision to former students, but it was a decision in favor of justice and equity.

Over a decade ago, Murphy (1993) spoke of a renewed interest in the need to prepare educational leaders to deal with equity issues due to the substantial demographic changes occurring in the United States. At about the same time, Beck and Murphy (1994) stated:

> As educators seek — at times frantically — to identify their role in the reconstruction of society, and, at the same time, to discover functional ways to deal with rapidly changing populations of students, they find themselves confronted with fundamental questions about equity, freedom, character, justice, and the like. (pp. 45, 46)

Caring

Noddings (1994) noted that "an ethic of care starts with a study of relation. It is fundamentally concerned with how human beings meet and treat one another" (p. 45). A caring principal develops meaningful relationships while inspiring others to excellence. Being thoughtful and sensitive, such principals recognize diversity and individualism in people. Whereas bureaucrats emphasize compliance with rules and regulations, caring principals above all else are uncritical, collegial, and supportive. They put people first and policy second (Glanz, 1998, p. 34). Kimbrough (1995) suggested that caring includes such actions as commitment, patience, knowledge of the needs and wants of others, tolerance, trust, hope, courage, and the ability to listen. He said that a caring school is where everyone counts, where all are heard, and where the principal works to ensure the personal growth and development of all.

Character, Commitment, and Formality

According to Palmour (1986), Aristotle defined *good character* as the life of right conduct — right conduct in relation to other persons and in relation to one's self. Character is closely associated with caring; if a principal is perceived to have a good character, then he has exhibited behavior such as honesty, courage, dependability, generos-

ity, and acceptable motivations. The principal should be of honorable repute in the eyes of the teachers and community (Kimbrough, 1995).

Commitment is related to character in that the principal must be committed to doing the right thing. Commitment is related to dependability. For example, if the principal is constantly late to meetings with the teachers, who always arrive on time, then her commitment as well as her dependability come into question. The teachers begin to question the principal's ethics. If the principal is not faithful or committed in little, then teachers begin to question her commitment in much.

Formality relates to commitment and, according to Kimbrough (1995), refers to being in compliance with accepted norms of behavior and ceremonies. Formality includes keeping personal appointments, promptness, courtesy, language, manners, and attention to individuals or ceremonies. Public display of professional, ethical behavior is at the center of formality.

Conflict of Interest

A conflict of interests is a situation in which the principal would have a competing professional or personal interest that would make it difficult to fulfill his duties fairly. In cases of a conflict of interest, the principal should recuse himself from the matter — not take part in, or influence in any way, the process. For example, if the principal's wife is hired and the principal is the evaluator who may or may not recommend her for a merit raise or job security, then the principal should recuse himself to avoid a conflict of interest.

At times, principals may be involved in situations with companies or private interests that promote student learning. An example situation occurs with the Channel One news program for teenagers, as described by Stark (2001). Stark stated that principals who engage in Channel One, which advertises commercial products, have put themselves into a kind of conflict of interest. Considering that principals and teachers are public officials, it stands to reason that teachers should make their official decisions — including those about allocating curricular time and classroom space — on their merits, according to the public interest, and not based on the school's need for private support. The Channel One example is not the most serious kind of conflict of interest. That would be the case when an official has the capacity to use her public role to benefit a private company in return for a personal payment. Instead, the Channel One arrangement resembles the milder form of conflict (but one still statutorily regulated at the federal level) in which officials take something of value from a private company not for themselves personally, but to help serve the purposes of their cash-strapped public school (Stark, 2001, p. 59).

The following are the most common forms of conflicts of interests:

1. Self-dealing, in which public and private interests collide; for example, issues involving family or privately held business interests

2. Outside employment, in which the interests of one job contradicts another

3. Accepting of benefits, including bribes and other gifts accepted to curry favor

4. Influence peddling — using one's position to influence other realms

5. Use of government, corporate, or legal property for personal reasons

6. Unauthorized distribution of confidential information

There are two kinds of conflicts of interests. In a *real conflict,* which is the type mentioned earlier, the competing interests are exploited for personal gain. In an *apparent conflict,* the parties involved acknowledge the conflict of interests and deal with it accordingly ("Conflict of Interest," 2004).

Loyalty

Loyalty generally refers to faithfulness, devotion, and allegiance to a leader, person, group, ideal, cause, or duty. A supervisor may ask the school principal to do something that the principal believes to be unethical. For example, the principal may be asked to place the superintendent's son in the gifted education program when in fact the child does not meet the criteria for placement. Of course, blind loyalty is extreme and produces negative results leading to unethical behavior. Principals who have blind loyalty may be viewed as "yes people."

Loyalty runs in both directions — to the supervisors as well as the supervised. Loyalty is developed and earned over time (Kimbrough, 1995). Is whistle-blowing an act of disloyalty? Kimbrough (1995) suggested that whether a whistle-blower acts from personal interest or from moral conscience, the principal must see that justice is done and consider the reported wrong, regardless of the source. Loyalty also implies openness and the feeling that one can share with the principal any serious violations that are observed.

Prudence

Prudence refers to the exercise of good judgment, common sense, and even caution, especially in the conduct of practical matters. Principals must remember that their actions have influence on people (Kimbrough, 1995). Prudence implies consequential thinking by the principal. If the principal does not think with prudence or consequentially, then the result may be harmful to the students and teachers. For example, during the budgeting process a principal may ask the superintendent for only one additional faculty member when, in fact, three faculty members are needed to handle the foreseen increase in students. If the principal is thus granted one faculty member, the principal will have to hire uncertified long-term substitutes to cover two classrooms. This outcome is ultimately injurious not only to student learning but also to continuous school improvement, due to the lack of permanent faculty members to plan and develop programs and carry out the mission and goals of the school.

Critique

According to Shapiro and Stefkovich (2001), "the ethic of critique is based on critical theory, which has, at its heart, an analysis of social class and its inequities," and it is "linked to critical pedagogy" (p. 14). They further claimed that critique is

> aimed at awakening educators to inequities in society and, in particular, in the schools. This ethic asks educators to deal with the hard questions regarding social class, race, gender, and other areas of difference, such as: Who makes the laws? Who benefits from the law, rule, or policy? Who has the power? Who are the silenced voices? This approach to ethical dilemmas then asks educators to go beyond questioning and critical analysis to examine and grapple with those possibilities that could enable all children, whatever their social class, race, or gender to have opportunities to grow, learn, and achieve. Such a process should lead to the development of options related to important concepts such as oppression, power, privilege, authority, voice, language, and empowerment. (Shapiro & Stefkovich, 2001, p. 15)

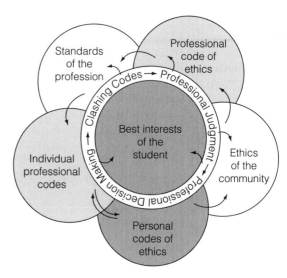

Figure 15.1

Shapiro and Stefkovich's Model of the Ethic of the Profession
Source: Adapted from *Ethical Leadership and Decision Making in Education: Applying Theoretical Perspectives to Complex Issues* (p. 23), by J. P. Shapiro & J. A. Stefkovich, 2001, Mahwah, NJ: Erlbaum.

Profession

Shapiro and Stefkovich (2001) described a paradigm for the profession. The ethic of their profession requires that principals develop and examine their own professional codes of ethics, which consider their own "individual personal codes of ethics, as well as standards set forth by the profession, and then calls on them to place students at the center of the ethical decision-making process" (p. 23). The authors stated that the ethic of the profession is "dynamic — not static — and multidimensional, recognizing the complexities of being an educational leader in today's society" (p. 23). In their model (Figure 15.1) for the ethic of the profession, Shapiro and Stefkovich (2001) demonstrate that all factors converge to create the professional paradigm. The circles depict (a) standards of the profession, (b) professional code of ethics, (c) ethics of the community, (d) personal codes of ethics, (e) individual professional codes, and (f) best interests of the student. The figure also

demonstrates that the ethic is affected by other factors, like clashing codes, professional judgment, and professional decision making. The authors' ethic of the profession raises questions to the principal posed by the other ethical paradigms or principles, but the principal must move further and "ask what the profession would expect and what is in the best interests of the students taking into account the fact that they may represent highly diverse populations" (Shapiro & Stefkovich, 2001, p. 25).

Moral Imperative

The moral imperative is an outward demonstration of morality that includes making hard choices when public opinion may be opposite, disturbing the status quo, and self-discipline. The worse situations become in schools, the greater the need for principals to exhibit this moral imperative. Moral leadership is not only about ethical decision making; it is about elements of the moral leadership process that are not directly covered in decision making (Covrig, 2000). The moral decision making and actions of a principal are strongly influenced by her values (Begley & Johanson, 1998; Irby, Brown, Duffy, & Trautman, 2002; Willower & Licata, 1997).

Sergiovanni (1992) also noted the influence of values, by including more characteristics of moral leadership that are akin to the spirit. He indicated that principals must appeal to their followers' sense of righteousness, obligation, and goodness as motivations for action and work. Additionally, principals must possess a personal sense of righteousness, obligation, and goodness. If the principal does not demonstrate these qualities, the question is, how could his followers be motivated to follow a moral path? Therefore, Sergiovanni said that the principal must have a moral position—a moral imperative.

Principals and Ethical Behavior in Schools

In the following section we outline some of the most controversial ethical components principals have to confront in schools. We also describe some specific school situations in which principals model and promote ethical behavior.

Principals Promoting Ethical Behavior in Athletic Programs

Conn and Gerdes (1998) stated that "the ethical standards or principles are immutable, regardless of the environment or circumstance in which they are implemented. As such, ethical decisions shape the nature of the sport experience for all participants, to include administrators, coaches, athletes, and parents" (p. 121). The community looks to high school and junior high school principals to monitor the ethical behavior of the coaches and players on their campuses. Principals as well as assistant principals pull duty for the games, where they monitor ethical behavior not only in the game but also on the sidelines and in the stands from the fans.

Why do campus principals need to monitor ethical behavior in athletics? According to Conn and Foshee (1993), there are coaches who (a) have students playing who are not eligible, (b) conduct out-of-season practices, (c) illegally recruit out-of-district players, (d) play injured players in order to win "championships," (e) leave players stranded on buses in a desert, (f) molest players, and (g) improperly desensitize (moderating the intense emotions and actions of competition) athletes post-contest and then resocialize them back into the mainstream.

Several ethics principles are undeniably linked to numerous core values upon which sports were founded several thousand years ago. Such principles are connected to character development or sportsmanship and not so much to the number of wins. Specific principles identified and linked to modern sports are that (a) athletes must always be considered ends and not means (Merriman & Hill, 1992); (b) the competition must be fair (Jones, Wells, Peters, & Johnson, 1988); (c) participation, leadership, resources, and rewards must be based on achievement rather than ascribed characteristics (Coakley, 1994); and (d) the activity must provide for the relative safety of the participants (Conn, 1997). Each principle sustains the inherent and traditional values of sport, reinforcing the "goodness" of the sports experience for players and coaches alike.

The National Federation of State High School Associations (2003) posts on its Web site an established code of ethics that is a valuable tool for principals and coaches. This code of ethics establishes mutually beneficial systems of conduct among members of the sport community such as coaches, players, spectators (fans), and vendors. Moreover, the code of ethics provides a publicly acceptable justification for actions and policies and serves as a benchmark for principals in assessing the actions and decision-making behavior of the coaches. The National Federation's code is based on the following statement: Each student-athlete should be treated as though he or she were the coaches' own, and his or her welfare should be uppermost at all times.

The principal can influence the coach; and discussing the principles of the code is as critical as observing what is happening in the coach's classroom. As the code indicates, the coach has a tremendous influence, for either good or ill, on the student-athletes' education and thus must never value winning above instilling the highest ideals of character. Coaches have great influence not only on athletes but on the entire student body. In all personal contact with student-athletes, officials, athletic directors, school administrators, the state high school athletic association, the media, and the public, the coach must strive to set an example of the highest ethical and moral conduct (National Federation of State High School Associations, 2003).

Principals Promoting Ethical Behavior Through Character Education

Principals have encouraged character education for three reasons. According to Lickona (1996), good character helps people become fully human and more capable of work and love by building strength of mind, heart, and will. Next, schools are better places "when they are civil and caring human communities that promulgate, teach, celebrate and hold students and staff accountable to the values on which good character is based" (p. 93). Finally, teaching character education is essential to the task of building a moral society. According to McBrien and Brandt (1997),

> character education involves teaching children about basic human values including honesty, kindness, generosity, courage, freedom, equality, and respect. The goal is to raise children to become morally responsible, self-disciplined citizens. Problem solving, decision making, and conflict resolution are important parts of developing moral character. Through role playing and discussions, students can see that their decisions affect other people and things. (pp. 17–18)

Principals can promote such activities within the curriculum that could enhance ethical behavior among teachers, staff, and students. Principals who facilitate parents, students, and community organizations make character education an integral part of the education process and teach students methods of critical reflection about situations and other moral dilemmas.

It is important to recognize that over the past two decades, character education has undergone some criticism. For example, Kohn (1997) stated, "What goes by the name of character education nowadays is, for the most part, a collection of exhortations and extrinsic inducements designed to make children work harder and do what they're told" (p. 429). Furthermore, Lockwood (1993) advised that "any program that intends to promote good behavior by teaching values rests on a shaky foundation" (p. 73). As for Kohn's attack on character education, Lickona (1997) indicated that it was not complex enough to be justified to guide the field, because it did not thoroughly discuss theories and accurately describe character education in schools.

On the other hand, character education is still promoted through national and state initiatives. Rod Paige, Secretary of Education, 2000–2004, said, "We have invested nearly $24 million in character education in FY 2003 because we believe that building strong character is as essential as reading, math and science" (Character Education Grants Awarded, 2003). The Partnerships in Character Education Program awards grants to eligible organizations to design and implement character education programs in areas such as citizenship, justice, respect, and responsibility for grades K–12. Grant recipients must show how they have integrated character education into classroom instruction and teacher training; and that they have involved parents, students, and the community in the process. Since 1995, a total of 93 state and local education agencies have received character education grants. Character education is a key feature of *No Child Left Behind*, the landmark education reform law designed to change the culture of America's schools by closing the achievement gap, offering more flexibility, giving parents more options, and teaching students based on what works. Under the act's strong accountability provisions, states must describe how they will close the achievement gap and ensure that all students, including those who are disadvantaged, achieve academic proficiency. In addition, states must produce annual state and school district report cards informing parents and communities about state and school progress. Schools that do not make progress must provide supplemental services, such as free tutoring or after-school assistance; take corrective actions; and, if still not making adequate yearly progress after five years, dramatically change the way their school is run.

As indicated by grants and legislation, in the latter part of the 1990s character education had become a prominent curriculum concern. For example, in 1996, one year after grant funds began to be applied to character education model programs, governors from Colorado, Iowa, Massachusetts, Michigan, New Hampshire, New Mexico, South Dakota, and Utah endorsed the *Character Education Manifesto,* written by Kevin Ryan, Karen E. Bohlin, and Judith O. Thayer. The *Manifesto* was the first document of its kind to define character education and to present to administrators, teachers, and parents seven guiding principles for school reform and to build character education (Center for the Advancement of Ethics and Character, 2003). The *Character Education Manifesto* principles could serve as a guide or map for principals and teachers to develop a campus manifesto on character education.

Principle 1: Education Is an Inescapable Moral Enterprise. Education in its fullest sense is inescapably a moral enterprise—a continuous and conscious effort to guide students to know and pursue what is good and what is worthwhile.

Principle 2: Parents. . . . Parents [are] the primary moral educators of their children and schools should build a partnership with the home. . . . [A]ll schools have the obligation to foster in their students personal and civic virtues such as integrity, courage, responsibility, diligence, service, and respect for the dignity of all persons.

Principle 3: Virtue. Character education is about developing virtues—good habits and dispositions which lead students to responsible and mature adulthood.

Principle 4: Teachers, Principals, Staff. The teacher and the school principal are central to this enterprise and must be educated, selected, and encouraged with this mission in mind. In truth, all of the adults in the school must embody and reflect the moral authority which has been invested in them by the parents and the community.

Principle 5: Community. Character education is not a single course, a quick-fix program, or a slogan posted on the wall; it is an integral part of school life. The school must become a community of virtue in which responsibility, hard work, honesty, and kindness are modeled, taught, expected, celebrated, and continually practiced. From the classroom to the playground, from the cafeteria to the faculty room, the formation of good character must be the central concern.

Principle 6: Curriculum. The human community has a reservoir of moral wisdom, much of which exists in our great stories, works of art, literature, history, and biography. Teachers and students must together draw from this reservoir both within and beyond the academic curriculum.

Principle 7: Students. Finally, young people need to realize that forging their own characters is an essential and demanding life task. And the sum of their school experiences—in successes and failures, academic and athletic, intellectual and social—provides much of the raw material for this personal undertaking.

This work is an example of the kinds of resources available to principals who are seeking to design or select curriculum to implement character education in their schools.

Policies and Procedures That Promote Ethical Behavior in Schools

The school principal is the most important person on the campus to promote and model ethical behavior and to implement policies that support an appropriate standard of conduct. As the principal goes, so goes the school. Principals can promote procedures that seek to enhance student learning by addressing the intellectual, emotional, and physical safety needs of students and staff. Principals can promote campus values in which all students receive a quality education that incorporates the teaching of respect for others and self, integrity, citizenship, and sense of commitment and obligation to the school and community—critical components for developing a safe and productive environment in which all students can learn and for contributing to the vitality of modern society. Principals and teachers should advance curricular activities that provide all students with an understanding of the necessity of ethical and legal conduct and a balancing of individual rights with the common good. It is first necessary for principals to work with teachers to advance moral and ethical leadership on the campus. "To be guides for the young in morality and ethics, teachers must understand the complex moral role that they occupy as ethical professionals and appreciate the significance of their own actions and decisions on the students in their care" (Campbell, 1997). It is important for the principal to ensure that all school personnel, board members, parents, students, and community agencies share a role in creating a safe and nurturing learning environment for all students and in helping to raise a generation of individuals who are respectful and responsible not only to themselves, but to others within their school and community.

Superintendents and School Boards Principals can work with the superintendent and local school board in developing ethical policies and subsequent procedures that assist all teachers and administrators in creating a safe learning environment that addresses every child's needs and embodies the belief that schools are designed to educate all young people. Specifically, principals can promote certain concepts with the superintendent and school board. It is crucial for superintendents and school boards to value the school climate as a critical component of effective learning and to provide resources to establish supportive, healthy school climates. Superintendents and school boards, with the principal, can review all disciplinary policies to ensure that they encourage children to stay in school rather than exclude them from school. Principals must ask superintendents and school boards to provide appropriate resources for a broad array of after-school activities to maximize the number of students involved in constructive,

adult-supervised activities. Superintendents and school boards, along with the principal, must ensure compliance with all health, safety, and equity standards pertaining to the school buildings, outdoor facilities, and curriculum so that every student has the maximum opportunity to learn in a healthy, safe, equitable, and nonhostile school environment.

School Actions Schools can take action to promote and teach ethical behavior and work toward better citizenship and the common good of the society. Some of those activities include engaging students in clubs, leadership activities, service learning, and peer mentoring. Additionally, the campus staff should monitor and supervise all areas of the school (e.g., classrooms, hallways and stairwells, cafeterias, playgrounds, shop areas, lavatories, and locker rooms) to ensure the safety of all students at all times. All members of the school community must identify acts of name-calling, teasing, bullying, exclusion, and harassment and take immediate action, based on a previously developed intervention plan, to intervene in those situations that are detrimental to students and the learning environment.

Other actions that schools can take to support ethical behavior revolve around the components of family involvement, mentors, volunteers, and curriculum. Support families to identify and address their critical role of assisting the school in providing a safe and productive learning environment. Mentors or buddies can be assigned to ensure that all students share a caring relationship with at least one adult in the school, in which regular, ongoing interactions occur. Each adult, including volunteers (this means training of volunteers is necessary), must (a) send a clear and consistent message to students that each has a duty to behave responsibly and respectfully toward others, (b) model the positive behaviors they hope to instill in their students, and (c) consistently enforce rules and provide opportunities to develop and foster ethical reasoning, self-control, and a generalized respect for others. Schools can incorporate the examination of and reflection upon ethical issues into the curriculum; they can teach conflict resolution skills to provide students with the capacity and commitment to solve conflicts in fair, nonviolent ways (an example of this is to train students as conflict managers, so they can assist with conflicts that arise between students during the lunch period).

Parents and Families   Parents and families are a child's first and most important teacher; therefore, family involvement is crucial in developing a child's sense of personal responsibility to others, or ethical behavior. Principals can facilitate parent-family involvement programs that focus on working with families to instill a sense of responsibility and empathy in every student. Concepts taught in involvement programs include (a) modeling and integrating ethical behavior into the everyday lives of the children; (b) providing consistent care and modeling pro-social behaviors; (c) setting strong examples; (d) correcting inappropriate actions (e.g., resolving conflicts peacefully, demonstrating tolerance and respect for individual differences, and encouraging lifelong learning); (e) becoming involved in school, community, and state events; and (f) taking an interest in national and global events.

Curriculum policies are also critical to the principal's ability to promote and ensure ethical behavior and decision making. When these policies are in place, principals have a foundation upon which to defend or enforce, if need be, the curriculum goals related to student respect and responsibility.

Curriculum   Principals must facilitate a curriculum that teaches students to take responsibility for observing state and national laws, campus and district policies and procedures, and school and classroom rules. It is critical to teach students to appreciate differences and to have respect for all other persons. Students, themselves, have a responsibility to contribute to a safe, productive school climate and to serve as positive role models in their school community as well as their local communities.

National and State Codes of Ethics for Principals

As Burns (2001) so aptly stated:

> Ethics are not unique to the profession of education. All professionals, from doctors and lawyers to carpenters to fry-cooks are expected to complete the duties of their jobs ethically. In order to ensure consistency of interpretation and understanding, many professions subscribe to a code of ethics. It is important to understand that a code of ethics in no way insures the ethical aptitude of school leaders. Much like a school vision or mission statement, a code of ethics is merely as strong as the commitment of the schools' leaders. (p. 19)

Walker (1999) indicated that a code of ethics is a simple map for professionals to follow that actually delineates a profession from a job. To truly constitute a profession, some type of effort must exist that seeks to enforce the code.

Arterbury, Crawford, and Moore (2001) reported three distinct reasons for a code of ethics:

1. Codes provide broad general guidelines and principles of conduct. They serve to educate the profession about sound practice and offer guidance. As a result of the code, educators should consider the ethical dimension of their actions and decisions.

2. Codes establish accountability and protect those served by the profession. In our profession this includes all of the stakeholders in public education.

3. Codes develop the aspiration dimension of the profession and serve as a catalyst to improve practice. The aspiration nature of the code means that ethical decision making is a continual process and that there are no pat answers. The professionals must be engaged in continual dialogue about what is ethical practice and informed judgment. (p. 13)

National Ethical Codes

In this section we discuss three national ethical codes. Presented first is the American Association of School Administrators code of ethics; next are the national principal associations, and finally, the general educator body, the National Education Association code of ethics.

American Association of School Administrators

In 1962, the American Association of School Administrators (AASA) created the AASA Code of Ethics to govern actions and behaviors of school administrators. Although AASA is an organization composed primarily of school superintendents, the code was designated for all administrators, from the assistant principal to the superintendent. Of course, in joining AASA or one of its state affiliates, one is expected to uphold the AASA Code of Ethics. The code states:

> Every member of a profession carries a responsibility to act in a manner becoming a professional person. This implies that each school administrator has an inescapable obligation to abide by the ethical standards of his profession. The behavior of each is the concern of all. The conduct of any administrator influences the attitude of the public toward the profession and education in general. (AASA, 1966, p. 16)

This AASA Code of Ethics was revised in 1976 and again in 1981, as follows:

> An educational administrator's professional behavior must conform to an ethical code. The code must be idealistic and at the same time practical so that it can apply reasonably to all educational administrators.
>
> The administrator acknowledges that the schools belong to the public they serve for the purpose of providing educational opportunities to all. However, the administrator assumes responsibility for providing professional leadership in the school and community. The responsibility requires the administrator to maintain standards of exemplary professional conduct. It must be recognized that the administrator's actions will be viewed and appraised by the community, professional associates, and students.
>
> To these ends, the administrator subscribes to the following statements of standards.
>
> The educational administrator:

1. Makes the well-being of students the fundamental value of all decision-making and actions.

2. Fulfills professional responsibilities with honesty and integrity.

3. Supports the principle of due process and protects the civil and human rights of all individuals.

4. Obeys local, state, and national laws and does not knowingly join or support organizations that advocate, directly or indirectly, the overthrow of the government.

5. Implements the governing board of education's policies and administrative rules and regulations.

6. Pursues appropriate measures to correct those laws, policies and regulations that are not consistent with sound educational goals.

7. Avoids using positions for personal gain through political, social, religious, economic or other influences.

8. Accepts academic degrees or professional certification only from duly accredited institutions.

9. Maintains the standards and seeks to improve the effectiveness of the profession through research and continuing professional development.

10. Honors all contracts until fulfillment, release or dissolution mutually agreed upon by all parties to contract. (AASA, 1981)

National Association of Elementary School Principals and National Association of Secondary School Principals

The National Association of Elementary School Principals adopted the same code of ethics as did AASA in 1976. The National Association of Secondary School Principals also adheres to the same code; it was approved in 1973 and revised in 2001. Revisions are slight with the body and meaning of the text remaining the same.

Polnick, Edmonson, and Fisher (2003) suggested a way to use such ethical codes in principal self-assessment and in faculty assessment of the principal. These authors suggested three tools for a principal to use in examining ethical behavior. One instrument, as seen in Figure 15.2, is a survey that examines ethical behaviors as they relate to faculty and staff; students, parents, and community members; communication; and general ethical characteristics. This tool can be used to compare staff perceptions with principal perceptions of which behaviors are valued with respect to ethical behavior.

Portrait of an Ethical Principal	
The following questionnaire is designed to assess faculty and staff perceptions of what behaviors and characteristics best exemplify an **ethical principal**.	
Directions: Please respond by selecting 10 items that most represent your perceptions of what an ethical principal should possess or exhibit.	
I think an ethical principal. . .	Please place a check by only 10 items.
INTERACTIONS WITH FACULTY AND STAFF	
is fair and consistent with his or her interactions with all teachers and staff	
treats all teachers and staff as professionals	
facilitates and offers assistance to others to enhance their knowledge and skills	
develops trust and confidence in teachers and staff	
shows respect for peers	
demonstrates high expectations and standards	
INTERACTIONS WITH STUDENTS, PARENTS, AND COMMUNITY MEMBERS	
is fair and consistent in his or her interactions with all students	
shows respect for students	
keeps students in mind as a priority	
is open to suggestions from everyone	
does not allow political pressure to negatively influence decisions	
is fair and consistent in his or her interactions with all parents and community members	
COMMUNICATION	
listens to others before speaking	
models and displays the characteristics you want to see in others	
does not talk about others or share gossip or use other people's names in discussions with other people	
effectively communicates personal values and beliefs	
effectively communicates values and beliefs of the school	
GENERAL CHARACTERISTICS	
displays confidence	
is open-minded	
is honest	
is knowledgeable	
is trustworthy and reliable	
exhibits professional behavior	

Figure 15.2

Portrait of an Ethical Principal

Source: Adapted from *The Ethical Administrator,* a paper presented by B. Polnick, S. Edmonson, & A. Fisher at the NCPEA Conference within a Conference, American Association of School Administrators, New Orleans, LA, 2003.

Figure 15.3 presents another tool that the principal can use to self-assess his own behaviors. This tool may also be used to build awareness of ethical standards and as a dialogue for discussion about what is ethical behavior by school principals and what is not.

National Education Association   The National Education Association (NEA) adopted its code of ethics in 1975. It mentions duty to the student and duty to the profession, in particular. The NEA Code of Ethics follows:

> The educator, believing in the worth and dignity of each human being, recognizes the supreme importance of the pursuit of truth, devotion to excellence, and the nurture of the democratic principles. Essential to these goals is the protection of freedom to learn and to teach and the guarantee of equal educational opportunity for all. The educator accepts the responsibility to adhere to the highest ethical standards.

NEA's code includes two principles: (1) commitment to the student and (2) commitment to the profession.

State Codes

Next we present three state codes of ethics. The first two codes specify guidelines for principal actions; the third specifies enforceable violations of the ethical code of conduct.

The New York State Code of Ethics for Educators   Although most states have a code of ethics for educators, the code may or may not be used in conjunction with disciplinary action toward educators. The case in New York is that the code cannot be used in any disciplinary action toward an employee. The New York code, adopted in 2002, is as follows:

> The Code of Ethics is a public statement by educators that sets clear expectations and principles to guide practice and inspire professional excellence. Educators believe a commonly held set of principles can assist in the individual exercise of professional judgment. This Code speaks to the core values of the profession. "Educator" as used throughout means all educators serving New York schools in positions requiring a certificate, including classroom teachers, school leaders and pupil personnel service providers. It maintains six principles.
>
> *Principle 1:* Educators nurture the intellectual, physical, emotional, social, and civic potential of each student.
>
> *Principle 2:* Educators create, support, and maintain challenging learning environments for all.
>
> *Principle 3:* Educators commit to their own learning in order to develop their practice.
>
> *Principle 4:* Educators collaborate with colleagues and other professionals in the interest of student learning.
>
> *Principle 5:* Educators collaborate with parents and community, building trust and respecting confidentiality.
>
> *Principle 6:* Educators advance the intellectual and ethical foundation of the learning community.

North Carolina Code of Ethics for Educators   The North Carolina State Board of Education adopted its Code of Ethics for educators in 1997. It has three principles related to responsibilities to the student, the school system, and the profession. The purpose of the North Carolina Code of Ethics is to define standards of professional conduct:

> The responsibility to teach and the freedom to learn, and the guarantee of equal opportunity for all are essential to the achievement of these principles. The professional educator acknowledges the worth and dignity of every person and demonstrates the pursuit of truth and devotion to excellence, acquires knowledge, and nurtures democratic citizenship. The educator exemplifies a commitment to the teaching and learning processes with accountability to the students, maintains professional growth, exercises professional judgment, and personifies integrity. The educator strives to maintain the respect and confidence of colleagues, students, parents and legal guardians, and the community, and to serve as an appropriate role model. To uphold these commitments, the educator must have (a) a commitment to the student, (b) a commitment to the School and School System, and (c) a commitment to the profession.

Self-Check for Ethical Behavior		
The purpose of this inventory is for the principal to self-assess his or her own ethical behavior.		
Have you ever. . .	**YES**	**NO**
1. given your son or daughter supplies bought with school funds?		
2. excluded a student from participating in a program because of their sex?		
3. refused to appoint someone for an honor because they filed a complaint against you?		
4. accepted the contract for a new assessment item bank from a friend who represents a new software company?		
5. created a special assignment for a young male teacher in the summer because he needed the money for his family?		
6. knowingly let your church group use the baseball equipment one Saturday without following the district policy and procedures?		
7. recorded that a student who dropped out of school was being homeschooled when you had no official documentation that this was true?		
8. overestimated the amount you should receive for reimbursement or expenses (because you were not reimbursed for a lost receipt last month)?		
9. offered a position to a friend even though you knew he or she wasn't as qualified as another candidate?		
10. knowingly run a red light on a deserted highway?		
11. not selected a person for an opportunity or a position because he or she was grossly overweight?		
12. misrepresented the facts regarding a student?		
13. won a $570.00 deer rifle from a Rotary Club raffle ($5.00 ticket) and did not report it to the IRS?		
14. knowingly given a student (with no authorization) an aspirin because he or she had a headache?		
15. knowingly recorded incorrect information on a student's records?		
16. used a friend's identification card to get your child into a game or access to an activity?		
17. allowed a student to consume alcohol in the presence of his uncle, who was an educator?		
18. shared details about a student's record with your family?		
19. taken advantage of your position as principal to get a discount?		
20. promised a co-worker dinner if he or she would go along with you regarding a professional decision?		

Scoring Rubric

If you marked yes for these questions:	*The following ethical areas were violated:*
1, 4, 8, 9, 19	*Financial Gain and Personal Benefit*
6, 7, 10, 12, 13, 15, 16	*Official Records and Policies*
2, 14, 17, 18	*Student Rights*
3, 5, 11, 20	*Personnel (Colleagues and Staff)*

Figure 15.3

Self-Assessment of Ethical Behavior

Source: Adapted from *The Ethical Administrator,* a paper presented by B. Polnick, S. Edmonson, & A. Fisher at the NCPEA Conference within a Conference, American Association of School Administrators, New Orleans, LA, 2003.

Box 15.1   Enforceable Standards from Texas

Texas Code of Ethics: Enforceable Standards

I. Professional Ethical Conduct, Practices and Performance.

Standard 1.1. The educator shall not knowingly engage in deceptive practices regarding official policies of the school district or educational institution.

Standard 1.2. The educator shall not knowingly misappropriate, divert or use monies, personnel, property or equipment committed to his or her charge for personal gain or advantage.

Standard 1.3. The educator shall not submit fraudulent requests for reimbursement, expenses or pay.

Standard 1.4. The educator shall not use institutional or professional privileges for personal or partisan advantage.

Standard 1.5. The educator shall neither accept nor offer gratuities, gifts, or favors that impair professional judgment or to obtain special advantage. This standard shall not restrict the acceptance of gifts or tokens offered and accepted openly from students, parents or other persons or organizations in recognition or appreciation of service.

Standard 1.6. The educator shall not falsify records, or direct or coerce others to do so.

Standard 1.7. The educator shall comply with state regulations, written local school board policies and other applicable state and federal laws.

Standard 1.8. The educator shall apply for, accept, offer, or assign a position or a responsibility on the basis of professional qualifications.

II. Ethical Conduct Toward Professional Colleagues.

Standard 2.1. The educator shall not reveal confidential health or personnel information concerning colleagues unless disclosure serves lawful professional purposes or is required by law.

Standard 2.2. The educator shall not harm others by knowingly making false statements about a colleague or the school system.

Texas Educator Code of Ethics   The Code of Ethics and Standard Practices for Texas Educators was rewritten in 2002 by the State Board for Educator Certification (SBEC), the entity responsible for enforcing the Code of Ethics. According to SBEC, it was difficult to enforce much of the old code because it was ambiguous. The new code endeavors to provide a more specific statement of the conduct that is expected from Texas educators.

The revised Texas code, shown in Box 15.1, outlines a comprehensive and enforceable set of ethical standards. (The statement of purpose, which is not enforceable, gives general ethical guidelines for educators.) The first two principles in the old code (Principle I, Professional Ethical Conduct, and Principle II, Professional Practices and Performance) have been merged into a new, broader principle, "Professional Ethical Conduct, Practices and Performance." Additionally, old Principle V (Ethical Conduct Toward Parents and Community) has been removed. The rationale for this was that the items in Principle V did not properly and clearly identify the standards of conduct required of educators in an enforceable manner.

Summary

1. The ethical principal is one who, in the face of adversity, ambiguity, and challenge, will reflect on what is right by some set standard or code and will act in a rational and caring manner to resolve problems and conduct business.

2. Ethical principals must be able to enable followers to use many of their innate talents in pursuing the school goals and mission.

Box 15.1   Continued

Standard 2.3. The educator shall adhere to written local school board policies and state and federal laws regarding the hiring, evaluation, and dismissal of personnel.

Standard 2.4. The educator shall not interfere with a colleague's exercise of political, professional or citizenship rights and responsibilities.

Standard 2.5. The educator shall not discriminate against or coerce a colleague on the basis of race, color, religion, national origin, age, sex, disability, or family status.

Standard 2.6. The educator shall not use coercive means or promise of special treatment in order to influence professional decisions or colleagues.

Standard 2.7. The educator shall not retaliate against any individual who has filed a complaint with the SBEC under this chapter.

III. Ethical Conduct Toward Students.

Standard 3.1. The educator shall not reveal confidential information concerning students unless disclosure serves lawful professional purposes or is required by law.

Standard 3.2. The educator shall not knowingly treat a student in a manner that adversely affects the student's learning, physical health, mental health or safety.

Standard 3.3. The educator shall not deliberately or knowingly misrepresent facts regarding a student.

Standard 3.4. The educator shall not exclude a student from participation in a program, deny benefits to a student, or grant an advantage to a student on the basis of race, color, sex, disability, national origin, religion, or family status.

Standard 3.5. The educator shall not engage in physical mistreatment of a student.

Standard 3.6. The educator shall not solicit or engage in sexual conduct or a romantic relationship with a student.

Standard 3.7. The educator shall not furnish alcohol or illegal/unauthorized drugs to any student or knowingly allow any student to consume alcohol or illegal/unauthorized drugs in the presence of the educator.

---

3. Ethical principals must be concerned with the following philosophical concepts: (a) rights, (b) freedom, (c) responsibility, (d) duty, (e) justice, (f) equity, (g) authority, (h) caring, (i) character, (j) commitment, (k) conflict of interest, (l) formality, (m) loyalty, and (n) prudence.

4. Ethical principals have a responsibility to respect the rights of others, as moral decision makers and as role models, but disagreement occurs about what rights should apply in a given situation or what constitutes violation of another person's rights.

5. The principal is responsible to all individuals on the campus to ensure the right of personal security.

6. Personal liberty is seen as an absolute right; however, in the case of schools it may become a prima facie right because it would be overridden if within the personal liberty there is potential harm or harassment to others or there is an endangerment of the equal rights of others.

7. Negative human rights are life, physical property, due process, privacy, autonomy, freedom of thought and expression; positive human rights include food, adequate housing, competent medical care, employment at a living wage, and education.

8. Particular rights are dependent upon specific circumstances; for example, a person who is promised a specific thing has the right to receive it.

9. Freedom is related closely to the exercise of rights and is aligned in Americans' minds with the notions of liberty, independence, and individuality.

10. Principals do not stand in a confidential relationship with others.

11. Authority is the power to influence the behavior of others.

12. Prima facie duties are (a) fidelity, (b) reparation, (c) gratitude, (d) justice, (e) beneficence, (f) self-improvement, and (g) non-maleficence. Other duties that may take precedence in the school arena over the prima facie duties are (a) duty to students, (b) duty to colleagues, (c) duty to discipline, (d) duty to the school team, (e) duty to the profession, (f) duty to funding sources, (g) duty to parents, and (h) duty to community.

13. There are concerns for principals in dealing with justice; such concerns include the equal treatment of non-equals or the unequal treatment of equals. Equity is the bending of the rules to fit the situation. This definition implies treating equals equally and non-equals unequally to level the playing fields, but not to the point of being unfair.

14. Caring principals develop meaningful relationships and inspire others to excellence. Character is closely associated with caring; if a principal is perceived to have a good character, then he or she has exhibited behavior such as honesty, courage, dependability, and generosity, and acceptable motivations.

15. Commitment is related to character in that the principal must be committed to doing the right thing. Commitment is related to dependability.

16. A conflict of interests is a situation in which the principal would have a competing professional or personal interest that would make it difficult to fulfill his or her duties fairly.

17. Loyalty generally refers to faithfulness, devotion, and allegiance to a leader, person, group, ideal, cause, or duty.

18. Prudence refers to the exercise of good judgment, common sense, and even caution, especially in the conduct of practical matters.

Principals must remember that their actions have influence on people.

19. The community looks to high school and junior high school principals to monitor the ethical behavior of the coaches and players on their campuses.

20. The *Character Education Manifesto* principles could serve as a guide or map for principals and teachers to develop a campus manifesto and curriculum on character education.

21. The school principal is the most important person on the campus to promote and model ethical behavior and to implement policies that support an appropriate standard of conduct. As the principal goes, so goes the school.

22. There are national and state codes of ethics. Most of these codes are unenforceable and serve as guides for ethical behavior by the principal.

Field-Based Activities

1. Look in back issues of the newspaper over the past several months, and find three examples of unethical or ethical behavior. Determine which principle or concept has been upheld or violated.

2. Review the curriculum at your school. Determine if character education is present and if the principles in the *Character Education Manifesto* are present. Design and conduct a study to determine if character education would be something that the community would support.

3. (a) Use the "Portrait of an Ethical Principal" (Figure 15.2) and conduct a self-assessment; then have teachers on your team complete it. How do the ratings compare? Is your team compatible in relation to ethical thought? (b) Review your state ethical codes for principals or educators. Are there enforceable codes for your state?

Suggested Readings

Beckner, W. (2003). *Ethics for educational leaders*. New York: Allyn & Bacon. The author recognizes that educational administrators are required to make decisions in problem situations without ideal solutions. In this book, Beckner provides a philosophical and theoretical base, along with practical suggestions and activities to use that foundation in making the best decisions possible in difficult situations. Case studies at the beginning and end of each chapter offer realistic examples of how chapter content applies to actual administrative practice.

Berger, R. (2003). *The ethic of excellence: Building a culture of craftsmanship in schools*. Portsmouth, NH: Heinemann. High expectations play a central role in encouraging student achievement. Berger describes his work with students and teachers and compares it to carpentry, where craftsmanship is valued as part of the culture. He gives us a vision of educational reform that transcends standards, curriculum, and instructional strategies and develops an ethic of excellence.

Haynes, F. (1998). *The ethical school*. New York: Routledge. This book applies traditional ethical theories to individual case studies of conflicts that arise frequently in school settings over such issues as dress codes, censorship, inclusivity, and punishment.

Nash, R. J. (1996). *Real world ethics*. New York: Teachers College Press. The author of this book demonstrates keen sensitivity to the real-world problems faced by professionals. He encourages reflective intuitive involvement in solving problems and develops a framework of three moral languages: (1) fundamental beliefs and values, (2) conceptions of moral character and professionally relevant virtues, and (3) rules and principles.

Rebore, R. W. (2000). *The ethics of educational leadership*. Upper Saddle River, NJ: Merrill/Prentice Hall. In treating the subject of ethics as it relates to educational leadership, the material and argumentation in this text are organized so that they support Standard 5.0, Ethics, of the Interstate School Leaders Licensure Consortium (ISLLC) Standards for School Leaders and Standard 5.0 of the ELCC. The works of important philosophers provide the basis for development of the ethical principles presented in this book. Two philosophers from the classical period are presented, along with six from the modern period and 15 from the contemporary period. These philosophers were chosen because their ideas and concepts are relevant to the American ethos and to the practice of educational leadership. The book has five parts. Part One, "The Ethical Administrator," contains Chapters 1 through 3 and is concerned with establishing the fundamental principles endemic to being an ethical person who is also an educational leader. Part Two, "The Ethical Practice of Educational Leadership," includes Chapters 4 and 5, which concentrate on the ethical practice of central office and school building administration. Part Three, "Equity and Educational Leadership," contains Chapters 6 and 7. These chapters deal with gender equity and how other kinds of equity issues can be addressed in a pluralistic society. In addition, this section discusses equity from the perspective of social justice and considers how public discourse can contribute to the development of educational administration policies. The epilogue constitutes the fourth part of this book, and sets forth some final thoughts about ethics. Last is the appendix, which contains a self-assessment instrument on ethical principles in relation to educational leadership activities.

Starratt, R. J. (1994). *Building an ethical school: A practical response to the moral crisis in schools*. London: Falmer Press. Starratt argues for much greater attention to ethical education and responds to skeptics who say that schools cannot be ethical in the face of a pluralistic, secular society that is badly fragmented over values. The author provides a conceptual foundation for ethical education broad enough for building consensus among teachers and parents, yet focused enough to provide guidance for highly specific learning activities. He presents a series of steps by which a school community might proceed in building an ethical school. The author shares exciting initiatives in ethical education.

Strike, K., Haller, E. J., & Soltis, J. F. (1998). *The ethics of school administration* (2nd ed.). New York: Teachers College Press. This book is designed to help teach a range of ethical concepts that are important to the practicing principal. It includes case studies and detailed analyses that include information and skills needed for a knowledgeable approach to thinking through the ethical problems encountered in schools.

Tough Decisions

Setting: Dr. Alice March, principal of Dover High School, is in the process of selecting a new chair for the English department at her school. This position is one of strong influence, because the chair sits on many standing committees in the district. In the past the chairperson has been a leader on the curriculum council and on the site-based decision-making (SBDM) committee.

Scenario: Dr. March is on the telephone, discussing the situation with Dr. Petrovsky, superintendent of schools.

"I have no idea who will apply for the position, Dr. Petrovsky," says Dr. March. "Yes, I realize that you have given the committee autonomy to decide who will be the next chair of the English department. I realize how important that role is, and we on the selection team will do our homework."

As she gets off the phone, Dr. March is almost beside herself. Two board members have already called her about this position. Now the superintendent has called to ask who is applying. It has been only an hour since she posted the expected vacancy on the bulletin board in the faculty room.

The principal thinks about which portions of the job description are most important to her: the required qualifications, the desired qualifications, and the performance responsibilities. Required and desired qualifications are valid teaching and supervisory certificates; at least six years of classroom teaching in high school English; experience in planning, developing, and evaluating the English program; and experience in preparing the budget. Performance responsibilities include contributing to a positive atmosphere, maintaining healthy relationships with colleagues, developing positive school-community relations to promote understanding and acceptance of the English program, assisting all English teachers in identifying and solving instructional-related problems, and assuming responsibility for acquiring knowledge, supervisory, and leadership skills necessary for fulfilling all assigned duties.

Dr. March recognizes that performance on the state test for reading and writing at the high school has not improved much in the last three years—except in grade 9. The poor test results certainly contributed to the current department chair's decision to retire.

Within two weeks, Dr. March receives three applications from her current staff. The applicants are all in-district veterans. Mary Worthy has been in the district for 20 years. She earned her master's degree and her certificate for instructional supervision in the year after graduating with her teacher's certificate. She has served as an English teacher for 12 years and as an English and Geography teacher for the last 8 years. She writes in her application that she "would cherish the opportunity to lead the English teachers." Mary notes that her experience includes curriculum writing; mentoring new teachers; assisting in the budget planning; and of course, teaching English to freshmen, sophomores, juniors, and seniors. Her style is steady and methodical. She prides herself on never failing to get an assignment done on time. She is quite knowledgeable and is well respected in the community.

The second applicant is Tim Cooke, a 10-year veteran whose experience is primarily with ninth-grade students. He is innovative, creative, enthusiastic, a hard worker, and very organized. His student teachers have truly enjoyed his classes. Scores on the state English test for the ninth grade have increased significantly since Tim introduced some new strategies to help all students improve their reading and writing. Teacher colleagues like him and his outgoing, easy manner. He has mentored two student teachers and has helped in the curriculum budget planning. He has just completed his master's degree in instructional supervision.

Dan Olenik, third applicant, also has 10 years of teaching experience at this campus. He has taught English at the sophomore and junior levels. He has some experience in curriculum writing and budgeting. He, too, has mentored two student teachers and has earned a master's in instructional supervision. (In Dr. March's mind, Dan can be somewhat unorganized. She could count on him coming to ask for an extra day to complete some of his lesson plans, particularly when he was working on his master's degree. Yet, to be fair, since then he has responded promptly to all her requests.) The current department chair thinks highly of him. Dan has sponsored the Literary Club, and he has trained debaters for interschool competition. He has done well in both; as a result, he is well known in the community. Of course, having the superintendent as his uncle has not hurt him.

The selection committee is composed of five members — two department chairs, those from Social Studies and Science, plus two English teachers and Dr. March. One of the English teachers serving on the committee has 6 years of experience, and the other has 15 years. Both of the women are competent but not outstanding teachers. Dr. March thinks that it will be interesting to hear their comments about the applicants. Dr. Peter Pharr, chair of the Social Studies department, is the most experienced member of the committee with 32 years in education. Phil Blalock, chair of the Science department, has 25 years of teaching experience.

Dr. March puts the applications aside and proceeds to review her mail for the day. The first letter she picks up is unsigned. It is addressed to her and to members of the selection committee.

> Dear Committee Members:
> There are a few things I think you ought to know. The teachers are all talking about who will get this job and betting on the side. You-know-who is their first guess for the next chair of the English department, because of his connections to the superintendent. I can tell you that this man is not the right choice. His professors never caught his plagiarism in papers written during his master's program; but as a fellow student, he boasted to me about it. His moral standing is questionable not only because of this, but because of his cheating on his wife. She does not know, but I have seen him several times in a hotel with another woman late at night. If you want someone with integrity, and one who can help with public relations, I would not select this person. I believe I have completed my duty in notifying you. — No Name

Normally, Dr. March thinks, I would pay no attention to an unsigned letter. Dr. Petrovsky knows this, too. Do I ignore it this time — especially because it refers to the superintendent's nephew? I wonder if this letter was sent to the other committee members. She does not have long to wonder, for at that moment her secretary appears in the doorway and says, "Dr. Pharr and Phil Blalock would like to see you. What shall I tell them?"

Dr. March meets with the department chairs, and after that with the two English teachers on the selection committee. The men say they have no problem with ignoring the letter; but both women say they can easily believe what the letter revealed and are not comfortable with selecting Dan as chair. Dr. March asks that the selection committee not pass judgment on such unfounded rumor. She explains her practice of ignoring unsigned mail. After more discussion, they also agree to proceed with the interviews as scheduled.

Before conducting the team interviews, committee members rate each applicant using a paper review. During the interviews, applicants are rated again based on the responses to 10 questions. All the applicants do well in the interview session, particularly Dan Olenik. His answers are outstanding. When all scores are tallied, Dan has scored a couple more points than either of the other two applicants have. Mary Worthy is ranked second, and Tim Cooke is rated last by only one point.

The results surprise Dr. March, but she has said that she is open to working and supervising any one of the three candidates. Just as the session is about to end, the two female teachers mention that they are afraid of what the superintendent might do if they do not select his nephew. Also, the women say, they are uncomfortable with the information in the unsigned letter and wish to state that they are upset because they have been pressured to proceed as if they had not received the letter.

Now Dr. March is not sure what to do. She did persuade the teachers to proceed as if they had not received the letter. Did they think she was pressuring them? Dr. March believes that ignoring any unsigned letters, in line with her consistent practice, has eliminated the possibility of subterfuge from someone with an invalid complaint. She is uncomfortable with the timing of the teachers' objection. Should she take the unsigned letter to the superintendent now, and use that as a tool to move Dan out of consideration? What is the right thing to do?

Questions

1. How can Dr. March remove any suspicion of a forced persuasion? Could she have acted earlier? If so, how?

2. If Dan were selected now, what effect might that have on committee members and ultimately on the department? How would you feel if you had been one of the members?

3. Is Dr. March putting loyalty above what might be truth? What can she say or do now to be perceived as an ethical leader?

4. Could the superintendent and board members be perceived as being unethical because of their phone calls to Dr. March? Explain your answer.

16. Political and Policy Context

> **Standard 6.0:** *Candidates who complete the program are educational leaders who have the knowledge and ability to promote the success of all students by understanding, responding to, and influencing the larger political, social, economic, legal, and cultural context.*

FOCUSING QUESTIONS

1 How does society affect policy and political occurrences in schools?

2 How is the principal's role impacted by the politics surrounding the creation and implementation of educational policies?

3 What is policy?

4 What is meant by politics?

5 What role does politics play in the relationship between the principal and the superintendent in the operation of a school district?

In this chapter, we respond to these questions concerning the principal's role in the political and policy context. We begin the chapter with a discussion of the connection between society and policy and political occurrences in schools. Then we examine more specifically the principal's role as it relates to politics and policy formulation and implementation. Next, we explore what is meant by policy. This is followed by a discussion of politics in general and the role of the principal in politics. Finally, we conclude the chapter with a discussion of politics within the school district, specifically the role that politics plays in principals' working relationship with their superintendents.

Society, Policy, and Politics

Because we address in this chapter both the encounters a principal may have with policy and politics within an ever-changing and diverse society and a framework for understanding policy and politics, we begin with a lengthy and relevant quote from John Dewey's *The School and Society* (1907). Even 100 years ago, Dewey viewed a changing society as directly connected with the policy and political occurrences in schools. Dewey's observations related to the politics of his day and still linger today within surmounting national and world events that impact schools daily. The cyclical relationship between society's needs, social justice, and education exists today as it did so many years ago. Consider that Dewey's thoughts were published at the turn of the 20th century; and 100 years later, at the turn of the 21st century, the context in which we find ourselves is, again as Dewey noted, a social revolution affecting education.

> Whenever we have in mind the discussion of a new movement in education, it is especially necessary to take the broader, or social view. Otherwise, changes in the school institution and tradition will be looked at as the arbitrary inventions of particular teachers; at the worst transitory fads, and at the best merely improvements in certain details— and this is the plane upon which it is too customary to consider school changes. The modification going on in the method and curriculum of education is as much a product of the changed social situation, and as much an effort to meet the needs of the new society that is forming, as are changes in modes of industry and commerce.
>
> It is to this, then, that I especially ask your attention: the effort to conceive what roughly may be termed the "New Education" in the light of larger changes in society. Can we connect this "New Education" with the general march of events?
>
> I make no apology for not dwelling at length upon the social changes in question. Those I shall mention are writ so large that he who runs may read. The change that comes first to mind, the one that overshadows and even controls all others, is the industrial one— the application of science resulting in the great inventions that have utilized the forces of nature on a vast and inexpensive scale: the growth of a world-wide market as the object of production, of vast manufacturing centers to supply this market, of cheap and rapid means of communication and distribution between all its parts. Even as to its feebler beginnings, this change is not much more than a century old; in many of its most important aspects it falls within the short span of those now living. One can hardly believe there has been a revolution in all history so rapid, so extensive, so complete. Through it the face of the earth is making over, even as to its physical forms; political boundaries are wiped out and moved about, as if they were indeed only lines on a paper map; population is hurriedly gathered into cities from the ends of the earth; habits of living are altered with startling abruptness and thoroughness; the search for the truths of nature is infinitely stimulated and facilitated and their application to life made not only practicable, but commercially necessary. Even our moral and religious ideas and interests, the most conservative because the deepest-lying things in our nature, are profoundly affected. That this revolution should not affect education in other than formal and superficial fashion is inconceivable. (Dewey, 1907, pp. 19–22)

To understand national, state, and local societal contexts as they relate to the politics of schooling, we believe that it is important for principals to consider an historical perspective first. Landmark events that have taken place in the latter part of the 20th century mark changes that force leaders to take notice and work within a more diverse system than that of the 1940s and early 1950s. *Brown vs. Board of Education of Topeka* is now a half-century old, and the marvel of it is that it forced schools to become the setting for change in the broader society related to civil rights. With the advent of Sputnik, the Soviet Union's earth-orbiting satellite program, a new era was launched for the educational leader. Prior to Sputnik, leaders were not forced to consider *differentiation within the curriculum* for students who excelled in science or math.

In 1964, the Civil Rights Act was passed. For principals of today, this act still beckons them daily to consider *equity* in educational curricular and extracurricular activities related not only to race, but also to religion, national origin, color, and sex. In the mid 1960s the federal Education and Secondary Education Act forced principals to pay attention and address issues revolving around those who are *socioeconomically disadvantaged* and as a result may be *academically disadvantaged*. Even students performing above the mark received little attention in terms of political and educational reforms.

Sputnik and the legislative and judicial acts passed in subsequent years launched the 1972 Marland definition of *gifted*— yet with minimal effect, as evidenced by the lack of federal legislation mandating a differentiated curriculum for gifted students. In the early 1970s, the Equal Rights Amendment was passed, but not ratified by all states until 1982; this legislation brought about more awareness related to another *equity* issue among leaders in education, who at that time were predominately male. Equity issues were added to the curricular and extracurricular issues related to *gender*. In the mid-1970s landmark legislation, Public Law 94-142, was passed; subsequent revisions have continued to develop. This law compelled leaders to adopt a different educational view of *children with disabilities* and to fully include these children in the public schools.

In the early 1980s, with the release of the landmark government report, *A Nation at Risk,* leaders were thrown into an age of *accountability and data-driven decision making* to an extent that had never before been experienced in schools. The 1990s brought about more change, with an influx of immigrants who spoke little or no English. The surge of immigrants affected principals in regard to curriculum, program choices, service delivery, and philosophical issues surrounding the *English language learner.*

The year 1999 and Columbine brought to the forefront school violence, jolting principals into strong consideration of safe school environments. September 11, 2001, followed soon after, and leaders tightened security to make schools even safer. Political events and social issues affecting education today have been evolving for over 50 years. These changes and events have created the more complex and politically charged school environments in which today's principals must lead.

Policy, Politics, and the Principal

Cooper, Fusarelli, and Randall (2004) stated that principals must be knowledgeable and cognizant of the politics surrounding the creation and implementation of educational policies. They must be aware of the macro-level forces and actors; this means that principals must be very conscious of national, state, and even local events as their foundation and range. The scope of policymaking and politics is large, considering that it includes the federal government with new administrations in the White House potentially every four years, the federal and state courts, 50 state legislatures, and local school boards. This does not include the 50 state educational and certification agencies that develop procedures for the policies and, in doing so, sometimes make additional and layered policies.

In describing principals and their involvement in the macro politics and policy, we could begin with "once upon a time," because once upon a time, prior to the 1990s, the principal was basically isolated from politics and dealt only with policy. In the 1990s things changed. School reforms began breaking up the isolation of principals within the four walls of their campuses. Principals became more connected, more involved. For example, under site-based decision making and management, a principal might find herself dealing directly with the city council or the legislators (Fowler, 2004). Thus enter policy and politics.

What Is a Policy?

Simply put, *policy* is the outgrowth of governmental actions. It is "courses of purposive action . . . directed towards the accomplishment of some intended or desired set of goals" (Harman, 1984, p. 13). Dye (1998) defined policy as what governments choose to do or not to do, which could indicate that what governments do not do is of equal importance in making policy. Ball (1994) defined policy as follows:

> Policy is both text and action, words and deeds, it is what is enacted as well as what is intended. . . . Policies are crude and simple. Practice is sophisticated, contingent, complex and unstable. Policy as practice is "created" in a trialectic of dominance, resistance, and chaos/freedom. Thus policy is not simple asymmetry of power. Control [or dominance] can never be totally secured, in part because of agency. It will be open to erosion and undercutting by action, an embodied agency of those people who are its object. (pp. 10–11)

Cooper and colleagues (2004) provided a comprehensive definition of policy as "a political process where needs, goals, and intentions are translated into a set of objectives, laws, policies, and programs, which in turn affect resource allocations, actions, and outputs, which are the basis for evaluation, reforms, and new policies" (p. 3).

According to Duemer and Mendez-Morse (2002), "Once an individual or policy-making body sets a policy, there is no guarantee that it will be implemented in the same way it was originally intended. The difference between institutions and individuals is central to understanding how policy can change from development to implementation" (p. 1). These authors discussed the connection of policy to implementation of a specific policy based on the role of the individual. The principal's connection to policy is at the local campus level, the district level, the state level, and to some extent the national level. The principal's role is related to policy in the following ways: (a) orientation, (b) degree, (c) resources, (d) activity, (e) autonomy, (f) societal values, (g) institutional values, (h) rationale, and (i) power relationship.

Duemer and Mendez-Morse (2002) explained each of these nine areas in the form of questions that could be asked of the principal with respect to his involvement in developing and adopting policy. The questions imply an active role for the principal in policy development and adoption—a role that has not often been observed in the past.

Orientation   Orientation refers to one's position with respect to attitude, judgment, inclination, or interest. Was the principal supportive, oppositional, or neutral toward the policy in question? Did the principal voice her stance on the policy?

Degree   Degree is the scale of intensity or amount. To what degree did the principal support or oppose the policy? Did the principal share his opposition or support with others in the organization? What means of communication did he use to do this? To whom did he communicate the stance on the policy? If the principal opposed the policy, to what degree did he attempt to obstruct or alter its implementation?

Resources   Resources refer to action, money, influence, information, expertise, or measures that can be brought to bear in order to influence or use. What resources were available to the principal that could be used to help or hinder implementation? What types of resources did the principal expend on this policy? What resources were specifically used in communicating the policy?

Activity   Activity is the specific deed, action, or function; use of force, influence, or process. What communication actions did the principal take to support or obstruct policy? How much communication activity did the principal expend to support or obstruct policy? With whom did the principal interact during these communication activities?

Autonomy   Autonomy relates to the degree of independence; how closely one has to adhere to prescribed guidelines. A high degree of support or opposition will not have had much impact on expense of energy and resources if the principal had little autonomy to exert influence on policy. What level of autonomy does the principal have in her position? How does the principal's position influence the communication modes available to her?

Societal Values   Societal values are the ideals or customs for which people have an affective regard. How did societal values influence implementation? To what extent did the principal accept or reject specific societal values that influenced implementation? How did the principal's actions or decisions change the societal climate?

Institutional Values   Institutional values refer to professional ideals or customs for which members have an affective regard. How did institutional values influence implementation? How are the institutional values communicated to the principal? To what extent did the principal accept or reject specific institutional values that influenced implementation? How did the principal's actions or decisions change the institutional climate? How did the institutional climate change the principal's actions or decisions?

Rationale   Rationale means the fundamental, underlying reasons to account for something. What explanation does the principal provide for his orientation toward the policy? Does the principal have superseding interests, loyalties, or values that conflict with the policy? What ethical concerns does the principal have related to the policy?

Power Relationship   Power relationship is the degree of status relative to the principal's position. What type of communication, both informal and formal, occurred between same or different power levels?

Principals must use the previous questions to:

1. Establish a framework that is informative about their perspectives toward policy and policy implementation
2. Establish a relationship to policy implementation on individual terms
3. Recognize that the relationship between the principal and the organization is reciprocal rather than unidirectional
4. Include issues of both informal and formal means of communication
5. Take into account societal and institutional contexts through investigating communication lines that influence principals
6. Consider that principals change institutions through actions, decisions, and participation in both informal and formal means of communication. (Duemer & Mendez-Morse, 2002)

The Examination of Policy

Principals are obligated to analyze and understand policy. Cooper and colleagues (2004) suggested that examining policy through multiple lenses and frameworks could assist principals in discussing policy, planning it, and implementing it in practice. This type of examination also aids in understanding the impact that practice, growing from policy, might have on individuals in a school. We present seven theories by which principals can examine policy.

Systems Theory   The analysis of policy through systems theory provides a holistic look at the policy itself. It allows principals to analyze the "policy 'inputs' including demands, needs, and resources, the 'throughputs' that involve the key actors who implement policy, and policy 'outputs' such as educated, civic-minded students or improved economic productivity" (Cooper et al., 2004, p. 9). Principals can use *systems theory* to analyze policy and its impact on student achievement in relation to the entire school unit and community, and they can analyze that relationship with respect to the whole school district and state and federal rules and regulations. A model of systems theory analysis at the local district level is seen in Figure 16.1.

Neopluralist Advocacy Coalition and Interest Group Theories   Neopluralist advocacy coalition and interest group theories are

> grounded in a political science perspective that seeks to answer "who gets what, when, and how" as key coalitions struggle to obtain from government the resources and support they believe necessary. These key actors (legislators, governors, mayors, superintendents, school boards, etc.) work out their interest group concerns in a variety of arenas, depending on the level in the federalist system (federal, state, county, city, school district, and individual schools). Bringing interest groups and their arenas together provides a useful means of understanding how laws are passed, shaped, implemented, and evaluated. (Cooper et al., 2004, p. 9)

Interest groups are organizations or groups that seek to influence the development and application of policy (Harman, 2001); they communicate needs to decision makers, structure alternative policy choices, act as buffers between government and the wider community, check demands made by others, and compartmentalize access to decision

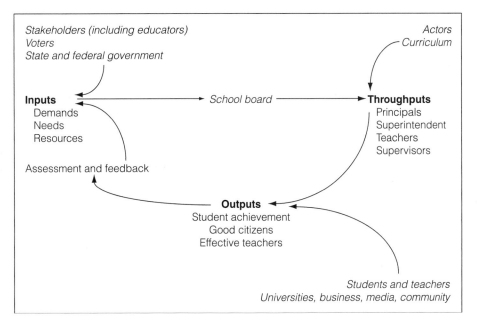

Figure 16.1

Model of Systems Theory Analysis of Policy

makers (Froman, 1966). During the policy process as the issues emerge and agendas are set; during the review of options and policy development; during the policy decision, authorization, and implementation; and during policy review, termination, replacement, or redirection, the potential for interest group influence is not only at a single key decision point, but during each stage in the policy process (Harman, 2001).

Under analysis of policy herein, the principal must pay careful attention to advocacy groups and become savvy to how various coalitions are playing the political game to achieve their policy objectives. The principal will need to be able to read the political groups and the actors to determine the impact of that conflict as policy is developed upon the degree to which, and the time in which, campus goals and objectives can be accomplished.

Neoinstitutional Theory   Neoinstitutional theory indicates that the "structure of societal and political organizations exerts independent effects on policy" (Cooper et al., 2004, p. 9). "This theory emphasizes routines, imitation, unreflective responses, custom and normative practices, and convergence of organizational forms; it deemphasizes power and conflict" (Perrow, 2002, p. 19). Neoinstitutional theory helps principals to understand why hegemonic practices may exist within the school or district. To understand policy, principals must understand the political institutions that enact and enforce the laws and regulations and the relationship to the schools and classrooms where the laws are carried out. The principal can work with his state legislative representatives to determine what policies are being proposed or enacted. He may even assist the legislator to understand the impact the policy may have at the local school level.

The principal needs to anticipate the change associated with new legislation, whether at the state or national level, but understand that under this theory the legislative body, the school board, or the district officials may not determine that alternatives to education are legitimate and may conform to customary organizational or societal norms and practices. At times, when the principal is up against this situation and at the same time is seeking to offer alternative inputs for new policy based on analysis and feedback of the learners, she may not have any fruition of her ideas. It may be a time when the principal's norms are not in line with that of the policymaking body, and it may be a time for the principal to seek employment in a district that is aligned with her own values. Therefore, this theory analysis has a by-product in that principals can determine their fit within the organization by understanding this theory within the framework of their school's policy development and adoption.

Critical Theory   Critical theory "questions the existing economic, political, and social purposes of schooling and examines policy through the lens of oppressed groups, with a normative orientation toward freeing disenfranchised groups from conditions of domination and subjugation" (Cooper et al., 2004, p. 9). This theory is concerned with equity and social justice analyses of policy. It tries to discover the "hidden uses of power through which policy is transformed into practice" (Cooper et al., 2004, p. 9). The principal can work to shape policy based on equitable power structures related to class, culture, ethnicity, and language; analyze policies related to the social structure of his campus; and engage in understanding how the policy reflects inclusion or exclusion.

Feminist Theory   "Feminist theory is concerned primarily with the often unequal effects of education policies on issues relating to gender and sexual difference, including how education policies are translated through institutional processes that serve to reinforce or encourage gender inequity" (Cooper et al., 2004, p. 9). The principal must seek to analyze policies and outgrowths of practice from the policies in relation to gender equities or inequities. Such analyses may include an examination of such issues as (a) salaries for male and female teachers, administrators, and coaches;

(b) job opportunities for both genders; and (c) sports equity for boys and girls with regard to facilities, spending, and opportunities.

Postmodernism   Postmodernism "argues that policy is contextually defined by those in authority and has little validity when separated from its setting" (Cooper et al., 2004, p. 9). This theory suggests that the scientific posturing in policy analysis only serves to perpetuate the highly racist, sexist, and class nature of most policies. Furthermore, it implies that schools do not progress due to the policies in place that support the privileged to maintain the status quo; this translates to keeping the upper-class, White, male leadership in power at the expense of the poor, women, people of color, and recent immigrants.

Scheurich (1994) provided direction for principals. He asked questions that can be asked and investigated by principals. "By what process did a particular problem emerge, or better, how did a particular problem come to be seen as a problem? What makes the emergence of a particular problem possible? Why do some 'problems' become identified as social problems while other 'problems' do not achieve that level of identification?" (p. 300). He focused principals on prior conditions of the policy—the politics of the policy.

Ideological Theories of Policymaking   Ideological theories "place policy into a partisan, politically value-laden structure, hoping to gain insight into the econo-political context surrounding key policies" (Cooper et al., 2004, p. 10). This theory seeks to determine if a policy is associated with the liberal left or the conservative right. Political parties and federal judges have used "ideological theories (rather than upon legitimate considerations of the quality of education) to justify racial assignments and the deprivation of true equal opportunity for all students, including the gifted students who have such great potential to enrich American life" (Hardaway, 1995, p. 149).

For this kind of analysis, the principal need only look at the political party platforms and those in power for national trends in policy. Lyndon Johnson promoted liberal policies, including compensatory education, equity, and help for disadvantaged, at-risk students; Reagan promoted the legislating of choice, markets, higher standards, and vouchers (Cooper et al., 2004). Locally, then, the principal should become familiar with the superintendent's and the school board members' agenda to anticipate potential policy changes and their impact on the campus.

Conceptual Framework for Understanding Policy

The previously discussed theories for examining policy help principals analyze their place and the school's place within policy, as well as to analyze the specific aspects of policies. To understand policies, principals can review the conceptual framework of four dimensions: (1) normative dimension, (2) structural dimension, (3) constituentive dimension, and (4) technical dimension (Cooper et al., 2004).

Normative Dimension   The *normative dimension* includes beliefs, values, and ideologies that drive societies to seek improvement and change. Diesing (1965) indicated there are four general criteria for judging the effect of a policy decision within a normative dimension: (1) the ability of the policy to reconcile or harmonize conflicting factors that blocked decision making; (2) the ability of the policy decision to increase toleration between various groups and their respective beliefs and values; (3) the decision's ability to establish balance between differing groups; and (4) the decision's ability itself to reject, repress, or otherwise exclude the threatening factors from the policy. Policies that are the expressed ideals of the society are considered to be normative in nature. Postmodernism and ideological theories are included in this dimension.

Structural Dimension   The *structural dimension* includes the "governmental arrangements, institutional structure, systems, and processes that promulgate and support policies in education" (Cooper et al., 2004, p. 43). The structural dimension

reflects the motivation, needs, and objectives expressed by political ideas and ideologies. Principals can attempt to define and promote ideas and influence structures; the community and groups can encourage or reply to ideas and confirm or reject structures through their participation—especially, but hardly exclusively, in the context of political democracy (Cyr, 1997, p. 10). The roles and effects of local, state, and federal governmental structures definitely influence the way educational policy is created. Neoinstitutional theory enlightens research in the structural dimension.

Constituentive Dimension   The *constituentive dimension* includes

> theories of networks, elites, masses, interest groups, ethnic/gender groups, providers and "end users," and beneficiaries who influence, participate in, and benefit from the policymaking process. Issues needing to be addressed in this dimension include who has access to power, how these interest groups make their needs felt, and the degree to which competing interests can work out a compromise solution or have their needs met. (Cooper et al., 2004, pp. 43–44)

In this dimension, the constituent groups either favor or oppose the policies developed. Neopluralist advocacy coalitions and interest group models, as well as critical and feminist theories, are the focus of this dimension.

Technical Dimension   The *technical dimension* "includes educational planning, practice, implementation, and evaluation—the nuts and bolts of policymaking. Systems theory is useful to understand developments in this dimension as we trace the technical and instrumental effects of policies" (Cooper et al., 2004, p. 44).

Figure 16.2 depicts how policy is formulated from an issue through these four dimensions to adoption, to implementation, and finally to evaluation.

Cooper and colleagues (2004) made a point that the framework must be concerned with ethics and social justice. Considerations of injustice and equity must be reviewed by the principal in observing how policies are made as well as how policies affect the students they serve. Principals must consider a policy in regard to its context, impact,

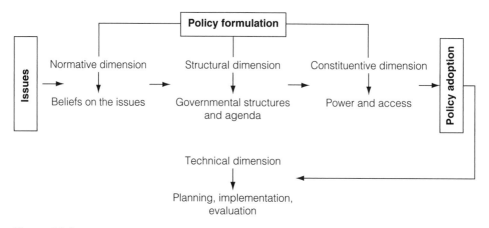

Figure 16.2

Policy Dimensions and Policy Process

and future implications. What is the policy likely to yield for those in our society who are most needy and vulnerable? This is but one of the questions principals must ask themselves as they develop and review and evaluate, for example, policies related to funding, student achievement, teacher quality, technology, special programs, and/or curriculum.

Just as ethics and social justice enter into a principal's evaluation of policy, so does the concept of moral purpose as described by Fullan (2001). He indicated that leaders (principals) contribute for the better or worse to moral purpose in the schools and in society as a whole. Because, as Fullan suggested, moral purpose is about how humans evolve over time, especially regarding how they relate to each other, the evaluation of policy as it affects others is critical for a higher moral purpose.

Following are several examples of how social justice must enter into the evaluation of policy. In Box 16.1 (pp. 380–381), we share first an excerpt from Berliner and Biddle (1995) as they discuss the concept of intelligence and gifted education. The principal must consider the social justice or inequities brought out in the excerpt.

An example of ethics and justice related to policy recently occurred in a suburban school district

and is still unresolved or unnoticed. A parent related to the authors that her daughter was participating in the high school band. She stated that there were numerous expenses incurred by this participation, in excess of $1,000. That was just the initial start-up fund for participation; there would be additional costs throughout the year, in addition to fund-raisers in which the child would be involved. So, what is the problem with ethics and justice in this school policy? The principal should be concerned with equity and justice under this policy. The parent who talked with us has the means to provide the extracurricular activity for her daughter; however, children who are, unfortunately, born into lesser financial conditions do not have this opportunity. The question becomes: Are there children from low-income families who are extremely talented and who would have their future in the musical field diminished via a public school policy that promotes and support a public school program giving benefits only to those with wealth who can afford it? The next question would be: What is the principal's role in promoting equal access to the band program for children of all financial circumstances? This policy, the way it currently is implemented, prohibits equal access and ultimately general access to future educational opportunities. This is similar to the arguments put forward by Berliner and Biddle (1995) in regard to gifted education and intelligence.

Another issue that mainly is identified by the time of adolescence is the issue of policy equity in counseling students. Both school policy and the students' own personal hindrances might prevent, for example, homosexual youth and rape or incest victims from being counseled. Traditionally, schools and communities are reluctant to broach such topics, admit such students' presence, or provide services for them. This presents a problem for the principals in that equitable services are negated by sheer neglect. Without the authority of explicit policy or law, individual school or social service personnel may fail to act because of moral or religious beliefs, fear of controversy, or being labeled "different" themselves (Lipkin, 1999). These types of controversial circumstances apply not only to policy but also to politics because the principal is, in each case, under the watchful eyes of the community in her implementation or interpretation of policy to her students, teachers, parents, and community constituents.

What Is Meant by *Politics*?

Politics and public education are inseparable. Since the mid 20th century, public education has been the setting for battles over race, class, and privilege. In *Webster's Dictionary*, the definitions of politics range from "the art and science of government" to "factional scheming for power." Elmore (1997) described politics as occurring in an arena of conflict, where competing interest groups with different resources and capacities vie for influence to shape policy in their own image. Education is an arena of conflicting priorities and interests where politics manifests itself.

Most definitions of politics are rooted in a system of governance. If governance is the system of directing affairs or political administration, politics is a by-product of that system. Our government is the structure, or machine, that we, the people, construct. The operation of the machine—the attempts to control the direction, speed, and

function of the machine—is determined through politics. The not-so-favorable interpretations of politics arise from the fact that many differing factions would like to control the machine of governance, and there are an infinite number of interpretations of how it can and should be driven (Learning Points Associates, n.d.b). Added to this, societal conditions and demands are ever-changing. Because politics is an integral part of the operation of public education and the school campus, it is important for principals to understand the political milieu in which they work—not just in the obvious ways like election of school board members or, in some districts, local school councils, but in more integral, day-to-day ways.

As principals work within that political landscape, they might find Apple's (2001) work instructive. He suggested there are hegemonic groups in society who have been influential in setting public educational policy. Those groups he classified as follows: (a) neoliberals who are relating schools to dollars and even marketing schools with voucher plans and tax credits; (b) neoconservatives who are deeply committed to establishing tighter mechanisms of control over knowledge, morals, and values through national or state curricula and national- or state-mandated reductive testing; (c) authoritarian populists who believe in a pedagogy that is based on traditional relations to authority where the teacher and the adults are always in control (they also believe that biblical authority should always supersede public policy); and (d) an upwardly mobile professional and managerial new middle class that thrives on managerialism and imposes policies of "steering at a distance" through national and state testing with tighter control through the use of industrial models, through cost/benefit analysis, and so on (this group is caught up in high-stakes testing). The bottom line is that these groups set agendas that establish connections between schools and the economy.

However, Apple also shared that there is another group, which he called "thick-visioned democrats" (not the political party). He indicated they are concerned with issues involving the power of collective local decision making of the

---

Box 16.1   Excerpt on Policy Implications for Gifted Education

Intelligence, Schooling, and Wealth. The implications of this revelation are disturbing. Consider, for example, the effects of wealth on intelligence. Rich parents in America often provide early experiences for their children that will make them smarter. Wealth allows those parents to purchase high-quality day care and to enroll their children in private preschools. It also permits them to purchase instructional toys, encyclopedias, computers, and first-rate health care—all of which are likely to improve a child's measured intelligence. This means that the sons and daughters of wealthy parents are likely to enter school with higher measured intelligence than that of the children of poor parents. This sounds bad if we believe in the ideal of equal opportunity for children, but there is worse. Since good schooling also leads to gains in intelligence, it follows that those children who attend "the best" schools will also gain the most. But since the quality of schools also varies greatly across the land, the growth of intelligence is not equal in America's schools. And in our country, children from rich families are much more likely than are children from poor families to attend "the best" schools—either because rich children are sent to private academies

or because they attend well-funded public schools in affluent suburbs—and this means they will gain more in intelligence than will the sons and daughters of middle- or working-class families. (Such inequities in school funding appear less often in other Western countries, where private schools are fewer and public schools more often receive equal funding based on student enrollment.) Thus, in America we also allow the rich to "buy" intelligence-test points for their children through unequal school funding.

What Are the Implications for Educational Policy? In recent years, for example, the Bush and Clinton administrations both urged the states to adopt programs that would provide enriched educational experiences for students who are "truly gifted," and various states have obliged by passing laws setting up such programs. But intelligence tests are widely used to select students who are "truly gifted," and this means that children of the rich are far more likely to participate in such programs than are children of the poor. Many children from poor families could also profit from enrichment programs, but they cannot enter those programs because of the mistake they made at birth—they "chose" to be

---

curriculum that is at the grass roots and that responds to the local needs, histories, and cultures of oppressed people, people of color, and economically disadvantaged people. This group advances a socially responsive pedagogy.

Schools and Politics   Chubb and Moe (1991) found that the most effective schools were characterized by a high level of professional autonomy at the individual building level, a condition that seldom exists in a highly politicized environment. In reality, the school is confronted with issues inextricably connected to their own political contexts. Too often, educational reform policy overlooks these connections, and educational innovations fail due to a lack of attention to the political context. The political context is often

interference in policy implementation by the school board—or, more specifically, by individual members of the school board. For example, a principal in a rural district was attempting to do her job and was effectively having children succeed on benchmark tests for the state exam. She did something that individual members of the school board did not like and consequentially was contacted by two individual members who suggested strongly that she resign. The board president contacted the principal and told her to disregard the two previous contacts because, of course, they were in violation of the law. However, this brief example points out the political context in which the school resides; and in this case, the resulting interruption of consistent, effective leadership during the time of this event.

Box 16.1   Continued

born to parents who were not wealthy! This is a problem for our democracy because we continue to preach that all people should have equal opportunities to rise through public schooling. Unfortunately, rising-through-schooling is probably happening less frequently in the present decade, in part because so many states have now instituted programs for the "truly gifted." The tests used to select students for these programs measure intelligence or other traits that reflect advantages that only wealthy parents can buy for their children. Such programs are inherently unfair. Other scholars have also made this point, of course, and we will have more to say later about special programs for "gifted" children. Here, we merely repeat that when high scores on intelligence tests are used to select students for enrichment programs, in the United States those programs always confer an unfair advantage on wealthy children. Our reasoning about wealth and intelligence also suggests that as the number of children living in poverty grows, as it did in the 1980s, the continuous rise in intelligence-test scores in this country is likely to stop. The cause for this will not be found in schools but in a society that imposes poverty on growing

numbers of its young people. We would be willing to bet, however, that some critics will try to blame public schools for the coming IQ decline.

Summary. What, then, can we conclude from these studies of measured intelligence? First, today's children are smarter, not dumber, than their parents. Furthermore, the parents of today's children were also more intelligent than were their own parents, the grandparents of today's youth. Second, intelligence is affected not only by inheritance and early childhood experiences; schooling also affects IQ test performance. More and better schooling in the U.S. and in other industrialized nations is the most likely reason for those nations' increases in IQ scores. High-quality instructional environments for toddlers, primary-school children, teenagers, and college students all seem to raise scores on IQ tests. Third, if wealthy people have better access than do poor people to high-quality education, as is the case so often in this country, then some children will do poorly and some will do well on IQ tests because of their parents' wealth rather than because of their genetic makeup or home environment.

Source: From *The Manufactured Crisis: Myths, Fraud, and the Attack on America's Public Schools* (pp. 49–50), by D. C. Berliner & B. Biddle, 1995, New York: Addison-Wesley.

Politics or Policy?   It is difficult at times to distinguish between policy and politics. For example, the No Child Left Behind (NCLB) Act placed teacher quality front and center for districts, campuses, and universities. Was it the politics or the policy? Whether teacher quality was an outgrowth of politics or not, there is no doubt that teacher quality is the single most important factor influencing student achievement (Darling-Hammond, 2000; Kaplan & Owings, 2001; Whitehurst, 2002); therefore, the policy now dictates to principals that each classroom must house a highly qualified teacher. For the principal, the teaching community, and scholars, an imperative outgrowth of this policy is to determine what constitutes a highly qualified teacher. NCLB indicates

that a highly qualified teacher is simply one who has a degree in the subject area and certification as defined by her respective state.

We now enter politics again with policy talk. Tyack and Cuban (1995) noted that there is a continual breach between *policy talk* and the world of daily school decisions. The authors argued that most reforms exist mainly in the realm of policy talk—which amounts to visionary and authoritative statements about how schools should be different; is carried on among scholars and policymakers; and usually involves callous conclusions about students, teachers, superintendents, and principals. However, according to Elmore (1997), *policy talk* can be influential in shaping public perceptions of the quality of schooling and what should be done about it; yet, policy talk hardly ever influences the deep-seated and enduring structures and practices of schooling, which he called the school's "instructional core."

Types of Educational Politics

Bryk, Sebring, Kerbow, Rollow, and Easton (1998) indicated that in the past local school politics may have been limited largely to face-to-face relations between a principal and individual teachers. Today, however, local school politics involve entirely new groups with very different interests. The following perspectives on school politics might be beneficial for principals to understand within their own political, school contexts: (a) pluralist maintenance politics, (b) adversarial politics, (c) strong democratic politics, (d) consolidated principal power, and (e) unitary politics.

Pluralist Maintenance Politics   The pluralist perspective on educational politics has several aspects: (a) group or individual interests are viewed as fixed and static, (b) pluralist bargaining often takes place in one-on-one negotiations, and (c) pluralist politics rarely brings about systemic change—which is why the authors call it "maintenance politics." Maintenance politics may be appropriate for "good" schools where little needs to change. However, in situations where deep change is needed, pluralist politics is not likely to bring about this kind of change (Bryk et al., 1998, p. 47).

Adversarial Politics   Bryk and colleagues (1998) recognized a form of community organizing that is adversarial by design. Some characteristics of this type of politics are as follows: (a) Adversarial politics often focuses on short-term goals; (b) adversarial politics exacerbates tensions between opposing groups; (c) adversarial groups tend to "personalize" the evils of an unfair system (e.g., in a particular principal rather than in the entire system); and (d) adversarial politics often seeks to organize and define one group against

other groups. Adversarial politics is likely to foster resentment among groups. The authors stated that deep, lasting reform is a long-term effort that requires trust, respect, collaboration, and a common commitment to goals; adversarial politics is not likely to provide the potential for reform.

Democratic Politics   There are four main characteristics of strong democratic politics: (1) Strong democratic politics fosters *sustained citizen participation* in the decision-making process and does not relegate decisions to representatives or "experts"; (2) there is an emphasis on *self-government and consensual politics,* in which the goal is to have citizens hammer out a common set of interests rather than merely try to accommodate or appease conflicting individual interests; (3) *public concern*, rather than individual interests, is the primary motivating force; and (4) core values and ideas are identified through *ongoing public debate*. Voting is less important than public talk that seeks to find common ground (Bryk et al., 1998).

The authors stated that democratic politics could serve as a lever for deep structural change by challenging entrenched, narrowly defined interests. Citizens who have a stake in schools, but have never really had a voice, can now hold educational professionals accountable. The authors also indicated that this kind of politics is probably a transitional state. Day-to-day school operations would get bogged down if strong democratic politics were the norm for every decision. In describing the role of principals within this political milieu, the authors said:

> Principals in schools with strong democracy display a distinctive leadership style. They support broad participation of both parents and faculty in the decision-making process and spend time promoting this involvement. They encourage a searching for new ideas that might help the school, and are also willing to challenge the status quo to implement them. (Bryk et al., 1998, p. 66)

Consolidated Principal Power   Bryk and colleagues (1998) identified two principal leadership styles for maneuvering through school politics: (1) autocratic—the principal brought order through fear, intimidation, or threats of reprisals, and control of the school originated with and was sustained by the principal; and (2) paternal/maternal—the principal treated school personnel as family. It was his job to take care of the family, and the principal fostered dependence on himself. The authors noted that a principal's ability to bring order to a chaotic situation often brings him a loyal following and allows him to hold onto his power despite reform legislation. This type of political context is much of what is observed prior to reform efforts. It is a more compliant form of politics in which the principal will engage.

Unitary Politics Bryk and colleagues (1998) observed the following in unitary politics: (a) a shared set of principles that provide a guiding framework for day-to-day operations; (b) a strong relational ethic, characterized by respect and trust; (c) small, stable communities where people have a common history, share a common vision of the future, and have ample opportunity to work together and get to know each other well (opportunities for substantive talk and collective planning are also critical); and (d) organizations that recruit like-minded individuals, or who aggressively socialize new members into group norms. The authors say that this form of politics is probably the norm in stable, high-performing schools. Unitary politics is more stable and efficient than strong democratic politics.

According to Kennedy (2000), educators have been told that they should stay out of political affairs, and that school people do not need to express opinions about such things in public. She indicated that such behavior is silent submission; the educators' reasoning was that while they were taking care of school, at another level, lawmakers were taking care of passing laws in educators' own interests and in the children's interests. Kennedy shared her own story as a young teacher. Her superintendent had warned her and other teachers that no teacher or principal was to get involved in the upcoming board of education election. They were not to donate money or make any visible show of support for a candidate. She admitted that even though she had an opinion about who should be elected to the board, she shared it with no one.

Kennedy (2000) pointed out that the voices of educators or principals can be heard in the hubbub of the political scene. For example, in 1999, an attempt to pass a collective bargaining bill in Missouri failed because of a concerted, organized opposition from elementary and secondary school principals. She indicated that the myriad of contacts received by lawmakers convinced them to defeat this bill despite support from the governor and house leadership. Kennedy provided another example from Michigan, where an amendment stating that every principal in the state would be an "at-will" employee generated more than 1,000 calls from principals and convinced legislators to defeat that amendment.

Kennedy (2000) made the following suggestions for principals as they become involved in making a difference through politics:

1. Use the resources of state and national principal-administrator associations. They have information about proposed legislation. For example, visit http://www.principals.org/s_nassp/sec_abstracts.asp?CID=28&DID=28.

2. Be sure you have correct information—don't contact a member of the House if the critical vote is in the Senate.

3. Be concise and accurate, and include a story in your message. You may use personal interest stories and leave students' names out, but tell the story. Talk about the effect the proposal will have on your students and your school.

4. Be alert. Follow the proposal as it moves through the process. Continue to push your issue between sessions of the legislature.

5. Get to know your senator and representative. Make frequent contacts.

6. Be sure to acknowledge those lawmakers who did support your issue. They appreciate a pat on the back.

7. Don't send a duplicated message. State and national lawmakers generally discount them.

8. Don't procrastinate.

Fowler (2004) added the following:

1. Identify and monitor your competitors.

2. Study the timing of elections and the concerns within the elections.

3. Look for windows of opportunity to impact policy when both politicians and the public support an issue.

4. Network and build coalitions.

5. Build relationships with educational professionals.

6. Build relationships with other governmental agencies.

Politics in the District: Working With the Superintendent and Other External Forces

Davis and Hensley (1999) put forth the notion that certainly politics plays a part in principals working with their superintendents. In particular, politics enters in during a principal's evaluation. The principal's job is multifaceted, with many demands from all directions—not just from above and below, but from outside—and this makes evaluation even more problematic (Brown & Irby, 2001). Davis and Hensley (1999) also observed that politics adds another important dimension to the issues of principal evaluation.

According to the *Synergistic Leadership Theory* (Irby, Brown, Duffy, & Trautman, 2003), a leader's perceived effectiveness is formed by factors beyond her leadership ability alone. Those factors include (a) the organizational structure; (b) the values, beliefs, and attitudes of the leader and of those with whom she works in the organization; and (c) in the case of politics, external forces. For the principal to be perceived as effective, all three of the factors would have to be aligned with the factor leadership behavior, and the factors would need to be harmonious most of the time. It is recognized that there will be bumps in the road; however, for the principal it is important to be able analyze synergistically all factors and get over the bump as quickly as possible.

Principals displaying this ability ensure that the perception of their role remains positive both inside and outside of the organization.

As Davis (1999) pointed out, most principals are faced with an increasingly contentious and diverse array of pressures from what Irby and colleagues (2003) called external forces—those within the school, the community, the district office, the judicial system, and society at large. Davis (1999) suggested that only rarely do the constantly shifting values, preferences, and needs of school constituents find themselves in perfect alignment. For example, he stated that in most districts the principal fits at midway in the management bureaucracy; at the same time, the principal is superordinate to teachers, staff, and students and subordinate to district office administrators. This situation may create incongruence among the factors of leadership behavior and external forces, as outlined in the synergistic leadership theory (Irby et al., 2003).

Davis (1998) found that poor interpersonal relationships and a lack of political acuity were far more likely to work toward the demise of a principal than was a lack of management skills or techniques. Principals who were weak in the areas of interpersonal relationships and political acuity failed to build confidence, trust, and support among constituent groups, or to effectively manage complex political influences. Davis's findings support the notion that many principals work within turbulent political environments that require skillful nurturing of interpersonal relationships and effective judgment about when and how to apply supportive leadership behaviors.

It appears that the balance between leadership behavior and external forces presents the most problems for principals; in Davis's (1998) research, the three critical areas cited by superintendents as highly related to a principal's performance failure were poor people skills, poor decision-making skills, and poor political skills. At the same time, most principals indicated particular concern about covert superintendent and/or board member agendas and perceptions. The principals believed that these factors, in concert with a few vocal or influential parents and teachers, could result in a negative evaluation. Principals also expressed concern about the increased number of parents and teachers who take their complaints directly to the superintendent or board members. Each of the principals complained that superintendents almost always overreacted to parent and/or teacher complaints about the principal or school. Another external force, unions, was a serious concern for principals, who thought the teachers' union had them under their influence and felt that principals, along with superintendents, were powerless to challenge the union.

Davis (1998) suggested the following strategies for principals when working within the political system and with their superintendents (we have integrated our strategies with his):

1. Focus on maintaining positive interpersonal relationships with parents, teachers, students, and supervisors. Project yourself as open, approachable, and caring. Be patient, listen well, and manage your anger (or frustration) when dealing with difficult circumstances. Learn to talk with, and not at, people. Distribute your attentions evenly and fairly among teachers, parents, the community, and students. Work on bringing people together in pursuit of common values and a clear vision for the school.

2. Maintain a sense of perspective relative to your status as principal. The days of principals acting like paternal or maternal authority figures are long gone. To survive, you need to know how to share power, empower others, and establish collaborative decision-making processes.

3. Know how others perceive you. Find out how teachers feel about you, and how parents and students perceive you. Without this feedback, you will never be certain how well you are doing in regard to maintaining positive relationships with others.

4. Know yourself. Assess your leadership style, your personality, and the way you interact with the world around you. Effective administrators tend to be self-reflective people who are honest about their shortcomings as well as their strengths; they are not afraid to seek assistance from others when confronted with complex problems or tasks. We suggest an analysis of your situation based upon the synergistic leadership theory, because it can assist you in understanding where there is misalignment.

5. Have a flexible leadership style. Develop the ability to apply different leadership styles as needed to address specific situations. Be willing and able to adapt to changing workplace conditions and environmental influences. Understand when to apply rational and logical perspectives to school issues and problems, when to focus on meeting individual needs, when to balance the competing interests of groups and individuals, and when to lead through the application of symbols and rituals.

6. Establish coalitions and partnerships with outside agencies; also establish professional relationships with statewide and national education associations.

7. Be proactive. Ask your superintendent to act as a mediator or broker between you and the community, to regularly communicate with the board about your school issues and outcomes, to redirect teacher and parent complaints to you, and to provide assistance or remediation if you are at risk early in your career.

8. As recommended by Brown and Irby (2001), complete an evaluation portfolio to critically analyze beliefs, experiences, understandings, and actions in the context of the school and district and to determine the impact of those actions upon student growth and the organization. As a tool for reflection, the portfolio can enhance the principal's ability to be cognizant of his or her place within the political context and the school.

As principals decide to move into the world of politics, probably the easiest route is through their superintendent. Principals and superintendents can influence board policy at the local level.

Box 16.2   Excerpts from Bellville Independent School District's Local Curriculum Policy (a political action by a school administrator)

Bellville Independent School District Local
Board Policy: Curriculum

Purpose: The Board recognizes the need and
value of a systematic, on-going program of
curriculum review and development. The Board
shall encourage and support the professional staff
in its efforts to investigate new curricular ideas,
develop and improve programs, and evaluate
results. In order to ensure quality control of the
curriculum and be responsive to the school
community and state requirements. . . .

Definition: Curriculum is defined as the
knowledge, skills, attitudes, and processes to be
taught and learned at the appropriate levels/areas
or in courses in the District schools.

Curriculum Philosophy: The curriculum of the
District shall be developed by teachers and administrators in cooperation with community, business,
and District educators to be responsive to the
demand of the real-world workplace. Students
shall possess competencies and skills to enable
them to be viable contenders in a global society.
Through equitable and quality authentic learning
experiences, all students shall demonstrate high
academic skills. The curriculum shall emphasize
the core knowledge and skills that are necessary
for profitably pursuing further education in college,
technical/vocational education, and productive and

responsible community membership. It shall be an
objective of the curriculum to enable each student to
obtain an education appropriate to his or her diverse
interests, ambitions, and abilities. The Board seeks
to ensure that each student receives the necessary
instruction to progress successfully through the
system. The Board requires that each student achieve
basic standards for satisfactory advancement,
particularly in progressing from elementary to junior
high school, and from junior high school to senior
high school. However, since initiative and flexibility
in instructional techniques are encouraged, teaching
methods may vary from campus to campus or from
class to class.

Alignment: The design and implementation of
the curriculum shall be aligned with the planned
and written curriculum as presented in the
curriculum guide, the taught curriculum as
presented to students by the teacher, and the tested
curriculum as determined by student assessments.
The teacher-made tests and standardized tests
shall be congruent with the written and taught
curriculum.

Board Adoption: The Board shall officially
adopt the curriculum that encompasses local
goals and objectives, skills that are identified by
state and federal guidelines, and mandates where
applicable.

First, the principal must become aware of local
board policies and develop an understanding of
"what is." Most board policies are divided into
the following or similar sections: (a) basic district
foundations, (b) local governance, (c) business
and support services, (d) personnel, (e) instruction, (f) students, and (g) community and governmental relations. Principals, working with their
superintendents, can influence the policies within
each section at the board level, most particularly
the policies dealing with personnel, instruction,
and students.

Barbara Polnick, a curriculum expert in Texas
(personal communication, September 5, 2004),

related the following incident about a school
administrator in Bellville Independent School
District. Based on the curriculum management audit work of Frase and English (1995), the school
administrator learned how to conduct curriculum
audits and how to lead audit and alignment efforts. His work within the political context of his
small district led to the development of a model
local curriculum board policy that was presented
to the board and subsequently adopted. For excerpts from that policy, see Box 16.2 (the full
policy is available at http://www.tasb.org/policy/
pol/private/008901/pol.cfm?DisplayPage=EG
(LOCAL).html).

Box 16.2   Continued

Accountability: The Superintendent shall be responsible for the implementation of the curriculum policy and shall serve as the primary mover of the curriculum management system. . . .

Principals: The building principal shall monitor the implementation of the curriculum, translating its importance to staff members on an on-going basis. The principal shall observe classes, monitor lessons, and evaluate teacher-made tests, using, as a minimum, the following strategies to monitor curriculum: (1) Classroom observations, (2) Interviews and conferences, (3) Confirmation of lesson plan alignment with curriculum.

Teachers: Teachers shall adhere to the curriculum philosophy of the District. They shall be responsible for teaching to the planned curriculum, testing their teaching, and accurately reporting results to parents.

Long-Range Planning: The curriculum process shall be aligned with the District Long-Range Plan.

Curriculum Direction: Subject-area written curriculum guides shall be developed locally for all grade levels or interdisciplinary subjects in the District. They shall be revised and readopted by the Board at least every five years. The guides shall contain or be based on the following: District mission statement; District philosophy of education; District curriculum philosophy; Belief statements related to the subject area and linked to appropriate exit expectations; Program goals

and objectives for each subject area; Instructional focus for the elementary and secondary levels; Correlation of objectives and activities to the state essential knowledge and skills and statewide assessments; A scope and sequence chart for use in designing instruction at the appropriate level of difficulty for all learners; Correlation and integration of activities to and/or with instructional resources, adopted texts, and supplemental material; Real-world activities derived from the program goals and objectives for all subject areas; Relevant modifications and enrichment activities; and a statement of the means of evaluation of each of the content areas, skills, and attitudes to be taught. In formatting curriculum, the Superintendent shall make appropriate use of a wide range of resources, including professional staff; lay members of the community; experience of other systems; programs of schools, colleges, and universities; and information prepared by the schools of education, research institutions, educational foundations, and state and federal governments. Copies of the curriculum guides in complete sets shall be available for all teachers and the public in each principal's office and in the public libraries of the community for parental review and reference. The Superintendent shall take steps to conduct a major review of one curriculum area per year. A report/presentation shall be organized for the Board, demonstrating

(continued)

Summary

1. Principals must be knowledgeable and cognizant of the politics surrounding the creation and implementation of educational policies.

2. Policy is the outgrowth of governmental actions.

3. Once policy is set, there is no guarantee that it will be implemented in the same way it was originally intended.

4. The principal could be related to policy in the following ways: (a) orientation, (b) degree, (c) resources, (d) activity, (e) autonomy, (f) societal values, (g) institutional values, (h) rationale, and (i) power relationship.

5. Principals can use theory to analyze policy. The analysis of policy through systems theory provides a holistic look at the policy itself. It allows principals to analyze the "policy 'inputs' including demands, needs, and resources, the 'throughputs' that involve the key actors who implement policy, and policy

---

Box 16.2   Continued

how this policy has been implemented, and making recommendations necessary for the improvement of pupil growth. The areas of review shall be: Mathematics; Language arts; Science; Social Studies (including geography, patriotism, government, and history); Health/safety; Fine arts; Vocational education; Special programs; Other languages; Technology; and Physical education. Other elective courses. The review process shall include a statement of instructional goals by grade level; assessment or testing trend data, as may be relevant; important new trends that are to be incorporated into the curriculum; recommended textbooks in the curriculum; and input from the teaching staff. The Superintendent shall employ one or more externally identified content area curriculum experts to critique the proposed or existing curriculum in light of available knowledge regarding appropriate curriculum in the areas being reviewed. Reports/critiques made by such experts shall be included in the report to the Board.

Review Committee: District-wide revisions in curriculum shall be considered by a District ad hoc committee in which a majority of the members have appropriate expertise to deal with the curriculum under consideration. The committee shall be composed of at least 50 percent teachers. The purpose of the committee shall be to provide the Superintendent and Board

with additional campus-level input regarding curriculum changes. The scope of the committee's work shall be limited to reviewing the following: Determination of adequate training and preparation of teachers and administrators for implementation of the proposed program; Determination of adequate funding for personnel and materials; and Determination of adequate lead time for implementation of the proposed curriculum change.

Curriculum Changes: Curriculum changes that do not alter course offerings or course objectives may be approved by the Superintendent after consideration by the curriculum review committee; the administration shall then direct the staff to implement such changes. Curriculum changes that may involve the addition or deletion of courses shall be made only after Board approval.

Resource Allocation: The Board shall adopt a budget annually that provides the monetary resources to fund the curriculum training, materials and resources, and testing necessary to implement effectively the aligned curriculum. The budget development process shall ensure that goals and priorities are considered in the preparation of budget proposals and that any decision related to reduction or increase in funding levels can be addressed in those terms.

'outputs' such as educated, civic-minded students or improved economic productivity."

6. Neopluralist advocacy coalition and interest group theories are grounded in a political science perspective that seeks to answer "who gets what, when, and how" as key coalitions struggle to obtain from government the resources and support they believe necessary.

7. Neoinstitutional theory indicates that the structure of societal and political organizations exerts independent effects on policy.

8. Critical theory questions the exiting economic, political, and social purposes of schooling and examines policy through the

lens of oppressed groups, with a normative orientation toward freeing disenfranchised groups from conditions of domination and subjugation.

9. Feminist theory is concerned primarily with the often unequal effects of education policies on issues relating to gender and sexual difference, including how education policies are translated through institutional processes that serve to reinforce or encourage gender inequity.

10. Postmodernism argues that policy is contextually defined by those in authority and has little validity when separated from its setting.

11. Ideological theories place policy into a partisan, politically value-laden structure, hoping to gain insight into the econo-political context surrounding key policies.

12. To understand policies, principals can review the conceptual framework of four dimensions: (a) normative dimension (beliefs and values), (b) structural dimension (organizational and governmental structures), (c) constituentive dimension (networks, interest groups, and end users), and (d) technical dimension (educational planning, implementation, and evaluation).

13. Just as ethics and social justice enter into a principal's evaluation of policy, so does the concept of moral purpose.

14. Politics and public education are inseparable. At times it is difficult to distinguish between policy and politics.

15. Most definitions of politics are rooted in a system of governance. If governance is the system of directing affairs or political administration, politics is a by-product of that system.

16. Five perspectives on school politics are beneficial for principals to understand within their own political, school contexts: (a) pluralist maintenance politics, (b) adversarial politics, (c) strong democratic politics, (d) consolidated principal power, and (e) unitary politics.

17. Politics plays a part in principal evaluation due to the multifaceted and complex nature of the job.

18. Principals should work with their superintendents to alter policy within the school district's political context.

Field-Based Activities

1. Discuss with the superintendent how policy is established within your school district. Ask how principals are involved in policy development. Try to ascertain how the policy development,

adoption, and implementation fit within the models presented in the chapter.

2. Review practices at your school campus. Can you identify any insidious policies that are in opposition to ethics and social justice? Talk with your principal about these policies, and determine a plan of action to remedy them.

3. Review the school board policies. (a) To what extent do the policies for curriculum adhere to the model policy presented? (b) Are policies inclusive of instruction? Personnel? Students? (c) Are the policies presented just?

Suggested Readings

Apple, M. W. (2001). *Educating the "right" way: Markets, standards, God, and inequality.* New York: Routledge/Falmer. Apple explores the "conservative restoration"—the rightward turn of a broad-based coalition that is making successful inroads in determining American and international educational policy. The author takes a pragmatic look at what critical educators can do to build alternative coalitions and policies that are more democratic. Apple urges this group to extricate itself from its reliance on the language of possibility in order to employ pragmatic analyses that address the material realities of social power.

Berliner, D. C., & Biddle, B. J. (1995). *The manufactured crisis: Myths, fraud, and the attack on America's public schools.* Reading, MA: Addison-Wesley. *The Manufactured Crisis* debunks the myths that test scores in America's schools are falling, that illiteracy is rising, and that better funding has no benefit. It shares the good news about public education. Winner of the American Educational Research Association book award, *The Manufactured Crisis* is the best source of facts and analysis for people who want to know what is really happening in our schools.

Brown, G., & Irby, B. J. (2001). *The principal portfolio* (2nd ed.). Thousand Oaks, CA: Corwin. Genevieve Brown and Beverly J. Irby update their best-selling *The Principal Portfolio* to offer the most comprehensive self-assessment guide available for principals. This easy-to-use resource sheds light on how a portfolio can help administrators and principals embrace and engage in the reflection and continued growth needed to create improved schools and learning. This revised edition includes

- A new section on electronic portfolios
- Expanded information on using portfolios for professional development
- Expanded information on using portfolios for evaluation
- New focus on academic growth in administrator preparation programs
- Current research and updated references
- New quotes and examples from successful principals in the field

Bryk, A. S., Sebring, P. B., Kerbow, D., Rollow, S., & Easton, J. Q. (1998). *Charting Chicago school reform: Democratic localism as a lever for change*. Boulder, CO: Westview. In 1989, Chicago began an experiment with radical decentralization of power and authority. This book tells the story of what happened to Chicago's elementary schools in the first four years of this reform. Implicit in this reform is the theory that expanded local democratic participation would stimulate organizational change within schools, which in turn would foster improved teaching and learning. Using this theory as a framework, the authors marshal massive quantitative and qualitative data to examine how the reform actually unfolded at the school level.

With longitudinal case study data on 22 schools, survey responses from principals and teachers in 269 schools, and supplementary system-wide administrative data, the authors identify four types of school politics: strong democracy, consolidated principal power, maintenance, and adversarial. In addition, they classify school change efforts as either systemic or unfocused. Bringing these strands together, the authors determine that in about a third of the schools, expanded local democratic participation served as a strong lever for introducing systemic change focused on improved instruction. Finally, case studies of six actively restructuring schools illustrate how under decentralization the principal's role is recast, social support for change can grow, and ideas and information from external sources are brought to bear on school change initiatives.

Few studies so completely intertwine extensive narratives and rigorous quantitative analyses. The result is a complex picture of the Chicago reform that joins the politics of local control to school change. This volume is intended for scholars in the fields of urban education, public policy, sociology of education, anthropology of education, and politics of education.

Chubb, J., & Moe, T. (1990). *Politics, markets, and America's schools*. Washington, DC: Brookings Institution. During the 1980s, widespread dissatisfaction with America's schools gave rise to a powerful movement for educational change, and the nation's political institutions responded with aggressive reforms. Chubb and Moe argue that these reforms are destined to fail because they do not get to the root of the problem. The fundamental causes of poor academic performance, they claim, are not to be found in the schools, but rather in the institutions of direct democratic control by which the schools have traditionally been governed. Reformers fail to solve the problem when the institutions are the problem. The authors recommend a new system of public education, built around parent-student choice and school competition, that would promote school autonomy and thus provide a firm foundation for genuine school improvement and superior student achievement.

Cooper, B. S., Fusarelli, L. D., & Randall, E. V. (2004). *Better policies, better schools: Theories and applications*. New York: Pearson. This is the most comprehensive book on educational policy. The authors weave together literature from numerous subfields to provide a unifying four-dimensional framework for approaching educational issues. They use the latest research on the policymaking process and theory and apply this information to key policy areas. Policy areas examined in the text include governance, curriculum and standards, accountability, labor relations, finance, and school choice. The authors examine these policy areas in a framework consisting of normative, structural, constituent, and technical dimensions.

Fowler, F. C. (2004). *Policy studies for educational leaders: An introduction* (2nd ed.). Upper Saddle River, NJ: Merrill/Prentice Hall. This comprehensive book encourages future educational leaders to be proactive rather than reactive, and arms them with an understanding of educational policy and the important political theories upon which it is based. Coverage addresses theory, analysis, development, and implementation of educational policy, with the knowledge base of the typical reader in mind. Fowler explores the reasons for change in educational policy, the ways to track its evolution, and the techniques for influencing its ultimate destination. The text includes updated statistics drawn from the 2000 census and explores economic changes expected from the business cycle downturn and the effect of war. Fowler includes news stories for analysis — related to chapter content as well as key current issues, including the No Child Left Behind Act of 2001; new case studies on the teaching of Darwinian evolution and on parent revolts against state testing programs; and an entire chapter devoted to policy values and ideology. There is extensive coverage on educational policy at the state level.

17. Legal Issues

Standard 6.0: *Candidates who complete the program are educational leaders who have the knowledge and ability to promote the success of all students by understanding, responding to, and influencing the larger political, social, economic, legal, and cultural context.*

FOCUSING QUESTIONS

1 What is the legal basis for education under which school principals operate?

2 How is the American judicial system of federal and state courts organized?

3 What are the major legal issues pertaining to schools and the state concerning compulsory school attendance, church-state relations, school fees, the curriculum, and state-mandated testing?

4 What are the major legal issues pertaining to students concerning freedom of expression, student appearance, extracurricular activities, student discipline, and students with disabilities?

5 What are the major legal issues pertaining to the school staff concerning certification, contracts, termination of employment, discrimination in employment, collective bargaining, and tort liability?

In this chapter, we address these questions concerning legal issues pertaining to the school principal's role in maintaining a safe and orderly environment for learning. We begin our discussion by examining the legal basis for public education. Then we discuss the American judicial system of federal and state courts. Next, we examine schools and the state pertaining to compulsory school attendance, church-state relations, school fees, the school curriculum, and state-mandated testing. This is followed by a discussion of legal issues pertaining to students, including freedom of expression, student appearance, extracurricular activities, student discipline, and students with disabilities. We conclude the chapter with a discussion of legal issues pertaining to school staff, including certification, contracts, termination of employment, discrimination in employment, collective bargaining, and tort liability.

Legal Basis for Public Education

Those involved in administering schools, particularly superintendents and principals, should ensure that their actions are lawful. Educational decisions may not be enforced arbitrarily or capriciously but must be based on appropriate legal principles. Laws affecting schools cover a wide range of legal subject matter, including the basic areas of contracts, property, torts, constitutional law, and other matters of law that directly impact the operation of public elementary and secondary schools. Due to the breadth of the subject matter involved, it is necessary for the school principal to be versed in certain fundamental concepts of the law and to be able to apply this knowledge to situations that daily affect school operation.

Sources of Law

A beginning point for ensuring lawful administrative conduct in the operation of schools is a systematic study of the sources of law under which school principals operate. Such a study follows and is designed to analyze sources of law that emanate from each level of government: federal, state, and local. This overview establishes a context for subsequent topics in which we more fully discuss legal principles as they apply to specific school situations.

Federal Level

At the federal level, the U.S. Constitution, federal statutes, federal administrative agencies, and case law all constitute sources of law under which school principals operate. We discuss each source in turn.

U.S. Constitution Although education is not specifically mentioned in the U.S. Constitution, the federal government has had a significant involvement in education. In fact, programs under various federal statutes regarding PK–12 education in

recent years have constituted more than 7% of the total expenditures for public elementary and secondary education (National Center for Education Statistics, 2004a). Of greater significance has been the pervasive force of the federal government in influencing educational policy. The federal judiciary has addressed education issues such as racial segregation in schools, equitable state financing of public schools, due process of students and teachers, church-state relations, search and seizure, and freedom of expression of students and teachers.

Particularly significant are the General Welfare Clause of the U.S. Constitution and the federal judiciary's interpretation of the Fourteenth Amendment to the Constitution. A brief examination of these percepts may be helpful to the school principal, based on their impact on the national well-being and the requirements for due process and equal protection of the law as they pertain to educational matters.

Under Article I, Section 8 of the Constitution, Congress has the power "to lay and collect taxes, duties, imposts and excises, to pay the debts and provide for the common defense and general welfare of the United States" (U.S. CONST. art. I, sec. 8). The General Welfare Clause has provided substantial federal support for research and instructional programs in the areas of reading, mathematics, science, special education, vocational education, career education, and bilingual education. Congress also has enacted legislation providing financial assistance for the school lunch program and for services to meet the needs of special groups of students, such as the educationally and culturally disadvantaged. Furthermore, Congress passed legislation pertaining to national health and safety concerns with the Asbestos School Hazard Detection and Control Act of 1980 and the Indoor Radon Abatement Act of 1988, which require the inspection of school buildings and, when necessary, corrective action to assure the safety of students and employees. Moreover, in an attempt to protect minor children's access to indecent material made available to them through the Internet, Congress passed the Children's Internet Protection Act of 2002;

see H.R. 5666 sec. 1721; U.S.C. sec. 9134 (f) (2002); 47 U.S.C. sec. 254 (h) (5) (2002). School principals need to abide by these provisions when operating their schools.

The Fourteenth Amendment is the most widely invoked constitutional provision in school litigation, because it specifically addresses state action. The U.S. Supreme Court has interpreted Fourteenth Amendment liberties as incorporating the personal freedoms contained in the Bill of Rights (*Cantwell v. Connecticut,* 310 U.S. 296, 303, 1940; *Gutlow v. New York,* 268 U.S. 652, 666, 1925). Consequently, the first 10 amendments, originally directed toward the federal government, have been applied to state action as well. In part, the Fourteenth Amendment stipulates, "No state shall . . . deprive any person of life, liberty, or property without due process of law; nor deny to any person within its jurisdiction the equal protection of the laws."

The Due Process Clause of the Fourteenth Amendment, which prohibits states from depriving citizens of life, liberty, or property without due process of law, has been significant in school cases. Compulsory school attendance laws confer on students a legitimate property right to attend school. The granting of tenure gives teachers a property right to continued employment. Liberty rights include interests in one's reputation and fundamental rights related to marriage, family, and personal privacy. The Equal Protection Clause, which prohibits states from denying to any person within its jurisdiction the equal protection of the laws, has played an important role in school litigation involving discrimination based on race, gender, ethnicity, and disabilities, as well as litigation calling for the equitable financing of schools.

Federal Statutes Congress has enacted many statutes that provide school principals with sources of law. The legal basis for this congressional involvement derives from the General Welfare Clause of the U.S. Constitution. Federal statutes enacted by Congress are designed to provide financial assistance to public schools and to clarify the scope of individual's civil rights.

Much of the federal legislation enacted has provided funds to assist school districts in attaining equity goals and other national priorities, including national defense (National Defense Education Act of 1958); vocational education (Vocational Education Act of 1963); elementary and secondary education (Elementary and Secondary Education Act of 1965); bilingual education (Bilingual Education Act of 1968); and children with disabilities (Education for All Handicapped Children Act of 1975, renamed the Individuals with Disabilities Act of 1990 and the Individuals with Disabilities Act of 1997).

The most comprehensive law offering financial assistance to schools was the Elementary and Secondary Education Act of 1965 (ESEA). In part, it supplied funds for compensatory education programs for economically disadvantaged students. In 2002, President Bush signed into law the No Child Left Behind Act (20 U.S.C. sec. 6301, 2002). The focus of the law is to improve the performance of public schools. The law pledges that no child will be left behind in a failing school. Specifically, the law requires that states develop both content standards in reading and mathematics and tests linked to the standards for grades 3 through 8, with science standards and assessments to follow. States must identify adequate yearly progress (AYP) objectives and disaggregate test results for all students and subgroups of students based on socioeconomic status, race and ethnicity, English language proficiency, and disability. Moreover, the law mandates that 100% of students must score at the proficient level on state tests by 2014. Furthermore, the No Child Left Behind Act requires states to participate every other year in the National Assessment of Educational Progress (NAEP) in reading and mathematics.

Federal legislation designed to clarify the scope of an individual's civil rights include the Civil Rights Act of 1964 (prohibits employment discrimination on the basis of race, color, sex, religion, or national origin); the Age Discrimination in Employment Act of 1967 (protects employees over 40 against age-based employment discrimination); Title IX of the Educational Amendments of 1972 (prohibits gender discrimination of participants in education programs); the Rehabilitation Act of 1973 (prohibits discrimination against otherwise qualified persons with disabilities); the Age Discrimination Act of 1975 (prohibits age-based discrimination in federally assisted programs); the Civil Rights Act of 1991 (prohibits race or ethnicity discrimination in making and enforcing contracts); and 42 U.S.C. sec. 1983, 2002 (provides the right of individuals to bring suit against any person who, acting under the authority of state law, impairs rights secured by the U.S. Constitution and federal legislation).

Federal Administrative Agencies   At the federal level, federal administrative agencies conduct the regulatory activities and structural details to implement broad legislative mandates. Originally established in 1867, the Office of Education became part of the Department of Health, Education, and Welfare in 1953. In 1980, the Department of Education was created. Its secretary is appointed by the president with the approval of the Senate and serves as a member of the president's cabinet.

The primary function of the Department of Education is to coordinate federal involvement in education. Regulations created by the Department of Education to implement federal legislation have had a significant impact on public elementary and secondary schools. The Department of Education administers regulations for more than 100 different programs. Other federal administrative agencies — including the Department of Agriculture, the Department of Defense, the Department of Health and Human Services, the Department of Justice, and the Department of Labor — administer the remaining educational programs. The Office of Civil Rights and the Equal Employment Opportunity Commission, through their regulatory activities, review claims of discrimination in public schools and initiate suits against school districts for noncompliance with civil rights laws. The Environmental Protection Agency regulates compliance with national health and safety concerns designed to assure the safety of students and employees.

Case Law   A fourth source of law is case law. Case law refers to principles of law established by the courts, as distinguished from the written law of constitutions, statutes, and administrative agencies. Case law frequently relies on earlier court decisions, which are called *precedents*. This practice is derived from the *doctrine of stare decisis*, meaning "let the decision stand." Under the doctrine of stare decisis, a court may stand by precedent and thereby not disturb an already settled point of law. Although courts generally rely on precedent, they are not bound by it in reaching a decision. A court may decide that the factual circumstances in the case being decided are not sufficiently similar to those of the precedent-setting case. Furthermore, the legal rationale used in reaching the precedent-setting case may not be applicable to the particular case under review.

Federal courts have contributed a significant body of case law, which has influenced educational policies governing the operation of public schools. Federal courts have addressed issues such as racial segregation, equitable methods of financing schools, separation of church and state, due process and equal protection concerns of students and teachers, freedom of expression of students and teachers, and dress and grooming standards of students and teachers. Precedents established by the federal courts regarding these issues provide school principals with an important source of law.

Case law is not always well settled, because occasionally federal district courts and courts of appeals render conflicting rulings within their jurisdictions. Consequently, school principals must follow case law rendered for their particular jurisdiction. The U.S. Supreme Court is the single court whose decisions affect the administration and operation of public schools across the nation. A decision of the U.S. Supreme Court may be modified only by another High Court decision or by an amendment to the constitution. Unfortunately, Supreme Court decisions have not always been followed by local school principals. Desegregation decisions and those dealing with Bible reading and reciting prayers during school hours are examples. It is vital for school principals to have a thorough understanding of well-settled case law and to enforce compliance with those decisions in operating their schools.

State Level

State-level sources of law include the state's constitution, state statutes, state administrative agencies, and case law. We discuss each source in turn.

State Constitutions   The Tenth Amendment to the U.S. Constitution stipulates that "the powers not delegated to the United States by the Constitution, nor prohibited by it to the states, are reserved to the states respectively, or to the people." Because education is not mentioned in the Tenth Amendment to the U.S. Constitution, it is left to the states to control. Therefore, state constitutions represent the basic source of law for individual states and generally require legislative bodies to make provision for a system of free public schools. Such provisions range from very specific educational provisions to broad mandates that direct the legislature of the state to provide funds for the support of a public school system. State constitutions also restrict the powers that legislative bodies may exercise.

State constitutions frequently address the same subject matter found in the federal Constitution, such as due process and/or equal protection of the law requirements, as well as separation of church and state. As a result, state courts are often asked to interpret these issues in an educational context. State constitutions may not contravene the federal Constitution.

State Statutes   The public schools of the United States are governed by state statutes enacted by state legislatures. State statutes represent an important source of law for school principals. The specificity of state statutes governing the operation of public schools varies from state to state and from subject to subject. Typically, however, state legislatures can raise revenue and distribute educational funds; prescribe curricular offerings; establish length of school day and year; mandate school attendance; establish pupil performance standards; set rules regarding suspension and expulsion of students; control teacher certification; establish procedures for tenure, retirement, collective bargaining, and fair dismissal procedures; create, alter, and abolish school districts and school boards; remove incumbent school board members and abolish their offices; set admission policies for local schools; impose penalties for noncompliance with state regulations; and regulate other specific aspects of public school operations, including state-funded charter schools and homeschooling.

State Administrative Agencies   State-level agencies typically include a State Board of Education, a Chief State School Officer, and a State Department of Education. Specific functions of these state administrative agencies vary considerably among the states. Nevertheless, these agencies individually and collectively provide an important source of law for school principals.

The primary function of state boards of education is to develop policies and regulations to implement legislation and constitutional requirements. One regulatory method used by state boards of education to compel local school districts to abide by their directives is accreditation. The most common accreditation models typically include the establishment of minimum standards in areas such as curriculum, instructional materials, teacher qualifications, and facilities. State funds may be withheld from school districts for noncompliance with accreditation requirements. Other areas dealt with by state boards of education include school district organization, school closings, reductions in professional staff, and state-level review of appeals from local school boards.

The chief state school officer (CSSO), variously designated as State Superintendent or Commissioner of Education, often acts as the executive head of the state's Department of Education. Typically, the CSSO's duties have been regulatory in nature; but they often include other activities such as research, long-range planning, and adjudicating educational controversies.

Each state also has established a state Department of Education, which may contain divisions for specialized services such as administration, finance, instruction, and research. State department personnel often collect data from local school districts to ensure that legislative requirements and State Board of Education policies are implemented; they also engage in activities to improve educational practices within the state.

Case Law State court decisions provide another source of law for school principals, where there is no policy direction from the state constitution, state statutes, or state administrative agencies. A decision of one state's highest court is not binding in another state. However, such a decision does provide school principals with the rationale of another state's highest court in an area of concern. And it should be noted that unless a federal issue is involved, there is no appeal of a decision of a state's highest court.

Courts have the final say on the meaning and effect of questioned laws. The power of individual courts to create law is illustrated in the cases appearing in later sections of this chapter. For example, among other things, courts determine issues involving whether a school principal lawfully exercised his or her authority or unlawfully abused administrative discretion.

Local Level

There are approximately 15,000 local school districts nationwide, ranging from a few students to several hundred thousand (National Center for Education Statistics, 2004b). Some states, particularly those with large numbers of school districts, like Texas, have created intermediate or regional service centers that perform regulatory or service functions for several school districts within a designated geographic area. School districts, acting through their local school boards, administer the public schools.

Local school board policies provide another source of law for school principals, as well as their individual school's rules or regulations. School board policies have the full force of the law as long as they do not contravene federal and state constitutions, federal and state statutes, or case law. Once these legal requirements are met, the school board as the delegated government at the local level may not violate its own policies. In many cases, school principals rely on this authority in dealing with such issues as administering corporal punishment, suspending or expelling a student, searching a student's locker or person, censorship of the school newspaper or yearbook, a student or teacher's refusal to participate in the Pledge of Allegiance or flag salute, use of the school building by the community, and dress and grooming standards of students and teachers.

State laws generally require that a school board can make official decisions only as a single corporate body, that is, as a whole at a duly convened official school board meeting (*Dugan v. Ballman,* 502 P. 2d 308, Fla. 1976; *Konovalchik v. Sch. Comm. of Salem,* 226 N.E. 2d 222, Mass. 1967; *State v. Consol. Sch. Dist.,* 281 S.W. 2d 511, Mo. 1955; *Whalen v. Minn. Spec. Sch. Dist.,* 2445 N.W. 2d 440, Minn. 1976). The school board meeting must be pursuant to proper public notification, attended by a quorum of board members, and open to the public (*Rathman v. Bd. of Dir. of Davenport Comm. Sch. Dist.,* 580 N.W. 2d 777, Ia. 1998). "Open meeting" or "sunshine" laws generally provide exceptions to open meeting requirements for school boards to meet in executive session to discuss the following issues:

1. Matters that threaten public safety or pending or current litigation (*Davis v. Churchhill Cty. Sch. Brd.,* 616 F. Supp. 1310, D. Nev. 1985; *Hanten v. Sch. Dist. of Riverview Gardens,* 13 F. Supp. 2d 971, E.D. Mo. 1998; *Racine Union Sch. Dist. v. Thompson,* 321 N.W. 2d 334, Wis. 1982)

2. Labor negotiations (*Bassett v. Braddock,* 262 So. 2d 425, Fla. 1972)

3. Potential land purchase (*Collinsville Comm. Unit Sch. Dist. No. 10 v. White,* 283 N.E. 2d 718, Ill. 1972)

4. Personnel matters (*McCown v. Patagonia Union Sch. Dist.,* 629 P2d 94 Ariz. 1981; *Sch.*

Dist. of the City of Royal Oak v. Schulman,
243 N.W. 2d 673, Mich. 1976)

Although discussion of these matters may take place in closed meetings, state statutes usually require that formal action must take place in open meetings (*Connelly v. Sch. Comm.,* 565 N.E. 2d 449, Mass. 1991.)

The American Judicial System

The United States judicial system consists of federal and state courts. The federal court system has its basis in the U.S. Constitution. State court systems have their basis in state constitutions or statutory laws. The federal courts have primary jurisdiction on federal law questions, whereas state courts have primary jurisdiction on laws of each respective state. Most school actions involve nonfederal questions and are decided by state courts. However, in the last several decades, federal courts have litigated an increasing number of school cases.

Federal Courts

In part, Article III, Section 1 of the U.S. Constitution provides that "The judicial power of the United States, shall be vested in one supreme court, and in such inferior courts as the Congress may from time to time ordain and establish" (U.S. CONST. art. III, sec. 1). Pursuant to this provision, Congress has created a network of courts. Presently, the federal court system in the United States includes district courts, circuit courts of appeal, and the Supreme Court (see Figure 17.1).

District Courts   At the lowest court level, district courts hear and decide lawsuits arising within their territorial jurisdictions. There is at least one district court in each state; many states have two or three; and California, New York, and Texas each have four. Cases adjudicated before district courts are usually presided over by one judge. Decisions of district courts may be appealed to federal circuit courts of appeal.

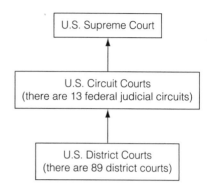

Figure 17.1

The Federal Court System

Circuit Courts of Appeal   Courts of appeal represent the intermediate appellate level of the federal court system. The primary function of the appellate court is to review appeals from district courts within the circuit to determine if errors of law were committed, such as procedural irregularities, constitutional misinterpretations, or inappropriate application of rules of evidence. Federal circuit courts have from 3 to 15 judges. Most circuit court decisions are rendered by a panel of the court, but in some instances the entire court will rehear a case. A federal circuit court decision is binding only in the states within that circuit, but such decisions often influence other appellate courts dealing with similar questions of law. The nation is divided into 13 federal circuit courts of appeal, comprising 11 regions and the District of Columbia Circuit and Federal Circuit (see Figure 17.2).

Supreme Court   The Supreme Court is the highest-level court in the federal court system, beyond which there is no appeal. It has been firmly established that the Supreme Court has the ultimate authority in interpreting federal constitutional provisions (*Marbury v. Madison,* 5 U.S. (1 Cranch) 137, 1803). If the constitutionality of a federal statute is contrary to legislative intent, such irregularities can be overturned only by an amendment to the Constitution or by subsequent ruling by the Supreme Court. Congress has done so with a number of civil rights laws in response

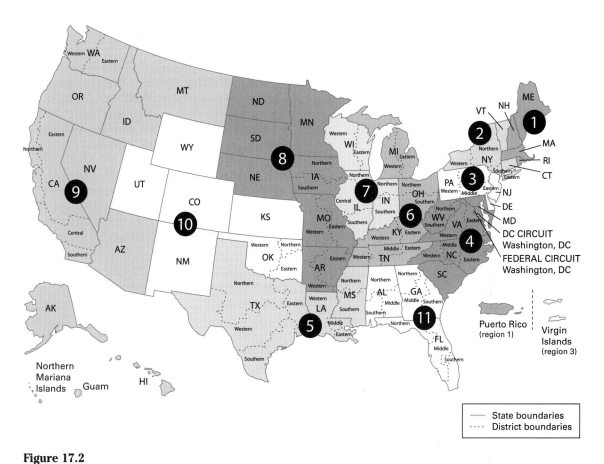

Figure 17.2

Geographical Boundaries of U.S. Courts of Appeals and U.S. District Courts

to Supreme Court rulings (*Grove City Coll. v. Bell*, 465 U.S. 555, 1984). Nine justices, including one chief justice, constitute the Supreme Court. The appointments of Supreme Court justices are for life.

State Courts

State constitutions prescribe the powers and jurisdiction of state courts. The structure of judicial systems varies among the 50 states, but all states have at least three or four levels of courts: courts of limited jurisdiction, courts of general jurisdiction,

intermediate appellate courts, and courts of last resort (see Figure 17.3).

Courts of Limited Jurisdiction Most states have trial courts, called courts of limited jurisdiction, that hear only certain types of cases (e.g., those concerning probate or criminal matters). These courts are referred to by a variety of names, including municipal, justices of the peace, probate, small claims, and traffic courts.

Courts of General Jurisdiction Courts of general jurisdiction are often referred to as circuit, chancery, district, superior, or juvenile courts.

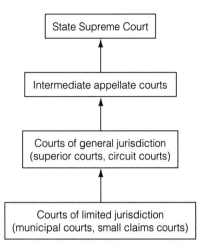

Figure 17.3

A Typical State Court System

Their jurisdiction covers all cases except those re-served for courts of limited jurisdiction. Decisions may be appealed from courts of general jurisdic-tion to intermediate appellate courts or, in some cases, to the court of last resort.

Intermediate Appellate Courts Most states have intermediate appellate courts. These courts have been established to hear appeals from trial courts or certain state agencies. The primary role of the intermediate appellate courts is to review proceedings from trial courts to determine if sub-stantive or procedural errors occurred in applying the law. The purposes of the intermediate appel-late courts and the courts of last resort are similar in this regard. The primary difference between the two courts is discretion. The intermediate appel-late court has less discretion in accepting cases than does the court of last resort.

Court of Last Resort All states have a court of last resort. In most states, the court of last resort is called the supreme court. The primary function of this court is to review lower court decisions on appeal. Nonfederal matters may not be appealed beyond a state's supreme court. However, if a federal question is involved, an appeal may be forwarded to the fed-eral courts or the U.S. Supreme Court.

Schools and the State

Education is a state function. In this section we focus on the extent of state and local authority in-volving such issues as compulsory school atten-dance, church-state relations, school fees, the curriculum, and state-mandated testing. A school principal needs to be knowledgeable about these issues in order to avoid lawsuits against the school district or administrative staff. Due to their lack of knowledge as regards the following important issues, many school principals have caused law-suits of sufficient severity to reach the Supreme Court.

Compulsory School Attendance

Every state has some form of compulsory school attendance law. These laws generally compel chil-dren between specified ages to attend school. Compulsory school attendance laws may be en-forced in the following ways:

1. By criminal prosecution of parents for child neglect
2. By judicially ordering children to return to school; see *In re J.B.*, 58 S.W. 3d 575 (Mo. Ct. App. 2001); *In re C.S.*, 382 N.W. 2d 381 (N.D. 1986); *State ex. rel. Estes v. Egnor*, 443 S.E. 2d 193 (W.Va. 1994)
3. By court removal of a child from a parent's custody; see *Scoma v. Ill.*, 391 F. Supp. 452 (N.D. Ill. 1974); *Matter of McMillan*, 226 S.E. 2d 693 (N.C. 1976)
4. By placing truants in custodial schools; see *In re T.V.P.*, 414 N.E. 2d 209 (Ill. 1974)

In *Pierce v. Society of Sisters*, 268 U.S. 510 (1925), the U.S. Supreme Court affirmed the man-date of compulsory school attendance. It also es-tablished the role of parochial and private schools in satisfying the state's requirement that children receive schooling. In essence, this landmark Supreme Court decision affirmed that parents do not have the right to determine *whether* their chil-dren are educated, but they do have the right to determine *where* such education takes place.

Most state statutes authorize home instruction programs that meet state standards; see *Deconte v. State,* 329 S.E. 2d 636 (N.C. 1985); *In re D.B.,* 767 P. 2d 801 (Col. Ct. App. 1988); *Tex. Educ. Agency v. Leeper,* 893 S.W. 2d 432 (Tex. 1994). However, courts do not agree that home schooling must be equivalent to public school instruction; see *Minnesota v. Newstrom,* 371 N.W. 2d 525 (Minn. 1985); *Mazanec v. N. Judson–San Pierre Sch. Corp.,* 798 F. 2d 230 (7th Cir. 1986); *Jeffrey v. O'Donnell,* 702 F. Supp. 516 (M.D. Pa. 1988); *Blackwelder v. Safnauer,* 866 F. 2d 548 (2d Cir. 1989). Since 1980, many states have changed their laws to ease restrictions on home instruction, and no state has strengthened such regulations (Hail, 2003; Klicka, 1996). However, most states require students educated at home to be subjected to state-prescribed tests to ensure that students are mastering basic skills; see *Murphy v. Arkansas,* 852 F. 2d 1039 (8th Cir. 1988).

Exemptions　State laws typically exempt from compulsory school attendance certain classes of children, such as emancipated youngsters (married or self-supporting students), children who must work to provide essential family support, and children with severe disabilities. In addition to statutory exemptions from compulsory school attendance laws, the Supreme Court, in *Wisconsin v. Yoder,* 406 U.S. 205 (1972), granted an exemption of First Amendment religious grounds to Amish children who have successfully completed eighth grade. However, the courts have denied most other religious exemption claims.

Residency Requirements　Each state constitution places an obligation on its legislature to provide for free public schooling, thus creating a state entitlement (property right) for all children to be educated at public expense. This state entitlement encompasses all school-age children, usually between the ages of 6 and 16, who are bona fide residents in that they live in the attendance district with their parents or legal guardians; are emancipated minors (married or self-supporting beyond a certain age); or are adult students who live independently from their parents. Furthermore, the U.S. Supreme Court, in *Plyer v. Doe,* 457 U.S. 202

(1982), held that school districts could not deny a free public education to resident children whose parents were illegal aliens.

Homeless children and state inter- and intra-district open enrollment plans may be subject to special rules. The federal Homeless Assistance Act of 1987 defines a homeless person as one who lacks a permanent nighttime residence or one whose residence is a temporary living arrangement. The law directs each state to adopt a plan for educating homeless children, including transportation and other school services; see 42 U.S.C.A. sec. 11302 (1987); *Harrison v. Sobel,* 705 F. Supp. 870 (S.D. N.Y. 1988); *G. Cooper Access to Education by Homeless Children,* 53 Ed. Law Rep. 757 (1989). Some states have enacted inter-district open enrollment plans, which allow students to apply for transfers to any public school district within the state. Transfer requests usually are subject to certain restrictions specified in the law, and participation by local districts may be optional under some plans. Most states now allow for some type of intra- or inter-district open enrollment plan; see *McMorrow v. Benson,* 617 N.W. 2d 247 (Wis. Ct. App. 2000). However, courts have rejected parents' claims that assignment to inadequate resident school districts was detrimental to their children's educational welfare; see *Ramsdell v. N. River Sch. Dist. No. 200,* 704 P. 2d 606 (Wash. 1985). Such claims may be more successful in the future in view of the federal No Child Left Behind Act of 2001. Under this federal legislation, students assigned to residence schools who have not met annual progress goals for two consecutive years must be provided other educational options, including transportation and all other school services; see 20 U.S.C. sec. 6316 (b) (2002).

Church-State Relations

The U.S. Supreme Court and lower federal courts have consistently declared that school-sponsored prayer during regular school hours and Bible reading for sectarian purposes are unconstitutional. These issues have provided a plethora of litigation focusing on church-state relations.

The First Amendment stipulates, in part, that "Congress shall make no law respecting an *establishment of religion,* or prohibiting the *free exercise thereof*" (U.S. CONST. Amendment I; emphasis added). The religious liberties of the First Amendment not only provide protection against actions by the Congress but also, when applied through the Fourteenth Amendment, protect the individual from arbitrary acts of the states (*Cantwell v. Connecticut,* 310 U.S., 296, 1940). Based on the Establishment and Free Exercise clauses of the First Amendment, courts must determine the constitutionality of such questions as allowing prayer and Bible reading in the public schools during normal school hours, prayer at graduations or football games, permitting religious clubs to meet on school grounds, disseminating religious materials, and observing religious holidays.

Prayer and Bible Reading   Two U.S. Supreme Court decisions in the 1960s established case law regarding prayer and Bible reading in the public schools. In *Engel v. Vitale,* 370 U.S. 421 (1962), the Court held that daily recitation of a New York State Board of Regents prayer in the presence of a teacher was unconstitutional and in violation of the Establishment Clause. In *Sch. Dist. of Abington Township v. Schempp,* 374 U.S. 203 (1963), the Court held that reading the Bible for sectarian reasons and reciting the Lord's Prayer in public schools during normal school hours were unconstitutional. The result of *Engel* and *Schempp* was that religious exercises in the public schools are clearly unconstitutional. Neither state, nor school, nor teacher can hold religious services of any type in the public schools. The Court did assert, however, that Bible study as part of a secular program of education for its literary and historic values would not be unconstitutional.

Silent Prayer   Since *Engel* and *Schempp,* the courts have decided a number of school prayer cases. Many state constitutions, statutes, and school board policies were changed, thereby permitting voluntary prayer in the public schools. Teachers and students both have maintained that the Free Exercise Clause of the First Amendment permits them to conduct prayers in the classroom. This issue was settled by the U.S. Supreme Court in *Wallace v. Jaffree,* 472 U.S. 38 (1985). The Court held that a period of silence for meditation or voluntary prayer in the public schools is unconstitutional. The Court ruled that the purpose of the 1981 Alabama silent prayer law was not secular and therefore violated the Establishment Clause. Courts have rejected most recent challenges to silent meditation or prayer.

Prayer at Graduation and Extracurricular Activities   Courts have been asked to render a decision on the constitutionality of prayers at graduation exercises and at other school-sponsored activities outside the classroom such as football games, team practices, and band concerts. The U.S. Supreme Court, in *Lee v. Weisman,* 505 U.S. 577 (1992), held that prayers organized by school officials at graduation exercises were unconstitutional. The Court opined that while some common ground of moral and ethical behavior is highly desirable for any society, for the state to advance a Judeo-Christian religious doctrine is "coercive" and can create great discomfort for students who do not believe in the particular religious precept that is being visited upon them. And in *Sante Fe Independent School District v. Doe,* 530 U.S. 290 (2000), the U.S. Supreme Court held that student-led, student-initiated prayer at football games violated the Establishment Clause. Thus *Santa Fe* joins a consistent array of precedents that enforce the secularization of public schools.

Equal Access Act   In 1984, Congress passed the Equal Access Act (EAA), which has since been amended in an attempt to clarify the unsettled area of law where students' free-speech rights compete with the rights of public schools to control access to the school as a forum for public discourse. The EAA, 20 U.S.C., Sec. 4071 (1988), as amended, states in part:

> It shall be unlawful for any public secondary school which received Federal financial assistance and which has a limited open forum to deny equal

access or a fair opportunity to, or discriminate against, any students who wish to conduct a meeting within that limited open forum on the basis of the religious, political, philosophical, or other content of the speech at such meetings.

A school has complied with the *fair opportunity* requirement if the meetings (a) are voluntary and student-initiated; (b) involve no school or government sponsorship; (c) allow the presence of school employees only in a nonparticipatory capacity; (d) do not materially and substantially interfere with the orderly conduct of educational activities within the school; and (e) are not directed, controlled, or regularly attended by nonschool persons; and the school cannot limit these groups to a specified size.

The U.S. Supreme Court, in *Bd. of Educ. of the Westside Community Schools v. Mergens*, 496 U.S. 226 (1990), upheld the constitutionality of the Equal Access Act. The Court ruled that if a school allows any noncurricular groups to meet, then a limited open forum is created, and any student-initiated group has the right to assemble. These groups would be allowed to convene during noninstructional times when other groups meet.

Released Time for Religious Instruction   The practice of releasing public school children during regular school hours for religious instruction first began in the United States at the beginning of the 20th century. Since then, two significant U.S. Supreme Court cases have addressed the issue of releasing public school students to receive religious instruction. In *McCollum v. Bd. of Educ. of School District No. 71*, 333 U.S. 203 (1948), the Court struck down a plan in which pupils were released to attend religious instruction in the classrooms of public school buildings. The Court asserted that the use of tax-supported property for religious instruction, the close cooperation between school officials and religious authorities, and the use of the state's compulsory education system all tended to promote religious education and, therefore, violated the First Amendment. In a second decision, *Zorach v. Clauson*, 343 U.S. 306 (1952), the Court upheld a plan whereby

students were released during public school hours to attend religious instruction off the school grounds. The Court found that the plan did not violate the First Amendment. The Court reasoned that whereas the Constitution forbids the government to finance religious groups and promote religious instruction, the First Amendment does not require the state to be hostile to religion. From the *Zorach* decision, it is clear that the Supreme Court does not prohibit some cooperation between public schools and churches; but the nature and degree of the cooperation are important in determining the constitutionality of the activity in question.

State Aid to Private Schools

Approximately 12% of all K–12 students in the United States attend private schools or home instruction (National Center for Education Statistics, 2004b). Despite state constitutional provisions to the contrary, several states provide state aid to private school students, including those enrolled in parochial schools. The primary types of aid provided are for transportation, the loan of textbooks, state-mandated testing programs, special education, and counseling services. Because the use of public funds for private, primarily sectarian education has raised serious questions about the proper separation of church and state under the First Amendment, their constitutionality has been examined by the U.S. Supreme Court.

Public funds to support religious schools dates back to 1930 when the U.S. Supreme Court, in *Cochran v. Louisiana State Bd. of Educ.*, 281 U.S. 370 (1930), held that a state plan to provide textbooks to parochial school students does not violate the Fourteenth Amendment. The decision in *Cochran* was rendered 10 years before the Supreme Court recognized in *Cantwell v. Connecticut*, 310 U.S. 296 (1940), that the fundamental concept of "liberty" embodied in the Fourteenth Amendment incorporates First Amendment guarantees and safeguards them against state interference. Since then, supreme courts have adopted the "child benefit" doctrine in many instances to defend the appropriation of public funds for private and parochial school use.

The U.S. Supreme Court, in *Everson v. Bd. of Educ.*, 330 U.S. 1 (1947), held that the use of public funds for transportation of parochial schoolchildren does not violate the First Amendment. The Court adopted the "child benefit" doctrine and reasoned that the funds were expended for the benefit of the individual child and not for religious purpose. Forty-one years later, the U.S. Supreme Court, in *Bd. of Educ. v. Allen*, 392 U.S. 236 (1968), applied the reasoning of the *Cochran* and *Everson* cases in ruling that the loan of textbooks to parochial school students does not violate the Establishment Clause of the First Amendment. The Court reasoned that because there was no indication the textbooks were being used to teach religion, and because private schools serve a public purpose and perform a secular as well as sectarian function, such an expenditure of public funds is not unconstitutional.

The Supreme Court's decision in *Allen* created many questions in the minds of public and parochial school administrators throughout the nation. The Court used the public purpose theory in the *Allen* case "that parochial schools are performing, in addition to their sectarian function, the task of secular education." Thus the Court reasoned that the state could give assistance to religious schools as long as the aid was provided only for secular services in the operation of parochial schools.

Many parochial school administrators interpreted this statement to mean that a state could provide funds to parochial schools for such things as teachers' salaries, operations, buildings, and so forth, as long as the parochial schools used the funds only for "public secular purposes." A plethora of bills flooded state legislatures to provide state support of parochial schools. Some were passed; others failed.

At around this time, the U.S. Supreme Court, in *Lemon v. Kurtzman*, 403 U.S. 602 (1971), was asked to rule on the constitutionality of two such statutes, one from Pennsylvania and another from Rhode Island. The Court invalidated both

statutes. The Pennsylvania statute provided financial support to nonpublic schools by reimbursing the cost of teachers' salaries, textbooks, and instructional materials. The Rhode Island statute provided a salary supplement to be paid to teachers dealing with secular subjects in nonpublic schools. The Court found that "secular purpose" standard to be inadequate and then added another standard of "excessive entanglement between government and religion." In *Lemon v. Kurtzman*, the Supreme Court first applied a three-part test to assess whether a state statute is constitutional under the Establishment Clause of the First Amendment. To withstand scrutiny under this test, often referred to as the Lemon test, governmental action must (a) have a secular purpose, (b) have a primary effect that neither advances nor impedes religion, and (c) avoid excessive government entanglement with religion.

In 1973 the Supreme Court delivered three opinions regarding financial aid to private schools after *Lemon*. The U.S. Supreme Court, in *Levitt v. Committee for Public Education and Religious Liberty*, 413 U.S. 472 (1973), invalidated a New York statute stipulating that nonpublic schools would be reimbursed for expenses incurred in administering, grading, compiling, and reporting test results; maintaining pupil attendance and health records, recording qualifications and characteristics of personnel; and preparing and submitting various reports to the state. The Court stated that such aid would have the primary purpose and effect of advancing religion or religious education and that it would lead to excessive entanglement between church and state. The U.S. Supreme Court, in *Committee for Public Education and Religious Liberty v. Nyquist*, 413 U.S. 756 (1973), struck down a New York statute that provided for the maintenance and repair of nonpublic school facilities, tuition reimbursement for parents of nonpublic school students, and tax relief for those not qualifying for tuition reimbursement. And the U.S. Supreme Court, in *Sloan v. Lemon*, 413 U.S. 825 (1973), invalidated a Pennsylvania statute that provided for parent reimbursement for nonpublic school students. The Court reasoned there was no constitutionally significant difference between

Pennsylvania's tuition-granting plan and New York's tuition-reimbursement scheme, which was held to violate the Establishment Clause in *Nyquist.*

The tripartite *Lemon* test was used consistently in Establishment Clause cases involving church-state relations issues until around 1992. A majority of the current justices, who are Reagan-Bush appointees to the U.S. Supreme Court, have voiced dissatisfaction with the test, and reliance on *Lemon* has been noticeably absent in the Supreme Court's recent Establishment Clause rulings. Support for church-state separation seems to be crumbling.

The Supreme Court has allowed increasing government support for parochial school students beginning in the 1980s. In 1980, the U.S. Supreme Court, in *Committee for Public Education and Religious Liberty v. Regan,* 444 U.S. 646 (1980), upheld government support for state-mandated testing programs in private schools. A few years earlier, the Supreme Court ruled, in *Levitt* and later in *Meek v. Pittenger,* 421 U.S. 349 (1975), that using state funds to develop and administer state-mandated as well as teacher-made tests was in violation of the Establishment Clause, because such tests could be used to advance sectarian purposes. In 1983 the U.S. Supreme Court, in *Mueller v. Allen,* 463 U.S. 388 (1983), upheld a state tax benefit for educational expenses to parents of parochial school students. Ten years later the Supreme Court, in *Zobrest v. Catalina Foothills Sch. Dist.,* 509 U.S. 1 (1993), held that providing state aid to sign-language interpreters in parochial schools is not a violation of the First Amendment. This decision represented a paradigm shift toward the use of public school personnel in sectarian schools.

The U.S. Supreme Court, in *Agostini v. Felton,* 521 U.S. 203 (1997), held that using federal education funds under Title I of the Elementary and Secondary Education Act (ESEA) of 1965 to pay public school teachers who taught in programs aimed at helping low-income, educationally deprived students within parochial schools was allowed. This decision overruled two earlier Supreme Court decisions announced 12 years earlier, which

had not allowed the practice; see *Aguilar v. Felton,* 423 U.S. 402 (1985) and *Grand Rapids School District v. Ball,* 473 U.S. 373 (1985). ESEA, which has gone through a number of reauthorizations since being enacted in 1965, requires that comparable services be provided for eligible students attending nonpublic schools. The most recent reauthorization of ESEA is P.L. 107-110, the No Child Left Behind Act of 2001, 20 U.S.C., sec. 6301 (2002). The Court in *Agostini,* for the first time, held that comparability can be achieved by permitting public school personnel to provide instructional services in sectarian schools. The Court further recognized that in *Zobrest* it abandoned its previous assumption that public school teachers in parochial schools would inevitably inculcate religion to their students or that their presence constituted a symbolic union between government and religion.

The U.S. Supreme Court, in *Mitchell v. Helms,* 530 U.S. 793 (2000), held that using federal aid to purchase instructional materials and equipment for student use in sectarian schools did not violate the Establishment Clause. Specifically, the decision permits the use of public funds for computers, software, and library books in religious schools under Title II of the ESEA federal aid program. The Court reasoned that the aid was allocated based on neutral, secular criteria that neither favored nor disfavored religion; was made available to both religious and secular beneficiaries on a nondiscriminatory basis; and flows to religious schools simply because of the private choices of parents. *Mitchell* overruled decisions in *Meek v. Pittenger,* 421 U.S. 349 (1975), and *Wolman v. Walter,* 433 U.S. 229 (1977), which barred state aid from providing maps, charts, overhead projectors, and other instructional materials to sectarian schools.

School Fees

In public schools there is a growing practice of charging "user fees" for select services and materials such as transportation, textbooks, course materials, and extracurricular activities. This practice has raised objections that charging fees violates a student's right to a free public education under state law. Whether or not fees may be charged depends partly on the wording in state statutes and partly on judicial interpretations as to which school activities should be considered part of a free public education.

Transportation   The law is clear that public schools cannot charge tuition to resident students who attend regular school year classes but may charge tuition to parents or legal guardians of nonresident students for such attendance. Some courts have distinguished between tuition charges and transportation charges, reasoning that transportation is not an essential part of students' property right to a free public education (*Kadrmas v. Dickinson Pub. Schs.*, 487 U.S. 450, 1988; *Salazar v. Eastin*, 890 P.2d 43, Cal. 1995). School board policies that have distinguished between resident and nonresident students pertaining to transportation fees have been upheld by the courts in *Fenster v. Schneider*, 636 F. 2d 765 (D.D. Cir. 1980), and courts have upheld policies that allow school districts to charge fees for summer school transportation (*Crim v. McWharter*, 252 S.E. 2d 421, Ga. 1979).

In *Kadrmas v. Dickinson Public Schools*, 487 U.S. 450 (1988), the U.S. Supreme Court held that a North Dakota statute allowing selected school districts to charge a transportation fee, not to exceed the school district's estimated cost of providing the service, does not violate a student's right to a free public education. The Court stated that unless mandated by state law, local school districts may refuse to provide school transportation services; thus, such services need not be free.

Whether or not reasonable school transportation fees can be imposed varies from state to state, depending on each state's classification of contested charges falling within or beyond the scope of that state's "free" public education. However, states do not have discretion regarding transportation for children with disabilities. Under federal and state laws, transportation is a related service that must be provided for free if necessary for a child with disabilities to participate in the educational program.

Textbooks, Courses, and Supplies   Some courts have upheld fees for textbooks, school supplies, and courses. Others have not. The U.S. Supreme Court has not invalidated textbook or other fees under federal equal protection guarantees; therefore, the legality of such fees depends on interpretations of state statutes and constitutions.

The Montana Supreme Court, in *Granger v. Cascade County Sch. Dist. No. 1*, 159 Mont. 516, 499 P.2d 780 (1972), applied a principle or test to determine whether a school district can or should charge fees for textbooks, courses, or supplies. The Montana Supreme Court interpreted "tuition-free" in their constitution to mean "free" as far as required courses were concerned and did not prohibit fees and charges for optional extracurricular or elective courses or activities. The Montana Supreme Court offered the following principle or test:

> We believe that the controlling principle or test should be stated in this manner: Is a given course or activity reasonably related to a recognized academic and educational goal or a particular school system? If it is, it constitutes part of the free, public school system commanded by Art. XI, Sec. 1 of the Montana Constitution and additional fees or charges cannot be levied, directly or indirectly, against the student or his parents. If it is not, reasonable fees or charges may be imposed.

The courts have consistently construed the language "without payment of tuition" or "tuition-free" or other such language to mean that a school district is prohibited from charging a fee for a pupil attending school. This language has also been construed as not prohibiting the charging of fees for textbooks or other educational materials. However, when state constitutions contain language such as "free public schools" or "free common schools" or similar language, the courts have generally held, with few exceptions, that this language contemplates furnishing textbooks and other educational materials free of charge, at least to the elementary schools.

An issue receiving increased attention in the public schools is that of charging fees for participation in extracurricular activities. The following court decisions will shed some light on this issue. School principals and other school officials should consult their state statutes.

Extracurricular Activities Several courts have ruled that public schools can charge students fees for participation in extracurricular activities. In *Paulson v. Minidoka County School District No. 331*, 463 P.2d 935, 938 (Idaho 1970), the Supreme Court of Idaho upheld a school district's policy that required students to pay for participation in extracurricular activities. The court reasoned that such activities are not necessary elements of a high school career. In *Bd. of Educ. v. Sinclair*, 222 N.W. 2d 143 (Wis. 1974) and in *Granger v. Cascade County Sch. Dist. No. 1*, 499 P.2d 780 (Mont. 1972), the Wisconsin and Montana Supreme Courts reached conclusions similar to that of Idaho. The courts ruled that school districts can charge fees for activities that are optional or elective. In *Attorney General v. E. Jackson Public Schools*, 372 N.W. 2d 638 (Mich. Ct. App. 1985), a Michigan appeals court upheld fees for playing on interscholastic teams. The court reasoned that interscholastic athletics are not considered an integral, fundamental part of the educational program, which would require providing them free to resident students. The Michigan court also noted the confidential waiver process available for students who could not afford to pay the fees. The court recognized that no students had been denied participation because of inability to pay the fees. Earlier, an Indiana federal district court, in *Carder v. Michigan City School Corporation*, 552 F. Supp. 869 (N.D. Ind. 1982), ruled that the state student disciplinary code and federal equal protection guarantees precluded school boards from suspending students for parents' failure to pay fees assessed for educational materials. The Ninth Circuit Court, in *Canton v. Spokane Sch. Dist. No. 81*, 498 F. 2d 840 (9th Cir. 1974), held that students have a constitutional right not to be subjected to embarrassment, humiliation, or other penalties for failure to pay fees for instructional materials. The Supreme Court of West Virginia, in *Vandevender v. Cassell*, 208 S.E. 2d 436 (W.Va. 1974), upheld waivers for students who could not afford to pay the assessed fees. And later, the U.S. Supreme Court, in *Kadrmas v. Dickinson Public Schools*, 487 U.S. 450 (1988), held that under the law, school districts have the discretion to waive any fee for families financially unable to pay fees assessed, and benefits such as diplomas and grades are not to be affected by nonpayment of fees. However, one year later, in *Association for Def. v. Kiger*, 537 N.E. 1292 (Ohio 1989), the Supreme Court of Ohio upheld state law that authorized school districts to withhold grades or credit if students failed to pay fees for educational materials.

Individual state laws may prohibit assessing students for participation in extracurricular activities. The Supreme Court of California, in *Hartzell v. Connell*, 679 P.2d 35, 44 (Cal. 1984), held that its state constitution prohibited charging students fees for participation in any extracurricular activities. The court stated that extracurricular activities are an integral part of the educational program and thus encompassed a guarantee of a free public education. The court further held that the fee violated the state administrative code, which stipulated that students shall not be required to pay any fees. Nevertheless, eight years later the same court, in *Arcadia Unified Sch. Dist. v. State Department of Education*, 825 P.2d 438 (Cal. 1992), held that school transportation fees were permissible under California law.

Given the fiscal constraints faced by school districts across the nation, an increasing number of school boards are likely to charge user fees for transportation, textbooks and other instructional materials, and extracurricular activities.

The School Curriculum

In view of the state's plenary power over education, the school curriculum is controlled primarily by states and local school boards. The federal government does influence the school curriculum through funds it provides for particular initiatives like "Reading First." Under the No Child Left Behind Act of 2001, states can apply for federal funds to strengthen reading instruction in the early grades; see (Reading First), 20 U.S.C. sec. 6362 (2002).

In all states, the local school district must offer a curriculum that state legislatures prescribe. In about half of the states, the local school district must offer the curriculum prescribed by state law. Even in those states where school districts retain some discretion, courses of study must be approved by the state board of education. Although states vary as to the specificity of course offerings, most states require instruction in American history and government, English, mathematics, drug education, health, and physical education. In addition, some state statutes specify the number, content, or quality of course offerings and what subjects will be taught at which grade levels. Many states have detailed legislation pertaining to vocational education, bilingual education, and special education.

Although states have substantial discretion in curricular matters, occasionally curriculum decisions by state legislatures have violated federal constitutional provisions. The U.S. Supreme Court, in *Epperson v. Arkansas,* 393 U.S. 97 (1968), held that preventing public school teaching of evolution simply because it conflicts with certain religious views is a violation of the First Amendment. Nearly two decades later, the U.S. Supreme Court, in *Edwards v. Aguillard,* 482 U.S. 578 (1987), struck down a Louisiana law requiring the teaching of creationism whenever evolution was introduced in the curriculum. The Court concluded that the law was a violation of the First Amendment because it unconstitutionally advanced religion.

The courts have generally enforced the view that the public schools should deal with secular matters and remain apart from sectarian affairs. The legal controversies that typically arise in this area generally involve some particular group seeking to impose particular religious and philosophical beliefs by restricting the school curriculum or demanding that certain books or courses be excluded from the instructional program. In response, the courts have traditionally upheld the "expansion of knowledge standard."

In *Board of Education v. Pico,* 457 U.S. 853 (1982), the U.S. Supreme Court reinforced the expansion of knowledge rule by prohibiting the removal of books by the local school board, which was responding to political pressure from a local school group of conservative parents. The Court reasoned that expansion of knowledge was an objective of education policy and stated that "the right to receive ideas is a necessary predicate to the recipient's meaningful exercise of his own right of speech, press, and political freedom." This general precedent, that the expansion of knowledge is paramount, was set in an earlier Supreme Court case in *Sweeney v. New Hampshire,* 354 U.S. 234 (1957). The Court said, "Teachers and students must always remain free to inquire, to study and then evaluate. . . . [The state cannot] chill that free play of the spirit which all teachers ought especially to cultivate and practice."

More recently, however, a new judicial pattern has emerged that may suggest a possible retreat from the "expansion of knowledge" rule. The present U.S. Supreme Court (Reagan-Bush appointees) has indicated its willingness to allow the final decision regarding the curriculum and the availability of books and materials to reside fully within the prerogative of the local school board, even though the result may be a contraction of the flow of information and a possible diminution of knowledge. This position was implied by the landmark 1988 Supreme Court decision involving students' free speech rights in *Hazelwood School District v. Kuhlmeier,* 484 U.S. 260 (1988). The Court declared that public school authorities can censor student expression in school-related activities, in this case the excision of two pages from a student newspaper, as long as it is "reasonably related to legitimate pedagogical concerns." Such a "reasonableness" standard is less definitive and gives local school authorities greater flexibility in determining whether to restrict or expand the curriculum. In this case, the

Court further justified restriction of curriculum content by concluding that "a school must be able to take into account the emotional maturity of the intended audience."

In following this precedent of greater latitude to local school boards in controlling curriculum, books, films, and materials, a Wisconsin court upheld a school district's ban on showing R-rated films in *Barger v. Bisciglia*, 888 F. Supp. 97 (E.D. Wis. 1995); an Eleventh Circuit Court upheld a Florida school board's decision to ban a humanities book in *Virgil v. School Board*, 862 F. 2d 1517 (11th Cir. 1989); and a California appeals court upheld a school board's censor of instructional materials in *McCarthy v. Fletcher*, 254 Cal. Rptr. 714 (Ct. App. 1989), but the court noted in this case that school board authority does have limits and prohibited the banning of materials purely for religious reasons.

State-Mandated Performance Testing

The state has the authority to establish standards for promotion and graduation. In recent years, states have begun to rely heavily on the standardized test as a criterion to determine students' proficiency in core subject areas. For example, in the mid-1970s, only a few states had enacted testing legislation pertaining to students' academic proficiency. Now all states have laws or administrative regulations regarding statewide performance testing, and most states require passage of a test as a condition of graduation. As long as such measures of academic attainment are reasonable and nondiscriminatory, the courts will not interfere. Courts have traditionally given teachers and administrators wide latitude in deciding on appropriate academic requirements. The courts adopted this position of nonintervention as early as 1913 in *Bernard v. Inhabitants of Shelburne*, 216 Mass. 19, 102 N.E. 1095 (1913). The court said, "So long as the school committee acts in good faith, their conduct in formulating and applying standards and making decisions touching this matter is not subject to review by any other tribunal." The U.S. Supreme Court reiterated this precedent in *Bd. of Curators v. Horowitz*, 435 U.S. 78 S. Ct. 948 (1978), when it said that "Courts are particularly ill-equipped to evaluate academic performance."

The federal government strongly supports statewide performance testing. The No Child Left Behind Act of 2001 mandates annual testing in grades 3 through 8 in reading and mathematics by 2006, and in science by 2007 at selected grades; the act also ties federal assistance and sanctions for schools to student test scores; see 20 U.S.C. sec. 6301 (2002). High-stakes testing shapes the instructional program, and states increasingly are evaluating teachers' and principals' performance based on their students' test scores. The American Evaluation Association (AEA) (2002) issued a statement opposing the use of tests as the sole or primary criterion for making decisions with serious negative consequences for students, educators, and schools. AEA joins a number of other professional organizations (e.g., American Educational Research Association, International Reading Association, National Council for Teachers of English, National Council for Teachers of Mathematics, National Council for the Social Studies, and National Education Association) in opposing the inappropriate use of tests to make high-stakes decisions. And claims have been made that teachers are limiting the curriculum to material covered on the tests (McNeil, 2000).

The major source of litigation regarding statewide performance testing stems from the movement of many states to competency tests as minimal criteria for awarding a high school diploma. The high school diploma represents a measure of attainment and is thus of special interest to the student. The diploma, therefore, meets the criteria for a property interest under the Due Process Clause of the Fourteenth Amendment, enunciated by the U.S. Supreme Court in *Bd. of Regents v. Roth*, 408 U.S. 564 (1972). The Court stated that "to have a property interest is a benefit, a person clearly must have more than an abstract need or desire for it. He must, instead, have a legitimate claim of entitlement to it." A high school diploma is a benefit that everyone needs, and when a student progresses academically for 12 years, one may assume that the diploma will be expected, contingent on the student's normal academic progress.

Litigation may occur when the competency tests used cause a risk of nonreceipt of the diploma and are the result of tests that do not measure the content they are supposed to measure. If tests do not measure the content they are supposed to measure, then the tests lack validity. Another important test concept is reliability, which requires that the test must yield consistent results.

These issues of due process and validity and reliability became the foci of the court in *Debra P. v. Turlington,* 644 F. 2d 397 (5th Cir. 1981), a case still widely cited as establishing the legal precedent pertaining to student proficiency tests. The court held that the property interest in receipt of a diploma necessitated sufficient notice of conditions attached to high school graduation and that an opportunity to satisfy the standards before a diploma can be withheld were not met (due process). Furthermore, the court held that the state may have administered an unfair test in that the test content did not match the material taught in the schools (validity). The state was enjoined from using the test as a diploma prerequisite for four years to provide time for the effects of prior school desegregation to be removed and to ensure that all minority students subjected to the test requirement started first grade under desegregated conditions. On remand, *Debra P. v. Turlington,* 564 F. Supp. 177 (M.D. Fla. 1983), affirmed 730 F. 2d 1405 (11th Cir. 1984), the district court ruled to lift the injunction, and the appeals court affirmed this decision. The state presented substantial evidence to the judiciary that the test was valid. Data also showed significant improvement among African American students during the six years the test had been administered. Thus the testing program could help remedy the effects of past racial discrimination.

Other courts have relied on *Debra P.* as precedent. A Texas federal district court, in *GI Forum v. Texas Education Agency,* 87 F. Supp. 2d 667 (W.D. Tex. 2000), struck down challenges to the Texas Assessment of Academic Skills (TAAS) test that has been administered to all Texas students since 1990. The court held that the test was valid in that the content of the test was congruent with the material taught in the schools, and students received adequate notice of the test requirement. The court noted that there was evidence of higher minority failure rates; but the passing-rate gap was narrowing (see Table 17.1), and the testing and remediation programs were addressing the effects of prior discrimination.

Two Texas federal district courts ruled differently with regard to students being allowed to participate in graduation exercises contingent on their passing the statewide proficiency test. In *Williams v. Austin Independent Sch. Dist.,* 796 F. Supp. 251 (W.D. Tex. 1992), the court ruled that students who failed the state's proficiency test have no constitutional right to participate in the graduation ceremony, because they had been given adequate notice of the test and were provided with the required courses to prepare for the test. In *Crump v. Gilmer Independent Sch. Dist.,* 797 F. Supp. 552 (E.D. Tex. 1992), the court struck down a school district's attempt to prevent students who had failed the state's proficiency test — but satisfied other graduation requirements — from participating in the graduation ceremony. The court reasoned that allowing students to graduate would provide no possible harm to the district from their participation, because their diplomas would be withheld until students passed the proficiency test. In another Texas federal district court case, *Hubbard v. Buffalo Independent Sch. Dist.,* 20 F. Supp. 2d 1012 (W.D. Tex. 1998), the court upheld a school district's requirement that all students who transfer from nonaccredited schools must take the state's proficiency test at their own expense.

Students with mental disabilities may be given a waiver from taking a proficiency test if the individualized education program (IEP) team agrees that the child is not likely to master the material covered on the test. And students with disabilities may be entitled to special accommodations in the administration of tests to ensure that their knowledge, rather than their disability, is being tested.

Table 17.1 Percentages of Students Passing the Texas Assessment of Academic Skills (TAAS) — English Version

	1994	1995	1996	1997	1998	1999	2000	Gain (in points)
All students								
Reading	74	76	77	80	83	86	87	13
Writing	76	79	79	82	84	88	88	12
Math	57	63	70	76	80	85	87	30
African American								
Reading	58	61	64	70	74	78	80	22
Writing	63	68	69	72	76	81	82	19
Math	36	42	52	60	66	72	76	40
Hispanic								
Reading	63	65	67	75	80	81	87	18
Writing	67	71	71	77	83	82	88	15
Math	45	50	60	73	80	83	87	38
White								
Reading	85	86	86	89	91	93	94	9
Writing	85	87	87	89	90	93	94	9
Math	70	76	81	85	88	92	93	23
Economically Disadvantaged								
Reading	61	64	65	70	74	78	80	19
Writing	65	69	69	72	75	81	81	16
Math	43	49	58	66	71	78	81	38
Limited English								
Reading	39	42	43	49	54	59	60	21
Writing	44	48	47	51	54	60	60	16
Math	30	35	44	53	59	68	69	39

The specific nature of the accommodations remains controversial.

Given mandatory testing provisions in the No Child Left Behind Act of 2001, statewide performance testing is likely to continue. Statewide proficiency testing programs will likely generate additional litigation in federal and state courts. School principals can take steps to minimize legal challenges by ensuring that (a) the proficiency tests are aligned with both curriculum and instruction, (b) students are advised upon entrance into high school that passage of the proficiency test is a prerequisite to receipt of a diploma, (c) tests are not intentionally discriminatory and do not perpetuate the vestiges of past school segregation, (d) students who fail the proficiency test are provided remediation and opportunities to retake the test, and (e) students with disabilities are provided with appropriate accommodations (Cambron-McCabe, McCarthy, & Thomas, 2004).

Students and the Law

Principals are given broad powers to adopt rules and regulations governing student conduct in the public schools. These powers are not absolute, and school authorities must implement rules and regulations within the scope of *reasonableness*. Generally, rules are thought to be reasonable in a school setting if they are necessary to maintain an orderly and safe environment conducive to learning. To protect the constitutional rights of students, courts have been diligent in determining the reasonableness and fairness of rules and regulations governing student conduct.

Court decisions in recent years pertaining to students' rights indicate that courts must often balance students' constitutional rights against the duty of school principals to maintain a safe and orderly environment for learning. To reduce legal confrontations pertaining to students' rights as well as to facilitate efficient and effective school operations, school principals should ensure that (a) the adoption of policies, rules, and regulations governing student conduct is legally and educationally sound; (b) the policies, rules, and regulations are clearly written; (c) the policies are adequately communicated to students and their parents; and (d) the policies are enforced in a fair and reasonable manner.

Freedom of Expression

Prior to the 1970s, courts generally upheld school principals' actions governing student conduct that simply satisfied the reasonableness standard. Public schools were perceived as possessing *in loco parentis* (in place of the parent) prerogatives (*State ex. rel. Burpee v. Burton,* 45 Wis. 150, 30 Am. Re. 706, 1878). Further, it was uncertain whether constitutional rights extended to students in school. However, in *Tinker v. Des Moines Independent Community Sch. Dist.,* 393 U.S. 503 (1969), the U.S. Supreme Court stated that students do not "shed their constitutional rights to freedom of speech or expression at the schoolhouse gate." Freedom of expression is derived from the First Amendment to the U.S. Constitution, which stipulates, in part, "Congress shall make no laws . . . abridging the freedom of speech, or of press or of the rights of peoples to peacefully assemble." The *Tinker* case confirmed that students are entitled to all First Amendment rights, subject only to the provision in which the exercise of these rights creates material and substantial disruption in the school. An excerpt from *Tinker* will help clarify the legal principles of the Court:

> School officials do not possess absolute authority over their students. Students in school as well as out of school are "persons" under our Constitution. They possess fundamental rights which the State must respect. . . . In the absence of a specific showing of constitutionally valid reasons to regulate their speech, students are entitled to freedom of expression of their views. (*Tinker v. Des Moines Independent Sch. Dist.,* 393 U. S. 503, 511, 1969)

The Court's decision in *Tinker* sent a clear message to the public school community that a student has the constitutional right of freedom of expression in school.

Subsequently, in *Goss v. Lopez,* 419 U. S. 565 (1975), the U.S. Supreme Court ruled that public school students possess liberty and property interests in their education, and therefore that constitutional principles of due process apply to school officials in dealing with regulations governing student conduct and other school-related activities. Due process of law is derived from the Fourteenth Amendment to the U.S. Constitution, which stipulates, in part, that "no state shall . . . deprive any person of life, liberty or property, without due process of law." Basically, due process is a procedure of legal proceedings following established rules that assure enforcement and protection of individual rights. The guarantees of due process require that every person be entitled to the protection of a fair hearing and a fair judgment. Following *Goss,* several significant federal laws also emerged in the early 1970s and extended through the early 1980s, further expanding the scope of students' rights. During this period, the courts often upheld students' legal challenges of school policies, rules, and regulations; many school principals perceived such rulings as an erosion of their authority.

By the mid-1980s, there was a noticeable shift in courts' tendency to uphold students' challenges. Two significant landmark Supreme Court decisions increased the public school principals' authority pertaining to students' freedom of expression and other issues concerning regulations that govern student conduct. In *Bethel School District No. 403 v. Fraser*, 478 U.S. 675 (1986), the U.S. Supreme Court stated that "the constitutional rights of students in public school are not automatically coextensive with the rights of adults in other settings" and may be limited by reasonable policies designed to take into account the special circumstances of the educational environment. The Court further noted that school principals have broad discretion to curtail lewd and vulgar student expression in school. In *Hazelwood Sch. Dist. v. Kuhlmeier*, 484 U.S. 260 (1988), the Supreme Court held that school principals can censor student expression in school newspapers and other school-related activities as long as the censorship decisions are based on legitimate pedagogical concerns.

Students have challenged local school policies or state statutes requiring their participation in patriotic exercises. In *Sherman v. Community Consolidated Sch. Dist. 21*, 980 F. 2d 437 (7th Cir. 1992) cert. denied, 508 U.S. 950 (1993), the court upheld a student's position not to participate in reciting the Pledge of Allegiance to the American flag. The Seventh Circuit Court's decision follows the rationale of other courts that have litigated this issue. Sensitive constitutional issues are being raised, following terrorist attacks on September 11, 2001, pertaining to reciting the Pledge of Allegiance and other patriotic exercises, such as displaying "God Bless America" and "In God We Trust" banners in schools. These school activities will likely result in new challenges to First Amendment rights to refrain from participation in patriotic exercises, to criticize school policies, or to raise church-state relations questions in

connection with these patriotic observances and displays in public schools.

Unprotected Expression　Courts have recognized that defamatory, obscene, and inflammatory communications are not protected by the First Amendment. Nor are these forms of expression protected in the public school setting.

Defamatory Expression　Defamation includes slander (verbal) and libel (written) statements that are false, expose another to ridicule, and are communicated to others. Courts have upheld school principals in banning libelous content from school publications and in sanctioning students for slanderous speech.

Unlike defamatory expression, comments about the actions of public figures that are neither false nor malicious are constitutionally protected. One example of the constitutionally protected speech of a public figure that received much media attention in the mid-1980s was litigated by the U.S. Supreme Court in *Hustler Magazine v. Falwell*, 485 U.S. 46 (1988). In the public school setting, school board members and superintendents are generally considered public figures for defamation purposes.

Obscene or Vulgar Expression　Courts have held that individuals are not protected by First Amendment rights for speaking or publishing obscene or vulgar language. This was confirmed in *Bethel School District v. Fraser* (1986), in which the Supreme Court granted the school principal considerable latitude in censoring obscene and vulgar student expression. The Supreme Court declared that speech protected by the First Amendment for adults is not necessarily protected for children, reasoning that the sexual innuendos contained in a student's speech during a student government assembly were offensive to students and inappropriate in the public school context. Other courts have struck down similar cases involving student expressions of obscene and vulgar language in the public schools.

Inflammatory Expression   Threats and fighting words made by students toward classmates or school personnel are not protected by the First Amendment. In determining whether a legitimate threat has been made, courts generally use a four-part test: (1) reaction of the recipient of the threat and other witnesses, (2) whether the person making the threat had made similar statements to the recipient in the past, (3) if the statement was conditional or communicated directly to the recipient, and (4) whether the recipient had reason to believe that the person making the threat would actually engage in violence (*Shoemaker v. State of Arkansas*, 343 Ark. 727, 2001; *United States v. Dinwiddie*, 76 f. 3d 193, 8th Cir. 1996). The courts as well as school principals are taking all threats seriously since the terrorist attacks on September 11, 2001.

Student Appearance

Despite continuing controversy over the years surrounding the issue of dress and grooming and the courts' frequent involvement, the U.S. Supreme Court has consistently declined to address the issue. Student dress and grooming as a form of freedom of expression are not viewed as significant as most other forms of free expression are. There is, however, a First Amendment constitutional right associated with them. School principals, however, may within reason prescribe rules governing student dress and grooming using the standard of reasonableness. The standard of reasonableness centers around well-established facts that (a) students have protected First Amendment constitutional rights, and (b) students' rights must be balanced against the legitimate right of school officials to maintain a safe and disruption-free learning environment. The courts now require school authorities to demonstrate the reasonableness of their rules before the courts will decide if the constitutional rights of students have been violated.

Dress and grooming generally are viewed as a form of self-expression, and a student must be afforded opportunities for self-expression.

Therefore, restrictions on student dress and grooming are justified when there is evidence of substantial disruption of the educational process. Justifiable reasons to restrict certain types of dress and grooming include violation of health and safety standards, gang-related dress, and controversial slogans.

The following restrictions have been upheld by the courts regarding dress and grooming (Essex, 2002):

1. School regulations necessary to protect the safety of students (e.g., wearing long hair or jewelry around shop and laboratories)

2. School regulations necessary to protect the health of students (e.g., requiring students to keep hair clean and free of parasites)

3. School regulations prohibiting dress and grooming that do not meet standards of community decorum (e.g., dressing in a manner that calls undue attention to one's anatomy)

4. Dress and grooming that result in material and substantial disruption of the maintenance of a safe and orderly environment for learning (e.g., wearing T-shirts containing vulgar, obscene, or defamatory language based on race, color, gender, national origin, or religion)

Health and Safety Standards   School officials may regulate certain types of dress and grooming that pose a threat to students' safety and health. For example, excessively long hair worn by students in shop classes, laboratories, or around dangerous equipment may pose a threat to their safety. School principals may take appropriate steps to regulate hair length in these situations. Students wearing fancy jewelry in shop classes, in laboratories, around dangerous equipment, and in physical education classes may pose a safety threat. School principals may take measures to regulate the type of jewelry worn in these situations.

School principals may require students to wash long hair for hygiene purposes. Similarly, school principals may take measures to address other hygiene problems related to dress. Efforts should always be made in these situations to ensure that the individual's dignity and rights are protected. The establishment of reasonable dress codes that are communicated to students and parents can curtail litigation regarding these issues.

Gang-Related Dress In recent years, school principals have witnessed an increase in the prevalence of gangs and hate groups in public schools. Gangs and hate groups pose serious problems for school authorities because the presence of such groups on a campus may contribute to substantial disruption of the educational process and threats to the safety of students. Members of such groups often wear clothing or symbols signifying their group membership. Such dress may be in violation of a school's dress and grooming codes but may be litigated to include violations of the First Amendment, gender discrimination, and racial discrimination. Examples of controversial student expression that may involve First Amendment protection include T-shirts depicting violence, drugs (e.g., marijuana leaves), or racial epithets; ripped, baggy, or sagging pants or jeans; colored bandanas, Confederate flag jackets, baseball or other hats; words shaved into the hair, brightly colored hair, distinctive haircuts or hairstyles, ponytails, and earrings for males; exposed underwear; Malcolm X symbols; Walkmans, cellular phones, or beepers; backpacks and baggy coats; tattoos, unusual-colored lipsticks, pierced noses, lips, and tongues; and decorative dental caps. Courts generally rule that such "expression" does not have constitutional protection under the First Amendment when there is evidence of gang activity in the school and community. Due to close scrutiny by parents, law enforcement officers, and school authorities, gangs will often change their appearances to become less recognizable. Today, many gang members wear professional sports team jackets, caps, and neutral T-shirts, making it difficult to detect them. School principals may take reasonable steps to minimize gang presence in school.

Controversial Slogans Slogans worn on T-shirts, caps, and other items of clothing that contain vulgar, lewd, or obscene pictures may be regulated by school principals. Suggestive clothing that draws undue attention to one's body may also be regulated. Banning controversial slogans and inappropriate attire generally has been upheld when there is evidence of disruption, when there is community sentiment regarding dress standards, and when the message is offensive to others based on race, gender, color, religion, or national origin (*Pyle v. South Hadley School Committee*, 861 F. Supp. 157, Mass. 1994).

School Uniforms The wearing of uniforms is gaining popularity in large city school districts, including Baltimore, Chicago, Cincinnati, Detroit, Houston, Los Angeles, Miami, New Orleans, New York, and Philadelphia (National Association of Elementary School Principals, 1998). Advocates assert that student uniforms provide easy identification of students, eliminate gang-related dress, promote discipline, reduce violence and socioeconomic distinctions, prevent unauthorized visitors from intruding on campus, and foster a positive learning environment. Typically, when school uniform dress codes are adopted, they apply to students in elementary and middle schools and may be either voluntary or mandatory. Many private and parochial schools have required uniforms for years.

Extracurricular Activities

It is clear that students have a property interest in their education and cannot be denied attendance without due process of law (*Goss v. Lopez*, 419 U.S. 565, 1975). But this property right does not extend to extracurricular activities. Courts generally hold that conditions can be attached to extracurricular participation, because such participation is a privilege rather than a right. The reasoning of the courts is that extracurricular activities, as the name implies, are usually conducted outside the classroom before or after regular school hours, usually carry no credit, are generally supervised by school officials or others, are academically nonremedial, and are of a voluntary nature for participants.

For these reasons, the courts have upheld the conditions typically attached to extracurricular participation. School principals may not be required by the Fourteenth Amendment to provide due process when denying students extracurricular participation, unless the school board has established policies for suspending or expelling students from extracurricular activities. Courts have upheld the suspension of students from interscholastic athletics for violating regulations prohibiting smoking and drinking, including off-campus and off-season conduct, providing the regulations so stipulate. Members of athletic teams and other extracurricular groups (drama, band, debate, cheerleading, and clubs) often are selected through a competitive process, and students have no property right to be chosen. Most state athletic associations prohibit students from involvement in interscholastic competition for one year after a change in a student's school without a change in the parent's address. Courts generally uphold age restrictions on extracurricular participation in an effort to equalize competitive conditions. Courts usually endorse rules limiting athletic eligibility to eight consecutive semesters, or four years after eighth grade. Several states have adopted "no pass, no play" provisions, which require students to maintain a 2.0 grade point average to participate in athletics (Hambrick, 2001). And the U.S. Supreme Court, in *Vernonia School District 4-7J v. Acton,* 515 U.S. 646 (1995), and in *Bd. of Educ. v. Earls,* 122 S. Ct. 2559 (2002), upheld school board policies requiring student athletes and those participating in other extracurricular activities to submit to random urinalysis as a condition of participation.

Student Discipline

School principals have not only the authority but the responsibility to maintain discipline in public schools. Although policies, rules, and regulations made at any level (e.g., classroom, building,

school board) cannot contravene federal and state laws, school principals and teachers are granted wide latitude in establishing and enforcing conduct codes that are necessary to maintain a safe and orderly environment for learning. In this section, we examine educators' prerogatives and students' rights in connection with suspensions and expulsions, corporal punishment, and search and seizure.

Suspensions and Expulsions Students may be excluded from school for violating school or district policy. Suspensions generally involve exclusion of a student from school for a brief, definite period of time, usually not exceeding 10 days. Courts have held that because students have a property interest in attending school, they must be provided due process before being excluded from school. Prior to 1975, procedural due process accorded to suspended students was poorly defined. Lower courts differed widely in their interpretation of the Fourteenth Amendment guarantees in suspension cases. In 1975, in *Goss v. Lopez,* 419 U.S. 565 (1975), the U.S. Supreme Court prescribed the minimum constitutional requirement in cases involving student suspensions of 10 days or less. The Court concluded that oral notice to the student of the reason for short suspensions, followed by an immediate, informal hearing by a local school official, would fulfill the due process requirement in brief suspensions. The Court specifically rejected the usual trial-type format including the involvement of attorneys and the presentation and cross-examination of adverse witnesses typical in criminal cases.

Somewhat related to suspensions are *disciplinary transfers* of students to a so-called alternative school. Generally, such transfers do not involve denial of public education, because students do not have an inherent right to attend a given school. Nevertheless, such transfers might implicate protected liberty or property interests due to the involuntary nature of the transfer for disciplinary reasons. Therefore, pupils facing involuntary disciplinary transfers are entitled to minimal due process, including (a) written notice to both the student and his or her parents; (b) a meeting involving school officials, parents, and the student during which the transfer may be discussed; and (c) a meeting during which evidence may be presented and witnesses examined.

From a practical standpoint, expulsion is the exclusion of a student from school for a period of time exceeding 10 days or more. Under common law, expulsion is vested exclusively in the board of education. Professional personnel may not expel students unless authorized by state statute.

Generally, courts have held that expulsion of students from school jeopardizes a student's property interests in an education. Thus students are guaranteed at least minimum due process under the Fourteenth Amendment. The following list enumerates suggested elements of recommended procedural due process in such cases:

1. A speedy and full notification of the charges should be given to the accused.

2. The accused should be provided an opportunity to answer the charges and to prepare an adequate defense.

3. The hearing should be conducted by an impartial tribunal.

4. The accused should be given the names of adverse witnesses, access to adverse evidence, and the right to introduce evidence.

5. The decision must be based on the evidence adduced at the hearing.

6. A prompt finding, giving the reasons for the decision and the evidence supporting it, should be delivered at the conclusion of the hearing.

7. The accused (or her counsel) should have the right to cross-examine adverse witnesses and introduce witnesses in her defense.

8. The accused has a right to representation by legal counsel.

9. A written record of the proceedings should be maintained.

10. The accused should have the right to appeal an adverse decision.

The Rehabilitation Act (Section 504), the Individuals with Disabilities Education Act (IDEA), and the Americans with Disabilities Act (ADA) provide special safeguards in the suspension and expulsion of children with disabilities. IDEA, in particular, assures all children with disabilities a free appropriate public education in the least restrictive environment. The Supreme Court in *Honig v. Doe*, 484 U.S. 305 (1988), has regarded expulsion and long-term suspension as a change in placement when children with disabilities are involved.

A crucial issue when suspending or expelling a disabled child is whether the misbehavior is related to the disability. Disabled students may be suspended for 10 days or less without inquiry into whether the student's misbehavior was caused by the disability (*Bd. of Educ. of Peoria v. Ill. State Bd. of Educ.*, 531 F. Supp. 148, C.D. Ill. 1982). Courts reasoned that short-term suspension is not a change of placement and therefore does not trigger the procedures of IDEA. Expulsions and suspensions of more than 10 days are changes of placement. They may not be used if there is a relationship between the misbehavior and the child's disability; see *S-1 v. Turlington*, 635 F. 2d 342 (5th Cir. 1891), *cert. denied*, 454 U.S. 1030 (1981). In these cases, transferring the child to a more restrictive environment is an option, after following change-of-placement procedures. If the misbehavior is not related to the disability, then expulsion and long-term suspension are permissible; but all educational services cannot be terminated. These special safeguards for the disciplining of disabled children do not apply to pupils who use illegal drugs or alcohol as stipulated in the ADA (29 U.S.C.A. sec. 706 (8) (West Supp., 1992).

Corporal Punishment   Although several states allow corporal punishment to be used as a means of student discipline, 27 states have now banned corporal punishment, and legislation is under way in many more (U.S. Department of Education, 2000). The American Academy of Pediatrics (2000) has recommended that corporal punishment be abolished in all states because of its detrimental effect on students' self-image and achievement as well as possible contribution to disruptive and violent behavior.

In the landmark Supreme Court decision *Ingraham v. Wright*, 430 U.S. 651 (1977), the Court held that corporal punishment of students does not violate the Eighth Amendment or the due process guarantees of the Fourteenth Amendment. The Court said that the Eighth Amendment's prohibition of cruel and unusual punishment applies to criminals only and is not applicable to the disciplining of students in public schools. The Court noted that "at common law a single principle has governed the use of corporal punishment since before the American Revolution: Teachers may impose reasonable but not excessive force to discipline a child." Regarding due process, the Court held that a student is not entitled to notice and a hearing prior to the imposition of corporal punishment.

Although the Supreme Court has held that the federal Constitution does not prohibit corporal punishment in schools, its use may conflict with state constitutions, state statutes, or local school board policies. Teachers can be disciplined or discharged for violating these state and local policies regulating corporal punishment.

Search and Seizure   The Fourth Amendment provides that "the right of people to be secure in their persons, houses, papers, and effects, against unreasonable searches and seizures shall not be violated, and no warrants shall issue, but upon probable cause." The clause has been involved in numerous criminal cases. Evidence obtained in violation of the amendment is inadmissible in court.

The introduction of drugs and other contraband in schools has placed school officials in the position of searching students' person or lockers, and students claim that such acts are a violation of their Fourth Amendment guarantees. A student's right to the Fourth Amendment's protection from unreasonable search and seizure must be balanced against the need for school officials to maintain discipline and to provide a safe environment conducive to learning. State and federal courts generally have relied on the doctrine of in loco parentis, reasoning that school officials stand in the place of a parent and are not subject to the constraints of the Fourth Amendment. In

New Jersey v. T.L.O., 469 U.S. 325 (1985), the U.S. Supreme Court held that searches by school officials in schools come within the constraints of the Fourteenth Amendment. The Court concluded that the special needs of the school environment justified easing the warrant and probable cause requirement imposed in criminal cases, provided that school searches are based on "reasonable suspicion."

In 1995, the U.S. Supreme Court rendered its decision in *Vernonia Sch. Dist. 4-7J v. Acton*, 515 U.S. 646 (1995), holding that a school district's random suspicionless drug testing of student athletes as a condition for participation in interscholastic athletics did not violate the Fourth Amendment's prohibition against unreasonable searches and seizures. In this particular case, however, the Court noted specific features including student athletes' decreased expectations of privacy, the relative unobtrusiveness of the search procedures, and the seriousness of the need met by this search. Regardless of the procedures, however, this case clearly lowered schools' previous legal search standard of reasonable suspicion as set forth by *New Jersey v. T.L.O.* in 1985.

The Supreme Court ruled on the issue of random suspicionless drug testing of students with its decision in *Bd. of Educ. v. Earls*, 122 S. Ct. 2559 (2002), a 10th Circuit case from Oklahoma in which drug testing of students in any extracurricular activities was determined to be unconstitutional. In a 5–4 decision, the Supreme Court upheld the school district's policy of random suspicionless drug testing of all students who participated in any extracurricular activities, not just athletics. Using *Vernonia* as a guideline, the 10th Circuit in *Earls* held that "before imposing a suspicionless drug testing program a school must demonstrate some identifiable drug abuse problem among a sufficient number of those to be tested, such that testing that group will actually redress its drug problem." In overturning the 10th Circuit's decision, the Supreme Court's majority in *Earls* stated that "a demonstrated drug abuse problem is not always necessary to the validity of a testing regime." Furthermore, the Court defends this stance by adding that "the need to prevent and deter the substantial harm of childhood drug use provides the necessary immediacy for a school testing policy." Thus, based on the *Earls* decision, random suspicionless drug testing of students does not violate the Fourth Amendment's protection from unreasonable searches and seizures.

Students With Disabilities

Historically, the prevailing attitude concerning the education of disabled students was that retarded, learning disabled, emotionally disturbed, deaf, blind, or otherwise disabled children were not the responsibility of the public schools. Consequently, many disabled children were exempted from compulsory school attendance laws either by parental choice or by school district design. Nationally, services for the disabled were either nonexistent or nonextensive. Very few school districts provided services; where such services existed, they were inadequate to meet even the minimal needs of this vulnerable minority group.

In recent years, substantial changes in attitude toward the disabled have occurred. Although disabled students do not comprise any "protected group" (such as race or gender) that is entitled to constitutional guarantees, federal statutes and state special education statutes were enacted to satisfy their constitutional rights. Lower court decisions and federal and state legislative enactments of the past three decades have mandated that all children, including the disabled, are entitled to admission to a school and placement in a program that meets their special needs. As summarized in the landmark Supreme Court school desegregation case, *Brown v. Bd. of Educ. of Topeka*, 347 U.S. 483 (1954), "education . . . is a right which must be made available to all on equal terms." Although the *Brown* decision dealt with the constitutional protections afforded minority children, its consent agreement implied a mandate that all students of legal age must be provided with appropriate school and classroom placement.

Two key court decisions outlined the legal framework for the constitutional protections of disabled children. In *Pennsylvania Association for Retarded Children (PARC) v. Commonwealth*, 334 F. Supp. 279 (E.D. Pa. 1977), a federal district court held that retarded children in Pennsylvania were entitled to a free public education and that, whenever possible, disabled children must be educated in regular classrooms and not segregated from other students. In *Mills v. Bd. of Educ. of the District of Columbia*, 348 F. Supp. 866 D.D.C. (1972), another federal district court expanded the *PARC* decision to include all school-age disabled children.

Subsequent to the *PARC* and *Mills* decisions, Congress passed two landmark pieces of legislation that led to the rapid development of comprehensive, nationwide educational programs for the disabled. Section 504 of the Rehabilitation Act of 1973 is a broad-based federal law that addresses discrimination against the disabled both in the workplace and in schools. The statute, as amended, stipulates:

> No otherwise qualified individual with handicaps . . . shall solely by reason of her or his handicap, be excluded from participation in, be denied the benefits of, or be subjected to discrimination under any programs or activity receiving Federal financial assistance. [29 U.S.C. sec. 794 (a) (1988)]

Thus Section 504 would cut off all federal funds from schools that discriminate against the disabled. The statute also provides that all newly constructed public facilities be equipped to allow free access by disabled individuals.

The Education for All Handicapped Children Act (EAHCA) of 1975, and currently the Individuals with Disabilities Education Act (IDEA), provide federal funds to school districts that comply with its requirements. The major thrust of the acts, however, was to ensure the right of all disabled children to a public education. Major provisions of the law include a free appropriate public education, an individualized education program, special education services, related services, due process procedures, and the least restrictive learning environment; see 20 U.S.C.A. sec. 1400 (a) (West Supp. 1992).

According to IDEA, all disabled children have the right to a "free appropriate public education."

An appropriate education for the disabled is defined as special education and related services. Special education refers to specially designed instruction at public expense, including a variety of opportunities on a spectrum from regular classroom instruction and special classes to placement in a private facility. Related services include transportation, physical and occupational therapy, recreation, and counseling and medical diagnosis. A written *individualized education program (IEP)* is another key element in a free appropriate public education. An IEP includes an assessment of the child's needs, specification of annual goals, strategies (methods, materials, interventions) to achieve the goals, and periodic evaluations of the child's progress. And finally, a disabled child must be educated in the least restrictive environment. That is, the placement must be tailored to the disabled student's special needs. In combination with related state laws, these federal statutes provide the guidelines for the education of the disabled.

In addition to the Rehabilitation Act, the disabled are now protected by the Americans with Disabilities Act of 1990 (ADA); see 42 U.S.C.A. sec. 12101–2213 (1990 & West Supp. 1992). This law prohibits discrimination in employment (and other situations) against any "qualified individual with a disability." Essentially it amplifies and extends prohibitions of Section 504 of the Rehabilitation Act of 1973. Coverage is not dependent on involvement of federal funds. A "reasonable accommodation" that would permit a qualified individual with a disability to perform the "essential functions" of a position (or other activity) must be provided.

The definition of a disabled person under ADA is somewhat different from that given in the Rehabilitation Act. Under the newer law, a "qualified individual with a disability" means "an individual with a disability who with or without reasonable modifications . . . meets the essential eligibility requirements for the receipt of services or the participation in programs or activities provided by a public entity"; see 42 U.S.C.A. sec. 12131 (2) (West Supp. 1992). To prevent conflict between the Rehabilitation Act and ADA, legislation requires that ADA be interpreted consistently with the older law. Thus court decisions interpreting Section 504 are not affected by the later law. Furthermore, the Rehabilitation Act looks to the terms of IDEA for resolution of most disputes concerning the education of the disabled; and compliance with IDEA will usually meet the requirements of ADA.

Of these three laws, IDEA has had the most significant impact on public schools. Congress reauthorized IDEA in 1997, adding some new amendments and extending federal funding for special education services. The purposes of the 1997 IDEA are (a) to assure that all children with disabilities are provided with a "free appropriate public education" that includes special education and related services tailored to their special needs, (b) to prepare them for employment and independent living, (c) to assure that the rights of children with disabilities are protected, and (d) to assist states in providing appropriate special education and related services (20 U.S.C. sec. 1401, 1997).

Teachers and the Law

A primary function of the state is to provide for an efficient system of public schools. The operation of public schools is governed by state statutory and regulatory policy. However, the actual administration of public school systems is delegated to state boards of education, state departments of education, and local school boards. These agencies adopt and enforce reasonable rules and regulations pursuant to state statutes for the operation of public school systems.

Although state statutes and regulatory policy are prominent in defining the employment conditions of public school personnel, they cannot be viewed independently of state and federal constitutional provisions, civil rights laws, and collective bargaining agreements between school boards and employee unions. These provisions may restrict or modify options stipulated in the state school code. In this section, we discuss licensure and certification, contracts, termination of employment, discrimination in employment, collective bargaining, and tort liability.

Licensure and Certification

The schools employ several categories of professional personnel: superintendents, principals, curriculum specialists, business managers, school psychologists, social workers, counselors, classroom teachers, and the like. To be eligible for employment in a professional position, the individual should possess a valid license or certificate issued according to statutory provisions of a given state. These statutes, varying from state to state, concern requirements and procedures for obtaining the different certificates. Generally, the legislature delegates the legal authority to issue and process certification to state boards and departments of education. In some states, however, the legislature delegates that authority to a local school district, as is the case in New York City and more recently in Chicago.

The preparation standards for each type of certificate are similar from state to state, with only a few exceptions. For example, every state requires applicants to have a college degree with a minimum number of credit hours in a prescribed curriculum. Besides educational requirements, other prerequisites may include evidence of good moral character, a minimum age, U.S. citizenship, and satisfactory performance on a state-administered examination.

The initial certification is usually issued for a specified period of time, including various designations such as temporary, emergency, conditional, standard, life, or permanent. It is the certificate holder's responsibility to keep it renewed. This may require evidence of additional coursework, professional experience in a public school, or passage of a standardized examination such as the National Teachers Examination (NTE). The U.S. Supreme Court, in *United States v. South Carolina*, 445 F. Supp. 1094 (D.S.C. 1977), *aff'd sub nom. National Education Association v. South Carolina*, 434 U.S. 1026 (1978), has upheld its use, even though the exam has been shown to disproportionately disqualify minority candidates. The Supreme Court of Texas, in *State v. Project Principle*, 724 S.W. 2d 387 (Tex. 1987), held that teachers possessing life certificates

may be required to pass a state examination as a condition of continued employment. Certificates also include specific endorsements (e.g., superintendent, principal, counselor, teacher), subject areas (e.g., English, social studies, mathematics, sciences), and grade levels (e.g., elementary, middle or junior high school, high school). A school board's failure to assign professional personnel to positions for which they are certified can result in loss of state accreditation and federal funding (Cambron-McCabe et al., 2004).

The state also has the power to revoke certification. Certification revocation is different from dismissal from employment by a local board of education. A local school board can legally dismiss a superintendent, principal, teacher, or other professional employee; but the state is generally the only government body that can revoke a certificate. Moreover, state statutes usually specify the grounds and procedures for certification revocation. For example, under the Kentucky statute, it is provided that "any certification . . . may be revoked by the Education Professional Standards Board for immorality, misconduct in office, incompetency or willful neglect of duty. . . . Before the certification is revoked defendant shall be given a copy of the charges against him and given an opportunity, upon not less than twenty (20) days' notice, to be heard in person or by counsel" (Kentucky Revised Statutes, Ch. 161.120, 2002).

Contracts

A certificate renders the holder eligible for employment in a state; it does not guarantee employment. Statutory law provides that local boards of education have the legal authority to enter into contracts with professional personnel. The relationship between a school board and its professional employees is contractual. The general legal principles governing contracts — offer and acceptance, competent parties, consideration, legal subject matter, and proper form — apply to this contractual relationship.

Offer and acceptance pertains to the job description, compensation level, and time of performance to which both parties have agreed. In most states, because only the board of education has the power to employ personnel, it must exercise that function itself. It cannot delegate the employment duty to the superintendent of schools or to individual members of the school board. Further, a local board of education is considered to be a legal body only as a corporate unit; therefore, for a board to enter into a valid contract with a teacher or other professional personnel, there must be a meeting of the board.

Competent parties means that, for a valid contract to exist, the parties must be authorized by law to enter into a contractual relationship. By law the school board possesses the legal authority to enter into contracts. A teacher or other professional employee is legally competent to contract, providing she possesses the necessary certification and meets other state requirements. An application of this element of contracts is found in a Kentucky case. A teacher lacked a certificate when she began teaching and was ineligible for one because she was under the state's minimum-age requirement for certification. Consequently, the contract between the parties was void, and the teacher was not entitled to receive a salary for the work she performed while a minor (*Floyd County Bd. of Educ. v. Slone*, 307 S.W. 23d. 912, Ky. 1957).

Consideration pertains to the promises bargained for and exchanged between the parties. Consideration is something of value — usually money or the equivalent. Promises to perform services gratuitously are not contracts, because they are not supported by consideration. To have valid consideration, each party must give up something of value. In the case of an employment contract, consideration consists of the exchange of promises between the employee and the school district. The employee promises to perform specified services, and the school board promises to pay a specified salary.

Legal subject matter refers to mutual assurance between the parties that the job and its performance would not be a violation of the law. Finally, *proper form* means that all legal requirements, as stipulated in the state's statutes, must be followed in order for a contract to be valid. The precise form for contracts may vary from one state to another, but in most states, the statute requires that contracts with professional personnel be written (*Jones v. Houston Independent School District*, 805 F. Supp 476, S.D. Tex. 1991, *aff'd*, 979 F. 2d 1004, 1992).

The policies and procedures of the local board of education, provisions of the state constitution and its statutes, and the collective bargaining agreement, if there is one, are considered part of the contract between the school district and the teacher or other professional employee. It is recommended therefore that the aforementioned inclusions to an employee's contract be referenced either in the body or on the face of the contract; they then become expressly part of the individual employment contract.

Termination of Employment

Local boards of education possess the legal authority to terminate the employment of school personnel. The U.S. Supreme Court bestowed on school boards this authority when it held that "school authorities have the right and the duty to screen the officials, teachers, and employees as to their fitness to maintain the integrity of the schools as part of ordered society" (*Adler v. Bd. of Educ.*, 342 U.S. 485, 1952). However, despite the legal authority of a board of education to terminate the employment, it cannot arbitrarily discharge personnel at any time.

Tenure Law   Tenure statutes protect teachers (and other school district personnel specifically enumerated in state statutes) from arbitrary actions by local boards of education. The courts have sustained the constitutionality of such statutes. Teachers' Tenure Act cases (*Teachers' Tenure Act Cases*, 329 Pa. 214, 197 A. 344, 1938) have concluded that tenure exists to protect competent teachers and other members of the teaching profession against unlawful and arbitrary board actions and to provide orderly procedures for the dismissal of unsatisfactory teachers and other professional personnel.

Tenure is attained by complying with specific provisions prescribed by state statutes. The nature of these provisions varies from state to state, but certain conditions are included in most legislation. Nearly all statutes require that teachers serve a probationary period before tenure becomes effective. Generally, the probationary period ranges from three to five years, during which time a teacher is employed on a term contract. On completion of the probation period, personnel acquire tenure either automatically or by school board action. Texas law is an exception and permits the local school board to choose between adopting continuing contracts and remaining under term contracts, in which case teachers do not have tenure (*White v. South Park Ind. Sch. Dist.,* 693 F. 2d 1163, 5th Cir. 1983).

Which positions are to be covered under tenure law is within the prerogative of state legislatures. In some jurisdictions, tenure legislation extends to selected administrative positions, but rarely to superintendents. Others afford tenure only to teachers. For example, in South Carolina, South Dakota, and Missouri, a school administrator possessing a teacher's certificate is a "teacher" within the meaning of tenure laws (*Snipes v. McAndrew,* 313 S.E. 2d 294, S.C. 1984; *Waltz v. Bd. of Educ.,* 329 N.W. 2d 131, S.D. 1983; *Fuller v. N. Kansas City Sch. Dist.,* 629 S.W. 2d 404, Mo. 1982). In Kentucky, "(t)he term 'administrator' for the purpose of (tenure) shall mean a certified employee, below the rank of superintendent . . ." (*Ky. Rev. Stat.,* Ch. 161.720, sec. 8, 2002).

Although principals and certain other supervisory personnel can acquire tenure either as teachers or as principals in states having tenure laws, superintendents are not generally covered by tenure in that position unless the statute specifically indicates such inclusions. For example, the Illinois Supreme Court ruled that because they are district employees who require certification, superintendents are covered by the tenure law, but that the tenure protection extended only to a teaching position and not to an administrative one (*Lester v. Bd. of Educ. of Sch. Dist. No. 119,* 230 N.E. 2d 893, Ill. 1967). On the other hand,

tenure can be acquired by superintendents in New Jersey (*N.J. Stat. Ann.,* sec. 18A:28–5(4), 2004).

In discussions of the termination of employment of teachers and supervisory personnel, the terms *nonrenewal* and *dismissal* are often used interchangeably. There is a substantial difference, however, in the manner in which the termination operates in each case. If not protected by tenure, a school employee may be nonrenewed for no reason or for any reason whatsoever, providing it does not violate an employee's substantive constitutional rights (e.g., free speech, protection against racial discrimination). Courts have reasoned in these cases that the contract has simply terminated and there is no "expectancy of continued employment." Dismissal, on the other hand, whether under tenure status or during an unexpired contract, is permissible only "for cause." Consequently, a tenured employee or a nontenured professional who is dismissed during a contract year is entitled to a due process hearing embodying all the statutory and constitutional safeguards.

Dismissal Procedures Most tenure laws provide specific procedures for dismissing tenured employees. The procedure typically includes three elements: notice by a specific date, specification of charges against the employee, and a hearing at which the charges are discussed. When state law describes a specific procedure for dismissal, it must be followed exactly to make the action legal.

Besides the procedures required under state law, tenure rights qualify for constitutional procedural protections encompassed within the concepts of *property* and *liberty interests* under the Due Process Clause of the Fourteenth Amendment. The holding of a teaching position qualifies as a property right if the employee has an unexpired contract or has acquired tenure. The aforementioned protections of the Fourteenth Amendment do not normally extend to nontenured employees. The Supreme Court in *Bd. of Regents v. Roth,* 408 U.S. 564 (1972), has affirmed the view of the courts that nontenured employees have no property or liberty interests in continued employment. In exceptional situations, courts have recognized "de facto tenure" where there was no tenure law, but tenure was acquired by custom and precedent (*Perry v. Sinderman*, 408 U.S. 593, 1972). However, de facto tenure is not possible where there is a well-established statewide system.

A liberty interest would be an issue in dismissal, and due process required, when evidence exists that a charge has been made that places a stigma on an employee's reputation, thus foreclosing future employment opportunities or seriously damaging his standing in the community (*Roth*). A liberty interest would not be a constitutional safeguard when school board members and school administrators refrain from making public statements or releasing information that is derogatory to the employee. Even when statements are made, if they simply describe unsatisfactory performance in general, normally they do not constitute a violation of the employee's Fourteenth Amendment rights.

Examples of charges against employees not involving stigma include ineffective teaching methods, inability to maintain classroom discipline, and inability to get along with administrators and colleagues. Failure to award tenure does not automatically create a stigma. Examples of stigmas that qualify for constitutional due process protection include the following charges: manifest racism, immoral conduct, serious mental disorder, a drinking or drug problem, willful neglect of duty, and responsibility for the deterioration of a school (Russo, 2004).

Causes for dismissal are generally specified in state statutes and differ from one state to another; however, there are similarities. For example, in Kentucky tenured employees can be dismissed for insubordination; immoral character or conduct; physical or mental disability; or inefficiency, incompetency, or neglect of duty (*Ky. Rev. Stat.*, Ch. 161.790, 2002). In Illinois cause for dismissal is specified as incompetency, cruelty, negligence, immorality or other sufficient cause, and whenever in the board's opinion a teacher is not qualified to teach or the best interests of the school require it (*Ill. Ann. Stat.*, Ch. 122, sec. 10–22.4, 2002). In

Connecticut cause is enumerated as inefficiency, incompetency, insubordination, moral misconduct, disability as shown by competent medical evidence, elimination of position, or for other due and sufficient cause (*Conn. Gen. Stat. Ann.*, Tit. 5A, sec. 10–151, 2003).

Discrimination in Employment

Recent federal laws intended to remove discrimination in employment have had a direct impact on school board employment practices. Such legislation includes Title VII of the Civil Rights Act of 1964, Title IX of the Education Amendments of 1972, the Rehabilitation Act of 1973, the Equal Pay Act of 1963, the Age Discrimination Act of 1986, the Pregnancy Discrimination Act of 1978, and the Americans with Disabilities Act of 1990 (ADA). In addition, guidelines and policies from such federal agencies as the Equal Employment Opportunities Commission (EEOC), the Office of Economic Opportunity (OEO), and 42 U.S.C. sec. 1983, in particular, have been applied in claims of employment discrimination. In this section we briefly discuss race and gender discrimination; sexual harassment; discrimination based on disabilities; and age, religious, and pregnancy discrimination.

Race and Gender Discrimination   Beginning in the early 1970s, the federal courts heard several cases challenging discrimination. In 1971 the U.S. Supreme Court, in *Griggs v. Duke Power Company*, 401 U.S. 424 (1971), determined that Title VII of the Civil Rights Act of 1964 (pertaining to hiring, promotion, salary, and retention) covered not only overt discrimination but also practices that are discriminatory in operation. The Court held that an employment practice is prohibited if the exclusion of minorities cannot be shown to be related to job performance. The case involved requiring job applicants to possess a high school diploma and make a satisfactory score on a general intelligence test as criteria for employment. The practice was shown to discriminate against Black applicants. During the same year, the Court, in *Phillips v. Martin Marietta Corporation,* 400 U.S. 542 (1971), handed down a decision relative to the disparate treatment of the sexes in the workplace. The Court ruled that discriminatory treatment of the sexes, by employment practices not necessary to the efficient and purposeful operation of an organization, is prohibited by the same federal legislation.

The effect of these two landmark decisions was to force employers to remove "artificial, arbitrary, and unnecessary" barriers to employment that discriminate on the basis of race and gender classification. In 1972, coverage of these provisions of Title VII, which previously had applied only to private employment, was extended to discriminatory employment practices in educational institutions. Subsequent to *Griggs* and *Phillips,* lower courts have applied these same legal standards to Fourteenth Amendment, Section 1983, and Title VII equal protection cases.

To establish a constitutional violation of equal protection, aggrieved individuals must prove that they have been victims of discrimination. In 1981, the Supreme Court, in *Texas Department of Community Affairs v. Burdine,* 450 U.S. 248 (1981), set forth the procedural steps to file a Title VII suit. The plaintiff has the initial burden of establishing a prima facie case of discrimination by showing the existence of five factors: (1) member in a protected group (e.g., minorities, women, aged, handicapped), (2) application for the position, (3) qualification for the position, (4) rejection for the position, and (5) employer's continued pursuit of applicants with the plaintiff's qualifications for the position. These factors constitute an initial, or prima facie, case of discrimination in any type of personnel decision. Once a prima facie case of discrimination is established, the defendant (employer) must articulate a nondiscriminatory reason for the action. If this is accomplished, the plaintiff (employee or applicant) then must prove that the explanation is a pretext for discrimination, the real reason for the personnel decision being based on the consideration of "impermissible factors" in employment (*McDonnell Douglas Corp. v. Green,* 411 U.S. 792, 1973). In 1993, the Supreme Court, in *St. Mary's Honor Center v.*

Hicks, 509 U.S. (1993), reiterated that the ultimate burden of proof in a discrimination suit lies with the plaintiff. The legal standards emanating from *Griggs, Phillips,* and *Hicks* in claims of discriminatory employment practices under Title VII have been applied also under civil rights legislation barring discrimination based on age. Title VII does not cover discrimination based on disabilities. Employees with disabilities in public schools must look to the Rehabilitation Act of 1973 (Section 504) and the Americans with Disabilities Act of 1990 (ADA).

Sexual Harassment   Charges of sexual harassment in the workplace have been litigated under Title VII of the Civil Rights Act of 1964 and Title IX of the Education Amendments of 1972. The regulations implementing Title VII define sexual harassment as follows:

> Unwelcome sexual advances, requests for sexual favors, and other verbal or physical conduct of a sexual nature constitute sexual harassment when (i) submission to such conduct is made either explicitly or implicitly a term or condition of an individual's employment, (ii) submission to or rejection of such conduct by an individual is used as the basis for employment decisions affecting such individual, or (iii) such conduct has the purpose or effect of unreasonably interfering with an individual's work performance or creating an intimidating, hostile, or offensive working environment. (29 C.F.R. sec. 1604.11(a), 1991)

In *Meritor Savings Bank v. Vinson,* 477 U.S. 57 (1986), the Supreme Court initiated this definition by identifying two different forms of sexual harassment: quid pro quo harassment and hostile environment harassment. *Quid pro quo sexual harassment* involves conditioning tangible employment benefits (e.g., promotion, demotion, termination) on sexual favors. *Hostile environment sexual harassment* involves a pattern of unwelcome and offensive conduct that unreasonably interferes with an individual's work performance or creates an intimidating or offensive work environment. The Court warned that "for sexual harassment to be actionable, it must be sufficiently severe or pervasive to alter the conditions of (the victim's) employment and create an abusive working environment." The Supreme Court, in *Harris v. Forklift Systems, Inc.*, 114 S. Ct. 367, 126 L. ed. 2d 295 (1993), elaborated further on the concept of the hostile environment form of sexual harassment, which creates a more difficult task for the courts to interpret than quid pro quo. In reaffirming the standard set in *Meritor,* the Court said that for sexual harassment to be actionable the conduct must cause "tangible psychological injury" rather than conduct that is "merely offensive." Courts determine this by examining such factors as frequency of the conduct, severity of the conduct, whether it is physically threatening or humiliating, and whether it unreasonably interferes with the employee's work performance.

Five kinds of sexual harassment include sexual bribery, sexual imposition, gender harassment, sexual coercion, and sexual behavior.

1. *Sexual bribery.* Sexual bribery is solicitation of sexual activity or other sex-linked behaviors by promise of rewards; the proposition may be either overt or subtle.

2. *Sexual imposition.* Examples of gross sexual imposition are forceful touching, feeling, grabbing, or sexual assault.

3. *Gender harassment.* Gender harassment means generalized sexist statements and behaviors that convey insulting or degrading attitudes about women. Examples include insulting remarks, offensive graffiti, obscene jokes, or humor about sex or women in general.

4. *Sexual coercion.* Sexual coercion means coercion of sexual activity or other sex-linked behavior by threat of punishment; examples include negative performance evaluations, withholding of promotions, threat of termination.

5. *Sexual behavior.* Sexual behavior means unwanted, inappropriate, and offensive sexual advances. Examples include repeated unwanted sexual invitations; insistent requests for dinner, drinks, or dates; persistent letters, phone calls, and other invitations. (Lowe & Strnadel, 1999)

School principals are strictly liable for quid pro quo sexual harassment under both Title VII of the Civil Rights Act of 1964 and Title IX of the Education Amendment of 1972. Therefore, school leaders need to take positive steps to prevent sexual harassment in the workplace.

School principals can take several positive approaches to preventing sexual harassment and maintaining a positive work environment.

Establish a no-tolerance policy   Declare that the employer will not stand for sexual harassment, discrimination, or retaliation in the workplace. Under the law, the employer has the affirmative duty to rid the workplace of sexual harassment and discrimination. All employees should know their employer's policy that forbids sexual harassment, discrimination, and retaliation.

Widely disseminate the policy   Everyone should have the policy readily available. This is important for both employer and employee.

Make it easy for employees to file complaints   Employees should be able to complain to someone other than their immediate superior. Someone outside the employee's chain of command, such as a human resource staff member, should be available to hear the complaint.

Investigate complaints promptly and objectively   Promptness and objectivity should be the standard response. If management has knowledge of discrimination or sexual harassment occurring, an investigation should be conducted. Prompt and objective investigation says to everyone that the complaint is serious.

Take appropriate remedial action to prevent a reoccurrence   Actions might include informal resolution between parties and disciplinary action against harassers. Offer the victim free counseling, if appropriate. Most important, provide training to all employees periodically.

Discrimination Based on Disabilities   The primary federal statutes that affect persons with disabilities are Section 504 of the Rehabilitation Act of 1973, 29 U.S.C. sec. 794 (2002), and the Americans with Disabilities Act of 1990 (ADA), 42 U.S.C. sec. 12101 *et seq.* (2003). These statutes prohibit discrimination based on disabilities against persons who are "otherwise qualified" for employment. These laws extend to all stages of employment, from recruiting and screening to hiring, promotion, and dismissal.

Section 504 and the ADA define a disabled person as one who has a physical or mental impairment that substantially limits one or more of such person's major life activities, has a record of such impairment, or is regarded as having such impairment. The ADA and Section 504, as recently amended, specifically exclude from the coverage of either law persons currently using illegal drugs and alcoholics whose use of alcohol interferes with job performance. But those in drug rehabilitation programs or who have successfully completed a program may be considered disabled.

The statutory definitions of a disabled person seem to include those with communicable diseases who are qualified to perform the job and whose condition does not threaten the health and safety of others. For example, the Supreme Court has ruled that the definition of a disabled person includes those with an infectious disease such as tuberculosis (*Sch. Bd. of Nassau Cty. Fla. v. Arline*, 480 U.S. 273, 1987). A lower court has extended coverage to teachers with AIDS (*Chalk v. U.S. District Court*, 840 F. 2d 701, 9th Cir., Cal. 1988).

The Supreme Court has said that an otherwise qualified disabled person is one who can meet all essential requirements of a job despite the disability. In determining whether a person with a disability is qualified to do a job, the central factors to consider are the nature of the disability in relation to the demands of the job. However, when a disabled person cannot meet all of the requirements of a job, an employer must provide "reasonable accommodation" that permits a qualified individual with a disability to perform the "essential functions" of a position. Furthermore, courts have ruled that Section 504 and the ADA protect otherwise qualified disabled individuals but do not require accommodations for persons who are not

qualified for the positions sought (*Southeastern Community College v. Davis*, 442 U.S. 397, 1979; *Beck v. James*, 793 S.W. 2d 416, Mo. Ct. App. 1990; *DeVargas v. Mason & Hanger-Silas Mason Co.*, 911 F 2d 1377, 10th Circ. 1990, *cert. denied*, 111 S. Ct. 799, 1991).

Age Discrimination   The Age Discrimination in Employment Act (ADEA), 29 U.S.C. sec. 621 *et seq.* (2002), was enacted to promote employment of older persons based on their ability and to prohibit arbitrary age discrimination in the terms and conditions of employment. The law covers public employees, including teachers and school administrators. Thus mandatory retirement for teachers is prohibited by law.

The act parallels Title VII in its application and operation. Litigation under ADEA thus follows the disparate treatment standard used for race and gender discrimination cases. A school district charged with age discrimination may defend itself by articulating nondiscriminatory reasons for the adverse employment decision, such as inferior qualifications or poor performance rather than age.

Religious Discrimination   Citizens' free exercise of religion is protected under the religion clauses of the First Amendment and the Equal Protection Clause of the Fourteenth Amendment. These clauses prohibit discrimination against any public school employee on the basis of religious beliefs. In addition to constitutional safeguards, public school employees are protected from religious discrimination under Title VII. In Title VII, as amended, Congress requires accommodation of "all aspects of religious observances and practices as well as belief, unless an employer demonstrates that he is unable to accommodate an employee's or prospective employee's religious observance or practice without undue hardship on the conduct of the employer's business" (U.S.C. sec. 2000e (j), 2002). The Equal Employment Opportunity Commission (EEOC) has developed guidelines with suggested accommodations for religious observance, such as assignment exchanges, flexible scheduling, job assignment changes, and using voluntary substitutes.

Pregnancy Discrimination According to the Pregnancy Discrimination Act (PDA), 42 U.S.C. sec. 2000e (k), (2002), which is an amendment to Title VII enacted in 1978, employers may not discriminate based on pregnancy, childbirth, or related medical conditions. Mandatory maternity leave policies have been the subject of litigation. In *Cleveland Bd. of Educ. v. LaFleur*, the Supreme Court held that a school board policy which required all pregnant teachers regardless of circumstances to take mandatory maternity leave for specified periods before and after childbirth was unconstitutional. The Court stated that it had long recognized that freedom of personal choice in matters of marriage and family choice liberties were protected under the Due Process Clause of the Fourteenth Amendment: "By acting to penalize the pregnant teacher for deciding to bear a child . . . can constitute a heavy burden on the exercise of these protected freedoms."

The U.S. Constitution still permits school boards to implement maternity leave policies that are not arbitrary and fulfill a legitimate goal of maintaining continuity of instruction in a school system. For example, a mandatory maternity leave beginning date for teachers set at the beginning of the ninth month of pregnancy was upheld on "business necessity" grounds by the Court of Appeals, Ninth Circuit (*deLaurier v. San Diego Unified Sch. Dist.*, 588 F 2d 674, 9 Cir. 1978). A New Jersey court has sustained a period of childbearing disability of four weeks before expected birth and four weeks following the actual date of birth for purposes of sick leave benefits (*Hynes v. Bd. of Educ. of Twp. of Bloomfield, Essex County*, 1190 N.J. Super. 36, 461 A. 2d 1184, 1983). A court found a male teacher not entitled to paid maternity leave for the purpose of caring for his disabled pregnant wife (*Ackerman v. Bd. of Educ.*, 287 F. Supp. 76, S.D. N.Y. 1974). However, childrearing leave must not be made available only to females. Such a provision in a collective bargaining agreement was declared to violate Title VII (*Shafer v. Bd. of Educ. of Sch. Dist. of Pittsburgh, PA*, 903 F. 2d 2443, 3d Cir. 1990).

A federal law, the Family and Medical Leave Act of 1993 (FMLA), P.L. 103-3, requires state and local government employers to provide up to 12 work weeks of unpaid leave during any 12-month period for the birth or adoption of a child. Upon return from FMLA leave, an employee must be restored to his or her original job, or to an equivalent job with equivalent pay and benefits. Other provisions of the act are requirements to provide 30 days' notice of leave, medical certifications supporting the need for leave, and reports regarding the employee's intention to return to work. Employees can bring civil action for employer violations of FMLA provisions.

Collective Bargaining

The labor union movement in the United States began in response to undesirable management practices in industry. It has spread to include employees in the public sector, such as teachers and government employees. Teachers represent the largest group of employees in an educational institution. Today, all but nine states have enacted statutes specifically establishing some rights of employees in public schools to bargain collectively with boards of education. These statutes range from very comprehensive laws controlling most aspects of collective bargaining to laws granting simply the right to meet and confer. Still other states, in the absence of legislation, rely on court decisions to define the basic rights of public employees in the labor relations area.

Prior to the 1960s, public school employees had been deprived of the right to organize and bargain collectively. In 1962, President Kennedy issued Executive Order 10988, which gave federal employees the right to form and join employee organizations. This Executive Order was a milestone for all public employees. The granting of organizational rights to federal employees provided the impetus for similar practices in the public schools. Nevertheless, statutes and regulations in some states prohibited union membership. These restrictions against union membership were challenged in the courts as violating association memberships protected by the First Amendment. In 1967, the U.S. Supreme Court in *Keyishian v.*

Bd. of Regents, 385 U.S. 589 (1967), held that public employment could not be conditioned on the elimination of free association rights.

The U.S. Constitution has been interpreted as protecting public employees' free association rights, but the right to establish and join a union does not guarantee the right to bargain collectively with a public employer. Collective bargaining is the process of negotiating between management and employees on the terms and conditions of employment. It is collective in the sense that the employees, as a unit, select representatives from their membership to meet with management to discuss issues that need to be resolved. The union bargains on items that represent the concerns of its membership. Management tries to advance the interests of the organization.

It is difficult to generalize about bargaining rights and practices, due to the diversity of labor laws among the states. A few states, such as New York, have a comprehensive collective bargaining statute that details specific bargaining rights of public employees. In contrast, negotiated contracts between teachers' organizations and school boards are prohibited in Texas. Under Texas law, any negotiated contract between a teachers' organization and a school board is void without express enabling legislation.

Bargaining Issues Collective bargaining agreements are complex and often lengthy, written contracts that are legally binding on both management and the union(s) representing its employees. A recent agreement between the Chicago Board of Education and the Chicago Teachers' Association is over 250 pages long (Chicago Board of Education, 2000). It is more streamlined than most. Although the specific provisions of collective bargaining agreements vary from one school district to another, the collective bargaining process and negotiated agreement generally address the following issues (Korney et al., 2000; Najita et al., 2001; Sharp, 1993).

Management rights During collective bargaining, unions strive to increase wages, protect job security, and improve the work conditions of employees. On the other hand, management tries to protect and clarify its rights as employer. Any rights not given to the union in the collective agreement are assumed to belong to management. These are called *management rights*. A strong management rights clause in the contract reinforces statutory rights of the board of education and aids in limiting the authority of an arbitrator in the grievance process. A common management rights clause is a lengthy list of specific management prerogatives, such as the right to supervise all operations; control all property and equipment; determine the size of the workforce; assign work to be done; introduce new methods, programs, or procedures; hire and fire employees; promote, demote, and transfer employees; and in general maintain an orderly, effective, and efficient operation.

Narrow grievance definition A grievance procedure is a formal system by which contract disputes are expressed, processed, and judged. The definition of a grievance in a written collective bargaining agreement determines which employee complaints are subject to binding grievance arbitration. A *narrow grievance definition* that limits employee complaints to the specific written agreement is recommended. Such an approach does not preclude other complaint procedures. It does limit what a grievance arbitrator can decide during the written terms of the negotiated agreement in force.

No-strike provision Federal law prohibits strikes by teachers. Most states have passed similar laws. Because teacher strikes occur despite the laws against them, additional protection is ensured through a *no-strike provision* in the collective bargaining agreement. Such a provision puts the union on record as being against strikes and involves the union in enforcement of the laws prohibiting them. In addition, a no-strike provision usually permits management to impose monetary damages on teachers who engage in an illegal strike.

Zipper clause A *zipper clause,* or waiver provision, stipulates that the written agreement is the complete and full contract between the parties and that neither party is required to bargain on other items during the term of the agreement. The purpose of such a provision is to avoid continuing negotiations after the contract has been ratified; when coupled with a strong management rights clause, the zipper clause limits the role of past practice used by grievance arbitrators.

Such a provision, however, does not preclude the parties from negotiating further if both agree. New bargaining strategies, including collaborative or win-win bargaining would be an exception to the use of a zipper clause. The idea of collaborative bargaining is that union and management negotiate continually during the year as problems arise.

Maintenance of standards   Management should avoid a *maintenance of standards* provision. Such a provision is routinely included in most union proposals and incorporates the school district's current practices on a wide range of items, many of which are not mandatory subjects of bargaining. Furthermore, a maintenance of standards provision leaves the district vulnerable to the role of past practice used by grievance arbitrators in settling contract disputes. It is the antithesis of a management rights provision and a zipper clause.

The following is an example of a maintenance of standards provision:

> All conditions of employment, including teaching hours, extra compensation for work outside regular teaching hours, relief periods, leaves and general working conditions shall be maintained at not less than the highest minimum standards, provided that such conditions shall be improved for the benefit of teachers, as required by the express provisions of this agreement. The agreement shall not be interpreted or applied to deprive teachers of professional advantages heretofore enjoyed, unless expressly states herein. (Gander, 1981, p. 22)

School boards and their designees should avoid such a provision.

Just cause   The term *just cause* is found in numerous collective bargaining agreements in public education and is routinely included in most union proposals. There is a danger in using such a term,

from management's standpoint, because *just cause* has no clear definition. If a collective bargaining agreement has binding arbitration as the last step in the grievance procedure, then an arbitrator will decide what the term means. The arbitrator's interpretation of the term may be different from what management had intended. For example, suppose a collective bargaining agreement contained the following provision: "No teacher will be disciplined without just cause." What does *just cause* mean in this case? It will likely mean something different to management than it does to employees. The point is that the meaning of *just cause* must either be spelled out clearly somewhere in the contract or be eliminated entirely.

Reduction in force   Nearly all collective bargaining agreements have some form of *reduction in force (RIF)* provision. Seniority, or length of continuous service within a certificated field, is the key factor used in employee layoff and recall. Some agreements allow for *bumping,* which means that a teacher laid off in one certificated field may replace another teacher in another certificated field who has less seniority in the field than the bumping teacher. A few RIF provisions stress other factors, such as affirmative action and teacher merit, that are more favorable to management but are opposed by most teachers' unions.

Wages and benefits   Much time at the bargaining table is devoted to wage increases and fringe-benefit improvements. Wage and salary increases are often stated as across-the-board salary increases for steps on a lockstep salary schedule and *cost-of-living adjustments (COLA)* based on the consumer price index in a designated geographic area. Besides salary increases, unions often demand improvements in various fringe benefits such as insurance programs (life, health, and dental); pension plans; merit pay; and sick leave, personal days, and paid religious holidays. Compensation costs in today's school districts often range from 75% to 85% of the total budget.

Other issues   Among other important bargaining issues are grievance arbitration, teacher evaluation, class size, and the school calendar. Binding grievance arbitration is not a problem, providing the rest of the agreement protects management prerogatives. Likewise, teacher evaluation, class size, and school calendar should not be overly restrictive on the school district.

The Bargaining Process   To bargain these issues, management and the union each select a negotiating team. Opinions vary widely on who should conduct management negotiations. In small school districts, the superintendent or a board member often conducts negotiations with the teachers' union. Experts advise against this practice, however (Booth, 1993). In large districts, a full-time administrator (director of employee relations, assistant superintendent, or director of personnel) usually serves as chief negotiator. Still other districts employ an outside negotiator — an attorney or labor relations specialist.

One of a superintendent's basic personnel decisions concerning collective bargaining is whether to have a labor relations specialist at the bargaining table to advise the school district during negotiations. When hiring a labor relations specialist, the superintendent must decide how much authority to give him or her.

One or more school principals (representing different school levels) often are included on management's negotiating team. These people live with the contract day to day; they know its weak and strong points; they will administer the new agreement; and they will likely give the contract greater support if they can participate in the changes made in it. The union team generally consists of the local union president and other members of the local membership. Its team may also include an attorney or a labor relations specialist from a regional unit that negotiates for other teachers' unions in the area.

Once each side has selected its negotiating teams, the bargaining process begins. The bargaining takes place between management and union representatives in face-to-face meetings, during which numerous proposals and counterproposals are exchanged. Several rounds of negotiations may be needed to reach agreement on all issues. When the two parties agree on the issues, a new negotiated contact is presented to the union membership and the board for a *ratification vote*. If both parties approve the agreement, each goes back to the bargaining table for another round of negotiations.

An *impasse* is said to exist when both parties are unable to reach agreement on a contract. State procedures vary when the union and the school board are deadlocked in negotiations. Most states have some provision for resolving impasses. Some states, like Wisconsin, have developed a procedure for resolving impasses. The procedure involves the following steps:

1. *Mediation.* The two contending parties meet with a neutral third person who attempts to persuade them to settle the remaining issues through discussion and by proposing compromise provisions to the contract. The mediator acts as a facilitator, however, and has no legal authority to force the parties to accept the suggestions offered.

2. *Fact finding.* The state appoints a group or committee to investigate and report the facts that are presented by each party. The fact-finding committee's recommendations are generally made public, which places additional pressure on the parties to come to agreement.

3. *Arbitration.* If the parties are still at an impasse, state law may require the union and the school board to submit to arbitration or binding arbitration. Guidelines for teachers' contracts in Wisconsin, for example, stipulate that arbitrators must choose the proposal of either the school board or the teachers' union, but not a compromise solution. This forces the two contending parties to bring their contract proposals closer together. The result has been a decrease in teacher strikes in Wisconsin (American Arbitration Association, 2004).

Bargaining Tactics   Negotiators have several tactics for improving their bargaining. Three tactics they typically use are counterproposals, trade-offs, and caucus (Korney et al., 2000; Najita et al., 2001; Neal, 1982; Sharp, 1993).

Counterproposals   Collective bargaining consists of the exchange of proposals and counterproposals in an effort to reach settlement between the negotiating parties. A proposal is an offer presented by one party in negotiations for consideration by the other party. A *counterproposal,* which is designed to bring the parties closer together on an issue, is an offer suggested as an alternative to the previous proposal by the other party. Because it is the union that is seeking improved conditions of employment, it introduces most of the proposals. Generally, management responds to the union's demands through counterproposals. Actually, there are at least two advantages to this approach for management: (1) The party that moves first on an issue is usually at a disadvantage because its negotiator invariably reveals some information helpful to the other negotiator; and (2) the union, as the initiating party, is forced to work for every concession it gets.

Trade-offs   Another bargaining tactic is the *trade-off,* which involves giving one issue in return for another. For example, the trade-off process works as follows: A teachers' union will make many proposals, such as (a) fair share, (b) salary increase, (c) increased sick leave, (d) increased personal days, (e) extra holiday(s), (f) hospitalization, (g) life insurance, (h) dental insurance, (i) maternity leave, (j) binding arbitration of grievances, (k) past practice provision, (l) reduction-in-force procedures, (m) teacher evaluations, (n) class size, (o) school calendar, and the like. Management then responds by stating that it will grant a 5% salary increase if the union withdraws its proposals for increased sick leave and personal days, hospitalization, life insurance, and dental insurance. Further, management will grant the past practice clause if the union drops its request for binding arbitration of grievances. All proposals are "packaged" in this manner until the teacher's union and the school board reach a settlement. Although neither party wants to give up its item, each may perceive the exchange as a reasonable compromise.

Caucus   A basic principle of negotiating is that only one person speaks at the bargaining table — the chief negotiator. Other members of the bargaining team must remain quiet at the bargaining table, which can be a frustrating demand. A *caucus* is a private meeting of a bargaining team to decide what action to take on a particular phase of negotiations. The caucus provides an opportunity to get needed input from other team members and to release built-up tensions that arise during stressful negotiations.

New Bargaining Strategies   Currently, 41 of the 50 states permit teachers to bargain collectively with school boards. Where such bargaining is allowed, almost all school districts employ traditional or adversarial bargaining. In recent years a new unionism, one that connects teacher participation in educational decisions to taking responsibility for outcomes, has become apparent. Studies of various collaborative efforts in union-management relations describe reform initiatives in Cincinnati, Ohio; Glenview, Illinois; Jefferson County, Kentucky; Pittsburgh, Pennsylvania; Rochester and Greece, New York; and other cities (Kerchner, Koppich, & Weeres, 1998; Troy, 2001). This research describes professional unionism and how it contrasts sharply with the beliefs and practices of traditional industrial unionism.

One consequence of professional unionism is the emergence of a new mode of principal leadership. Although they vary in personal style, gender, and ethnicity, professional unions share similar management styles. They empower the people with whom they work. They use a hands-on approach. They are entrepreneurs; they gather and redistribute resources and encourage others to do so. They abide by a common realization that the best leaders are those who develop the talents of others and gain commitment rather than compliance with organizational rules.

Consistent with professional unionism is collaborative bargaining (also known as win-win bargaining). Typically, collaborative bargaining focuses on ongoing problem solving rather than dealing with a buildup of issues presented at the bargaining table. Both management and union keep a "tickler file" of problems encountered in administering the current contract. Joint committees deal with the problems encountered. Then when contract language is finally discussed, the parties present specific notes to support their positions. Both parties establish agreed-on ground rules and specific time limits for negotiations; write trust agreements and memoranda of understanding; and carefully select respected, credible members of negotiating teams. These procedures can help establish trust and a sense of collaboration to solve mutual problems throughout the school year and at the bargaining table.

Tort Liability

A *tort* is a civil wrong, not including contracts, for which a court will award damages. The three major categories of torts are intentional interference, strict liability, and negligence. Instances of intentional interference and strict liability in school-related injuries are rare and will not be pursued in this section. Accordingly, we examine the elements of negligence and the defenses against liability. We also address liability under Section 1983 of the Civil Rights Act.

Elements of Negligence To establish a legal cause for action in tort, four essential elements must exist: The individual has a duty to protect others against unreasonable risks; the individual failed to exercise an appropriate standard of care; the negligent act is the proximate cause of the injury; and there is a physical or mental injury, resulting in actual loss or damage to the person (Alexander & Alexander, 2005; Cambron-McCabe et al., 2004; Fischer, Schimmel, & Kelly, 2003; LaMorte, 2002; Russo, 2004; Valente & Valente, 2001).

Duty School employees have a *duty* to protect students entrusted to their care from being injured. Specifically, these duties include adequate supervision and instruction, maintenance of premises and equipment, and foreseeability. The test of foreseeability is whether under all circumstances the possibility of injury should have been reasonably foreseen and that supervision likely would have prevented the injury. For example, a teacher was found guilty of negligence when an eighth-grade pupil was injured from pebble throwing during a morning recess (*Sheehan v. St. Peter's Catholic School*, 291 Minn. 1, 188 N.W. 2d 868, 1971). Similarly, in a New Jersey suit, an elementary school principal was held liable for injuries suffered when a pupil was struck by paper clips shot from a rubber band by another child before the classrooms opened. The court found the principal had acted improperly by announcing no rules on the conduct of students before entering classrooms, by not assigning teachers to assist him in supervising the pupils before school, and by engaging in activities other than overseeing the pupils' activities (*Titus v. Lindberg*, 49 N.J. 66, A. 2d 65, 1967).

Standard of care Failure of a school employee to act in a manner that conforms to an appropriate *standard of care* can render said employee negligent. The standard of care is that which a reasonable and prudent person would have exercised under similar circumstances. For example, the Oregon Supreme Court said "Negligence . . . is . . . the doing of that thing which a reasonably prudent person would not have done, in like or similar circumstances" (*Biddle v. Mazzocco*, 284 P. 2d 364, Ore. 1955). The model for the reasonable and prudent person has been described as one who possesses "(1) the physical attributes of the defendant himself, (2) normal intelligence, (3) normal perception and memory with a minimum level of information and experience common to the community, and (4) such superior skill and knowledge as the actor has or holds himself out to the public as having" (Alexander & Alexander, 2005, p. 502).

The standard of care required would depend on such circumstances as the age, maturity, and experience of students; the type of activity; the environment; and the potential for danger. The amount of care owed to children increases with their immaturity. A higher standard of care is required in shop, physical education, and laboratory classes and in situations and environments that pose a greater threat of danger (e.g., school field trips).

Proximate cause There must be a connection between the action of school personnel and the resultant injury sustained by the student. Courts will ask, "Was the failure to exercise a reasonable standard of care the *proximate cause* of the injury?" The cause of the injury first must be established. Then it must be shown that there was some connection between the injury and the employee's failure to exercise a reasonable standard of care.

As in determining whether an appropriate standard of care has been exercised, the test of foreseeability is used in establishing proximate cause. For proximate cause to be established, it is not necessary to have foreseen a particular injury. If reasonable precautions are taken and an intervening injury not foreseen occurs, no negligence exists. Such was the case when a student returned to his desk and sat on a sharpened pencil placed there by another student. School authorities were not held liable for the injury (*Swaitkowski v. Bd. of Educ. of City of Buffalo*, 36 A.D. 2d 685, N.Y. 1971).

Injury There must be proof of actual loss or damage to the plaintiff resulting from the *injury*. If the injury suffered is caused by more than one individual, damages will be apportioned among the defendants (Cambron-McCabe et al., 2004). A school district may be required to compensate an injured party for negligent conduct of an officer, agent, or employee of the district. Individual school board members or employees (superintendents, principals, teachers) may also be liable personally for torts that they commit in the course of their duties.

Defenses Against Negligence Several defenses can be invoked by a defendant (school board, superintendent, principal, teacher) in a tort action. These defenses include contributory negligence, assumption of risk, comparative negligence, and government immunity.

Contributory negligence If it is shown that a student's own negligence contributed to the injury, the law in many states would charge the student with *contributory negligence*. However, a student cannot be charged with contributory negligence if

he is too immature to recognize the risks: A standard of care that is adequate when dealing with adults generally will not be adequate when dealing with children. For example, in about a dozen states, courts have ruled that students under 7 years of age cannot be prohibited from recovery of damages because of negligence. In other states, the age has been set at 4, 5, or 6 years. And for older children up to the age of 14, there is a "rebuttable presumption" that they are incapable of contributory negligence (Fischer et al., 2003).

Assumption of risk Another commonly used defense in tort actions is the doctrine of *assumption of risk*. It is based on the theory that one who knowingly and willingly exposes oneself to a known danger may be denied tort recovery for injury sustained. Requisite to invoking a defense of assumption of risk is that there be knowledge and appreciation of the danger. Thus it was held that a child who was cut by submerged broken glass while playing in a high school sandpit did not assume the risk of injury because he did not know the glass was in the sandpit (*Brown v. Oakland*, 124 P. 2d 369, Cal. 1942). On the other hand, the Oregon Supreme Court found an assumption of risk in the injury of a high school football player when he was injured in a scheduled football game (*Vendrell v. Sch. Dist. No. 26C, Malheur Cty.*, 233 Ore. 1, 376 P. 2d 406, 1962). As with contributory negligence cases, courts will consider the age and maturity level of students when assessing a defense of assumption of risk in tort.

Comparative negligence Where the common-law rule of contributory negligence and assumption of risk is followed, plaintiffs whose own negligence contributed to an injury are barred completely from recovery. This harsh rule has been modified. Some states have adopted the doctrine of *comparative negligence*. Under the comparative negligence doctrine, a plaintiff can obtain a proportionate recovery for injury depending on the amount of negligence she contributed to the injury. Specific statutory provisions vary from state to state (Valente & Valente, 2001).

Government immunity The origin of the doctrine of *government immunity* from tort liability can be traced to two early cases, one in England in 1788 and the other in Massachusetts in 1812 (*Russell v. Men of Devon*, 100 Eng. Rep. 359, 2 T.R. 667, 1788; *Mower v. Leicester*, 9 Mass. 237, 1812). The courts held that the government could not be sued for negligence; thus, the precedent of the immunity of school districts from tort liability was established and remained in effect until the passage of the Federal Tort Claims Act of 1946. Subsequently, the doctrine of state immunity in tort has been abrogated or modified by state legislatures. However, tort law does extend certain immunity to teachers and administrators in the scope and performance of their duties. One example is administering corporal punishment in schools (*Ingraham v. Wright*, 430 U.S. 651, 1977).

School board members also have some degree of immunity in the scope and performance of their duties. However, Section 1983 of the Civil Rights Act, rooted in 1871, changed the status of the immunity of school board members regarding their activities. This section provides that every person who subjects any citizen of the United States to the deprivation of any rights secured by the U.S. Constitution be liable to the (injured) party in an action at law (42 U.S.C. sec. 1983, 1871). A plethora of court cases have been litigated under the act, primarily dealing with First and Fourteenth Amendment rights. The tort liability of school board members was further extended under Section 1983 to students by the Supreme Court decision in *Wood v. Strickland*, 420 U.S. 308 (1975). The Court held that school board members could be sued individually by students whose constitutional rights were denied. The case involved a denial of due process of students in a suspension hearing.

Summary

1. All three levels of government — federal, state, and local — exercise some degree of authority and control over public education.

2. At the federal level, the U.S. Constitution, federal statutes, federal administrative agencies, and case law all constitute sources of law under which school principals operate.

3. State-level sources of law under which school principals operate include the state's constitution, state statutes, state administrative agencies, and case law.

4. At the local level, local school board policies provide another source of law for school principals, as well as their individual school's rules and regulations.

5. The American judicial system consists of federal and state courts. The federal court system has its basis in the U.S. Constitution. State court systems have their basis in state constitutions or statutory laws. The federal courts have primary jurisdiction on federal law questions, while state courts have primary jurisdiction on laws of each respective state.

6. Litigation has reached both federal and state courts in the areas of compulsory school attendance, church-state relations, school fees, the curriculum, and state-mandated testing.

7. U.S. Supreme Court decisions have been prevalent in such student-related issues as freedom of expression, corporal punishment, search and seizure, suspensions and expulsions, and students with disabilities.

8. U.S. Supreme Court decisions have been prevalent also in such staff-related issues as certification and licensure, contracts, termination of employment, discrimination in employment, sexual harassment, and tort liability.

9. Most states permit teachers and other employee groups to bargain collectively with boards of education. The term *labor relations* refers to dealing with employees when they are organized into a union. Management (school board and its designee) must engage in collective bargaining with the union in an effort to reach agreement on a contract. The most recent approaches to collective bargaining are referred to as "win-win bargaining."

Field-Based Activities

1. Litigation has reached both federal and state courts in the areas of compulsory school attendance, church-state relations, school fees, the curriculum, and state-mandated testing. Consult school board policies in your district and interview your building principal, and your school district's attorney, concerning each of the issues just listed. Record your responses in your journal.

2. U.S. Supreme Court decisions have been prevalent in such student-related issues as freedom of expression, corporal punishment, search and seizure, suspensions and expulsions, and students with disabilities. Consult school board policies in your district and interview your building principal, and your school district's attorney, concerning each of the student-related issues. Record your responses in your journal.

3. U.S. Supreme Court decisions have been prevalent also in such staff-related issues as certification and licensure, contracts, termination of employment, discrimination in employment, sexual harassment, and tort liability. Consult school board policies in your district and interview your building principal, and your school district's attorney, concerning each of the staff-related issues. Record your responses in your journal.

Suggested Readings

Alexander, K., & Alexander, M. D. (2005). *American public school law* (6th ed.). West/Thomson Learning. This book is intended for graduate students studying education or students in law schools who desire a comprehensive view of the law that governs the public school system of America. The legal precedents presented and discussed herein deal with the multitude of issues occurring in a country that has developed an extraordinary reliance on the public schools as a mechanism for social and economic justice and improvement.

Cambron-McCabe, N. H., McCarthy, M. M., & Thomas, S. B. (2004). *Public school law: Teachers' and students' rights* (5th ed.). Boston: Allyn & Bacon. The text addresses legal principles applicable to practitioners in a succinct but comprehensive manner. It blends a detailed treatment of landmark cases with a thorough discussion of the legal context, trends, and generalizations to guide all school personnel in their daily activities. Information in this text will help alleviate concerns voiced by educators who either don't know the legal concepts that govern schools or feel that the scales of justice have been tipped against them.

Essex, N. L. (2002). *School law and the public schools: A practical guide for educational leaders* (2nd ed.). Boston: Allyn & Bacon. This book was written to provide practical knowledge to practicing and prospective educational leaders, students of educational leadership, and policymakers at all educational levels. The author thoroughly yet succinctly covers legal issues, discussing them in an informative, entertaining, and useful way so that the audience can effectively perform professional duties within the boundaries of constitutional, statutory, and case law.

Fischer, L., Schimmel, D., & Stellman, L. (2003). *Teachers and the law* (6th ed.). Boston: Allyn & Bacon. Clearly written and useful to both teachers and school administrators, this text focuses on the legal issues that are most important to educators today. The authors designed the text to help school professionals avoid unnecessary litigation by educating them about their legal rights and responsibilities and explaining how and why the courts reached the decisions in pertinent cases.

Imber, M., & von Geel, T. (2000). *Education law* (2nd ed.). Mahwah, NJ: Erlbaum. In this second edition, the authors of *Education Law* provide a comprehensive survey of the legal problems and issues that confront school administrators and policymakers. The greater the likelihood of litigation or error in a particular area of professional practice, the more extensive the discussion. In response to student feedback, the new edition contains about half as much case material and about twice as much commentary as the first edition. Landmark cases and cases that best illustrate major principles of education law have been retained and surrounded by expanded discussion and analysis. Students who want additional cases can easily access them via the Internet.

LaMorte, M. W. (2002). *School law: Cases and concepts* (7th ed.). Boston: Allyn & Bacon. Clearly and interestingly written, this book examines the laws educators need to know to operate in a legally defensible and educationally sound manner. In addition to providing historical perspective, this new edition examines policies and litigation pertaining to church and state issues, legal rights and restrictions applicable to students and teachers, desegregation, school finance, vouchers and charter schools, developments in disabilities law, and harassment of students.

Russo, C. J. (2004). *Reutter's the law of public education* (5th ed.). New York: Foundation Press. This fifth edition of *The Law of Public Education* is designed to provide basic knowledge of the laws affecting public education in the United States. The text covers principles and patterns of law applied to various aspects of public education. Citations now include references to West's *Education Law Reporter,* thereby making it easier for instructors and students to locate cases.

A Case for
the Attorney

Setting: Knowland High School is the second high school in the Eisenhower School District. Knowland lies across town from Dover High School and is known as the "country" high school because of its location at the edge of the city. Many of the students attending this school reside in several very small communities that recently have been incorporated by the city. When Knowland is compared to Dover High School, the most glaring difference is the larger number of disadvantaged students.

Scenario: As he comes down the hall to his office at Knowland, Principal Gary Jones hears his secretary say, "If you would only wait for a few minutes, Ms. Freer, I am sure that Mr. Jones will see you about this urgent matter."

Mr. Jones rounds the corner to the waiting room and greets Ms. Freer, saying, "Good morning, Ms. Freer. How are you today?"

"You wouldn't ask if you knew what I was going to say, Mr. Jones. I need to see you right away, and privately." She looks pointedly at the secretary, who immediately resumes processing the daily mail.

After getting Ms. Freer settled in his office, Mr. Jones inquires, "What is your urgent concern, Ms. Freer?"

"Well," she huffs, "I believe I saw Coach White having a beer with one of our students in a café in the neighboring town. I went in to see about a carryout meal, and there they were big as life, just sitting at the bar looking into each other's eyes. Each of them had a mug of beer in one hand. They were so engrossed with each other, they didn't even see me."

"Are you sure you saw Coach White? And what was the name of the student you saw?"

"I am sure the man was Coach White. He was still in his coaching shirt and shorts with our school colors. Can you imagine that? Bringing such disgrace on our high school! I have no idea who the girl was. She was mighty pretty and so was the gold jewelry she was wearing! Now what are you going to do about such a scene?"

"I'll look into the situation and take the appropriate action, Ms. Freer. Please trust me to handle this in an appropriate way."

As soon as Ms. Freer leaves the office, Mr. Jones calls the athletic director, Steve Hill, and asks him to come to his office. He tells Director Hill what has been reported and asks if he has seen or heard anything about Coach White dating one of the high school students.

"No, but I will tell you that I have heard rumors about him being associated with some gold jewelry disappearing in the locker room. I never could get anyone, students or staff, to tell me any more, so I let it go. I figured that if someone had valuable jewelry stolen, he or she would report it and then we could investigate. Oh, and one more thing, one of the girls seemed pretty upset last week. She was crying and wanted to talk to Coach White, but I never could get her to tell me anything. It seems to me that at one time she was Coach White's student trainer when he was coaching the girls' basketball team. Maybe you could talk to her and find out more."

"What is her name, Steve?"

"Clara Garcia is her name, and she is a junior."

When Clara comes into Mr. Jones's office, she is visibly upset. Mr. Jones starts the conversation by asking about her activities and her work as a student trainer. She shares that she had enjoyed working with Coach White.

"Why, then, were you so upset last week?" asks Mr. Jones.

At first Clara denies being upset; but after learning that the athletic director has seen her crying, she admits that she is in turmoil. She has lost her gold necklace and her gold bracelet. Her father gave both items to her when she turned 16.

"Where do you think you lost your jewelry?" asks Mr. Jones.

Clara's answer surprises the principal. "I gave my jewelry to Coach White for safekeeping, and he says he lost it."

Mr. Jones tells Clara that he will check for her missing jewelry and asks her to bring him a detailed description. He also tells her that she should keep alert to rumors and possible sightings of her jewelry.

About two weeks later, Steve Hill, the athletic director, visits Mr. Jones in the office and says, "I think I know who the current girlfriend is. I think I also know who Coach White's ex-girlfriend is — Clara Garcia." He continues, saying that he overheard a couple of the boys talking about Clara and how stuck up she was now that she had had an affair with Coach White. "The new girl is a senior, 17 years old, going on 25 in looks. Her name is Sara Blitz."

Just then Mr. Jones's secretary buzzes him to let him know that Clara Garcia is outside wanting to see him right away. He asks Director Hill to leave via the back door to his office and invites Clara to come in and sit down. Immediately Clara blurts out, "I saw it, Mr. Jones. Sara Blitz is wearing my jewelry. Please help me get my jewelry back. My Dad will kill me if he finds out that I lost it!" Mr. Jones calms Clara and sends her on her way, assuring her that action will be taken.

He calls in Sara Blitz, who is indeed wearing a beautiful gold necklace and bracelet. He asks her where she got them and she says, "They are gifts from my boyfriend."

"Who is your boyfriend?"

"Someone you don't know."

"May I have a closer look at the jewelry? It is beautiful."

After noting the make and marks, Mr. Jones knows that this jewelry belongs to Clara Garcia and presses Sara to tell him more. She resists at first, but eventually confesses that Coach White is her boyfriend. With that confession, Mr. Jones takes her into the counselor's office and tells her to remain there until he comes for her. Mr. Jones takes a few minutes to call Dr. Petrovsky, superintendent, to inform him of the facts. He promises to visit personally to brief Dr. Petrovsky about all the details as soon as the current crisis is addressed.

Now Mr. Jones knows that he must confront Coach White about sexual abuse and sexual harassment of Clara Garcia and Sara Blitz. He must also confront Coach White about what appears to be a clear case of theft of Clara's jewelry. He knows that he must give due process to Coach White, but at the moment he is so angry that he can hardly think straight. He needs time to organize his thoughts, but he knows that both Sara and Clara are waiting. He also knows that he must ask both students about the extent of their involvement with Coach White, and he must report all of this to the parents of the students.

Upon questioning each girl independently, first Sara and then Clara, Mr. Jones learns that both girls have been intimate with Coach White. He also learns that neither set of parents has a clue about what has been an ongoing set of affairs with Coach White. He understands better than ever before in his tenure as principal that being knowledgeable about the law is critical to any administrative role.

Questions

1. What laws have been violated? What school board policies have been violated? What "good causes" for termination of Coach White will most likely be pursued?

2. What due process must the district provide?

3. What are the students' legal rights in a situation such as this?

4. What court or courts could possibly end up hearing the case?

5. What kind of liability does Mr. Jones possibly have in this case? Steve Hill, the athletic director? The school district?

▪ References

AASA. (1996). AASA's code of ethics. *The School Administrator, 53*(9), 16.

AASA. (1981). *AASA's statement of ethics for school administrators.* Retrieved November 2003 from http://www.aasa.org/about/ethics.htm

Abrell, R. (2004). *Preventing communication breakdowns.* Reston, VA: National Association of Secondary School Principals.

Acheson, K. A. (1985). The principal's role in instructional leadership. *OSSC Bulletin, 28*(8), 1–25.

Acheson, K. A., & Gall, M. D. (2003). *Techniques in the clinical supervision of teachers: Preservice and inservice applications* (5th ed.). White Plains, NY: Longman.

Acheson, K. A., & Smith, S. C. (1986). *It is time for principals to share the responsibility for instructional leadership with others.* Eugene, OR: Oregon School Study Council. (ERIC Document Reproduction Service No. ED267510)

Achilles, C. M. (1997, October). Small classes, big possibilities. *American Association of School Administrators Online, 9*(54). Retrieved November 21, 2003, from http://www.aasa.org/ publications/sa/1997_10/achilles.htm

Ackerman v. Board of Education

Adair, J. (2003). *Effective decision making: A guide to thinking for management success.* London: Pan Macmillan.

Adams, P. W., et al. (2004). *Introduction to computers for teachers* (2nd ed.). Charlotte, NC: CPI Training Solutions.

Addams, J. (1910). *Twenty years at Hull-House: With autobiographical notes.* New York: Macmillan.

Adey, P. S. (1997, April). *Factors influencing uptake of a large scale curriculum innovation.* Paper presented at the annual meeting of the American Educational Research Association, Chicago. (ERIC Document Reproduction Service No. ED408672)

Adler v. Board of Education

AERA position statement concerning high-stakes testing in prek–12 education (2000). Retrieved August 10, 2003, from http://www.aera.net/ about/policy/stakes.htm

Agostini v. Felton

Aguilar v. Felton

Aguinis, H. (2004). *Test-score bonding in human resource selection: Legal, technical, and social issues.* Westport, CT: Greenwood.

Alexander, K., & Alexander, M. D. (2005). *American public school law* (6th ed.). Belmont, CA: West/Thomson Learning.

Alkire, P. (2004). *Strategies to improve teacher evaluations.* Washington, DC: National School Boards Association.

Allen, D. (1995a). *Resources for teacher-constructed curriculum.* Unpublished manuscript, ATLAS Seminar, Providence, RI.

Allen, D. (1995b). *The tuning protocol: A process for reflection* (Studies on Exhibitions Monograph No. 15). Providence, RI: Coalition of Essential Schools, Brown University.

Allen, D., & McDonald, J. (2003). *The tuning protocol: Process for reflection on teacher and student work.* Retrieved November 3, 2004, from http://www.essentialschools.org/cs/resources/view/ ces_res/54

Allison, G. S. (2004). *How to prevent and safely manage physical aggression and property destruction.* Austin, TX: PRO-ED.

Alvesson, M. (2002). *Understanding organizational culture.* Thousand Oaks, CA: Sage.

Alvy, H. B., & Robbins, P. (1998). *If I only knew: Success strategies for navigating the principalship.* Thousand Oaks, CA: Corwin.

American Academy of Pediatrics. (2000, August). Corporal punishment in schools. *Pediatrics, 106,* 343.

American Arbitration Association. (2003). *An inside look at collective bargaining.* New York: Author.

American Institute of Certified Public Accountants. (2000). *Understanding audits and the auditor's report: A guide for financial statement users.* Jersey City, NJ: Author.

American Management Association. (2004). *Present-day administrative and financial controls.* New York: Author.

American Society for Testing and Materials. (2004). *Nondestructive testing.* West Conshohocken, PA: Author.

Andryzewski, T. (2004). *Terrorism in America.* Brookfield, CT: Millbrook Press.

Apple, M. W. (1990). *Ideology and curriculum.* New York: Routledge.

Apple, M. W. (2001). *Educating the "right" way: Markets, standards, God, and inequality.* New York: Routledge/Falmer.

Arcadia Unified School District v. State Department of Education

Arfstrom, K. (1998). Keeping the feds out of your airspace. *School Administrator, 55,* 39.

Argyris, C. (1985). *Strategy, change, and defense routines.* Boston: Pitman.

Arter, J., et al. (2000). *Scoring rubrics in the classroom: Using performance criteria for assessing and improving student performance.* Thousand Oaks, CA: Corwin.

Arterbury, E., Crawford, C., & Moore, D. (2001). Is there an ethic complaint in your future? *Insight, 15*(1), 13–41.

Ash, R., & Persall, M. (2002). Instructional leadership. In G. Brown, J. G. DeZwaan, D. L. Gray, R. C. Hill, B. J. Irby, L. A. Kirby, P. L. Pickles, J. Whatley, & J. D. Wills (Eds.), *Developing the effective principal.* Gaithersburg, MD: Aspen.

Aspen Publishers Staff. (2004). *Safety and security administration in school facilities: Forms, checklists, and guidelines.* New York: Aspen.

Association for Def. v. Kiger

Attorney General v. East Jackson Public Schools

Ausubel, D. (1968). *Educational psychology: A cognitive view.* New York: Holt, Rinehart & Winston.

Babbit, N. (2001). *Adolescent drug and alcohol abuse: How to spot it, stop it and get help for your family.* Cambridge, MA: O'Reilly & Associates.

Baca, L. M., & Cervantes, M. T. (1989). Background and rationale for bilingual special education. In L. M. Baca & H. T. Cervantes (Eds.), *The bilingual special education interfaces* (2nd ed., pp. 1–21). Columbus, OH: Merrill.

Backlund, P., & Ivy, D. K. (2003). *Exploring genderspeak: Personal effectiveness in gender communication.* New York: McGraw-Hill.

Baerdwell, I., et al. (2001). *Human resource management: A contemporary approach.* Englewood Cliffs, NJ: Prentice Hall.

Bagin, D., & Gallagher, D. R. (2001). *The school and community relations* (7th ed.). Boston: Allyn & Bacon.

Bailey, G. D., & Littrell, J. H. (1981). A blueprint for curriculum development: Establishing a systemic design. *NASSP Bulletin, 65,* 22–28.

Baker, B. D., & Richards, C. E. (2004). *The ecology of educational systems: Data, models, and tools for improvisational leading and learning.* Upper Saddle River, NJ: Merrill/Prentice Hall.

Baker, J. (1988). *Causes of failure in performance appraisal and supervision: A guide to analysis and evaluation for human resources professionals.* Westport, CT: Greenwood.

Baker, S. B. (2004). *School counseling for the 21st century.* Columbus, OH: Merrill/Prentice Hall.

Baldwin, J. R., Perry, S. D., & Moffitt, M. A. (2003). *Communication theories for everyday life.* Boston: Allyn & Bacon.

Ball, S. (1994). *Education reform—A critical and post-structural approach.* Philadelphia: Open University Press.

Banham, R. (1994). Lead poisoning: Who is liable? Who pays? *Independent Agent, 14,* 22–30.

Banks, J. A. (1988). *Multiethnic education: Theory and practice* (2nd ed.). Boston: Allyn & Bacon.

Banks, J. A., & C. A. Banks (Eds.). (1995). *Handbook of research on multicultural education.* New York: Simon & Schuster Macmillan.

Barger v. Bisciglia

Barker, L. (1991). *Listening behavior.* New Orleans: Spectra.

Baron, R. S., et al. (2003). *Group process, group decisions, group action.* New York: Taylor & Francis.

Barrow, R. (1984). *Giving teaching back to teachers: A critical introduction to curriculum theory.* London, ON: Althouse Press.

Barth, R. S. (2003). *Lessons learned: Shaping relationships and the culture of the workplace.* Thousand Oaks, CA: Corwin.

Barth, R. S. (2004). *Learning by heart.* New York: Wiley.

Barton, E. A. (2001). *Leadership strategies for safe schools.* Glenview, IL: Pearson Professional Development.

Barton, P. E. (2003). *Parsing the achievement gap.* Princeton, NJ: Educational Testing Service. Retrieved March 1, 2004, from http://www.ets.org/research/pic/parsing.pdf

Basham, V., & Lunenburg, F. C. (1989). Strategic planning, student achievement, and school district financial and demographic factors. *Planning and Changing, 20,* 158–171.

Bass, B. M. (1985). *Leadership and performance beyond expectations.* New York: Free Press.

Bass, B. M. (1997). *A new paradigm of leadership: An inquiry into transformational leadership.* Mahwah, NJ: Erlbaum.

Bass, B. M., & Avolio, B. J. (1994). *Improving organizational effectiveness through transformational leadership.* Thousand Oaks, CA: Sage.

Bassett v. Braddock

Baylor, A. L., Kitsantas, A., & Chung, H. (2001). The Instructional Planning Self-Reflective Tool (IPSRT): A method for promoting effective lesson planning. *Educational Technology, 41*(2), 56–59.

Beaty, J. L. (2004). *Safety in preschool programs.* Englewood Cliffs, NJ: Prentice Hall.

Beauchamp, G. A. (1981). *Curriculum theory.* Itasca, IL: Peacock.

Beck v. James.

Beck, I., & McKeown, M. (1988). Toward meaningful accounts in history texts for young learners. *Educational Researcher, 17*(6), 31–39.

Beck, L. G., & Murphy, J. (1994). *Ethics in educational leadership programs: An expanding role.* Thousand Oaks, CA: Corwin.

Beckner, W. (2004). *Ethics for educational leaders.* Boston: Pearson.

Begley, P. T., & Johansson, O. (1998, July). The values of school administration: Preferences, ethics, & conflicts. *Journal of School Leadership, 9*(4), 399–422.

Begun, R. W., & Huml, F. J. (Eds.). (2003). *Ready-to-use violence prevention skills: Lessons and activities for secondary students.* New York: Wiley.

Bell, D. (1989, Spring). The third technological revolution. *Dissent,* 164–176.

Bellinger, D. (1987). Longitudinal analysis of prenatal and postnatal lead exposure and early cognitive development. *New England Journal of Medicine, 316,* 1037–1043.

Bennett, N., & Dunne, E. (1992). *Managing small groups.* New York: Simon & Schuster.

Bennis, W. G. (1966). *Changing organizations.* New York: McGraw-Hill.

Bennis, W. G. (2000). *Managing the dream: Reflections on leadership and change.* Cambridge, MA: Perseus.

Bennis, W., & Nanus, B. (1985). *Leaders: The strategies for taking charge.* New York: Harper & Row.

Benward, B., & Kolosick, T. J. (1995). *Ear training: A technique for listening.* Madison, WI: Brown and Benchmark.

Berliner, D. C., & Biddle, B. (1995). *The manufactured crisis: Myths, fraud, and the attack on America's public schools.* New York: Addison-Wesley.

Bermúdez, A. B., & Márquez, J. A. (1996). An examination of a four-way collaborative to increase parental involvement in the schools. *The Journal of Educational Issues of Language Minority Students,* Special Issue, 16, 1–16.

Bermúdez, A. B., & Padrón, Y. M. (1988). University-school collaboration that increases minority parent involvement. *Educational Horizons, 66*(2), 83–86.

Bernard v. Inhabitants of Shelburne

Bernardin, H. J. (2002). *Human resource management: An experiential approach.* New York: McGraw-Hill.

Bernd, M. (1992). Shared decision making requires effective instructional leadership. *NASSP Bulletin, 76,* 64–69.

Bernhardt, V. L. (1999). *The school portfolio: A comprehensive framework for school improvement* (2nd ed.). Larchmont, NY: Eye on Education.

Bernhardt, V. L. (2003). *Using data to improve student learning in elementary schools.* Larchmont, NY: Eye on Education.

Bethel School District No. 403 v. Fraser

Betts, G. T., & Kercher, J. K. (1999). *Autonomous learner model: Optimizing ability.* Greeley, CO: ALPS.

Beveridge, M., & Jerrams, A. (1981). Parental involvement in language development: An evaluation of a school-based parental assistance plan. *British Journal of Educational Psychology, 51,* 259–269.

Bhushan, N., et al. (2003). *Strategic decision making.* New York: Springer-Verlag.

Biddle v. Mazzocco

Birman, B. F., & Ginsburg, A. L. (1983). Introduction: Addressing the needs of language-minority children. In K. A. Baker & A. A. deKanter (Eds.), *Bilingual education: A reappraisal of federal policy* (pp. ix–xxi). Lexington, MA: Lexington Books.

Black, S. (2001). Heavy metal. *American School Board Journal, 188,* 62.

Blackstone, W. (1941). *Blackstone's commentaries on the laws of England (1765–1769)* (B. C. Gavit, Ed.). Washington, DC: Washington Law Book Co.

Blackwelder v. Safnauer

Blank, R. K. (1987). The role of principal as leader: Analysis of variation in leadership of urban high schools. *Journal of Educational Research, 81*(2), 69–80.

Blanton, C. K. (1999). *The strange career of bilingual education: A history of the political and pedagogical debate over language instruction in American public education.* 1890–1990. (Doctoral dissertation, Rice University, 1999). UMI Services, 9928507.

Blase, J., & Blase J. (1997). *The fire is back: Teachers sharing school governance.* Thousand Oaks, CA: Corwin.

Blase, J., & Blase, J. (2003). *Handbook of instructional leadership: How successful principals promote teaching and learning.* Thousand Oaks, CA: Corwin.

Blauvelt, P. D. (2001). *Making school safe for students: Creating a proactive school safety plan.* Thousand Oaks, CA: Corwin.

Bloom, B. S. (1956). *Taxonomy of educational objectives: Book I, Cognitive domain.* New York: Longman.

Bluestein, J. (2002). *Creating emotionally safe schools: A guide for educators and parents.* Deerfield Beach, FL: Health Communications.

Board of Curators v. Horowitz

Board of Education v. Allen

Board of Education v. Earls

Board of Education v. Pico

Board of Education v. Sinclair

Board of Education of Peoria v. Ill. State Board of Education

Board of Education of the Westside Community Schools v. Mergens

Board of Regents v. Roth

Bobbitt, F. (1918). *The curriculum.* Boston: Houghton Mifflin.

Bonstingl, J. J. (2001). *Schools of quality* (3rd ed.). Thousand Oaks, CA: Corwin.

Booth, R. R. (1993). *Collective bargaining and the school board member.* Springfield, IL: Illinois Association of School Boards.

Bor, R. (1993). *Managing and evaluating counseling services.* New York: Cassell.

Boschee, F., & Baron, M. (1994). OBE: Some answers for the uninitiated. *Clearing House, 67* (March/April), 193–196.

Boyd, W. L., & Miretzky, D. (Eds.). (2003). *American educational governance on trial: Change and challenges.* Chicago: University of Chicago Press.

Boyer, E. L. (1991). *Ready to learn: A mandate for the nation.* Princeton, NJ: Carnegie Foundation for the Advancement of Teaching.

Boyer, E. L. (1995). *The basic school: A community for learning.* Princeton, NJ: Carnegie Foundation for the Advancement of Teaching.

Bracey, G. (1997). *The truth about America's schools: The Bracey reports, 1991–1997.* Bloomington, IN: Phi Delta Kappa Educational Foundation.

Bracey, G. W. (2002). *The war on public schools: Privatizing schools, commercializing education.* Boston: Allyn & Bacon.

Bransford, J., Brown, A., & Cocking, R. (Eds.). (1999). *How people learn: Brain, mind, experience, and school.* Washington, DC: National Academy Press.

Bratton, J. (2003). *Human resource management: Theory and practice.* Gordonsville, VA: Palgrave Macmillan.

Bringing the Constitution to life; now is a good time to teach the hows and whys of liberty. (2003, March 24). *The Washington Times,* p. A23. Retrieved September 4, 2004, from Questia database, http://www.questia.com

Brock, S. T., Sandoval, J., & Lewis, S. (1996). *Preparing for crisis in the schools.* Brandon, VT: Clinical Psychology.

Brogan, B. R. (1995). *The case for teacher portfolios.* Paper presented at the 47th annual meeting of the American Association of Colleges for Teacher Education, Washington, DC. (ERIC Document Reproduction Service No. ED381516)

Bronfenbrenner, U. (1974). *A report on longitudinal evaluations of preschool programs, Vol. II: Is early intervention effective?* (ERIC Document Reproduction Service No. ED09301)

Brookover, W., Beady, C., Flood, P., Schweitzer, J., & Wisenbaker, J. (1979). *School social systems and student achievement: Schools can make a difference.* Brooklyn, NY: J. F. Bergin.

Brooks, J. G., & Brooks, M. G. (2003). *In search of understanding: The case for constructivist classrooms.* Alexandria, VA: Association for Supervision and Curriculum Development.

Brophy, J. (1983). Classroom organization and management. *The Elementary School Journal, 83,* 265–85.

Brophy, J. (1998). *Motivating students to learn.* Boston: McGraw-Hill.

Brophy, J. (1999). *Teaching.* Educational Practice Series 1. International Academy of Education and International Bureau of Education. Retrieved September 3, 2003, from http://www.ibe.unesco.org/International/Publications/EducationalPractices/EducationalPracticesSeriesPdf/prac01e.pdf

Brophy, J., & Alleman, J. (1991). Activities as instructional tools: A framework for analysis and evaluation. *Educational Researcher, 20*(4), 9–23.

Brophy, J. E., & Good, T. L. (1986). Teacher behavior and student achievement. In M. C. Wittrock (Ed.), *Handbook of research on teaching* (3rd ed, pp. 328–375). New York: Macmillan.

Browder, L. H. (2001). Coping with children on their own. In T. Kowalski (Ed.) & G. Perreault (Assoc. Ed.), *21st century challenges for school administrators.* Lanham, MD: Scarecrow Press.

Brown v. Board of Education of Topeka

Brown v. Oakland

Brown, B., & Merritt, R. (2002). *No easy answers: The truth behind death at Columbine.* New York: Lantern Books.

Brown, C. A., Smith, M. S., & Stein, M. K. (1995). *Linking teacher support to enhanced classroom instruction.* Paper presented at the annual meeting of the American Educational Research Association, New York City.

Brown, C. N. (1997). Gifted education is a constitution issue. *Roeper Review, 19,* 3.

Brown, G., & Irby, B. J. (1997). *The principal portfolio.* Thousand Oaks, CA: Corwin Press.

Brown, G., & Irby, B. J. (2000). *The career advancement portfolio.* Thousand Oaks, CA: Corwin.

Brown, G., & Irby, B. J. (2001). *The principal portfolio* (2nd ed.). Thousand Oaks, CA: Corwin.

Brown, G., & Irby, B. J. (2002). Documenting continuing professional education requirements using the professional development portfolio. *Texas Study, XI*(2), 13–16.

Brown, G., Irby, B. J., & Fisher, A. (2001). The leadership framework: Facilitating reflection for 21st century leaders. In T. Kowalski & G. Perreault (Eds.), *21st century challenges for school administrators.* Lanham, MD: Scarecrow Press.

Brown, M. (2003). *Assessment for learning and teaching in secondary schools.* Arlington, VA: Learning Matters.

Brown, P. C. (1989). Involving parents in the education of their children. *ERIC Digest.* (ERIC Document Reproduction Service No. ED308988)

Brown, W. B., & Moberg, D. J. (2004). *Organization theory and management* (8th ed.). New York: Wiley.

Bruce, K., Lara-Alecio, R., Parker, R., Hasbrouck, J. E., Weaver, L., & Irby, B. (1997). Inside transitional bilingual classrooms: Accurately describing the language learning process. *Bilingual Research Journal, 21*(2–3), 123–145.

Brunner, C. C. (1999). Power, gender and superintendent selection. In C. C. Brunner (Ed.), *Sacred dreams: Women and the superintendency.* Albany, NY: State University of New York Press.

Bryk, A. S., & Schneider, B. (2002). *Trust in schools: A core resource for improvement.* New York: Sage.

Bryk, A. S., Sebring, P. B., Kerbow, D., Rollow, S., & Easton, J. Q. (1998). *Charting Chicago school reform: Democratic localism as a lever for change.* Boulder, CO: Westview.

Bryson, J. M. (2004). *Strategic planning for public and nonprofit organizations: A guide to strengthening and sustaining organizational achievement* (4th ed.). San Francisco: Jossey-Bass.

Bubnicki, Z. (2003). *Analysis and decision making in uncertain systems.* New York: Springer-Verlag.

Bullard, P., & Taylor, B. O. (1994). *Keepers of the dream.* Chicago: Excelsior.

Burke, R. J., et al. (2003). *Leading in turbulent times.* Williston, VT: Blackwell.

Burko, C. (1991, May 19). Jury out on risk from power lines. *Chicago Tribune,* p. 26.

Burns, H. (2001). *Decision making and ethics: A study of Texas superintendents* (Doctoral dissertation, Sam Houston State University, Huntsville, TX). UMI Dissertation Services DAI, 62, no. 07A (2001), p. 2294.

Burns, J. (1978). *Leadership.* New York: Harper & Row.

Bushweller, K. (2000). Schools curtail pesticide use. *American School Board Journal, 187,* 53.

Calabrese, R. L. (2001). *Leadership for safe schools: A community-based approach.* Lanham, MD: Rowman & Littlefield.

Calabrese, R. L. (2003). *A companion guide to leadership for safe schools.* Lanham, MD: Rowman & Littlefield.

Calbom, L. M. (2003). *Education financial management: Weak internal controls led to instances of fraud and other improper payments.* New York: DIANE.

Cambron-McCabe, N. H., McCarthy, M. M., & Thomas, S. B. (2004). *Public school law: Teachers' and students' rights* (5th ed.). Boston: Allyn & Bacon.

Campbell, D. E. (1996). *Choosing democracy: A practical guide to multicultural education.* Upper Saddle River, NJ: Prentice Hall.

Campbell, E. (1997). Connecting the ethics of teaching and moral education. *Journal of Teacher Education, 48*(4), 255+. Retrieved December 6, 2004, from Questia database, http://www.questia.com

Campbell, J. R., Hombo, C. M., & Mazzeo, J. (2000). *NAEP 1999 trends in academic progress: Three decades of student performance* (NCES No. 2000–469). Washington, DC: National Center for Educational Statistics.

Canton v. Spokane School District No. 81

Cantwell v. Connecticut

Capper, C. A. (1996). We're not housed in an institution, we're housed in the community: Possibilities and consequences of neighborhood-based interagency collaboration. In J. Cibulka & W. J. Kritek (Eds.), *Coordination among schools, families, and communities: Prospects for educational reform* (pp. 299–322). Albany: State University of New York Press.

Carder v. Michigan City School Corporation

Carisson-Paige, N., & Levin, D. E. (2004). *Before push comes to shove: Building conflict resolution skills with children.* St. Paul, MN: Redleaf Press.

Carlson, R. V., & Awkerman, G. (1991). *Educational planning: Concepts, strategies, and practices.* New York: Longman.

Carmichael, D. R., et al. (2004). *PPC's guide to audits of financial institutions.* Fort Worth, TX: Practitioners.

Carnall, C. A. (2003). *Managing change in organizations.* Englewood Cliffs, NJ: Prentice Hall.

Carnegie Task Force on Teaching as a Profession. (1986). *A nation prepared: Teachers for the 21st century.* Washington, DC: Author.

Carr, J. F., & Harris, D. E. (2001). *Succeeding with standards: Linking curriculum, assessment, and action planning.* Alexandria, VA: Association for Supervision and Curriculum Development.

Carter, P. J., et al. (2003). *More psychometric testing: 100 ways to assess your personality, creativity, intelligence, and lateral thinking.* New York: Wiley.

Castallo, R. (2001). *Focused leadership: How to improve student achievement.* Lanham, MD: Scarecrow Press.

Castetter, W. B., & Young, I. P. (2000). *The human resource function in educational administration.* Columbus, OH: Merrill/Prentice Hall.

Center for the Advancement of Ethics and Character Education. (2003). *Character education manifesto.* Retrieved November 7, 2004, from http://www.bu.edu/education/caec/files/manifesto.htm

Centers for Disease Control. (1999). *Strategic plan for the elimination of childhood lead poisoning* (rev. ed.). Washington, DC: U.S. Government Printing Office.

Chalk v. U.S. District Court

Chamot, A. U., & Stewner-Manzanares, C. (1985). *A summary of current literature on English as a second language* (Part C: Research agenda). Rosslyn, VA: InterAmerica Research Associates, 1985. (ERIC Document Reproduction Service No. ED261539)

Character education grants awarded. (2003, September 29). Retrieved November 4, 2004, from http://www.ed.gov/news/pressreleases/2003/09/09292003.html

Chavkin, N. F., & Williams, D. L. (1988). Critical issues in teacher training for parental involvement. *Educational Horizons, 6*(2), 87–89.

Chavkin, N. F., & Williams, D. L. (1989). Low-income parents' attitudes toward parents' involvement in education. *Journal of Sociology & Social Welfare, 16,* 17–28.

Cheney, G., Christensen, L. G., Zorn, T. E., & Ganesh, S. (2003). *Organizational communication in an age of globalization: Issues, reflections, practices.* Prospect Heights, IL: Waveland.

Cheung, D., Clemente, B., & Pechman, E. (2000). *Protecting the privacy of student records: Guidelines for education agencies.* New York: DIANE.

Chicago Board of Education (2000)

Chowdhury, A., & Kirkpatrick, C. (1994). *Development policy and planning: An introduction to models and techniques.* New York: Routledge.

Chrispeels, J. H. (2002). Effective Schools—the California Center for Effective Schools: The Oxnard School District Partnership. *Phi Delta Kappan, 83*(5), 382. Retrieved August 19, 2004, from Questia database, http://www.questia.com

Christian, D. (1994). *Two-way bilingual education: Students learning through two languages.* Santa Cruz, CA: National Center for Research on Cultural Diversity and Second Langage Learning.

Christie, K. (2000). Stateline—Leadership comes around again. *Phi Delta Kappan, 82*(2), 105. Retrieved August 19, 2004, from Questia database, http://www.questia.com

Chubb, J., & Moe, T. (1991). *Politics, markets, and America's schools.* Washington, DC: Brookings Institution.

Cihon, P. J., & Castagnera, J. O. (2001). *Employment and labor law* (4th ed.). Belmont, CA: South-Western/Thomson Learning.

Clair, N. (1995). Mainstream teachers and ESL students. *TESOL Quarterly, 29,* 189–196.

Clair, N. (1998). Teacher study groups: Persistent questions in a promising approach. *TESOL Quarterly, 32,* 465–492.

Clair, N., & Adger, C. T. (1999). *Professional development for teachers in culturally diverse schools.* Washington, DC: ERIC Clearinghouse. (ERIC Document Reproduction Service No. ED435185)

Clark, C., & Dunn, S. (1991). Second-generation research on teacher planning. In H. C. Waxman & H. J. Walberg (Eds.), *Effective teaching: Current research.* Berkeley, CA: McCuthan.

Clark, C. & Peterson, P. (1986). Teacher's thought process. In M. C. Wittrock (Ed.), *Handbook of research on teaching* (pp. 255–296). New York: Macmillan.

Clark, R. M. (1988). Parents as providers of linguistic and social capital. *Educational Horizons, 6*(2), 93–95.

Clegg, A. (1968). In J. S. Maclure, *Curriculum innovation in practice: Report of the Third International Curriculum Conference*. London: Her Majesty's Stationery Office.

Cleveland Board of Education v. La Fleur

Coakley, J. J. (1994). *Sport in society: Issues and controversies* (5th ed.). St. Louis, MO: Times Mirror/Mosby.

Cobia, D. C., et al. (2002). *Handbook of school counseling*. Englewood Cliffs, NJ: Prentice Hall.

Cochran v. Louisiana State Board of Education

Cogan, M. (1961). *Supervision at the Harvard-Newton summer school*. Cambridge, MA: Harvard Graduate School of Education.

Cogan, M. (1973). *Clinical supervision*. Boston: Houghton Mifflin.

Cohen, D. K. (1988, September). *Teaching practice: Plus ca change . . .* (Issue Paper 83-3). East Lansing: Michigan State University, The National Center for Research on Teacher Education.

Cohen, D. K., & Hill, H. (1997). *Instructional policy and classroom performance: The mathematics reform in California*. Paper presented at the annual meeting of the American Educational Research Association, Chicago.

Cohen, D. L. (1995, May 3). Joining hands. *Education Week*, 35–38.

Cohen, D. M., March, J. G., & Olsen, J. D. (1972). A garbage can model of organizational choice. *Administrative Science Quarterly, 17*, 1–25.

Colby, A., Kohlberg, L., & DeVries, R. (1987). *The measurement of moral judgment* (2 vols.). New York: Cambridge University Press.

Cole, K. B., Struyk, L. R., Kinder, D., Sheehan, J. K., & Kish, C. K. (1997). Portfolio assessment: Challenges in secondary education. *High School Journal, 80*(4), 261–272.

Coleman, M. R., & Gallagher, J. (1992). *Report on state policies related to the identification of gifted students*. Chapel Hill, NC: University of North Carolina, Gifted Education Policy Studies Program.

Collier, V. P. (1992). A synthesis of studies examining long-term language minority student data on academic achievement. *Bilingual Research Journal, 16*, 187–212.

Collins, J. C., & Porras, J. (1989, July). Purpose, mission, vision. *Stanford Business School Magazine.*

Collins, J., & Porras, J. I. (2002). *Built to last: Successful habits of visionary companies (Harper business essentials)*. New York: Harper Collins.

Collinsville Community Unit School District No. 10 v. White

Colvin, R. L. (2002, February). What hath 9/11 wrought? In the aftermath, school leaders see shifts in thinking, priorities, and curricular emphases. *School Administrator, 59*, 42+. Retrieved August 28, 2004, from Questia database, http://www.questia.com

Comer, J. P. (1984). Home-school relationships as they affect the academic success of children. *Education and Urban Society, 51*, 259–269.

Comer, J. P. (1986). Parent participation in the schools. *Phi Delta Kappan, 67*, 442–446.

Commission on the Reorganization of Secondary Education. (1918). *Cardinal principles of secondary education* (Bulletin No. 35). Washington, DC: U.S. Government Printing Office.

Committee for Public Education and Religious Liberty v. Nyquist

Committee for Public Education and Religious Liberty v. Regan

Commonwealth of Virginia. (1992). *Design and technology: Teacher's guide for high school technology education*. Richmond, VA: Virginia Department of Education.

Conflict of interest. (2004). Retrieved September 4, 2004, from http://www.worldhistory.com/wiki/c/conflict-of-interest.htm

Conley, D. J. (2003). *Who governs our schools? Changing roles and responsibilities*. New York: Teachers College Press.

Conley, D. T. (1991). Lessons from laboratories in school restructuring and site-based decision making. *Oregon School Study Council Bulletin, 34*(7), 1–61.

Conlon, E. J., & Short, L. O. (1984). Survey feedback as a large-scale change device: An empirical examination. *Group and Organization Studies, 9*, 339–416.

Conn, J., & Foshee, D. (1993). Artificial turf injuries, economics, emotion, and ethics. In P. J. Graham (Ed.), *Sports business: Operational and theoretical aspects* (pp. 132–142). Dubuque, IA: Wm. C. Brown.

Conn, J. H., & Gerdes, D. A. (1998, Fall). Ethical decision-making: Issues and applications to American sport. *Physical Educator, 55*(3), 121–126.

Conn. Gen. Stat. Ann. (2003)

Connelly v. School Committee

Convery, A., & Coyle, D. (1993). *Differentiation—taking the initiative.* London: Centre for Information on Language Teaching and Research. (ERIC Document Reproduction Service No. ED382025)

Conzemius, A., & O'Neill, J. (2001). *Building shared responsibility for student learning.* Alexandria, VA: Association for Supervision and Curriculum Development.

Cook, W. J. (1995). *Bill Cook's strategic planning for America's schools.* Arlington, VA: American Association of School Administrators.

Cooper, B. S., Fusarelli, L. D., & Randall, E. V. (2004). *Better policies, better schools: Theories and applications.* Boston: Allyn & Bacon.

Cooper, H. (1994). *The battle over homework: An administrator's guide to setting sound and effective policies.* Thousand Oaks, CA, Corwin.

Cooper, H. M., & Good, T. L. (1983). Classroom expectations: Definitions, past research, and the research model. In H. Cooper & T. Good (Eds.), *Pygmalion grows up: Studies in the expectation communication process.* New York: Longman.

Cooper, T. L. (1982). *The responsible administrator.* Port Washington, NY: Kennikat Press.

Corrigan, D. (1995). *Teacher education and interprofessional collaboration: Creation of family-centered, community-based integrated service systems.* Paper presented at the National Congress on Teacher Education, Dec. 10–12, 1995, Washington, DC.

Costa, A. L., & Garmston, R. J. (1994). *Cognitive coaching: A foundation for renaissance schools.* Norwood, NJ: Christopher-Gordon.

Cotton, K. (1995). *Effective schooling practices: A research synthesis.* 1995 Update. School Improvement Research Series. Portland, OR: Northwest Regional Educational Laboratory.

Cotton, K. (2003). *Principals and student achievement: What the research says.* Alexandria, VA: Association for Supervision and Curriculum Development.

Council for Exceptional Children. (2000). *Safe schools—school-wide discipline practices.* Reston, VA: Author.

Council for School Performance. (1998). *Staff development and student achievement: Making the connection in Georgia schools.* Atlanta: Author; School of Policy Studies, Georgia State University.

Council of Chief State School Officers. (1996). *Interstate school officers, interstate school leaders licensure consortium: Standards for school leaders.* Washington, DC: Author.

Covrig, D. M. (2000). The organizational context of moral dilemmas: The role of moral leadership in administration in making and breaking dilemmas. *Journal of Leadership Studies, 7*(1), 40. Retrieved September 6, 2004, from Questia database, http://www.questia.com

Coy, D. R. (2004). *Developmental guidance and counseling in today's schools.* Alexandria, VA: National Association of Secondary School Principals.

Craig, R. P. (1999). Ethical frameworks to guide action. In L. W. Hughes (Ed.), *The principal as leader* (2nd ed.). Upper Saddle River, NJ: Prentice Hall.

Crawford, J. (1989). *Bilingual education: History, politics, theory and practice.* Trenton, NJ: Crane.

Crawford, J. (1997). The campaign against proposition 227: A post mortem. *Bilingual Research Journal, 21*(1), 1–29.

Creel, J. R. (2000). *A study of the implementation of a standardized dress code and student achievement of African American students in a suburban high school: A companion study.* Unpublished doctoral dissertation, Sam Houston State University, Huntsville, TX.

Creemers, B., & Scheerens, J. (Eds.). (1989). Developments in school effectiveness research. *International Journal of Educational Research* (Oxford, UK), *13,* 685–825.

Creighton, T. (2004). *Leading from below the surface: A non-traditional approach to the principalship.* Thousand Oaks, CA: Corwin Press.

Crim v. McWharter

Crone, D., Horner, R., & Hawken, L. S. (2003). *Responding to problem behavior in schools: The behavior education program.* New York: Guilford.

Crow, G. M., Hausman, C. S., & Scribner, J. P. (2002). Reshaping the role of the school principal. In J. Murphy (Ed.), *The educational leadership challenge: Redefining leadership for the 21st century* (pp. 189–210). Chicago: University of Chicago Press.

Crowson, R. L. (1998). Community empowerment and the public schools: Can educational professionalism survive? *Peabody Journal of Education, 73*(1), 56–68.

Crump v. Gilmer Independent School District

Cruz, B. C. (2003). *School shootings and school violence: A hot issue.* Berkeley Heights, NJ: Enslow.

Cuban, L., & Usdan, M. (Eds.). (2003). *Powerful reforms with shallow roots: Improving America's urban schools.* New York: Teachers College Press.

Cyr, A. (1997). *After the cold war: American foreign policy, Europe, and Asia American foreign policy.* Basingstoke, UK: Macmillan.

Czaja, M., & Lowe, J. (2000). Preparing ethical leaders. *AASA Professor, 24*(1), 7–12.

Daft, R. L. (1993). *Management* (2nd ed.). New York: Dryden.

Daft, R. L. (2004). *Organizational theory and design.* Belmont, CA: South-Western/Thomson Learning.

Daley, D. M. (2001). *Strategic human resource management: People and performance management in the public sector.* Englewood Cliffs, NJ: Prentice Hall.

Danielson, C. (2002). *Enhancing student achievement: A framework for school improvement.* Alexandria, VA: Association for Supervision and Curriculum Development.

Darling-Hammond, L. (1995). Restructuring schools for students success. *Daedalus, 124*(4), 153+.

Darling-Hammond, L. (1996). What matters most: A competent teacher for every child. *Phi Delta Kappan, 78*(3), 193–200.

Darling-Hammond, L. (1997). *The right to learn: A blueprint for creating schools that work.* San Francisco: Jossey-Bass.

Darling-Hammond, L. (1998). *Investing in quality teaching: State-level strategies, 1999.* Denver, CO: Education Commission of the States.

Darling-Hammond, L. (2000). Teacher quality and student achievement: A review of state policy evidence. *Education Policy Analysis Archives, 8*(1). Retrieved November 1, 2003, from http://epaa.asu.edu/epaa/v8n1/

Davidson, J. E., et al. (2003). *The psychology of problem solving.* New York: Cambridge University Press.

Davidson-Taylor, C. M. (2002). Is instruction working? *Principal Leadership, 3*(2), 30–35.

Davis v. Churchill County School Board

Davis, L. (2004). *Education and conflict: Complexity and chaos.* London: Routledge.

Davis, M. E. (2002). *Standards-based counseling in the middle school.* New York: First Books Library.

Davis, S. H. (1998, November). Why do principals get fired? *Principal, 78*(2), 34–39.

Davis, S. H., & Davis, P. B. (2003). *The intuitive dimensions of administrative decision making.* Blue Ridge Summit, PA: Rowman & Littlefield.

Davis, S. H., & Hensley, P. A. (1999, September–October). The politics of principal evaluation. *Thrust for Educational Leadership, 29*(1), 22–26.

Dawson, P. (2003). *Reshaping change: A processual perspective.* Florence, KY: Routledge.

Deal, T. E., & Kennedy, A. A. (1984). *Corporate cultures: The rites and rituals of corporate life.* Reading, MA: Addison-Wesley.

Deal, T. E., & Peterson, K. D. (2000). *The leadership paradox: Balancing logic and artistry in schools.* San Francisco: Jossey-Bass.

Deal, T. E., & Peterson, K. D. (2003). *Shaping school culture: The heart of leadership.* San Francisco: Jossey-Bass.

Debra P. v. Turlington

Decker, G. (2003). Using data to drive student achievement in the classroom and on high-stakes tests. *THE Journal (Technological Horizons in Education), 30*(6), 44+. Retrieved August 19, 2004, from Questia database, http://www.questia.com

Deconte v. State

DeGroof, J., et al. (2003). *Special education.* Dordrecht, The Netherlands: Kluwer Law International.

DeLaurier v. San Diego Unified School District

Deming, W. E. (1988). *Out of the crisis.* Cambridge, MA: Massachusetts Institute of Technology.

Dempsey, D. F. (1999). The principal push for technology. *The High School Magazine, 7*(1), 30–33.

Dempster, F. (1991). Synthesis of research on reviews and tests. *Educational Leadership, 48*(7), 71–76.

DeNavas-Walt, C., Proctor, B. D., & Mills, R. J. (2003). *Income, poverty, and health insurance coverage: Coverage in the United States.* Current Population Reports. Washington, DC: U.S. Government Printing Office.

Denham, C., & Lieberman, A. (Eds.). (1980). *Time to learn.* Washington, DC: National Institute of Education.

Dessler, G. (2002). *Human resource management* (8th ed.). Englewood Cliffs, NJ: Prentice Hall.

DeVargas v. Mason & Hanger-Siles Mason Co.

Devine, C., & Hansen, C. R. (1999). *Human rights: The essential reference.* Phoenix, AZ: Oryx Press.

Dewey, J. (1907). The school and social progress. In *The school and society* (pp. 19–44). Chicago: University of Chicago Press.

Dewey, J. (1938). *Experience and education.* New York: Collier Books.

Dewey, J. (1966). *Democracy and education.* New York: Macmillan/Free Press. (Originally published in 1916)

Dias de Figueiredo, A. (1995, July). *What are the big challenges of education for the XXI century? Proposals for action.* Invited contribution for the preparation of the White Book on Education and Training for the XXI Century, Eurydice, The Education Information Network in the European Unit, Department of Informatics Engineering University of Coimbra, Portugal. Retrieved July 2003 from http://eden.dei.uc.pt/~adf/whitebk.htm

Diesing, P. (1965). Bargaining strategy and union-management relationships. In J. D. Singer (Ed.), *Human behavior and international politics.* Chicago: Rand McNally.

Digest of education statistics, (1999). Retrieved June 2003 from http://nces.ed.gov/pubs2000/digest99/d99t053.asp

Doh, J. C. (1971). *The planning-programming-budgeting systems in three federal agencies.* Manchester, NH: Irvington.

Dollarhide, C. T., et al. (2002). *School counseling in the secondary school: A comprehensive process and program.* Boston: Allyn & Bacon.

Donahue, P. L., Voelkl, K. E., Campbell, J. R., & Mazzeo, J. (1999). *The NAEP 1998 reading report card for the nation and the states.* Washington, DC: National Center for Educational Statistics (NCES No. 1999–500).

Dorn, M. S. (2003). *School/law enforcement partnerships: A guide to police work in schools.* Dallas, TX: Ram Publishing.

Dornbusch, S. M., & Ritter, P. L. (1988). Parents of high school students: A neglected resource. *Educational Horizons, 66*(2), 75–77.

Doud, J. L. (1989a). The K–8 principal in 1988. *Principal, 68,* 6–12.

Doud, J. L. (1989b). The K–12 principal in 1988. *Principal, 68,* 6–12.

Doyle, W. (1986). Classroom organization and management. In M. C. Wittrock (Ed.), *Handbook of research on teaching* (3rd ed., pp. 392–431). New York: Macmillan.

Drake, T. L., & Roe, W. H. (2003). *The principalship* (6th ed.). Upper Saddle River, NJ: Merrill/Prentice Hall.

Driver, R., & Bell, B. (1985, March). Students' thinking and the learning of science: A constructivist view. *School Science Review,* 443–456.

Drucker, P. F. (2001). *Leading in a time of change: What will it take to lead tomorrow?* New York: Wiley.

Drucker, P. F. (2004). *Managing for results* (3rd ed.) New York: HarperCollins.

Dryfoos, J. (2002). Partnering—full-service community schools: Creating new institutions. *Phi Delta Kappan, 83*(5), 393. Retrieved August 28, 2004, from Questia database, http://www.questia.com

Duarte, D. L., et al. (2003). *Strategic innovation.* Florence, KY: Routledge.

Dubois, D. D. (2004). *Competency-based human resource management.* Palo Alto, CA: Consulting Psychologists Press.

Duemer, L. S., & Mendez-Morse, S. (2002, September 23). Recovering policy implementation: Understanding implementation through informal communication. *Education Policy Analysis Archives, 10*(39). Retrieved March 25, 2004, from http://epaa.asu.edu/epaa/v10n39.html

Dues, M. (2003). *Boxing Plato's shadow: The study of human communication.* New York: McGraw-Hill.

Duffy, F. M. (2003). *Courage, passion, and vision: A guide to leading systemic school improvement.* Lanham, MD: Scarecrow Press.

Duffy, F. M. (2004). *Moving upward together: Creating strategic alignment to sustain school improvement.* Lanham, MD: Scarecrow Press.

DuFour, R. P., & Eaker, R. (1998). *The professional learning community at work: Best practices for enhancing student achievement.* Lanham, MD: Scarecrow Press.

Dugan v. Ballman

Duhon-Sells, R. M., & Agard-Jones, L. (2004). *Educators leading the challenge to alleviate school violence.* Lewiston, NY: Mellen.

Duke, D. L. (2002). *Creating safe schools for all children.* Boston: Allyn & Bacon.

Duke, D. (2004). *The challenges of educational change.* Boston: Allyn & Bacon.

Dunn, D. (1990). Environmental health hazards move indoors. *Midwest Real Estate News, 14,* 1–5.

Dunn, R., & Dunn, K. (1992a). *Teaching elementary students through their individual learning styles: Practical approaches for grades 3–6.* Needham Heights, MA: Allyn & Bacon.

Dunn, R., & Dunn, K. (1992b). *Teaching elementary students through their individual learning styles: Practical approaches for grades 7–12.* Needham Heights, MA: Allyn & Bacon.

Dye, T. R. (1998). *Understanding public policy* (9th ed.). Upper Saddle River, NJ: Simon & Schuster.

Edmonds, R. (1979, October). Effective schools for the urban poor. *Educational Leadership,* 15–24.

Educational Policies Commission. (1940). *Learning the ways of democracy.* Washington, DC: National Education Association.

Educational Research Service. (2004). *Report: Evaluating teacher performance* (rev. ed.). Arlington, VA: Author.

Edwards v. Aguillard

Eisenberg, E. M. (2003). *Organizational communication.* New York: Bedford/Saint Martin's Press.

Eisner, E. W. (1985). *The art of educational evaluation: A personal view.* Barcombe, UK: Falmer.

Eisner, E. W. (1991). Should America have a national curriculum? *Educational Leadership, 49,* 76–81.

Electromagnetic fields: Are they a cause of concern? *Winnetka Report, 11,* 1–2.

Elmore, R. F. (1997, Fall). The politics of education reform. *Issues in science and technology online.* Retrieved March 20, 2004, from http://www.issues.org/issues/14.1/elmore.htm

Elmore, R. F. (2000). *Building a new structure for leadership.* New York: Albert Shanker Institute.

Emmer, E. T., et al. (2003). *Classroom management for secondary schools* (6th ed.). Boston: Allyn & Bacon.

Emmer, R. (2001). *School activities.* New York: Rosen.

Engel v. Vitale

English, F. W. (2000). *Deciding what to teach & test: Developing, aligning, & auditing the curriculum.* Thousand Oaks, CA: Corwin.

English, F., & Steffy, B. (2001). *Deep curriculum alignment.* Lanham, MD: Scarecrow Press.

Epperson v. Arkansas

Epstein, J. (1983). *Effects on parents of teacher practices in parent involvement.* Baltimore, MD: Center on Families, Communities, Schools and Children's Learning, Johns Hopkins University.

Epstein, J. L. (1995). School/family/community partnership: Caring for the children we share. *Phi Delta Kappan, 76,* 701–712.

Epstein, J. L. (1997, September–October). Six types of school-family-community involvement [electronic version]. *Harvard Education Letter, Research Online.* Retrieved December 13, 2003, from http://www.edletter.org/past/issues/1997-so/sixtypes.shtml

Epstein, J. L. (2001). *School, family, and community partnerships: Preparing educators and improving schools.* Boulder, CO: Westview.

Erchul, W. P., et al. (2002). *School consultation: Conceptual and empirical bases of practice.* Dordrecht, The Netherlands: Kluwer Academic Publishers.

Erford, B. T. (2003). *Transforming the school counseling profession.* Columbus, OH: Merrill/Prentice Hall.

Essex, N. L. (2002). *School law and the public schools: A practical guide for educational leaders* (2nd ed.). Boston: Allyn & Bacon.

Estler, S. E. (1988). Decision making. In N. J. Boyan (Ed.), *Handbook of research on educational administration* (pp. 305–319). New York: Longman.

Everson v. Board of Education

Evertson, C. M. (2003). *Classroom management for elementary teachers* (6th ed.). Boston: Allyn & Bacon.

Fairholm, G. W. (2000). *Capturing the heart of leadership spirituality and community in the new American workplace.* Wesport, CT: Praeger.

Farr, B., & Trumbull, E. (2000). *Grading and reporting student progress in an age of standards.* Norwood, MA: Christopher-Gordon.

Fashola, O. S. (2001). *Building effective after-school programs.* Thousand Oaks, CA: Corwin.

Fawcett, G., Brobeck, D., Andrews, S., & Walker, L. (2001). Principals and beliefs-driven change. *Phi Delta Kappan, 82,* 405–410.

Federal Register (1998, March 18), *63,* 52.

Feiman-Nemser, S. (1990). Teacher preparation: Structural and conceptual alternatives. In W. Robert Houston (Ed.), *Handbook of research on teacher education,* (pp. 212–233). New York: Macmillan.

Feldman, R. S. (2004). *Applications of nonverbal behavioral theories and research.* Mahwah, NJ: Erlbaum.

Fenster v. Schneider

Fernald, G. M. (1943). *Remedial techniques in basic school subjects.* New York: McGraw-Hill.

Ferrandino, V. (2001). Challenges for 21st century elementary school principals. *Phi Delta Kappan, 82,* 440–442.

Fertakis, J. P. (1999). *The design and implementation of administrative controls: A guide for financial executives.* Westport, CT: Greenwood Press.

Findley, D., & Findley, B. (1992). Effective schools: The role of principal. *Contemporary Education, 63*(2), 102–104.

Fine, M. (1993). [Ap]parent involvement: Reflections on parents, power, and urban public schools. *Teachers College Record, 94,* 682–710.

Fink, D. (2000). *Good schools/real schools: Why school reform doesn't last.* San Francisco: Jossey-Bass.

Fink, E., & Resnik, L. B. (2001). Developing principals as instructional leaders. *Phi Delta Kappan, 82*(8), 598–600.

First, F., & Cooper, G. R. (1989). Access to education by homeless children. *West's Educational Law Reporter, 53,* 757–765.

Fischer, L., Schimmel, D., & Kelly, C. (2003). *Teachers and the law* (6th ed.). New York: Addison-Wesley Longman.

Fishbaugh, M. S., Schroth, G., & Berkeley, T. R. (Eds.). (2003). *Ensuring safe school environments: Exploring issues, seeking solutions.* Mahwah, NJ: Erlbaum.

Flaxman, E., & Inger, M. (1991). Parents and schooling in the 1990s. *ERIC Review, 1*(3), 2–6.

Florida Department of Education. (1999). *Impact of staff development* (Issue brief). Tallahassee: Author.

Florio, J. J. (1988). Asbestos in the schools: New requirements take effect. *PTA Today, 14,* 31–32.

Floyd County Board of Education v. Slone

Foot, M., et al. (2002). *Introductory human resource management.* Englewood Cliffs, NJ: Prentice Hall.

Ford, D., & Thomas, A. (1997, June). *Underachievement among gifted minority students: Problems and promises. ERIC EC Digest.* (ERIC Document Reproduction Service No. E544)

Forgang, W. G. (2004). *Strategy-specific decision making: A guide for executing competitive strategy.* New York: Sharpe.

Foshee, D. P., & Conn, J. H. (1991). Artificial turf: Injuries, economics, emotions and ethics. *Journal of Legal Aspects of Sports, 1*(1), 36–49.

Fowler, F. C. (2004). *Policy studies for educational leaders: An introduction* (2nd ed.). Upper Saddle River, NJ: Merrill/Prentice Hall.

Frase, L., et al. (2003). *School management by wandering around.* Lanham, MD: Scarecrow Press.

Frase, L. E., & English, F. W. (1995). *The curriculum management audit: Improving school quality.* Lancaster, PA: Technomic.

Fredrikson, N., Mislevy, R. J., & Bejar, I. I. (Eds.). (2002). *Test theory for a new generation of tests.* Hillside, NJ: Erlbaum.

Froman, L. A., Jr. (1966). Some effects of interest group strength in state politics. *American Political Science Review, 60*(4), 952–962.

Fryklund, V. C. (1970). *Analysis techniques for instructors.* Milwaukee, WI: Bruce.

Fullan, M. (1993). *Change forces: Probing the depths of educational reform.* London: Falmer Press.

Fullan, M. (1999). *Change forces: The sequel.* Bristol, PA: Falmer Press.

Fullan, M. J. (2001). *Leading in a culture of change.* San Francisco: Jossey-Bass.

Fullan, M., & Hargreaves, A. (1992). *What's worth fighting for? Working together for your school.* Toronto: Elementary Teachers Federation of Ontario.

Fullan, M. J., & Miles, M. B. (1992). Getting reform right: What works and what doesn't. *Phi Delta Kappan, 73,* 745–752.

Fuller v. North Kansas City School District

Fyack, C. D. (2004). *Hiring sourcebook: A collection of practical samples.* Alexandria, VA: Society for Human Resource Management.

Gagné, R. M. (1964). The implications of instructional objectives for learning. In C. M. Lindvall (Ed.), *Defining educational objectives* (pp. 35–48). Pittsburgh, PA: University of Pittsburgh Press.

Gagne, R. (1985). *The conditions of learning* (4th ed.). New York: Holt, Rinehart & Winston.

Galanes, G. J., Brilhart, J., & Adams, K. (2004). *Effective group discussion: Theory and practice* (11th ed.). New York: McGraw-Hill.

Gale Research Staff. (2003). *Drugs and controlled substances for students.* Farmington Hills, MI: Gale Group.

Gander, P. O. (1981). *Collective bargaining.* Arlington, VA: American Association of School Administrators.

Gardner, H. (1985). *Frames of mind: The theory of multiple intelligences.* New York: Basic Books.

Gardner, H. (1993). *Frames of mind: The theory of multiple intelligences.* New York: Basic Books.

Gardner, H. (1999). *Intelligence reframed: Multiple intelligences for the 21st century.* New York: Basic Books.

Garner, C. W. (2004). *Education finance for school leaders: Strategic planning and administration.* Upper Saddle River, NJ: Merrill/Prentice Hall.

Garrett, A. G. (2002). *Keeping America safe: A handbook for parents, students, educators, law enforcement personnel, and the community.* Jefferson, NC: McFarland.

Garrett, J. E. (2002). Cultural diversity: Applying technology. *National Social Science Journal, 19,* 55–60.

Garrett, J. E., & Morgan, D. E. (2002). Celebrating diversity by educating all students: Elementary teacher and principal collaboration. *Education, 123*(2), 268–275.

Gelatt, H. B., et al. (2003). *Creative decision making* (rev. ed.). Menlo Park, CA: Crisp Publications.

Gempel, J. (1999, October 3). Hispanic growing in numbers, clout. *Washington Times,* p. C1.

George, P. (1992). *How to untrack your school.* Arlington, VA: Association for Supervision and Curriculum Development.

GI Forum v. Texas Education Agency

Gilbert, M. B. (2004). *Communicating effectively: Tools for educational leaders.* Lanham, MD: Scarecrow Press.

Gilligan, C. (1982). *In a different voice: Psychological theory and women's development.* Cambridge, MA: Harvard University Press.

Ginsberg, J. (2003). *Motivation matters: A workbook for school change.* New York: Wiley.

Ginsberg, R. (1988). Principals as instructional leaders: An ailing panacea. *Education and Urban Society, 20*(3), 276–293.

Glantz, J. (1998, October). Autocrats, bureaucrats, and buffoons: Images of principals. *AASA: The School Administrator.* Retrieved November 1, 2004, from http://www.aasa.org/publications/sa/1998_10/Glanz.htm

Glickman, C. (1993). *Renewing America's schools: A guide for school-based action.* San Francisco: Jossey-Bass.

Glickman, C. D. (2002). *Leadership for learning: How to help teachers succeed.* Alexandria, VA: Association for Supervision and Curriculum Development.

Glickman, C. D., Gordon, S. P., & Ross-Gordon, J. M. (2004). *Supervision and instructional leadership: A developmental approach* (6th ed.). Boston: Allyn & Bacon.

Goldhammer, R. (1969). *Clinical supervision.* New York: Holt, Rinehart & Winston.

Goldhammer, R., Anderson, R. H., & Krajewski, R. J. (1969). *Clinical supervision.* San Diego, CA: Harcourt Brace.

Goldhammer R., Anderson, R. H., & Krajewski, R. J. (1980). *Clinical supervision: Special methods for the supervision of teachers.* New York: Holt, Reinhart & Winston.

Goldman, P., Dunlap, D. M., & Conley, D. T. (1991, April). *Administrative facilitation and site-based school reform projects.* Paper presented at the annual meeting of the American Educational Research Association, Chicago.

Goldring, E. B. (1990). Elementary school principals as boundary spanners: Their engagement with parents. *Journal of Educational Administration, 28*(1), 53–62.

Goldring, E., & Greenfield, W. (2002). Understanding the evolving concept of leadership in education: Roles, expectations, and dilemmas. In J. Murphy (Ed.), *The educational leadership challenge: Redefining leadership for the 21st century* (pp. 1–19). Chicago: University of Chicago Press.

Goldstein, A. P., & Conoley, J. C. (Eds.). (2004). *School violence intervention: A practical handbook.* New York: Guilford.

Good, T. L., & Brophy, J. E. (2003). *Looking into classrooms* (9th ed.). Boston: Allyn & Bacon.

Goodlad, J. (1958). Toward a conceptual system for curriculum problems. *School Review, 66,* 391–401.

Goodlad, J. (1984). *A place called school.* New York: McGraw-Hill.

Goodlad, J. (1990). *Teachers for our nation's schools.* San Francisco: Jossey-Bass.

Goodson, I. (1987). *School subjects and curriculum change.* London: Falmer Press.

Goodson, I. (1991). Studying curriculum: Towards a social constructionist perspective. In I. Goodson & M. Mangan (Eds.), *Qualitative educational research studies: Methodologies in transition* (pp. 49–90). Research Unit on Classroom Learning and Computer Use in Schools (RUCCUS). London, ON: Faculty of Education, University of Western Ontario.

Goodson, I., & Mangan, I. (1991). An alternative paradigm for educational research. In I. Goodson & M. Mangan (Eds.), *Qualitative educational research studies: Methodologies in transition* (pp. 9–48). Research Unit on Classroom Learning and Computer Use in Schools (RUCCUS). London, ON: Faculty of Education, University of Western Ontario.

Gordon, E. W. (1999). *Education and justice: A view from the back of the bus.* New York: Teachers College Press.

Goss v. Lopez

Government of Ontario. (1989). *Ministry of Education action plan: 1989–1994.* Toronto, ON: Queen's Printer.

Grand Rapids School District v. Ball

Granger v. Cascade County School District No. 1

Greenberg, K. R. (2002). *Group counseling in schools: A handbook for school counselors.* Boston: Allyn & Bacon.

Greenburg, P. (1989). Parents as partners in young children's development and education: A new American fad? Why does it matter? *Young Children, 44*(4), 61–75.

Greenfield, W. D. (1988). Moral imagination, interpersonal competence, and the work of school administrators. In D. E. Griffiths, R. T. Stout, & P. B. Forsyth (Eds.), *Leaders for America's schools* (pp. 207–232). Berkeley, CA: McCutchan.

Greenwald, E. A., Persky, H. R., Campbell, J. R., & Mazzeo, J. (1999). *The NAEP 1998 writing report card for the nation and states.* Washington, DC: National Center for Educational Statistics (NCES No. 1999–462).

Greim, C., & Turner, W. (1991). Breathing easy over air quality. *American School Board Journal, 178,* 29–32.

Greiner, L. E. (1967, May–June). Patterns of organizational change. *Harvard Business Review, 126.*

Greve, H. R. (2003). *Managing change and innovation.* New York: Cambridge University Press.

Griffin, R. W. (2003). *Management* (6th ed.). Boston: Houghton Mifflin.

Griffin, R. W., & Woodman, R. W. (1985). Utilizing task redesign strategies within organization development programs. In D. D. Warrick (Ed.), *Contemporary organization development: Current thinking and applications* (pp. 308–319). Glenview, IL: Scott Foresman.

Griggs v. Duke Power Co.

Grimes, F., et al. (2002). *School violence: What is being done to combat school violence? What should be done?* Congressional Hearing. New York: DIANE.

Grove City College v. Bell

Guenther, D. A. (2004). *Financial planning and analysis.* New York: McGraw-Hill.

Guilford, J. P. (1967). *The nature of human intelligence.* New York: McGraw-Hill.

Gulledge, J., Trump, K. S., & Beard, S. (2001). *Preventing school violence: Resource guide to safe schools.* New York: Aspen.

Gullickson, A. R. (2002). *The student evaluation standards: How to improve evaluations of students.* Thousand Oaks, CA: Corwin.

Guskey, T. R. (2003). *How's my kid doing? A parents' guide to grades, marks, and report cards.* New York: Wiley.

Guskey, T. R., et al. (2000). *Developing grading and reporting systems for student learning.* Thousand Oaks, CA: Corwin.

Gutlow v. New York

Gutman, A. (2000). *EEO law and personnel practices.* Thousand Oaks, CA: Sage.

Hail, D. W. (2003). *The impact of state regulation upon the home schooling movement as measured by specific descriptive factors.* Unpublished doctoral dissertation, Sam Houston State University, Huntsville.

Hall, D. T. (1986). *Career development in organizations.* San Francisco, CA: Jossey-Bass.

Hall, G. E., & Hord, S. M. (2001). *Implementing change: Patterns, principles, potholes.* Boston: Allyn & Bacon.

Hallinan, M. T., Gamoran, A., Kubitacheck, W., & Loveless, T. (Eds.). (2003). *Stability and change in American education: Structure, process, and outcomes.* Clinton Corners, NY: Eliot Werner.

Hallinger, P., & Heck, R. H. (1996). Reassessing the principal's role in school effectiveness: A review of empirical research, 1980–1995. *Educational Administration Quarterly, 32*(1), 5–44.

Hallinger, P., & Murphy, J. F. (1987). Assessing and developing principal instructional leadership. *Educational Leadership, 45*(1), 54–61.

Hambrick, J. G. (2001). *Principals' perceptions of the influence of extracurricular activities on selected student academic performance factors: The impact of the no pass–no play rule.* Unpublished doctoral dissertation, Sam Houston State University, Huntsville.

Hammond, T. H., & Knott, J. H. (1980). *Zero-based look at zero-based budgeting.* New Brunswick, NJ: Transaction.

Hansen, R. (1995a). The curriculum studio concept in technological education teacher development. *Technology Teacher, 54*(4), 43–48.

Hansen, R. E. (1995b). Five principles for guiding curriculum development: The case of technological teacher education. *Journal of Industrial Teacher Education, 32*(2), 30–50.

Hansen, R., Fliesser, C., Froelich, M., & McClain, J. (1992). *Teacher development project: Technological education.* Final report of the Teacher Development Project. London, ON: Faculty of Education, University of Western Ontario.

Hanten v. School District of Riverview Gardens

Hardaway, R. M. (1995). *America goes to school: Law, reform, and crisis in public education.* Westport, CT: Praeger.

Hardman, D., et al. (2003). *The international handbook of reasoning and decision making.* New York: Wiley.

Hargis, C. H. (2003). *Grades and grading practices: Obstacles to improving education and to help at-risk students.* Springfield, IL: Charles Thomas.

Harman, G. (1984). Conceptual and theoretical issues. In J. R. Hough (Ed.), *Educational policy: An international survey* (pp. 13–29). London: Croom Helm.

Harman, G. (2001). The politics of quality assurance: The Australian quality assurance program for higher education, 1993–1995. *Australian Journal of Education, 45*(2), 168+. Retrieved September 1, 2004, from Questia database, http://www.questia.com

Harrington-Lucker, D. (1990). Are pesticides the latest peril facing your schools? *Executive Educator, 12,* 21–23.

Harris and Associates. (2004). *The metropolitan life survey of the American teacher: Violence in America's public schools—The family perspective.* New York: Author.

Harris v. Forklift Systems, Inc.

Harrison v. Sobel

Harrow, A. J. (1972). *A taxonomy of the psychomotor domain.* New York: Longman.

Hartsock, N. (1987). Foucoult on power: A theory for women. In L. J. Nicholson (Ed.), *Feminism/postmodernism* (pp. 157–175). London: Routledge Press.

Hartzell v. Connell

Hasday, J. L. (2003). *Columbine high school shooting: Student violence.* Berkeley Heights, NJ: Enslow.

Hassell, K. P. (2002). *Body language.* Portsmith, NH: Heinemann.

Haughey, M. (1992). Distance education in schools: Implications for teacher education. *Canadian Journal of Educational Communication, 21*(2), 123–140.

Havelock, R. G., & Sashkin, M. (1983). Help scores: A guide to promoting change in groups and organizations. In H. H. Blumberg, A. P. Hare, V. Kent, & M. Davis (Eds.), *Small groups and social interaction* (Vol. 2). New York: Wiley.

Hawley, W. D., & Rollie, D. L. (Eds.). (2002). *The keys to effective schools: Educational reform as continuous improvement.* Thousand Oaks, CA: Corwin.

Haycock, K. (1998). *Good teaching matters.* Washington, DC: Education Trust.

Hazelwood School District v. Kuhlmeier

Hearne, J., & Maurer, B. (2002). *Gifted education: A primer.* New Horizons for Learning. Retrieved September 6, 2004, from http://www.newhorizons.org/spneeds/gifted/hearne.htm

Heck, R. H. (1992). Principals' instructional leadership and school performance: Implications for policy development. *Educational Evaluation and Policy Analysis, 14*(10), 21–32.

Hedwig, L. (2000). *Body language: A guide for professionals.* Thousand Oaks, CA: Sage.

Herschbach, D. R. (1992). Technology and efficiency: Competencies as content. *Journal of Technology Education, 3*(2), 17–28.

Herzberg, F. (1987). One more time: How do you motivate employees? *Harvard Business Review, 65,* 109–120.

Hess, G. A. (1991). *School restructuring, Chicago style.* Newbury Park, CA: Corwin.

Hester, J. P. (2004). *Public school safety: A handbook with a resource guide.* Jefferson, NC: McFarland & Company.

Hickson, M. L. (2002). *Nonverbal communication: Studies and applications.* New York: Roxbury.

Hill, D. T. (2004). *Crisis and the classroom.* Springfield, IL: Thomas.

Hirsch, G. D. (2000). *A report cards handbook: A guide to grade reporting using the Mac school student information system.* Hancock, NH: Sugar Hill Press.

Hitchner, K., et al. (2002). *Counseling today's secondary students: Practices, strategies, techniques, and materials for the school counselor.* New York: Wiley.

Holbrook, S. F. (1994). *Effective planning* (6th ed.). Princeton, NJ: Princeton Management Associates.

Hollingsworth, P. M., & Hoover, K. H. (1991). *Elementary teaching methods.* Needham Heights, MA: Allyn & Bacon.

Holmes Group. (1986). *Tomorrow's teachers: A report of the Holmes Group.* East Lansing, MI: Author.

Honig v. Doe

Hopfenberg, W. S. (1995). *The accelerated school resource guide.* San Francisco: Jossey-Bass.

Hord, S. M. (2003). *Learning together, leading together: Changing schools through professional learning communities.* New York: Teachers College Press.

Houlihan, T. (2002, July). *Reporting for No Child Left Behind: What's the impact on education?* Opening remarks at Stats-DC 2002 NCES Forum and Summer Data Conference, Common Data Common Goals, Washington, DC.

Hovell, J. P., & Dorfman, P. W. (1986). Leadership and substitutes for leadership among professional and nonprofessional workers. *Journal of Applied Behavioral Science, 22,* 29–46.

Howe, L. (1994). Political immunology: Political subjectivity (subjection) in the information age. *New Political Science, 30/31,* 77–97.

Hoy, A. W., & Hoy, W. K. (2003). *Instructional leadership: A learning-centered guide.* Boston: Allyn & Bacon.

Hubbard v. Buffalo Independent School District

Huberman, M. (1993). Linking the practitioner and researcher communities for school improvement. *School Effectiveness and School Improvement, 4*(1), 1–16.

Huddleston, J., Claspell, M., & Killion, J. (1991). Participative decision making can capitalize on teacher expertise. *NASSP Bulletin, 75,* 80–89.

Huffman, J. B., & Hipp, K. K. (2003). *Reculturing schools as professional learning communities.* Lanham, MD: Scarecrow Press.

Hunkins, F. P. (1995). *Teaching thinking through effective questioning.* Norwood, MA: Christopher-Gordon.

Hunsucker, G. (2000). *Attention deficit disorder* (rev. ed.). Ft. Worth, TX: Forrest Publishing.

Hurdeman, A. A. (2004). *The worldwide history of telecommunications.* New York: Wiley.

Hustler Magazine v. Falwell

Hynes v. Board of Education of Township of Bloomfield, Essex County

Illinois Ann. Statutes (2002)

Illinois Association of School Boards

Inger, M. (1992). *Increasing the school involvement of Hispanic parents. ERIC Digest,* No. 80. Washington, DC: Clearinghouse on Urban Education.

Ingraham v. Wright

International Curriculum Management Center. (n.d.). Retrieved October 20, 2003, from http://www.pdkintl.org/profdev/icmac/whatis.htm

Iowa Association of School Boards. (n.d.). *Professional development: A key strategy for improving student learning.* Retrieved November 24, 2003, from http://www.iasb.org/studnetachievement/staffdevelopment.asp

Irby, B., & Brown, G. (1996, October). *Administrative portfolio evaluation system training.* Paper presented at Judson Independent School District, San Antonio, TX.

Irby, B. J., & Brown, G. (2000). *The career advancement portfolio.* Thousand Oaks, CA: Corwin.

Irby, B. J., & Brown, G. (2003). Promoting authentic assessment: Portfolios in early childhood education. In *The DLM early childhood express.* Atlanta, GA: SRA McGraw-Hill.

Irby, B. J., Brown, G., Duffy, J., & Trautman, D. (2002). The synergistic leadership theory. *Journal of Educational Administration, 40*(4), 304–322.

Irby, B. J., & Lara-Alecio, R. (2001). Educational policy and gifted/talented, linguistically diverse students. (2001). In J. A. Castellano & E. Díaz (Eds.), *Reaching new horizons: Gifted and talented education for culturally and linguistically diverse students* (pp. 265–281). Needham Heights, MA: Allyn & Bacon.

Ivancevich, J. M. (2003). *Human resource management* (8th ed.). New York: McGraw-Hill.

Jackson, M. C. (2003). *Creative systems thinking: A complete approach to successful management.* New York: Wiley.

Janis, I. L. (1982). *Groupthink: Psychological studies of policy decisions and fiascoes* (2nd ed.). Boston: Houghton Mifflin.

Jantzi, D., & Leithwood, K. (1996). Toward an explanation of variation in teachers' perceptions of transformational leadership. *Educational Administration Quarterly, 3*(4), 512–538.

Jeffrey v. O'Donnell

Johnson, D. (1992, April). *Principal vision, environmental robustness, and teacher autonomy at the high school.* Paper presented at the annual meeting of the American Educational Research Association, San Francisco.

Johnson, D., & Johnson, R. (1994). *Learning together and alone: Cooperative, competitive, and individualistic learning* (4th ed). Boston: Allyn & Bacon.

Johnson, J. F., Jr. (1998, October). *Improving public schools in Texas, 43*(2), from http://www.c-b-e.org/articles/texas.htm

Johnson, L., et al. (2003). *Absolute honesty: Building a corporate culture that values straight talk and rewards integrity.* New York: AMACOM.

Jones v. Houston Independent School District

Jones, B., Wells, L., Peters, R., & Johnson, D. (1988). *Guide to effective coaching principles and practice.* Newton, MA: Allyn & Bacon.

Jones, G. R. (2003). *Organizational theory, design, and change.* Englewood Cliffs, NJ: Prentice Hall.

Jones, R. (1999). Waste not, want not. *American School Board Journal, 186,* 16–19.

Joyce, B. (1990). *Changing school culture through staff development. The 1990 ASCD yearbook.* Alexandria, VA: Association for Supervision and Curriculum Development.

Joyce, B., & Showers, B. (1988). *Student achievement through staff development.* New York: Longman.

Joyce, B., & Showers, B. (2002). *Student achievement through staff development* (3rd ed.). Arlington, VA: Association for Supervision and Curriculum Development.

Kadrmas v. Dickinson Public Schools

Kampwirth, T. J. (2002). *Collaborative consultation in the schools: Effective practices for students with learning and behavior problems.* Englewood Cliffs, NJ: Prentice Hall.

Kane, W., Avila, M. M., & Quiroz, H. C. (2002). *Step-by-step to safe schools: The program planning guide—preventing bullying, harassment, hazing, hate-motivated behavior, and violence.* New York: ETR Associates.

Kaplan, L. S., & Owings, W. A. (2001). Enhancing teacher and teaching quality: Recommendations for principals. *NASSP Bulletin, 85*(628), 64–73.

Karr v. Schmidt

Katz, R. L. (1974). Skills of an effective administrator. *Harvard Business Review, 52*, 90–102.

Katzan, H. (1989). *Quality circle management: The human side of quality.* Blue Ridge Summit, PA: TAB Books.

Kaufman, R. A. (2003). *Strategic planning for success: Aligning people, performance, and payoff.* New York: Wiley.

Kaufman, R., & Herman, J. (1990). *Strategic planning in education: Rethinking, restructuring, revitalizing.* Lancaster, PA: Technomic.

Kelleher, J. (2003). A model for assessment-driven professional development. *Phi Delta Kappan* (June), 751–756.

Kemp, L., & Hall, A. H. (1992). *Impact of effective teaching research on student achievement and teacher performance: Equity and access implications for quality education.* Jackson, MS: Jackson State University. (ERIC Document Reproduction Service No. ED348360)

Kennedy, C. (2000). Principal: Too quiet, too long. *High School Magazine, 7*(6), 20–23.

Kennedy, M. M. (2002). Knowledge and teaching. *Teachers and Teaching, 8*, 355–370.

Kentucky Revised Statutes, Chapter 160. 593. (2002).

Kepner, C. H., & Tregoe, B. B. (2004). *The new rational manager* (rev. ed.). New York: Kepner-Tregoe.

Kerchner, C. J., Koppich, J., & Weeres, J. G. (1998). *Taking charge of quality; how teachers and unions can revitalize schools: An introduction and companion to united mind workers.* San Francisco: Jossey-Bass.

Kerr, S., & Jermier, J. M. (1978). Substitutes for leadership: Their meaning and measurement. *Organizational Behavior and Human Performance, 22*(3), 375–403.

Keyishian v. Board of Regents

Keyton, J., et al. (2006). *Case studies for organizational communication: Understanding communication processes.* New York: Roxbury.

Kidder, R. M. (1995). *How good people make tough choices.* New York: Fireside, Simon & Schuster.

Kimbrough, R. (1985). *Ethics: A course of study for educational leaders.* Arlington, VA: American Association of School Administrators.

Kimbrough, R. B. (1995). *Ethics.* Arlington, VA: American Association of School Administrators.

King, R. A., Swanson, A. D., & Sweetland, S. R. (2003). *School finance: Achieving high standards with equity and efficiency* (3rd ed.). Boston: Allyn & Bacon.

Kirton, M. J. (2003). *Adaption-innovation: In the context of change and diversity.* Brandon, VT: Psychology Press.

Klesse, E. J. (2004). *Student activities in today's schools: Essential learning for all youth.* Lanham, MD: Scarecrow Press.

Klicka, C. J. (1996). *Home schooling in the United States: A legal analysis.* Paconian Springs, VA: Home School Legal Defense Association.

Kliebard, H. M. (1992). Constructing a history of the American curriculum. In P. W. Jackson (Ed.), *Handbook of research on curriculum* (pp. 157–184). New York: Macmillan.

Kmetz, J. T., & Willower, D. J. (1982). Elementary school principals work behavior. *Educational Administration Quarterly, 18*, 62–78.

Knapp, M. (1995). *Teaching for meaning in high-poverty classrooms.* New York: Teachers College Press.

Knapp, M. L., & Hall, J. (2001). *Nonverbal behavior in human interaction.* Belmont, CA: Wadsworth.

Knowles, M. (1980). *The modern practice of adult education.* Englewood Cliffs, NJ: Cambridge Adult Education.

Kohlberg, L. (1989). *A study of three democratic high schools.* New York: Teachers College Press.

Kohlberg, L., & Lickona, T. (1986). *The stages of ethical development: From childhood through old age.* New York: HarperCollins.

Kohn, A. (1997). How not to teach values: A critical look at character education. *Phi Delta Kappan, 78*(6), 429–437.

Konovalchick v. School Community of Salem

Korney, R. C., et al. (2000). *Labor relations in the public sector.* New York: Marcel Dekker.

Koutsoukis, N. S. (2003). *Decision modelling and information systems: The information value chain.* Dordrecht, The Netherlands: Kluwer Academic Publishers.

Kouzes, J. M., & Posner, B. Z. (2002). *Encouraging the heart: A leader's guide to rewarding and encouraging others.* San Francisco: Jossey-Bass.

Kramer, M. (1990). Curriculum reform: Rules of engagement. *Change, 22*(4), 54.

Kramer, M. W. (2003). *Managing uncertainty in organizational communication.* Mahwah, NJ: Erlbaum.

Kramer, R. (1976). *Maria Montessori.* New York: G.P. Putman's Sons.

Kramer, R. (1988). *Maria Montessori: A biography.* Reading, MA: Perseus.

Krathwohl, D. R., Bloom, B. S., & Masia, B. B. (1964). *Taxonomy of educational objectives,*

Book 2—Affective domain. New York: Longman.

Kraus, W. A. (1992). *Collaboration in organizations: Alternatives to hierarchy.* New York: Human Sciences Press.

Kreitner, R. (2004). *Management* (7th ed.). Boston: Houghton Mifflin.

Krieger, R. (2000). Policing pests. *American School Board Journal, 187,* 52–54.

Lambert, C. (2004). *The complete book of supervisory training* (6th ed.). New York: Wiley.

Lambert, L. (1998). *Building leadership capacity in schools.* Alexandria, VA: Association for Supervision and Curriculum Development.

Lambert, L. (2002). Beyond instructional leadership. *Educational Leadership, 59*(8), 37–40.

Lambert, L. (2003). *Leadership capacity for lasting school improvement.* Alexandria, VA: Association for Supervision and Curriculum Development.

LaMorte, M. W. (2002). *School law: Cases and concepts* (7th ed.). Boston: Allyn & Bacon.

Landrum, M. S., Katsiyannis, A., DeWaard, J. (1998). A national survey of legislative policies and mandates in gifted education: The impact of the National Excellence Report. *Journal for the Education of the Gifted, 21*(3), 352–371.

Langdon, T. P., et al. (2004). *Financial planning applications.* New York: American College.

Langer, G. M., Colton, A. B., & Goff, L. S. (2003). *Collaborative analysis of student work: Improving teaching and learning.* Alexandria, VA: Association for Supervision and Curriculum Development.

Lanphear, B. P. (2001, April 30). *Blood levels below acceptable value linked with IQ deficits.* Paper presented at the Pediatric Academic Societies, Cincinnati, OH.

Laosa, L. M. (1977). Socialization, education, and continuity: The importance of the sociocultural context. *Young Children, 32*(5), 21–27.

Laosa, L. M. (1978). Maternal teaching strategies in Chicano families of varied educational and socioeconomic levels. *Child Development, 49*(4), 1129–1135.

Laosa, L. M. (1982). School, occupation, culture, and family: The impact of parental schooling on the parent-child relationship. *Journal of Educational Psychology, 74*(6), 791–827.

Lara-Alecio, R., Bass, J., & Irby, B. J. (2001). Science of the Maya: Teaching ethnoscience in the classroom. *Science Teacher, 68*(3), 48–51.

Lara-Alecio, R., Galloway, M., Mahadevan, L., Mason, B., Irby, B. J., Brown, G., & Gomez, L. (2004). *Texas dual language cost analysis.* College Station, TX: Language Diversity Network.

Retrieved March 1, 2005, from http://ldn.tamu.edu/Archives/CBAReport.pdf

Lara-Alecio, R., Irby, B. J., & Ebener, R. (1997). Developing academically supportive behaviors among Hispanic parents: What elementary school teachers and supervisors can do. *Preventing School Failure, 42,* 27–32.

Lara-Alecio, R., & Parker, R. (1994). A pedagogical model for transitional English bilingual classrooms. *Bilingual Research Journal, 18*(3–4), 119–133.

Larson, R., et al. (2004). *Organized activities as contexts of development: Extracurricular activities after-school and community programs.* Mahwah, NJ: Erlbaum.

Lauda, D. P. (1994). *Global education: Internationalizing the curriculum.* Paper presented at the International Technology Education Association 56th Annual Conference, Kansas City, MO.

Laurea, A. (1989). *Home advantage: Social class and parental intervention in elementary education.* Philadelphia: Falmer Press.

Lawrence-Brown, D. (n.d.). *Differentiated instruction: Inclusive strategies for standards-based learning that benefit the whole class.* Retrieved September 4, 2002, from http://sched.sbu.edu/faculty/dbrown/DI-forASE.htm

Layton, D. (1993). *Technology's challenge to science education: Cathedral, quarry, or company store?* Buckingham: Open University Press.

Lazarus, P. J., Brock, S., & Feinberg, T. (1999). Dealing with the media in the aftermath of school shootings. *NASP Communiqué, 28*(1).

Lazarus, P. J., & Gillespie, B. L. (1996, February). Critical actions in aftermath of natural disasters. *School Administrator, 53,* 35.

Learning Points Associates. (n.d.a). *Implementing the No Child Left Behind Act: Implications for rural schools and districts.* North Central Regional Educational Laboratory. Retrieved January 20, 2004, from http://www.ncrel.org/policy/pubs/html/implicate/intro.htm

Learning Points Associates. (n.d.b). *Viewpoints: From the statehouse to the classroom: Governing America's schools.* North Central Regional Educational Laboratory. Retrieved October 25, 2004, from http://ncrel.org/policy/pubs/html/viewpt/define.htm

Lee v. Weisman

Lee, G. V. (1991). Instructional leadership as sense-making. *Theory into Practice, XXX*(2), 83–90.

Leithwood, K. A. (1992). The move toward transformational leadership. *Educational Leadership, 49,* 8–12.

Leithwood, K. A. (1994). Leadership for school restructuring. *Educational Administration Quarterly, 30*(4), 498–518.

Leithwood, K., Aitken, R., & Jantzi, D. (2001). *Making schools smarter: A system for monitoring school and district programs* (2nd ed.). Thousand Oaks, CA: Corwin.

Leithwood, K., & Duke, D. L. (1999). A century's quest to understand school leadership. In J. Murphy & K. S. Louis (Eds.), *Handbook of research on educational administration* (pp. 45–72). San Francisco: Jossey-Bass.

Leithwood, K., & Louis, K. S. (2000). *The learning school and school improvement: Linkages and strategies.* Lisse, The Netherlands: Swets and Zeitlinger.

Leithwood, K. A., & Montgomery, D. J. (1982). The role of the elementary school principal in program improvement. *Review of Educational Research, 52*(3), 309–339.

Lemon v. Kurtzman

Leonard, B. (2000). *Creating safe schools and drug-free schools: An action guide.* New York: DIANE.

Lester v. Board of Education of School District No. 119 (1967)

Lester, W. (1999, September 15). New census report illustrates nation's expanding diversity. *Houston Chronicle,* p. 2.

Levine, D. U., & Lezotte, L. W. (1990). *Unusually effective schools: A review and analysis of research and practice.* Madison, WI: National Center for Effective Schools Research and Development, University of Wisconsin–Madison.

Levitt v. Committee for Public Education and Religious Liberty

Lewin, K. (1975). *Field theory in social sciences: Selected theoretical papers.* Westport, CT: Greenwood Press. (Original work published 1951)

Lewis, A. (1989). *Wolves at the schoolhouse door: An investigation of the condition of public school buildings.* Washington, DC: Education Writers Association.

Lewis, T. (1993). Valid knowledge and the problem of the practical arts. *Curriculum Inquiry, 23*(2), 175–202.

Lezotte, L. W. (1997). *Learning for all.* Okemos, MI: Effective Schools Products.

Licata, J. W., & Harper, G. W. (2001, February). Organizational Health and Robust School Vision, *Educational Administration Quarterly, 37*(1), 5–26.

Licata, J. W., Teddlie, C. B., & Greenfield, W. B. (1990). Principal vision, teacher sense of autonomy, and environmental robustness. *Journal of Educational Research, 84*(2), 93–99.

Lichtenstein, R., et al. (2004). *How to prepare for and respond to crisis.* Arlington, VA: Association for Supervision and Curriculum Development.

Lickona, T. (1996). Eleven principles of effective character education. *Journal of Moral Education, 25*(1), 93–100.

Lickona, T. (1997). The case for character education. *Tikkun, 21*(1), 22–30.

Lieberman, A., & Miller, L. (1986). School improvement: Themes and variations. In A. Lieberman (Ed.), *Rethinking school improvement: Research craft and concept.* New York: Teachers College Press.

Lightfoot, S. L. (1978). *Worlds apart: Relationships between families and schools.* New York: Basic Books.

Likert, R. (1961). *New patterns of management.* New York: McGraw-Hill.

Likert, R. (1967). *The human organization: Its management and value.* New York: McGraw-Hill.

Likert, R. (1979). From production and employee-centeredness to systems 1–4. *Journal of Management, 5,* 147–156.

Likert, R. (1987). *New patterns of management.* New York: Garland.

Lincoln, M. (2003). *Conflict resolution communication: Patterns promoting peaceful schools.* Lanham, MD: Rowan & Littlefield.

Lindblom, C. E. (1993). *The science of muddling through.* New York: Irvington.

Lindquist, A. K., & Metzger, E. G. (2004). *Teacher recruitment consortium.* Washington, DC: National School Boards Association.

Lipkin, A. (1999). *Understanding homosexuality, changing schools: A text for teachers, counselors, and administrators.* Boulder, CO: Westview.

Lissitz, R. W., & Schafer, W. D. (2002). *Assessment in educational reform: Both means and ends.* Boston: Allyn & Bacon.

Liston, D. P., et al. (2003). *Teaching, learning, and loving: Reclaiming passion in educational practice.* Florence, KY: Routledge.

Little, J. W. (1993). Teachers' professional development in a climate of education reform. *Education Evaluation and Policy Analysis, 15,* 129–151.

Little, M. E. (2001). Successful school improvement using classroom-based research. *Educational Leadership, 2*(1), 41–44.

Little, M. E., & Houston, D. (2003). Research into practice through professional development. *Remedial and Special Education, 95*(1), 3–10.

Loader, D. (2003). *Controls, procedures, and risk.* San Francisco: Elsevier Science and Technology Books.

Lockard, J., et al. (2004). *Computers for twenty-first century educators.* Boston: Allyn & Bacon.

Locke, E. A., & Latham, G. P. (1995). *A theory of goal setting and task performance* (2nd ed.). Englewood Cliffs, NJ: Prentice Hall.

Lockwood, A. L. (1993). A letter to character educators. *Educational Leadership, 51,* 72–75.

Louis, K. S., & Kruse, S. (2000). Creating community in reform: Images of organizational learning in urban schools. In K. Leithwood & K. S. Louis (Eds.), *Organizational learning and strategies.* Lisse, The Netherlands: Swets and Zeitlinger.

Lovejoy, S. (1992). *Getting results: A systematic approach.* Brookfield, VT: Ashgate.

Lovell, J. T., & Wiles, K. (1983). *Supervision for better schools.* Englewood Cliffs, NJ: Prentice Hall.

Lowe, J., & Strnadel, K. (1999). *Sexual harassment: Approaches to a more positive work environment.* Unpublished paper, Sam Houston State University.

Lundy, J., et al. (2003). *Strategic human resource management.* Belmont, CA: Wadsworth/Thomson Learning.

Lunenburg, F. C. (1992). The urban superintendent's role in school reform. *Education and Urban Society, 25,* 37–48.

Lunenburg, F. C. (1994). *Strategic planning: A manual for school administrators* (4th ed.). South Orange, NJ: Educational Consultants.

Lunenburg, F. C. (1995). *The principalship: Concepts and applications.* Columbus, OH: Prentice Hall.

Lunenburg, F. C. (2002). Cocking lecture: Improving student achievement: Some structural incompatibilities. In G. Perreault & F. C. Lunenburg (Eds.), *The changing world of school administration* (pp. 5–27). Lanham, MD: Scarecrow Press.

Lunenburg, F. C. (2003). The post-behavioral science era: Excellence, community, and justice. In F. C. Lunenburg & C. S. Carr (Eds.), *Shaping the future: Policy, partnerships, and emerging perspectives* (pp. 36–55). Lanham, MD: Scarecrow Press.

Lunenburg, F. C., & Irby, B. J. (1999). *High expectations: An action plan for implementing goals 2000.* Thousand Oaks, CA: Corwin.

Lunenburg, F. C., & Ornstein, A. O. (2004). *Educational administration: Concepts and practices* (4th ed.). Belmont, CA: Wadsworth Thomson.

Luthans, F. (2004). *Organizational behavior: Performance and productivity* (9th ed.). New York: McGraw-Hill.

Maanum, J. L. (2004). *The general educator's guide to special education: A resource handbook for all who teach students with special needs.* Minnetonka, MN: Peytral Publications.

MacKenzie, D., & Wajcman, J. (Eds.). (1985). *The social shaping of technology: How the refrigerator got its hum.* Philadelphia, PA: Open University Press.

Maeroff, G. I. (1993). *Team building for school change: Equipping teachers for new roles.* New York: Teachers College Press.

Majkowski, C. (2000). The essential role of principals in monitoring curriculum implementation *NASSP Bulletin, 85(613),* 76–83.

Marbury v. Madison

March, J. G. (1978). Bounded rationality, ambiguity, and the engineering of choice. *Bell Journal of Economics, 9,* 587–608.

March, J. K., & Peters, K. H. (2002). Effective Schools—Curriculum development and instructional design in the effective schools process. *Phi Delta Kappan, 83(5),* 379. Retrieved August 21, 2004, from Questia database, http://www.questia.com

Marcoux, J. S., Rodriguez, L., Brown, G., & Irby, B. J. (2001). Enhancing teacher quality: How portfolios can help. *Insight, 15(2),* 24–25.

Marczely, B., & Marczely, D. W. (2002). *Human resource and contract management in the public school: A legal perspective.* Lanham, MD: Scarecrow Press.

Margolis, H. (2004). *Understanding resistance to change.* Reston, VA: National Association of Secondary School Principals.

Marland, S. P. (1971). *Education of gifted and talented* (2 vols.). Washington, DC: U.S. Government Printing Office.

Marotto, P. F. (2004). *A monograph on the subject of school violence, violence prevention, and mediation efforts in post-Columbine world.* South Windsor, CT: Allegory Mediation Service.

Marshall, C. (1992, August). School administrators' values: A focus on atypicals. *Educational Administration Quarterly, 28(3),* 368–386.

Marshall, M. J. (2003). *Response to reform: Composition and the professionalization of teaching.* Carbondale, IL: Southern Illinois University Press.

Martin, W. J., & Willower, D. J. (1981). The managerial behavior of high school principals. *Educational Administration Quarterly, 17,* 69–90.

Martin-Kniep, G. O. (2003). *Developing learning communities through teacher expertise.* Thousand Oaks, CA: Corwin.

Martocchio, J. J. (2002). *Employee benefits: A primer for human resource professionals.* New York: McGraw-Hill.

Martocchio, J. J. (2003). *Strategic compensation: A human resource management approach.* Englewood Cliffs, NJ: Prentice Hall.

Marzano, R. J., Pickering, D. P., & Pollock, J. E. (2001). *Classroom instruction that works: Research-based strategies for increasing student achievement.* Alexandria, VA: Association for Supervision and Curriculum Development.

Mason, S. A. (2002, July). *Data for learning: The role of data in professional learning communities.* Unpublished AERA Conference proposal.

Mathison, S. (2004). *Encyclopedia of evaluation.* Thousand Oaks, CA: Sage.

Matter of McMillan (1976)

Mauka Lani Elementary School. (2004). *Vision/mission.* Retrieved June 4, 2004, from http://community.hei.com/civiled/mauka-vision.html

Mazanec v. N. Judson–San Pierre School Corporation

McAdams, R. P. (1998). The principalship: An international perspective. *Principal, 77*(3), 10–16.

McAuliffe Elementary School. (2003). *Vision and mission statements.* Retrieved December 3, 2003, from http://www.mcauliffe.cps.k12.il.us/mcaulif-fevision.htm

McBrien, J. L., & Brandt, R. S. (1997). *The language of learning: A guide to education terms.* Alexandria, VA: Association for Supervision and Curriculum Development.

McCabe, N. H., McCarthy, M. M., & Thomas, S. B. (2004). *Public school law: Teachers' and students' rights* (5th ed.). Boston: Allyn & Bacon.

McCann, J. T. (2004). *Threats in schools: A practical guide for managing violence.* Binghamton, NY: Haworth.

McCarthy v. Fletcher

McCollum v. Board of Education of School District No. 71

McCormick, R. (1990, October). *The evolution of current practice in technology education.* Paper presented at the NATO Advanced Research Workshop: Integrating Advanced Technology into Technology Education, Eindhoven, The Netherlands.

McCown v. Patagonia Union School District

McCune, S. D., & Brandt, R. (1986). *Guide to strategic planning for educators.* Alexandria, VA: Association for Supervision and Curriculum Development.

McDill, E. L., & Rigsby, L. (1973). *Structure and process in secondary schools: The academic impact of educational climates.* Baltimore, MD: Johns Hopkins University Press.

McDonnell Douglas Corp v. Green

McDonnell, L. M. (2004). *Politics, persuasion, and educational testing.* Cambridge, MA: Harvard University Press.

McGreal, T. L. (1980). Helping teachers set goals. *Educational Leadership 37*(5, February), 414–419.

McKeon, D. (1987). Different types of ESL programs. *ERIC Digest.* Washington, DC: ERIC Clearinghouse on Languages and Linguistics. (ERIC Document Reproduction Service No. ED289360)

McKerrow, K. (1997). Ethical administration: An oxymoron? *Journal of School Leadership, 7,* 210–225.

McLaughlin, M. W. (1990). Embracing contraries: Implementing and sustaining teacher evaluation. In J. Millman & L. Darling-Hammond (Eds.), *The new handbook of teacher evaluation* (pp. 403–415). Newbury Park, CA: Sage.

McLaughlin, M. W., & Shields, P. M. (1987). Involving low-income parents in the schools: A role for policy? *Phi Delta Kappan, 69,* 156–160.

McLoughlin, J. A., et al. (2005). *Assessing students with special needs.* Columbus, OH: Merrill/Prentice Hall.

McMillan, E. (2004). *Complexity, organizations, and change.* Florence, KY: Routledge.

McMorrow v. Benson

McNabb, M. L. (2004). *Perspectives about education.* North Central Regional Educational Laboratory. Retrieved November 4, 2004, from http://www.ncrel.org/tandl/change.htm

McNeil, J. (1996). *Curriculum—a comprehensive introduction* (5th ed.). New York: Harper-Collins.

McNeil, L. M. (2000). *Contradictions of school reform: Educational costs of standardized testing.* New York: Routledge.

Meece, J. L., & Kurtz-Costes, B. (2001). Introduction: The schooling of ethnic minority children and youth. *Educational Psychologist, 36,* 1–7.

Meek v. Pittenger

Meeks, L. B., et al. (2000). *Violence prevention: Totally awesome teaching strategies for safe and drug-free schools.* Chicago: Everyday Learning.

Meichenbaum, D., & Biemiller, A. (1998). *Nurturing independent learners: Helping students take charge of their learning.* Cambridge, MA: Brookline.

Meier, D. (2003). *In schools we trust: Creating communities of learning in an era of testing and standardization.* Boston: Beacon.

Meritor Savings Bank v. Vinson

Merriam School. (2003). *Merriam's mission and vision statements.* Retrieved December 3, 2003, from http://merriam.ab.mec.edu/ foundat/vision

Merriman, J., & Hill, J. (1992). Ethics, law and sport. *Journal of Legal Aspect of Sport, 2(2),* 56–63.

Mescon, M. H., Albert, M., & Khedouri, F. (2004). *Management* (6th ed.). New York: HarperCollins.

Metcalfe, J. S., et al. (2003). *Change, transformation, and development.* Heidelberg, Germany: Physica-Verlag.

Meyer, J. W., & Rowan, B. (1977). Institutionalized organizations: Formal structure as myth and ceremony. *American Journal of Sociology, 83,* 440–463.

Michel, G. (1995). Ethical and legal responsibilities of principals. In J. S. Kaiser (Ed.), *The 21st century principal.* Mequon, WI: Stylex.

Millennium Development Goals. (2003a). Retrieved from http://www.developmentgoals.org/ Education.htm

Millennium Development Goals: A compact among nations to end human poverty. (2003b). Retrieved from http://www.undp.org/hdr2003/pdf/hdr03_overview.pdf

Miller J., & Seller, W. (1985). *Curriculum perspectives and practice.* New York: Longman.

Miller, L. D., et al. (2002). *Integrating school and family counseling: Practical solutions.* Washington, DC: American Counseling Association.

Mills, M. (2002). *Challenging violence in schools.* New York: Open University Press.

Mills v. Board of Education of the District of Columbia

Millward, R., & Gerlach, G. (1991). *Pre-teacher assessment: An innovative concept in pre-teacher evaluation.* Indiana, PA: Indiana University of Pennsylvania.

Minaya-Rowe, L. (1996). Bilingual teachers involving parents in the teaching-learning process: A practicum experience. *Journal of Educational Issues of Language Minority Students, 16,* 57–76.

Miner, J. B. (2002). *Organizational behavior: Foundations, theories, and analyses.* New York: Oxford University Press.

Minnesota v. Newstrom

Mitchell, B. L., & Cunningham, L. L. (1986). State policy and the pursuit of instructional leadership. *Theory Into Practice, XXV(3),* 207–213.

Mitchell v. Helms

Mohondie, K. (2003). *School violence threat management: A practical guide for educators, law enforcement, and mental health professionals.* San Diego, CA: Specialized Training Services.

Molloy, J. T. (1993). *Dress for success.* New York: Warner.

Molloy, J. T. (1996). *New women's dress for success.* New York: Warner.

Mondy, R. W., et al. (2004). *Human resource management.* Englewood Cliffs, NJ: Prentice Hall.

Mooney, G., et al. (2002). *National directory of drug and alcohol abuse treatment programs.* New York: DIANE.

Moore, M. H., et al. (2003). *Deadly lessons: Understanding lethal school violence.* Washington, DC: National Academy Press.

Moran, C. (1993). Content area instruction for students acquiring English. In J. Villareal & A. Ada (Eds.), *The power of two languages.* New York: Macmillan/McGraw-Hill.

Mort, P. R. (2004). *Public school finance: Its background, structure, and operation.* Temecula, CA: Textbook Publishers.

Mosley, D. C., Megginson, L. C., & Pietri, P. H. (2004). *Management: Concepts and applications* (6th ed.). New York: HarperCollins.

Mosline, S. R. (2001). *Drug abuse and teens.* Berkeley Heights, NJ: Enslow.

Moulton, J. C., Curcio, J. L., & Fortune, J. C. (1999). Structurally sound? *American School Board Journal, 186,* 38–40.

Moustakas, C. (1990). *Heuristic research: Design, methodology, and applications.* Newbury Park, CA: Sage.

Mower v. Leicester

Mowry, C. (1972). *Investigation of the effects of parents participation in Head Start: Nontechnical report.* Washington, DC. (ERIC Document Reproduction Service No. ED080216)

Mueller v. Allen

Murphy v. Arkansas

Murphy, C. U., & Lick, D. W. (2001). *Whole-faculty study groups: Creating student-based professional development* (2nd ed.). Thousand Oaks, CA: Corwin.

Murphy, J. (1988). The instructional leadership role of the school principal. An analysis. *Educational Evaluation and Policy Analysis, 10(2),* 71.

Murphy, J. (1991). *Restructuring schools.* New York: Teachers College Press.

Murphy, J. (1993). Restructuring schooling: The equity infrastructure. *School Effectiveness and School Improvement, 4(2),* 111–130.

Murphy, J. (2002a). Reculturing the profession of educational leadership. In J. Murphy (Ed.), *The educational leadership challenge: Redefining leadership for the 21st century* (pp. 65–82). Chicago: University of Chicago Press.

Murphy, J. (2002b). Reculturing the profession of educational leadership: New blueprints. *Educational Administration Quarterly, 39*(2), 176–191.

Murphy, J., & Datnow, A. (2003). *Leadership lessons from comprehensive school reforms.* Thousand Oaks, CA: Corwin.

Murphy, J., Hallinger, P., Weil, M., & Mitman, A. (1983). Instructional leadership: A conceptual framework. *Planning and Changing,* 137–149.

Murphy, K. R., & Cleveland, J. N. (2004). *Performance appraisal: An organizational perspective* (4th ed.). Boston: Allyn & Bacon.

Murray, M. M. (1991). *Goal performance system: A complete guide to achieving strategic goals* (2nd ed.). Plantation, FL: Center for Human Work Flow Dynamics, Inc.

Muscott, H. S., & O'Brien, S. T. (1999). Teaching character education to students with behavioral and learning disabilities through mentoring relationships. *Education & Treatment of Children, 22*(3), 373. Retrieved September 4, 2004, from Questia database, http://www.questia.com

Najita, J. M., et al. (2001). *Collective bargaining in the public sector: The experience of eight states.* New York: Sharpe.

Narayanan, M. P. (2004). *Finance for strategic decision making.* New York: John Wiley & Sons.

Nata, R. (2003). *Progress in education.* Hauppauge, NY: Nova Science Publishers.

Natale, J. A. (1991). Tainted water, poison paint. *American School Board Journal, 178,* 24–28.

National Alliance for Safe Schools. (2004). *Safe schools—better schools.* Eastsound, WA: Author.

National Association for Schools of Excellence & Northwest Regional Educational Laboratory. (1999). *Leading America's schools: The critical role of principal.* Portland, OR: Author. (ERIC Document Reproduction Service No. ED432835)

National Association of Elementary School Principals. (1998). *Backgrounder on public school uniforms.* Alexandria, VA: Author.

National Association of Secondary School Principals. (1996). *Breaking ranks: Changing an American institution.* Reston, VA: Author.

National Association of Secondary School Principals. (2002). *Professional development and assessment programs.* Reston, VA: Author.

National Association of State Directors of Education Plant Services. (1989). *Projection of population by states, 1988–2010.* Washington, DC: Author.

National Board for Professional Teaching Standards. (n.d.). *Five core propositions.* Retrieved October 1, 2004, from http://www.nbpts.org/about/coreprops.cfm.

National Center for Education Statistics. (n.d.). *NAEP 1992, 1994 national reading assessments—Data almanac—Grade 4: Teacher questionnaire weighted percentages and composite proficiency means (Public school).* Retrieved November 5, 2003, from http://www.Nces.ed.gov/nationsreportcard/y25alm/almanac.shtml

National Center for Education Statistics. (1994). *Data compendium for the NAEP 1992 reading assessment of the nation and the states: 1992 NAEP trial state assessment.* Washington, DC: U.S. Department of Education.

National Center for Education Statistics. (2003a). *Status and trends in the education of Hispanics.* Retrieved February 20, 2004, from http://nces.ed.gov/pubs2003/hispanics/

National Center for Education Statistics. (2003b). *The nation's report card.* Retrieved February 20, 2004, from http://nces.ed.gov/nationsreportcard/

National Center for Education Statistics. (2004a). *Revenues and expenditures for public elementary and secondary education.* Washington, DC: U.S. Department of Education. Retrieved November 5, 2004, from http://nces.ed.gov/pubs

National Center for Education Statistics. (2004b). *Digest of education statistics.* Washington, DC: U.S. Department of Education.

National Center for Effective Schools Research and Development. (2000). *The triumph of effective schools: A review and analysis of research and practice.* Madison, WI: Wisconsin Center for Education Research, University of Wisconsin, the National Center for Effective Schools Research and Development.

National Commission on Excellence in Education. (1983). *A nation at risk.* Washington, DC: U.S. Government Printing Office.

National Commission on Teaching and America's Future. (1996). *What matters most: Teaching for America's future.* New York: Author.

National Conference of State Legislatures. (1993). *Legislative requirements under the Clean Air Act of 1990.* Denver, CO: Author.

National Conference of State Legislatures. (1999). *Legislative guidance for comprehensive state groundwater protection program.* Denver, CO: Author.

National Council for the Accreditation of Teacher Education. (1995). *Curriculum guidelines for school administrators.* Washington, DC: Author.

National Crime Survey. (2004). *Crimes committed on school grounds.* Washington, DC: Author.

National Education Association v. South Carolina

National Education Association. (1975). *Code of ethics for the education profession.* Retrieved March 24, 2005, from http://www.nea.org/code.html

National Education Association. (2002). *NEA and teacher recruitment: An overview.* Retrieved December 23, 2002, from http://www.nea.org/recruit/minority/overview.html

National Education Goals Panel. (2000). *The national education goals report: Building a nation of learners.* Washington, DC: Author.

National Federation of State High School Associations. (2003). *Coaches code of ethics.* Retrieved March 24, 2005, from http://www.nfhs.org

National Policy Board for Educational Administration. (2002a). *Standards for advanced programs in educational leadership.* Retrieved August 15, 2003, from http://www.ascd.org/aboutascd/ELCC_Instructions.html

National Policy Board for Educational Administration. (2002b). *The Educational Leadership Constituent Council standards for advance programs in educational leadership.* Arlington, VA: Author.

National School Boards Association. (2004). *National education policy reference manual.* Alexandria, VA: Author.

National School Boards Association Council of School Attorneys Staff. (2001). *Safe schools, safe communities.* Alexandria, VA: Author.

National School Public Relations Association. (n.d.). *Getting a public relations program started.* Retrieved November 24, 2003, from http://www. nspra.org

National School Safety Center. (2004). *School violence overview: National statistics report.* Malibu, CA: U.S. Department of Education and Pepperdine University.

National Staff Development Council. (2000). *Code of ethics.* Retrieved September 19, 2003, from http://www.nsdc.org/connect/about/ethics.cfm

Neal, R. G. (1982). *Bargaining tactics.* Manassas, VA: Richard Neal Associates.

Neber, H., Finsterwald, M., & Urban, N. (2001). Cooperative learning with gifted and high-achieving students: A review and meta-analysis of 12 studies. *High Ability Studies, 12*(1), 199–214.

Needleman, H. L. (1992). Childhood exposure to lead: A common case of school failure. *Phi Delta Kappan, 74,* 35–37.

Nelson, J. (2004). *The art of focused conversation for schools: Over 100 ways to guide clear thinking and promote learning.* Gabriola Island, BC: New Society.

New Jersey v. T. L. O.

New Jersey Statutes Ann. (2004)

New York City Board of Education. (2004). *Report on school violence in the New York City Public Schools.* New York: Author.

Newman, F. M., Smith, B., Allensworth, E., & Bryk, A. S. (2001). Instructional program coherence: What it is and why it should guide school improvement policy. *Educational Evaluation and Policy Analysis, 23*(4), 297–321.

Newmann, F. (1990). Qualities of thoughtful social studies classes: An empirical profile. *Journal of Curriculum Studies, 22,* 253–275.

Newstrom, J. W., & Davis, K. (2004). *Human behavior at work: Organizational behavior* (12th ed.). New York: McGraw-Hill.

Nichols, J. O., et al. (2000). *The department guide and record book for student outcomes, assessment, and institutional effectiveness.* New York: Algora.

Nicolau, S., & Ramos, C. L. (1990). *Together is better: Building strong relationships between schools and Hispanic parents.* Washington, DC: Hispanic Policy Development Project.

Nicoletti, J., & Spencer-Thomas, S. (2003). *Violence goes to school.* Bloomington, IN: National Educational Service.

No Child Left Behind Act of 2001. (n.d.). Retrieved from http://www.ed.gov/offices/OESE.esca/

Noble, P. V. (2003). *Safe and drug free schools.* Hauppauge, NY: Nova Science Publishers.

Noddings, N. (1994). Caring: A feminist perspective. In K. Strike & P. Ternasky (Eds.), *Ethics for professionals in education* (pp. 43–53). New York: Teachers College Press.

Noddings, N. (1997). Thinking about standards. *Phi Delta Kappan, 78*(3), 184+. Retrieved August 19, 2004, from Questia database, http://www.questia.com

Norris, C. J., Barnett, B. G., Basom, M. R., & Yerkes, D. M. (2002). *Developing educational leaders: A working model: The learning community in action.* New York: Teachers College Press.

North Carolina State Board of Education. (1997, June 5). *Code of Ethics for North Carolina Educators.* Retrieved November 2, 2004, from http://www.coe.ecu.edu/OCE_files/Code%20of%20Ethics.htm

North Central Regional Educational Laboratory. (1996). *Critical issue: Realizing new learning for all students through professional development.* Retrieved November 19, 2003, from http://www.ncrel.org/sdrs/areas/issues/educatrs/profdevl/pd200.htm

Oakes, J. (1985). *Keeping track: How schools structure inequality.* New Haven, CT: Yale University Press.

Oakes, J. (1992). *Keeping track.* New York: McGraw-Hill.

Odden, A. R., & Picus, L. O. (2004). *School finance: A policy perspective.* New York: McGraw-Hill.

Olembo, J. O., Wanga, P. E., & Karagu, N. M. (1988). *Management in education.* Kijabe, Kenya: A. I. C. Kijabe Printing Press.

Oliva, P. F. (1997). *Developing the curriculum* (4th ed.). New York: Longman.

Oliva, P. F. (2001). *Developing the curriculum* (5th ed.). New York: Longman.

Oliver, S. (2004). *Special education needs and the law.* Las Vegas, NV: Jordan Publishing.

O'Malley, J. M., & Waggoner, D. (1984). Public school teacher preparation and the teaching of ESL. *TESOL Newsletter, 18*(1), 18–22.

O'Neill, J. (2000, February). SMART goals, SMART schools. *Educational Leadership, 57,* (5), 46–50.

Ornstein, A. C. (1986). How do educators meet the needs of society? How are education's aims determined? *NASSP Bulletin, 70,* 36–47.

Ornstein, A. C., & Cienkus, R. C. (1990). The nation's school repair bill. *American School Board Journal, 177,* 1–4.

Ornstein, A. C., & Hunkins, F. P. (2004). *Curriculum: Foundations, principles, and issues* (4th ed.). Boston: Allyn & Bacon.

Ornstein, A. C., & Lasley, T. J. (2004). *Strategies for effective teaching* (4th ed.). New York: McGraw-Hill.

Orr, T. (2004). *Violence in our schools: Halls of hope, halls of fear.* Danbury, CT: Scholastic Library.

Ortiz, V., & Gonzalez, A. (1989). Validation of a short form of the WISC-R with accelerated and gifted Hispanic students. *Gifted Child Quarterly, 33,* 152–155.

Osher, D., et al. (2004). *Safe, supportive, successful schools step by step.* Longmont, CO: Sopris West.

Ovando, C. J., & Collier, V. P. (1998). *Bilingual education and ESL classrooms* (2nd ed.). Boston, MA: McGraw-Hill.

Palmour, J. (1986). *On moral character: A practical guide to Aristotle's virtues and vices.* Washing-ton, DC: Archon Institute for Leadership Development.

Pardo, E. B., & Tinajero, J. V. (1993). Literacy instruction through Spanish: Linguistic, cultural, and pedagogical considerations. In J. Villareal & A. Ada (Eds.), *The power of two languages.* New York: Macmillan/McGraw-Hill.

Parker, R., Lara-Alecio, R., Ochoa, S., Bigger, M., Hasbrouck, J., & Parker, W. (1996). School improvement ideas: Guidance from parents and students from three ethnic groups. *Journal of Educational Issues of Language Minority Students, 16,* 149–178.

Parker, S. A., & Day, V. P. (1997). Promoting inclusion through instructional leadership: The roles of the secondary school principal. *NASSP Bulletin, 81*(587), 83–89.

Parnes, S. J. (1992). *Source book for creative problem solving.* Buffalo, NY: Creative Foundation Press.

Parsad, B. (2003). *High school guidance counseling.* Washington, DC: U.S. Government Printing Office.

Parsons, B. A. (2002). *Evaluative inquiry: Using evaluation to promote student success.* Thousand Oaks, CA: Corwin.

Pascale, R. T. (1985). The paradox of corporate culture: Reconciling ourselves to socialization. *California Management Review, 27,* 26–41.

Pascarella, S. V., & Lunenburg, F. C. (1988). A field test of Hersey and Blanchard's situational leadership theory in a school setting. *College Student Journal, 21,* 33–37.

Pasmore, W. A. (1985). A comprehensive approach to planning an OD/QWL strategy. In D. D. Warrick (Ed.), *Contemporary organization development: Current thinking and applications* (pp. 195–205). Glenview, IL: Scott Foresman.

Passow, A. H., & Rudnitski, R. (1994). Transforming policy to enhance educational services for the gifted. *Roeper Review, 16,* 271–275.

Paulson v. Minidoka County School District No. 331 (1970)

Peery, A. (2002). Beyond inservice. *Principal Leadership, 3*(3). Retrieved November 4, 2003, from http://www.principals.org/news/pl_beyondsvc_1102.html

Pennsylvania Association for Retarded Children (PARC) v. Commonwealth

Pepperl, J. C., & Lezotte, L. W. (2000). *What the effective schools research says: Safe and orderly environment.* Okemos, MI: Effective Schools.

Peragoy, S., & Boyle, O. (1993). *Reading, writing, and learning in ESL: A resource book for K–8 teachers.* New York: Longman.

Perkins, S. J. (1998). On becoming a peer coach: Practices, identities, and beliefs of inexperienced coaches. *Journal of Curriculum and Supervision, 13,* 235–254.

Perrow, C. (2002). *Organizing America: Wealth, power, and the origins of corporate capitalism.* Princeton, NJ: Princeton University Press.

Perry v. Sinderman

Peters, T. J., & Waterman, R. H. (2004). *In search of excellence.* New York: Harper Business Essentials.

Peterson, K. D. (2000). *Teacher education* (2nd ed.). Thousand Oaks, CA: Corwin.

Phelps, V. W., & Warren, E. F. (2004). *Refining common sense: Moving from data to information.* Lanham, MD: Scarecrow Press.

Phenix, P. (1962). The use of the disciplines as curriculum content. *The Educational Forum, 26*(3), 273–280.

Phi Delta Kappa. (2004). *International curriculum management center.* Retrieved October 28, 2004, from http://www.pdkintl.org/icmc/whatis.htm

Phillips v. Martin Marietta Corp.

Phinney, A. (2004, September). *Preparedness in America's schools: A comprehensive look at terrorism preparedness in America's twenty largest school districts.* America Prepared Campaign. Retrieved September 3, 2004, from http://www.americaprepared.org/pdf/SchoolsAssessment_0904.pdf

Piaget, J. (1950). *The psychology of intelligence.* New York: Harcourt.

Piaget's theory. (1970). In P. Mussen (Ed.), *Carmichael's manual of child psychology* (Vol. 1, pp. 703–732). New York: Wiley.

Pierce v. Society of Sisters

Pinar, W. F., Reynolds, W. M., Slattery, P., & Taubman, P. M. (1996). *Understanding curriculum: An introduction to the study of historical and contemporary curriculum.* New York: Peter Lang.

PITS, et al. (2004). *Psychology in the schools: Implementing the safe schools/healthy students projects.* New York: Wiley.

Plake, B. S., Impara, J. C., & Spies, R. A. (2003). *The fifteenth mental measurements yearbook.* Lincoln, NE: Buros Institute of Mental Measurements.

Plecki, M. L., & Monk, D. H. (2004). *School finance and teacher quality: Exploring the connections.* Larchmont, NY: Eye on Education.

Plyer v. Doe

Polnick, B., Edmonson, S., & Fisher, A. (2003, March). *The ethical administrator.* A paper presented at the NCPEA Conference within a Conference, American Association of School Administrators, New Orleans, LA.

Poole, M., Van de Ven, A., Dooley, K., & Holmes, M. (2000). *Organizational change and innovation processes: Theory and methods for research.* Oxford: Oxford University Press.

Popham, W. J. (1998). Farewell, curriculum: Confessions of an assessment convert. *Phi Delta Kappan, 79*(5), 380+. Retrieved August 19, 2004, from Questia database, http://www.questia.com

Popham, W. J. (2003a). *Educational evaluation* (5th ed.). Boston: Allyn & Bacon.

Popham, W. J. (2003b). *Test better, teach better: The instructional role of assessment.* Alexandria, VA: Association for Supervision and Curriculum Development.

Portin, B. S., & Shen, J. (1998). The changing principalship: Its current status, variability, and impact. *Journal of Leadership Studies, 5*(3), 93.

Possin, C. C. (2004). *Key principal behaviors for successful school change.* Atlanta, GA: American Association of School Administrators.

Pratt, D. (1980). *Curriculum design and development.* New York: Harcourt Brace Jovanovich.

Pratt, D. (1989). Characteristics of Canadian curricula. *Canadian Journal of Education, 14*(3), 295–310.

Pratt, D. (1994). *Curriculum planning: A handbook for professionals.* Toronto, ON: Harcourt Brace.

Prawat, R. S. (1992). From individual differences to learning communities—Our changing focus. *Educational Leadership, 49*(7), 9–13.

Pressley, M., & Beard El-Dinary, P. (Guest Eds.). (1993). Special issue on strategies instruction. *Elementary School Journal, 94,* 105–284.

Pring, R. (1976). *Knowledge and schooling.* London: Open Books Publishing.

Probst, T. (1990). Case study: Asbestos encapsulation. *Executive Educator, 12,* 11A–12A.

Proctor, B. D., & Dalaker, J. (2003). *Poverty in the United States: 2002. Current Population Reports.* Washington, DC.: U.S. Government Printing Office.

Pyle v. South Hadley School Committee

Racine Union School District v. Thompson

Raebeck, B. (2002). *The teacher's gradebook: Strategies for student success.* Lanham, MD: Rowman & Littlefield.

Ramirez, J. D. (1992). Executive summary. *Bilingual Research Journal, 16*(1–2), 1–62.

Ramsdell v. North River School District

Rathman v. Board of Directors of Davenport Community School District

Rebore, R. W. (2000). *The ethics of educational leadership.* Upper Saddle River, NJ: Merrill/Prentice Hall.

Reid, W. A. (1999). *Curriculum as institution and practice: Essays in the deliberative tradition.* Mahwah, NJ: Erlbaum.

Reiser, R. A., & Dick, W. (1996). *Instructional planning: A guide for teaching* (2nd ed.). Needham Heights, MA: Allyn & Bacon.

Rennie, J. (1993). *ESL and bilingual program models.* Washington, DC: Clearinghouse on Language and Linguistics. (ERIC Document Reproduction Service No. ED 362-072)

Renyi, J. (1996). *Teachers take charge of their learning: Transforming professional development for student success.* New York: National Foundation for the Improvement of Education.

Renzulli, J. (1985). *The schoolwide enrichment model.* Mansfield Centre, CT: Creative Learning Press.

Renzulli, J., Sand, J., & Reis, S. S. (1986). *Systems and models for developing programs for the gifted and talented* (J. S. Renzulli, Ed.). Mansfield Centre, CT: Creative Learning.

Rettig, M. A. (1999). Schools must develop comprehensive plans that anticipate and prepare for every imaginable crisis. *Principal, 79,* 10–13.

Reuter, P. H., et al. (2002). *Options for restructuring the safe and drug-free schools and communities act: Report with background papers and focus group summary.* Santa Monica, CA: Rand.

Reynolds, C. R., et al. (2004). *Concise encyclopedia of special education: A reference for the education of the handicapped and other exceptional children and adults.* New York: Wiley.

Richardson, J. (1997). *Teachers can be leaders of change.* Retrieved November 5, 2004, from www.nsdc.org/library/innovator/inn3-97rich.html

Richardson, V. (2000). The dilemmas of professional development. *Phi Delta Kappan, 84*(5), 401–406.

Richman, L. S. (1988, June 6). Why throw money at asbestos? *Fortune,* 155–170.

Riley, R. (2000, March 15). *Excelencia para todos—excellence for all—the progress of Hispanic education and the challenges of a new century.* Washington: Bell Multicultural High School. Retrieved October 26, 2004, from http://www.ed.gov/Speeches/03-2000/000315.html

Rist, M. C. (1989). Schools by design. *American School Board Journal, 176,* 42–48.

Robbins, S. P. (2004a). *Management* (5th ed.). Englewood Cliffs, NJ: Prentice Hall.

Robbins, S. P. (2004b). *Organization theory: Structure, design and applications* (6th ed.). Englewood Cliffs, NJ: Prentice Hall.

Roberts, S. M., & Pruitt, E. Z. (2003). *Schools as professional learning communities.* Thousand Oaks, CA: Corwin.

Rodgers, F. A. (1975). *Curriculum and instruction in the elementary school.* New York: Macmillan.

Rogers, B. (1999). Conflicting approaches to curriculum: Recognizing how fundamental beliefs can sustain or sabotage school reform. *Peabody Journal of Education, 74*(1), 29–67.

Rogers, C. R. (1942). *Counseling and psychotherapy.* Boston: Houghton Mifflin.

Rogers, C. R., & Farson, R. F. (n.d.). *Active listening.* Chicago: Industrial Relations Center, University of Chicago.

Rosenshine, B. (1968). To explain: A review of research. *Educational Leadership, 26,* 275–280.

Rosenshine, B., & Meister, C. (1992). The use of scaffolds for teaching higher level cognitive strategies. *Educational Leadership, 49,* 26–33.

Rosenstengel, W. E. (2004). *School finance: Its theory and practices.* Temecula, CA: Textbook Publishers.

Ross, D. M. (2004). *Childhood bullying, teasing, and violence: What school personnel, other professionals and parents can do.* Arlington, VA: American Counseling Association.

Rowan, B. (1990). Commitment and control: Alternative strategies for the organizational design of school. *Review of Research in Education, 16,* 353–389.

Rowe, M. (1986). Wait time: Slowing down may be a way of speeding up! *Journal of Teacher Education, 37,* 43–50.

Rubin, H. (2002). *Collaborative leadership: Developing effective partnerships in communities and schools.* Thousand Oaks, CA: Corwin.

Rueda, R. (1998). *Standards for professional development: A sociocultural perspective* (Research Brief No. 2). Santa Cruz, CA: University of California, Center for Research on Education, Diversity & Excellence.

Russell v. Men of Devon (1788)

Russo, C. J. (2004). *Reutter's the law of public education* (5th ed.). New York: Foundation Press.

S–1 v. Turlington

Saaty, T. L. (1990). *Multicriteria decision making: The analytic hierarchy process: Planning, priority setting, resource allocation* (2nd ed.). New York: RWS Publications.

Sack, J. L. (2000). Riley endorses "dual immersion" programs. *Education Week, 19,* 28.

Sadker, M., & Sadker, D. (1995). *Failing at fairness: How America's schools cheat girls.* New York: Scribner.

St. John, W. (2004). *How to plan an effective school communications program.* Reston, VA: National Association of Secondary School Principals.

St. Mary's Honor Center v. Hicks

Salazar v. Eastin

Sanders, M. (1990). Selecting and developing communication activities. In J. A. Liedtke (Ed.), *Communication in technology education. Council on Technology Teacher Education 39th yearbook* (pp. 115–138). Mission Hills, CA: Glencoe/McGraw-Hill.

Sandu, D. S. (2001). *Elementary school counseling in the new millennium.* Washington, DC: American Counseling Association.

Sante Fe Independent School District v. Doe

Sarason, S. B. (1998). *The case for a change.* San Francisco: Jossey-Bass.

Sarason, S. B. (2004). *And what do you mean by learning?* Portsmith, NH: Heinemann.

Sashkin, M., & Huddle, G. (1986). *A synthesis of job analysis research on the job of the school principal.* Washington, DC: Office of Educational Research and Improvement, U.S. Department of Education.

Savage, E., & Sterry, L. (1990). A conceptual framework for technology education—part 1. *Technology Teacher, 50*(1), 6–11.

Savage, S. L. (2003). *Decision making with insight.* Belmont, CA: Wadsworth Thomson.

Saylor, J. G., Alexander, W. M., & Lewis, A. J. (1981). *Curriculum planning: For better teaching and learning.* New York: Holt, Rinehart, and Winston.

Schein, E. H. (1996). *Organizational culture and leadership* (3rd ed.). San Francisco: Jossey-Bass.

Schein, E. H. (1999). *Process consultation: Its role in organization development* (4th ed.). New York: Addison-Wesley Longman.

Scheurich, J. J., & Skrla, L. (2003). *Leadership for equity and excellence.* Thousand Oaks, CA: Corwin.

Schiller, P., Clements, D., & Lara-Alecio, R. (2003). *Home connections resource guide.* Columbus, OH: DLM Early Childhood Express, SRA, McGraw-Hill.

Schmitt, N., & Cohen, S. A. (1990). *Criterion-related validity of the National Association of Secondary School Principals' assessment centers.* Reston, VA: National Association of Secondary School Principals.

Schmoker, M. M. (1996). *Results: The key to continuous school improvement.* Alexandria, VA: ASCD.

Schmoker, M. (2001). *The results fieldbook: Practical strategies from dramatically improved schools.* Alexandria, VA: Association for Supervision and Curriculum Development.

Schneider, K. (1993, 24 March). Battling radon: Changing targets. *New York Times,* p. C19.

Schoderbeck, P. B., Cosier, R. A., & Aplin, J. C. (2004). *Management* (6th ed.). San Diego, CA: Harcourt Brace Jovanovich.

Schonfeld, D. J., et al. (2003). *How to prepare for and respond to a crisis.* Arlington, VA: Association for Supervision and Curriculum Development.

School Board of Nassau County, Florida v. Arline

School District of Abington Township v. Schempp

School District of the City of Royal Oak v. Schulman

Schriesheim, C. A., & Neider, L. L. (Eds.). (2003). *New directions in human resource management.* Greenwich, CT: Information Age.

Schwab, J. (1972). The practical: A language for curriculum. In D. Purpel & M. Belanger (Eds.), *Curriculum and the cultural revolution* (pp. 79–99). Berkeley, CA: McCutchan.

Sciarra, D. T. (2004). *School counseling: Foundations and contemporary issues.* Belmont, CA: Brooks/Cole Thomson.

Sclafani, S. (2001). Using an aligned system to make real progress in Texas students. *Education and Urban Society, 33*(3), 305–312.

Sclan, E. M. (1994). *Performance evaluation for experienced teachers: An overview of state policies.* Washington, DC: ERIC Clearinghouse on Teaching and Teacher Education. (ERIC Document Reproduction Service No. ED373054)

Scoma v. Illinois (1974)

Scott, P. (1987). *A constructivist view of learning and teaching in science.* Children's Learning in Science Project. Leeds: The University of Leeds, Centre for Studies in Science and Mathematics Education.

Seaburg, V. (Ed.). (1991). *The 1990 state of the states gifted and talented education report.* Augusta, ME: Council of State Directors of Programs for the Gifted.

Searfoss, L. W., & Enz, B. J. (1996). Can teacher evaluation reflect holistic instruction? *Educational Leadership, 53*(6), 38–41.

Sedlak, A. J., & Broadhurst, D. D. (1996, September). *Third national incidence study of child abuse and neglect.* U.S. Department of Health and Human Services Administration or Children and Families Administration on Children, Youth and Families, National Center on Child Abuse and Neglect. Retrieved May 2002 from http://nccanch.acf.hhs.gov/

Senge, P. (1990). *The fifth discipline: The art and practice of the learning organization.* New York: Doubleday.

Senge, P. (1994). *The fifth discipline: Strategies and tools for building a learning organization.* New York: Doubleday Dell Publishing.

Senge, P. (2001). *Schools that learn.* New York: Doubleday.

Sergiovanni, T. J. (1992). *Moral leadership.* San Francisco: Jossey-Bass.

Sergiovanni, T. J. (1994). *Building community in schools.* San Francisco: Jossey-Bass.

Sergiovanni, T. J. (2000). *Moral leadership: Getting to the heart of school improvement.* San Francisco: Jossey-Bass.

Sergiovanni, T. J. (2004). *The principalship: A reflective practice perspective* (5th ed.). Boston: Pearson Education.

Seyfarth, J. T. (2001). *Human resource management for effective schools.* Boston: Allyn & Bacon.

Shafer v. Board of Education of School District of Pittsburgh, PA

Shanteau, J., et al. (2004). *Psychological explorations of competent decision making.* New York: Cambridge University Press.

Shapiro, J. P., & Stefkovich, J. A. (2001). *Ethical leadership and decision making in education: Applying theoretical perspectives to complex issues.* Mahwah, NJ: Erlbaum.

Sharkey, N. S., & Murnane, R. J. (2003). Learning from student assessment results. *Educational Leadership, 61*(3), 77–81.

Sharp, W. L. (1993). *Collective bargaining in the public schools.* Madison, WI: Brown & Benchmark.

Sharp, W. L. (2003). *Winning at bargaining: Strategies everyone can live with.* Lanham, MD: Scarecrow Press.

Sharp, W. L., & Walter, J. K. (2003). *The principal as school manager* (2nd ed.). Lanham, MD: Scarecrow Press.

Sheehan v. St. Peter's Catholic Church

Shelley, G. B., et al. (2004). *Teachers discovering computers: Integrating technology in the classroom.* Boston: Course Technology, Inc.

Sherman v. Community Consolidated School District No. 21

Sheurich, J. (1994). Policy archeology: A new policy studies methodology. *Journal of Education Policy, 9*(4), 297–316.

Shockley-Zalabak, P. (2002). *Fundamentals of organizational communication: Knowledge, sensitivity, skills, values.* Boston: Allyn & Bacon.

Shoemaker v. State of Arkansas

Shor, I. (1992). *Empowering education: Critical teaching for social change.* Chicago: University of Chicago Press.

Shuell, T. J. (1993). Toward an integrated theory of teaching and learning. *Educational Psychologist, 28*(4), 291–312.

Shuell, T. J. (1996). Teaching and learning in a classroom context. In D. Berlinger & R. Calfee (Eds.). *Handbook of Educational Psychology* (pp. 726–764). New York: Macmillan.

Siegel, M. A., et al. (2001). *Illegal drugs and alcohol: Hurting American society.* Farmington Hills, MI: Gale Group.

Simon, H. A. (1982). *Models of bounded rationality.* Cambridge, MA: MIT Press.

Simon, H. A. (1997). *Models of bounded rationality: Empirically grounded economic reason.* Cambridge, MA: MIT Press.

Sims, S. J., et al. (2003). *Managing school system change: Charting a course for renewal.* Greenwich, CT: Information Age.

Sioukas, T. (2003). *The solution path.* New York: Wiley.

Slattery, P. (1995). *Curriculum development in the postmodern era.* New York: Garland.

Slavin, R. (1990). *Cooperative learning: Theory, research, and practice.* Englewood Cliffs, NJ: Prentice Hall.

Sleeter, C. E. (2002). State curriculum standards and the shaping of student consciousness. *Social Justice, 29*(4), 8+. Retrieved August 21, 2004, from Questia database, http://www.questia.com

Sloan v. Lemon

Smith, D. (2004). *Bulletproof vests versus the ethic of care: Which strategy is your school using?* Lanham, MD: Rowman & Littlefield.

Smith, L. (1992). *Jean Piaget: Critical assessments.* 4 vols. London: Routledge.

Smith, S. C., & Stolp, S. (1995). Transforming a school's culture through a shared vision. *Oregon School Study Council Report, 35*(3), 1–6.

Smith, W. F., & Andrews, R. L. (1989). *Instructional leadership: How principals make a difference.* Alexandria, VA: Association for Supervision and Curriculum Development.

Smylie, M. A., Conley, S., & Marks, H. (2002). Building leadership into the roles of teachers. In J. Murphy (Ed.), *The educational leadership challenge: Redefining leadership for the 21st century* (pp. 162–188). Chicago: University of Chicago Press.

Snipes v. McAndrew

Snyder, K. J., Krieger, R., & McCormick, R. (1984). School improvement goal setting: A collaborative model. *NASSP Bulletin, 68,* 60–65.

Social context of education, The. (1997). Washington, DC: National Center for Education Statistics.

Soleo, K. (2004). *New directions for evaluation.* New York: Wiley.

Southeastern Community College v. Davis

Sowell, E. J. (2000). *Curriculum: An integrative introduction* (2nd ed.). Upper Saddle River, NJ: Merrill/Prentice Hall.

Sparks, D., & Hirsch, S. (1997). *A new vision for staff development.* Alexandria, VA, and Oxford, OH: Association for Supervision and Curriculum Development and National Staff Development Council.

Sparks, D., & Loucks-Horsley, S. (1992). *Five models of staff development for teachers.* Oxford, OH: National Staff Development Council.

Sparks, D., & Richardson, J. (1997). *What is staff development anyway?* Oxford, OH: National Staff Development Council.

Speck, M., & Knipe, C. (2001). *Why can't we get it right? Professional development in our schools.* Thousand Oaks, CA: Corwin.

Stake, R. E. (2003). *Standards-based and responsive evaluation.* Thousand Oaks, CA: Sage.

Stallings, A. W. (2000). *A study of the implementation of a standardized dress code and student achievement of Hispanic students in a suburban high school: A companion study.* Unpublished doctoral dissertation, Sam Houston State University, Huntsville.

Stamm, B. V. (2003). *What changes are occurring in your school: Managing innovation, design, and creativity.* New York: Wiley.

Stark, A. (2001, August/September). Pizza Hut, Domino's, and the public schools. *Policy Review Online, 108.* Retrieved November 5, 2004, from http://www.policyreview.org/AUG01/stark.html

Starratt, R. J. (1994). *Building an ethical school.* London: Falmer Press.

State Board for Educator Certification. (2002). *The code of ethics and standards practices for Texas educators.* Retrieved October 25, 2004, from http://info.sos.state.tx.us/pls/pub/readtac$ext.Tac Page?sl=R&app=9&p_dir=&p_rloc=&p_tloc= &p_ploc=&pg=1&p_tac=&ti=19&pt=7&ch= 247&rl=2

State ex. rel. Burpee v. Burton

State ex. rel. Estes v. Egnor

State v. Consolidated School District

State v. Project Principle

Steege, M., & Watson, T. S. (2004). *Conducting school-based functional assessments: A practitioner's guide.* New York: Guilford.

Stern, H. P., et al. (2003). *Communication system design.* Englewood Cliffs, NJ: Prentice Hall.

Sternberg, R. (1985). *Beyond IQ: A triarchic theory of human intelligence.* New York: Cambridge University Press.

Sternberg, R. J. (1994). Commentary: Reforming school reform. Comments on multiple intelligences: The theory in practice. *Teachers College Record, 95,* 561–569.

Stevens, L. J. (2003). *A critical incident planning and development guide: An administrative handbook.* Lanham, MD: Rowman & Littlefield.

Stiggins, R. J. (2000). *Student-involved classroom assessment* (3rd ed.). Englewood Cliffs, NJ: Prentice Hall.

Stirling, W. C. (2003). *Satisficing games and decision making.* New York: Cambridge University Press.

Stivers, C. (2001). *Democracy, bureaucracy, and the study of administration.* Boulder, CO: Westview.

Stolp, S. (1994). Leadership for school culture. *Education Digest, 91.* Retrieved August 2003 from http://www.ericfacility.net/ericdigests/ed370198.html

Stone, J. A. F. (1968). Risky and cautious shifts in group decision: The influence of widely held values. *Journal of Experimental Social Psychology, 4,* 442–459.

Stoner, J. A. F., & Wankel, C. (2004). *Management* (8th ed.). Englewood Cliffs, NJ: Prentice-Hall.

Straus, D. (2002). *How to make collaboration work: Powerful ways to build consensus, solve problems, and make decisions.* Williston, VT: Berrett-Koehler.

Streifer, P. (2002). *Using data to make better decisions.* Lanham, MD: Scarecrow Press.

Strong, R. W., Silver, H. F., & Perini, M. J. (2001). *Teaching what matters most: Standards and strategies for raising student achievement.* Alexandria, VA: Association for Supervision and Curriculum Development.

Supik, J. D. (1998). Evaluating Title VII programs: An update of biennial evaluations. *Intercultural Development Research Association Newsletter,* p. 3.

Swaitkowski v. Board of Education of City of Buffalo

Sweeney v. New Hampshire

Sybouts, W., & Wendel, F. C. (1994). *The training and development of school principals: A handbook.* Westport, CT: Greenwood Press.

Taba, H. (1962) *Curriculum development: Theory and practice.* New York: Harcourt Brace.

Taba, H. (1971). *Teacher's handbook for elementary social studies*. Reading, MA: Addison-Wesley.

Tannenbaum, R., & Schmidt, W. (1973). How to choose a leadership pattern. *Harvard Business Review, 51,* 162–180.

Taylor, B. M., Pearson, D., Clark, K., & Walpole, S. (1999). Effective schools, accomplished teachers. *Reading Teacher, 53*(2), 156–159.

Teachers' Tenure Act Cases (1938)

Teddlie, C., & Stringfield, S. (1993). *Schools make a difference: Lessons learned from a 10–year study of school effects*. New York: Teachers College Press.

Texas Department of Community Affairs v. Burdine

Texas Education Agency. (1997). *The professional development appraisal system handbook*. Austin, TX: Author.

Texas Education Agency v. Leeper

Tharp, R., & Gallimore, R. (1988). *Rousing minds to life: Teaching, learning, and schooling in social context*. Cambridge, UK: Cambridge University Press.

Thayer-Bacon, B. (2003). *Introduction of luncheon speaker, Olga Welch*. Presented at the Fall Conference of the American Educational Research Association's Research on Women and Education Special Interest Group, Knoxville, TN.

Theobold, D. (2000). *Before and after school activities*. Atlanta, GA: Humanics Publishing Group.

Thomas, W. P. (1992). An analysis of the research methodology of the Ramirez study. *Bilingual Research Journal, 16*(1–2), 213–245.

Thomas, W. P., & Collier, V. (1997). *School effectiveness for language minority students*. Washington, DC: National Clearinghouse for Bilingual Education.

Thomerson, J. (2003a). *School violence: Sharing student information*. Denver, CO: National Conference of State Legislatures.

Thomerson, J., et al. (2003b). *School violence: What works to keep schools safe*. Denver, CO: National Conference of State Legislatures.

Thompson, R. (2002). *School counseling: Best practices for working in the school*. London: Routledge.

Tileston, D. W. (2000). *10 best teaching practices*. Thousand Oaks, CA: Corwin.

Tinker v. Des Moines Independent School District

Titus v. Lindberg

Tizard, J., Schofield, W. N., & Hewison, J. (1982). Collaboration between teachers and parents in assisting children's reading. *British Journal of Educational Psychology, 52,* 1–15.

Tomlinson, C. A. (2003). *Fulfilling the promise of the differentiated classroom: Strategies and tools for responsive teaching*. Alexandria, VA: Association for Supervision and Curriculum Development.

Tomlinson, C. A., & Allan, S. D. (2000). *Leadership for differentiating schools & classrooms*. Alexandria, VA: Association for Supervision and Curriculum Development.

Tomlinson, C. A., & Kalbfleisch, M. L. (1998, November). Teach me, teach my brain: A call for differentiated classrooms. *Educational Leadership, 52–55.*

Torr, J. D. (2004). *Computers and education*. Farmington Hills, MI: Gale Group.

Torrington, D., et al. (2002). *Human resource management*. Englewood Cliffs, NJ: Prentice Hall.

Tourish, D., et al. (2004). *Key issues in organizational communication*. London: Routledge.

Troy, L. (2001). *Beyond unions and collective bargaining*. New York: Sharpe.

Trueba, H. (1979). Bilingual education models: Types and designs. In H. Trueba & C. Barnett-Mizrahi (Eds.), *Bilingual multicultural education and the professional: From theory to practice*. Rowley, MA: Newbury House.

Tschannen-Moran, M., Uline, C., Hoy, A. W., & Mackley, T. (2000). Creating smarter schools through collaboration. *Journal of Educational Administration, 38*(3), 247–271.

Tsoukas, H., & Mylonopoulos, N. (2003). *Organizations as knowledge systems: Knowledge, learning, and dynamic capabilities*. Gordonville, VA: Palgrave Macmillan.

Turk, W. (2004). *School crime and policing*. Englewood Cliffs, NJ: Prentice Hall.

Tushman, M. L., et al. (2004). *Managing strategic innovation and change: A collection of readings*. New York: Oxford University Press.

Tyack, D., & Cuban, L. (1995). *Tinkering towards Utopia: A century of public school reform*. Cambridge, MA: Harvard University Press.

Tyler, R. W. (1949). *Basic principles of curriculum and instruction*. Chicago: University of Chicago Press.

Tyler, R. W. (1969). *Basic principles of curriculum and instruction*. Chicago: University of Chicago Press.

Ubben, G. C., Hughes, L. W., & Norris, C. J. (2004). *The principal: Creative leadership for effective schools* (5th ed.). Boston: Allyn & Bacon.

U.S. Agency for Toxic Substances. (1988). *The nature and extent of lead poisoning in children in the United States.* Washington, DC: U.S. Government Printing Office.

U.S. Bureau of Census. (2000). *Minority economic profiles.* Retrieved March 1, 2002, from http://www.census.gov/population/socdemo/hispanic/p20-535/p20-535.pdf

U.S. Bureau of Census. (2001). *The Hispanic population: Census 2000l brief.* Retrieved May 20, 2005, from http://64.233.167.104/search?q=cache:0lYPRZHS5NIJ:www.census.gov/prod/2001pubs/c2kbr01-3.pdf+hispanic+population+houston+2000&hl=en

U.S. Constitution, art. I, sec. 8. Available online at http://www.house.gov/Constitution/Constitution.html

U.S. Department of Education. (n.d.). *The mission and principles of professional development.* Retrieved December 13, 2003, from http://www.ed.gov/G2K/bridge.html

U.S. Department of Education. (1989). *Radon in schools.* Bulletin No. 520. Washington, DC: U.S. Government Printing Office.

U.S. Department of Education. (1995). *School facilities condition of American schools, Report to congressional requesters.* Washington, DC: U.S. Government Printing Office.

U.S. Department of Education. (1996). *Achieving the goals: Goal 4: Teacher professional development.* Retrieved December 12, 2003, from http://www.ed.gov/pubs/AchGoal4/index.html

U.S. Department of Education. (2000). *1998 elementary and secondary school civil rights compliance report no. 614/221–8829.* Washington, DC: U.S. Government Printing Office.

U.S. Department of Education. (2001a). *The condition of education, 2000.* Washington, DC: U.S. Government Printing Office.

U.S. Department of Education. (2001b). *Digest of education statistics, 2000.* Washington, DC: U.S. Government Printing Office.

U.S. Department of Education. (2002a). *The condition of education, 2002.* Washington, DC: U.S. Government Printing Office.

U.S. Department of Education. (2002b, January 8). *No child left behind act: Public law 107–110.* Washington, DC: Office of English Language Acquisition, Language Enhancement and Academic Achievement of Limited English Proficient Students.

U.S. Department of Education. (2004a). *Report of the taskforce on school violence.* Washington, DC: Author.

U.S. Department of Education. (2004b). *Safe, disciplined, drug-free schools: A report.* Washington, DC: Author.

U.S. Department of Education, National Center for Education Statistics. (2005). *School safety and discipline survey.* Washington, DC: Author.

U.S. Department of Health and Human Services. (2003). Help for children of addicted parents. *SAMHSA News, XI* (2). Retrieved July 2003 from http://alt.samhsa.gov/samhsa_news/VolumeXI_2/article5.htm

U.S. Department of Health and Human Services. (2004a). *Current violence in U.S. public high schools.* Washington, DC: Author.

U.S. Department of Health and Human Services. (2004b). *Current tobacco, alcohol, marijuana, and cocaine use among high school students.* Washington, DC: Author.

U.S. Department of Labor, Bureau of Labor Statistics. (2005). *Employment and earnings.* Washington, DC: U.S. Government Printing Office.

U.S. Environmental Protection Agency. (2000). *The cost of asbestos removal in the nation's schools.* Washington, DC: Author.

United States v. Dinwiddie

United States v. South Carolina

Urban Institute. (2000, February 1). *A new look at homelessness in America.* Retrieved August 2003 from http://www.urban.org

Valente, W. D., & Valente, C. M. (2001). *Law in the schools* (5th ed.). Upper Saddle River, NJ: Merrill/Prentice Hall.

Valesky, T. C. (2002). *Training for quality school-based decision making: The total teamwork system.* Blue Ridge Summit, PA: Rowman & Littlefield.

Van de ven, A. H., et al., (2004). *Organizational change and innovation processes: Theory and methods for research.* New York: Oxford University Press.

Vandevender v. Cassell (1974)

Vansciver, J. H. (2004). *Components of a good interview process.* Atlanta, GA: American Association of School Administrators.

VanTassel-Baska, J. (1994). *Comprehensive curriculum for gifted learners.* Boston: Allyn & Bacon.

Vendrell v. School District No. 26C Malheur County

Vasquez, H., Myhand, M. N., & Creighton, A. (2004). *Making allies, making friends: A curriculum for making peace in middle schools.* New York: Hunter House.

Vernonia School District 4-7J v. Acton (1995)

Virgil v. School Board

Vroom, V. H. (1994). *Work and motivation.* San Francisco: Jossey-Bass.

Vroom, V., Yetton, P., & Jago, A. (1988). *The new leadership: Managing participation in organizations.* Englewood Cliffs, NJ: Prentice Hall.

Wald, P. J., & Castleberry, M. S. (2000). *Educators as learners: Creating a professional learning community in your school.* Alexandria, VA: Association for Supervision and Curriculum Development.

Waldron, N., & McLeskey, J. (2001). An interview with Nancy Waldron and James McLeskey. *Intervention and School & Clinic, 36*(3), 175–183.

Walker, D. F., & Soltis, J. F. (1997). *Curriculum and aims.* New York: Teachers College Press.

Walker, H. M., & Eaton-Walker, J. (2000). Key questions about school safety: Critical issues and recommended solutions. *NASSP Bulletin, 84*(614), 46–55.

Walker, K. S. (1999). *Decision making and ethics: A study of California superintendents* (Doctoral dissertation, University of La Verne, 1999). *UMI Dissertation Services, 9944527.*

Wallace v. Jaffree

Wallace, J. (1998). Collegiality and teachers' work in the context of peer supervision. *Elementary School Journal, 99,* 81–98.

Walsh, D. J. (2003). *Employment law and human resource practice.* Mason, OH: South-Western.

Walsh, J. A., & Sattes, B. D. (2000). *Inside school improvement: Creating high-performing learning communities.* Lanham, MD: Scarecrow Press.

Waltz v. Board of Education

Wang, M., Haertel, G., & Walberg, H. (1993). Toward a knowledge base for school learning. *Review of Educational Research, 63,* 249–294.

Wanko, M. A. (2002). *Safe schools: Crisis prevention and response.* Lanham, MD: Rowman & Littlefield.

Wanzare, Z., & DaCosta, J. L. (2001). Rethinking instructional leadership roles of the school principal: Challenges and prospects. *Journal of Educational Thought, 35*(3), 269–295.

Wasley, P., Hampel, R., & Clark, R. (1996). *The puzzle of whole school change.* Providence, RI: Coalition of Essential Schools, Brown University.

Wasson, B., Ludvigsen, S., & Hopper, U. (2003). *Designing for change in networked learning environments.* Dordrecht, The Netherlands: Kluwer Academic Publishers.

Watson, J. (2002). *The martyrs of Columbine: Faith and the politics of tragedy.* Gordonsville, VA: Palgrave Macmillan.

Watson, R. J., et al. (2003). *The school as a safe haven.* Westport, CT: Greenwood Publishing.

Webb, L. D., & Norton, M. S. (2004). *Human resources administration: Personnel issues and needs in education* (4th ed.). Columbus, OH: Merrill/Prentice Hall.

Webber, J. A. (2004). *Failure to hold: The politics of school violence.* Lanham, MD: Rowman & Littlefield.

Weber, M. (1947). *The theory of social and economic organization* (T. Parsons, Trans.). New York: Oxford University Press.

Webster, W. G. (1994). *Learner-centered principalship: The principal as teacher of teachers.* Westport, CT: Praeger Publishers.

Weckmueller, B. L., et al. (1998). *Student records management: A handbook.* Westport, CT: Greenwood Publishing Group.

Weick, K. E. (1976). Educational organizations as loosely coupled systems. *Administrative Science Quarterly, 21,* 1–19.

Weick, K. E. (1982). Administering education in loosely coupled systems. *Phi Delta Kappan, 63*(10), 673–676.

Weick, K. E., & McDaniel, R. R. (1989). How professional organizations work: Implications for school organization and management. In T. J. Sergiovanni & J. H. Moore (Eds.), *Schooling for tomorrow: Directing reforms to issues that count* (pp. 330–355). Boston: Allyn & Bacon.

Weinstein, C., & Mayer, R. (1986). The teaching of learning strategies. In M. C. Wittrock (Ed.), *Handbook of research on teaching* (3rd ed., pp. 315–327). New York: Macmillan.

Weiss, E. M., & Weiss, S. G. (1998). New directions in teacher evaluation. *ERIC Digest.* (ERIC Document Reproduction Service No. ED429052)

Wellman, C. (1999). *The proliferation of rights: Moral progress or empty rhetoric?* Boulder, CO: Westview.

Wessler, S., & Preble, W. (2003). *The respectful school: How educators and students can conquer hate and harassment.* Arlington, VA: Association for Supervision and Curriculum Development.

WestED. (1996). *Planning schoolwide program change.* Retrieved July 20, 2003, from http://www.ed.gov/pubs/Idea_Planning/Step_2.html

Whalen v. Minnesota Special School District

Wheatley, M. J. (1994). *Leadership and the new science.* San Francisco, CA: Barrett-Koehler.

White v. South Park Independent School District

Whitehurst, G. J. (2002). Scientifically based research on teacher quality: Research on teacher preparation and professional development. Presented to White House Conference on Preparing Tomorrow's Teachers, March 5, 2002. Published as Appendix C of *Improving teacher quality state grants. Title II, Part A. Non-regulatory draft guidance.* Washington, DC: U.S. Department of Education. Retrieved November 6, 2004, from http://www.ed.gov/offices/OESE/SIP/TitleIIguidance2002.doc

Wiggins, G. (1992). Creating tests worth taking. *Educational Leadership, 49,* 26–33.

Wiggins, G. (1993). *Assessing student performance: Exploring the purpose and limits of testing.* San Francisco: Jossey-Bass.

Wiggins, G. P. (1999). *Assessing student performance: Exploring the purpose and limits of testing.* New York: Wiley.

Wilde, J. (2003). *Anger management in schools: Alternatives to school violence.* Lanham, MD: Rowman & Littlefield.

Wilde, J. (2004). *Peace in the halls: Stories and activities to manage anger and prevent school violence.* New York: LGR Publishing.

Wildy, H., & Dimmock, C. (1993). Instructional leadership in primary and secondary schools in Western Australia. *Journal of Educational Administration, 31*(21), 43–61.

Wiles, J., & Bondi, J. (2002). *Curriculum development: A guide to practice.* Upper Saddle River, NJ: Merrill/Prentice Hall.

Wiles, J., & Bondi, J. (2004). *Supervision: A guide to practice* (6th ed.). Upper Saddle River, NJ: Merrill/Prentice Hall.

Wiley, D., & Yoon, B. (1995). Teacher reports of opportunity to learn: Analyses of the 1993 California Learning Assessment System. *Educational Evaluation and Policy Analysis, 17*(3), 355–370.

Williams, B. (Ed.). (2003). *Closing the achievement gap: A vision for changing beliefs and practices* (2nd ed.). Alexandria, VA: Association for Supervision and Curriculum Development.

Williams, K. M. (2004). *The peace approach to violence prevention: A guide for administrators and teachers.* Lanham, MD: Scarecrow Press.

Williams, S. S. (2002). *Effective practices in shared decision making.* Northglenn, CO: Adams Twelve Five Star Schools.

Williams v. Austin Independent School District

Willower, D. J., & Licata, J. W. (1997). *Values and valuation in the practice of educational administration.* Thousand Oaks, CA: Corwin.

Wisconsin Center for Education Research. (2001). *Teacher research spurs professional development.* Retrieved November 23, 2003, from http://www.wcer.wisc.edu/publications/archives/feature/may00.asp

Wisconsin v. Yoder

Wolman v. Walter

Wood v. Strickland

Woodall, J., Lee, M., & Stewart, J. (Eds.). (2004). *New frontiers in human resource development.* London: Routledge.

Worzbyt, J. C., et al. (2004). *Elementary school counseling: A commitment to caring and community building.* Independence, KY: Taylor & Francis.

Wotherspoon, T. (1987). Introduction: Conflict and crisis in Canadian education. In T. Wotherspoon (Ed.), *The political economy of Canadian schooling* (pp. 1–15). Toronto, ON: Methuen.

Wright, H. (1989). Radon gas: New threat in schools. *USA Today, 21,* p. 1A.

Xavier University. (2000). *School violence studies.* Cincinnati, OH: Author.

Yeh, S. S. (2001). Tests worth teaching to: Constructing state-mandated tests that emphasize critical thinking. *Educational Researcher, 30*(9), 12–17.

Yudof, M. G., Kirp, D. L., Levin, B., & Moran, R. E. (2002). *Education policy and the law* (4th ed.). Belmont, CA: West/Thomson Learning.

Zey, M. (1992). *Decision making: Alternatives to rational choice models.* Thousand Oaks, CA: Sage.

Zimmerman, B. J. (1999). Attaining self-regulation: A social cognitive perspective. In M. Boekaerts, P. Pintrich, & M. Seidner (Eds.), *Self-regulation: Theory, research and applications.* Orlando, FL: Academic Press.

Zobrest v. Catalina Foothills School District

Zorach v. Clauson

Zuga, K. F. (1993). A role for alternative curriculum theories in technology education. *Journal of Industrial Teacher Education, 30*(4), 48–67.

Name Index

Abrell, R., 230
Acheson, K. A., 314
Adair, J., 206
Adams, P. W., 7
Addams, J., 326
Agard-Jones, L., 280
Aguinis, H., 302
Airasan, P. W., 118
Aitken, R., 8, 106
Albert, M., 178
Alexander, K., 239, 257, 258, 433, 436
Alexander, M. D., 239, 257, 258, 433, 436
Alexander, William, 60
Alkire, P., 315
Allan, C. A., 69–70, 85
Alleman, J., 110
Allen, D., 63
Allensworth, E., 90
Allison, G. S., 280, 288
Alvesson, M., 10
Anderson, L. W., 118
Anderson, R. H., 114, 314
Andryzewski, T., 281
Aplin, J. C., 180
Apple, M. W., 379, 389
Arfstrom, K., 270
Argyris, C., 240
Aristotle, 350
Arter, J., 143, 148
Arterbury, E., 357
Ash, Mary Kay, 11
Ausubel, D., 109
Avila, M. M., 281
Avolio, B. J., 6
Awkerman, G., 45

Babbit, N., 277
Baca, L. M., 165
Backlund, P., 230
Baerdwell, I., 298
Bagin, D., 325
Bailey, G. D., 38
Bailey, J. M., 169
Baker, B. D., 136, 137, 138, 139, 183

Baldwin, J. R., 230
Ball, S., 372
Banks, C. A., 91
Banks, J. A., 78, 91
Barker, L., 233
Barnett, B. G., 6
Baron, R. S., 54, 212
Barrera, Dr. John, 90–91
Barth, R. S., 10, 12, 18, 47, 239, 247, 251, 252
Barton, E. A., 27, 281
Basham, V., 252
Basom, M. R., 6
Bass, B. M., 6, 91, 193
Baylor, A. L., 87, 88
Beard, S., 281
Beard El-Dinary, P., 110
Beaty, J. L., 71, 288
Beauchamp, G. A., 56–58
Beck, I., 109
Beck, L. G., 350
Beckner, W., 346, 347, 348, 349, 365
Begley, P. T., 353
Begun, R. W., 280, 288
Bejar, I. I., 147
Bell, D. L., 47
Bennett, N., 110
Bennis, W. G., 104, 190, 193
benShea, N., 236
Benward, B., 233
Berger, R., 365
Berkeley, T. R., 277, 294
Berliner, D. C., 332, 378, 389
Bermúdez, A. B., 329, 330
Bernardin, H. J., 298
Bernd, M., 203
Bernhardt, V. L., 143
Beveridge, M., 329
Bhushan, N., 203
Biddle, B. J., 332, 378–379, 389
Biemiller, A., 109, 110
Bigger, M., 330
Birman, B. F., 165
Blackstone, J. A., 347
Blase, J., & Blase, J., 14, 18, 33, 102, 103

Blauvelt, P. D., 281
Bloom, B. S., 54, 57, 74–75, 143
Bluestein, J., 282
Bobbitt, F., 55
Bohlin, K. E., 355
Bondi, J., 17, 62, 82, 106, 288, 289, 313, 315
Bonstingl, J. J., 252
Booth, R. R., 317, 431
Bor, R., 139
Boschee, F., 54
Boyd, W. L., 239
Boyer, E. L., 58, 61, 62
Boyle, O., 165
Bracey, G., 239, 332
Brandt, R. S., 252, 354
Bratton, J., 296
Brimley, V., 274
Broadhurst, D. D., 27
Brock, S. T., 333, 334
Brogan, B. R., 126
Bronfenbrenner, U., 330
Brookover, W., 71
Brooks, J. G., 105
Brooks, M. G., 105
Brophy, J., 108, 109, 110, 111, 112, 113, 290
Browder, L. H., 28–29
Brown, A., 122
Brown, B., 281
Brown, G., 6, 32–33, 110, 111, 113, 125, 126, 128–130, 131, 133, 154, 166, 194, 195, 330, 353, 384, 385, 390
Brown, M., 143
Brown, W. B., 209
Bruce, K., 165
Brunner, C. C., 6
Bryk, A. S., 90, 382, 383, 390
Bryson, J. M., 252
Bubnicki, Z., 210
Burke, R. J., 245, 252
Burko, C., 273
Burns, H., 357
Burns, J., 6
Burns, J. M., 193

Burstyn, J. N., 293
Bush, President George W., 380
Bushweller, K., 272

Calbom, L. M., 261
Calderón, M. E., 169
Cambron-McCabe, N. H., 411,
    433, 436. *See also*
    McCabe, N. H. C.
Campbell, D. E., 73
Campbell, E., 356
Campbell, J. R., 27
Capper, C. A., 325
Carisson-Paige, N., 288
Carlson, R. V., 45
Carmichael, D. R., 261
Carnall, C. A., 245
Carr, J. F., 17, 103, 105, 106
Carter, P. J., 145
Caseau, D., 237
Castallo, R., 14
Castangnera, J. O., 239
Castetter, W. B., 296, 300, 301,
    304, 305, 306, 319
Castleberry, M. S., 6, 8, 10, 11
Cervantes, M. T., 165
Chamot, A. U., 167
Chavkin, N. F., 329
Cheney, G., 226
Cheung, D., 141
Chowdhury, A., 46
Christensen, L. G., 226
Christie, K., 71
Chubb, J., 380, 390
Chung, H., 87
Cienkus, R. C., 265
Cihon, P. J., 239
Clair, N., 122
Clark, C., 87, 108, 109
Clark, R., 63, 330
Claspell, M., 211
Clemente, B., 141
Clements, D., 329, 330
Cleveland, J. N., 309
Clinton, President William J., 380
Coakley, J. J., 353
Cobia, D. C., 136, 137, 138, 139
Cocking, R., 122
Cogan, M., 114, 313, 314
Cohen, D. K., 105, 211
Cohen, D. L., 325
Cohen, D. M., 183
Cohen, S. A., 303
Cole, K. B., 62

Coleman, M. R., 154
Collier, V. P., 166, 167
Collins, J. C., 32
Colton, A. B., 14, 103
Colvin, R. L., 327
Comer, J. P., 329
Conley, S., 5–6, 8, 247, 251, 252
Conlon, E. J., 250
Conn, J. H., 353
Conoley, J. C., 280, 288
Convery, A., 92
Cook, W. J., 252
Cooper, B. S., 239, 249, 251,
    372, 373, 374, 375, 376,
    377, 390
Cooper, H., 87, 110
Cooper, T. L., 349
Cordeiro, P. A., 220
Corrigan, D., 58, 61–62
Cosier, R. A., 180
Costa, A. L., 116
Cotton, K., 15, 103, 107
Covey, S., 47
Covrig, D. M., 353
Coyle, D., 92
Craig, R. P., 346
Crawford, C., 357
Crawford, J., 167, 329
Creel, J. R., 288
Creemers, B., 111
Creighton, T., 90–91
Crone, D., 141
Crow, G. M., 5–6
Crowson, R. L., 324, 325
Cruikshank, K. A., 118
Cruz, B. C., 277
Cuban, L., 16, 254, 381
Cunningham, W. G., 220
Curcio, J. L., 265
Cyr, A., 377
Czaja, M., 346

Daft, R. L., 44
Dalaker, J., 26, 27
Daley, D. M., 298, 305, 309,
    315
Danielson, C., 14, 106
Darling-Hammond, L., 87, 107,
    121, 122, 381
Datnow, A., 5, 8, 191, 192, 239
Davidson, J. E., 206
Davidson-Taylor, C. M., 115
Davis, L., 229, 233
Davis, P. B., 136, 206, 210, 220

Davis, S. H., 136, 206, 210, 220,
    384, 385
Dawson, P., 247
Deal, T. E., 10, 11, 12, 18, 239
DeGroof, J., 150
DeKlerk, F. W., 25
Deming, W. E., 196
Dempster, F., 110, 111
DeNavas-Walt, C., 26
Denham, C., 109
Dessler, G., 296, 300, 301, 304,
    305, 306, 307
Devine, C., 347
DeWaard, J., 154
Dewey, J., 66, 84, 326, 370–371
Dias de Figueiredo, A., 28
Dick, W., 87–88
Diesing, P., 377
Dimmock, C., 71
Doh, J. C., 263
Dollarhide, C. T., 136
Donahue, P. L., 27
Dooley, K., 246
Dorfman, P. W., 5
Dorn, M. S., 280, 281, 283
Dornbusch, S. M., 329
Doud, J. L., 184, 189, 210
Doyle, W., 109
Draft, R., 224, 226, 227
Drake, T. L., 265
Drucker, P. F., 9, 252
Dryfoos, J., 326
Duarte, D. L., 245
Dubois, D. D., 301, 309, 315
Duemer, L. S., 373
Dues, M., 231
Duffy, F. M., 14
Duffy, J., 6, 194, 195, 353, 384
DuFour, R. P., 6, 8, 10, 11, 190
Duhon-Sells, R. M., 280
Duke, D. L., 102, 106, 239, 281,
    288, 293
Dunlap, D. M., 8
Dunn, D., 272
Dunn, K., 99–101
Dunn, R., 99–101
Dunne, E., 110
Dutton, J., 49
Dye, T. R., 372

Eaker, R., 6, 8, 10, 11, 190
Early, L., 254
Easton, J. Q., 382, 390
Eaton-Walker, J., 285

Ebener, R., 292, 330
Edmonds, R., 71, 103, 104, 107
Edmonson, S., 358
Einstein, Albert, 25
Eisenberg, E. M., 223
Eisner, E. W., 62, 68–69
Elmore, R. F., 8, 15, 16, 211, 379, 381
Emmer, E. T., 149, 150, 290
English, F. W., 15, 17, 81, 84, 386
Enz, B. J., 113
Epstein, J. L., 106, 107, 193, 325, 328, 329
Erford, B. T., 138
Essex, N. L., 239, 414, 436
Evertson, C. M., 290

Farr, B., 147, 148, 149
Farson, R., 233
Fashola, O. S., 149
Fawcett, G., 184, 210
Feinburg, T., 333
Feldman, R. S., 235
Ferrandino, V., 184, 210
Fertakis, J. P., 261
Fine, M., 325
Fink, D., 16
Fink, E., 114
Finsterwald, M., 92
Fischer, L., 239, 433, 436
Fishbaugh, M. S. E., 277, 280, 287, 288, 294
Fisher, A., 32–33, 84, 118, 358
Flaxman, E., 329, 330
Flood, P., 71
Foot, M., 296
Ford, D., 160
Ford, Henry, 11, 193
Forgang, W. G., 205
Fortune, J. C., 265
Foshee, D. P., 353
Fowler, F. C., 183, 372, 384, 391
Frase, L., 229, 386
Fredrikson, N., 147
Froman, L. A., 375
Fuhrman, S. H., 254
Fullan, M., 17, 125, 133, 200, 239, 254, 378
Fusarelli, L. D., 239, 249, 251, 372, 390
Fyack, C. D., 298, 300, 301, 302, 309

Gagné, R., 92–94, 95
Galanes, G. J., 212
Gall, M. D., 314
Gallagher, D. R., 325
Gallagher, J., 154
Gallimore, R., 110
Galloway, M., 166
Gamoran, A., 239
Ganesh, S., 226
Gardner, H., 101–102, 118, 153, 157
Garfield, R. R., 274
Garmston, R. J., 116
Garner, C. W., 239, 256, 260, 263, 264, 267, 268
Garrett, A. G., 162, 164, 281, 288
Gelatt, H. B., 207
Gempel, J., 162
Gerdes, D. A., 353
Gerlach, G., 303
Ghatala, E., 84
Gilbert, M. B., 229, 231, 236
Gillespie, B. L., 327, 328
Gilligan, C., 98
Ginsberg, J., 239
Ginsburg, A. L., 165
Glickman, C., 7, 14, 15, 16, 17, 102, 125, 190, 288, 289, 315
Goff, L. S., 14, 103
Goizueta, R., 193
Goldhammer, R., 114, 314
Goldman, P., 8
Goldring, E. B., 5, 325
Goldstein, A. P., 280, 288
Gómez, L., 166
Gonzalez, A., 154
Good, T. L., 87, 109, 110, 111, 113, 290
Goodlad, J., 55, 69
Goodson, I., 55
Gorbachev, M., 25
Gordon, E. W., 102
Gordon, S. P., 288, 315
Greenfield, W. D., 5, 33
Greenwald, E. A., 27
Greim, C., 272
Greiner, L. E., 247
Gresham, F. M., 294
Greve, H. R., 245
Griffin, R. W., 179, 251
Grimes, F., 277, 288
Guenther, D. A., 260, 263, 264, 268

Guilford, J. P., 94, 101
Gulledge, J., 281, 288
Gullickson, A. R., 147, 148
Guskey, T. R., 147, 149, 169

Haertel, G., 109
Hall, A. H., 108
Hall, G. E., 105
Hall, J., 235
Haller, E. J., 365
Hallinan, M. T., 239
Hallinger, P., 87
Hamilton, R., 84
Hampel, R., 63
Hansen, C. R., 347
Hansen, R., 55
Hanson, E. M., 200
Hanson, K. L., 220
Hardaway, R. M., 376
Hardman, D., 207
Hargis, C. H., 148
Hargreaves, A., 125, 254
Harman, G., 374, 375
Harper, G. W., 33
Harrington-Lucker, D., 270
Harris, D. E., 17, 103, 105, 106
Harris and Associates, 278–279
Harrow, A. J., 143
Hartsock, N., 6
Hasbrouck, J. E., 165, 330
Hasday, J. L., 281
Hassell, K. P., 235
Hausman, C. S., 6
Havelock, R. G., 246
Hawley, W. D., 14
Haycock, K., 107
Haynes, C., 348
Haynes, F., 365
Hearne, J., 160
Heck, R. H., 87
Hedwig, L., 235
Hensley, P. A., 384
Herman, J., 44
Herzberg, F., 251
Hess, G. A., 192
Hester, J. P., 280, 283, 288
Hewison, J., 329
Hickson, M. L., 235
Hill, D. T., 277, 287, 288
Hill, J., 353
Hipp, K. K., 6, 8, 10, 11, 102, 105
Hirsch, S., 122, 134, 147
Hitchner, K., 136

Holbrook, S. F., 44
Holmes, M., 246
Hombo, C. M., 27
Hopfenberg, W. S., 12
Hopper, U., 245
Hord, S. M., 6, 8, 10, 11, 18–19, 105
Houlihan, T., 89
Houston, D., 124
Hovell, J. P., 5
Howe, L., 162
Hoy, A. W., 17, 106
Hoy, W. K., 17, 106, 220
Hoyle, J., 47–48
Huberman, M., 15
Huddle, Gene, 187
Huddleston, J., 211
Huffman, J. B., 6, 8, 10, 11, 102, 105
Hughes, L. W., 184, 210, 265
Huml, F. J., 280, 288
Hunkins, F. P., 62, 78–79, 84, 288, 291

Iacocca, Lee, 11, 193
Imber, M., 436
Impara, J. C., 146
Inger, M., 329, 330
Irby, B. J., 6, 9, 16, 32–33, 63–66, 91, 110, 111, 113, 125, 128–130, 131, 133, 153, 154, 159–160, 165, 166, 183, 194, 195, 211, 239, 277, 289, 292, 326, 330, 353, 384, 385, 390
Ivancevich, J. M., 296, 300, 304, 305, 306, 307
Ivy, D. K., 230

Jackson, P. W., 84, 245
Jago, A., 213, 214
Janis, I. L., 212
Jantzi, D., 8, 33, 106
Jermier, J. M., 5
Jerrams, A., 329
Jobs, S., 193
Johansson, O., 353
Johnson, D., 33, 110, 353
Johnson, J. F., Jr., 46–47
Johnson, L., 230, 231
Johnson, President Lyndon B., 263, 376
Johnson, R., 110
Johnson, S., 336–337

Jones, B., 353
Joyce, B., 14, 16, 103, 105, 125, 133, 240, 308

Kaagan, S. S., 133
Kalbfleisch, M. L., 92
Kampwirth, T. J., 141
Kane, W., 281
Kaplan, L. S., 381
Katsiyannis, A., 154
Katz, R. L., 185
Katzan, H., 252
Kaufman, J. M., 294
Kaufman, R., 44, 183, 252
Kegan, R., 236
Kelleher, J., 123, 128
Kelly, C., 433
Kemp, L., 108, 210
Kennedy, A. A., 11, 12
Kennedy, C., 383
Kennedy, M. M., 308
Kennedy, President John F., 428
Kepner, C. H., 204
Kerbow, D., 382, 390
Kerchner, C. J., 317, 432
Kerr, S., 5
Keyton, J., 223
Khedouri, F., 178
Kidder, R. M., 346
Killion, J., 211
Kimbrough, R. B., 346, 349, 350, 351
Kinder, D., 62
King, R. A., 256, 260, 267, 268, 274
Kirkpatrick, C., 46
Kirp, D. L., 240
Kirton, M. J., 206
Kish, C. K., 62
Kitsantas, A., 87
Kleiner, A., 49
Klesse, E. J., 149, 150, 169
Kmetz, J. T., 184, 210
Knapp, M., 110, 235
Knipe, C., 14
Knowles, M., 122
Koehler, M., 134
Kohlberg, L., 96–98
Kohn, A., 354
Kolosick, T. J., 233
Koppich, J., 317, 432
Korney, R. C., 317, 429, 431
Kottler, E., 169
Kottler, J. A., 169

Koutsoukis, N. S., 212
Kouzes, J. M., 7, 184, 200
Krajewski, R., 114, 314
Kramer, M., 25, 230
Krathwohl, D. R., 118, 143
Krieger, R., 43, 271
Kruse, S., 6, 190, 191
Kubitacheck, W., 239
Kurtz-Costes, B., 27

Lahey, L. L., 236
Lambert, L., 6, 7, 14, 19, 72, 102, 200, 217
LaMorte, M. W., 240, 433, 436
Landrum, M. S., 154
Langdon, T. P., 263, 264
Langer, G. M., 14, 103
Laosa, L. M., 330
Lara-Alecio, R., 91, 111, 153, 154, 159–160, 165, 166, 292, 329, 330
Larson, R., 149, 150
Lasley, T. J., 288, 289, 291, 315
Latham, G. P., 9, 36, 251, 315
Laurea, A., 330
Lawrence-Brown, D., 92
Lazarus, P. J., 327, 328, 333, 334
Lee, M., 301
Leithwood, K. A., 6, 8, 15, 33, 106, 193, 194
Leonard, B., 281, 288
Lester, W., 162
Levin, B., 240, 241
Levin, D. E., 288
Levin, H. M., 274
Levine, D. U., 5, 43
Lewis, A., 60, 265, 267
Lewis, S., 333
Lezotte, L. W., 5, 43, 105, 280, 287, 288
Licata, J. W., 33, 353
Lichtenstein, R., 283
Lick, D. W., 14
Lickona, T., 96, 354
Lieberman, A., 72, 109
Lightfoot, S. L., 329
Likert, R., 191–192
Lindblom, C., 210
Lindquist, A. K., 299
Lipkin, A., 379
Lipton, M., 254
Lissitz, R. W., 106
Liston, D. P., 239, 247, 251, 252
Little, J. W., 122

Little, M. E., 124, 125
Littrell, J. H., 38
Loader, D., 261
Lockard, J., 7
Locke, E. A., 9, 36, 251, 315
Lockwood, A. L., 354
Lombardi, Vince, 12
Loucks-Horsley, S., 125
Louis, K. S., 6, 8, 15, 190, 191
Loveless, T., 239
Lowe, J., 346
Lucas, T., 49
Ludvigsen, S., 245
Lundy, J., 298, 305
Lunenburg, F. C., 8, 9, 15, 16,
    17, 39, 63–66, 91, 102,
    103, 183, 189, 191, 197,
    207, 211, 239, 252, 277,
    289, 291, 299, 302, 307,
    308
Luthans, F., 189, 226, 234

Maanum, J. L., 150
Maeroff, G. I., 250
Majkowski, C., 71
Mandela, Nelson, 25
Manning, S., 254
March, J., 63, 183, 209, 211
Marcoux, J. S., 125, 126
Marczely, B., 297, 319
Marczely, D. W., 297, 319
Margolis, H., 243
Marks, H., 5–6
Marland, S. P., 372
Marotto, P. F., 277, 283, 288
Márquez, J. A., 329, 330
Marshall, C., 346
Marshall, M. J., 247, 251, 252
Martin, W. J., 184, 210
Martin-Kniep, G. O., 6, 8, 10, 11
Martocchio, J. J., 309
Marzano, R. J., 15, 118, 169
Masia, B. B., 143
Mason, S. A., 89
Mathison, S., 143
Maurer, B., 160
Mayer, R. E., 110, 118
Mazzeo, J., 27
McBrien, J. L., 354
McCabe, N. H. C., 49, 240. See
    also Cambron-McCabe
McCann, J. T., 277, 280, 283,
    288
McCarthy, M. M., 240, 411, 436

McCauley, Joyce, 61–62
McCormick, Robert, 43
McCune, S., 252
McDaniel, R. R., 5
McDill, E. L., 329
McDonnell, L. M., 145, 154
McEwan, P. J., 274
McKeon, D., 167–168
McKeown, M., 109
McKerrow, K., 346
McLaughlin, M. L., 169
McLaughlin, M. W., 113, 329
McLeskey, J., 92
McMillan, E., 240
McNabb, M. L., 61
McNeil, J., 54, 409
Meece, J. L., 27
Meeks, L. B., 281, 287, 292
Megginson, L. C., 180
Meichenbaum, D., 109, 110
Meier, D., 239, 247, 251, 252
Meister, C., 96, 110
Mendez-Morse, S., 373
Merriman, J., 353
Merritt, R., 281
Mescon, M. H., 178
Metcalfe, J. S., 246
Metzger, E. G., 299
Meyer, J. W., 183
Michel, G., 346
Miller, J., 62
Miller, L., 72, 147
Mills, M., 281
Mills, R., 26
Millward, R., 303
Minaya-Rowe, L., 169, 330
Miner, J. B., 181
Miretzky, D., 239
Mislevy, R. J., 147
Moberg, D. J., 209
Moe, T., 380, 390
Moffitt, M. A., 230
Mohondie, K., 280, 281, 283
Molloy, J. T., 235
Mondy, R. W., 301
Monk, D. H., 260, 268, 275
Montessori, Maria, 25
Moore, D., 357
Moore, M. H., 277
Moore, S., 254
Moran, C., 166
Moran, R. E., 240
Morgan, D. E., 162, 164
Mort, P. R., 260

Mosley, D. C., 180
Mosline, S. R., 277
Moulton, J. C., 265
Moustakas, C., 209
Mowry, C., 329
Murnane, R. J., 89–90
Murphy, C. U., 14
Murphy, J., 5, 8, 106, 189, 191,
    192, 239, 350
Murphy, K. R., 309
Murray, M. M., 38
Mylonopoulos, N., 246

Najita, J. M., 429, 431
Nanus, B., 49, 104
Narayanan, M. P., 205
Nash, R. J., 365
Nata, R., 239
Neal, R. G., 431
Neber, H., 92
Neider, L. L., 298
Nelson, J., 230, 231
Newmann, F., 90, 110
Newstrom, J. W., 229, 233
Nicolau, S., 330
Nicoletti, J., 277, 281
Noble, P. V., 277, 288
Noddings, N., 73, 350
Nolet, V., 169
Norris, C. J., 6, 8, 10, 11, 184,
    210, 265
Norton, M. S., 296, 306, 320

Oakes, J., 103, 105
Oaks, J., 254
Ochoa, S., 330
Odden, A., 256, 260, 262, 267,
    268, 274
Oliva, P. F., 62
Oliver, S., 150
Olsen, J., 183, 211
O'Malley, J. M., 167
O'Neill, J., 36
Ornstein, A. C., 8, 9, 16, 17, 62,
    66–68, 78–79, 84, 103,
    183, 189, 191, 207, 211,
    239, 265, 288, 289, 291,
    299, 302, 308, 315
Orr, T., 277, 281
Ortiz, V., 154
Osher, D., 283, 288
Ovando, C. J., 166, 167
Owings, W. A., 381
Ownen, R. G., 200

Padrón, Y. M., 329
Paige, R., 354
Palmour, J., 350
Pardo, E. B., 167
Parker, D. A., 236
Parker, R., 111, 165, 330
Parker, W., 330
Parnes, S. J., 161
Parsad, B., 136
Parsons, B. A., 143
Pascale, R. T., 12
Pascarella, S. V., 307
Passow, A. H., 154
Pearson, D., 108
Pechman, E., 141
Peery, A., 124
Pepperl, J. C., 280, 287, 288
Peragoy, S., 165
Perini, M. J., 17
Perkins, S. J., 308
Perry, S. D., 230
Persky, H. R., 27
Peters, K. H., 63
Peters, R., 353
Peters, T., 193, 209
Peterson, K. D., 10, 11, 12, 18, 239, 313
Peterson, P., 87, 109
Phelps, V. W., 104
Phenix, P., 54
Phinney, A., 347
Piaget, J., 25, 96, 98, 105
Pickering, D., 15, 118
Picus, L., 256, 260, 262, 267, 268, 274
Pietri, P. H., 180
Pinar, W. F., 62
Pintrick, P. R., 118
Plake, B. S., 146, 302
Plecki, M., 260, 268, 275
Pollock, J. E., 15, 118
Polnick, B., 358, 386
Poole, M., 246
Popham, W. J., 17, 19, 73–74, 106, 145
Porras, J., 32
Portin, B. S., 325
Posner, B. Z., 7, 184, 200
Possin, C. C., 249
Powell, R. G., 237
Prawat, R. S., 71
Preble, W., 280, 294
Pressley, M., 110

Proctor, B. D., 26, 27
Pruit, E. Z., 6, 8, 11

Quartz, K. H., 254
Quiroz, H. C., 281

Raebeck, B., 149
Ramirez, J. D., 165–166
Ramos, C. L., 330
Ramsey, E., 294
Ramsey, R. D., 237
Randall, E. V., 239, 249, 251, 372, 390
Raths, J., 118
Reagan, President Ronald, 377
Rebore, R. W., 346, 365
Reid, W. A., 65
Reis, S. S., 161
Reiser, R. A., 87–88
Rennie, J., 165, 167
Renyi, J., 122
Renzulli, J., 159, 161
Resnik, L. B., 114
Rettig, M. A., 285
Reuter, P. H., 288
Reynolds, W. M., 62, 150
Richards, C. E., 183
Richardson, J., 121
Richetti, C. T., 221
Richman, L. S., 266
Rigsby, L., 329
Riley, R., 166
Rist, M. C., 268
Ritter, P. L., 329
Robb, L., 134
Robbins, S. P., 175, 207
Roberts, S. M., 6, 8, 11
Rodgers, F. A., 96
Rodriguez, L., 125, 126
Roe, W. H., 265
Rogers, C., 139, 233
Rollie, D. L., 14
Rollow, S., 382, 390
Rosenshine, B., 96, 109, 110
Rosenstengel, W. E., 260
Ross-Gordon, J. M., 288, 315
Rowan, B., 183
Rowe, M., 110
Rubin, H., 106, 107
Rudnitski, R., 154
Russo, C. J., 257, 258, 424, 433, 436
Ryan, K., 355
Ryan, S., 254

Saaty, T. L., 37
Sack, J. L., 162
Sand, J., 161
Sandoval, J., 333
Sandu, D. S., 136
Sarason, S. B., 8, 15, 19, 254
Sashkin, M., 187, 246
Sattes, B. D., 6, 8, 10, 11
Savage, E., 212
Saylor, Galen, 60
Schafer, W. D., 106
Scheerens, J., 111
Schein, E. H., 11, 250
Scheurich, J. J., 14, 102, 376
Schiller, P., 329, 330
Schimmel, D., 239, 433, 436
Schlechty, P. C., 255
Schmidt, W., 216
Schmitt, N., 303
Schmoker, M. M., 36, 102, 103
Schneider, K., 270
Schoderbeck, P. B., 180
Schofield, W. N., 329
Schonfeld, D. J., 281
Schriesheim, C. A., 298
Schroth, G., 277, 294
Schwarzkopf, General Norman, 44
Schweitzer, J., 71
Sciarra, D. T., 136, 137, 138, 139
Sclafani, S., 15
Sclan, E. M., 113
Scriven, M., 6, 84, 118
Seaburg, V., 154
Searfoss, L. W., 113
Sebring, P. B., 382, 390
Sedlak, A. J., 27
Seller, W., 62
Senge, P. M., 6, 8, 10, 11, 15, 30, 49, 251, 252, 306
Sergiovanni, T. J., 7, 12, 102, 109, 184, 200–201, 353
Seyfarth, J. T., 296, 298, 305, 320
Shanteau, J., 205
Shapiro, J. P., 221, 346, 347, 349, 352
Sharkey, N. S., 89–90
Sharp, W. L., 8, 317, 429, 431
Sheehan, J. K., 62
Shelley, G. B., 7
Shen, J., 325
Shields, P. M., 329
Shockley-Zalabak, P., 227, 228

Short, L. O., 250
Showers, B., 14, 16, 103, 105, 125, 133, 308
Shuell, T. J., 86, 110, 111, 118
Silver, H. F., 17
Simon, H., 209
Sims, S. J., 239, 245
Sioukas, T., 204
Skrla, L., 14, 102
Slattery, P., 58, 61–62
Slavin, R., 110
Sleeter, C. E., 63
Sloan, A., 193
Smith, B., 49, 90
Smith, D., 280
Smith, L., 98
Smith, R. E., 320
Smith, S. C., 28, 33
Smutny, J. F., 170
Smylie, M. A., 5–6
Snyder, Karolyn J., 43
Soder, R., 201
Soleo, K., 143, 148
Soltis, J. F., 62, 365
Sowell, E. J., 288
Sparks, D., 122, 125, 134
Speck, M., 14
Spencer-Thomas, S., 277, 281
Spies, R. A., 146
Stake, R. E., 143
Stallings, A. W., 288
Stamm, B. V., 245, 247
Stark, A., 350, 351
Starratt, R. J., 345
Steege, M., 139
Steffy, B., 15, 17
Stefkovich, J. A., 346, 347, 349, 352
Stellman, L., 436
Stern, H. P., 230
Sternberg, R., 157
Stevens, L. J., 281
Stewart, J., 301
Stewner-Manzanares, C., 167
Stiggins, R. J., 111, 143, 148
Still, Suzanne, 12
Stirling, W. C., 209
Stivers, C., 190
St. John, W., 224
Stolp, S., 28, 33
Stoner, J. A. F., 178, 212
Straus, D., 211
Streifer, P., 104, 221
Strike, K., 365

Stringfield, S. C., 84–85, 111, 118
Strong, R. W., 17
Stronge, J. H., 320
Struyk, L. R., 62
Swanson, A. D., 256, 267, 274
Sweetland, S. R., 256, 267, 274
Sybouts, W., 331, 348

Taba, Hilda, 54, 58–60, 99
Tannenbaum, R., 216
Tarter, C. J., 220
Taubman, P. M., 62
Taylor, B. M., 108
Teddlie, C. B., 33, 84–85, 111, 118
Tharp, R., 110
Thayer, Judith, 355
Thayer-Bacon, B., 71
Theobold, D., 149, 150
Thomas, A., 160
Thomas, S. B., 240, 411, 436
Thomas, W. P., 166, 167
Thomerson, J., 280, 288
Thompson, D. C., 275
Thompson, R., 136, 137
Tileston, D. W., 112, 119
Tinajero, J. V., 167
Tizard, J., 329
Tomlinson, C. A., 16, 69–70, 85, 92, 103, 105, 106, 237
Torr, J. D., 7
Torrington, D., 298
Tourish, D., 224
Trautman, D., 6, 194, 195, 353, 384
Tregoe, B. B., 204, 221
Troy, L., 317, 432
Trueba, H., 165
Trumbull, E., 147, 148, 149
Trump, K. S., 281
Tsoukas, H., 246, 251
Tucker, P. D., 320
Turk, W., 280, 281
Turner, W., 272
Tushman, M. L., 246
Tyack, D., 381
Tyler, R. W., 55–56, 76–78

Ubben, G. C., 184, 210, 265
Urban, N., 92
Usdan, M., 16

Valente, C. M., 433
Valente, W. D., 433

Valesky, T. C., 211
Van de Ven, A. H., 246
Vansciver, J. H., 301
VanTassel-Baska, J., 160
Vasquez, H., 288
Voelkl, K. E., 27
von Geel, T., 436
Vroom, V., 10, 213, 214
Vygotsky, Lev, 25

Waggoner, D., 167
Walberg, H., 109
Wald, P. J., 6, 8, 10, 11
Waldron, N., 92
Walker, D. F., 62
Walker, H. M., 285, 294
Walker, K. S., 357
Wallace, J., 308
Wallace, R. C., 49
Walpole, S., 108
Walsh, D. J., 297
Walsh, J. A., 6, 8, 10, 11
Walton, Sam, 12
Wang, M., 109
Wankel, C., 178
Wanko, M. A., 281, 288
Warren, E. F., 104
Wasley, P., 63
Wasson, B., 245
Waterman, R., 193, 209
Watson, J., 277
Watson, R. J., 281, 287, 288
Watson, T., 11
Watson, T. S., 139
Weaver, L., 165
Webb, L. D., 296, 306, 320
Webber, J. A., 281
Weber, M., 190
Weckmueller, B. L., 141, 142
Weeres, J. G., 317, 432
Weick, K. E., 5, 183
Weinstein, C., 110
Weiss, E. M., 113
Weiss, S. G., 113
Welch, J., 193
Wellman, C., 347
Wells, L., 353
Wendel, F. C., 331, 348
Wessler, S. L., 280, 294
Wheatley, M. J., 29
Whitehurst, G. J., 381
Wiggins, G., 62, 111, 143
Wilde, J., 280, 288
Wildy, H., 71

Wiles, J., 17, 62, 82, 106, 288, 289, 313, 315
Williams, B., 16, 103, 105, 106
Williams, D. L., 329
Williams, K. M., 280, 288
Williams, S., 213
Willower, D. J., 184, 210, 353
Wisenbaker, J., 71

Wittrock, M. C., 118
Woodall, J., 301, 304, 305, 306, 307
Woodman, R. W., 251
Wood, R. C., 275
Worzbyt, J. C., 136

Yeh, S. S., 17
Yerkes, D. M., 6

Yetton, P., 213, 214
Young, I. P., 296, 300, 301, 304, 305, 306
Young, P., 319
Yudof, M. G., 240

Zey, M., 209
Zimmerman, B. J., 88
Zorn, T. E., 226

Subject Index

Absolute rights, 347
Abuse, child, 27
Academics. *See also* Education
  academic concept, of curriculum, 54
  disadvantaged students and, 372
  factors in improving, 47
  goals, 287–288
Accelerated Schools Model, 12
Accountability, in delegation process, 177
Accounting, reporting, 226
Accounts receivable, 262
Achievement
  evidence-driven decisions, 90–91
  improving, 72
  NCLB and, 89–90
  recognition of, 12
  standards, 196
  tests, 146–147
Action plans
  goal setting and, 40
  NSPRA public relations process and, 336
Action research, 125, 127
Active listening, 233–234
Activity, principals' roles in policy, 373
Actuating. *See* Leadership
ADA (Americans with Disabilities Act), 417, 420, 424, 427
ADA (average daily attendance), 90
Adaptive mode, of organization, 5
Additive approach, curriculum integration, 78
ADEA (Age Discrimination in Employment Act), 394, 427
Adequate Yearly Progress (AYP), 142, 394
Administration
  bilingual education, 164–165
  ELCC standards, 3
  functions of, 182–183
  gifted education, 156–157

goal setting and, 42
principals' demand relating to, 210
school safety, 286
Administrative roles, 184–185
  oral communicative ability, 185
  variety, fragmentation, and brevity of task, 185
  workload of principals, 184–185
Administrators
  effective vs. ineffective, 188–189
  hierarchy of goals and, 38
  relationship of skills to administrative levels, 186
Adult learning, 122
Adversarial politics, 382
Affective domain, testing programs, 143
Affirmative action programs, 298
African Americans
  cultural bias in testing, 303
  gifted ed programs, 154
  school violence, 278
Age
  equal employment opportunities, 297
  as factor in school violence, 278
  teachers' protections against age discrimination, 427
Age Discrimination Act, 424
Age Discrimination in Employment Act (ADEA), 394, 427
Air quality, environmental hazards, 271–272
Alcohol and drug use
  drug testing, 418
  eliminating, 279–280
  research on, 279
  search and seizure and, 289, 418
Alignment process (curriculum, instruction, and assessment), 17, 80, 204

All-channel network, of communication, 228
Alternative schools
  disciplinary transfers, 416–417
  serving violence-prone youths, 284
  transferring violent students to, 282–283
American Arbitration Association, 13
American Association of Colleges for Teacher Education (AACTE), 2
American Association of School Administrators (AASA), 2, 358
American Educational Research Association, 79
American Red Cross, 327
American Society for Testing and Materials, 145
Americans with Disabilities Act (ADA), 417, 420, 424, 427
Analysis. *See* Assessment/analysis
Analysis-for-the-top, change agents, 245
Anticipatory set, in learning, 290
Apparent conflicts of interest, 351
Appearance, student
  dress codes, 288–289
  regulations and rights, 414–415
Applicative model (Taba), curriculum, 58–60
Aptitude tests, 146
Arbitration, collective bargaining, 431
Arts, fine, 111
Asbestos, environmental hazards, 269
Asbestos School Hazard Detection and Control Act, 393
ASBO (Association of School Business Officials), 257

Assessment/analysis. *See also* Evaluation; Performance appraisal
  aligning curriculum, instruction, and assessment, 17, 204
  of curriculum, 65–66
  frequency of, 106
  goal setting and, 10, 41
  of guidance/counseling services, 138
  instructional planning and, 89
  restructuring content and, 198
  reward and control systems, 13
  self-assessment for ethical behavior, 361
  student learning, 15–16
  student progress, 142–143
  teacher awareness of need for, 113
  tools for, 80
  Twelve Principles of Effective Teaching (Brophy), 111
Assessment centers, 303–304
Association for Supervision and Curriculum Development (ASCD), 2
Association of School Business Officials (ASBO), 257
Associations, in Gagné's conditions for learning, 93
Assumption of risk, negligence, 434
Athletic programs, 353–354. *See also* Extracurricular activities
Attendance
  compulsory attendance, 400–401
  contrasting ways of looking at, 90–91
  records, 140–142
Attending behavior, 291
Attitudes
  staff development and, 306
  in synergistic leadership theory, 194
  vision development and, 30–31
Audits
  curriculum, 81
  financial, 261–262
Authority
  delegation process and, 177

discipline and, 416
hierarchy of, 5, 190
postmodernism and, 376
responsibility and, 349
Autobiographical section, in cumulative record, 141
Autocratic leadership, 383
Autonomy, principals' role in policy, 373
Average daily attendance (ADA), 90
Awards, recognition of achievement, 12
AYP (Adequate Yearly Progress), 142, 394

Balance, in counseling services, 140
Beepers, banning from school environment, 289
Behavior
  reports in cumulative record, 141
  school culture and, 11
  staff development and, 307
Beliefs. *See also* Values
  culture and, 28
  decision making and, 203
  normative dimension of policy, 377
  in synergistic leadership theory, 194
  vision development and, 30–31
Benchmarks
  curriculum and, 80–81
  planning and, 88, 183
Benefits, in collective bargaining, 430
Biases. *See also* Prejudice
  cultural bias in testing, 303
  in teacher appraisal, 313
Bible reading, in public schools, 402
Bilingual education, 162–168
  administration of, 164–165
  models for, 163, 165–168
  overview of, 161–162
  resources for, 164
  state guidelines, 163–164
  student population and, 164
Bilingual Education Act, 394
Bill of Rights, 394

Bodily kinesthetic intelligence, multiple intelligences (Gardner), 101
Body language, nonverbal communication, 235
Bolstering the alternative, rational decision making (Bubnicki), 210
Brown v. Board of Education of Topeka, 371
Budgets, 256–264
  auditing, 261–262
  challenges to state financing, 258
  expenditures, 257
  fiscal independence and dependence of school districts, 258
  internal controls, 261
  overview of, 256
  PPBS (planning-programming-budgeting system), 263–264
  process of, 259–261
  revenues, 257–258
  in single-use plans, 46
  suggested readings, 274–275
  zero-based, 262–263
Bureaucracy
  building bureaucratic linkages, 188
  effectiveness of, 191
  negative features of, 189–191
Business community, participation in goal setting, 40

California Achievement Test (CAT), 81
Campus Improvement Plan (CIP), 18
Capital outlays, schools, 257
Careers
  career ladder for teachers, 13
  counselors' role in planning, 137
  lifelong careers in bureaucracies, 190
Caring relationships, 350
Carnegie Task Force on Teaching as a Profession, 13, 176
Case law
  federal, 395–396
  state, 397
Cash flow, auditing, 262

Catastrophes
  community support during, 326–328
  natural disasters, 286
CAT (California Achievement Test), 81
Caucus, collective bargaining, 432
CCSSO (Council of Chief State School Officers), 2
Centers for Disease Control (CDC), 270
CENTRAL (Coordinating Existing Networks to Reach All Learners), 124
Central tendency errors, in teacher appraisal, 312
Certification, of teachers, 421
Certified public accountants (CPA), 261–262
CFO (chief financial officer), 259–260
Chain networks, of communication, 227
Chains or sequences of responses, in Gagné's conditions for learning, 93
Challenge, balancing with realism in goal setting, 39
Change, 238–255
  agents of, 245–247
  behaviors promoting, 249
  factors in success of, 244
  forces against, 249
  forces for, 239–240
  managing, 191
  nature of organizational change, 238–239
  overcoming resistance to, 240–243
  principals as agents of, 244–245
  process of, 247–249
  strategies, 249–251
  structural strategies, 251–253
  suggested readings, 254–255
  understanding resistance to, 243–244
Change agents, 245–247
  characteristics of successful, 246–247
  principals as, 6, 244–245

roles of, 245–246
  types of, 245
Character
  education, 354–355
  ethics and, 350
Character Education Manifesto, 355
Chief financial officer (CFO), 259–260
Chief state school officer (CSSO), 396
Children
  abuse, 27
  with disabilities, 28, 372
  early development, 112
  Education for All Handicapped Children Act, 394, 419
  homeless, 401
  parents' involvement with education of, 329–330
Children's Internet Protection Act, 393–394
Church-state relations, 401–403
CIP (Campus Improvement Plan), 18
Circle network, of communication, 228
Circuit court of appeals, 398
Citizens, development of effective, 112
Civil Rights Act of 1964
  discrimination in employment, 424
  federal statutes regarding education, 394
  liability and, 433
  sexual harassment, 425
Civil Rights Act of 1991, 395
Clarity
  effective goal setting, 38
  synergistic decision making and, 218–219
Class distinctions, 292
Classical model, curriculum (Tyler), 55–56
Classification, curriculum objectives, 74
Class period, bilingual programs, 167
Classroom
  class size and, 112
  practices, 112–113
  principals' visits to, 315
  time management in, 109

Classroom observation
  decision making and, 203
  as evaluation model, 114
Clergy, community involvement with schools, 326
Clinical supervision, 114, 314
Closure, learning and, 291–292
Clubs, 149–150
Coaching
  decision making and, 203
  ethics and, 353–354
Cocaine, 279. See also Alcohol and drug use
Cocurricular activities. See Extracurricular activities
Codes of ethics
  national, 357–360
  reasons for, 357
  state, 360–362
Coercion
  overcoming resistance to change, 243
  sexual coercion, 426
Cognition, in Guilford's structure of intellect model, 95
Cognitive domain, 143
Cognitive theories, 98–99
COLA (cost-of-living adjustments), in collective bargaining, 430
Collaboration. See also Leadership
  community involvement with schools, 328
  culture of, 194
  in ELCC standards, 4
  principals' role in encouraging, 15
  productivity improved by, 43
  professional learning communities and, 7
Collective bargaining
  issues, 429–431
  overview of, 428–429
  process of, 431
  tactics and strategies, 431–433
  union-management relations, 317
Columbine incident, 372
Commitment
  ethics and, 350
  goal creation supporting, 9
Common sense, 351

Communication, 222–237
    ability for, 231
    active listening and, 233–234
    articulating the vision, 33
    barriers to, 226, 229–231
    community and schools and,
        328, 332
    facilitating student communi-
        cation, 286
    feedback and, 234–235
    flow of, 224–227
    of goals, 10
    grapevine, 228–229
    implementing decisions,
        206–207
    improving effectiveness of, 231
    networks, 227–228
    nonverbal, 235
    overcoming resistance to
        change, 242
    power and, 374
    principals' abilities, 185
    process of, 222–224
    public relations and, 336
    receivers' responsibilities, 233
    school-wide communication
        program, 224
    senders' responsibilities,
        231–233
    storytelling as part of school
        culture, 12
    suggested readings, 236–237
Community, 324–345
    academic improvement and, 47
    case study, 342–344
    catastrophes and, 326–328
    change process and, 249
    character education and, 355
    comprehensive partnerships,
        328–329
    curriculum development and,
        64–65
    family involvement, 329–331
    goal setting and, 39–40
    internal and external publics,
        333
    involvement in schools,
        325–326
    media and, 333–334
    overview of, 324
    principals as boundary span-
        ners with, 325
    public relations programs of
        schools, 334–338

    safe, risk free, 112
    school-community relations,
        331–332
    student learning and, 108–109
    suggested readings, 340–341
    types of, 328
    violence spilling over into
        schools, 277
Community services, school
    expenditures, 257
Comparative negligence, 434
Complacency, as obstacle to
    vision development, 34
Comprehension, in Guilford's
    structure of intellect model,
    95
Comprehensive partnerships,
    328–329
Compulsory school attendance
    exemptions, 401
    law enforcement and, 400–401
    residency requirements, 401
Concepts, in Gagné's conditions
    for learning, 93
Conceptual skills
    developing, 306
    as management skills,
        185–186
Concrete operational stage
    (Piaget's stages of cognitive
    development), 99
Conditioning, as barrier to com-
    munication, 231
Conferences, family involvement,
    331
Conflict of interest
    forms of, 351
    overview of, 350–351
Conflicts
    adversarial politics, 382
    upward communication and,
        226
Consensual politics, 382
Consolidated power, in educa-
    tional politics, 382–383
Constituentive dimension, of pol-
    icy, 377
Construction, financing school
    construction, 267–268
Constructivism, 105
Constructivist theories
    learning styles, 99–101
    multiple types of intelligence,
        101–102

Consulting role, of change agents,
    245
Content
    of applicative curriculum,
        59–60
    Campbell on course content, 73
    emphasizing structure and
        connections in presentation
        of, 109
    professional development of
        teachers and, 124
    relationship to objectives,
        75–76
    restructuring, 197–198
    what vs. how, 66
Contextual model of curriculum,
    69–70
Contracts, teachers' rights, 315,
    421–422
Contributions approach, to inte-
    gration of curriculum, 78
Contributory negligence, 434
Control, in reward and control
    systems, 13
Conventional level, Kohlberg's
    levels of moral develop-
    ment, 97
Convergent thinking, in Guil-
    ford's structure of intellect
    model, 95
Cooperation, counseling services
    and, 140
Cooperative learning, 197
Co-optation, overcoming resist-
    ance to change, 242–243
Coordinating Existing Networks
    to Reach All Learners
    (CENTRAL), 124
Corporal punishment, 417–418
Corrective feedback, in communi-
    cation process, 234
Cost constraints, in decision mak-
    ing, 208
Cost-efficiency, 196
Cost-of-living adjustments
    (COLA), in collective bar-
    gaining, 430
Council of Chief State School
    Officers (CCSSO), 2
Counseling/guidance services
    aims of, 136–137
    counselors, 137
    directive counseling, 138–139
    eclectic counseling, 139

evaluating, 139–140
nondirective counseling, 139
overview of, 138
policy and, 379
types of, 137–138
Counterproposals, collective bargaining, 432
Course materials, education law and, 403–405
Court of last resort, 400
Court rulings
church-state relations, 401–402
compulsory school attendance, 400–401
corporal punishment, 417–418
curriculum, 408–409
disability discrimination, 419–420, 427
extracurricular activities, 406–407, 415–416
freedom of expression, 412–414
prayer and Bible reading, 401–402
pregnancy discrimination, 428
race and gender discrimination, 424–425
religious instruction, 403
school transportation, 406
search and seizure, 418–419
sexual harassment, 425–426
slogans, 415
state aid to private schools, 403–405
state-mandated performance testing, 409–411
suspensions and expulsions and, 416–417
tenure law, 422–424
termination of school personnel, 422
textbooks, courses, and supplies, 406–407
tort liability, 433–435
Courts, 398–400
federal, 398
state, 399–400
Courts of general jurisdiction, 399–400
Courts of limited jurisdiction, 399
CPA (certified public accountants), 261–262

CPTED (Crime Prevention Through Environmental Design), 285
Creative Problem Solving (Parnes), 161–162
Crime Prevention Through Environmental Design (CPTED), 285
Crimes, at or near schools, 277–278
Crisis management, 285–287
Critical theory, policy and, 376
Critical thinking, 17
Criticism
ethics of, 352
methods for improving communication, 233
principles for improving delegation, 177
CSSO (chief state school officer), 396
Cultural diversity. See Ethnic background
Culture
barriers to communication, 231
collaborative, 194
diversity of world culture, 26
social and economic in ELCC standards, 4–5
Culture, school
building cultural linkages, 187–188
characteristics, 10–11
communications networks (storytelling), 12
decentralization and, 179
in ELCC standards, 3
heroes and heroines, 11–12
integrating with instruction and programs in curriculum, 66
maintaining, 12–14
overview, 10
school vision and, 8
traditions and rituals and, 12
vision development and, 28–29
Cumulative record, of students, 141–142
types of information in, 141
uses of, 141–142
Current expense category, of school expenditures, 257

Curriculum, 53–85
adapting to student ability, 105
aligning with instruction and assessment, 17, 80, 204
auditing, 81
Beauchamp model, 56–58
benchmarking, 80–81
character education in, 355
cohesiveness of, 109
concepts, 54
content restructuring, 198
counselors' role in, 136
education law and, 407–409
Eisner model, 68–69
ethics in, 357
gifted education, 161–162
goals of, 73–74
instructional differentiation in, 81
instruction and, 69–70
Irby and Lunenburg model, 63–66
mapping, 80
models, 55, 61–63
needs assessment and, 78–80
objectives of, 74–78
Ornstein model, 66–68
planning, 88
principal's role in, 71–72
Saylor model, 60
suggested readings, 84–85
Taba model, 58–60
teacher support and, 16
Tyler model, 55–56
vision and mission and, 82–83

Dana Center studies, 46–47
Data-driven decision making, 372
Day care, 288
Debt service, school expenditures, 257
Decentralization
characteristics for measuring, 178
of organizational structure, 178–179
rationale for, 193
Decision making, 202–221
community involvement in, 328
data-driven, 90, 372
decision-making patterns (Tannenbaum & Schmidt), 216–217

Decision making *(continued)*
  Decision Tree Model (Vroom, Yetton, & Jago), 213–216
  democratic politics and, 382
  effective leaders and, 7
  evaluating alternatives, 206
  evaluating effectiveness of decisions, 207
  evidence-driven, 90
  faculty involvement in, 8
  generating alternatives, 205
  identifying problems, 204–205
  implementing decisions, 206–207
  nature of, 202–204
  principals' success dependent on, 384
  process of, 204
  rational, 207–211
  SBDM (site-based decision making), 103
  selecting among alternatives, 206
  shared, 211–213
  suggested readings, 220–221
  synergistic, 217–219
Decision-making patterns (Tannenbaum & Schmidt), 216–217
Decision Tree Model (Vroom, Yetton, & Jago), 213–216
Decoding/encoding, in communication process, 223, 229
Defamatory expression, 413–414
Degree, principals' role in policy, 373
Delegation, 176–178
  decentralization compared with, 178
  effectiveness of, 177–178
  overview of, 176–177
  steps in delegation process, 177
Delphi Dialog Technique, 43–44
Democracy
  characteristics of democratic politics, 382
  development of effective citizens, 112
  extracurricular activities supporting democratization process, 150
  globalization and, 26
Demographics, U.S., 26–27
Departmentalization, in organizational structure, 176

Dependence, resistance to change, 239
Descriptive method, of reporting student progress, 148
Design, in system model of curriculum, 60
Developmental problems, counseling for, 136
Differentiated instruction, for different student levels, 81, 91–92
DIP (District Improvement Plan), 18
Directive counseling, 138–139
Disability
  children with, 28, 372
  discrimination protections, 426–427
  Education for All Handicapped Children Act, 394, 419
  equal employment opportunities, 297
  Individuals with Disabilities Acts, 394
  legal rights of disabled students, 419–420
  state-mandated performance testing and, 410
Disadvantaged students, socioeconomic and academic, 372
Disciplinary transfers, 416–417
Discipline
  data on discipline problems, 280
  legal rights of students and, 416
  in public schools, 280
  removing student privileges, 284
  rules and procedures, 288–289
  school-wide plan for, 286
Disease, globalization, 26
Dismissal procedures, tenured employees, 423–424
Disputes, upward communication and, 226
District courts, 398
District Improvement Plan (DIP), 18
Divergent questions, 291
Divergent thinking, in Guilford's structure of intellect model, 95

Division of labor (job specialization), 175–176, 189, 297
Doctrine of no surprises (English & Steffy), 17
Doctrine of *stare decisis*, 395
Dominant values, in school culture, 11
Downward flow, of communication in organizations, 224–225
Dreams, in vision development, 30
Dress codes, 288–289, 415. *See also* Appearance, student
Drugs. *See* Alcohol and drug use
Dual immersion bilingual programs, 166
Dual language, bilingual programs, 166
Due Process Clause, Fourteenth Amendment, 394, 423
Duties, ethics and, 349
Duty, tort liability and, 433

EAA (Equal Access Act of 1984), 402
EAHCA (Education for All Handicapped Children Act), 394, 419
Early exit bilingual programs, 165
Early Warning/Timely Response Guide, 286–287
Eclectic counseling, 139
Economics, as external force for change, 239
Education. *See also* Academics
  alternatives to traditional models, 28
  bilingual. *See* Bilingual education
  character education, 354–355
  counselors' role in, 137
  federal statutes regarding, 394
  federation role in public education, 28
  gifted. *See* Gifted education
  overcoming resistance to change, 242
  politics, 382–384. *See also* Politics
  quality of education as factor in school violence, 279
  special, 150–153

Educational Leadership Constituent Council (ELCC)
  descriptions of Standards 1.0 through 7.0, 2–5
  role of NPBEA in creating, 2
Educational needs standard, 258
Educational Testing Service (ETS), 2
Education Amendment of 1972, 424, 426
Education for All Handicapped Children Act (EAHCA), 394, 419
Education law
  church-state relations, 401–403
  compulsory attendance, 400–401
  curriculum, 407–409
  extracurricular activities, 407
  performance testing, 409–411
  school fees, 405–406
  state aid to private schools, 403–405
  student rights. *See* Students, legal rights
  teacher rights. *See* Teachers, legal rights
  textbooks, courses, and supplies, 406–407
  transportation, 406
Educators, participation in goal setting, 39
EEOC (Equal Employment Opportunity Commission), 297, 424, 427
EEO (equal employment opportunity), 297
Effective Instructional Practices (EIP), 124
Effective Schools Model
  correlation of opportunity to learn with time on task, 105–106
  high expectations, 104–105
  home-school relations, 107
  instructional leadership, 104
  mission statements, 104
  monitoring and assessment, 106
  overview of, 102–104
  safe, orderly environment, 106–107
Eighth Amendment, 418

EIP (Effective Instructional Practices), 124
ELCC (Educational Leadership Constituent Council)
  descriptions of Standards 1.0 through 7.0, 2–5
  role of NPBEA in creating, 2
Electromagnetic fields (EMFs), environmental hazards, 272–273
Elementary and Secondary Assessment of Teaching Skills (ESATS), 302
Elementary and Secondary Education Act (ESEA), 394
ELL (English language learner)
  bilingual education and, 163
  immigration and, 372
  programs for, 154
  statistics regarding, 27
Emergencies, policies and procedures, 286
Emerging reading tests, 145
EMFs (electromagnetic fields), environmental hazards, 272–273
Emotional elements, learning styles (Dunn & Dunn), 100
Empathy
  communication breakdowns and, 230
  methods for improving communication, 233
  successful change agentry and, 246
Employment, legal rights regarding termination of, 422–424
Empowerment, effective leaders and, 7
Encoding/decoding, in communication process, 223, 229
Energy costs, school infrastructure, 266
English as second language (ESL), 163, 167
English immersion bilingual programs, 166
English language, globalization and, 26
English language learner (ELL). *See* ELL (English language learner)
Enrichment Triad Model (ETM), 161

Environment
  conditions for learning, 111
  orderly, 106–107
  safe, 106–107, 277
Environmental elements, learning styles (Dunn & Dunn), 99–100
Environmental hazards, 268
  air quality, 271–272
  asbestos, 269
  EMFs, 272–273
  lead, 270–271
  radon gas, 269–270
Environmental Protection Agency (EPA), 269
Equal Access Act of 1984 (EAA), 402
Equal Employment Opportunity Commission (EEOC), 297, 424, 427
Equal employment opportunity (EEO), 297
Equal Pay Act, 424
Equal Protection Clause, Fourteenth Amendment, 394, 427
Equal Rights Amendment, 372
Equity
  Effective Schools Model and, 102–103
  Equal Rights Amendment and, 372
  ethics and, 349–350
  justice and, 349
  policy and, 379
ESATS (Elementary and Secondary Assessment of Teaching Skills), 302
ESEA (Elementary and Secondary Education Act), 394
ESL (English as second language), 163, 167
Ethics
  athletic programs and, 353–354
  caring, 350
  case study, 367–369
  character, commitment, and formality, 350
  character education, 354–355
  codes of, 357
  conflict of interest, 350–351
  critique, 352
  curriculum and, 357
  duty, 349

Ethics (continued)
    ELCC Standards, 4
    equity, 349–350
    freedom, 348
    justice, 349
    loyalty, 351
    moral imperative, 352–353
    national code, 357–360
    overview of, 345–346
    parents and families and,
        357
    policy, 355–356, 378
    principals' promotion of,
        353–356
    procedures for, 355–356
    professional, 132, 352
    prudence, 351
    responsibility and authority
        and, 348–349
    rights, 347–348
    school support for, 356–357
    state codes, 360–362
    suggested readings, 365–366
    superintendents and school
        boards and, 356
Ethnic background. See also Prej-
        udice; Race
    disaggregation of test scores,
        103, 106
    instructional planning and,
        91–92
Ethnoinstruction, 91
ETM (Enrichment Triad Model),
        161
ETS (Educational Testing Ser-
        vice), 2
Evaluation. See also
        Assessment/analysis; Per-
        formance appraisal
    bureaucracies and, 190
    of counseling/guidance service,
        139–140
    decision making and, 206, 207
    in Eisner's curriculum model,
        69
    in Guilford's structure of intel-
        lect model, 95
    in NSPRA public relations
        process, 336
    in Ornstein's curriculum
        model, 68
    performance appraisal,
        313–315
    staff development, 306–307

in system model of curricu-
        lum, 60–61
    teacher development, 125–126
Evaluation models, 113–116
    classroom observation, 114
    formative and summative,
        113–114
    overview of, 113
    peer coaching, 116
    walk-through observation,
        114–116
Evaluation services, 142–147
    criteria for, 143
    overview of, 142
    purposes of, 142–143
    tests for, 143–147
Evidence-driven decision making,
        90–91, 112
Excellence, vision development, 8
Expectations
    Effective Schools Model,
        104–105
    restructuring content and,
        197–198
    Twelve Principles of Effective
        Teaching (Brophy), 111
Expenditures
    auditing, 262
    budgeting, 257
Experience and Education
        (Dewey), 66
Expulsions
    legal rights of students,
        416–417
    violent students, 282
External audits, 261
External public, of schools, 333,
        337–338
Extracurricular activities,
        149–150
    charging for, 407
    functions of, 149–150
    relationship to education,
        149
    student rights and, 415–416

Facilitation. See also Leadership
    overcoming resistance to
        change, 242
    principals as facilitators, 6
    teachers as facilitators, 112
Facilities, 264–273
    air quality and, 271–272
    asbestos and, 269

construction financing,
        267–268
    for counseling service, 140
    crisis management planning,
        286
    EMFs and, 272–273
    environmental hazards, 268
    infrastructure costs, 265–267
    lead and, 270–271
    overview of, 264–265
    radon gas and, 269–270
    suggested readings, 274–275
Fact finding, collective bargain-
        ing, 431
Faculty. See also Teachers
    decision making, 8
    mission statements, 7
    school culture and, 14
    self-analysis, 63
    traditions and rituals reinforc-
        ing, 12
    value statements, 8–9
    vision development, 7–8
Fairness, 349
Fair opportunity, Equal Access
        Act, 403
Family
    academic improvement and, 47
    ethics and, 357
    involvement with schools,
        329–331
Fear, as barrier to improvement,
        197
Federal government
    agencies, 395
    courts, 398
    legal statutes, 394–395
    role in public education, 28
    school revenues, 257
Federal law
    agencies, 395
    case law, 395–396
    hiring practices and, 297–298
    statutes, 394–395
    U.S. Constitution, 393–394
Feedback
    art of giving, 234–235
    barriers to communication,
        229, 231
    downward communication
        and, 225
    goal setting and, 43
    school systems receiving,
        181–182

student learning and, 109–110
teachers need for, 106
Feelings
    listing techniques and,
        233–234
    school culture and, 11
Fees, public schools, 405–406
Females. *See* Gender
Feminist theory, policy, 376
Fields of experience, psychosocial
    barriers to communication,
    230
*Fifteenth Mental Measurements
    Yearbook* (Plake, Impara, &
    Spies), 146
Finances/accounting budgets.
    See Budgets
Fine arts, 111
Fingerprint identification,
    juvenile justice system,
    285
Firefighters, community involve-
    ment with schools, 326
First Amendment
    released time for religious
        instruction, 403
    religious discrimination and,
        427
    religious freedom guaranteed
        by, 402
First impressions, teacher
    appraisal, 313
Fiscal independence/dependence,
    of school districts, 258
Fiscal neutrality standard, state
    financing, 258
Fixed assets, auditing, 262
Flexibility, of counseling services,
    140
Folklore, 13
Follow-up services,
    guidance/counseling serv-
    ices, 138
Force-field analysis (Levin),
    240–241
Formality, ethics and, 350
Formal operational stage (Piaget's
    stages of cognitive develop-
    ment), 99
Formative evaluation
    limitations of, 90
    of teaching, learning,
        113–114

Fourteenth Amendment
    applying Bill of Rights to
        states, 394
    corporal punishment of stu-
        dents, 418
    Due Process Clause, 394, 423
    Equal Protection Clause, 394,
        427
    federal role in education, 393
    search and seizure and, 289,
        418
    suspensions and expulsions
        and, 416
Fourth Amendment, 289, 418
Frames of reference, in teaching,
    291
Freedom, as ethical concept, 348
Freedom of expression, 412–414
    court rulings regarding,
        412–413
    Equal Access Act of 1984,
        402–403
    ethics, 348
    unprotected expression,
        413–414
Full Circle Literacy (McCauley),
    62
Future, vision development and,
    25

Gangs
    gang-related dress, 415
    graffiti and, 289
    needs for belonging and, 286
    school violence and, 277–278
    zero tolerance for, 106
Garbage-Can model, decision
    making, 210–211
Gates-MacGinitie Reading Tests,
    145
Gender
    discrimination protections,
        395, 424–425
    equal employment opportuni-
        ties, 297, 298
    feminist theory of policy, 376
    harassment, 426
    moral development and, 98
    orderly environment and, 292
General Welfare Clause, of U.S.
    Constitution, 393–394
Gifted education, 153–162
    administration of, 156–157
    curriculum models, 161–162

defining giftedness, 156–160
    equity and, 372
    overview of, 153–156
    policy and, 379–380
    principal's role, 160–161
Global society
    curriculum responding to,
        65
    vision development and, 26
Goals
    academic, 287–288
    change strategies and, 251
    criteria for effective, 38–40
    curriculum, 73–74
    decision making and, 208
    downward communication as
        means of implementing,
        224
    establishing, 9–10
    hierarchy for setting, 36–37
    instructional planning, 88
    learning supported by, 109
    monitoring, 111
    obstacles to setting, 41–43
    performance appraisal and,
        315
    in PPBS, 263
    process oriented vs. results ori-
        ented, 36
    public relations, 338
    results from use of, 46–47
    setting, 40–42, 44
    as system outputs, 182
Gossips, in school culture, 12
Governance. *See* Politics
Government
    federal. *See* Federal govern-
        ment
    immunity, tort liability, 435
    laws/regulations as external
        force for change, 239
    participation of groups and
        officials in goal setting, 40
    state. *See* States
Grade point average (GPA), 302
Grades, 147–148
Graffiti, 289
Grants/foundation funds, 112
Grapevine, 227–229
Groups
    constituent groups in policy,
        377
    decision making, 211, 217
    group learning, 15, 110

Groups (continued)
heterogeneous grouping in
schools, 197
political, 379
resistance to change, 239
Groupthink, 212
Guidance services. See Counsel-
ing/guidance services
Guns. See Weapons, in school

Halo effect, in teacher appraisal,
312
Handicaps. See Disability
Harvard Training Program, 314
Head Start, 288
Health insurance, minority
profiles, 27
Health, student appearance and,
414–415
Heroes/heroines
as role models, 13–14
in school culture, 11–12
Heuristics, rational decision mak-
ing, 209
Hierarchy
organization of schools and, 8
principalship and, 5
High-Intensity Language Training
(HILT), 167
HILT (High-Intensity Language
Training), 167
Hispanics
bilingual education and, 162
cultural bias in testing, 303
family involvement with
schools, 329–330
gifted ed programs and, 154
school violence and, 278
U.S. society and, 27
HIV/AIDS, 26
Holmes Group
on alternatives to job specialization, 176
on job mastery, 13
Homeless Assistance Act of 1987,
401
Homelessness, 27
Homes, student
family involvement with
schools, 331
home-school relations, 107,
147
learning at home, 328
Honesty, 230

Horizontal flow, of communication in organizations, 227
Humanistic concept, of curriculum, 54
Human resources, 295–323
assessment centers, 303–304
case study, 321–323
interviews, 299–302
overview of, 295–296
people as internal force for
change, 239
performance appraisal. See
Performance appraisal
principals as, 187–189
process of, 296
recruiting, 296–299
selecting, 299
staff development, 304–309
suggested readings, 319–320
testing applicants, 302–303
union-management relations,
316–317
Human rights, 347–348
Human skills (people skills)
developing, 306
management as, 186–187
principals' success dependent
on, 384

IAQ (indoor air quality),
271–272
IDEA. See Individuals with Dis-
abilities Act (IDEA)
Identification learning, in Gagné's
conditions for learning, 93
Ideological theories, policy,
376–377
IEPs (individual education plans),
16
Imagination, role in creating
vision, 25
Immigration
ELL (English language learner)
and, 372
U.S. society and, 26–27
Impasse, in collective bargaining,
317
Impersonality, of bureaucracies,
190
Incentives, delegation, 177
Incrementalizing, rational deci-
sion making, 210
Individual education plans (IEPs),
16

Individualized education program
(IEP), 420
Individuals with Disabilities Act
(IDEA), 135–136
appropriate free public education, 419–420
disciplining children with disabilities, 152–153
due process protections,
151–152
federal statutes regarding education, 394
impact on public schools, 151
related services, 151
safeguards against expelling
children with disabilities,
417
Indoor air quality (IAQ),
271–272
Indoor Radon Abatement Act,
393
Induction period, beginning
teachers, 307–308
Inflammatory expression, 414
Information processing theory,
92–102
cognitive theories, 98–99
conditions of learning, 92–94
constructivist theories, 99–102
stages of moral development,
96–98
structure of intellect, 94–96
theoretical frames for learning,
92
Information services,
guidance/counseling serv-
ices, 138
Infrastructure costs, 265–267
Initiating questions, 291
Injury, tort liability, 434
Innovation
goal categories, 39
reflection leading to, 72
Inputs, to school systems, 181
Institutional values, principals'
role in policy, 373–374
Instruction. See also Curriculum;
Teaching
academic improvement and,
47
aligning with curriculum and
assessment, 204
differentiated instruction, 81,
91–92

ethnoinstruction, 91
integrating with culture and
    curriculum programs, 66
in Ornstein's curriculum
    model, 66
principals and, 17, 71–72
relationship to curriculum,
    69–70
school expenditures, 257
Instructional leadership
Effective Schools Model and,
    102, 104
principal as, 14
Instructional objectives, 74
Instructional planning
applying student data, 89
cultural backgrounds of stu-
    dents and, 91–92
evidence-driven decision mak-
    ing for improving, 90–91
information processing theory.
    See Information processing
    theory
NCLB requirements for
    improving achievement,
    89–90
principal's role in, 87–88
reflection promoted in, 88–89
Instructional Planning Self-Reflec-
    tive Tool (IPSRT), 88
Intellect
stages of development, 98–99
structure of, 94–96
types of, 101–102
Intelligence
definitions of, 157–160
giftedness and, 157
Intelligence tests, 146
Interest groups, 374–375
Interest payments, school expen-
    ditures, 257
Interest tests, 146
Intermediate appellate courts, 400
Internal audits, 261–262
Internal controls, budgets, 261
Internal public, of schools, 333,
    337–338
Internet, Children's Internet Pro-
    tection Act, 393–394
Internship, in ELCC Standards, 5
Interpersonal intelligence, 102,
    159
Interstate School Leaders Licen-
    sure Consortium (ISLLC), 2

Interview process, in applicant
    selection, 299–302
components of good interview,
    301
improving, 300–301
overview of, 299
problems to avoid, 299–300
questions, permissible and
    impermissible, 301–302
Intradepartmental communica-
    tion, 227
Intrapersonal intelligence, multi-
    ple intelligences (Gardner),
    102, 159
Intuition, decision making and,
    210
Inventory, auditing, 262
Iowa Association of School
    Boards, 128
Iowa Test of Basic Skills (ITBS),
    81
IPSRT (Instructional Planning
    Self-Reflective Tool), 88
ISLLC (Interstate School Leaders
    Licensure Consortium), 2
Isolation, of teachers, 8, 15
ITBS (Iowa Test of Basic Skills),
    81

Japan
quality circles, 252
TQM, 196
Jobs, 176
description, 297
downward communication as
    vehicle for job instruction,
    225
enlargement and enrichment,
    176
familiarity in interview
    process, 299
performance appraisal and, 309
recruitment process and,
    296–297
redesigning as change strategy,
    251–252
rotating, 176
specialization, 175–176, 189,
    297
teachers mastering, 13
Journals, supporting family
    involvement, 331
Judgmental methods, perform-
    ance appraisal, 310–312

Judicial system, 398–400
Just cause, in collective bargain-
    ing, 430
Justice
policy and, 378
types of, 349
Juvenile justice system, 283, 285

Key area focus, goal setting, 38–39

Labor markets, as external force
    for change, 239
Languages, globalization and, 26
LAST (Liberal Arts and Science
    Test), 302
Late-exit bilingual programs, 166
Law enforcement
catastrophes and, 327
compulsory school attendance,
    400
improving juvenile justice sys-
    tem, 285
reporting violent offenders to,
    283
Law, federal
agencies, 395
case law, 395–396
hiring practices, 297–298
statutes, 394–395
U.S. Constitution, 393–394
Law, state and local
agencies, 396–397
education. *See* Education law
local, 397–398
state constitutions, 396
statutes, 396
Lead, environmental hazards,
    270–271
Leadership. *See also* Principals
ability basis of, 5–6
autocratic, 383
creating positive climate for,
    42
functions of, 182
leading, 184
monitoring, 184
moral imperative and,
    352–353
organizing, 183–184
paternal/maternal, 383
planning, 182
politics of, 382–383
principal's role in curriculum,
    71–72

Leadership *(continued)*
    professional development and,
        123–124, 127
    sharing, 6
    in SLT, 194
    styles, 385
    in TQM, 196
Leadership framework (Brown &
    Irby), 32–33, 130
Leading, as basic leadership func-
    tion, 184
Leading from Below the Surface
    (Creighton), 90
Learner characteristics, of stu-
    dents, 89
Learning. *See also* Teaching
    about vs. how, 59
    active learning, 198
    analyzing, 15–16
    anticipatory set in, 290
    assisting low performance, 16
    change as, 244
    closure and, 291–292
    community of learners, 71–72
    conditions for, 92–94,
        111–112
    correlating with time on task,
        105–106
    group learning, 15
    information processing theory.
        See Information processing
        theory
    instructional planning. *See*
        Instructional planning
    principals' role in, 14–15
    professional learning commu-
        nity. *See* Professional learn-
        ing community
    relationship to objectives, 76
    schools as place of, 14
    staff development and, 307
    theoretical frames for, 92
    traditions and rituals reinforc-
        ing, 12
Learning experiences, 76–78
Learning Points Associates, on
    NCLB, 28
Learning readiness test, 46
Learning styles (Dunn & Dunn),
    99–101
Lee-Clark Emerging Reading
    Test, 145
Legal issues
    case study, 438–440

education law. *See* Education
    law
federal law. *See* Law, federal
judicial system, 398–400
law enforcement. *See* Law
    enforcement
legal basis for public educa-
    tion, 393
overview of, 392
recruitment process and,
    297–298
sources of law, 393
state and local law. *See* Law,
    state and local
suggested readings, 436–437
LEP (limited English proficient),
    163–164
Letter method, of reporting stu-
    dent progress, 148
Liability, tort liability, 433
Liberal Arts and Science Test
    (LAST), 302
Licensure, of teachers, 421
Lifelong careers, bureaucracies,
    190
Limited English proficient (LEP),
    163–164
Line positions
    conflicts with staff positions,
        180–181
    overview of, 179
    staff communicating with, 227
Linguistic intelligence, multiple
    intelligences (Gardner),
    101, 159
Linking pins, in System 4, 192
Listening
    ability, 231
    methods for improving com-
        munication, 233
    synergistic decision making
        and, 218
Literacy, globalization, 26
Loans, auditing, 262
Local laws, 397–398. *See also*
    Law, state and local
Logical-mathematical intelli-
    gence, multiple intelligences
    (Gardner), 101, 156, 159
Loyalty, ethics of, 351

Maintenance of standards provi-
    sion, in collective bargain-
    ing, 430

Males. *See* Gender
Management. *See also* Leadership
    ability basis of, 5–6
    conceptual skills, 185–186
    human skills, 186–187
    rights in collective bargaining,
        429
    technical skills, 187
    top management as obstacle to
        goal setting, 41
Management Information System
    (MIS), 205
Managerial model (Beauchamp),
    56–58
Managing the Dream (Bennis),
    190
Mapping
    curriculum, 80
    planning and, 88
Marijuana, 279. *See also* Alcohol
    and drug use
Marketplace, as external force for
    change, 239
Maternal/paternal leadership,
    383
Maternity leaves, 428
Mathematics
    minority profiles, 27
    National Council of Teachers
        of Mathematics, 73
Means-ends chains, in goal set-
    ting, 42
Media
    community relations and,
        333–334
    school liaison with, 332
Mediation, collective bargaining,
    431
Medium, of communication, 223,
    229
Memory, in Guilford's structure
    of intellect model, 95
Men. *See* Gender
Mentoring beginning teachers,
    308
Merriam School, mission state-
    ment, 35–36
Message
    in communication process,
        223
    distortion of, 230
    vehicle of, 230–231

Minorities. *See also individual types of minorities*
in gifted education programs, 154
U.S. society and, 26–27
MIS (Management Information System), 205
Mission
curriculum and, 65, 82–83
Effective Schools Model, 104
employing in day-to-day work, 10
parts of mission statement, 35
principal's role in creating mission statement, 7
professional development of teachers, 121–122
vision development and, 35–36
Models
Accelerated Schools Model, 12
bilingual education, 163, 165–168
decision-making, 210–211, 213–216
Enrichment Triad Model (ETM), 161
evaluation, 113–116
organizational, 5, 191
Models, curriculum
Beauchamp's managerial model, 56–58
Eisner's model, 68–69
Irby and Lunenburg model, 63–66
modern models, 61–63
Ornstein's model, 66–68
overview of, 55
Saylor and colleagues' systems model, 60
Taba's applicative model, 58–60
Tyler's classical model, 55–56
Models, effective schools. *See* Effective Schools Model
Monitoring, as leadership function, 184. *See also* Performance, monitoring
Montessori schools
public access to, 112
respect in, 31
Moral development, 96–98. *See also* Ethics
Moral imperative, 352–353

Motivation, goal creation and, 10
Moving, in force-field analysis (Levin), 242
Multiple Intelligence Theory (Gardner), 101–102, 153
Murphy-Durrell Emerging Reading Analysis, 145
Musical intelligence, multiple intelligences (Gardner), 101, 159

NAEP (National Assessment of Educational Progress), 27, 394
Naively egoistic orientation, Kohlberg's levels of moral development, 97
Narrow grievance definition, in collective bargaining, 429
National Assessment of Educational Progress (NAEP), 27, 394
National Association of Elementary School Principals (NAESP), 2, 358–360
National Association of Secondary School Principals (NASSP), 2, 303–304
National Board for Professional Teaching Standards (NBPTS), 113
National Center for Effective Schools Research and Development, 5, 104, 107
National Commission on Teaching and America's Future (NCTAF), 113
National Council for the Accreditation of Teacher Education (NCATE), 2
National Council of Professors of Educational Administration (NCPEA), 2
National Council of Teachers of Mathematics, 73
National Defense Education Act, 394
National Education Association (NEA)
code of ethics, 360
on lack of minority teachers, 27

National ethics code, 357–360
AASA, 358
National Association of Elementary School Principals, 358–360
NEA, 360
National Merit Schools, 12
National Organization for Victims Assistance, 327
National Policy Board for Educational Administration (NPBEA), 2
National School Boards Association (NSBA), 2
National School Public Relations Association (NSPRA)
example plan, 334–336
four-step process for public relations, 336
guidelines for school-community relations, 331–333
planning process, 337–338
National Staff Development Council, 132
National Teachers Examination (NTE), 302, 421
Nation at Risk, A, 1, 372
Native Americans, in gifted ed programs, 154
Natural disasters, 286
Naturalistic intelligence, multiple intelligences (Gardner), 102, 159
Naysaying, as obstacle to vision development, 33–34
NBPTS (National Board for Professional Teaching Standards), 113
NCLB. *See* No Child Left Behind Act (NCLB)
NCREL (North Central Regional Educational Laboratory), 127
NCTAF (National Commission on Teaching and America's Future), 113
NEA (National Education Association)
code of ethics, 360
on lack of minority teachers, 27
Needs assessment
curriculum, 78–80
staff development, 305
Negative rights, 347

Negligence
    defenses, 434
    tort liability, 433
Negotiation, overcoming resist-
    ance to change, 242
Neoinstitutional theory, policy
    examination, 375–376
Neopluralist advocacy coalition,
    policy examination,
    374–375
Networks, communication,
    227–228
Newsletters, family involvement
    with schools, 330
News reporters, 333–334. See
    also Media
New York State Code of Ethics
    for Educators, 360
No Child Left Behind Act
    (NCLB), 28
    bilingual education, 162
    character education, 354
    disaggregation of test scores,
        103
    evaluating student progress,
        142
    instructional planning based
        on, 89–90
    performance in public schools,
        394
    performance testing, 409, 411
    residency requirements and,
        401
    standards as basis of improve-
        ment, 128, 196
    teacher quality emphasized in,
        381
Noise, in communication process,
    223, 231
Nonclassroom activities. See
    Extracurricular activities
Nondirective counseling, 139
Nonjudgmental methods, per-
    formance appraisal,
    309–310
Non-programmed charges, school
    expenditures, 257
Nonverbal communication, 234,
    235
Normative dimension, policy,
    377
Norms, in school culture, 11
North Carolina Code of Ethics
    for Educators, 360

North Central Regional Educa-
    tional Laboratory
    (NCREL), 127
No-strike position, in collective
    bargaining, 429
NPBEA (National Policy Board
    for Educational Adminis-
    tration), 2
NSPRA. See National School
    Public Relations Associa-
    tion (NSPRA)
NTE (National Teachers Exami-
    nation), 302, 421

Obedience-punishment orienta-
    tion, Kohlberg's levels of
    moral development, 97
Objectives
    curriculum, 59, 74–78
    downward communication for
        implementing, 224
    instructional planning, 88–89
    learning supported by, 109
    public relations, 338
    staff development, 305–306
    as system outputs, 182
Object language, nonverbal com-
    munication, 235
Obscene expressions, freedom of
    expression and, 413–414
Occupational Safety and Health
    Administration (OSHA),
    272
OECD (Organization for Eco-
    nomic Co-operation and
    Development), 274–275
Office of Economic Opportunity
    (OEO), 424
Ombudsperson, 226
Open-door policy, 226
Open systems, 181–182
    feedback, 181–182
    inputs, 181
    outputs, 181–182
    overview of, 181
    transformational process,
        181–182
Operational plans, 44–45
Order, school environments
    anticipatory set and, 290
    attending behavior and, 291
    beepers and pages, banning,
        289
    closure and, 291–292

    dress codes, 288–289
    frames of reference, 291
    graffiti, 289
    importance of, 106–107
    questioning techniques, 291
    race, class, and gender issues,
        292
    reinforcement and, 290–291
    rules and procedures, 288
    school design, 289
    search and seizure and, 289
    teacher-student relations, 289
Organic model, of organization,
    5
Organizational communication,
    224–229. See also Commu-
    nication
    downward communication,
        224–225
    grapevine, 228–229
    horizontal communication,
        227–228
    overview of, 224
    upward communication and,
        225–227
Organization for Economic
    Co-operation and Develop-
    ment (OECD), 274–275
Organizations, 174–201
    administrative roles, 184–185
    alternative models to hierar-
        chical, 5–6
    bureaucracy and, 189–191
    change agents, 245
    decentralization, 178–179
    delegation, 176–178
    departmentalization, 176
    goal setting and, 42
    hierarchy in role of principals,
        5
    job specialization, 175–176
    leadership functions, 182–184
    line and staff positions,
        179–181
    management skills, 185–187
    models, 191
    nature of organizational
        change, 238–239
    open systems and, 181–182
    overview of, 174–175
    politics, 180
    principals, 187–189
    professional development and,
        123

school vision and, 8
site-based management, 192–193
span of management, 179
suggested readings, 200–201
synergistic leadership, 194–196
in synergistic leadership theory, 195
System 4 design, 191–192
total quality management, 196–198
transformational leadership, 193–194
Organizing, as leadership function, 183–184
Orientation
    of beginning teacher, 307–308
    family involvement with schools, 330
    principals' role in policy, 373
    of staff, 13
OSHA (Occupational Safety and Health Administration), 272
Outputs, from school system, 181–182
Outside pressure, change agents, 245
Ownership, vision development, 34

Packages, goal setting, 42
Pagers, banning, 289
Paperwork, as obstacle to goal setting, 41
Paralanguage, 235
Parents
    building trust with, 12
    character education and, 355
    community involvement with schools, 325, 328
    ethics, 357
    involvement with education of children, 329–330
    participation in goal setting, 39
    report in cumulative record, 141
Participation. See also Shared decision making
    democratic politics, 382
    overcoming resistance to change, 242
    reinforcement and, 290–291

Paternal/maternal leadership, 383
PDAS (professional development and appraisal system), 125–126
Pedagogy, 198. See also Teaching
Peer coaching
    as evaluation model, 116
    importance of, 88
    induction of beginning teachers, 308
Peer collaboration, 126
Peer sharing, 308
People. See Human resources
People-change-technology, 245
People skills (human skills)
    developing, 306
    management as, 186–187
    principals' success dependent on, 384
Percentage method, of reporting student progress, 148
Percentile method, of reporting student progress, 148
Performance
    curriculum, 65–66
    downward communication for giving feedback, 225
    goal basis of, 10
    reward and control systems, 13
    standards, 79–80
    state-mandated tests, 409–411
    student learning, 15–16
    upward communication for reporting, 226
Performance appraisal, 309–316. See also Assessment/analysis; Evaluation
    defined, 296
    error sources, 312–313
    goal setting and, 315
    improving, 315–316
    judgmental methods, 310–312
    nonjudgmental methods, 309–310
    overview of, 309
    reviewing, 305
    supervision and evaluation, 313–315
    techniques, 309, 313
Performance, monitoring
    Effective Schools Model, 106
    goal setting and, 40

Twelve Principles of Effective Teaching (Brophy), 111
Personal data sheet, students, 141
Personal development goals, 39
Personal growth, counselors' role in, 137
Personal notes, family involvement with schools, 331
Personnel, 298–299. See also Human resources; Staff
Pesticides, air quality, 271–272
Philosophy, in school culture, 11
Phone calls, family involvement with schools, 331
Physical barriers, to communication, 229–230
Physical elements, learning styles (Dunn & Dunn), 101
Physical facilities. See Facilities
Placement services, guidance/counseling services, 138
Planning. See also Instructional planning
    as basic leadership function, 182
    curriculum, 66, 69
    importance of, 88
    operational plans, 44–45
    professional development, 127, 130–131
    single-use plans, 46
    standing plans, 45–46
    strategic plans, 44
    tactical plans, 44
Planning-programming-budgeting system (PPBS), 263–264
Pluralist politics, 382
Police, community involvement with schools, 326
Policy, 370–379
    conceptual framework for, 377–379
    emergencies, 286
    ethics, 355–356
    gifted students, 379–381
    local school districts, 397
    overview of, 372–373
    politics distinguished from, 381–382
    principals' role in, 373–374
    sexual harassment, 426
    society and, 370–372
    in standing plans, 45

Policy (continued)
suggested readings, 389–391
theories for examining, 374–377
Policy talk, 381–382
Politics, 379–387
distinguishing from policy, 381–382
educational, 382–384
organizational, 180
overview of, 379–380
principals' success dependent on political skill, 384
school, 380
school districts, 384–387
society, 370–372
suggested readings, 389–391
Positive rights, 347
Postconventional level, Kohlberg's levels of moral development, 97–98
Postmodernism, 376
Poverty
gifted students and, 380–381
globalization and, 26
U.S. society and, 27
Power
communication and, 374
consolidated in educational politics, 382–383
power over vs. power to, 6
principals' role in policy, 374
PPBS (planning-programming-budgeting system), 263–264
Prayer, constitutionality of school prayer, 401–402
Precedents, in case law, 395
Preconventional level, Kohlberg's levels of moral development, 96–97
Pregnancy Discrimination Act, 424, 428
Prejudice. See also Ethnic background
bias in interview process, 300
differentiated instruction reduces, 92
guidelines for avoiding in interviews, 301–302
Preoperational stage (Piaget's stages of cognitive development), 98–99
Pressure groups, in goal setting, 40

Pre-Teacher Assessment Program (Millward & Gerlach), 303–304
Prevention, in TQM approach, 196
Pride, in TQM approach, 197
Priests, in school culture, 12
Primacy/recency effect, rational decision making, 209
Primary school, global enrollment statistics, 26
Principals
as administrator, 184–185, 187–189
aligning curriculum, instruction, and assessment, 17
as boundary spanners between school and external constituencies, 325
case study, 21–23
catastrophes and, 326–328
as change agents, 241, 244–245
character education and, 355
collaboration encouraged by, 15
communication, 223–224, 226, 231–233
community of learners, 72
curriculum leadership by, 63, 71–72
decentralization and, 179
decision-making, 202–204
decision-making patterns, 216–217
decision-making process, 204–207
decision-making styles, 214
delegation by, 177
ELCC Standards, 2–5
ethics promoted by, 353–356
evaluating teachers, 315–316
family involvement supported, 329–331
gifted education and, 160–161
goal setting, 9–10, 42
human resource activities of, 187–189
instructional leadership by, 14, 104
instructional planning by, 87–88
internal and external publics and, 333

leadership styles, 382–383
learning as focus of, 14–16
as media coordinator, 333
mission statements, 7
new approach to, 5–6
organizational structures and, 191
overview of role of, 1–2
personal development of, 128
policy and politics and, 372–374
political strategies of, 385–386
professional learning community encouraged by, 6–7
sexual harassment and, 426
shared decision making, 213
skills needed by, 384
span of management, 179
suggested readings, 18–19
supporting beginning teachers, 308–309
tasks in job of, 187
teacher development, 120–122
teacher support, 16–17
teaching role of, 86–87
value statements, 8–9
vision development, 7–8, 30–32
Principles, in Gagné's conditions for learning, 93
Private schools, state aid to, 403–405
Problem identification, decision-making, 204–205
Problems
accepting as friends, 244
indicators of people problems, 239
upward communication and, 226
Problem solving
Creative Problem Solving (Parnes), 161–162
in Gagné's conditions for learning, 93
goal categories, 39
group approach to, 194
intradepartmental, 227
team-based approach to, 161–162
Procedures
bureaucracies, 190
downward communication in implementation of, 225

emergencies, 286
ethics, 355–356
instructional planning, 89
order based on, 288
standing plans, 45–46
Process barriers, to communication, 229
Process consultation, as change strategy, 250
Processes, as internal force for change, 239
Process strategies, for change, 249–251
Productivity, improving with collaboration, 43
Professional development, 120–134. *See also* Staff
artifacts and reflections related to, 131–132
ethics of, 132, 352
leadership framework (Brown & Irby), 130
plan for, 130–131
principal's role in personal development, 128
principal's role in teacher development, 120–122
Professional Development Portfolio (Brown & Irby), 128–130
quality of, 122
resources required for, 127
suggested readings, 133–134
Ten Principles, 123–128
Professional development and appraisal system (PDAS), 125–126
Professional Development Portfolio (Brown & Irby), 128–130
Professional learning community
as alternative to hierarchical organizations, 5
goal creation, 9–10
mission statements, 7
principals as valued participant in, 190
principal's role in creating, 6–7
sharing leadership and, 6
value statements, 8–9
vision development, 7–8
Professional skills, goals, 39
Projects, in single-use plans, 46

Proximate cause, tort liability, 433–434
Prudence, 351
Psychological distance, barriers to communication, 230
Psychomotor domain, 143
Psychosocial barriers, to communication, 230–231
Public debate, in democratic politics, 382
Public education. *See also* Education law
appropriate free public education, 419–420
legal basis for, 393
role of federal government in, 28
Public relations
NSPRA (National School Public Relations Association), 331–333
school programs, 334–338
Pull-out, bilingual programs, 167
Purpose, consistency of (in Deming), 196

Quality
Effective Schools Model and, 102
of professional development, 122
Quality circles, 252
Quality of Work Life (QWL), 251
Quantification, as obstacle to goal setting, 41–42
Questionnaires, methods for improving communication, 226
Questions
in discourse-based learning, 109–110
methods for improving communication, 233
permissible and impermissible in jog interviews, 301–302
teaching techniques, 291
for understanding resistance to change, 243–244
Quotas, in TQM approach, 197
QWL (Quality of Work Life), 251

Race. *See also* Ethnic background
equal employment opportunities, 297

legal rights of teachers and, 424–425
orderly environment and, 292
Radon gas, environmental hazards, 269–270
Rank method, of reporting student progress, 148
Ratification vote, in collective bargaining, 317
Rating teachers, 310–312
Rational decision making, 207–211
assumptions, 207–208
bolstering the alternative, 210
Garbage-Can model, 210–211
heuristics, 209
incrementalizing and, 210
intuition and, 210
limits to rationality, 209
primacy/recency effect, 209
satisficing, 209
Rationale, principals' role in policy, 374
Reading
emerging reading test, 145
minority profiles and, 27
Real conflicts of interest, 351
Realism, goal setting, 39
Receivers, of communication, 223, 229, 233
Recency of events errors, in teacher appraisal, 313
Records
for counseling service, 140
cumulative record of students, 141–142
Recruitment process, human resources, 296–299
defined, 296
job analysis, 296–297
legal constraints, 297–298
personnel sources, 298–299
teacher recruitment consortium, 299
Red Cross, 327
Reduction in force (RIF) provision, in collective bargaining, 430
Reflection
instructional planning and, 88–89
leading to innovation, 72
professional development and, 131–132
in vision development, 30

Reflection Cycle (Brown & Irby), 131–132
Refreezing, in force-field analysis (Levin), 242
Rehabilitation Act
  discrimination in employment and, 424
  federal statutes, 395
  prohibitions on discrimination based on disabilities, 427
  student with disabilities and, 420
  suspensions and expulsions and, 417
Reinforcement
  participation and, 290–291
  synergistic decision making and, 218
Relationships
  caring, 350
  cooperative, 137
  principals maintaining positive, 385
Reliable tests, 303
Religion
  in education law, 401–403
  equal employment opportunities and, 297
  First Amendment and, 402
  legal rights of teachers, 427
  released time for religious instruction, 403
  state aid to private schools, 403–405
Reporting services, 147–149
  grades, 147–148
  methods, 148–149
  overview of, 147
Research
  action research, 125
  in NSPRA public relations process, 336
  professional development and, 124, 127
Researchers
  as change agents, 246
  participation in goal setting, 39
Residency requirements, school attendance, 401
Resistance, to change
  overcoming, 240–243
  reasons for, 240
  understanding, 243–244

Resources. See also Human resources
  change and, 244, 249
  delegation of, 177
  principals' role in policy, 373
  safety and, 284–285
Respect
  in Montessori school, 31
  rights of others and, 347–348
Responding, synergistic decision making and, 218
Response learning, in Gagné's conditions for learning, 93
Responsibility
  as balance to rights and freedom, 348–349
  in delegation process, 177
Responsive feedback, in communication process, 234
Restructuring content, in schools, 197–198
Revenues
  auditing, 262
  budgeting, 257–258
Rewards
  linking to goals, 39
  reward and control system, 13
  successful change agentry and, 246
RIF (reduction in force), in collective bargaining, 430
Rights
  absolute, 347
  Bill of Rights in U.S. Constitution, 394
  Civil Rights Act of 1964, 394, 424–425, 433
  Civil Rights Act of 1991, 395
  ethics of respect, 347–348
  management rights in collective bargaining, 429
  negative/positive, 347
  positive rights, 347
  of students. See Students, legal rights
  of teacher. See Teachers, legal rights
Rituals
  reinforcing folklore, 13
  in school culture, 12
Role models
  consistency of, 13–14
  in matrix of school performance, 15

Roles
  change agents, 245–246
  communication breakdown based on role perception, 230
  leadership based on ability rather than, 5–6
Rules
  as negative feature of bureaucracies, 190
  orderly environment and, 288
  in school culture, 11
  in standing plans, 46

Safe Schools, Better Schools, 280–281
Safety, 276–294
  alcohol and drug use, 277, 279–280
  creating safe environment, 277
  crisis management planning, 285–287
  drills, 286
  juvenile justice system and, 285
  orderly environment conducive to learning. See Order, school environments
  overview of, 276
  predicting violence, 280–281
  preventing violence, 281–284
  principals' responsibility for, 347
  resources needs for, 284–285
  in school environment, 106–107
  student appearance and, 414–415
  suggested readings, 293–294
  violence and, 277–278
Satisficing, rational decision making, 209
SBDM (site-based decision making), 103
SBM (site-based management), 5–6, 192–193
SBS (sick building syndrome), 271
Scaffolds, techniques for bridging abilities and goals, 96
School and Society, The (Dewey), 372
School-based budgeting, 259–261

School boards
    ethics promoted by, 356
    local school districts, 397
    mission statements, 104
    principals' strategies for work-
        ing with, 386
School districts
    actions to make schools safer,
        283–284
    equal employment opportuni-
        ties, 298
    local policy, 397
    politics, 384–387
    testing applicants, 302
School handbook, 330–331
Schools
    budgets. See Budgets
    communication program for,
        224
    as community of learners,
        71–72
    community relations. See
        Community
    cooperative relationship with
        students, 137
    culture. See Culture, of
        schools
    design of, 289
    ethics promoted by, 356–357
    facilities. See Facilities
    home-school relations, 107
    law. See Education law
    as open systems, 181–182
    as place of learning, 14
    politics, 380
    as professional learning com-
        munities, 5
    safety. See Safety
    technology incorporated into
        teaching, 113
School supplies, in education law,
    406–407
School uniforms, 415
Science, minority profiles and, 27
Science of Muddling Through,
    The (Lindblom), 210
Scorn, as obstacle to vision devel-
    opment, 33
Search and seizure, student rights
    and, 289, 418–419
Security. See Safety
Selection process, human
    resources
    assessment centers, 303–304

defined, 296
interviews, 299–302
overview of, 299
testing applicants, 302–303
Self-perception, communication
    and, 230
Self-regulation, teacher support
    for, 110
Semantic barriers, to communica-
    tion, 230
Senders, of communication, 223,
    229–233
Sensory motor stage, Piaget's
    stages of cognitive develop-
    ment, 98
Sexual behavior, 426
Sexual bribery, 426
Sexual coercion, 426
Sexual harassment, legal rights of
    teachers, 425–427
Sexual imposition, 426
Shared decision making, 211–213
    advantages/disadvantages,
        212–213
    effective practices, 213
    methods for improving com-
        munication, 226
    overview of, 211
Sheltered English or content-based,
    bilingual programs, 167
Short-range thinking, as obstacle
    to vision development, 34
Sick building syndrome (SBS), 271
Sincerity, in communication
    process, 230
Single-dimension errors, in
    teacher appraisal, 312
Single-use plans, 46
Site-based budgeting, 259–261
Site-based decision making
    (SBDM), 103
Site-based management (SBM),
    5–6, 192–193
Skills
    developing, 306
    ITBS (Iowa Test of Basic
        Skills), 81
    management skills, 185–187
    professional skills, 39
    work skills, 112
Slogans
    restrictions regarding contro-
        versial, 415
    in TQM approach, 197

SLT. See Synergistic leadership
    (SLT)
Social action approach, curricu-
    lum, 78
Socialization, 225
Social reconstructionist concept,
    of curriculum, 54
Society
    global, 26
    policies and politics, 370–372
    values, 373
Socioeconomics, disadvantaged
    students, 372
Sociogram, in cumulative record,
    141
Sociological elements, learning
    styles (Dunn & Dunn),
    100–101
Span of management, in
    organizational structure,
    179
Spatial intelligence, multiple
    intelligences (Gardner),
    101
Special education, 150–153
    discipline, 152–153
    due process protections,
        151–152
    overview of, 150–151
    related services, 151
Specialization. See Division of
    labor (job specialization)
Specificity, effective goal setting,
    38
Speech, freedom of. See Freedom
    of expression
Spies, in school culture, 12
Stability, in counseling services,
    140
Staff. See also Professional devel-
    opment
    breaking down barriers
        between, 197
    character education for, 355
    decentralization, 179
    hiring, 12–13
    line positions, 180–181, 227
    National Staff Development
        Council, 132
    staff positions, 180–181
    support staff in schools, 112
Staff development, 304–309
    assessing needs, 305
    defined, 296

Staff development *(continued)*
   Effective Schools Model, 103, 105
   evaluating program for, 306–307
   methods, 306
   objectives, 305–306
   orientation and induction of beginning teacher, 307–308
   overview of, 304
   support for beginning teacher, 308–309
Stakeholders
   goal creation, 9–10
   mission statement, 7
   role in developing school culture, 11
   value statement creations, 8–9
   vision development and, 34
Standard of care, tort liability, 433
Standards
   achievement based on, 196
   achievement tests, 147
   AYP standards, 142
   curriculum analysis, 65–66
   ELCC, 2–5
   ISLLC, 2
   performance, 10, 79–80
Standing plans, 45–46
State Board of Education, 396–397
State Department of Education, 396–397
States
   agencies, 396–397
   aid to private schools, 403–405
   applying Bill of Rights to, 394
   Center for the Prevention of School Violence, 285
   church-state relations in education law, 401–403
   constitutions, 396
   courts, 399–400
   education law. *See* Education law
   ethics codes, 360–362
   financing, 258
   school revenues, 257
   statutes, 396
Statutes, legal
   federal, 394–395
   state, 396
Storytelling, in school culture, 12

Strategic planning, 252–253
   overview of, 44–45
Strategies, in Gagné's conditions for learning, 93
Strictness/leniency errors, in teacher appraisal, 312
Structural dimension, policy, 377
Structural strategies, for change, 251–253
Structured English immersion, bilingual programs, 167
Structure of intellect model (Guilford), 94
Students
   attendance, 90–91
   character education, 355
   cooperative relationship with school, 137
   culture of school and, 14
   cumulative record, 141–142
   curriculum responding to needs of, 65
   differentiated instruction for, 91–92
   diversity of, 198
   in exemplary school, 7–8
   guiding, 136, 140
   hierarchy of goals and, 38
   identifying students at risk for violent behavior, 286–287
   instructional planning, 89
   learning analysis, 15–16
   learning focus, 14–15
   level/learner characteristics, 89
   participation in goal setting, 39
   participation in mission statement, 7
   planning as means of addressing weaknesses of, 88
   problem students, 280
   student-counselor ratio, 140
   success of, 63
   teacher quality impacting achievement of, 381
   teacher-student relations, 289
   traditions and rituals reinforcing learning, 12
   violent students, 282–283
Student services, 135–173
   attendance and records, 140–142
   bilingual education. *See* Bilingual education

case study, 171–173
counseling/guidance. *See* Counseling/guidance services
evaluation. *See* Evaluation
extracurricular activities, 149–150
gifted education. *See* Gifted education
overview of, 135–136
reporting to parents and families, 147–149
special education, 150–153
suggested readings, 169–170
Students, legal rights, 412–420
   appearance, 414–415
   corporal punishment, 417–418
   disabled students and, 419–420
   discipline, 416
   extracurricular activities, 415–416
   freedom of expression, 412–414
   overview of, 412
   search and seizure, 418–419
   suspensions and expulsions, 416–417
Subject matter. *See* Content
Submersion, bilingual programs, 166
Suggested readings
   budgets, 274–275
   change, 254–255
   communication, 236–237
   community, 340–341
   curriculum, 84–85
   decision making, 220–221
   ethics, 365–366
   facilities management, 274–275
   human resource management, 319–320
   legal issues, 436–437
   organizational structure, 200–201
   policy, 389–391
   politics, 389–391
   principals, 18–19
   professional development, 133–134
   safety, 293–294
   student services, 169–170

teaching/learning, 118–119
vision, 48–49
Suggestion box, family involvement with schools, 331
Suggestions, upward communication, 226
Summative evaluation, of teaching/learning, 113–114
Superintendents
  ethics promoted by, 356
  principals' strategies for working with, 385–386
Supervision, performance appraisal, 313–315
Support
  for beginning teacher, 308–309
  principals' support for teachers, 16–17
  professional learning communities, 6
Supportive relationships, in System 4, 191
Support services, school expenditures, 257
Supreme courts
  federal, 398–399
  state, 400
Supreme Court, U.S., 417
  church-state relations, 401–402
  collective bargaining, 428–429
  corporal punishment, 417–418
  curriculum, 408
  desegregation case, 419
  discrimination based on disabilities, 427
  Equal Access Act of 1984 (EAA), 403
  prayer and Bible reading in public schools, 402
  pregnancy discrimination, 428
  race and gender discrimination, 425
  school transportation, 403–405
  search and seizure, 418
  sexual harassment, 425–426
  state aid to private schools, 403–405
  state-mandated performance testing, 409–410

suspensions and expulsions, 416–417
tenured employees, 422–424
Survey feedback, as change strategy, 250
Suspensions, legal rights of students, 416–417
Synergistic decision making, 217–219
Synergistic leadership theory (SLT), 194–196
  factors in, 194–195
  overview of, 194
  value of, 196
Synergistic Leadership Theory (Irby, Brown, Duffy, & Trautman), 384
System 4 design, 191–192
  linking pins, 192
  overview of, 191
  supportive relationships, 191
Systemic vision, 29
Systems, 181. See also Open systems
Systems model (Saylor and colleagues), curriculum, 60
Systems theory, policy, 374

Tactical plans, 44
Task forces, on school violence, 284–285
Tasks
  correlation of opportunity to learn with time on task, 105–106
  demands on principals, 210
  principals' job, 185, 187
Taxonomy, curriculum objectives, 74
TBE (transitional bilingual education), 165
Teacher Expectation and Student Achievement (TESA), 103
Teacher of the Year awards, 12
Teacher recruitment consortium, 299
Teachers. See also Faculty
  career ladder, 13
  character education, 355
  collaboration, 15
  counselors assisting, 136–137
  development of, 103, 121–123, 194

effective teaching practices, 107–111
empowering, 6
evaluation, 113
as facilitators, 112
feedback from monitoring process, 106
hierarchy of goals and, 38
identifying problem teachers, 281
isolation of, 8
minority teachers, 26–27
mission statements and, 7
rating, 310–312
student achievement and, 381
success of, 63
support mechanisms for, 16–17
teacher-student relations, 289
training in goal setting, 42
violence in schools and, 278–279
Teachers, legal rights, 420–435
  age discrimination, 427
  collective bargaining, 428–433
  contracts, 421–422
  licensure and certification, 421
  overview of, 420
  pregnancy discrimination, 428
  race and gender discrimination, 424–425
  religious discrimination, 427
  sexual harassment, 425–427
  termination of employment, 422–424
  tort liability, 433–435
Teaching. See also Instruction; Learning
  classroom practices, 112–113
  conditions for learning, 111–112
  diverse approach to pedagogy, 198
  Effective Schools Model. See Effective Schools Model
  evaluation models, 113–116
  frames of reference, 291
  information processing theory. See Information processing theory
  instructional planning. See Instructional planning
  learning focus vs. teaching focus, 14–15

Teaching *(continued)*
practices, 107–111
principal's role in, 86–87
questions as teaching technique, 291
suggested readings, 118–119
Teams
building teams as change strategy, 250
decision-making, 211
Safe Schools, Better Schools, 281
schools as community of learners, 71
teacher teams, 15
team-based approach to problem solving, 180
Technical dimension, policy, 377–379
Technical skills, 187, 306
Technological concept, of curriculum, 54
Technological society, 28
Technology
as external force for change, 239
semantic barriers to communication, 230
viewing as tool or resource, 198
Ten Principles of Professional Development, 123–128
Tenure law, 422–423
Termination of employment, legal rights of teachers, 422–424
TESA (Teacher Expectation and Student Achievement), 103
Tests, 143–147
American Educational Research Association on, 79
components of testing programs, 145–147
creating effective, 143–145
criteria for, 143
in cumulative record, 141
disaggregation of test scores, 103, 106
establishing criteria to be tested, 143
job applicants, 302–303
nationally standardized, 81
purposes of, 144–145
Texas Education Code, 163–164

Texas Educator Code of Ethics, 362
Textbooks
as basis of curriculum, 73
critical examination of, 63–64
in education law, 406–407
Thinking critically, 17
Three-group method, of reporting student progress, 148
Time
constraints in decision making, 208
group decision making and, 213
as resource for learning, 198
Time frames, effective goal setting, 38
Time management, in classroom, 109
Tort liability, 433–435
Total quality management (TQM), 196–198
TQM (Total quality management), 196–198
Trade-offs, collective bargaining, 432
Traditions
barriers to communication, 231
folklore and, 13
as obstacle to vision development, 33
in school culture, 12
Training
change and, 249
interviewers, 300
on job, 196
principals and teachers in goal setting, 42
staff. *See* Staff development
in TQM approach, 197
Training role, of change agents, 245
Transactional leadership, 193
Transformational leadership, 193–194
goals of, 194
models, 193
overview of, 193
principals' role and, 6
Transformational process, students into graduates, 181–182
Transformation, in TQM approach, 197

Transformative approach, to integration of curriculum, 78
Transitional bilingual education (TBE), 165
Transportation, in education law, 406
Trial courts, 399
Trust
academic improvement and, 47
resistance to change, 239
value of, 31–32
T-score method, of reporting student progress, 148–149
Tuning protocol, teacher feedback, 63
Twelve Principles of Effective Teaching (Brophy), 108–111, 112
Two-way, bilingual programs, 166

Uncertainty, resistance to change, 239
Unfreezing, in force-field analysis (Levin), 241–242
Uniforms, school, 415
Unions
collective bargaining, 428
contracts governing teacher evaluation, 315
methods for improving communication, 227
relations with school management, 316–317
Unitary politics, 383–384
University Council for Educational Administration (UCEA), 2
Upward flow of communication, in organizations, 225–227
U.S. Constitution
Bill of Rights, 394
Eighth Amendment, 418
employee rights of free association, 429
federal involvement in education, 393–394
First Amendment, 402, 403, 427
Fourteenth Amendment. *See* Fourteenth Amendment
Fourth Amendment, 289, 418
maternity leaves, 428
state powers in, 396

User fees, public schools,
    405–406
U.S. society, 26–28
U.S. Supreme Court. *See* Supreme
    Court, U.S.

Valid tests, 303
Values. *See also* Beliefs
    adherence to, 13
    creating value statements, 8–9
    culture and, 28
    dominant, in school culture, 11
    normative dimension of pol-
        icy, 377
    in synergistic leadership the-
        ory, 194
    vision development and, 30–31
Vandalism, 266, 289
Violence
    alternatives to, 286
    collecting and analyzing data,
        280
    dealing with violent students,
        282–283
    plain clothes police officers in
        schools, 284
    predicting, 280–281
    preventing, 281–284
    research on, 277–278
    size of school as factor in, 278
    teachers and educational
        climate as factors in,
        278–279
Virtue, character education, 355
Vision, 24–52
    articulating, 33
    case study, 50–52
    creating, 29–30
    curriculum and, 65, 82–83
    detractors, 33–34
    developing, 7–8
    in ELCC Standards, 2

employing in day-to-day
    work, 10
global society and, 26
goal criteria, 38–40
goal-setting process, 40–44
goal-setting results, 46–47
goal statements, 36–38
imagination in, 25
leadership framework, 32–33
maintainers, 34–35
mission statements, 35–36
operational plans, 44–45
principal's role in creating,
    30–32
professional learning commu-
    nity sharing, 6
promoting change with, 249
school culture and, 28–29
sharing, 72
single-use plans, 46
standing plans, 45–46
strategic plans, 44
suggested readings, 48–49
systemic vision, 29
tactical plans, 44
U.S. society and, 26–28
Visionaries, 25
Vision detractors, 33–34
Vision maintainers, 34–35
Vocational Education Act, 394
Volunteer programs
    community involvement with
        schools, 325, 328
    conditions for learning, 112
Vulgar expressions, freedom
    of expression and,
    413–414

Wages, in collective bargaining,
    430
Walk-through observation,
    114–116

Water, globalization, 26
Wealth, policy and, 380–381
Weapons, in school
    school violence and,
        277–278
    search and seizure and,
        289
    toughening laws regarding,
        281–282
    zero tolerance for, 106
Weariness, as obstacle to vision
    development, 34
Weather, school infrastructure
    costs, 266
We-they attitudes, barriers to
    communication, 230
What, of curriculum content,
    66
Wheel network, of communica-
    tion, 228
Whisperers, in school culture,
    12
Women. *See* Gender
Workload, of principals,
    184–185
Work skills, 112

Y network, of communication,
    228

Zero-based budgets (ZBB),
    262–263
    developing decision packages,
        262–263
    identifying decision units,
        262
    overview of, 262
    PPBS compared with, 263
    ranking decision packages,
        263
Zipper clause, in collective bar-
    gaining, 429–430